East Africa

a travel survival kit

Geoff Crowther

East Africa – a travel survival kit
  1st edition

Published by
  Lonely Planet Publications
  Head Office: PO Box 88, South Yarra, Victoria 3141, Australia
  Also: PO Box 2001A, Berkeley, California 94702, USA

Printed by
  Colorcraft, Hong Kong

Photographs
  Rona Abbott (RA)
  Geoff Crowther (GC)
  Hugh Finlay (HF)
  Linda Henderson (LH)
  Jane Siegel (JS)

  Cover photo of a Maasai women GC; East Africa faces page photos 1 & 3 LH, 2 & 4 JS, 5 GC;
  animals pages GC, HF, LH; other photos as indicated.

Cartoons by
  Tony Jenkins

Published
  September 1987

**Although the author and publisher have tried to make the information as
accurate as possible, they accept no responsibility for any loss, injury or
inconvenience sustained by any traveller using this book.**

National Library of Australia
Cataloguing in Publication Data

Crowther, Geoff
  East Africa, a travel survival kit.

  Includes index.
  ISBN 0 86442 005 6.

  1. Africa, East – Description and travel – 1981- – Guide-books. I. Title

916.7'6044

The Author

Geoff Crowther was born in Yorkshire, England and started his travelling days as a teenage hitch-hiker. Later, after many short trips around Europe, two years in Asia and Africa and short spells in the overgrown fishing village of Hull and on the bleak and beautiful Cumberland fells, Geoff got involved with the London underground information centre BIT. He helped put together their first, tatty, duplicated overland guides and was with them from their late '60s heyday right through to the end.

With Lonely Planet Geoff has written or collaborated on guides to Africa, India, South America, Malaysia, Korea and Taiwan as well as this book. Geoff now lives with Hyung Pun, whom he met in Korea, on an old banana plantation in the rainforests near the New South Wales/Queensland border. In between travel he spends his time pursuing noxious weeds, cultivating tropical fruits, trying to get a house built and brewing mango wine.

Lonely Planet Credits

Editor	Richard Everist
Maps	Geoff Crowther
Design & Illustrations	Peter Flavelle
Cover	
& Additional Maps	Todd Pierce
Typesetting	Alison Porter

Thanks must also go to Debbie Lustig for map keys and other support work and Ann Jeffree for support typesetting.

Acknowledgements

This book is partially the result of feedback from overburdened travellers who were becoming rebellious about having to carry around 700-plus-pages of *Africa on a Shoestring*, when all they needed was part of it and that part they needed in greater detail. I'd be the first to admit that, like any guidebook, *Africa on a Shoestring* isn't perfect or totally comprehensive but it's as up to date as African conditions allow.

Many travellers who wrote to Lonely Planet in response to *Africa on a Shoestring* and others that I met on the road while I was there have contributed to this new book. So have a number of people who live in northern New South Wales, Australia, who have never seen the inside of a *matatu*. Without wishing to list them in any order of preference, I would like to thank the following people very sincerely for their help, encouragement, friendship, hospitality and constructive criticism:

Rowland Burley and Helen Crowe of Nairobi, Kenya, who laid out the red carpet for us, warmly welcomed us to their home, gave us lots of space, and shared what was probably the most memorable safari (to the Jade Sea) that I shall ever experience. Rowland is a former president of the Kenya Mountain Climbing Club and Helen works as a nurse for the US Peace Corps. Many, many thanks!

Kireli Leseelah of Wamba, Kenya, a member of the Samburu tribe and a ranger for the Kenya National Parks who guided us through the Mathew's Range. Kireli knows this area like the back of his hand and he showed us many things we would otherwise have missed.

Arthur Stern (USA) who accompanied us through much of Uganda and who ended up acquiring a very unexpected and unwelcome insight into another dimension of that country, namely Idi Amin's former hell-hole, Luzira jail – luckily Amin had long since gone.

The RSI (Repetitive Strain Injury) Rescue Squad of northern New South Wales peopled by Debbie Woods, Graeme Cook, Bob Bathie, John and Rolly Hocking (in various combinations) who halted work on several occasions with cases of Swan Lager.

Jes Ford and Alison Lescure (UK) who, since they started their African adventure well over a year ago, have written countless long and very detailed letters which have been of immense help in putting this volume together and in keeping *Africa on a Shoestring* up to date.

Mike and Jean Whittinghill (USA) for their friendship and good humour whilst in Malindi and Lamu.

Dave Schwarz (Australia) for his unstinting help with the map-work and for fitting a new output transformer in the inverter before it burnt out the computer. May your solar trackers prosper.

Said M Famao (Uganda) for keeping the best hotel in Uganda – the *Saad* in Kasese.

For the technically minded and those interested in the possibilities of living without another Chernobyl, this book was written on a solar-powered computer using a Kaypro 4 microprocessor, four Solarex X100 GT solar panels, a Santech 1000 watt inverter and 12 ex-Telecom 2v 500 AH lead-acid batteries. It works like a treat! The last book I wrote (the 1986 edition of *South America on a Shoestring*) was done utilising the same computer but on the English 240v AC grid system. Whilst it was being done the local power station burnt down and there was a labour dispute. Both incidents led to a power shut-down without warning and both resulted in me losing half a day's work with no re-call possible. On solar power I get at least two weeks warning of a shut-down and the only disputes I have to contend with are about who is going to cook dinner!

The Next Edition
Things change, prices go up, good places go bad and bad ones go bankrupt. So if you find things better, worse or simply different please write and tell us about it. As usual good letters will be rewarded with a free copy of the next edition or an alternative Lonely Planet guidebook.

Contents

Introduction

If your vision of Africa is of elephants crossing the plain below Kilimanjaro, an Arab dhow sailing into Zanzibar, a million pink flamingos, a Maasai tribesman guarding his cattle – East Africa is where this vision becomes reality.

This book covers a small group of countries of absorbing interest and diversity. Whatever your interests, East Africa has plenty to see, experience and consider.

Kenya and Tanzania are the heart of African safariland. Some of the most famous reserves are found here and in a trip to these countries you will probably see everything from rhinos to lions, hippos to baboons, wildebeeste to flamingos. Safaris are an experience in themselves, but some of the reserves are also spectacular – such as the Ngorongoro park in Tanzania which is in the crater of a colossal extinct volcano or the Amboseli park in Kenya which has Mt Kilimanjaro as a spectacular backdrop.

The reserves of Kenya and Tanzania are the region's best known natural attractions but far from the only ones. The superb Ruwenzori Mountains sprawl across the border between Uganda and Zaire, further south are some of the most active volcanoes in Africa, particularly in the Parc National des Volcans in Rwanda. And Rwanda is, of course, famous for its scattered groups of mountain gorillas which you can also visit. Scuba divers will find plenty to interest them along the coast and around the offshore islands, while other visitors may find lazing on the beach and collecting a suntan quite enough exercise.

If lazing isn't a word in your vocabulary then East Africa offers some wonderful mountains to climb. If you're fit an assault on Mt Kenya or, best of all, snow-capped Mt Kilimanjaro, the highest mountain in Africa, is within your reach.

East Africa isn't just wildlife and scenery – there are also people, cultures and politics. Politically the region offers as wide a span of Africa's problems and aspirations as you could ask for. At one extreme there's Kenya where Africa really works and where stability and progress have been the norm, a situation very different from so many other African nations. Tanzania illustrates where the best of African intentions can go disastrously awry while Zaire is one of the best examples of pure, untrammelled greed. Burundi is a painful example of the horrors of tribal animosity, and while Idi Amin may be gone Uganda has far from forgotten him.

The cultures and people of the region are equally interesting. Along the coast and particularly on islands like Zanzibar and Lamu you can observe the strong influence of the Arabs who came first as traders and later as slavers and remained in the region for centuries. Everywhere you'll see the many and varied tribes of the region, particularly the colourful and strong-minded Maasai of Kenya. Go there, it's a wonderful region.

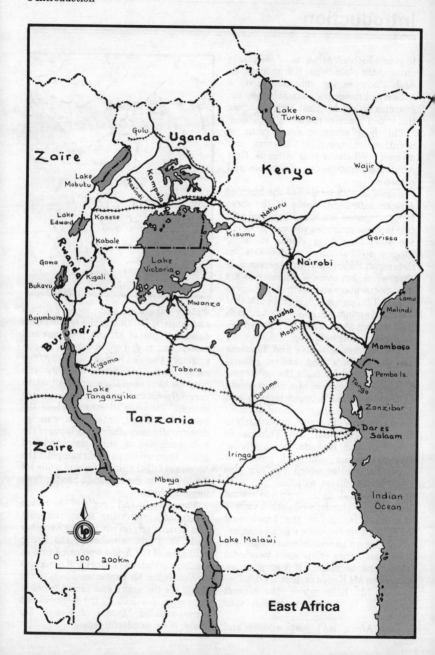

East Africa

Facts for the Visitor

PAPERWORK

The essential documents are a passport and an International Vaccination Card. If you already have a passport, make sure it's valid for a reasonably long period of time and has plenty of blank pages on which stamp-happy immigration officials can do their stuff. If it's half full then get a new one before you set off. This way you won't have to waste time hanging around in a capital city somewhere while they issue you with a new one. In some countries there is the option of getting a normal sized passport or a 'jumbo' passport. Get the larger one. US nationals can have extension pages stapled into otherwise full passports at any of their embassies.

Whoever supplies you with your vaccinations will provide you with a Vaccination Card and the necessary stamps.

If you're taking your own transport or you're thinking of hiring a vehicle to tour certain national parks, get hold of an International Driving Permit before you set off. Any national motoring organisation will fix you up with this, provided you have a valid driving licence for your own country. The cost of these permits is generally about US$5.

An International Student Identity Card or the graduate equivalent is also very useful in many places and can save you a considerable amount of money. Some of the concessions available include airline tickets, train and riverboat fares and reduced entry charges to museums and archaeological sites. If you're not strictly entitled to a student card, it's often possible to get one if you book a flight with one of the 'bucket shop' ticket agencies that have proliferated in certain European and North American cities. The deal usually is that you buy an airline ticket and they'll provide you with a student card. Another possibility is to buy a fake card (average price around US$10). There always seems to be someone selling these wherever travellers collect in numbers, but examine them carefully before buying, as they vary a great deal in quality.

Another useful thing to have is a Youth Hostel Association membership card, particularly for Kenya. Some of the hostels will allow you to stay without a card but others will insist you join up first. Concessions which are possible with an International Student Card or a YHA membership card are mentioned in the appropriate chapters.

VISAS

A visa is a stamp in your passport permitting you to enter a country and stay there for a specified period of time. They are obtained from the embassy or consulate of the appropriate country either before you set off or along the way. It's best to get them along the way, especially if your travel plans are not fixed, but keep your ear to the ground regarding the best places to get them. Two different consulates of the same country may have completely different requirements; the fee may be different, one consulate might want to see how much money you have whereas another won't, one might demand an onward ticket while another won't even mention it, one might issue visas while you wait, and another might insist on referring the application back to the capital (which can take weeks).

Whatever you do, don't turn up at a border without a visa unless you're absolutely sure visas aren't necessary or you can get one at the border. If you get this wrong you'll find yourself tramping back to the nearest consulate and, in some countries, this can be a long way.

You'll occasionally come across some tedious, petty-power freak at an embassy or consulate whose sole pleasure in life appears to be making as big a nuisance of himself/herself as possible and causing you the maximum amount of delay. If you bite the carrot and display your anger or frustration, the visa will take twice as long to issue. There's one of these creeps born every minute but if you want that visa don't display any emotion, pretend you have all day to waste.

Consular officials sometimes refuse point-blank to stamp a visa on anything other than a completely blank page, so make sure your passport has plenty of them. Zaïre demands that you produce a letter of recommendation from your own embassy before they will issue a visa. Embassies are aware of this bureaucratic nonsense and will have form letters available for the purpose, but you may have to pay for these – British embassies charge almost as much for these letters as the visa itself costs.

Another important fact to bear in mind about visas is their sheer cost. Very few of them are free and some are outrageously expensive. Unless you carry a passport from one of the Commonwealth or European Economic Community countries, you'll probably need quite a few visas, and if you're on a tight budget the cost of them can make a hole in your pocket. It's a good idea to make a rough calculation of what the visa fees are going to amount to before you set off, and allow for it. Make sure you have plenty of passport-size photographs for visa applications – 24 should be sufficient.

Some countries, it seems, are so suspicious about your motives for wanting to pay a visit that they demand you have a ticket out of the country before they will let you in. So long as you intend to leave from the same place you arrived at, there is no problem, but if you want to enter at one point and leave from another, this can sometimes be a headache. Fortunately, few East African countries demand that you have an onward ticket, although I was asked for one when I applied for a Zaïre visa. If they do insist on you having one but you want to spend the minimum possible – and have it refunded without problems – try buying an MCO (Miscellaneous Charges Order) from an international airline for, say, US$100.

An MCO is similar to having a deposit account with an airline and the beauty of it is that it looks like an airline ticket, but it isn't for any specific flight. It can be refunded in full or exchanged for a specific flight either with the airline you bought it from or with any other airline which is a member of IATA. Most consular and immigration officials accept an MCO as an onward ticket. The other way to get around having an onward ticket is to buy the cheapest ticket available out of the country and then get it refunded later on. If you do this, make sure you can get a refund without having to wait months. Don't forget to ask specifically where it can be refunded since some airlines will only refund tickets at the office where you bought them; some only at their head office.

Most East African countries take a strong line against South Africa to the point of refusing entry to nationals of that country. They are also not keen on people whose passports show that they have visited South Africa. If that's the case they may refuse to issue you with a visa or refuse entry when you get to the border. Tanzania is inordinately keen about this so if your passport has South African stamps in it or even the stamps of border crossing points to or from Botswana, Zimbabwe, Lesotho or Swaziland you'll have to get rid of it and have a new one issued.

MONEY

It's very difficult to predict what a trip to Africa is going to cost since so many factors are involved: how fast you want to travel, what degree of comfort you consider to be acceptable, how much sight-seeing you want to do, whether you intend to hire a vehicle to explore a game park or rely on other tourists to give you a lift, whether you're travelling alone or in a group, whether you will be changing money on the street or in banks, and a host of other things.

There's only one thing which remains the same in Africa and that's the pace of change – it's fast. Inflation and devaluations can wreak havoc with your travel plans if you're on a very tight budget. You should budget for at least US$10 per day in the cheaper countries and US$20 per day in the more expensive ones. This should cover the cost of very basic accommodation, food in local cafés and the cheapest possible transport. It won't include the cost of getting to Africa, safaris in game parks or major purchases in markets. On the other hand, if you stay in one place for awhile and cook your own food you can reduce daily costs considerably since you won't be paying for

IM JUST **VERY** HAPPY TO BE HERE...

actual Zairois customs official

On Entering Zaire with underwear full of blackmarket currency — (for naught, as it transpires; the customs men ~~SELL~~ blackmarket money on the spot!)

transport and you'll get a better deal on the cost of accommodation.

It doesn't matter which currency you take if you only intend to use banks when you change it. If, however, you want to take advantage of the black market (usually cash only) then take a well-known currency – US dollars, £ sterling, French francs, DM – otherwise no-one will know what the current exchange rate is or they'll offer you a very poor rate.

Travellers' Cheques & Cash

For maximum flexibility, take the larger slice of your money in travellers' cheques and the rest in cash – say up to US$500. American Express, Thomas Cook and Citibank cheques are the most widely used and they generally offer instant replacement in the event of loss or theft. Keep a record of the cheque numbers and the original bill of sale for the cheques in a safe place in case you lose them. Replacement is a whole lot quicker if you can produce this information. Even so, if you don't look clean and tidy, or they don't believe your story for some reason or another, replacement can take time since quite a few travellers have sold their cheques on the black market, or simply pretended to lose them, and then demanded a replacement set. This is particularly so with American Express cheques. You should avoid buying cheques from small banks which only have a few overseas branches, as you'll find them very difficult if not impossible to change in many places.

Make sure you buy a good range of denominations when you get the cheques – US$10, US$20, US$50 and US$100 – so you don't get stuck changing large denomination bills for short stays or for final expenses. Don't carry too many small cheques, however. Having a credit card and a personal cheque-book is another way of having secure funds to hand. With these you can generally withdraw up to US$50 in cash and US$500 (sometimes US$1000) in travellers' cheques per week from any branch of the credit card company. This way you can avoid having to carry large wads of travellers' cheques. If you don't have a personal cheque-book but you do have a credit card there's usually no problem. Simply present your card and ask for a counter-cheque.

Credit Cards

American Express, Diner's Club, Visa and MasterCharge are all widely recognised credit cards. The National Westminster card is particularly useful in Africa since National Westminster has many branches in British ex-colonies. They also have a small booklet containing the addresses of all their African branches. With a personal cheque-book this is useful because you can get an exact amount of money rather than have to change a large travellers' cheque.

Credit cards also have their uses when 'sufficient funds' are demanded by immigration officials before they will allow you to enter a country. It's generally accepted that you have 'sufficient funds' if you have a credit card.

The Black Market

You cannot always change travellers' cheques in small places or, of course, when the banks are closed. This is one reason why you should bring some cash with you but the major reason is that it allows you to take advantage of any street rate of exchange (black market). Sometimes you can change travellers' cheques on the black market but this isn't always the case.

There are four countries in East Africa where you can get considerably more for your hard currency on the streets than you can in the banks. In Tanzania and Uganda the difference is little short of spectacular. If you don't take advantage of this you are going to find these countries very expensive whereas if you do they'll be relatively cheap. Some people regard the black market as

morally reprehensible. It's certainly predatory but some countries overvalue their currency to a degree that is totally unrealistic. The decision is yours but it's unusual to find anyone who doesn't use the black market where it's worth the effort.

If you're setting off from Europe the Credit Suisse bank at the Zurich airport will change paper money from any country in the world at very reasonable rates and they will also issue paper money in all currencies. Their rates for some currencies are about the same as the black market rate.

When changing on the black market have the exact amount you want to change available – avoid pulling out large wads of notes. Be very wary about sleight of hand and envelope tricks. Insist on personally counting out the notes that are handed to you. Don't let anyone do this for you and don't hand over your money until you're satisfied you have the exact amount agreed to. If at any point you hand the notes back to the dealer (because of some discrepancy, for example) count them out again when they're handed back to you, because if you don't you'll probably find that all but the smallest notes have been removed. Some operators are so sharp they'd have the shoes off your feet while you were tying up the laces. Don't allow yourself to be distracted by supposed alarms like 'police' and 'danger.' In many countries you won't have to take part in this sort of mini-drama, as money is generally changed in certain shops or with merchants at a market, so it's a much more leisurely process. Indeed, in many places it's very unwise to change on the street as you may be set up by a police undercover agent.

You should treat all the official and black market rates given in this book as a guide only. They are correct at the time the book goes to press, but coups, countries defaulting on their external debt repayments, devaluations and IMF strictures can alter the picture dramatically. You must check out all prices and exchange rates with your fellow travellers along the way. They are your best source of current information.

Currency Forms

Kenya, Tanzania and Uganda issue currency declaration forms on arrival. On these forms you must write down how much cash and travellers' cheques you are bringing into the country. Tanzania checks these very thoroughly when you leave at its southern borders with Zambia and Malawi and if there are any discrepancies you're in the soup. At the northern borders they apparently couldn't care less. Kenya certainly collects them when you leave but they are not scrutinised. Uganda doesn't even issue them at minor border crossings and rarely asks for them when you leave. Make sure you get one on arrival, though, because you cannot change money at a bank without one. Zaïre abolished currency forms in mid-1986.

If you intend using the black market you must declare less than you are bringing in and hide the excess. More details about the forms can be found in the appropriate country chapters.

Money Safety

There is no 'safe' way to keep your money while you're travelling, but the best place is in contact with your skin where, hopefully, you'll be aware of an alien hand before your money disappears. One method is to wear a leather pouch hung around your neck and kept under a shirt or dress. If you do this, incorporate a length of old guitar string into the thong which goes around your neck (the D string should be thick enough). Many thieves carry scissors but few carry wire cutters.

Another method is to sew an invisible pocket inside the front of your trousers. Others prefer a money-belt. Ideally your passport should be in the same place but this isn't always possible as some are either too thick or too stiff. Wherever you decide to put your money, it's a good idea to enclose it in a plastic bag. Under a hot sun that pouch or pocket will get soaked with sweat – repeatedly – and your cash or cheques will end up looking like they've been through the laundry.

Money Transfers

If you run out of money while you're abroad and need more, ask your bank back home to send a draft to you (assuming you have money back home to send!). Make sure you specify the city and the bank branch. Transferred by cable or telex money should reach you within a few days. If you correspond by mail the process will take at least two weeks, often longer. Remember that some countries will only give you your money in local currency, and others will let you have it in US dollars or another hard currency. Find out what is possible before you request a transfer. You could lose a fair amount of money if there's an appreciable difference between the official and unofficial exchange rates. Kenya is probably the best place to transact this sort of business.

Bargaining

Many purchases involve some degree of bargaining. This is always the case with things bought from a market, street stall or craft shop. Bargaining may also be necessary for hotels and transport in some places, although these are often fairly standard and you won't be paying any more than the local people. Food and drink bought at restaurants don't usually involve any bargaining. The prices will be written on the menu.

Where bargaining is the name of the game, commodities are looked on as being worth what their owners can get for them. The concept of a fixed price would invoke laughter. If you cop out and pay the first price asked, you'll not only be considered a half-wit but you'll be doing your fellow travellers a disservice since this will create the impression that all travellers are equally stupid and are willing to pay outrageous prices. You are expected to bargain, it's part of the fun of going to Africa. All the same, no matter how good you are at it, you'll never get things as cheaply as local people do. To traders, hotel and café owners you represent wealth – whatever your appearance.

In most cases bargaining is conducted in a friendly, sometimes exaggeratedly extrovert manner, although there are occasions when it degenerates into a bleak exchange of numbers and leaden head-shakes. Decide what you want to pay or what others have told you they've paid, and start off at a price about 50% lower than this. The seller will inevitably start off at a higher price, sometimes up to 100% higher, than he or she is prepared to accept. This way you can both end up appearing to be generous. There will be times when you simply cannot get a shopkeeper to lower the prices to anywhere near what you know the product should be selling for. This probably means that a lot of tourists are passing through and if you don't pay those outrageous prices, some mug will. Don't lose your temper bargaining. If you get fed up, go home and come back the next day. Or go to a different shop.

BOOKS

You can walk into any decent bookshop in Europe, America or Australasia and find countless books on western and eastern history, culture, politics, economics, religion/philosophy, craft and anything else you care to name. Finding the same thing for Africa is much more difficult except where it relates to European or American history and much of that is pure ethnocentric rubbish clothed in the racist cliches of colonialism. Until recently, Africa was treated as a lost world full of Stone-Age savages and hardly worthy of scholastic inquiry. You would be even harder pressed to find a good selection of novels by contemporary African authors.

Yet such books do exist, although you need to be a sleuth to track them down outside Kenya and a few major cities in Europe and America.

General Books

There are some excellent but expensive hardbacks with many colour plates which you may prefer to look for in a library. They include *Journey though Kenya* by Mohammed Amin, Duncan Willets and Brian Tetley (Bodley Head 1982). There is a companion volume entitled *Journey through Tanzania* by the same authors and publisher.

Other colourful books on the region include *Africa Adorned* by Angela Fisher (Collins, 1984), *Ivory Crisis* by Ian Parker and Mohammed Amin (Chatto & Windus 1983), *Isak Dinesen's Africa* by various authors (Bantam Books, 1985), *Africa: A History of a Continent* by Basil Davidson (Weidenfield & Nicolson, 1966) and *Through Open Doors: A View of Asian Cultures in Kenya* by Cynthia Salvadori (Kenway Publications, Nairobi, 1983).

History

There are numerous books on the history of Africa starting with *The Penguin Atlas of African History* by Colin McEvedy (Penguin, 1980) and *A Short History of Africa* by Roland Oliver and J D Fage (Penguin, 1962). *The Story of Africa* is by Basil Davidson (Mitchell Beazley/Channel Four, 1984).

For the colonial period try *The Portuguese Period in East Africa* by Justus Strandes (East African Literature Bureau, 1961) or *How Europe Underdeveloped Africa* by Walter Rodney (Bogle L'Ouverture, 1976).

Worthwhile contemporary accounts include the extremely readable but rather discouraging *The Africans* by David Lamb (Vintage Books/Random Books, 1984). Or there's *The Making of Contemporary Africa* by Bill Freund (Indiana, 1984) and *A Year in the Death of Africa* by Peter Gill (Paladin, 1986). *Africa*

Review is an annual production by World Almanac Publications which gives you all the facts and figures and a brief update of recent events.

Other Books

Dian Fossey's research with the mountain gorillas of Rwanda is recounted in her book *Gorillas in the Mist* (Penguin, 1983). *The White Nile* by Alan Moorehead (Penguin, 1973) is a superbly evocative recounting of the exploration of the upper Nile.

Journey to the Jade Sea by John Hillaby (Paladin, 1974) recounts this redoubtable walker's epic trek to Lake Turkana in northern Kenya. Other books to look for include *Initiation* by J S Fontaine (Penguin, 1985), *A Bend in the River* by V S Naipaul (Penguin, 1979) and *Travels in the Congo* by Gide (Penguin, 1927).

Two women's accounts of life in East Africa earlier this century have been recent best sellers. *Out of Africa* by Karen Blixen (Isak Dinesen) is published by Penguin books and has also been made into a hugely popular movie. *West With the Night* by Beryl Markham (North Point Press) has also been a major best seller.

African Fiction

Heineman's African Writers Series probably has the greatest range of contemporary African authors. There's a list of their writers on the first page of each of their books. Two of Kenya's best authors are Ngũgĩ wa Thiongo and Meja Mwangiwhose and their books will introduce you to what's happening in East African literature at present. Titles worth reading by Ngũgĩ wa Thiongo include *Petals of Blood* (1977) and *A Grain of Wheat* (1967). Titles by Meja Mwangiwhose include *Going Down River Road, Kill me Quick* (1974) and *Carcass for Hounds* (1974). Ngũgĩ is considered dangerously subversive by the Kenyan Government and lives in exile in London yet, curiously, his books can be found for sale in any bookshop in Kenya!

Another author who is worth trying is Chinua Achebe, a Nigerian. Perhaps his most famous title is *Things Fall Apart* (1958).

Guidebooks

Africa on a Shoestring by Geoff Crowther (Lonely Planet, 1986) covers more than 50 African countries, concentrating on Practical information for budget travellers.

Durch Africa by Klaus & Erika Darr (Darr Publications) is in German. It's principally for travellers taking their own vehicles and covers a number of routes through Africa. *Insight Kenya* edited by Mohammed Amin and John Eames (APA Productions, 1985) is another of the popular coffee-table guidebook series with many excellent photographs.

Guide to Mt Kenya & Kilimanjaro edited by Iain Allan (Mountain Club of Kenya, Nairobi, 1981) has been written and added to over the years by dedicated enthusiasts. What isn't in this book isn't worth knowing. It contains trail descriptions, maps, photographs, descriptions of fauna and flora, climate and geology, even mountain medicine. It's a must for anyone thinking of spending some time in Kenya or Tanzania. Pick up your copy from the club's HQ at Wilson Airport, Nairobi, or from PO Box 45741, Nairobi.

Field Guides

A Field Guide to the Larger Animals of Africa by Jean Dorst and Pierre Dandelot (Collins, 1970) together with *A Field Guide to the Birds of East Africa* by J G Williams and N Arlott (Collins, 1963) should suffice for most people's purposes in the national parks and wildlife reserves.

MAPS

Most travellers take the Michelin map *Southern Africa* (No 155) to East Africa. It's usually fairly accurate and certainly better than the Bartholomew's map of the same area. Nevertheless, you shouldn't rely on it too much for detail in Eastern Zaïre or on the borders between Zaïre and Rwanda or Burundi.

There are other maps which some travellers say are better than the Michelin series. One which has often been recommended is the Freytag & Berndt map of *East Africa* (1:2,000,000) which is published in four languages and includes rainfall averages and a distance chart. It's available throughout Europe and perhaps in America, too. Another is the *East Africa/Ostafrika* (1:2,000,000) published by Ravenstein which is also a very good, detailed map.

HEALTH

Two useful books are *The Traveller's Health Guide* by Dr A C Turner (Lascelles, London) and *Preservation of Personal Health in Warm Climates* published by the Ross Institute of Tropical Hygiene, Keppel St, London WC1. Another helpful book on health is David Werner's *Where There is No Doctor: a village health care handbook* (Macmillan Press, London).

Vaccinations

Before you're allowed to enter most African countries you must have a valid International Vaccination Card as proof that you're not the carrier of some new and exotic plague. The essential vaccinations are cholera (valid for six months) and yellow fever (valid for 10 years). In addition, you're strongly advised to be vaccinated against typhoid (valid for one year), tetanus (valid for five to 10 years), tuberculosis (valid for life) and polio (valid for life). Gamma globulin shots are also available for protection against infectious hepatitis (Type A) but they are ineffective against serum hepatitis (Type B). Protection lasts three to six months. There is a vaccine available for Type B but it's only recommended for individuals at high risk. It's expensive, and the series of three injections takes six months to complete.

You need to plan ahead for these vaccinations, as they cannot all be given at once and typhoid requires a second injection about two or three weeks after the first. Cholera and typhoid jabs usually leave you with a stiff and sore arm for two days afterwards if you've never had them before. The others generally don't have any effect. Tetanus requires a course of three injections.

If your vaccination card expires whilst you're away, there are a number of medical centres in African cities where you can be re-vaccinated. There's usually a small fee for these but sometimes they are free. The centres that we know of are listed in the chapters on the respective countries.

Avoid turning up at borders with expired vaccination cards, as officials may insist on you having the relevant injection before they will let you in and the same needle may be used on a whole host of people.

Your local physician will arrange a course of injections for you or in most large cities there are vaccination centres which you can find in the telephone book:

Belgium
    Ministere de la Santé Publique et de la Famille, Cité Administrative de l'Etat, Quartier de l'Esplanade, 1000 Brussels
    Centre Médical du Ministere des Affaires Etrangeres, 9 Rue Brederode, 1000 Brussels
France
    Direction Départmentale d'Action Sanitaire et Sociale, 57 Boulevard de Sevastopol, 75001 Paris (tel 508 9690)
    Institut Pasteur, 25 Rue du Docteur Roux, 75015 Paris (tel 566 5800)
Holland
    Any GGD office or the Academical Medical Centre, Amsterdam.
Switzerland
    L'Institut d'Hygiene, 2 Quai du Cheval Blanc, 1200 Geneva (tel 022-43 8075)
United Kingdom
    Hospital for Tropical Diseases, 4 St Pancras Way, London, NW1 (tel 01 387 4411). Injections here are free but they're often booked up about a month ahead.

West London Designated Vaccination Centre, 53 Great Cumberland Place, London W1 (tel 01 262 6456). No appointment is necessary; the fees vary depending on the vaccine.

British Airways Immunisation Centre, Victoria Terminal, Buckingham Palace Rd, London, SW1 (tel 01 834 2323). Try to book a few days in advance, or you might have to wait around for a few hours before they can fit you in.

British Airways Medical Centre, Speedbird House, Heathrow Airport, Hounslow, Middlesex (tel 01 759 5511).

Medical Insurance

Get some! You may never need it, but if you do you'll be very glad to have it. Medical treatment in East Africa is not free and public hospitals are often very crowded. Don't expect the same quality of medical treatment in an East African public hospital as you get back home either. There are many different travel insurance policies available and any travel agent will be able to recommend one.

Before you choose one collect several different policies and read through them for an hour or two, as the cost of a policy and the sort of cover offer can vary considerably. Many pitch themselves at the family package tour market and are not really appropriate for a long spell in Africa under your own steam. Usually medical insurance comes in a package which includes baggage insurance and life insurance, etc. You need to read through the baggage section carefully as many policies put a ceiling on how much they are prepared to pay for individual items which are lost or stolen.

General Health

Get your teeth checked and treated if necessary before you set off. Dentists are few and far between in Africa and treatment is expensive.

The main things which are likely to affect your general health while you're abroad are diet and climate. Cheap food from cafés and street stands tends to be overcooked, very starchy (mainly maize and millet) and lacking in protein, vitamins and calcium. Supplement your diet with milk or yogurt (where it's available and pasteurised) and fresh fruit or vitamin/mineral tablets. Avoid untreated milk and milk products – in many countries herds are not screened for brucellosis or tuberculosis. Peel all fruit. Read up on dietary requirements before you set off. And watch out for grit in rice and bread – a hard bite on the wrong thing can lead to a cracked tooth.

In hot climates you sweat a great deal and lose a lot of water and salt. Make sure you drink sufficient liquid and have enough salt in your food to make good the losses (a teaspoon of salt per day is generally sufficient). If you don't make good the losses, you run the risk of suffering from heat exhaustion and cramps. Heat can also make you impatient and irritable. Try to take things at a slower pace. Hot, dry air will make your hair brittle, so oil it often with, say, refined coconut oil. Take great care of cuts, grazes and skin infections otherwise they tend to persist and get worse. Clean them well with antiseptic or mercurochrome. If they're weeping, bandage them up since open sores attract flies. Change bandages daily and use an antibiotic powder if necessary.

A temporary but troublesome skin condition from which many people from temperate climates suffer initially is prickly heat. Many tiny blisters form on one or more parts of your body – usually where the skin is thickest, such as your hands. They are sweat droplets which are trapped under your skin because your pores aren't large enough or haven't opened up sufficiently to cope with the greater volume of sweat. Anything which promotes sweating – exercise, tea, coffee, alcohol – makes it worse. Keep your skin aired and dry, reduce clothing to a loose-fitting minimum and keep out of direct sunlight. Calamine lotion or zinc oxide-based talcum powder helps to soothe the skin. Apart from that, there isn't much else you can do. The problem is one of acclimatisation and shouldn't persist more than a few days.

Adjustment to the outlook, habits and social customs of different people can take a lot out of you too. Many travellers suffer from some degree of culture shock. This is particularly true if you fly direct from your own country to an African city. Under these conditions, heat can aggravate petty irritations which would pass unnoticed in a more temperate climate. Exhausting all-night, all-day bus journeys over bad roads don't help if you're feeling this way. Make sure you get enough sleep.

Drinking Water

Avoid drinking unboiled water anywhere it's not chlorinated, unless you're taking it from a mountain spring. Unboiled water is a major source of diarrhoea and hepatitis, as are salads that have been washed in contaminated water and unpeeled fruit that has been handled by someone with one of these infections.

Avoiding contaminated water is easier said than done, especially in the desert and in parts of Zaïre, and it may be that you'll have to drink water regardless of where it came from. This is part of travelling and there is no way you can eliminate all risks. Carrying a water bottle and a supply of water-purifying tablets is one way around this. Halazone, Potable Aqua and Sterotabs are all good for purifying water but they have little or no effect against amoebas or hepatitis virus. For this you need a 2% tincture of iodine – five drops per litre in clear water and 10 drops per litre in cloudy water. Wait 30 minutes and it's safe to drink.

Malaria

Malaria is caused by a blood parasite which is spread by certain species of night-flying mosquito (anopheles). Only the female insects spread the disease but you can contract it through a single bite from an insect carrying the parasite. Start on a course of anti-malarials before you start and keep it up as you travel.

The drugs are fairly cheap in some place but horrendously expensive in others – the USA and Scandinavia in particular. There are basically two types: Proguanil (or Paludrine) which you take daily and Chloroquine which you take once or twice per week (depending on its strength). Both are marketed under various trade names. In some areas of Africa the parasite is beginning to acquire immunity to some of the drugs. This is particularly true in East and Central Africa. Here you will need to take Maloprim in addition to Chloroquine. You would be very unlucky to contract malaria if you are taking one or more of these drugs but they are not a 100% guarantee.

If you do develop malarial symptoms – high fever, severe headaches, shivering – and are not within reach of medical advice, the treatment is one single dose of four tablets (600 mg) of Chloroquine followed by two tablets (300 mg) six hours later and two tablets on each following day. As an alternative (or in Chloroquine-resistant areas) take a single dose of three tablets of Fansidar.

Other than the malaria hazard, mosquito bites can be troublesome and although it's probably useless to say this, *don't scratch the bites*. If you do, and they don't heal quickly, there's a chance of them becoming infected with something else. You'll come across people in Africa pock-marked with angry sores which started out as insignificant mosquito bites – the owners couldn't resist the urge to scratch them. Don't join them. Will-power works wonders, as does antihistamine cream. To keep the mosquitoes off at night, use an insect repellent or sleep under a fan. Mosquitoes don't like swift-moving currents of air and will stay on the walls of the room in these circumstances.

There is not yet a vaccination against malaria. Take those pills.

Bilharzia

This is caused by blood flukes (minute worms) which live in the veins of the bladder or the large intestine. The eggs which the adult worms produce are discharged in urine or faeces. If they reach water, they hatch out and enter the bodies of a certain species of fresh-water snails where they multiply for four or more weeks and are then discharged into the surrounding water. If they are to live, they must find and invade the body of a human being where they develop, mate and then make their way to the veins of their choice. Here they start to lay eggs and the cycle repeats itself. The snail favours shallow water near the shores of lakes and streams and they are more abundant in water which is polluted by human excrement. They particularly like reedy areas. Generally speaking, moving water contains less risk than stagnant water but you can never tell.

Bilharzia is quite a common disease in Africa so stay out of rivers and lakes. If you drink water from any of these places, boil it or sterilise it with chlorine tablets. The disease is painful and causes persistent and cumulative damage by repeated deposits of eggs. If you suspect you have it, seek medical advice as soon as possible – look for blood in your urine or faeces that isn't associated with diarrhoea. The only body of water in Africa which is largely free of bilharzia is Lake Malawi. Keep out of lakes Victoria, Tanganyika, Mobutu Sese Seko, Edward (Idi Amin) and Kivu and the River Nile. As the intermediate hosts (snails) live only in fresh water, there's no risk of catching bilharzia in the sea.

Trypanosomiasis (Sleeping Sickness)

This is another disease transmitted by biting insects, in this case by the tsetse fly. Like malaria, it's caused by minute parasites which live in the blood. The risk of infection is very small and confined to areas which are only a fraction of the total area inhabited by the tsetse fly. The flies are only found south of the Sahara but the disease is responsible for the absence of horses and cattle from large tracts of central Africa particularly central and eastern Tanzania.

The fly is about twice the size of a common housefly and recognisable from the scissor-like way it folds its wings while at rest. The disease is characterised by irregular fevers, abscesses, local oedema (puffy swellings caused by excess water retained in body tissues), inflammation of the glands and physical and mental lethargy. It responds well to treatment.

Yellow Fever

Yellow fever is endemic in much of Africa. Get that vaccination before you set off and you won't have to worry about it.

Hepatitis

Hepatitis is a liver disease caused by a virus. There are basically two types – infectious hepatitis (known as Type A) and serum hepatitis (known as Type B). The one you're most likely to contract is Type A. It's very contagious and you pick it up by drinking water, eating food or using cutlery or crockery that's been contaminated by an infected person. Foods to avoid are salads (unless you know they have been washed thoroughly in purified water) and unpeeled fruit that may have been handled by someone with dirty hands. It's also possible to pick it up by sharing a towel or toothbrush with an infected person.

An estimated 10% of the population of the Third World are healthy carriers of Type B but the only ways you can contract this form are by having sex with an infected person or by being injected with a needle which has previously been used on an infected person.

Symptoms appear 15 to 50 days after infection (generally around 25 days) and consist of fever, loss of appetite, nausea, depression, complete lack of energy and pains around the base of your rib cage. Your skin will turn progressively yellow and the whites of your eyes yellow to orange. The easiest way to keep an eye on the situation is to watch the colour of your eyes and urine. If you have hepatitis, the colour of your urine will be deep orange no matter how much liquid you've drunk. If you haven't drunk much liquid and/or you're sweating a lot, don't jump to conclusions. Check it out by drinking a lot of liquid all at once. If the urine is still orange then you'd better start making plans to go somewhere you won't mind convalescing for a few weeks. Sometimes the disease lasts only a few weeks and you only get a few really bad days, but it can last for months. If it does get really bad, cash in that medical insurance you took out and fly back home.

There is no cure as such for hepatitis except rest and good food. Diets high in B vitamins are said to help. Fat-free diets have gone out of medical fashion, but you may find that grease and oil make you feel nauseous. Seeking medical attention is probably a waste of time and money although you are going to need a medical certificate for your insurance company if you decide to fly home. There's nothing doctors can do for you that you can't do for yourself other than run tests that will tell you how bad it is. Most people don't need telling; they can feel it! Wipe alcohol and cigarettes right off the slate. They'll not only make you feel much worse, but alcohol and nicotine can do permanent damage to a sick liver.

Think seriously about getting that gamma globulin vaccination.

Diarrhoea

Sooner or later most travellers get diarrhoea, so you may as well accept the inevitable. You can't really expect to travel halfway around the world without succumbing to diarrhoea at least once or twice, but it doesn't always mean that you've caught a bug. Depending on how much travelling you've done and what your guts are used to, it can be merely the result of a change of food. If you've spent all your life living out of sterilised, cellophane-wrapped packets and tins from the local supermarket, you're going to have a hard time until you adjust.

If and when you get a gut infection, avoid rushing off to the chemist and filling yourself with antibiotics. It's a harsh way to treat your system and you can build up a tolerance to them with over-use. Try to starve the bugs out first. Eat nothing and rest. Avoid travelling. Drink plenty of fluids. Have your tea with a little sugar and no milk. Diarrhoea will dehydrate you and may result in painful muscular cramps in your guts. The cramps are due to a bad salt balance in your blood, so take a small amount of salt with your tea. If you can find it, tincture of opium (known as 'paregoric' and often mixed with kaolin – a stronger version of Milk of Magnesia) will relieve the pain of cramps. Something else you may come across, called RD Sol, also helps to maintain a correct salt balance and so prevent cramps. It's a mixture of common salt, sodium bicarbonate, potassium chloride and dextrose. Two days of this regime should clear you out.

If you simply can't hack starving, keep to a *light* diet of curd, yogurt, toast, dry biscuits, rice and tea. Stay away from butter, milk, sugar, cakes and fruit.

If starving doesn't work or you really have to move on and can't rest for a couple of days, try Pesulin (or Pesulin-O which is the same but with the addition of a tincture of opium). The dosage is two teaspoons four times daily for five days. Or try Lomotil – the dosage is two tabs three times daily for two days. Avoid over-use of Lomotil.

If you have no luck with either of these, change to antibiotics or see a doctor. There are many different varieties of antibiotics and you almost need to be a biochemist to know what the differences between them are. They include tetracycline, chlorostep, typhstrep, sulphatriad, streptomagma and thiazole. If possible, have a word with the chemist about their differences. Over-use will do you more harm than good but you must complete the course otherwise the infection may return and then you'll have even more difficulty getting rid of it.

Dysentery

Dysentery is, unfortunately, quite prevalent in some places. It's characterised by diarrhoea containing blood and lots of mucus, and painful gut cramps. There are two types. Bacillary dysentery is short, sharp and nasty but rarely persistent – it's the most common variety. Amoebic dysentery is, as its name suggests, caused by amoebic parasites. This variety is much more difficult to treat and often persistent.

Bacillic dysentery comes on suddenly and lays you out with fever, nausea, painful cramps and diarrhoea but, because it's caused by bacteria, responds well to antibiotics. Amoebic dysentery builds up more slowly and is more dangerous. You cannot starve it out and if it's untreated it will get worse and permanently damage your intestines. If you see blood in your faeces persistently over two or three days, seek medical attention as soon as possible.

Flagyl (metronidazole) is the most commonly prescribed drug for amoebic dysentery. The dosage is six tablets per day for five to seven days. Flagyl is both an antibiotic and an anti-parasitic as well. It is also used for the treatment of giardia and trichomoniasis. Flagyl should not be taken by pregnant women. If you get bacillic dysentery, the best thing for slowing down intestinal movements is codeine phosphate (30-mg tablets – take two once every four hours). It's much more effective than Lomotil or Imodium and cheaper. Treatment for bacillic dysentery consists of a course of tetracycline or bactrim (antibiotics).

Giardia

Giardia is prevalent in tropical climates and is characterised by swelling of the stomach, pale-coloured faeces, diarrhoea and, after a while, depression and sometimes nausea. Many doctors recommend Flagyl – seven 250 mg doses over a three-day period should clear up the symptoms, repeated a week later if not. Flagyl, however, has many side effects and some doctors prefer to treat giardia with Tinaba (tinadozole). Two grams taken all at once normally knocks it right out but if not you can repeat the dosage for up to three days.

AIDS

AIDS, also known as 'Slim' in East Africa, is prevalent in Uganda, Rwanda, Burundi and Eastern Zaïre, although less so in Kenya and Tanzania. Most of those who have it are not aware of the fact, and hospitals (if they ever get to them) are likely to diagnose their symptoms as something more mundane. The obvious way to pick it up is to have sex with someone who has the disease. The obvious way to avoid it is to be celibate. Not everyone can do this so if you do have sex make sure you cut the risk as far as you can by using condoms. You are still a long way from 100% safe if you do this.

There are two other ways you can pick it up. The first is if you need a blood transfusion. Blood donors in East Africa are rarely screened for AIDS and if you receive blood from an infected donor you will be exposed to the virus. Your options are probably limited if you get into the sort of strife which requires a transfusion. It is also possible to pick up the virus if you are injected with an unsterilised needle. If you do have an injection in Africa try to ensure the needle is either new or properly sterilised.

Tropical Ulcers

These are sores which often start from some insignificant scratch or blister which doesn't seem to heal up. They often get worse and spread to other areas of the body and they can be quite painful. If you keep clean and look after any sores which you get on your arms and legs (from ill-fitting shoes, accidents to your feet, or from excessive scratching of insect bites) then it's unlikely you will be troubled by them. If you do develop sores which won't clear up then you need to hit the antibiotics quickly. Don't let them spread.

Fellow Travellers

Unwanted passengers you're likely to come across are fleas, lice and bed bugs. There isn't a lot you can do about fleas. They vary considerably in numbers from one season to another; some places have a lot, others none at all. The less money you pay for a bed or a meal, the more likely you are to encounter them.

You can generally avoid lice by washing yourself and your clothes frequently. You're most likely to pick them up in crowded places like buses and trains, but you might also get them by staying in very cheap hotels. You'll occasionally meet tribespeople whose hair is so matted and so unwashed that it's literally crawling with lice. However, it takes a while for lice to get stuck into you so you should get a companion to have a look through your hair about once a week to see if you've acquired any eggs. They are always laid near the base of the hairs. If you find any, you can either pick them out one by one (very laborious) or blitz them with insecticide shampoo like Lorexane or Suleo. We've had letters from people who have doused their hair in petrol or DDT. You're certainly guaranteed total wipe-out this way but it does seem mildly hysterical!

With luck you won't come across bed bugs too often. These evil little bastards live in the crevices of walls and the framework of beds where they hide during the day. They look like lice but they move like greased lightning once you become aware of their presence and switch on the light to see what's happening. Look for tell-tale bloodstains on the walls near beds in budget hotels. If you see them, find another hotel.

Don't Panic

This section might seem long and off-putting. It isn't meant to be. Most travellers arrive healthy and leave even healthier. If you do pick up something, however, it's useful to know what to do about it.

POST

Have letters sent to you c/o Poste Restante, GPO, in whatever city/town you will be passing through. Alternatively you can use the mail-holding service operated by American Express offices and their agents if you have their cheques or one of their credit cards. Most embassies no longer hold mail and will forward it to the nearest poste restante. Plan ahead. It can take up to two weeks for a letter to arrive even in capital cities and it sometimes takes much longer in smaller places.

The majority of poste restantes are pretty reliable though there are exceptions. Mail is generally held for four weeks – sometimes more, sometimes less – after which it is returned to sender. The service is free in most places but in others, particularly ex-Belgian colonies, there is a small charge for each letter collected. As a rule you need your passport as proof of identity. In large places where there's a lot of traffic the letters are generally sorted into alphabetical order, but in smaller places they may all be lumped together in the one box. Sometimes you're allowed to sort through them yourself; sometimes a post office employee will do the sorting for you.

If you're not receiving expected letters, ask them to check under every conceivable combination of your given name, surname, any other initials and even under 'M' (for Mr, Ms, Miss, Mrs). This sort of confusion isn't as widespread as many people believe, though most travellers have an improbable story to tell about it. If there is confusion, it's generally because of bad handwriting on the envelope or language difficulties. If you want to make absolutely sure that the fault won't be yours, have friends address letters with your surname in block capitals and even underlined.

Avoid sending currency notes through the post. They'll often be stolen by post office employees no matter how cleverly you disguise the contents. There are all sorts of ways of finding out whether a letter is worth opening up. Still, some people do still successfully get cash sent through the mail.

When sending letters yourself, try to use aerograms (air letters) rather than ordinary letters. If you send stamped letters it's sometimes necessary to ensure the stamps are franked in front of you. There's a chance that unfranked stamps will be steamed off, re-sold and the letter thrown away. Having said that, I've posted ordinary letters, parcels and postcards back home from all the countries which are covered in this book and all of them have arrived – and not all of them were franked in front of me.

There's little point in having any letter sent by Express Delivery (called Special Delivery in the UK), as they won't get there any quicker, on average, than an air letter.

ACCOMMODATION

Except in Burundi and Rwanda where options for cheap accommodation are very limited, you can usually find somewhere cheap to stay, even in the smallest towns. Options range from a wide choice of budget hotels, youth hostels (Kenya only), religious missions and Sikh temples, to campsites. Some of these places (religious missions and Sikh temples) may be free but, if they are, please leave a donation otherwise it won't be long before they no longer welcome travellers – as has happened in other parts of Africa.

In budget hotels what you get depends largely on what you pay for although, in general, they're good value. You can certainly expect clean sheets and showers in all of them, but you don't always get a fan or mosquito net and, if you're paying rock-bottom prices, the showers will be cold. Pay a little more and you can expect hot showers. Very cheap hotels often double as brothels (or sperm palaces, as an American companion was fond of calling them) but so do many other more expensive hotels. If you're not used to that familiar crescendo of groans and sighs filtering through thin walls, you soon will be.

Theft from hotel rooms generally isn't a problem, although only a fool would tempt fate by leaving money and other valuables lying around unattended for hours at a time. If a place looks safe, it generally is. Check door locks and the design of keys. Many cheap hotels in Kenya also have a full-time doorman and even a locked grille and they won't let anyone in who is not staying there. Obviously, you need to take care in dormitory-type accommodation since you can't lock anything up (unless there are lockers). All in all, the chances of you being mugged in a dark alley at night in a dubious part of a city or along a deserted stretch of beach are far greater than having your gear stolen from a hotel room.

There are campsites of a sort all over East Africa but they vary tremendously in what facilities they offer. Some are nothing more than a patch of dirt without even a tap. Others are purpose-built. Where there's nothing, religious missions will often allow you to camp in their compounds – usually for a small fee. Don't simply camp out in the bush or on a patch of waste land in a town or city, however. You are asking for problems and if you leave your tent unattended, there'll be nothing left in it when you get back. In remote small villages, ask permission first from the village elder or chief.

WHAT TO BRING

Take the minimum possible. An overweight bag will become a nightmare. A rucksack/backpack is preferable to an overnight bag since it will stand up to rougher treatment and is easier to carry. Choose a pack which will take some rough handling – overland travel destroys packs rapidly. Make sure the straps and buckles are well sewn on and strengthened if necessary before you set off. Whether you take a pack with or without a frame is up to you but there are some excellent packs on the market with internal frames (eg Berghaus). Probably the best stockists in Britain are the YHA Adventure Centre, 14 Southampton St, London WC2 (tel 01 836 8541). Take a strong plastic bag with you that will completely enclose the pack. Use it on dusty journeys whether your pack is in the luggage compartment of a bus or strapped onto the roof. If you don't, you'll be shaking dust out of your pack for the next week.

A sleeping bag is more or less essential. Deserts get very cold at night and, if you'll be visiting mountainous areas, you'll need one there as well. You'll also be glad of it on long bus or train journeys as a supplement to the wooden seats or sacks of potatoes. A sheet sleeping bag – similar to the ones used in youth hostels – is also good when it is too hot to use a normal bag. It's cool and keeps the mosquitoes off your body. It also means you don't have to use hotel sheets if they look dubious.

Take clothes for both hot and cold climates, including at least one good sweater for use at night in the mountains and the desert. Gloves and a woolly hat are very useful if you are planning on climbing mountains. You needn't go overboard however, and take everything in your wardrobe. Things like T-shirts, cotton shirts and sandals are very cheap in most places and it's usually more economical to buy these things along the way.

In some places, Tanzania for example,

it's prohibited to wear clothes that reveal large areas of your body. This includes shorts, short skirts and see-through garments. The rules are relaxed at beach resorts of course. It's inadvisable for women to wear anything short or overly revealing in Muslim areas (the coastal areas of Kenya and Tanzania and the Comoros Islands) otherwise they may well come in for a lot of hassling by local men or youths. Muslim women in these areas all wear the *bui bui* (the equivalent of the *chador* or *burqa* in other Muslim countries) though, in East Africa, it doesn't cover the face and is worn with considerably more panache.

Some people take a small tent and a portable stove. These can be very useful and save you a small fortune, but they do add considerably to the weight of your pack. Camping equipment can be rented in several places in Kenya and in Arusha (Tanzania).

Don't forget the small essentials: a combination pocket knife or Swiss Army knife, needle and cotton and a small pair of scissors, pair of sunglasses, towel and tooth brushes, oral contraceptives, tampons and one or two good novels. Most toiletries – toilet paper, toothpaste, shaving cream, shampoo, suntan lotion, etc – are available in capital cities and large towns, except in Uganda where there's hardly anything. A water bottle (fabric covered) is very useful when it's hot or for walking in the mountains. It also enables you to give those dubious water holes a miss and so cut down your chances of getting hepatitis.

TRAVELLING COMPANIONS

Travelling overland is rarely a solo activity unless you want it that way. Even if you set off travelling alone you'll quickly meet other travellers who are heading in the some direction, as well as others who are returning. Crossroads where travellers congregate are good places to meet other people and team up with someone. The best are Arusha, Dar es Salaam, Lamu, Malindi, Mombasa, Nairobi and Zanzibar.

If you'd prefer to find someone before you set off, check the classified advertisements in national newspapers or the notice-boards at colleges and universities before the summer holidays come up. If you're in London, England, very good places to look are *Time Out, TNT* magazine and the notice-board at *Trailfinders*, 48 Earls Court Rd, London, W8. In New York, USA, try the New York Student Centre, Hotel Empire, Broadway and 63rd St (tel 212 695 0291), or get hold of something like the *Village Voice*. The *Lonely Planet Newsletter* also sometimes carries travel companion notices.

LANGUAGE

You will be able to get by in most of East Africa if you can speak English and French – English for Kenya, Tanzania and Uganda and French for Burundi, the Comoros Islands, Rwanda and Eastern Zaïre.

It helps a lot, however, to have a working knowledge of Swahili which is rapidly becoming the *lingua franca* of much of Kenya and Tanzania and is even useful in parts of Uganda and Eastern Zaïre. This is especially so in the rural areas where the local people may only have a smattering of education, if any, and are unlikely to be able to speak any English or French. Local people will always warm to any attempt to speak their language no matter how botched the effort.

There are scores of tribal languages spoken only in certain areas. Any particular one may be totally unintelligible even to a tribesperson from a neighbouring tribe. It's unlikely you will have time to pick up too much of these while you're travelling, but phrase books do exist if you are interested. The best place to find them is in the bookshops of Nairobi. A *Swahili Phrasebook* by Robert Leonard is in the works to join the Lonely Planet language survival kit series.

SWAHILI
Pronunciation

Vowel pronunciation is as follows:

a is pronounced like the 'a' sound in 'father'.
e is pronounced like the 'e' sound in 'better'.
i is pronounced like the 'ee' sound in 'bee'.
o is pronounced like the 'a' sound in 'law'.
u is pronounced like the 'oo' sound in 'too'.

Double vowels, or any two vowels together, are pronounced as two separate syllables. Thus *saa* (time/hour) is pronounced 'sa-a', and *yai* (egg) is pronounced 'ya-i'. There are no diphthongs as in English.

General rules

Swahili is a prefixed language; adjectives change prefix according to the number and class of the noun. Thus *mzuri, wazuri, vizuri* and *kizuri* are different forms of the word 'good.'

Verbs use a pronoun prefix:

I	*ni*
you	*u*
he/she	*a*
we	*tu*
you	*m*
they	*wa*

and a tense prefix:

present	*na*
past	*li*
future	*ta*
infinitive	*ku*

giving you:

We are going to Moshi.
    Tunakwenda Moshi.
Shall I take a picture?
    Nitapiga picha?

Juma spoke much.
   Juma alisema sana.

Useful Words

hello*	*jambo* or *salama*
welcome	*karibu*
thank you	*asante*
thanks very much	*asante sana*
how are you?	*habari?*
I'm fine, thanks	*mzuri*
what's your name?	*unaitwa nani?*
it is ...	*ninaitwa ...*
how was the journey?	*habari ya safari?*
goodbye	*kwaheri*
yes	*ndiyo*
no	*hapana*
how much/ how many?	*ngapi*
money	*pesa*
where?	*wapi*
today	*leo*
tomorrow	*kesho*
guest house	*nyumba ya wageni*
toilet	*choo*
eat	*kula*
sleep	*lala*
want	*taka*
come from	*toka*
is	*ni*
there is	*kuna*
there isn't	*hakuna*
white people	*wazungu*

* There is also a respectful greeting used for elders: *shikamoo*. The reply is *marahaba*.

Food

food	*chakula*
rice	*mchele*
bananas	*ndizi*
bread	*mkate*
vegetables	*mboga*
water	*maji*
salt	*chumvi*
meat	*nyama*
goat	*mbuzi*
beef	*ng'ombe*
chicken	*kuku*
fish	*samaki*
egg(s)	*(ma)yai*
milk	*maziwa*

Numerals

1	*moja*
2	*mbili*
3	*tatu*
4	*nne*
5	*tano*
6	*sita*
7	*saba*
8	*nane*
9	*tisa*
10	*kumi*
11	*kumi na moja*
20	*ishirini*
30	*thelathini*
40	*arobaini*
50	*hamsini*
60	*sitini*
70	*sabini*
80	*themanini*
90	*tisini*
100	*mia*
½	*nusu*

Getting There

Many travellers get to East Africa overland as part of a much lengthier journey through the continent. Due to the civil war in Sudan, however, it is no longer possible to go overland down the Nile valley between Egypt and either Uganda or Kenya. The furthest you will get coming down from the north is Khartoum. From there to Kenya or Uganda you will have to fly. This means that there are only two overland routes open at present – the one from Zaire into Burundi, Rwanda or Uganda and the one from Zambia or Malawi into Tanzania.

Flights from Cairo to Nairobi are not at all cheap, count on US$350 one-way. This is almost as much as a one-way London-Nairobi ticket bought in the UK with a possible stop-over in Cairo! A Khartoum-Nairobi ticket would be cheaper but not by a large margin. There's no advantage, either, in going first to Juba (the only major southern Sudan city in government hands) since you'll have to both fly in and fly out again.

Trying to find a passage on a ship to Africa these days is virtually a waste of time. There are no regular passenger services and you won't get onto a freight ship without a seaman's ticket.

AIR

Unless you are coming overland, flying is just about the only – and the most convenient – way of getting to East Africa. Nairobi is the main hub for flights and the route you are most likely to get a relatively cheap ticket on.

Buying an ordinary economy-class ticket is not the most economical way to go, although it does give you maximum flexibility and the ticket is valid for 12 months.

Students and those under 26 can often get discounted tickets so it's worth checking first with a student travel bureau to see if there is anything on offer. Another option is an APEX (advanced purchase excursion ticket) which is usually between 30 and 40% cheaper than the full economy fare although it does have restrictions. You must purchase your ticket at least 21 days in advance (sometimes more) and you must stay away for a minimum period (usually 14 days) and return within 180 days (sometimes less). The main disadvantage is that stop-overs are not allowed and if you have to change your dates of travel or destination then there will be extra charges to pay. Standby fares are another possibility. Some airlines will let you travel at the last minute if there are seats available just before departure. These tickets cost less than the economy fare but are usually not as cheap as APEX fares.

Of all the options, however, the cheapest way to go is via the so-called 'bucket shops'. These are travel agents who sell discounted tickets. Airlines only sell a certain percentage of their tickets through bucket shops so the availability of seats can vary widely, particularly in the high season. You have to be flexible with these tickets although if the agents are sold out for one flight they can generally offer you something similar in the near future.

Most of the bucket shops are reputable organisations but there is always the occasional fly-by-night operator who sets up shop, takes your money for a bargain-basement ticket and then either disappears or issues you with an invalid or unusable ticket. Check carefully what you are buying before you hand over money although I've used bucket shops for years and been handed the most weird and wonderful tickets – for example, tickets issued in East Berlin but bought in London for a flight from London to

Malaysia with stop-overs in New Delhi, Bangkok and Kuala Lumpur. They've all been sweet.

Bucket shops generally advertise in newspapers and magazines and there's a lot of competition and different routes available so it's best to telephone first and then rush round if they have what you want. In Europe, the market for these sort of tickets to American and Asian destinations has been well developed over many years, but little has been available to African destinations south of the Sahara until fairly recently. Fares are becoming more flexible but the options are still limited. Luckily, Nairobi is one of the few destinations that does have plenty of options.

FROM NORTH AMERICA

In the USA, the best way to find cheap flights is by checking the Sunday travel sections in the major newspapers such as *The Los Angeles Times* or *San Francisco Examiner-Chronicle* on the west coast and *The New York Times* on the east coast. The student travel bureaus are also worth trying – STA or Council Travel.

North America is a relative newcomer to the bucket shop traditions of Europe and Asia so ticket availability and the restrictions attached to them need to be weighed against what is on offer on the more normal APEX or full economy price tickets.

It may well be cheaper in the long run to fly first to London from the east coast of the USA using Virgin Atlantic (for around US$225 one-way or US$560 return), or standby on the other airlines for a little more, and then buy a bucket shop ticket from there to East Africa with or without stop-overs. But you must do your homework to be sure of this. All the main magazines which specialise in bucket shop advertisements in London will mail you copies so you can study current prices before you decide on a course of action.

FROM EUROPE

You can find bucket shops by the dozen in London, Paris, Amsterdam, Brussels, Frankfurt and a few other places too. In London, there are several magazines with lots of bucket shop ads which will give you a good idea of current fares:

Trailfinder is a paper put out quarterly by Trailfinders (tel 01-603 1515 from 9 am to 6 pm), 42-48 Earls Court Rd, London W8 6EJ. It's free if you pick it up in London but if you want it mailed it costs £6 for four issues in the UK or Eire and £10 or the equivalent for four issues in Europe or elsewhere in the world (airmail). Trailfinders can fix you up with all your ticketing requirements. They've been in business for years and can be highly recommended.

Time Out (tel 01 836 4411), Tower House, Southampton St, London WC2E 7HD is London's weekly entertainment guide and it's available from all bookshops and newsagents. Subscription enquiries should be addressed to Time Out Subs, Unit 8 Grove Ash, Bletchley, Milton Keynes MK1 1BZ, UK.

TNT Magazine (tel 01 937 3985), 52 Earls Court Rd, London W8 is a free magazine which you can pick up from most London underground stations and though the news it carries is oriented towards Australians and New Zealanders living in the UK, it carries pages of travel advertising.

In these magazines you will come across fares from London to Nairobi for as little as £190 one-way and £330 return. Most of them use Aeroflot and other Eastern European and Middle Eastern airlines. There is no advantage in buying a one-way ticket to Nairobi and then another one-way ticket back to Europe from there. You'll end up paying more than buying a return ticket in the first place. The cheapest one-way tickets from Nairobi to various northern European cities is Sh 4600 which equals about US$285 or £190, *but* in order to buy them you have to produce bank receipts for the value of a full economy class ticket or pay in hard currency.

Don't take the advertised fares as gospel truth. To comply with truth in advertising laws UK companies must be able to offer *some* tickets at their cheapest quoted price but they might only have one or two of them each week. If you are not one of the lucky ones, you may find yourself looking at tickets which cost up to £50 more (one-way or return). The best thing to do, therefore, is to start looking into tickets well before your intended departure date so you have a very good idea what is available.

Flights from Europe to Uganda, Tanzania, Rwanda or Burundi will generally be more expensive than to Kenya.

If you are starting from France or don't mind going there first then it's worth checking out Point Air-Mulhouse (popularly known by travellers as 'Le Point'). This company operates some of the cheapest no-frills flights to Ouagadougou (Burkina Faso) and Bangui (CAR) and they are expanding so they may soon have similar flights to an East African destination. Their addresses are: 4 Rue des Orphelins, 68200 Mulhouse (tel 89-42 4461), and 54 Rue des Ecoles, 75006 Paris.

FROM ASIA

There are no longer any passenger ships from India or Pakistan to East Africa. Don't believe any rumours that there are such ships. There are about four or five Arab dhows which do the journey between Zanzibar/Mombasa to Karachi/Bombay each year via Somalia, South Yemen and Oman, but they are extremely difficult to locate and to get onto. The days of the dhows were numbered decades ago; if you can find a dhow in Mombasa harbour it will only be plying between Lamu, Mombasa, Pemba and Zanzibar.

You may safely assume that flying is the only feasible way of getting between the Indian sub-continent and East Africa. There are bucket shops of a sort in New Delhi, Bombay and Calcutta. In New Delhi I'd recommend Tripsout Travel, 72/7 Tolstoy Lane behind the Government of India Tourist Office, Janpath.

From East Africa to India, the best place to buy your ticket is Nairobi where there are a lot of bucket shops offering tickets to Karachi, Islamabad, New Delhi, Bombay and Calcutta. You are looking at around US$260 for a one-way Nairobi-Bombay ticket.

FROM AUSTRALASIA

There are no longer tight constraints on ticket discounting in Australia, but for Australians and New Zealanders there are simply very few route options to Africa. Apart from the SAA flight from Perth to Johannesburg, due to be suspended as this goes to press, there's only the Qantas flight from Perth to Harare (Zimbabwe). Sydney-Harare costs around US$700 one-way (or almost A$1100).

It obviously makes sense for Australasians to think in terms of a round-the-world flight ticket or an Australia/New Zealand-Europe round ticket with stop-overs in Asia and Africa. It shouldn't be too much trouble for a travel agent to put together a ticket which includes various Asian stop-overs plus a Nairobi stop-over. It's still possible to pick up round-the-world air tickets ex-Australia for A$1800 with various stopovers. The best publications for finding good deals are the daily newspapers such as the *Sydney Morning Herald* and *The Age* or try travel agents like the student travel people at STA.

Getting Around

Most African countries offer a choice of railways, buses, minibuses (generally called *matatus*), taxis (whether shared or private) and trucks.

AIR
There are some internal airlines in East Africa, particularly in Kenya, and limited connections between the various countries of the region.

ROAD
Roads in far-flung rural areas of all East African countries may well be in a bad state of repair so break-downs and getting stuck, especially in the wet season, are a regular feature of any journey. Desert roads in north and north-east Kenya may just be a set of tyre tracks left in the sand or dust by previous trucks. Don't pay any attention to red lines drawn on maps in places like this. Many roads are impassable in the wet season and on some of them a convoy system may be in operation so that you can only travel at certain times of day.

Buses, Matatus & Taxis
Buses are usually quicker than going by rail or truck. In Kenya, where there is a good network of sealed roads, you may have the choice of going by so-called 'luxury' bus or by ordinary bus over certain routes. The 'luxury' buses cost more but are not always quicker than the ordinary buses. In Tanzania and Uganda they are all ordinary buses and in Tanzania they are somewhat unreliable because of fuel and spare parts shortages. There are very few full-size buses in Burundi and Rwanda – minibuses are the rule. In Zaïre, buses and minibuses are few and far between.

Most East African countries rely heavily for transport on minibuses *(matatus)*. They're generally more expensive than ordinary buses, but quicker. In Kenya, Tanzania and Uganda you can expect them to be packed to bursting point. In Rwanda and Burundi this isn't the case and travelling in *matatus* is quite a civilised way of moving around.

Most countries also have shared taxis (which take up to five passengers and leave when they're full) and private taxis. You can forget about private taxis if you're on a budget, but shared taxis should definitely be considered. They can cost up to twice the price of the corresponding bus fare, but in some places they're only slightly more expensive than a matatu and they're certainly quicker and more comfortable. They're also considerably safer than *matatus* whose drivers are often reckless.

You may have to pay an additional fee for your baggage on some buses, *matatus* and shared taxis but this isn't usually the case.

Trucks
For many travellers, trucks are the favoured means of transport. They may be the *only* form of transport in some areas. They're not only the cheapest way of getting from A to B as a rule, but you can get an excellent view from the top of the load. Free lifts are the exception rather than the rule though it depends on the driver. You may well have to wait a long time until a free lift comes along and it's often not worth bothering. Hitching is a recognised form of public transport in much of Africa and local people expect to pay for it. So should you. Most of the time you will be on top of the load, though you can sometimes travel in the cab for about twice what it costs on top.

For most regular runs there will be a 'fare' which is more or less fixed and you'll be paying what the locals pay – but check this out before you agree to a price.

Sometimes it's possible to get the truckie to lower the price if there's a group of you (form an impromptu group where possible). Trucks are generally cheaper than buses over the same distance.

There are trucks to most places on main routes every day, but in the more remote areas they may only run once or twice a week. Many lifts are arranged the night before departure at the 'truck park' – a compound/dust patch that you'll find in almost every African town of any size. Just go there and ask around for a truck which is going the way you want to go. If the journey is going to take more than one night or one day, ask whether the price includes food and/or water.

Hitching

In Kenya, but less so in the other countries of East Africa, resident expatriates, international aid workers and the like who are driving their own vehicles seem to be reasonably generous about offering (free) lifts. It may be the only way of getting to some of the Ugandan national parks since there's rarely any public transport right up to the entrance gates. Don't expect too much in the way of lifts from expatriate workers. They have a tendency to regard budget travellers as a lesser form of humanity. Remember that sticking out your thumb in many African countries is the equivalent of an obscene gesture, although allowances are generally made for foreigners. Wave your hand vertically up and down instead.

A word of warning about lifts in private cars. Smuggling across borders does go on, and if whatever is being smuggled is found, you may be arrested even though you knew nothing about it. Most travellers manage to convince police that they were merely hitching a ride and had nothing to do with the smuggler (passport stamps are a good indication of this), but the convincing can take days. It's unlikely they'll let you ring your embassy during this time, and even if you do, you shouldn't count on their ability to help you. If you're worried about this, get out before the border and walk through.

RAIL

Kenyan trains are excellent and are the preferred method of transport where they are available. Tanzanian trains are considerably slower but they are still the preferred method of transport across the centre of the country between Dar es Salaam and Kigoma and if you are heading south to Malawi or Zambia. Ugandan trains are slower still and you probably wouldn't use them in the eastern part of the country, but they are the most convenient way of going west between Kampala and Kasese. Burundi, Rwanda and Eastern Zaïre have no railways.

Third class is usually very crowded and uncomfortable and you may have thieves to contend with so it's not generally recommended. Second class is preferable and will cost you about the same as a bus over the same distance. Travelling 1st class will cost you about double what a bus would cost.

BOAT

There are quite a few possibilities for travelling by boat either on the lakes inland or along the coast. In particular there are some amazingly venerable old steamships operating on the lakes. A trip on the *MV Liemba* on Lake Tanganyika is quite an experience. Along the coast there are some regular shipping services and with persistence you can get rides on dhows.

Kenya

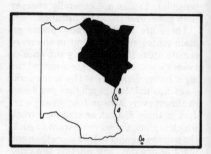

Kenya is becoming a magnet for the adventurous traveller in search of something exotic, fascinating and quite different from the well-trodden routes in the Americas and Asia. Sitting astride the equator, it's a spectacularly beautiful land of contrasts, ranging from the balmy shores of the Indian Ocean with their uncluttered white-sand beaches and coral reefs to the snow-capped peaks of Mt Kenya (Africa's second highest mountain) to the wild and vast scrub deserts of the north.

Because of its prolific wildlife, Kenya has for decades been synonymous with the safari. The country is well provided with national parks and game reserves and safaris are well within the range of even budget travellers. The people are friendly and there is none of the suspicion of foreigners sometimes encountered in African countries with a history of instability and military government. In few other African countries will you come across such a diversity of incredibly colourful tribespeople, many of whom still continue to live according to their centuries-old traditions. Times are changing but many of these people remain hardly affected by the 20th century.

There is a similar diversity of towns, ranging from Nairobi, a modern capital city where you can find all the amenities you would expect to find in a western city, to Lamu, a living Omani-African museum of narrow, twisting alleyways, donkeys – and not a car in sight.

HISTORY
The Birthplace of Humanity

The Rift Valley, which runs through the centre of Kenya, has been established as the 'cradle of mankind' as a result of the now famous digs of the Leakey family in Olduvai Gorge (Tanzania) and around Lake Turkana (Kenya). Their discoveries of several hominoid skulls, one of which is estimated to be 3½ million years old, have radically altered the accepted theories on the origin of humans.

Before the East African digs, the generally accepted theory was that there were two different species of the ancestors of modern humans: the ape-like *Australopithecus africanus* and *Australopithecus robustus*. It was believed one of these died out while the other gave rise to *Homo sapiens*. The Leakey discoveries suggested that there was a third contemporary species, *Homo habilis*, and that it was this one which gave rise to modern humans while both the *Australopithecus* species died out, leaving no descendants.

The Tribes

This area of Africa has a large diversity of peoples – Kenya is home to almost every major language stock in Africa. Even Khoisan, the 'click' language spoken by the Bushmen and Hottentots in southern Africa, has its representatives, although these days they are only a tiny community close to the Tana River near the coast. This diversity is clear evidence that Kenya has been a major migratory pathway over the centuries.

The first wave of immigrants were the tall, nomadic Cushitic people from

Ethiopia who began to move south around 2000 BC. They were pastoralists and depended on good grazing land for their cattle and goats, so when the climate began to change and the area around Lake Turkana became more arid, they were forced to resume their migration south. They were to reach as far as central Tanzania. A second group of pastoralists, the Eastern Cushitics, followed them around 1000 BC and occupied much of central Kenya. The rest of the ancestors of the country's melée of tribes arrived from all over Africa between 500 BC and 500 AD though there was still much movement and rivalry for land right up to the beginning of the 20th century. Even today it hasn't ended completely.

The Eastern Cushitics eventually gave rise to the Sam people whose numerous sub-groups include the Rendille, who herd camels in the semi-desert between Marsabit and Mt Kulal, and the Boni, who are hunter-gatherers on the mainland opposite Lamu.

The ancestors of the Kalenjin tribes – the Kipsigis, Nandi, Marakwet and Tugen which today are the fourth largest group in Kenya – arrived between 2000 and 2500 years ago from the Nile Valley – hence their general classification as Nilotics. They were originally pastoralists but gradually began to cultivate sorghum and millet. These days they occupy the highland regions from Kericho north to Kitale and beyond.

Splinter groups include the Pokot, who have remained pastoralists and occupy the lower and drier lands north of Lake Baringo, and the Okiek, who live by hunting and gathering wild plant foods and honey, and who are scattered throughout the highland forest regions of western and central Kenya. The Okiek trade with the Maasai who are keen to acquire their wild honey, for making an alcoholic beverage, and ivory for ornaments.

One of the best known tribes of East Africa – the Maasai – are also descended from Nile Valley migrants. These tall, proud pastoralists with their warrior traditions were greatly influenced by the Eastern Cushitics on their migration through the Lake Turkana region and it's thought that they picked up many of their social and cultural traditions from them. By the 14th century the Maasai had moved further south to occupy much of the Rift Valley down through Kenya and into Tanzania and the adjacent highlands. They were much feared and admired by other tribes and only in the late 19th century was their power finally broken by the British, and then only after a disastrous civil war, famine and disease had decimated their numbers. They were confined by the colonial authorities to reservations south of the Mombasa to Uganda railway line but their cousins, the Samburu, still occupy much of the land between Isiolo and Lake Turkana. The Maasai currently number some 250,000.

Another war-like Nilotic tribe which arrived on the western shores of Lake Turkana in the 16th century were the Turkana. These pastoralists had, by the mid-19th century, pushed the Samburu, Rendille and Pokot out of the land west of the lake and begun to take over the land south and east of the lake too. They were finally subdued by troops of the colonial authorities.

The remaining major Nilotic tribal group, numbering about 2¼ million, are the Luo who migrated south from the southern Sudan to reach western Kenya in the 16th century. In the process, they absorbed or displaced the Bantu tribes and eventually settled along the north-eastern shores of Lake Victoria.

At about the same time as the Kalenjin were arriving in north-west Kenya, waves of Bantu were pouring out of south-eastern Nigeria and spreading throughout central and southern Africa. They are the dominant group in many of the countries of that region today. In Kenya they are represented by the Kikuyu, the Kamba

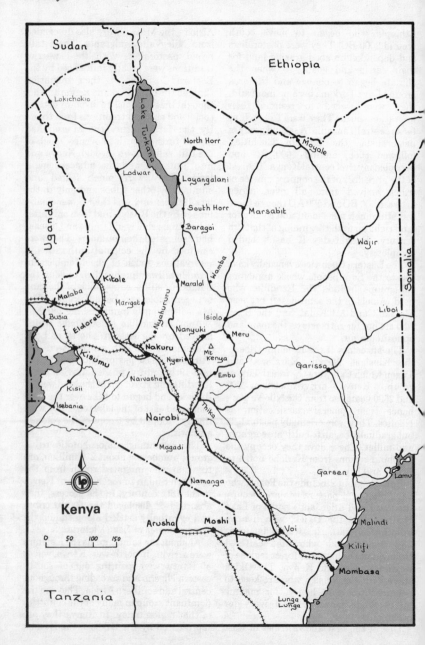

Kenya

0   50   100   150

Sudan

Ethiopia

Lokichokio

Lake Turkana

North Horr

Moyale

Lodwar

Loyangalani

South Horr

Marsabit

Baragoi

Wamba

Wajir

Uganda

Kitale

Maralal

Malaba

Marigat

Ngahururu

Isiolo

Liboi

Busia

Eldoret

Nanyuki

Meru

Somalia

Kisumu

Nakuru

Nyeri

Mt Kenya

Naivasha

Embu

Garissa

Kisii

Isebania

Nairobi

Thika

Magadi

Garsen

Lamu

Namanga

Arusha

Moshi

Voi

Malindi

Kilifi

Mombasa

Tanzania

Lunga Lunga

and the Meru, totalling some 6½ million people in all. They live mainly on the fertile slopes of Mt Kenya where most of the country's food and export crops are produced. Related groups of Bantu who have been much influenced by their Kalenjin and Nilotic neighbours are the Luyha, Gusii and Kuria who occupy land close to Lake Victoria around the towns of Bungoma, Kakamega and Kisii. They number over 3½ million.

The Bantu also spread to the coastal area where they traded with the Persians and Arabs who came in search of slaves and ivory. One major consequence of this interaction was the Swahili language spoken today by some 60 million people in East Africa. The language is essentially Bantu, but contains numerous Arabic, Asian and European words.

A related group of Bantu, the Mijikenda, who occupy a long strip of land just inland from the coast stretching from the Tana River down into Tanzania, previously lived in what is now Somalia but were pushed out of there by marauding Galla pastoralists from the north sometime in the past. The Galla are a branch of the Boran and their descendants who live in Kenya today are known as the Oromo.

If you are interested in learning more about these tribes there is an excellent series of illustrated booklets under the general title of *Kenya's People*, published by Evans Brothers (London & Nairobi). You can find them in any reasonable bookshop in Kenya. Titles include *People of the Plains: Maasai, Akamba, Mijikenda, People of the Rift Valley: Kalenjin, People round the Lake, People of the Coast, Okiek* and *People round Mt Kenya: Kikuyu*. They each cost around Sh 30 (about US$2).

The Arabs

While all these migrations and inter-tribal struggles were going on in the interior, Muslims from the Arabian Peninsula and Shirazis from Persia (now Iran) began to visit the East African coast from the 8th century AD onwards. They came to trade, convert and settle, rather than conquer, as they had done in North Africa and Spain. Their dhows would head down on the north-east monsoon bringing glassware, ironware, textiles, wheat and wine and return with ivory, slaves, tortoise shell and rhino horn.

This trade soon extended right across the Indian Ocean to India and beyond. Even China entered the fray at one point early in the 15th century, with a fleet of 62 ships and an escort of some 37,000 men, after the king of Malindi had sent the Chinese emperor a gift of a giraffe! Many of the traders stayed to settle and inter-marry with the Africans. As a result, a string of relatively affluent and Islamic-influenced coastal towns sprang up along the East African coast from Somalia to Mozambique, acting as entrepôts for the cross-Indian Ocean trade. Though there was natural rivalry between these towns, until the 16th century life was relatively peaceful. The Portuguese arrival rudely shattered that peace.

The Portuguese

While the Spanish Crown was busy backing expeditions to the Americas, the Portuguese were determined to circumvent the Ottoman Turks' grip on trade with the Far East, particularly the trade in spices which were worth more than their weight in gold in Europe. Throughout the 15th century, the Portuguese had been exploring further and further down the western coast of Africa until, in 1498, they finally rounded the Cape of Good Hope and headed up the eastern coast under the command of Vasco da Gama.

They were given a hostile reception both at Sofala on the Mozambique coast and at Mombasa but were lucky to find a friendly sultan at Malindi who provided them with a pilot who knew the route to India. Da Gama was back again with another expedition in 1502, after selling the first expedition's cargo of spices in Portugal and earning a small fortune.

The main Portuguese onslaught began with Francisco d'Almeida's armada of 23 ships and some 1500 men in 1505. Sofala was burned to the ground and looted, Kilwa was occupied and garrisoned and Mombasa was taken after a naval bombardment and fierce street fighting. Mombasa was sacked again by Nuña da Cunha in 1528. The Arab monopoly of Indian Ocean trade had been broken. Though the Ottoman Turks attempted to wrest it back from the Portuguese in 1585 and again in 1589 they were unsuccessful.

After the original onslaught, there followed two centuries of harsh colonial rule. Tribute was demanded and levies were imposed on all non-Portuguese ships visiting the coastal towns. Severe retribution was the reward for the slightest offense. Economic exploitation came hand in hand with a drive to convert the local population to Catholicism but they never had much success at this and, whenever they abandoned an outpost, those who had been 'converted' reverted back to Islam. Mombasa came to be their principle outpost following the construction of Fort Jesus there in 1593.

The Portuguese task was made easier since they were able to play one sultan off against another, but their grip over the East African coast was always tenuous since their outposts had to be supplied from Goa in India, where the Viceroy had his headquarters. Delays were inevitable. The colonial bureaucracy also became moribund because of the sale of offices to the highest bidder. And, in the final analysis, Portugal was too small a country with insufficient resources to effectively hold onto a world-wide empire.

The beginning of the end came in 1698 when Fort Jesus fell to the Arabs after a siege lasting 33 months and, by 1720, the Portuguese had packed up and left the Kenyan coast for good.

The Omani Dynasties

The Arabs were to remain in control of the East African coast until the coming of the British and Germans in the late 19th century. The depredations of the Portuguese period, however, had exacted a heavy price and the constant quarreling among the Arab governors who succeeded them led to a decline in the trade and prosperity which the East African coast had once enjoyed. Political and economic recovery had to wait until the beginning of the 19th century.

Throughout the 18th century, Omani dynasties from the Persian Gulf entrenched themselves along the East African coast. They were nominally under the control of the Sultan of Oman but this control was largely ineffective until Seyyid Said came to the Omani throne in 1805. The Omanis had gradually built up a relatively powerful navy during the latter part of the 18th century and Seyyid Said decided to use this to bring the East African dynasties into line. In 1822 he sent an army to subdue Mombasa, Paté and Pemba, which were then ruled by the Mazrui clan.

The Mazruis appealed to Britain for help. The following year this was provided in the form of two warships on a survey mission. The commander of one of these ships, Captain Owen, decided to act first and ask questions later, so the British flag was raised over Fort Jesus and a protectorate was declared. A small garrison was left in charge, but three years later the British government repudiated the protectorate and the flag was hauled down. Seyyid Said re-asserted his control the following year, garrisoned Fort Jesus and began to lay out clove plantations on Zanzibar. In 1832, he moved his court to Zanzibar.

19th Century Colonialism

By the mid-19th century, several European nations were showing an interest in the East African coast, including the British and the Germans. The British were interested in the suppression of the slave trade and when Seyyid Said moved to Zanzibar they set up a consulate at his court. Later an agreement was reached between the British and the Germans as to their spheres of interest in East Africa. Part of the deal was that the Sultan of Zanzibar would be allowed to retain a 16 km wide strip of the Kenyan coastline under a British Protectorate. It remained as such right up until independence when the last Sultan of Zanzibar, Seyyid Khalifa, ceded the territory to the new government.

Penetration of the Kenyan interior, and particularly of the Rift Valley and the Aberdare highlands, by outsiders was delayed until the 1880s since it was occupied by the Maasai pastoralists. Their reputation as a proud warrior tribe had been sufficient to deter Arab slavers and traders and European missionaries and explorers up to that date. But with the rest of Africa being combed by European explorers Kenya's turn was soon to follow.

Notable early explorers who lived to tell the tale were Gustav Fischer (a German whose party was virtually annihilated by Maasai at Hell's Gate on Lake Naivasha in 1882), Joseph Thomson (a Scot who reached Lake Victoria via the Rift Valley lakes and the Aberdares in 1883), and Count Teleki von Szek (an Austrian who explored the Lake Turkana region and Mt Kenya in 1887). James Hannington, an Anglican bishop who set out in 1885 to set up a diocese in Uganda, wasn't quite so fortunate. Though he discovered Lake Bogoria (known as Lake Hannington during colonial days) he was killed when he reached the Nile.

By the late 19th century, the Maasai were considerably weakened and their numbers reduced by years of civil war between two opposing factions, the Ilmaasai and the Iloikop. The dispute was about which of the two were the true descendants of Olmasinta, the legendary founder of the tribe. Rinderpest (a cattle disease), cholera, smallpox and famine had also taken their toll between 1880 and

1892. Because of this, the British were able to negotiate a treaty with Olonana (these days known as Lenana), the *laibon* (chief, or spiritual leader of the Maasai). Armed with this treaty, the British were able to construct their Mombasa to Uganda railway through the heart of the Maasai grazing lands. The approximate half-way point of this railway is where Nairobi stands today.

White Settlement

With the railway completed and the headquarters of the colonial administration moved from Mombasa to Nairobi, white settlers began to move into the fertile highlands north of Nairobi in search of farming lands. Their interests naturally clashed with those of the Maasai, prompting the colonial authorities to pressure Olonana into restricting the Maasai to two reserves, one on either side of the new railway. Though this was a blow to Maasai independence, worse was to follow since the white settlers soon wanted the northern reserve as well. In 1910-11 those Maasai who lived there were forced to trek south, despite Olonana's objections.

The Maasai have lived in the southern reserve and in northern Tanzania ever since but, these days, they have to share their grazing land with two of Kenya's national parks. This has led to many disputes between the Maasai and the game wardens since the Maasai prefer to graze their cattle along certain routes as they lead them to water. This method of cattle grazing often leads to soil erosion which, in turn, seriously effects all of the human and animal inhabitants of the area. There is no easy answer to this since the Maasai are one of the tribes least affected by, or interested in, the mainstream of modern Kenya and it is hard to persuade them to alter their traditional ways. Times are changing but only very slowly for the Maasai.

Though it's probably true that it was the Maasai who had the greatest amount of land taken from them by the white settlers, the Kikuyu, a Bantu agricultural tribe which occupied the highlands around the western side of Mt Kenya, also suffered. It was the Kikuyu who came to nurse a particular grievance about the alienation of land by white settlers later on in the 20th century. Many of the numerically larger tribes such as the Luo and Luyha and the tribes of the north-east were hardly affected, if at all, by white settlement.

White settlement in the early years of the 20th century was led by Lord Delamere, a pugnacious gentleman farmer from Cheshire, England. Since he was not familiar with the land, its pests and its wildlife, his first ventures – into sheep farming and, later, wheat growing – were a disastrous failure. By 1912, however, following the move to the highlands, Delamere and his followers had put the colony onto a more realistic economic footing by establishing mixed agricultural farms. Other European settlers established coffee plantations about the same time, including Karen von Blixen and her hunter husband, Bror. Her memoirs are to be found in the book *Out of Africa*, recently made into a very successful film.

WW I interrupted settlement of Kenya for four years during which time some two-thirds of the 3000 white settlers formed impromptu cavalry units and went off in search of Germans in neighbouring Tanganyika, leaving their wives behind to manage the farms. They were not entirely successful but they did eventually manage to drive the German forces into Central Africa with assistance from Jan Smut's South African units. However, Vorbeck's intrepid unit of 155 Germans and 3000 Africans remained undefeated when the armistice was signed in November 1918. Under the Treaty of Versailles, Germany lost Tanganyika and the British were given a mandate by the League of Nations to control the territory.

Settlement of Kenya resumed after the war under a scheme where veterans of the European campaign were offered land in the highlands, either at rock-bottom prices or on long-term loans. The effect of this was to raise the white settler population to around 9000 by 1920. By the 1950s it had reached 80,000.

African Nationalism

While all this was going on, more and more Kikuyu were migrating to Nairobi or being drawn into the colonial economy in one way or another. They weren't at all happy about the alienation of their land and this led to the formation of a number of associations whose principle concern was the return of land to the Kikuyu.

One of the early leaders of the Kikuyu political associations was Harry Thuku. Shortly after he was arrested for his activities by the colonial authorities in March 1922, a crowd of Africans gathered outside the Nairobi Central Police Station where he was being held. Reports differ as to what happened next but by the time the police had stopped shooting, between 21 and 100 people had been killed. Thuku was eventually exiled to Kisimayo and was only finally released from jail in 1930 after he had agreed to cooperate with the colonial authorities. His cooperation cost him his leadership of the Kikuyu movement since he was thenceforth regarded as something of a collaborator. This early Sharpeville led to the politicisation of the Kikuyu and was the start of a sustained campaign for political, social and economic rights.

While Harry Thuku's star was on the wane, that of another member of the tribe was on the rise. His name was Johnstone Kamau, later changed to Jomo Kenyatta, who was to become independent Kenya's first president. Kenyatta was born in 1892 in the highlands north of Nairobi, the son of a peasant farmer. He spent the early years of his life as a shepherd tending his father's flocks. When he was in his teens he ran away to a nearby Church of

Scotland mission school where he picked up an education.

At the age of 29 he moved to Nairobi. He worked there as a court interpreter and water-meter reader but his real skills lay elsewhere – as an orator. He soon became the propaganda secretary of the East Africa Association which had been set up to campaign for land reform, better wages, education and medical facilities for Africans. At this time, Africans were barred from hotels and restaurants and were only considered for the most menial jobs within the colonial administration. Although it was official British government policy to favour African interests over those of the settlers in the event of conflicts, this was often ignored in practice because of the dominance of Lord Delamere's lobby in the whites-only Legislative Council which had been formed after the protectorate became a colony. Recognising this, Kenyatta soon moved to the more outspoken Kikuyu Central Association as its secretary-general.

Shortly afterwards, in 1929, with money supplied by Indians with communist connections, he sailed for London to plead the Kikuyu case with the British colonial secretary. Though the colonial secretary declined to meet him, Kenyatta teamed up with a group called the League Against Imperialism which took him to Moscow and Berlin and then back again to Nairobi. He returned to London the following year and remained there for the next 15 years. He spent his time perfecting his oratory with Trafalgar Square crowds, studying revolutionary tactics in Moscow, visiting cooperative farms in Scandinavia and building up the Pan-African Federation with Hastings Banda (who later became the president of Malawi) and Kwame Nkrumah (who later became the president of Ghana). By the time he returned to Kenya in 1946, he was the recognised leader of the Kenyan liberation movement.

During WW II, the Belgian, British, French and Italian governments all recruited African troops to fight. The over-all effect on Africans (as well as soldiers from other colonised peoples) was a realisation that the Europeans were not omnipotent. They could be defeated or, at the least, forced to come to terms with African aspirations for the same benefits and opportunities as their European overlords. Africans had also been trained in the use of arms. When the war ended, therefore, the returning soldiers were in no mood to accept the status quo and began to actively campaign for changes.

The main African political organisation involved in the confrontation with the colonial authorities was the Kenya African Union (KAU), first headed by Harry Thuku and then by James Gichuru who himself stood down in favour of Kenyatta on the latter's return from Britain. The Kikuyu Central Association had been banned in 1940 along with many other similar organisations.

The Mau Mau Rebellion

As the demands of the KAU became more and more strident and the colonial authorities less and less willing to make concessions, oath-taking ceremonies began to spread among various tribes like the Kikuyu, Maasai and Luo. Some of these secret oaths bound the participants to kill Europeans and their African collaborators.

The first blow was struck early in 1953 with the killing of a white farmer's entire herd of cattle. This was followed, a few weeks later, by the massacre of 21 Kikuyu loyal to the colonial government. The Mau Mau rebellion had started. The government declared an emergency and began to herd the tribespeople into 'protected villages' surrounded by barbed wire and booby-trapped trenches which they were forbidden to leave during the hours of darkness. Some 20,000 Kikuyu 'Home Guards' were recruited to assist British army units brought in to put down the rebellion and to help police the 'protected villages'. By the time it came to an end in 1956 with the defeat of the Mau Mau, the death toll stood at over 13,500 Africans – Mau Mau guerrillas, civilians and troops – and just over 100 Europeans, only 37 of which were settlers. In the process an additional 20,000 Kikuyus had been thrown into detention camps.

Only a month after the rebellion started, Kenyatta and several other KAU leaders were arrested and put on trial for allegedly being the leaders of the Mau Mau. It's very doubtful that Kenyatta had any influence over the Mau Mau commanders, let alone that he was one of their leaders, but he was, nevertheless, sentenced to seven years jail in the remote Turkana region after a trial lasting five months. He was released in 1959 but was immediately sent to Lodwar under house arrest.

The rebellion shook the settlers to the roots and gave rise to a number of white political parties with opposing demands, ranging from partition of the country between blacks and whites to the transfer of power to a democratically elected African government. It should have been obvious to anyone with eyes to see that the latter view would have to prevail in the end, but it wasn't adopted as official policy until the Lancaster House Conference in London in 1960. The rebellion did lead, however, to an exodus of white settlers who packed their bags and headed off to Rhodesia, South Africa and Australia. At the conference, independence was scheduled for December 1963 and the British government agreed to provide the new Kenyan government with US$100 million in grants and loans so that it would be able to buy out European farmers in the highlands and restore the land to the tribes from whom it had been taken.

In the meantime a division occurred in the ranks of KAU between those who wanted a unitary form of government with firm centralised control in Nairobi and the others who favoured a federal set-up in order to safeguard the rights of minorities. The former renamed their party the Kenya African National Union (KANU) and the latter split off under the leadership of Ronald Ngala to become the Kenya African Democratic Union (KADU). Many of the white settlers, who had come to accept the inevitable, supported KADU.

Kenyatta was released from house arrest in mid-1961 and assumed the presidency of KANU. Despite his long period of incarceration by the colonial authorities he appeared to harbour no resentment of the whites and indeed set out to re-assure the settlers that they would have a future in the country when independence came. At a packed meeting of settlers in Nakuru Town Hall in August 1963, he asked them to stay, saying that the country needed experience and that he didn't care where it came from. He assured them of the encouragement and protection of the new government and appealed for harmony, saying that he wanted to show the rest of the world that different racial groups were capable of living and working together. It did the trick. Kenyatta's speech transformed him, in the eyes of the settlers, from the feared and reviled spiritual leader of the Mau Mau into the venerable *mzee* (respected elder) of the post-independence years.

Most of the white settler farms have been bought out by the government over the years and the land divided up into small subsistence plots which support 15 to 20 people. This may well have appeased the pressure for land redistribution in a country with the world's highest birth rate but it has led to a serious decline in agricultural production (and therefore a diminishing tax base for the government) and has threatened to damage the region's delicate ecology. By 1980, Kenya was forced to import half its grain needs whereas in 1975 it was self-sufficient in these. The government is keen to halt the break-up of the 100-odd settler farms which remain but the prospects of being able to do this in a land-hungry nation are not good.

Independence

Independence came on 12 December 1963 with Kenyatta as the first president. He was to rule Kenya until his death in 1978. Under Kenyatta's presidency, Kenya developed into one of Africa's most stable and prosperous nations. Unlike many other newly independent countries, there was no long string of coups and counter-coups, military holocausts, power-crazy dictators and secessionist movements. It wasn't all plain sailing but he left the country in a much better state than he found it and, although there were excesses, they were minor by African standards. By the time he died, there were enough Kenyans with a stake in their country's continued progress to ensure a relatively smooth succession to the presidency. Violence and instability would have benefited few people. Kenyatta's main failings were that he was excessively biased in favour of his own tribe and that he often regarded honest criticism as tantamount to treason.

Control of the government and large sectors of the economy still remain in the hands of the Kikuyu, to the social and financial detriment of other ethnic groups. Corruption in high places remains a problem and once prompted J M Kariuki, a former Mau Mau fighter and later an assistant minister in the government, to remark that Kenya had become a nation of '10 millionaires and 10 million beggars'. There are indeed great disparities in wealth. Many destitute squatters and unemployed people, especially in Nairobi, have little hope of ever finding employment – but this is hardly a problem peculiar to Kenya.

In 1964, Kenya effectively became a one-party state following the voluntary dissolution of the opposition KADU party. With it died the party's policy of regionalism and the two-chamber Legislature became a single chamber, the National Assembly. However, when Oginga Odinga, a Luo, was purged from the KANU hierarchy in 1966 over allegations that he was plotting against the government, he resigned from the vice-presidency and formed his own opposition party, the Kenya People's Union. The party was later banned and Odinga was jailed. He was released when he agreed to rejoin KANU, but was imprisoned again in 1969 on spurious charges. Even today, his son is subjected to police harassment.

Similarly, Tom Mboya, an intelligent young Luo who was widely regarded as future presidential material, was murdered by a Kikuyu gunman in 1969. The ambitious Mboya was feared by influential Kikuyu who felt that he might have designs on succeeding Kenyatta as president. J M Kariuki, a very popular Kikuyu who spoke out stridently and often about the new black elite and their corrupt practices, met a similar fate. He was assassinated in 1975. Other politicians who opposed Kenyatta – however mildly – found themselves arrested and held for long periods, often without trial.

Kenyatta was succeeded by Daniel arap Moi, a member of the Tugen tribe and regarded by Kikuyu power brokers as a suitable front man for their interests. Lacking the charisma of Kenyatta and the cult-following which he enjoyed, Moi was even less willing to brook criticism of his regime and his early years were marked by the arrest of dissidents, the disbanding of tribal societies and the frequent closure of the universities. There were allegations of conspiracies to overthrow the government whose details were often so labyrinthine they could have come straight out of a modern spy novel. Whether these conspiracies were real or just a convenient facade to justify Moi's consolidation of power is hard to tell since rarely were all the details released.

Sedition: Seven arrested in toilet

By ODHIAMBO-ORLALE
and
JOHN MBURU

Police arrested seven employees of a Thika textile manufacturing firm on Tuesday after they were found in a crowded toilet reading a copy of a publication by the clandestine Mwakenya group.

Nairobi newspaper headline

What certainly was real was the attempted coup by the Kenyan Air Force in August 1982. It was put down by forces loyal to the government but, by the time it was over, about 120 people had been killed and there was widespread looting of the major shopping areas. Twelve ring-leaders were subsequently sentenced to death and 900 others received jail sentences. The entire Kenyan Air Force was disbanded and replaced by a new unit.

Since then, other alleged conspiracies have come to light but, again, rarely are the details made known. The latest story doing the rounds and providing the newspapers with headlines is the *Mwakenya* 'movement', centred around lecturers at Nairobi University and involving the distribution of a supposedly subversive publication. The exiled novelist and political activist, Ngũgĩ wa Thiongo, has been accused of being involved. Precisely what seditious things this publication is supposed to be encouraging is virtually impossible to

ascertain since there is no discussion of it whatsoever in the newspapers, merely reports of arrests and people being sent to jail.

Kenya Today

The reasons why there might be such clandestine groups is fairly easy to understand. Ever since independence, opportunist politicians (especially Kikuyu ones) have amassed fortunes and put together property empires. Many people have been pushed aside or ignored and enemies have been made. There is a ground swell of discontent but this is due to many factors and isn't simply a function of corruption. The world-wide economic depression of the early 1980s led to increasing social problems and there is resentment among many black Kenyans against the extensive control which Asians have over the economy.

India's connections with East Africa go back centuries to the days when hundreds of dhows used to make the trip between Bombay or the Persian Gulf and the coastal towns of East Africa every year. In those days, however, the Indians came as traders and only a very few stayed to settle. This all changed with the building of the Mombasa to Uganda railway at the turn of the century. In order to construct it, the British colonial authorities brought in some 32,000 indentured labourers from Gujarat and Punjab. When their contracts expired, many of them decided to stay and set up businesses. Their numbers were augmented after WW II with the encouragement of the British.

Since they were an industrious and economically aggressive community they quickly ended up controlling large parts of the economies of Kenya, Tanzania and Uganda as merchants, artisans and financiers. Not only that, but they kept very much to themselves, regarding the Africans as culturally inferior and lazy. Few gave their active support to the black nationalist movements in the run-up to independence despite being urged to do so by Nehru, the Prime Minister of India. And when independence came, like many of the white settlers, they were very hesitant to accept local citizenship, preferring to wait and see what would happen. To the Africans, therefore, it seemed they were not willing to throw their lot in with the newly independent nations and were there simply as exploiters.

As is well known, Idi Amin used this suspicion and resentment as a convenient ruse to enrich himself and his cronies. Uganda's economy collapsed shortly afterwards since Amin's henchmen were incapable of running the industries and businesses which the Asians had been forced to leave. Asians have fared somewhat better in Tanzania though nationalisation of many of their concerns has considerably reduced their control over the economy. It is in Kenya that they have fared best of all. Here they have a virtual stranglehold over the service sector (the smaller hotels, restaurants, bars and road transport and the tourist trade), the textile trade, book publishing and book shops, and they are very important in the construction business.

For a time in the 1970s, it seemed that there was little future for them in Africa. Governments were under heavy pressure to 'Africanise' their economies and job markets. Even in Kenya, thousands of shops owned by Asians who had not taken out Kenya nationality were confiscated in the early 1970s and they were forbidden to trade in the rural areas. Those days appear to have passed and African attitudes towards them have mellowed. What seemed like a widespread demand that they should go 'home' has been quietly dropped and the Asians are there to stay. The lesson of what happened to the economy of Uganda when the Asians were thrown out is one reason for this.

POPULATION
Kenya's population is something over 16 million and increasing rapidly since Kenya's birth rate is the highest in the world. There are a wide diversity of tribal groups in Kenya plus an economically influential Asian minority.

ECONOMY
Kenya is still a predominantly agricultural country although there is an industrial sector and tourism is important.

GEOGRAPHY
Kenya's 582,646 square km is spread over a wide variety of topographies ranging from the sandy deserts of the far north to the mountainous highlands of the south. In between there are fine beaches along the Indian Ocean coast, the rolling central plains and the lakes of the Great Rift Valley.

FESTIVALS & HOLIDAYS
1 January, Maundy Thursday (pm only), Good Friday, Easter Monday, 1 May, 1 June, Id-el-Fitr (end of Ramadan), 20 October, 15 December, 25 December, 26 December.

LANGUAGE

Swahili and English are the official languages though there is a movement afoot to make Swahili the sole official language. It will be a long time, however, before most urban Kenyans stop using English in their normal, everyday conversations. On the other hand, it is extremely useful to have a working knowledge of Swahili, especially outside urban areas and if you are going on safari to remote areas. You won't meet many tribal people out in the bush who can speak English, particularly those who have had little exposure to tourism, but most of them can speak *some* Swahili whatever their first language might be. Other major languages are Kikuyu, Luo and Kikamba.

VISAS

Visas are required by all except nationals of Commonwealth countries (except nationals of Australia and Sri Lanka and British passport holders of Indian, Pakistani and Bangladeshi origin), Denmark, Ethiopia, West Germany, the Irish Republic, Italy, Norway, Spain, Sweden, Turkey and Uruguay. Those who don't need visas are issued on entry with a Visitor's Pass valid for a stay of up to six months. Three months is the average but it depends what you ask for.

Visas can be obtained from Kenyan embassies or High Commissions in:

Australia
    33 Ainslie Avenue, Canberra
Austria
    Rotenturmstrasse 22, 1010 Vienna
Belgium
    Avenue d'Auderghem 40-48, 1040 Brussels
Canada
    Gillia Building, Suite 600, 141 Laurier Avenue, West Ottawa, Ontario
Egypt
    8 Medina Munawara St, PO Box 362, Dokki, Cairo
Ethiopia
    Fikre Miriam Rd, PO Box 3301, Addis Ababa
France
    3 Rue Cimarose, 75116 Paris
West Germany
    53 Bonn-Bad Godesburg 2, Micael Plaza, Villichgasse 23, Bonn
India
    66 Vasant Marg, Vasant Vihar, New Delhi
Italy
    Casella Postalle 10755, 00144 Rome
Japan
    24-20 Nishi-Azobu 3-Chome, Minato-Ku, Tokyo
Nigeria
    53 Queens Drive, Ikoyi, PO Box 6464, Lagos
Rwanda
    Boulevard de Nyabugogo just off the Place de l'Unite Nationale, Kigali
Saudi Arabia
    PO Box 6347, Jeddah
Somalia
    Km IV Via Mecca, PO Box 618, Mogadishu
Sweden
    Birger Jarlsgatan 37, 2st 111 45 Stockholm
Tanzania
    NIC Investment House, Samora Machel Avenue, Dar es Salaam
Uganda
    Plot No 60, Kira Rd, Kampala
UK
    45 Portland Place, London W1N 4AS
USA
    2249 R St NW, Washington DC 20008
USSR
    Bolshaya Ordinka, Dom 70, Moscow
Zaïre
    Plot No 5002, Avenue de l'Onganda, BP 9667, Gombe, Kinshasa
Zambia
    Harambee House, 5207 United Nations Avenue, Lusaka
Zimbabwe
    95 Park Lane, Harare

Where there is no Kenyan embassy or high commission, visas can be obtained from the British embassy or high commission.

The cost of visas generally increases with the distance from Kenya and so do the hassles of getting them. We've had cliff-hanger stories from Australia where the high commission took 1½ months to issue a visa. All this time they hung on to the person's passport and he got it back (with a visa) *one* day before he was due to fly out. This is not at all typical but it does indicate that you should apply well in advance if you're flying direct.

In New York visas cost US$10, and you must have two photographs and an onward ticket or a letter from your bank saying you have at least US$2000 in your account. They're issued in 24 hours and are valid for a stay of six months. In London they cost £5, you do not need photographs or onward tickets, and they are issued in 15 minutes.

Closer to Kenya things are generally simpler and less time consuming:

Rwanda In Kigali they cost RFr 400, you need two photographs, no onward ticket is required, and they are issued in 15 minutes to one hour.

Tanzania In Dar es Salaam they cost TanSh 120, you need one photograph, and they can be issued the same day if you get your application in early in the day (visa applications are only accepted in the mornings).

Uganda In Kampala, Uganda (tel 31861), they cost UgSh 3500, no photographs are required and they are issued in 24 hours.

Zambia In Lusaka they cost Kw 15, two photographs and are issued in 24 hours. No onward ticket is required.

If you enter Kenya through a land border no-one will ever ask you for an onward ticket or 'sufficient funds'. This isn't always the case if you enter by air. A lot depends on what you look like, whether you're male or female, what you write on your immigration card and which immigration officer you deal with. Don't worry too much about it; Kenya is a very civilised country. If it's fairly obvious that you aren't intending to stay and work then you'll generally be given the benefit of the doubt. Put yourself in a strong position on arrival: look smart and put an expensive hotel under 'accommodation' on your immigration card.

Single women have been told at times that 'sufficient funds' in the absence of an onward ticket were suspect 'because women lose money easily'! Perhaps the appropriate rejoinder should be that 'men spend money faster'. To balance these experiences, it should be said that we've never heard of anyone being refused entry to Kenya even if, as a last resort, they've had to buy a refundable onward ticket.

So long as your visa remains valid you can visit either Tanzania or Uganda and return without having to apply for another visa. This does not apply to visiting any other countries. There is, however, a charge at the border for doing this – usually US$4.

Visas can be renewed in Nairobi at Immigration (tel 33 2110), Nyayo House (ground floor), on the corner of Kenyatta Avenue and Uhuru Highway or at the office in Mombasa (tel 31 1745) during normal office hours. A single re-entry permit costs US$8 and a multiple-entry permit US$40. You must pay in foreign currency. No onward tickets or 'sufficient funds' are demanded. Remember that you don't need a re-entry permit if you're only going to visit Tanzania or Uganda *so long as your visa remains valid*. The staff here are friendly and helpful.

Visas for Other Countries

Since Nairobi is a common gateway city to East Africa and the city centre is easy to get around, many travellers spend some time here picking up visas for other countries which they intend to visit. If you are going to do this you need to plan ahead because some embassies only accept visa applications in the mornings, others only on certain days of the week. Some take 24 hours to issue, others 48 hours. Some visas (Sudan, for instance) may have to be referred to the capital city but this is rare. The visa story in Nairobi is as follows:

Burundi Visas The embassy is on the 14th floor,

Development House, Moi Avenue (tel 338 7350). It's open Monday to Thursday from 8.30 am to 12.30 pm and 2 to 5 pm. Single entry visas cost Sh 50 (two-day transit) and Sh 100 (30-day tourist), require two photographs and take 24 hours to issue, but they will only issue visas on Tuesdays and Thursdays so you must put in your application on either Monday or Wednesday. The staff are friendly and there are tourist leaflets available.

Egypt Visas The embassy is at Chai House, Koinange St (tel 25991). It's open Monday to Friday from 9 am to 1.30 pm. One-month, single-entry visas cost Sh 170 (though New Zealanders report they are charged Sh 325) and double-entry visas cost Sh 200, require one photograph and take 24 hours to issue.

Ethiopia Visas The embassy is on State House Avenue (tel 72 3035). It's open Monday to Friday from 8.30 am to 12.30 pm and 2.30 to 5 pm. No visa is necessary if you are going to stay less than 72 hours. A one-month tourist visa costs Sh 80 and is issued in 48 hours. Entry is by air only and you must have an onward ticket.

Madagascar Visas There is no Malagasy embassy/consulate as such in Nairobi but there is a consular official who comes into Nairobi every Monday and will accept visa applications at the Air Madagascar office in the Hilton Hotel block (City Hall Way). Visas cost Sh 170, require four photographs and an onward ticket. The official takes the application forms to Antananarivo on Mondays and returns on Thursdays when the visas are issued. Very occasionally it's possible to get a visa in 24 hours.

Rwanda Visas The embassy is on the 12th floor, International House, Mama Ngina St (tel 33 4341). It's open Monday to Friday from 8.30 am to 12.30 pm and 2 to 5 pm. One-month visas cost Sh 200, require two photographs and take 24 hours to issue. On the application form it will ask you the date when you want to enter Rwanda. Think carefully about this as the visa will run from then.

Somalia Visas The embassy is at International House, Mama Ngina St (tel 24301). Visa applications are only accepted on Mondays. One-month visas cost Sh 200, require two

photographs and are issued in 24 hours. You may well be asked which country you come from before they will give you the application forms and if there is a Somali embassy in the country you name they may refuse to give you the forms saying you have to apply in your own country. If this happens, tell them you are a permanent resident in a different country.

Sudan Visas The embassy is on the 7th floor, Minet ICDC House, Mamlaka Rd (tel 72 0853). A one-month visa costs Sh 100, requires one photograph and takes between 24 hours and three weeks to issue – longer if it's necessary to refer the application to Khartoum. An onward ticket is necessary.

Tanzania Visas The high commission is on the 4th floor, Continental House, on the corner of Harambee Avenue and Uhuru Highway (tel 33 1056). It's open Monday to Thursday from 9 am to 12.30 pm and 2 to 5 pm, but visa applications are only accepted in the mornings. The cost of a visa varies considerably, depending on your nationality, but they are issued in 48 hours as a rule. Be very careful when filling in the application form since there is a US$80 per day minimum 'sufficient funds' rule – which is enforced. If you want one month you must write down at least US$2400. No-one actually wants to see it and if they do, well, it's in the hotel safe. The woman on the reception counter here is training for a job with the KGB. And you are a filthy dissident. Expect maximum unpleasantness.

Uganda Visas The high commission is on the 5th floor, Baring Arcade, Phoenix House, Kenyatta Avenue. A two-week visa costs an incredible Sh 330, and requires two photographs, but they are issued in one hour. Thank God for small mercies!

Zaïre Visas The embassy is in Electricity House, Harambee Avenue (tel 29771). It's open Monday to Friday from 10 am to 12 noon. One-month, single entry visas cost Sh 160, two-month, multiple entry visas cost Sh 280 and three-month, multiple entry visas cost Sh 360, plus you need four photographs, a letter of recommendation from your own embassy, an 'onward ticket' (which doesn't have to start from Zaïre) and vaccination certificates. They're issued in 24 hours and the staff are helpful. Letters of recommendation are issued free by some embassies but at others there is a charge.

Zambia Visas The high commission is on Nyerere Rd next door to the YWCA (tel 72 4799). One-month, single entry visas cost Sh 35, require three photographs and take 48 hours to issue. Double entry visas cost Sh 52.80.

French-speaking Countries The French embassy (Embassy House, Harambee Avenue (tel 33 9783) issues visas for French-speaking countries which don't have embassies in Nairobi – Chad and Central African Republic, for instance.

MONEY

US$1 = Sh 16.50

The unit of currency is the Kenyan Shilling (Sh), which is made up of 100 cents. The following official bank rates fluctuate according to the international currency markets but not by a great deal. The Kenyan shilling is virtually a hard currency especially in surrounding countries.

Import/export of local currency is allowed up to Sh 100 and, when you leave the country, customs officials will ask you if you are carrying any. If you say you are not that's generally the end of the matter. If you're only leaving the country for a short while and intend to return and don't want to convert all your Kenyan shillings into another currency you can leave any excess at a border post against a receipt and pick it up again when you get back.

You will probably meet people (especially in Nairobi) who offer to buy US dollars and £ sterling from you at a rate which you almost can't refuse (Sh 20-25 for the US dollar). It's more than likely you are being set up for a rip-off. There is no way *anyone* is going to give you Sh 25 to the US dollar. You can, by changing on the street market, get one or two more shillings to the dollar than what the banks offer but that's the extent of it. Most of the time it's not worth it since the people you will have to deal with are generally more interested in ripping you off than buying dollars.

Travellers' cheques attract a 1% commission at some banks but none at all at others (at Barclays there's generally no commission). Barclays is probably the best bank to change cheques at since there's hardly any red tape and the transaction takes just a few minutes. Avoid Standard Chartered banks where possible as there is a lot of form-filling and it can take more than half an hour to change a cheque. Banking hours are Monday to Friday from 8 or 9 am to 2 pm and on the first and last Saturdays of the month from 9 to 11 am.

Currency declaration forms are usually issued on arrival although you may have to ask for one at the Namanga border between Kenya and Tanzania. These are collected when you leave, but not scrutinised. You cannot change travellers' cheques without a currency form so it's to your advantage to make sure you get one. If for any reason you don't, they can be obtained from the Central Bank of Kenya, Kencom House (7th floor), City Hall Way, Nairobi, without any fuss (it takes about 10 minutes). Currency forms and bank receipts have to be produced when buying international flight tickets in Kenya. If you are intending to do this plan ahead because if you leave the country and then return you will no longer have your original currency form and you will have lost credit for the money which you changed on your first visit. See the Getting There section in this chapter for further details on how this affects you.

If you have money transferred from your home country for collection in Kenya, you can pick it up entirely in US dollar travellers' cheques but these may be stamped 'Non-negotiable in the Republic of South Africa'. If you intend to go there, this is going to cause problems. It is, after all, your money and not the bank's. Some travellers regard this sort of interference as totally unacceptable and have spent the best part of a day arguing with bank officials. Some have been successful. Barclays Bank does this, which is nonsense since they have scores of branches in South Africa.

It used to be possible, and still may be, to cash US dollar travellers' cheques at banks in Kenya and get US dollars cash for them but it's getting harder. At most banks you'll be met with a flat 'No' but some people are successful. Certainly you have to prove that you are leaving the country within 48 hours (air ticket/dated visa) and you generally need a convincing story about why you need cash dollars. You can get cash dollars with no problems if you make a withdrawal against your home account using a Visa card at Barclays Bank. So long as you don't want more than US$150 to US$200 per day it takes about 20 minutes. One traveller reported that she was able to get US$1000 in cash though that required a telex to the bank in her home country. Asked why she wanted that amount, she told them she was going to Tanzania where hotel bills and national park entry fees had to be paid in hard currency. Several other travellers have used the same explanation with success.

At the Bank of Kenya's Bureau de Change at Kenyatta Airport, Nairobi, you can exchange shillings for cash dollars up to any amount so long as you have bank receipts to cover the transaction. The facility is obviously meant for those who are leaving the country and have excess shillings (which you can't legally export) but they don't ask to see your air ticket at the time so presumably anyone could do this.

COSTS

The cost of budget accommodation in Kenya is very reasonable so long as you're happy with communal showers and toilets. Clean sheets are invariably provided and sometimes you'll also get

soap and a towel. For this you're looking at US$3 a single and US$4.50 a double and up. It can be slightly cheaper on the coast, especially at Lamu. If you want your own bathroom costs rise to around US$5 a single and US$8 a double and up. Again, it can be slightly cheaper on the coast but more expensive in Nairobi.

There are plenty of small cafés in every town, usually in a certain area. They cater to local people and you can get a traditional meal for about US$1. Often the food isn't up to much but sometimes it can be excellent. For a little more the Indian restaurants are great value. Many offer all-you-can-eat lunches for around US$2. They're not only tasty but you won't need to eat for the rest of the day either. A splurge at a better class restaurant is going to set you back between US$5 and US$10.

Soft drinks are very cheap at around US$0.15 and locally produced beer (Tusker, White Cap, Pilsener and Premium) costs US$0.55-60 depending on whether you want it cold or warm and where you buy it. Locally produced brandy *(konyagi)* is cheap and powerful.

Public transport is very reasonable and the trains are excellent value. To get from one end of Kenya to the other (Mombasa to Malaba) on the train in 2nd class is going to cost you about US$17. In 3rd class it's less than half of that. Buses are priced about half way between the 3rd and 2nd class rail fares.

The thing that is going to cost you most in Kenya is safaris. A safari for three nights and four days, for instance, by companies which cater for budget travellers is priced around US$120 to US$130. This includes transport, food, hire of tents, national park entry fees, camping fees and the wages of the guides and cooks. In other words, more or less everything except a few drinks and tips. A six night/seven day safari would be around US$180 minimum. Car hire is even more expensive and is probably out of reach of many budget travellers. A

four-wheel-drive Suzuki will cost around US$340 per week, with unlimited mileage and petrol.

CLIMATE

Although Kenya lies astride the equator, much of the country consists of a high plateau and mountains so the weather is generally warm and pleasant. March to May (the long rains) and October/November (the short rains) are generally wet periods throughout the country but downpours occur mostly in the late afternoons, the earlier part of the day being warm and sunny. Violent storms may well be encountered during the wet seasons in the Lake Turkana region, especially around Mt Kulal.

On the coast, the hottest months are September and October and between December and April but cool monsoon breezes make these months very pleasant. At other times it is hot and humid but not unbearably so. Kisumu on Lake Victoria has a similar climate because of the influence of the lake. The northern area, which is semi-desert, remains hot and dry throughout the year apart from the occasional downpour. Temperatures in Nairobi range from 11°C to 23°C in July and 13°C to 28°C in February. Nairobi and the highlands can get cold especially in the evenings during July and August.

NEWSPAPERS & MEDIA

Newspapers and magazines are published mainly in English and Swahili. There are radio services in English, Swahili, Hindi and various regional African languages. Kenya also has television broadcasting in English and Swahili.

FILM & PHOTOGRAPHY

Kenya actively encourages tourism and, unlike some neighbouring countries such as Rwanda, Zaïre and even Tanzania, they couldn't care less what you take photographs of. This doesn't mean that you can – or should – poke a camera into local peoples' faces. There are things called dignity, respect and consideration. If you want 'mug shots', ask first. It's unlikely you will meet with hostility but you may be refused unless you have the time to talk with whoever it is for a while.

On the other hand, the Maasai and, to some extent, the Samburu and Turkana tribespeople have come to terms with tourism. They'll willingly pose for photographs – for a fee. Fair enough! If you can afford to travel thousands of km to see them, you can afford to give them a few shillings. People who do this for a living in the west often make fortunes. But do negotiate a reasonable price.

This isn't difficult with Samburu and Turkana, for instance, but it's virtually impossible with Maasai. They've been in the game so long that the rates are now almost standard. Sh 100 wouldn't be unusual! And if you don't want to pay that, don't, under any circumstances, point a camera at them. Some people have had spears through the side of their vehicles for doing this. Paying for shots, on the other hand, is usually going to guarantee you better photographs than trying to take them on the run with a telephoto lens. There are trade-offs.

Kenya is one of the best places in Africa to buy film if you haven't brought enough with you. There's a wide range of film available in Nairobi and Mombasa and it's not that expensive. Prices for 36-frame colour negative Kodak/Agfa were: ASA 100 (US$4.93); ASA 200 (US$6.56); ASA 400 (US$7.18). For Kodak/Agfa slide film (not including developing) they were: ASA 100 (US$8.12); ASA 200 (US$10.62); ASA 400 (US$11.25). Fuji film prices were about 12% lower.

If you don't have enough film for your projected needs, buy it in a large city. Don't wait until you get to a game lodge. Most of them carry film for sale but the range is very limited and their prices are often up to 50% higher than you would pay in Nairobi.

It gets very bright in the arid areas of Kenya during the middle of the day and you might be tempted to over-use a polarising filter or simply leave it attached the whole time. If you do you may be looking at some pretty disappointing photographs when you get home. The flamingoes on Lake Nakuru, for instance, just don't take to it. To be sure, take shots with and without a polariser. Film, after all, is the least expensive of your outlays.

HEALTH

Most of Kenya enjoys a very healthy climate and malaria is rare in Nairobi or in the highlands, but it is endemic in the hot and humid coastal areas and the bush so you need to take precautions against it. Mosquitoes are only very rarely a nuisance in urban areas. You are advised not to swim in lakes or rivers because of the risk of contracting bilharzia. Lake Turkana, a soda lake with a barren shoreline, is probably free of this parasite (and of the snail which is the intermediate host). What you have to watch for here are the crocodiles!

Tap water in urban areas is usually safe to drink unless you are told otherwise though only rarely will you see expatriate residents doing this. During the rainy season you'd be advised to avoid it – take a look at what floats down the Nairobi River when there's a flood!

If you are planning on taking off into the bush on safari for lengthy periods of time it might be worth taking out temporary membership in the Flying Doctor Service (tel 50 1301), PO Box 30125, Nairobi. The monthly fee is negligible – around US$2.

If you need to renew vaccinations (for the purposes of your International Vaccination Certificate) you can do this at the City Hall Clinic, Mama Ngina St, Nairobi. You'll get a clean needle each time here. They do cholera injections from Monday to Friday from 8.30 am to 12 noon and yellow fever, tetanus and typhoid on the same days from 8.30 to 11 am. Yellow fever costs Sh 25 and cholera Sh 20. The others are free of charge.

GENERAL INFORMATION
Post

The Kenyan postal system is usually very reliable. I sent a lot of parcels back from Kenya and only one parcel of books failed to arrive. Poste restante is likewise well-organised and reliable Parcel postage rates are as follows:

Surface
    100 gm to 1 kg – Sh 64.50; 1 kg to 3 kg – Sh 104; 3 kg to 5 kg – Sh 144; 5 kg to 10 kg – Sh 232.
Air
    Up to 200 gm – Sh 81; each additional 200 gm – Sh 21.50.

Time

Greenwich Mean Time plus three hours.

Business Hours

General government business hours are 8 or 8.30 am to 12.45 pm and 2 pm to 4.30 or 5 pm. Some offices open on Saturday mornings from 8 am to 12.30 pm.

INFORMATION

There is no national tourist organisation in Kenya but the Ministry of Tourism does maintain offices overseas:

France
    Kenya Tourist Office, 5 Rue Volney, Paris 75002
West Germany
    Kenya Tourist Office, Hochstrasse 53, 7 Frankfurt
Sweden
    Kenya Tourist Office, Birger Jarlsgatan, S 102 95 Stockholm
Switzerland
    Kenya Tourist Office, Bleicherweg 30, CH-8039 Zurich
UK
    Kenya Tourist Office, 13 New Burlington St, London WIX IFF
USA
    Kenya Tourist Office, 9100 Wilshire Boulevard, Doheney Plaza Suite 111, Beverly Hills CA 90121

Kenya Tourist Office, 60 East 56th St, New York NY 10022

GETTING THERE

You can enter Kenya by air, road, lake ferry and possibly dhow. There are railways in Kenya but, although the tracks are continuous with the Tanzanian and Ugandan systems, there are no international services.

Air

Kenyatta International Airport in Nairobi is the main gateway to East Africa. It is served by Aeroflot, Air Afrique, Air Canada, Air Djibouti, Air France, Air India, Air Madagascar, Air Malawi, Air Mauritius, Air Tanzania, Air Zaïre, Air Zimbabwe, Alitalia, British Airways, Cameroon Airlines, Egyptair, El Al, Ethiopian Airlines, Iberia, Japan Airlines, Kenya Airways, KLM, Lufthansa, Nigeria Airways, Olympic Airways, PIA, Pan Am, Royal Swazi Airways, Sabena, SAS, Saudia, Somali Airlines, Sudan Airways, Swissair, Uganda Airlines, Varig and Zambia Airways.

Airline Tickets Nairobi is the best city in East Africa (and perhaps in the whole of Africa) to pick up cheap airline tickets for international flights. There is a lot of competition between travel agents so most of them lean over backwards to give you whatever discounts they can. They are the equivalent of 'bucket shops' in Europe. Only a few of the airlines sell discounted tickets through these agents and none of them sell them directly from their own offices. The most common discounters are Aeroflot, Ethiopian Airlines, Olympic Airways and Sudan Airways and most of the cheap tickets available are for flights to Europe, although there are others to India or Pakistan and to Madagascar, Mauritius, Réunion.

Tickets are paid for in local currency but to comply with government regulations it's usually necessary to produce your currency declaration form and bank receipts for the full amount you would pay if you bought the ticket direct from the airline concerned. It's important to bear this in mind if you are going to be leaving Kenya for a while and then returning later to buy your ticket, since your currency form will be collected at the border so you will lose the exchange credits recorded on it. The best thing to do in these circumstances is to buy your ticket just before you leave Kenya for the first time. You can also pay for your ticket in foreign currency in which case you don't need bank receipts.

A Nairobi-London ticket on Aeroflot or Sudan Air currently goes for Sh 4600 to Sh 4800 (about US$287 to US$300) but you may have to produce bank receipts for Sh 11,600 to Sh 13,600 (about US$725 to US$850). If you're lucky you may find an agency which only wants to see bank receipts for the price of the ticket. Olympic Airways on the same route generally costs more – expect Sh 6200 (about US$387). A Nairobi-Bombay ticket (on PIA) goes for Sh 4200 (about US$262) and you have to produce bank receipts for Sh 5830 to Sh 6110 (about US$364 to US$380). Again, you may find an agency which doesn't want to see bank receipts.

Similarly, there are deals on Air Madagascar and Air Mauritius. Bought from an agent, it's possible to have a 21-day excursion fare 'doctored' to give you as much as eight to 10 weeks for the same price. On this basis a Nairobi-Antananarivo-Nairobi ticket would cost about Sh 4250 (about US$265) and Nairobi-Comoros Islands-Mauritius-Réunion-Madagascar-Nairobi ticket with stop-overs in each place would be around Sh 6640 (US$415).

You may think that the fares quoted above are hardly 'cheap' if you're sitting in a northern European city (especially London, Amsterdam or Frankfurt) where there are hundreds of bucket shops selling discounted international airline tickets.

You'd be right. If you buy a return ticket from London to Nairobi, for instance, it will cost you around US$560 so you won't be saving anything if you buy a one-way ticket from Europe to Nairobi and another ticket from Nairobi back to Europe. But if you haven't got a return ticket – if you came overland from Europe or flew in from India for example – then you won't beat Nairobi prices. Other African capital cities are about twice as expensive.

Airport Tax The airport departure tax for international flights is US$10. You must pay this in foreign currency. Kenyan shillings are not accepted.

To/From Somalia

Air There are flights twice a week in either direction between Nairobi and Mogadishu, one by Somali Airlines and the other by Kenya Airways. The fare is Sh 1638 one-way and Sh 2623 return. Keep anything of value in your cabin luggage or it will probably have disappeared by the time you get your luggage back in Mogadishu. The baggage handlers there are notorious for their light fingers.

Road By road, the first part of the journey involves taking a bus from Nairobi to Garissa. There are buses from Garissa to Liboi (the border village) from the Mobil station on the road out of town to the north at 9 am on Tuesday, Thursday and Saturday. In the opposite direction they travel Wednesday, Friday and Sunday. The actual departure time depends on when the military escort is ready – there has been trouble with *shifta* (bandits) in the past but this has decreased dramatically since the buses were provided with an armed escort. The bus costs Sh 70 and takes about six hours. It's also fairly easy to hitch since a lot of government vehicles also cover this route and they often have spare seats. Lifts are often free.

When you get to Liboi you must report to the police. The immigration official

Top: Nairobi, Kenya (RA)
Left: Malindi, Kenya (GC)
Right: Omani ruin, Gedi near Malindi, Kenya (GC)

can be tiring. Changing money in Liboi used to be a good idea as the rate for Somali shillings was excellent. The January 1985 devaluation and subsequent float of the Somali shilling has virtually killed the black market but you are still going to need enough shillings to get you as far as Kisimayo or Mogadishu.

The next morning, very early, a bus will take you to the Somali Liboi (about 20 km) and from there to Kisimayo there is usually one bus per day in either direction either direct or via Afmadu. The cost is SomSh 300 (plus a small baggage charge) and the trip takes about 10 hours. The 'road' is just a sandy track through the scrub and there are numerous security checks which involve baggage searches and document checks. They're mainly concerned with Somalis smuggling goods in from Kenya and don't normally hassle western travellers. Make sure you ask for a currency declaration form at the Somali border. Banks won't change money without one so if you don't have one you'll have to go chasing around town to get one.

Liboi is an important staging post in the *qat* (known as *miraa* in Kenya) trade (which is now illegal in Somalia). At least two light planes arrive here from Nairobi daily, drop their load and return – always empty. It's relatively easy to hitch a ride with them and it's usually free, but you must be at the airstrip as they don't hang around very long. Picking up these planes in Nairobi to fly to Liboi is much more difficult.

Sea It's possible to find dhows in Lamu going up the coast to Kiunga (about 18 km from the Somali border) and even to Chiamboni (just over the border – you'd need a Somali visa for this). There are very few onward connections going north from Chiamboni, however. Dhows to Kisimayo and Mogadishu are very infrequent and you would have to wait a long time before finding one. If this is where you'd like to go, ask Mr Mwanjala

at the customs office in Lamu if he knows of anyone going that way.

There is also a fairly regular schooner, the *El Mansur*, captained by Omar Baqshweni, which sails from Lamu to Kisimayo. It's a three-day trip which costs Sh 600 including food. On the return trip it costs SomSh 600 (making the return trip much cheaper). You sleep on deck.

Between Mombasa and Kisimayo (Somalia) it's worth making enquiries down at the old dock with the Registrar of Dhows about the *MV Tawakal* which occasionally makes this run. The fare is Sh 400 which includes food and water, although you're advised to bring some of your own too. They journey takes about 48 hours. Bring sun-tan lotion with you or you'll be burnt alive.

To/From Sudan

Air The only way to get to Sudan from either Kenya or Uganda at present is to fly either to Juba or Khartoum – and if you fly into Juba you'll have to fly out again as it's virtually the only enclave in the south still controlled by the central government.

Road The best way of getting to Sudan used to be to go to Uganda and then take the main road from Kampala north to Juba via the Nimule border post. It used to be possible to go direct from Kenya via Lodwar, Lokichoggio, Kapoeta and Torit and on to Juba but it's a much rougher route which took at least six days.

The civil war in Sudan is now in full swing again and this has put the whole southern part of the country virtually off-limits to overland travel. You'd be very foolish to attempt it, even with official permission from the Sudanese authorities, which probably won't be forthcoming anyway.

To/From Tanzania

Road There are several points of entry into Tanzania but the main overland routes

are from Nairobi to Arusha via Namanga and from Mombasa to Tanga or Dar es Salaam via Lunga Lunga. Other lesser used routes are from Kisii to Musoma via Isebania in the north-west and Voi to Moshi via Taveta. There's also the Lake Victoria ferry from Kisumu to Musoma and Mwanza.

Until recently, there were international buses by several different companies from Nairobi to Arusha and Dar es Salaam and from Mombasa to Tanga and Dar es Salaam but, because of uneconomic fees imposed on commercial vehicles at the Tanzanian border, these were mostly suspended in mid-1986. It appears that the services have now been restored – certainly there are buses between Mombasa and Tanga or Dar es Salaam. At the time they were running, Goldline, Rombo Investments and Hood, among others, were all providing services from Nairobi.

Goldline and Hood were operating from Mombasa, usually at least twice a week from either end. Nairobi to Dar cost Sh 345 and took about 24 hours. To Arusha cost Sh 100-120 depending on the company. We know for certain that both Cat Bus, Kenyatta Avenue (Monday, Wednesday, Friday and Sunday at 5 pm), and Maranzana Bus, Kenyatta Avenue (daily at 4 pm) provide a Mombasa-Tanga-Dar service. The cost is Sh 200 and the journey takes about 14 hours.

Taking an international bus, however, is an expensive way of getting to Tanzania. You can save quite a lot of money by doing the journey in stages and changing at the border and it won't take that much longer either, if you are only going as far as Arusha (from Nairobi) or Tanga (from Mombasa). Both Namanga and Lunga Lunga are easy-going borders which you can get through in less than 30 minutes. You might be subjected to a cursory baggage search on the Tanzanian side but currency declaration forms are treated as so much waste paper.

From Nairobi there are frequent buses,

matatus and shared taxis to Namanga. Buses cost Sh 30 but they take up to four hours. It's much more convenient to take a shared taxi from East African Road Services at the bottom of Ronald Ngala St. They cost Sh 50 per person but take only two hours (five passengers per car). From the Tanzanian side of the border there are frequent buses (TanSh 60), *matatus* (TanSh 150) and shared taxis to Arusha which take less than two hours. The two border posts are right next to each other at Namanga. Assuming there are no delays at the border, therefore, you can be in Arusha about 4½ hours after leaving Nairobi.

Similarly, there are frequent buses (Sh 30), *matatus* and shared taxis from the southern side of the Likoni ferry in Mombasa to Lunga Lunga which take about 1½ hours and then *matatus* and shared taxis from there to Tanga for TanSh 100 which take about one hour. There is a six km gap between the Kenyan and Tanzanian border posts at Lunga Lunga. If you get there early enough in the day there will be pick-ups available to transport you between the two posts. Later on in the day you may have to hitch.

There's usually plenty of transport if you're crossing the border between Voi and Moshi but up in the north between Kisii and Musoma you may well get stuck and have to do a considerable amount of walking.

Boat – Lake Victoria Ferries Across Lake Victoria the *MV Bukoba* connects Kisumu in Kenya with Musoma, Mwanza and Bukoba in Tanzania. It's operated by the Tanzanian Railways Corporation so all services on the boat have to be paid for in Tanzanian shillings. It may be possible to pay for the boat fare in Tanzanian shillings you have previously changed and it would work out much cheaper this way if you bought your Tanzanian shillings on the street market at around US$1 = TanSh 160 as opposed to the

official rate of about TanSh 20. There's no need to book in advance as there are few passengers between Kisumu and Musoma. The schedule is:

day	port	arrive	depart
Mon	Mwanza	–	9 pm
Tues	Musoma	6 am	9 pm
Wed	Mwanza	6 am	–
Thurs	Mwanza	–	9 am
Thurs	Musoma	7 pm	9 pm
Fri	Kisumu	6 am	9 pm
Sat	Musoma	6 am	9 am
Sat	Mwanza	6 pm	9 pm
Sun	Bukoba	7 am	9 pm
Mon	Mwanza	7 am	–

Kisumu-Mwanza fares are: TanSh 571 (1st class), TanSh 453 (2nd class), TanSh 206 (3rd class). First class is a cabin with four bunks on the top deck, 2nd class is a cabin with four bunks on the lower deck, and 3rd class is wooden benches only. As there are usually few passengers between Kisumu and Musoma, 3rd class would be adequate if you have your own bedding since by the time you reach Musoma it will be daylight. Meals are available on the boat for TanSh 80 (main course only) and TanSh 150 (three-course meal). They're not exactly cordon bleu but they're not bad either.

In the past, it used to be necessary to visit Kenyan Immigration in Kisumu (Alpha House, Oginga Odinga Rd) before boarding the boat. This may now have changed so that all formalities are completed in the customs building just inside the port entry gate.

Boat - Dhows From the old harbour in Mombasa you can find dhows going south to the islands of Pemba and Zanzibar in Tanzania. There are no regular schedules although usual price to Zanzibar is Sh 200, including fish caught en route and cooked on deck. The journey takes two days and one night – you sleep on deck in the harbour at Pemba where you also clear Tanzanian immigration. The boat can get very crowded between Pemba and Zanzibar but you'll probably end up with half a dozen invitations to stay in Zanzibar.

To/From Uganda
Road & Rail The two crossing points into Uganda are Malaba and Busia. The former is the most popular but it's just as easy to cross the border at Busia. There is a choice of train (three times per week) or bus/matatu.

Trains depart Nairobi on Tuesday, Friday and Saturday at 3 pm, arriving at 8.30 am the next day. In the opposite direction they depart Malaba on Wednesday, Saturday and Sunday at 4 pm and arrive at 9.30 am the next day. The fares are: 1st class – Sh 336; 2nd class – Sh 145; 3rd class – Sh 63.

Buses are operated daily in either direction by several companies between 7 and 7.30 pm. The fare is Sh 110 and they arrive the next morning about 5.30 to 6 am. If you don't want to travel at night you can do it in stages through Nakuru and Eldoret to Malaba.

In the opposite direction from Malaba to Nairobi, you can do the journey by day if you first take a matatu from Malaba to Bungoma (Sh 15, about 45 minutes), stay the night in Bungoma (plenty of budget hotels) and then take one of the many buses to Nairobi the following morning at about 8 am. They arrive in Nairobi about 5 pm and cost Sh 90.

From the Kenyan border post it is about one km to the Ugandan post and you will have to walk (there's no transport). Both border posts are easy-going though there may be a very cursory baggage search at Ugandan customs. You also have to visit the currency declaration office (see the Money section in the Uganda chapter for further details). There are frequent daily matatus from the border to Tororo (Sh 600, less than one hour) and to Jinja and Kampala (Sh 9000, about 3½ hours).

If your starting point in Kenya is

Kisumu then Busia is your nearest border post. There are frequent *matatus* to Busia and others from there to Jinja and Kampala (by-passing Tororo).

GETTING AROUND
Air

Kenya Airways, the national carrier, connects the main cities of Nairobi, Mombasa, Kisumu and Malindi and seats are usually readily available. There are also a number of private airlines which connect the main cities with smaller towns and certain national parks. The main ones are Cooper Skybird and Pioneer Airlines. Both of these companies connect Mombasa with Malindi and Lamu and the latter also fly to Garissa, Hulugho, Kunga, Liboi, Maasai Mara, Mandera, Marsabit, Moyale, Ukunda and Wajir. It's worth considering these companies if your time is very limited and/or the roads are bad.

Road

Kenyan roads in the south-western part of the country – west of a line drawn through Malindi, Isiolo and Kitale – are excellent. In fact they're some of the best in Africa. North and north-east of this line and in the national parks they are all gravel roads, usually in a reasonable state of repair if you consider *piste* (corrugated gravel) to be a reasonable state of repair. Driving on these, at the necessary speed to avoid wrecking a vehicle, can be agony on your kidneys after several hours, especially if you're on a bus which has had a double set of unyielding springs fitted to it. Naturally, there are wash-outs on some of these during the rainy seasons and, under these circumstances, journey times can be considerably longer.

Right up in the north on the eastern side of Lake Turkana, especially in the Kaisut and Chalbi deserts, you can make good headway in the dry season and the roads (which would be better described as tracks) are often surprisingly smooth and in good condition. This is certainly true of

the road from Wamba to North Horr via Parsaloi, Baragoi, South Horr and Loyangalani. After rain, however, it's another story, particularly on the flat parts of the deserts. They turn into treacherous seas of mud, often as much as a metre deep in places. Only a complete fool would attempt to drive in these circumstances without four-wheel-drive, sand ladders, adequate jacking equipment, shovels, a tow rope/wire, drinking water and spare metal jerrycans of fuel. This is especially true of the stretches of track between North Horr and Maikona and on any of the tracks leading off the Marsabit-Isiolo road to South Horr.

To get out of the mud, if you're really stuck, you're going to be entirely dependent on the small number of vehicles which *may* pass by and *may* stop and help (they won't want to get stuck either), or a passing herd of camels. It's going to cost you money either way. Not only that but you can sometimes drive for hours only to find that it's impossible to cross a river, which may not even exist in the dry season, and have to drive all the way back again. Fuel is very difficult to find in this region and is usually only available at mission stations at up to three times what you would pay for it in Nairobi – and they'll only sell you a limited amount. Make adequate preparations if you are driving your own vehicle.

Driving If you are bringing your own vehicle to Kenya you should get a free three-month permit at the border on entry, so long as you have a valid carnet de passage for it. If you don't have a carnet you should be able to get a free one-week permit at the border on entry after which you must get an 'Authorisation permit for a foreign private vehicle' which costs Sh 3900 (about US$244). Before you do this, however, get in touch with the Automobile Association in Nairobi.

When you are driving your own vehicle there are certain routes in north-east

Kenya where you must obtain police permission before setting out. This is just a formality but there will be a road-block to enforce this. The main stretch where this applies is between Isiolo and Marsabit where all transport must travel in convoy at a particular time of day.

Hiring a Vehicle Hiring a car in Kenya is an expensive affair but it does give you freedom of movement and the ability to go places which tours don't go to. For visiting the most popular of the national parks (Amboseli, Masai Mara, Tsavo East and West and Lake Nakuru) it's probably cheaper and you will see more if you go on an organised camping tour. Two of the main reasons for this are that the tour company organises the catering and their guides who take you out on game viewing trips generally have a good idea where to find the animals. In your own vehicle you might drive round all day and not see anywhere near as much as you would on a tour. However, it's probably worth hiring a car to explore northern Kenya and particularly the Lake Turkana area.

Ordinary cars are cheaper to rent than four-wheel-drive vehicles but the whole point about hiring a vehicle is that it will enable you to get off the beaten track. It's not worth hiring anything that isn't four-wheel-drive. A four-seater, Suzuki Safari four-wheel-drive will cost you around Sh 240 per day plus Sh 80 insurance and Sh 3 to Sh 3.50 per km. Or US$325 per week with unlimited mileage but excluding petrol. A six to eight-seater Isuzu Trooper, Land-Rover or Toyota Land Cruiser will cost you about Sh 500 per day plus Sh 120 insurance plus Sh 5.30 to Sh 6.20 per km. Or US$540 per week with unlimited mileage but excluding petrol.

You will also have to pay a returnable deposit of between Sh 3000 and Sh 5000 unless you take out accident waiver insurance. Petrol costs about Sh 8 per litre on average (from a pump). It can cost up to three times this price in remote areas, if you can find it. Take lots of jerrycans with you!

Before you hire a car, go round as many companies as you can find and ask what their rates are. The daily and weekly fixed charges generally only vary by up to Sh 50 but the mileage charges can vary by much more. Don't forget to ask what the insurance covers – a smashed windscreen? burst tyres? theft? accident damage? Some companies have minimum age limits which can be 23 or 25 years old with a minimum of two years' experience. You only need a driving licence from your own country or an international driving permit. Some firms offer special low season rates between the beginning of March and the end of May. See the Nairobi section for rental agency information.

Bus & Matatu Kenya has a network of regular buses, *matatus* (normally mini-buses or saloon cars which you share with others) and private taxis. The cheapest form of transport are buses, next *matatus* and lastly private taxis (expensive). There's not a lot to choose in terms of journey times between normal buses and *matatus* but there is a lot in terms of safety. Most *matatu* drivers are under a lot of pressure from their owners to maximise profits so they tend to drive recklessly and overload their vehicles. They also put in long working days. Stories about *matatu* smashes and overturnings in which a few people are killed and many injured can be found almost daily in the newspapers. Of course, many travellers use them and, in some cases, there is no alternative, but if there is (such as a bus or train) then take that in preference. The Mombasa-Nairobi road is notorious for smashes.

As in most East African countries, you can always find a *matatu* which is going to the next town or further afield so long as it's not too late in the day. Simply ask around among the drivers at the park. Sometimes it's shared with the bus station. They leave when full and the

fares are fixed. It's unlikely you will be asked for more money than other passengers are paying.

Bus fares are generally about half way between what you would pay on the railways in 2nd and 3rd class and the journey times are quicker. Unlike the trains, which usually travel at night, many buses travel during the day so you may prefer to take a bus if you want to see the countryside. All the bus companies are privately owned and some of them run better buses than others. Coastline Safari, Goldline and Tana River Bus Company are about the best of the bunch. Mawingo Bus Service and Akamba Bus Service are cheaper but their buses are older. On a long journey you're only looking at about US$1 difference in the fare.

Some Kenyan towns (Bungoma, Eldoret, Malindi, Naivasha) have bus stations, although these are often nothing more than a dirt patch. In most places each bus company will have its own terminus though these are often close to each other. There are exceptions and these are indicated on the street maps. *Matatu* and taxi lines sometimes share the same stations as buses but this isn't always the case, especially in Nairobi.

Hitching Hitching is usually good on the main roads and may well be preferable to travelling by *matatu*, but if you are picked up by an African driver and are expecting a free lift then make this clear from the outset. Most will expect a contribution at least. Hitching to the national parks, on the other hand, can be very difficult since most people either go on a tour or hire their own vehicle. Apart from that, once you get to the park lodges or camping areas, you will be entirely dependent on persuading other tourists with their own vehicles to take you out with them to view game since walking in the parks is forbidden.

Rail
Kenyan Railways are excellent; they're a very popular way of travelling, generally run on time and they're considerably safer than travelling by bus or *matatu*. The main railway line runs from Mombasa to Malaba on the Kenya/Uganda border via Voi, Nairobi, Nakuru and Eldoret with branch lines from Nakuru to Kisumu, Nairobi to Nanyuki, Voi to Taveta and Eldoret to Kitale. There are no passenger services on the Nairobi-Nanyuki or Eldoret-Kitale branches. Although the tracks are continuous with both the Tanzanian and Ugandan systems, there are no international services at present.

First class consists of two-berth compartments with a wash basin, drinking water, a wardrobe and a drinks service. There's a lockable door between one compartment and the adjacent one so, if there are four of you travelling together, you can make one compartment out of two, if you wish. They're spotlessly clean.

Second class consists of four-berth compartments with a hand basin and drinking water supply. Third class is seats only. All the compartments have fans. Sexes are separated in 1st and 2nd class unless you book the whole compartment. Third class can get a little wearing on the nerves on long journeys especially if they are overnight (which most are). Second class is more than adequate in this respect and 1st class is definitely a touch of luxury as far as budget travel goes.

You must book in advance for both 1st and 2nd class – two to three days is usually sufficient – otherwise you'll probably find that there are no berths available and will have to go 3rd class. If you're in Malindi and planning on taking the Mombasa-Nairobi train, bookings can be made with an agent in Malindi. Compartment and berth numbers are posted up about 30 minutes prior to departure. Bedding (sheets, pillow and

blanket) is available for Sh 25 if you don't have a sleeping bag – attendants will come round to ask you if you want bedding before the train departs.

There is a dining car on most trains offering dinner and breakfast (two sittings). Dinner on the Nairobi-Mombasa or Mombasa-Nairobi runs is an East African experience you should not miss at any price, but try to go to the second sitting as you can hang around afterwards and continue your conversation. The food is excellent, plentiful. You are served four courses on starched white linen and silver-plated cutlery by immaculately-dressed waiters. One time I was on this run I found myself seated with the black Anglican Bishop of Mombasa in his mauve cassock and a very scantily dressed and very attractive woman who lived with a white planter up in the Aberdares. The conversation was, to the say the least, convoluted and somewhat bizarre but thoroughly enjoyable. Dinner costs just Sh 60 and breakfast is Sh 35.

Boat
Lake Victoria Ferries Ferries service ports on the small Kenyan part of the lake and others connect Kisumu with the Tanzanian ports of Musoma, Mwanza and Bukoba.

Dhows Sailing on a dhow along the East African coast is one of Kenya's most worthwhile and memorable experiences. There's nothing quite like drifting along the ocean in the middle of the night with the moon up high, the only sounds the lapping of the waves against the side of the boat and subdued conversation. It's enjoyable at any time of day, however, even when the breeze drops and the boat virtually comes to a standstill.

There are no creature comforts aboard these dhows so when night comes you simply bed down wherever there is space. You'll probably get off these boats smelling of fish since fish oil is used to condition the timbers of the boat – nothing that a shower won't remove! Take drinking water and some food with you although fish is usually caught on the way and cooked up on deck over charcoal. Lamu is one of the best places to pick up a dhow and many people take them down to Mombasa.

Nairobi

Mark Knopfler could almost have been singing about Nairobi when he wrote *Telegraph Road*. Until the late 1900s there was nothing there. It was just a watering hole for the Maasai. Then came the Mombasa-to-Uganda railway complete with its 32,000 indentured Indian labourers from Gujarat and Punjab along with their British colonial overlords intent on beating the German colonial push for the Ugandan heartland. Being approximately half-way between Mombasa and Uganda and a convenient place to pause before the arduous climb into the highlands it quickly became tent city.

Much of the area was still a foul-smelling swamp at this time and game roamed freely over the adjoining plains yet by 1900 it had become a town of substantial buildings and five years later succeeded Mombasa as the capital of the British East Africa Protectorate. Since then it has gone from strength to strength and is now the largest city between Cairo and Johannesburg. The tower blocks of Nairobi can be seen for miles as you crest the hills which surround the plain on which it sits. Yet, in terms of the world's largest cities, Nairobi is still small with a population of just over ¾ million. You can walk from one end of the central business district to the other in 15 minutes. And where else in the world would you be able to see lion, cheetah, rhino and giraffe roaming free with the tower blocks of a city as a backdrop?

It's a very cosmopolitan place, lively, interesting, pleasantly landscaped and a good place to get essential business and

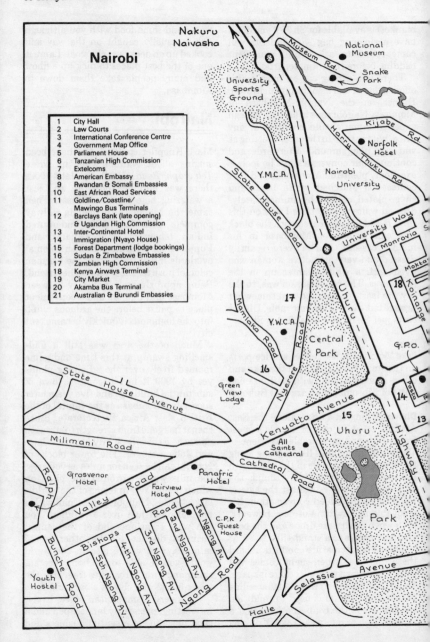

Nairobi

1 City Hall
2 Law Courts
3 International Conference Centre
4 Government Map Office
5 Parliament House
6 Tanzanian High Commission
7 Extelcoms
8 American Embassy
9 Rwandan & Somali Embassies
10 East African Road Services
11 Goldline/Coastline/
   Mawingo Bus Terminals
12 Barclays Bank (late opening)
   & Ugandan High Commission
13 Inter-Continental Hotel
14 Immigration (Nyayo House)
15 Forest Department (lodge bookings)
16 Sudan & Zimbabwe Embassies
17 Zambian High Commission
18 Kenya Airways Terminal
19 City Market
20 Akamba Bus Terminal
21 Australian & Burundi Embassies

Nakuru
Naivasha

Museum Rd.

National
Museum

Snake
Park

University
Sports
Ground

Kijabe Rd.

Norfolk
Hotel

Harry Thuku Rd.

Y.M.C.A.

State House Road

Nairobi
University

University Way

Monrovia S

Moktar

Koinange

18

Uhuru

17

Mamlaka Road

Y.W.C.A.

Nyerere Road

Central
Park

G.P.O.

16

Green
View
Lodge

Posta

14

13

Kenyatta Avenue

State House Avenue

15

Uhuru

Highway

All
Saints
Cathedral

Milimani Road

Grosvenor
Hotel

Valley Road

Panafric
Hotel

Fairview
Hotel

Cathedral Road

Park

Ralph

Bunche Road

Bishops Road

5th Ngong Av.

4th Ngong Av.

3rd Ngong Av.

2nd Ngong Av.

1st Ngong Av.

Ngong Road

C.P.K.
Guest
House

Selassie

Avenue

Youth
Hostel

Haile

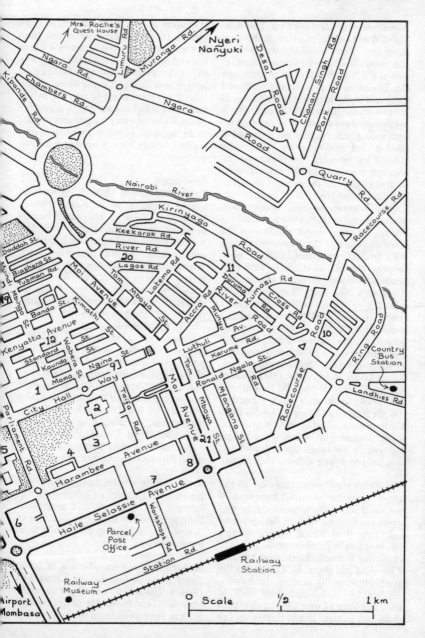

bureaucratic matters sewn up. This is no Third World capital city though there are some very overcrowded shanty towns on the outskirts and even across the other side of the Nairobi River from Kirinyaga Rd. The latter are periodically bulldozed away and burnt down by the City Council *askaris*, in the interests of hygiene but it takes only days for them to regenerate! Like most cities, Nairobi has its crowded market and trading areas, its middle class/office workers' suburbs and its spacious mansions and beautiful flower-decked gardens for the rich and powerful. The first is an area full of local colour, energy, aspirations and opportunism where manual workers, exhausted *matatu* drivers, the unemployed, the devious, the down-and-out and the disoriented mingle with budget travellers, whores, shop keepers, high school students, food stall vendors, drowsy security guards and those with life's little illicit goodies for sale. It's called River Rd – though, of course, it spans more than just this road itself. One of the funniest yet most poignant yarns I have ever read about an area such as this is to be found in a novel by Kenyan author Meja Mwangi called, *Going Down River Road* (Heinemann: African Writers Series). I'd recommend this book to anyone and especially travellers passing through Nairobi. Even if you are not staying in this area you should make a point of getting down there one evening just to see how the other half lives on the wrong side of Tom Mboya St.

Elsewhere in Nairobi there are all the sort of things that you won't have seen for months if you've been hacking your way across the Central African Republic and Zaire from West Africa, making do with the shortages in Zambia and Tanzania or wandering through the cultural vacuum of Rwanda and Burundi. Things like the latest films on big screens, bookshops, restaurants, cafés and bars full of travellers from all over the world, offices where you can get things done with the minimum of fuss, banks where you can change travellers' cheques in less than five minutes and a poste restante where you sort out your own letters from the pile so you don't end up with that feeling that letters have been put in the wrong pigeon hole. It's a great place to stay for awhile but if you stay too long it gets expensive because almost everyone you meet wants to do the same as you did when you first arrived – binge, rage, whatever word you use for it!

Information

Tourist Information There is no national tourist organisation in Kenya though there is a place in the small square between the Nairobi Hilton and Moi Avenue which used to be one but now it only has information on expensive hotels, safaris and Kenya Airways/charter flights. It has nothing of interest for budget travellers but they do not charge for making hotel reservations and there are a number of other services. Mr Butt is particularly helpful.

There is also a leaflet called, *Tourist's Kenya* (PO Box 40025; tel 337169) published every two weeks. It is free of charge and available from most large hotels – the Thorn Tree Café is the most convenient place to find it. It contains most of what you'll need to know – hotels, restaurants, airlines, tour and safari operators – but it doesn't bend over backwards to keep its factual information up to date or even comprehensive.

Banks At Kenyatta International Airport, Nairobi, the Bureau de Change is open 24 hours a day, seven days a week. The Kenyatta Avenue branch of Barclays in Nairobi is open Monday to Saturday from 9 am to 4.30 pm.

Bookshops The best selection of book-shops are to be found along Kimathi St (Select Bookshop and New Stanley Bookshop) and Mama Ngina St (Prestige Books). For second hand books, there is a

used paperback book store on Market St just down from the American Snack Bar and Khima Chappati Corner. They have a good selection of novels, a fairly fast turn-over and will take back their own books and refund you half what you paid for them. All the foreign cultural organisations have libraries which are open to the public and are free of charge.

Maps There are many maps of Nairobi available in the bookshops but probably the best is the *City of Nairobi: Map & Guide* in English, French and German published by the Survey of Kenya (Sh 45) in a red front cover with partially coloured photographs on the back cover. It covers the suburbs as well as having a detailed map of the central area. If you're going to be staying for a long time, however, the *A to Z: Guide to Nairobi* (Sh 40) by D T Dobie (Kenway Publications) is worth buying.

Post Poste restante in Nairobi is at the old main post office on Kenyatta Avenue. There is no charge for collecting letters and they give you the whole pile of your

letter of the alphabet to sort through. If expected letters are not in the appropriate pigeon hole they're more than willing to let you look through others.

The post office on Kenyatta Avenue, Nairobi, doesn't handle parcel post (other than very small parcels such as newspapers and magazines) and if you do put small parcels into the public posting box here they probably won't arrive. The one parcel of books which I sent and did not arrive was posted here. The parcel post office is the huge new building on Haile Selassie Avenue.

Safety You may hear rumours about Nairobi being a dangerous city at night as far as robberies go. I've certainly had enough letters from people whom this has happened to but I've been there quite a few times and I've never once felt even threatened walking back to my hotel. Perhaps it's just that I don't do crazy things like walk across Uhuru Park late at night or stumble from pillar to post, drunk as a skunk, alone up River Rd, or pull out my wallet when someone asks me for a few shillings down a dark alley. Be careful! It's no worse than many other cities in the world but, as in every other, you must be vigilant. You should definitely not walk from the centre to the Youth Hostel or through Uhuru Park or along Uhuru Highway/Waiyaki Way anywhere between Westlands and the roundabout with Haile Selassie Avenue at night. You are asking for trouble. And if you meet anyone claiming to be a Ugandan student/refugee with a hard luck story, you'll know it's bogus.

Vaccinations You can get these at City Hall Clinic, Mama Ngina St. Yellow fever is done from 8.30 to 11 am Monday to Friday (Sh 25), cholera from 8.30 am to 12 noon Monday to Friday (Sh 20) and tetanus and typhoid from 8.30 to 11 am Monday to Friday (free). If you want a gamma globulin shot (for hepatitis) go to Dr Meyerhold, 3rd floor, Bruce House,

Standard St. They cost Sh 150. This doctor has his own pathology laboratory if you need blood or stool tests. It will cost you Sh 120 per consultation plus laboratory fees. Otherwise go to the Nairobi Hospital which has the same scale of charges. Avoid like the plague Kenyatta Hospital since, although it's free, treatment here is possibly worse than the ailment according to local residents.

Photography For passport size photographs, the cheapest place to go is the machine under the yellow and black sign 'Photo Me', a few doors up Kenyatta Avenue from the New Stanley Bookshop. It costs Sh 15 for four prints and takes about three minutes. You can also get them from the photography shop in Kimathi House opposite the New Stanley Hotel but here they cost Sh 35 for three prints.

For camera repairs or equipment rental the Camera Maintenance Centre (tel 26920) in the Hilton Arcade is definitely not cheap. Make sure you get a quote beforehand as quite a few people have felt they've been ripped off here. Alternatively try Camera Experts (tel 337750), KCS House, Mama Ngina St. They can also process film overnight.

Embassies Apart from embassies in neighbouring countries mentioned under Visas others include:

Algeria
    Matungulu House, Mamlaka Rd (tel 334227)
Australia
    Development House, Moi Avenue (tel 334666/334670)
Austria
    City House, Wabera St (tel 28281/2)
Belgium
    Silopark House, Mama Ngina St (tel 20501)
Canada
    Comcraft House, Haile Selassie Avenue (tel 334033)

Denmark
    HFCK Building, Koinange St (tel 331088)
Finland
    International House, Mama Ngina St (tel 334777/8)
West Germany
    Embassy House, Harambee Avenue (tel 26661/2/3)
Ghana
    International House, Mama Ngina St (tel 27231)
India
    Jeevan Bharati Building, Harambee Avenue (tel 22566)
Irish Republic
    Maendeleo Building, Monrovia St (tel 26771/4)
Italy
    Prudential Assurance Building, Wabera St (tel 21615)
Japan
    ICEA Building, Kenyatta Avenue (tel 332955)
South Korea
    Kencom House, City Hall Way (tel 333581/2)
Lesotho
    International House, Mama Ngina St (tel 337493)
Liberia
    Bruce House, Standard St (tel 22604)
Libya
    Jamahiriya House, Loita St (tel 29814)
Malawi
    Bruce House, Standard St (tel 21174)
Netherlands
    Uchumi House, Nkrumah Lane (tel 27111)
Nigeria
    Kencom House, Moi Avenue (tel 28321)
Norway
    Rehani House, Kenyatta Avenue (tel 337121)
Swaziland
    Silopark House, Mama Ngina St (tel 20468)
Sweden
    International House, Mama Ngina St (tel 29042)
Switzerland
    International House, Mama Ngina St (tel 28735)
UK
    Bruce House, Standard St (tel 335944)
USA
    corner Haile Selassie Avenue & Moi Avenue (tel 334141)

Top: Cat & Mouse rocks, near Wamba, Kenya (GC)
Left: Kenyatta Conference Centre, Nairobi, Kenya (GC)
Right: Old dhow dock, Mombasa, Kenya (GC)

USSR
   Lenana Rd (tel 722462)

Airlines

Aeroflot
   International House, Mama Ngina St (tel 20746)
Air Canada
   Kimathi House, Kimathi St (tel 21024)
Air France
   Chai House, Koinange St (tel 335325). They also handle Air Djibouti
Air India
   Jeevan Bharati Building, Tumaini House, Moi Avenue & Harambee Avenue (tel 334788)
Air Madagascar
   Nairobi Hilton, Mama Ngina St & Moi Avenue (tel 252860)
Air Mauritius
   Union Towers, Moi Avenue (tel 29166)
Air Malawi
   Mitchell Cotts House, City Hall Way (tel 340212)
Air Zaire
   Shretta House, Kimathi St (tel 25625)
Air Zimbabwe
   International House, Mama Ngina St (tel 20106)
Alitalia
   Nairobi Hilton, Mama Ngina St & Moi Avenue (tel 24361)
British Airways
   Prudential Building, Wabera St (tel 334362)
Cameroon Airlines
   HFCK Building, Kenyatta Avenue (tel 337788)
Egyptair
   Shankardass House, Moi Avenue (tel 2681)
Ethiopian Airlines
   Bruce House, Standard St (tel 26631)
El Al
   Sweepstake House, Mama Ngina St (tel 28123)
Iberia
   Nairobi Hilton, Mama Ngina St & Moi Avenue (tel 338623)
Japan Airlines
   International House, Mama Ngina St (tel 20591)
Kenya Airways
   Airways Terminal, Koinange St (tel 29291)
KLM
   Fedha Towers, Muindi Mbingu St (tel 332673)

Lufthansa
   IPS Building, Kimathi St (tel 335819)
Nigeria Airways
   Nairobi Hilton, Mama Ngina St & Moi Avenue (tel 336555)
Olympic Airways
   Nairobi Hilton, Mama Ngina St & Moi Avenue (tel 338441)
Pakistan International Airlines
   ICEA Building, Banda St (tel 333900)
Pan Am
   Nairobi Hilton, Mama Ngina St & Moi Avenue (tel 23581)
Royal Swazi
   Reinsurance Plaza, Taifa Rd (tel 339300)
Saudia
   Jamia Mosque, Kigali Rd (tel 331456)
Sabena
   International House, Mama Ngina St (tel 22185)
SAS
   Grindlays Building, Kimathi St (tel 338347)
Somali Airlines
   Bruce House, corner Standard St & Muindi Mbingu St (tel 335409)
Sudan Airways
   York House, Moi Avenue (tel 21326)
Swissair
   Corner House, Kimathi St (tel 331012)
TWA
   New Stanley House, Standard St (tel 24036)
Uganda Airlines
   corner Kenyatta Avenue & Muindi Mbingu St (tel 21354)
Varig
   Eagle House, Kimathi St (tel 20961)
Zambia Airways
   Nairobi Hilton, Mama Ngina St & Moi Avenue (tel 24722)

Airline Tickets Always get several quotes. One of the most popular agents is Hanzuwan-el-Kindly Tours & Travel (tel 26810 or 33 8729), Rajab Manzil Building (4th floor, room 3), Tom Mboya St. It's run by a man called Fehed A S H el-Kindly though he's known to everyone as Eddie. Budget travellers have been using his services for years. He's very friendly and helpful and offers some of the best deals in Nairobi.

Equally well recommended are Prince Travel, Kenyatta Conference Centre (especially for flights to Cairo); Crocodile Travel, Tom Mboya St, in the same block as the Ambassadeur Hotel; and Falcon Travel, International House, Mama Ngina St. Banko Travel, Latema Rd, are also very friendly and offer similar deals. Others which are worth checking out are Let's Go Travel on Standard St close to the junction with Koinange St, Appel Travel, Tamana Tours and Kambo Travel.

Foreign Cultural Organisations

Alliance Francçaise (tel 340054), ICEA Building, ground floor, Kenyatta Avenue. Open Monday to Friday from 10 am to 1 pm and 2 to 5.15 pm and on Saturday from 9.30 am to 12 noon. There is a good French restaurant here, too, which is open in the evenings.

American Cultural Center (tel 337877), National Bank Building, Harambee Avenue. Open Monday to Friday from 10 am to 5 pm and on Saturday from 10 am to 1 pm. There is a fairly large library here which is open to the public.

British Council (tel 334855), ICEA Building, mezzanine floor, Kenyatta Avenue. Open Monday to Friday from 10 am to 5 pm and on Saturday from 9 am to 12 noon. Like the American centre, there is a fairly large library here which is open to the public.

French Cultural Centre (tel 336263), Maison Francáise, corner Monrovia & Loita Sts. Open Monday to Friday from 10 am to 5 pm and on Saturday from 10 am to 1 pm.

Goethe-Institut (tel 24640) Maendeleo House, corner Monrovia & Loita Sts (tel 24640). Open Monday to Friday from 10 am to 6 pm.

Italian Cultural Institute (tel 21615) Prudential Building, Wabera St. Open Monday to Friday from 8.30 am to 1 pm and 2.30 to 5 pm.

Japan Information Centre (tel 331196), Matungulu House, Mamlaka Rd. Open Monday to Friday from 10 am to 12 noon and 2.10 to 4.30 pm.

National Museum

The National Museum is on Museum Rd off Museum Hill which itself is off Uhuru Highway. The museum has a good exhibition on prehistoric man, an incredible collection of native birds, mammals and tribal crafts as well as a new section on the culture, history and crafts of the coastal Swahili people. Opening hours are 9.30 am to 6 pm daily and admission is Sh 30 and Sh 10 for students. The local bird-watching club meets at the museum every Wednesday at 9 am. Visitors are welcome.

Snake Park

Across the road from the museum the Snake Park has living examples of most of the snake species found in East Africa – some of them are in glass cages, others in open pits. There are also tortoises and crocodiles. Hours and entry charges are the same as for the museum.

Railway Museum

The Railway Museum is on Station Rd – follow the railway tracks until you are almost at the bridge under Uhuru Highway or walk across the small piece of waste ground just next to the Uhuru Highway/Haile Selassie Avenue roundabout. In addition to old steam engines and rolling stock it will give you a good idea of Kenya's history since the beginning of the colonial period. The curator here is very friendly if there's anything you want to ask him about the exhibits. It's open Monday to Friday from 8.30 am to 6.30 pm and on Saturday from 8.30 am to 3.30 pm and entry is Sh 5 (Sh 3 for students).

Parliament House

Like to take a look at how democracy works in Kenya? If so, you can get a permit for a seat in the public gallery at Parliament House on Parliament Rd or, if Parliament is out of session, you can tour the buildings by arrangement with the Sergeant-at-Arms. Phone 21291 ext 254/5.

Nairobi National Park

This park is the most accessible of all Kenya's game parks being only a few km from the city centre. You should set aside a morning or an afternoon to see it. As in all the game parks, you must visit them in a vehicle. Walking is prohibited. This means you will either have to arrange a lift at the entrance gate with other tourists or go on a tour. Entry to the park costs Sh 30 per person.

There are many companies offering tours of Nairobi National Park and there's probably not much to choose between them. They usually depart twice a day at 9.30 am and 2 pm for a four-hour tour and cost Sh 150. Most of the tour companies also offer a day-long combined tour of the national park with a visit to the Bomas of Kenya and including a gargantuan lunch at The Carnivore for Sh 450. Most of the wild animals found in Kenya except elephant can be seen in the park. If driving your own vehicle to the park it will cost Sh 30 entry per person plus Sh 35 per car. Bus Nos 24 or 25 from Moi Avenue will get you to the park entrance.

Langata Giraffe Centre

The Langata Giraffe Centre is on Gogo Falls Rd near the Hardy Estate Shopping Centre in Langata, about 18 km from Nairobi centre. Here you can observe and hand-feed Rothschild giraffes from a raised circular wooden structure which also houses a display of information about giraffes. It's open during school term from 4 to 5.30 pm Monday to Friday and 10 am to 5.30 pm on Saturday and Sunday. During school holidays and public holidays it's open from 11 am to 5.30 pm. Admission costs Sh 30 (free to children). To get there from the centre take bus No 24.

The Bomas of Kenya

The Bomas of Kenya at Langata – a short way past the entrance to the national park on the right hand side – is a cultural centre. Here you can see traditional dances and hear songs from the country's 16 ethnic groups amid authentically recreated surroundings. There are daily performances at 2 and 4.30 pm. Entry costs Sh 60 or Sh 30 for students. If you are not on a tour, bus No 24 from outside Development House, Moi Avenue, will get you there in about a half hour.

Karen Blixen Museum

This is the farm house which was formerly the residence of Karen Blixen, author of *Out of Africa*. It's open daily from 9.30 am to 6 pm and entry costs Sh 30 or Sh 10 for students. It's right next door to the Karen College on Karen Rd between the residential areas of Karen and Langata. To get there, take public bus No 27 from the central bus station, the GPO or from the corner of Ralph Bunche Rd and Ngong Rd or No 24 from Moi Avenue. Bus No 111 will also get you most of the way but you'll have to change to No 24 at the Karen Shopping Centre.

Great Views

The revolving restaurant on the 28th floor of the **Kenyatta Conference Centre** may be closed but you can still go up to the viewing level if you ask the officials on duty in the main hall where the lifts are situated. It is East Africa's tallest building with superb views over Nairobi, the Athi Plains and out to Mt Kenya and Kilimanjaro on a fine day. Whoever takes you up may well expect a tip. You can take photographs from the top – no restrictions.

For other excellent views over Nairobi and down into the Rift Valley, go up to the Ngong Hills. Take a bus to Ngong Town from the centre and walk up to the top from there (about 1½ hours). Don't go alone and beware of muggers, especially at weekends.

Places to Stay – bottom end

There is a very good selection of budget hotels in Nairobi and the majority of

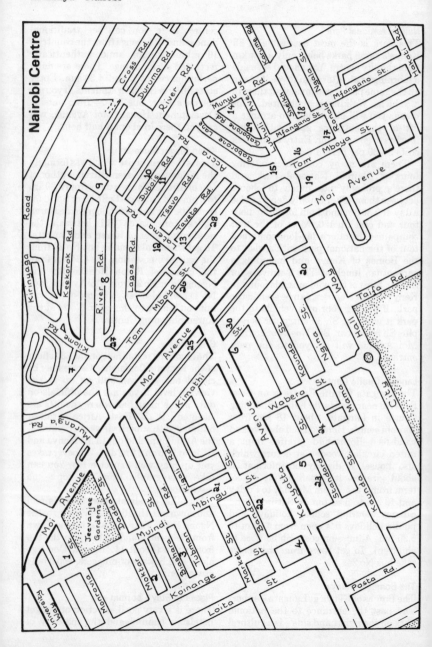

Nairobi Centre

1	Garden Guest House & Park View Hotel
2	Terminus Hotel
3	Embassy Hotel
4	Excelsior Hotel
5	680 Hotel
6	New Stanley Hotel & Thorn Tree Cafe
7	Kambirwa Boarding & Lodging
8	Mombasa Rest House
9	New Kenya Lodge
10	New Safe Life Lodging
11	Bujumbura Lodge & Africana Hotel
12	Sunrise Lodge & Modern Green Bar
13	Iqbal Hotel
14	Al Mansura Hotel
15	Hotel Salama
16	Hotel Solace
17	Gloria Hotel
18	Dolat Hotel
19	Ambassadeur Hotel
20	Hilton Hotel
21	Blukat Restaurant
22	African Heritage Cafe
23	The Pub & Japanese Restaurant
24	Trattoria
25	Satkar Vegetarian Restaurant
26	Growers' Cafe & Lobster Pot
27	Mayur Restaurant (Supreme Hotel)
28	Mandarin Restaurant
29	Malindi Dishes
30	Supermac

them, except for two very popular places outside of the city centre, are between Tom Mboya St and River Rd so if you find that one is full another is nearby.

In the Centre The *New Kenya Lodge* (tel 22202), River Rd at the junction with Latema Rd, is a legend among budget travellers and still one of the cheapest. There's always a wild and interesting bunch of people from all over the world staying here. Some even build humpies on the roof and live there for weeks. Accommodation is very basic and there are cold showers only. It costs Sh 25 for a bed in a shared room (four beds per room) and Sh 65 for a double. If it's full you can sleep on the roof or in the lobby for Sh 15. The staff are very friendly and baggage is safe here.

Sharing the legend is the *Iqbal Hotel* (tel 20914), Latema Rd, which has been popular for years. It was refurbished from top to bottom a couple of years ago and is still very pleasant and excellent value for money. The latest improvements include hot showers 24 hours a day. It costs Sh 29 for a bed in a room with four beds, Sh 34.50 for a bed in a room with three beds and Sh 69 a double. Baggage is safe here and there's a store room where you can leave excess gear (Sh 3 per day) if you are going away for a while. Get there early in the day if you want to be sure of a room.

If the above two are full there are three others on Dubois Rd, just off Latema Rd. The *Bujumbura* is very basic but clean and quiet and very secure – locked grille at the entrance. The toilets and showers are clean and there is hot water 24 hours a day. Clothes left to dry on the line will be there when you return. It costs Sh 50 a single – only two of these – and Sh 60 a double. The *New Safe Life Lodging* is very similar and the staff are cheerful. It costs Sh 60 a single and Sh 80 a double though they sometimes offer a discount on these rates if they're not busy. The *Nyandarwa Lodging* is very clean, quiet and comfortable and you can get a large double room for Sh 70. They also have single rooms but they're just glorified cupboards and not such good value for money.

Another similar place is the *Kambirwa Boarding & Lodging*, River Rd close to the junction with Tom Mboya St. They have good double rooms for Sh 70. *Naseem's Lodgings*, River Rd, is also recommended by quite a few travellers. It's very friendly, has plenty of hot water and costs Sh 105 a double for bed and breakfast. They will store baggage safely here.

About the same price is the *Sunrise Lodge*, Latema Rd opposite the Iqbal. It's clean, secure and friendly and there is usually hot water in the evenings and mornings. Rooms cost Sh 70 a single and

Sh 100 a double. The front two rooms overlooking the street are the largest and they have a balcony but they are right next door to the Modern Green Bar which rages 24 hours a day, 365 days a year so if you want a quiet room take one of those at the back of the hotel. If, on the other hand, you want enough material to write a novel of the type, 'One Day in the Life of .... ' then stay in one of the front rooms.

The *Al Mansura Hotel*, Munyu Rd, also used to be popular but it's just a filthy, squalid hole these days and very poor value at Sh 57.50 a double. Baggage is not safe left in the rooms here.

Away from the Centre There are two very popular places away from the city centre. *Mrs Roche's*, 3rd Parklands Avenue opposite the Aga Khan Hospital, is, like the New Kenya and the Iqbal, a legend. Mrs Roche has been making travellers welcome for at least 15 years and it's a favourite with campers and those with their own vehicle as well as those who don't particularly want a room in the city centre. It's situated in a very pleasant area amongst trees and flowering shrubs and is a very mellow place to stay.

The good lady now has more room as a result of recent building extensions and there are hot showers. Camping costs Sh 30 per night. A bed in a shared room costs Sh 35 or Sh 25 on the floor. Because it's so popular you may have to sleep on the floor for the first night until a bed is available. Breakfast is available for Sh 15 (two eggs, unlimited toast, butter, jam and coffee). If you go up the road about 200 to 300 metres there's a café called *Stop n' Eat* where you can get a tomato and onion omelette for Sh 9.50. There's also a place across 3rd Parklands Avenue next to the supermarket which offers vegetable samosas and Indian sweets.

Mrs Roche's two dogs, Curly and Bruno, which once acquired a reputation for eating clothes left to dry on the washing lines are now getting too old for

those antics. You can leave baggage for Sh 20. To get to Mrs Roche's, take a *matatu* (Sh 2) from the junction of Latema Rd and Tom Mboya St. They will have 'Aga Khan' in the front windscreen. Tell the driver you're heading for Mrs Roche's Guest House. It's well known.

The other very popular place is the *Youth Hostel* (tel 21789), Ralph Bunche Rd between Valley Rd and Ngong Rd. It's often very crowded here so it's a good place to meet other travellers. It's very clean, well-run, stays open all day and there's always hot water in the showers. Dave, the warden, is very friendly and will lock up gear safely for you for up to two weeks. On a day-to-day basis there are lockers to keep your gear in when you go out. The notice board here (for messages, things for sale, etc) is one of the best in Africa. A bed in a shared room costs Sh 35 but you must have a YHA membership card to stay. If not, you'll have to join the association for Sh 150 plus a photograph.

Any *matatu* or bus which goes down either Valley Rd or Ngong Rd will drop you at Ralph Bunche Rd. The No 8 *matatu* which goes down Ngong Rd is probably the most convenient. You can pick it up either outside the Hilton Hotel or the main post office on Kenyatta Avenue. If you're returning to the Youth Hostel after dark don't be tempted to walk back from the centre of the city. Many people have been robbed. Always take a *matatu* or taxi.

There are three *YMCAs* (tel 337468) and one *YWCA* (tel 338689). The former are all on State House Rd and the latter on Mamlaka Rd off Nyerere Rd. The YMCAs all cost Sh 100 per person for bed and breakfast in a dormitory or shared room plus they have more expensive private rooms (around Sh 240 with your own bathroom) but baggage left in the rooms is definitely not safe here and the prime culprits are fellow travellers. Meals at the YMCAs are excellent value. The YWCA is reluctant to take short-term visitors. It prefers to take people who are going to stay at least one month and the room rates are geared towards this. It does, however, take couples as well as single women.

Some travellers have recommended the *Dutch Volunteer Service Guest House*, Ngong Rd just past Kenyatta Hospital, which is a large old house surrounded by a garden. A bed here costs Sh 50 and there are cooking facilities. Whether this place is for volunteers alone isn't clear so it would be best to stay somewhere else initially until you can check it out.

Japanese travellers have recommended the *River House Hotel* at the west end of Kirinyaga Rd near the junction with River Rd but it's for Japanese only and costs just Sh 18 for a bed in a dormitory. They serve Japanese food here.

Places to Stay – middle

There are several mid-range hotels in the same area as the bulk of the budget hotels. One of the cheapest is the *Dolat Hotel*, Mfangano St, which is very clean and quiet and costs Sh 93.60 for singles or Sh 140.40 for doubles, both with own shower and toilet. Quite a few travellers stay here.

Another is the *Gloria Hotel*, Tom Mboya St at Ronald Ngala St, which costs Sh 110 a single, Sh 135 a double and Sh 200 a triple with own bathroom and including breakfast. It's clean and there are hot showers. In the same block is the *Hotel Solace* (tel 331277), Tom Mboya St, which costs Sh 165 a single, Sh 215 a double and Sh 330 a triple.

More expensive is the *Hotel Salama* (tel 25898), Tom Mboya St at Luthuli Avenue, but it's a little on the pricey side at Sh 195-292 a single and Sh 260-339 a double for bed and breakfast in self-contained rooms. It's fairly good value. Tom Mboya St is a very busy road so, depending on which room you are given, the Gloria, the Solace or the Salama can be noisy.

Outside of this area, the best value for money is the *Hotel Terminal* (tel 28817), Moktar Daddah St between Koinange St and Muindi Mbingu St and close to the Kenya Airways city terminus. It's very clean and quiet here and the rooms are pleasant and airy. It costs Sh 145 a single and Sh 175 a double with own shower and toilet. There's always hot water available and there's an overnight laundry service at reasonable rates. It's quite a popular place for travellers to stay.

Not such good value but reasonable all the same is the *Embassy Hotel* (tel 24087), Biashara St/Tubman Rd between Koinange St and Muindi Mbingu St. Rooms here cost Sh 152-175 a single and Sh 237 a double with own shower and toilet. Hot water is available 24 hours a day. If the Embassy is full then try either the *Garden Guest House* or the *Parkview Hotel*, next to each other on Monrovia St at Muindi Mbingu St overlooking Jeevanjee Gardens. Room prices are about the same as at the Embassy.

Outside of the city centre, one of the cheapest is the *Green View Lodge* (tel 720908), off Nyerere Rd. It's at the top of the gravel road which runs at the back of the Minet ICDC House and other high-rise offices and there's a sign for the hotel on Nyerere Rd. It's an older style lodge surrounded by a garden and fairly quiet. Rooms cost Sh 130 a single and Sh 240 a double including breakfast. The lodge has its own bar and restaurant.

Another place worth trying in this price range is the *CPK Guest House*, Bishops Rd between Valley Rd and Ngong Rd. This is an Anglican guest house and they're not too keen on taking non-religious people but it's very good value at Sh 160 per day including three meals morning and afternoon tea. The food is very good. The missionaries who stay here can tell you a lot about what's happening right out in the sticks.

At the top end of the mid-range is the *Fairview Hotel* (tel 723211), Bishops Rd off 2nd Ngong Avenue. This place is popular with university post-graduates and other students who are looking for long-term accommodation. It costs Sh 230-320 a single and Sh 370-470 a double for bed and breakfast with own shower and toilet. The rooms all have their own radio and television.

Places to Stay – top end
In a city the size of Nairobi there are naturally many top-range hotels, some of them in the city centre itself and others outside this immediate area. The *Hotel Ambassadeur* (tel 336803), Moi Avenue, is right in the city centre and costs Sh 400 for singles, Sh 500 for doubles, including breakfast. Also in the centre the *Excelsior Hotel* (tel 26481), corner Kenyatta Avenue and Koinange St, costs Sh 375 single or Sh 475 double including breakfast.

The *Hotel Boulevard* (tel 27567) is on Harry Thuku Rd off University Way. Rooms are Sh 350 a single and Sh 500 a double without breakfast.

At any of the other top range hotels you are looking at Sh 810-1325 a single and Sh 1020-1470 a double. The circular *Hilton International* (tel 334000), Mama Ngina St and Moi Avenue, has all mod cons including a rooftop swimming pool. The *Hotel InterContinental* (tel 335550), City Hall Way, is centrally located and all rooms are air-con and have balconies. The *Nairobi Serena Hotel* (tel 720760) in Central Park is noted for its beautiful garden setting.

The *New Stanley Hotel* (tel 333233), Kimathi St and Kenyatta Avenue, was built in 1907 and despite numerous subsequent renovations still carries that colonial air. The Thorn Tree Café is a popular attraction here. The *Norfolk Hotel* (tel 3355422), Harry Thuku Rd, is even older – it was built in 1904. It too has plenty of colonial style and safari atmosphere.

Places to Eat
For most people with limited means, lunch is the main meal of the day and this is what the cheaper restaurants cater for. That doesn't mean that they're all closed in the evening (though quite a few are). It does mean, however, that what is available in the early evening is often what is left over from lunch time and the choice is limited. If you want a full meal in the evening it generally involves a splurge.

Nairobi is replete with restaurants offering cuisines from all over the world – Italian, Spanish, Japanese, Chinese, Indian, Lebanese, steak houses, sea food specialists, etc – and at many of them the prices are surprisingly reasonable. For US$5 per person you could eat well at quite a few of them. For US$10 per person you could eat very well at almost all of them and if you spent that much at some of them you'd hardly need to eat anything the next day.

The revolving restaurant at the top of the Kenyatta Conference Centre tower is presently closed. This happens fairly regularly, the reason apparently being that the rates are too high so it's difficult to make a profit there.

Cheap Eats There are a lot of very cheap cafés and restaurants in the Latema Rd/River Rd area where you can pick up a very cheap, traditional African breakfast of *mandazi* and tea/coffee. Most of these places would also be able to fix you up with eggs and the like. Since many of them are Indian-run, they also have traditional Indian breakfast foods like *samosa* and *idli* with a sauce.

If you'd like something more substantial (or don't like Indian food) then the *Grower's Café*, Tom Mboya St, is deservedly popular with both local people and travellers and the prices are reasonable. They have such things as eggs (boiled or fried), sausages and other hot foods, fruit salads with or without yoghurt and good coffee.

The *Bull Café*, round the corner from the New Kenya Lodge on Ngariama Rd, is a pleasant place and popular with people staying on Latema Rd.

If you're staying at Mrs Roche's you can get good, cheap food at *Tom's Shack* which is up the road to the first junction and then turn left. His place is on the right hand side. Good Indian food can be found at *Bimpy's*, 5th Parklands Avenue – a short walk from Mrs Roche's.

Fish & Chips That well-known English staple, fish & chips, has caught on in a big way in Nairobi and there are scores of places offering it. They're all cheap but the quality varies from instant nausea to excellent.

I would suggest you avoid like the plague the one on the corner of Moktar Daddah St and Muindi Mbingu St on the opposite side of the road from Jeevanjee Gardens. The 'food' here tastes and smells terrible and after getting a glimpse of the 'kitchen' I'm not surprised. On the other hand, my friend and long-time resident of Nairobi, Rowland Burley, totally disagrees. He says it's his usual haunt when his lady friend is out for the night.

My own recommendation for a lunch of fish & chips would go to *Supermac*, Kimathi St directly opposite the Thorn Tree Café on the mezzanine floor of the high-rise there. It's very popular at lunch times and deservedly so. They not only do some of the best fish & chips in Nairobi but also offers sausages, salads and fruit juices. Get there early if you don't want to queue.

Other travellers have recommended *Monty's Fish & Chips*, Tubman Rd at Muindi Mbingu St. Like Supermac, they offer fish, chips and sausages to take away or eat there. You'll undoubtedly come across others which are either good or ought to be closed down.

Good Breakfasts If you're staying at the *Hotel Terminal* then the attached restaurant on the ground floor is a good place to pick up breakfast. For a breakfast splurge, try the restaurant on the ground floor of the *Ambassadeur Hotel*, Moi Avenue, which offers the full range of western breakfast dishes. It's not cheap so do treat it as a splurge. Similar is the breakfast buffet at the *New Stanley Hotel*.

Big Lunches Kenya is the home of all-you-can-eat lunches at a set price and Nairobi has a wide choice of them, most offering Indian food. One of the best is the *Supreme Restaurant* at the junction of Tom Mboya St and River Rd. It offers excellent Indian vegetarian food at Sh 35 to Sh 55, depending on whether you want the ordinary or the 'delux' lunch, and superb fruit juices.

Similar is the *Blukat Restaurant*, Muindi Mbingu St between Banda St and Kigali Rd. It offers both vegetarian and meat set lunches for around Sh 35 to Sh 45. The day's specials are chalked up on a blackboard outside the restaurant. You'll see quite a few travellers eating here. The *New Flora Restaurant*, Tsavo Rd just off Latema Rd, is said by some travellers to have the best barbecued chicken in Africa and prices are very reasonable. They also offer other dishes.

The *Kamana Restaurant Co* at the back of the Good Hope Hotel, River Rd just before Accra St, has excellent mixed-grill lunches for Sh 20 which you'll be hard pressed to finish and they do pots of tea for Sh 4. Similar is the *Njogu-ini-Rwathia Hotel*, Mfangano St near to the Dolat Hotel. The servings here are enormous. Ideal if you've just got off a bus from Somalia or are otherwise famished. The *Lidos Bar & Restaurant*, Latema Rd at Lagos Rd, has a similar set up and offers such things as mutton curry (Sh 17), chicken masala, tandoori dishes, chappati and nan but I can't recommend it. The last time I attempted to eat there the food was inedible.

The restaurant on the ground floor of the *Iqbal Hotel* is a much better place for Indian curries. It's popular with people who are staying at the hotel. For traditional coastal Swahili dishes (made with coconut/coconut milk) try one of the restaurants on Gaborone Rd off Luthuli Avenue.

More Expensive Restaurants Going up-market, you can get an excellent western-style lunch for Sh 35-60 in the restaurant section of *The Pub*. It's on Standard St between Koinange St and Muindi Mbingu St, directly opposite the British High Commission. It's open daily from 12 noon to 2 pm and 6 to 11 pm. They do such things as grilled steaks, chops, goulash and chicken all served with salad and chips. Soup and sweets are extra.

The *Lamu Restaurant*, just opposite The Pub in the bottom floor of Bruce House, is very similar. This is one of the few places where you can eat cheapish western-style food out of doors at lunchtime. The food is mediocre but at least you can sit out in the sunshine. You should also try a Sh 70 set lunch (choice of menu) at the *African Heritage Café*, Banda St between Koinange St and Muindi Mbingu St. The best time to go is on Saturdays since there's a live band which plays most of the afternoon.

Indian Food Remember that Indian vegetarian restaurants generally don't serve alcohol and tend to close early in the evening (around 9 pm). For South Indian vegetarian food you probably can't beat the *Satkar Restaurant* (tel 337197), Moi Avenue. The entrance is in the first alleyway on the left hand side past Kenyatta Avenue walking towards Jeevanjee Gardens. If you order a full dinner here you probably won't be able to finish it if you ate lunch. A *masala dosa*, on the other hand, though delicious, won't satisfy a hungry person and two would cost more than a full dinner. A dinner with fruit juice will cost about Sh 50-60 per person.

Similar is the *Mayur Restaurant* (tel 25241) on the 1st floor of the Supreme Restaurant (mentioned earlier regarding

lunches). It's open daily for lunch and dinner but closed on Tuesdays. We must also mention the *Minar Restaurant*, Banda St close to the junction with Kimathi St, which serves Kashmiri food. There's a good choice on the menu, prices are very reasonable and the staff is friendly.

Chinese Food The *Mandarin Restaurant*, Tom Mboya St, is supposedly the best Chinese restaurant in Nairobi and a meal here will cost about Sh 150 for two people sharing a choice of dishes. The *Hong Kong Restaurant* (tel 28612), Koinange St, is also good.

Italian Food For Italian food there is really only one place to go and that is the very popular *Trattoria* (tel 340855), corner Wabera St and Kaunda St, which is open daily from 8.30 am to 11.30 pm. Both the atmosphere and the food here are excellent and there's a wide choice on the menu but the service tends to be supercilious. A soup, main course, salad, dessert and a carafe or two of house chianti will relieve you of up to US$10. As you might expect, the ice cream here is superb. It's well worth it!

Other National Cuisines The only Spanish restaurant in town is *El Patio* (tel 340114), Reinsurance Plaza Building, mezzanine floor, Nkrumah Lane. Similarly, there's only one Japanese restaurant, the *Akasaka*, which you'll find next to The Pub on Standard St between Koinange and Muindi Mbingu St. It's definitely on the expensive end of a splurge.

Seafood & Steak For seafood, try the *Lobster Pot* (tel 20491), corner Tom Mboya St and Cabral St, which offers fish, prawn and lobster dishes as well as charcoal-grilled meats. The best seafood restaurant in Nairobi is the *Tamarind*, off Harambee Avenue, but it's astronomically expensive.

For steak eaters who haven't seen a decent door-step since they left Argentina, Australia, Uruguay or America and are looking for a gut-busting extravaganza then there's no better place than *The Carnivore*, out at Langata just past Wilson Airport (bus Nos 14, 24 and 124). Tell the conductor where you are going and it's a one km signposted walk from where you are dropped off. It's easy to hitch back into the centre when you're ready to go. Whether it's lunch or dinner you take there's always beef, pork, lamb, ham, chicken, sausages and at least one game meat (often wildebeeste or zebra). The roasts are barbecued on Maasai spears and the waiters carve off hunks onto your plate until you tell them it's enough. Prices include salads, bread, desserts and coffee. Lunch costs Sh 150 (12.30 till 2.30 pm) and dinner costs Sh 162. Where else could you eat so much for US$10?

Hotel Smorgasbords Many of the large hotels in Nairobi offer all-you-can-eat smorgasbord lunches and dinners often with barbecued steaks and the like for a set price at the weekends. Sunday lunches are popular. Check out which hotels are doing them at present.

Entertainment & Activities

Cinema Nairobi is a good place to take in a few films and at a price considerably lower than in the west. The cleanest/least noisy of the cinemas are *The Nairobi* (behind The Kenya) and *20th Century*, Mama Ngina St. The noisier ones – which generally feature Bruce Lee, James Bond, Rambo and the like – are on Latema Rd. There are also two good drive-ins if you have the transport, both have snack bars and bars. Nairobi is also a good place to see an Indian film. If you've never seen one of these then treat yourself one evening. If you have seen them before, you won't need persuading! Check with local papers to see what's on.

Theatre At the *Phoenix Theatre*, Parliament Rd, the auditorium is small and the acting professionally competent but it's very expensive (around Sh 120). Check with local papers to see what's on.

Discos There are three main discos in the centre of Nairobi. The *New Florida Bar* is on Koinange and Banda Sts and is a most unusually shaped building. The *Starlight Disco* is next to the Panafric Hotel at the junction of Milimani Rd and Valley Rd. *Visions* on Kimathi St is owned by the same people who run the Trattoria Italian restaurant. They all cost Sh 100 entrance unless you get hold of a discount card entitling you (usually) to a 50% discount. If you eat at the Trattoria you'll get one automatically. Otherwise, these cards get handed out on the street when business is slack. With drinks, they're all a pretty expensive night out.

Live Music The *African Heritage Café* on Banda St is a popular place any Saturday afternoon.

Bars The most popular bar among travellers is probably the *Thorn Tree Café*, part of the New Stanley Hotel on Kimathi St, although you could die of thirst at times waiting for your beer to arrive. This is an outdoor bar and café with tables, chairs and Martini umbrellas where you can sit and watch the world go by. You'll meet people here that you haven't seen since Zaïre and if you are arranging to meet someone in Nairobi then this is the place to do it. Everyone knows where the Thorn Tree is and there's a notice board where you can leave personal messages (but not advertisements of any kind – things for sale, looking for people to join a safari, etc). The Thorn Tree is a restaurant as well as a bar and it does breakfasts, lunches and dinners but it's expensive and you don't get much for your money. Between around 11.30 am and 2 pm they won't serve you a beer unless you are also eating.

Another very popular bar (where you don't have to buy a meal in order to have a beer) is *The Pub*, Standard St between Koinange and Muindi Mbingu Sts. It's designed to resemble an English pub and is open daily from 12 noon to 2 pm and 6 to 11 pm. It attracts a remarkable cross-section of the population and is one of *the* places to go if you're a single man looking for some action. There are always plenty of good-looking girls in this place but that doesn't mean it's solely a pick-up joint. The Pub is part of the *Six Eighty Hotel* which has another open-air bar (the Terrace Bar) on the 1st floor above the entrance lobby. The Terrace is open all day, unlike The Pub.

For an unparalleled spit-and-sawdust binge put aside a whole evening to join the beer-swilling, garrulous hordes at the *Modern Green Bar*, Latema Rd next to the Sunrise Lodge. This place rages 24 hours a day, 365 days a year and the front door has never been closed since 1968. All human life is here – *miraa*-chewing teenage girls, hustlers, whores, dope dealers and what one traveller once described as 'lowlife whites'. The juke box is always on full blast with screaming Indian vocalists or African reggae and the bar is completely encased in heavy-duty wire mesh with a tiny hole through which money goes first and beer comes out afterwards. It's a great night out if you have the stamina but definitely not for the squeamish.

Those looking for more genteel surroundings in which to sip their beer should try either the *Grosvenor Hotel*, Ralph Bunche Rd at the junction with Lenana Rd and close to the Youth Hostel, or the lawn of the *Fairview Hotel*, Bishops Rd close to 3rd Ngong Avenue. For fading touches of the colonial era, try the terrace bar at the *Norfolk Hotel* which is open at lunch times and in the evening from 5 to 11 pm. Friday nights is when the young white population of Nairobi descends on

this bar to drink itself leg-less. If you have transport, local residents also recommend the intimate atmosphere of the *Hurlingham Hotel*, Argwings Kodhek Rd about three km from the centre of town. They also offer very good, very cheap pub meals. You can eat lunch out in the garden.

Remember that the prices of beer and soft drinks are government controlled so it costs roughly the same to drink in the dirtiest dive as it does in the Hilton Hotel. 'Roughly' because the government stipulates *maximum* prices only – bars are free to charge less than this figure so there can be a difference of up to Sh 2 if you drink in the roughest bars.

Clubs & Societies For something with more intellectual and less alcoholic content there are a lot of specialist clubs and societies in Nairobi, many of which welcome visitors. Most of the foreign cultural organisations have film and lecture evenings (usually free of charge) at least once or twice a week. Give them a ring and see what they have organised. In addition to these, some local clubs you may be interested in contacting include:

Mountain Club of Kenya (tel 501747), PO Box 45741, Nairobi. The club meets every Tuesday at 8.30 pm at the clubhouse at Wilson Airport. Members frequently organise climbing weekends at various sites around the country. Information on climbing Mt Kenya and Kilimanjaro is available on the same evening.

African Cultural Society (tel 335581), PO Box 69484, Nairobi. This society organises cultural festivals and events, lectures and theatre.

East African Wildlife Society (tel 27047), Nairobi Hilton, PO Box 20110, Nairobi. This society is in the forefront of conservation efforts in East Africa and it publishes an interesting monthly magazine. Membership costs Sh 150 but entitles you to certain reductions in the national parks.

Nairobi Chess Club (tel 25007), PO Box 50443, Nairobi. The club meets every Thursday after 5.30 pm at the French Cultural Centre, Monrovia and Loita Sts.

Nairobi Photographic Society (tel 337129), PO Box 49879, Nairobi. Members meet at 8.30 pm on the first and third Thursdays of each month at St John Ambulance Headquarters behind the Donovan Maule Theatre.

Sports For sporting facilities, contact one or other of the following: Impala Club (tel 568573), Ngong Rd; Nairobi Club (tel 336996), Ngong Rd; Nairobi Gymkhana (tel 20087), Rwathia/Forest Rds; Parklands Sports Club (tel 742829), Ojijo Rd. They all offer facilities for tennis, squash, cricket and some of them also play football and hockey.

Swimming Most of the international tourist hotels have swimming pools which can be used by non-residents for a daily fee of Sh 25. The YMCA on State House Rd also has a large pool with spring board which you can use for Sh 20.

Getting There

Air Nairobi is the major entry and exit point in all of East Africa for international flights. See the introductory Getting There section for more details. It's also the best place in the region for buying international airline tickets. See the Nairobi Information section for airline addresses and for recommended travel agents.

The airport departure tax for international flights is US$10. You must pay this in foreign currency. Kenyan shillings are not accepted.

Internally Kenya Airways flies to Mombasa 47 times per week, to Malindi 10 or 11 times per week and to Kisumu nine times per week.

Pioneer Airlines fly from Lamu to Nairobi daily at 2 pm (1½ hours, Sh 1050 one-way). Other flights are Nairobi-Garissa daily at 7 am, Garissa-Nairobi at 3.30 pm (1¼ hours, Sh 1150 one-way); Garissa-Wajir daily at 8.30 am, Wajir-Garissa at 1 pm (2 hours); Wajir-Mandera daily at 10 am, Mandera-Wajir at 12 am (1¼ hours). Flying Nairobi-Wajir costs Sh 1400 one-way, and Nairobi-Mandera costs Sh 2000 one-way. Return tickets are double the cost of one-way tickets. Flights to Marsabit and Moyale depend on demand. There are two flights daily in either direction between Nairobi and Masai Mara (departing at 10 am and 2 pm from Nairobi and 11 am and 3 pm from Masai Mara, one hour, Sh 1050 return).

Pioneer Airlines' main office in Nairobi (tel 21177 and 33 9557) is in the Baring Arcade (2nd floor), Kenyatta Avenue.

Cooper Skybird, which has flights Mombasa-Malindi-Lamu, has an office in Nairobi at Bunsons Travel (tel 21992/3/4), Standard St.

Bus In Nairobi most bus stations are along Accra Rd near the junction with River Rd except for Akamba on Lagos Rd between Latema Rd and Tom Mboya St.

Travelling Nairobi-Mombasa there are many departures daily in either direction (mostly in the early morning and late evening) by, among others, Akamba, Coastline Safari, Goldline and Mawingo. The trip costs Sh 100 and takes seven to eight hours including a lunch break about half way.

Travelling to Garissa, en route to Somalia, there is a direct bus which leaves from outside the Munawar Hotel opposite the Kenya Bus Depot in Eastleigh, Nairobi, on Monday, Wednesday, Friday and Sunday at 8 am. The depot is a 10-minute *matatu* ride from Ronald Ngala St (Route No 9). The fare is Sh 80 and the journey takes about eight hours.

Rent-a-Car Vehicle rental companies which travellers have used over a number of years and found to be consistently reliable and cost competitive are:

Market Service Station
   corner Koinange St and Banda St, Nairobi (this is the Mobil station) (tel 25797 or 33 5735)
Habib's Cars
   Agip House, Haile Selassie Avenue, Nairobi (tel 20463 or 23816)
Polay's Car Hire
   NCM House, 1st floor, Tom Mboya St, Nairobi (tel 33 4207 or 33 1681)
Let's Go Travel
   Caxton House, Standard St, Nairobi (tel 29539 or 29540)
Oddjobs
   corner Koinange St and Monrovia St, Nairobi (tel 21375 or 23110)
Others worth checking:
   InterRent (tel 34 0684), IPS Building, 1st floor, Kimathi St, Nairobi
   Birds Paradise Tours & Travel (tel 25898), PO Box 22121, Nairobi
   Crossways (tel 23949), Banda St, Nairobi

Hitching For Mombasa, take bus No 13 or 109 as far as the airport turn-off and hitch from there. For Nakuru/Kisumu, take bus No 23 from the Hilton to the end of its route and hitch from there. Otherwise start from the junction of Waiyaki Rd and Chiromo Rd (the extension of Uhuru Highway) in Westlands. For Nanyuki/Nyeri take bus No 45 or 145 from the central bus station up Thika Rd to the entrance to Kenyatta College and hitch from there. Make sure you get off the bus at the college entrance not the exit. It's very difficult to hitch from the latter. Otherwise, start from the roundabout where Thika Rd meets Forest Rd and Muranga Rd.

Rail Trains run Nairobi-Mombasa every day in both directions at 5 and 7 pm. The journey takes about 13 hours. The fares are: 1st class – Sh 321; 2nd class – Sh 138; 3rd class – Sh 60. If you're travelling alone and want a 1st class compartment to yourself it costs Sh 420.

Nairobi-Malaba there are trains on Tuesday, Friday and Saturday at 3 pm arriving at 8.30 am the next day. In the opposite direction they depart Malaba on Wednesday, Saturday and Sunday at 4 pm and arrive at 9.30 am the next day. The fares are: 1st class – Sh 336; 2nd class – Sh 145; 3rd class – Sh 63.

Nairobi-Kisumu trains depart daily at 6 pm arriving at Kisumu at 8 am the next day. In the opposite direction they depart daily at 6.30 pm arriving at Nairobi at 7.35 am the next day. Depending on demand there is usually an additional train ('express') at 5.30 pm from Nairobi daily for the first week of every month (and sometimes for the second week too) which arrives at Kisumu at 6 am the next day. The fares are: 1st class – Sh 242; 2nd class – Sh 104; 3rd class – Sh 45. As a rule, the carriages used on the Kisumu run are older than those used on the Nairobi-Mombasa run and are not such good value.

Getting Around

Airport Transport To Jomo Kenyatta International Airport the Kenya Airways bus leaves the Airlines Terminal, Koinange St, daily at 8, 9, 10 and 11.30 am, 12.45, 2.30, 4.45, 6.45 and 8 pm. The fare is Sh 40 and the journey takes about a half hour. A taxi will cost Sh 150 for the car (shared by up to four people). You can also take public bus No 34 from outside the Ambassadeur Hotel. It costs just Sh 5 but takes considerably longer.

To Wilson Airport (for small aircraft to Malindi, Lamu, etc) take buses No 14, 24 or 124 from in front of Development House, Moi Avenue, and elsewhere. The fare is Sh 2 off-peak.

Bus & Taxi Buses are the cheapest way of getting around Nairobi. Taxis cannot usually be hailed on the street, there are taxi ranks at the railway station, the museum and the main hotels. The drivers are not very enthusiastic about using their meters so agree fares in advance.

The Coast

LAMU

In the early 1970s Lamu acquired a reputation as the Kathmandu of Africa – a place of fantasy, mystery and other-worldliness. It drew all self-respecting seekers of the miraculous, globe-trotters, and that much maligned, supposedly drug, sex and rock n' roll-crazed bunch of people called hippies. The attraction was obvious. Both Kathmandu and Lamu were remote, unique and fascinating self-contained societies which had somehow escaped the depredations of the 20th century with their culture, their centuries-old way of life and their architecture intact.

Though Kathmandu is now over-run with well-heeled tourists and the hippies have retired to the rural purity of Pembrokeshire, northern California and Nimbin, Lamu remains much the same as it has always been. Access is still exclusively by diesel-powered launch from the mainland and the island has yet to see a motor-powered vehicle. The streets are far too narrow and winding to accommodate anything other than pedestrians or donkeys. Men still wear the full-length white robes known as *khanzus* and the *kofia* caps, and women cover themselves with the black wrap-around *bui bui* as they do in other Islamic cultures, although here it's a liberalised version which often hugs their bodies, falls short of the ankles and dispenses completely with the dehumanising veil in front of the face. Local festivals still take place as though nothing had ever changed. The beach at Shela is still magnificent and uncluttered and nothing happens in a hurry. Lamu is one of the most relaxing places you will ever have the pleasure to visit.

History

It has not always been that way and, indeed, Lamu has only ever been of minor importance in the string of Swahili towns which stretched from Somalia to Mozambique. Although it was a thriving port by the early 1500s, it surrendered without a fight to the early Portuguese mariners and was generally politically dependent on the more important Sultanate of Paté which, at the time, was the most important island port in the archipelago. It did manage to avoid, until the late 1700s, the frequent wars between the sultanates of Paté, Mombasa and Malindi following the decline of Portuguese influence in the area.

After that there followed many years of internecine strife between the various island city-states of Lamu, Paté, Faza and Siyu which only ended in 1813 when Lamu defeated the forces of Paté in a battle at Shela. Shortly afterwards Lamu became subject to the Sultanate of Zanzibar which nominally controlled the whole of the coastal strip from Kilwa to the Somali border (under a British Protectorate from 1890) until Kenya became independent in 1963.

In common with all the other Swahili coastal city-states Lamu had a slave-based economy until the turn of the 20th century when the British forced the Sultan of Zanzibar to sign an anti-slaving agreement and subsequently intercepted dhows carrying slaves north from that island. All that cheap labour fuelled a period of economic growth for Lamu and traders grew rich by exporting ivory, cowries, tortoise shell, mangroves, oil seeds and grains, and importing oriental linen, silks, spices and porcelain. When it came to an end in 1907 with the abolition of slavery the economy of the island rapidly went into decline and stayed that way until very recently when increased receipts from tourism gave it a new lease of life. That decline, and the lack of interest in importing western technology and consumerism, is what has preserved the Lamu you see today. No other Swahili town can offer you such an uninterrupted tradition and an undisturbed traditional

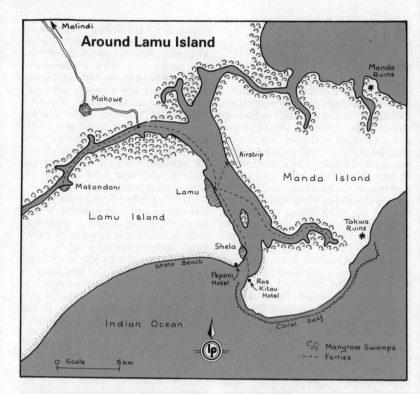

Around Lamu Island

Malindi

Mokowe

Matondoni

Lamu Island

Lamu

Shela

Shela Beach

Peponi Hotel

Ras Kitau Hotel

Indian Ocean

Airstrip

Manda Island

Manda Ruins

Takwa Ruins

Coral Reef

Mangrove Swamps
Ferries

0 Scale 5 km

style of architecture, though the old stone town of Zanzibar might come close.

Information

Books There are some excellent books about Lamu and the Swahili civilisation if you are interested in digging deeper into this fascinating period of East African history and culture. The best general account is *The Portuguese Period in East Africa*, Justus Strandes (East African Literature Bureau, Nairobi, 1971). This is a translation of a book originally published in German in 1899 with up-to-date notes and appendices detailing recent archaeological findings, some of which contradict Strandes' opinions. It's very readable.

Lamu: A Study of the Swahili Town,

Usam Ghaidan (East African Literature Bureau, Nairobi, 1975), is a very detailed study of Lamu by an Iraqi who was formerly a Lecturer in Architecture at the University of Nairobi and has since devoted his time to research into the Swahili architecture of the north Kenyan coast. You can find both of them in most good bookshops in Nairobi or Mombasa and the latter at the museum in Lamu.

If you're going to spend long in Lamu the leaflet-map *Lamu: Map & Guide to the Archipelago, the Island & the Town* is worth buying at the museum bookshop.

Bank The Standard Chartered Bank on the harbour front is the only bank in Lamu. It's open Monday to Friday from 8.30 am to 1 pm and Saturday from 8.30 to

11 am. In the low season, cashing a cheque can take as little as half an hour but in the high season it can take considerably longer.

Lamu Town

The town dates back to at least the late 14th century when the Pwani Mosque was built. Most buildings date from the 18th century, but the lower parts and basements are often considerably older. The streets are narrow, cool and quiet and there are many small 'squares' and intimate spaces enclosed by tall coral walls. Since the mosques have no minarets. little outward decoration and few doors and windows opening onto the street they are often hard to distinguish from domestic buildings. One of the most outstanding features of the houses here, as in old Zanzibar, is the intricately carved doors and lintels which have kept generations of carpenters busy. Sadly, many of them have disappeared in recent years but there is now an active conservation movement which should prevent further losses. In any case, the skill has not been lost. Walk to the far end of the harbour front in the opposite direction to Shela and you'll see them being made.

Lamu Museum

An hour or two in the Lamu Museum, on the waterfront next to Petley's Inn, is an excellent introduction to the culture and history of Lamu. It's one of the most interesting small museums in Kenya. There's a reconstruction of a traditional Swahili house, charts, maps, ethnological displays, model dhows and two examples of the remarkable and ornately-carved ivory *siwa* – a wind instrument peculiar to the coastal region which is often used as a fanfare at weddings. Entry costs Sh 10.

There's also a good bookshop at the museum. If the museum stokes your interest then you should also visit their **Swahili House** (see street map for location) which was restored by the National Museums of Kenya.

Shela & Matondoni Villages

You'll see many dhows anchored in the harbour at the south end of town but if you want to see them being built or repaired you can do this at Shela or Matondoni villages. The latter is perhaps the best place to see this and you have a choice of walking there (about two hours walking, or you could hire a donkey), or hiring a dhow and sailing there. If you choose the dhow it will cost Sh 150-200 for the boat (so you need a small group together to share the cost) but it usually includes a barbecued fish lunch.

If you want to walk, leave the main street of Lamu up the alleyway by the side of Kenya Cold Drinks and continue in as straight a line as possible to the back end of town. From here a well-defined track leads out into the country. You pass a football pitch on the right hand side after 100 metres. Follow the touch line of the pitch and continue in the same direction past the paddock/garden on the left hand side and then turn left onto another track. This is the one to Matondoni. The football pitch has telephone wires running above it. These go to Matondoni and they're almost always visible from the track so if you follow them you can't go wrong. If you don't cut across the football pitch you'll head off into the middle of nowhere and probably get lost – although this can be interesting (old houses, wells, goats, etc).

Set off early if you are walking. It gets very hot later on in the day. There are no cafés in Matondoni but if you ask around tea and *mandazi* usually turn up. There's also nowhere to stay unless you can arrange a bed or floor space in a private house.

Beach

The beach is just past Shela village, a 40-minute walk from Lamu. To get there, follow the harbour-front road till it ends and then follow the shore line. You will pass a new hospital being built by the Saudi Arabian government and a ginning factory before you get to Shela. If the tide is out, you can walk along the beach most of the way. When it's in, you may well have to do a considerable amount of wading up to your thighs and deeper. If that doesn't appeal, there is a track all the way from Lamu to Shela but there are many turn-offs so stay with the ones which run closest to the shore (you may find yourself in a few cul-de-sacs doing this as a number of turn-offs to the left run to private houses and end there). There are also dhows between Lamu and Shela, usually for Sh 10 one-way.

The best part of the beach (if you want surf) is well past Peponi's – there's no surf at Peponi's because you're still in the channel between Lamu and Manda islands. In the past there have been robberies and, at one time, a couple of rapes further along the beach but we haven't heard of anything like that for two or three years now. There was a big police crack-down following these incidents. It's possible to hire a wind surfing rig at Peponi's but it won't be cheap (they're free to residents).

Dhow Trips
See the following Islands Around Lamu section for details about dhow trips.

Places to Stay
Lamu has been catering for budget travellers for well over a decade and there's a good choice of simple, rustic lodges, rooftops and whole houses to rent. Don't believe a word anyone tells you about there being running water 24 hours a day at any of these places. There isn't. Water is not an abundant commodity in Lamu and restrictions are in force most of the year. It's usually only available early in the morning and early in the evening which, in most cases, means bucket showers only and somewhat smelly toilets. The prices are all very similar – Sh 25-35 a single and Sh 50-70 a double – though they may go up a little in the high season (August and September). If a lodge is full

when you arrive but you like it a lot and want to be first in line for a room, they'll usually let you sleep on the roof or elsewhere for about Sh 15 per person.

Where you stay will probably depend largely on what sort of room you are offered and who meets you getting off the ferry from the mainland. Most of the young men who meet the ferries have no connection with any of the lodges other than the hope of a tip (from travellers) or a small commission (from the hotel management). Some of them can be very insistent.

If you plan on staying in Lamu for a while it's worth making enquiries about renting a house, so long as there's a group of you to share the cost. On a daily basis it won't be much cheaper (if at all) than staying at a lodge but on a monthly basis you are looking at Sh 3000 a month in the low season and Sh 5000-6000 a month in the high season. You can share this with as many people as you feel comfortable with or have space for. They're available in Lamu town itself but also at Shela and between Lamu and Shela. Some of them can be excellent value and very spacious. You need to ask around and see what is available. It's possible to find some remarkably luxurious places especially around Shela.

Places to Stay – bottom end
Lamu Town The popular *Dhow Lodge, Pole Pole Guest House* and *Kisiwani Guest House* are all owned by Ali who was once a DJ in Mombasa. He has a good collection of contemporary music. All his lodges have a fridge, cooker for the use of residents, showers (when available) and toilet paper is provided. The Dhow Lodge has a small library.

The *Castle Lodge* overlooks the main 'square' and the fortress and picks up sea breezes since it's fairly high up. The *Bahati Lodge* is similar. One of my own favourites is the *Full Moon Guest House* so long as you can get one of the better rooms overlooking the harbour. It has an

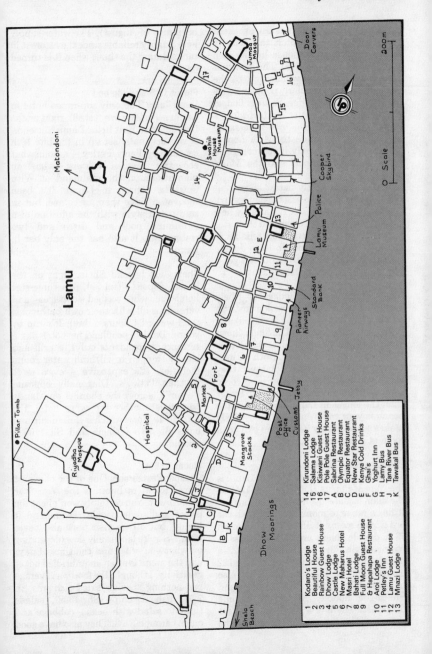

Lamu

- Matondoni
- Pillar Tomb
- Riyadha Mosque
- Hospital
- Jumaa Mosque
- Swahili House Museum
- Door Carvers
- Cooper Skybird
- Lamu Police
- Lamu Museum
- Standard Bank
- Pioneer Airways
- Fort
- Market
- Mangrove Stacks
- Post Office
- Customs
- Jetty
- Dhow Moorings
- Shela Beach

Scale
0   200m

1   Kodaro's Lodge
2   Beautiful House
3   Rainbow Guest House
4   Dhow Lodge
5   Castle Lodge
6   New Maharus Hotel
7   Masri Hotel
8   Bahati Lodge
9   Full Moon Guest House
    & Hapahapa Restaurant
10 Aroi Lodge
11 Petley's Inn
12 Lamu Guest House
13 Mnazi Lodge
14 Kirundoni Lodge
15 Salama Lodge
16 Kisiwani Guest House
17 Pole Pole Guest House

A   Sabrina Restaurant
B   Olympic Restaurant
C   Equator Restaurant
D   New Star Restaurant
E   Kenya Cold Drinks
F   Ghai's
G   Yoghurt Inn
H   Lamy Bus
J   Tana River Bus
K   Tawakal Bus

upstairs balcony which is an excellent place to relax and watch the activity below and the guest house has its own restaurant (the Hapahapa). The *Beautiful House* also has rooms which overlook the harbour. Other particularly popular lodges are the *Kirundoni Lodge, Salama Lodge, Rainbow Guest House* and *Kadara's Lodge*. Other lodges – not necessarily second best – include the *Aroi Lodge, Mnazi Lodge* (but only if you can get a room on the top floor) and the *Masri Hotel*.

If you want slightly better accommodation than the bare essentials then try the *Lamu Guest House*. It's a fairly new place, good value and clean and the water supply tends to be a little more reliable. It costs Sh 50 a single and Sh 100 a double though in the low season you can get a room for less if you negotiate.

Shela There are also lodges at Shela including the *Samahane* which costs Sh 50 a double (more in the high season) and has a good water supply. The *Shela Guest House* will quote up to Sh 200 a double (bargain down from there). Both of these lodges will often quote whatever they think you might pay so you need to do some hard bargaining. They're no better than the lodges in Lamu itself but if the beach is your main interest it obviously makes sense to stay here if you can get a room at a reasonable price.

Places to Stay – middle

The only real mid-range hotel in Lamu is the *New Maharus Hotel* (tel 1 or 125) on the main 'square' overlooking the fortress. It has a range of rooms starting with the 3rd class B rooms at Sh 49 a single and Sh 73 a double. Next are the 3rd class A rooms at Sh 73 a single and Sh 122 a double and the 2nd class rooms at Sh 122 a single and Sh 173 a double. They also have 1st class rooms at Sh 173 a single and Sh 294 a double. All prices include breakfast. There is a discount on these prices in the low season (April to the

beginning of August). The water supply here is fairly reliable since they store it in tanks during the times when it is turned on.

Places to Stay – top end

Lamu Town The only top-range hotel in Lamu is *Petley's Inn* (tel 48), right on the harbour front next to the Lamu Museum. It was originally set up in the late 19th century by Percy Petley – a somewhat eccentric English colonist who ran plantations on the mainland at Witu until he retired to Lamu. It's been renovated since then, of course, but in traditional style with the addition of a swimming pool and disco and two restaurants. It also has the only bar in Lamu.

Shela Just beyond Shela, right on the beach, *Peponi's* (tel 29), is a three-star hotel of whitewashed cottages and verandahs all with their own bathrooms (and water 24 hours a day). It's run by young Danish people. The hotel has a restaurant (residents only), a grill and bar (both open to all) and water sports facilities. It's expensive – even more so than Petley's. Diagonally opposite Peponi's, across the channel on Manda Island, is another top-range hotel, the *Ras Kitau Hotel* which is Italian-run and costs Sh 750 a single and Sh 1100 a double.

Places to Eat

Cheaper Restaurants One of the cheapest places to eat in Lamu is the *New Star Restaurant*. You certainly won't beat the prices and some people recommend it highly, but others visit once and never return. Service is certainly slow (depending on what you order and the time of day) and the menu is often an unbridled act of creativity. I thought the food was average but nothing special. Fried fish was Sh 7.50, fish & chips Sh 13.50, salads (tomato salad with beans, cabbage and onion) around Sh 8. They also have good yoghurt. Similar in price is the *Sabrina Restaurant* which serves mainly Indian food for main courses and western breakfasts but they do offer very reasonably-priced lobster, prawn and crab dishes. The staff are very friendly.

For consistently reliable good food at a reasonable price there are three very popular restaurants. The first is the *Olympic Restaurant* on the waterfront overlooking the dhow moorings. Here you can get pancakes with various fillings, grilled fish and salad for Sh 25 and a daily 'special' of soup, main course and fruit juice for Sh 40

The *Yoghurt Inn* has also been popular for years – it has an attractive garden with individual outside tables each with a grass roof. It offers dishes like crab with cheese and chips (Sh 30), prawns or kebabs (Sh 25), grilled fish (Sh 22), barbecued lobster (Sh 45) plus there are daily 'specials'. They also have (as you might expect) yoghurt (Sh 3.50), *lassi* (Sh 10) and banana pancakes with wild honey (Sh 10). The food is excellent and well-presented. It's open daily from 7 am to 9.30 pm except on Fridays when it's 7 am to 12 noon and 4 to 9.30 pm.

The *Hapahapa Restaurant* on the ground floor of the Full Moon Guest House is also very good and offers a similar range of dishes. You may also come across a man popularly called 'Ali Hippy' who, for several years now, has been offering travellers meals at his house for an average price of Sh 25. Quite a few people have recommended him.

At Shela the café at the Shela Guest House (usually called the *Stop Over*) is right on the beach. They have fruit juices, yoghurt and snacks as well as simple meals for about Sh 15.

More Expensive Restaurants For a splurge there are several places you can try. *Ghai's*, on the waterfront next to the Cooper Skybird office, is very well known. Ghai may be somewhat eccentric but he considers himself to be the best seafood

cook on the island. He may well be right. The food is excellent and the service is impeccable. A three course meal here with tea will set you back Sh 60 to Sh 150 depending on what you order.

Also excellent is the *Equator Restaurant* which is usually only open in the evenings. It's run by a 'quaint English gentleman' (as one traveller described him) called Ron Partridge. The set-up here is very relaxing (classical music and oldies) but it's *very* popular so book a table in advance if possible. It can be more expensive than Ghai's but it's well worth the little extra.

Lastly, there is, of course, the restaurant at *Petley's Inn*. There are actually two restaurants here: the barbecue/ice cream garden across the alley from the main building and the restaurant proper which has both inside tables and others on the verandah overlooking the harbour. The prices of food ordered from the main menu are, as you might expect, high (although the cuisine is excellent) but you can also order much less expensive dishes (such as grilled lobster) from the barbecue across the alley.

For a splurge at Shela try the *BBQ Grill* at Peponi's which is open to non-residents and offers delicious food. There's a choice of menu but the fish is superb – grilled fish and salad will cost Sh 45.

Snacks & Drinks For fruit juices and other cold drinks and snacks (such as samosas) make sure you pay at least one visit to *Kenya Cold Drinks* at the back of the Lamu Museum. It's been deservedly popular for years.

There are only two places (unless you get an invitation to the police canteen) where you can get a beer on Lamu Island. One is *Petley's Inn* which sports an English-style pub, the entrance to which is in the alley between the hotel and the barbecue garden opposite. It's a popular watering hole and is open to non-residents. The beer is often lukewarm (usually because of demand) and often 'runs out' around 9 pm. It doesn't actually 'run out' at all– it's just the hotel's way of rationing the supply so that they always have enough for their guests and those who eat in the restaurant. Beer is delivered by freighter regularly and if you're here when it arrives you'll get some idea of the prodigious thirst which must prevail on this island!.

Peponi's is a mandatory watering hole en route to or from Shela beach. The bar is on the verandah overlooking the channel and beach. Unlike Petley's, they don't seem to have problems of supply and you can be guaranteed of an ice-cold beer anytime of day.

Getting There

Air Cooper Skybird flies Mombasa-Lamu daily, departing at 8.30 am and arriving at 9.30 am (Sh 600 one-way). The Malindi-Lamu flights depart daily at 9 am and 3 pm (Sh 400 one-way). Return tickets are twice the price of one-way tickets.

Pioneer Airlines fly Nairobi-Lamu daily at 10 am (1½ hours, Sh 1050 one-way); Mombasa-Lamu daily at 8.30 am and 2.30 pm (1½ hours, Sh 600 one-way); Malindi-Lamu daily at 9 am and 3 pm (half an hour, Sh 400 one-way). Return tickets are double the cost of one-way tickets. Pioneer's phone number is 139.

Bus The bus companies – Tana River Bus Company, Lamy Bus and Tawakal Bus Company – which service the Lamu-Malindi-Mombasa route all maintain offices in Lamu Island so you can book tickets in advance. It's advisable to book in advance though you can often find seats if you turn up early enough on the morning of departure.

If you don't want to stop at Malindi you can travel by bus or *matatu* direct from Mombasa to Lamu but very few people do this. The best company to travel with from Malindi to Lamu is the Tana River Bus Company which goes to Lamu on Monday, Wednesday and Friday and

returns the following day. Other companies making this trip are Lamy Bus and Tawakal.

If you go with Tana River try to go on one of their Isuzu buses. The road is rough but you won't notice it too much on these buses. On the Leyland buses – forget it! The fare is Sh 85 and journey takes about six hours. There are two ferry crossings on this route and, like everyone else, you'll have to get down and haul away on the ropes. The buses stop on the mainland and from there you board a ferry to Lamu (for which you must pay another Sh 5).

Dhow Lamu is one of the best places for dhow trips and many people take them down to Mombasa – a journey of one night and two days on average. Prices vary according to your negotiating powers but should be around Sh 140 to Sh 150 including food. Before you set off you need to get permission from the district commissioner. His office is on the harbour front close to the post office and opposite the main quay. It's best if you can persuade the captain of the dhow to take you along here and guide you through the formalities. It shouldn't take more than 1½ hours in that case. Usually they will do this without charging you money but be prepared to pay if the captain is unwilling.

Getting Around

Boat There are frequent ferries between Lamu and the bus terminus on the mainland (Mokowe). The fare is Sh 5. Ferries also operate between Lamu and Manda Island where the airstrip is located.

ISLANDS AROUND LAMU

A popular activity while you're in Lamu is to take a dhow trip to one of the neighbouring islands. You need a small group (six to eight people) to share costs if you're going to do this but it's very easy to put a group like that together in Lamu. Just ask around.

Since taking tourists around the archipelago is one of the easiest ways of making money for dhow owners in Lamu, there's a lot of competition and you'll be asked constantly by different people if you want to go on a trip. You'll also see many notices in the café. You must bargain hard since many people will try to charge you as much as they think you will pay. You'll come across people who paid, say, Sh 200 and others who paid Sh 400 for the same trip. Don't take the first offer unless it's a particularly good one and check if food is included. Dhow trips are usually superb whoever you go with so it's impossible to make any specific recommendations of boats or boatmen.

Takwa is the easiest place to get to from Lamu and the return trip takes only a morning or an afternoon. You shouldn't pay more than Sh 200 for the boat although food won't be included. Trips to Paté, Faza and Siyu will be considerably longer and will involve being away for the night. Have a word with the man at the Lamu Museum first if you want to go there.

Paté Island

Paté, Siyu and Faza are three ruined Swahili cities on Paté island. Founded in the 15th century, Siyu had a brief period of fame in the middle of the 19th century as the last upholder of coastal independence though it was generally dependent on the town of Paté. Outside of town few people see the substantial fort Seyyid Said built in about 1843.

Lamu Archipelageo

Faza has had a chequered history. It was destroyed by Paté in the 13th century and refounded in the 16th century only to be destroyed again by the Portuguese in 1586. It was subsequently rebuilt and became an ally of the Portuguese against Paté during the 17th century but declined into insignificance during the 18th and 19th centuries. These days it is the centre of a sub-district which includes Paté, Ndau and part of the Kenya mainland to the north.

The origins of Paté are disputed. There are claims that it was founded in the 8th century by refugees from Oman, but recent excavations have produced nothing earlier than the 15th century. Certainly by the time the Portuguese arrived it was of no great importance but by the 17th century it had become the focus of resistance to the Portuguese and in the 18th century it was at war with Mombasa for control of the coastal region. It lost all importance, however, after the ruling family were driven out by Seyyid Majid in 1865 to set up the short-lived Sultanate of Witu on the mainland. A number of interesting buildings remain, including the gate through the former city wall, the palace and several mosques.

Manda Island

The extensive ruins of Takwa, another old Swahili city, are at the head of a creek on Manda Island opposite Shela. They consist of a large mosque and a number of houses surrounded by a town wall, although it appears that the site was only occupied briefly from the end of the 15th century until the end of the 16th century. It's presently maintained by the Archaeological Survey of Kenya so entry costs Sh 30.

Kiwayu Island

The other place of interest, Kiwayu Island in the Kiunga Marine National Reserve, is a two-day, one-night trip which will cost you about Sh 200 per person including food. Contact a man called Saidi at the Hapahapa Restaurant after 8 pm any day. The coral reefs off the island are one of the best snorkelling spots on the whole Kenyan coast. The variety of marine life is incredible but few people get to see it.

MALINDI

Malindi, a popular port of call for travellers either heading north from Mombasa or south from Lamu, is for sybarites, bacchanalians and beach lovers; it rivals the coast north and south of Mombasa for the title of Kenya's premier tourist resort. In many ways it's superior to the latter since it has developed from a town which existed before the tourist boom. It has a recognisable centre where commerce, business and everyday activities, which aren't necessarily connected with the tourist trade, still continue. Cotton growing and processing, sisal production and fishing are still major income earners.

In the beach resort hotels south of Mombasa you're more or less isolated from everyday African life and you could be almost anywhere if it wasn't for the fact that most of the staff at the hotels are black Kenyans. The beach at Malindi, too, is superior if you prefer surf with your ocean – there's a break in the coral reef at this point along the coast. Sharks are not a problem. The absence of a coral reef prevents the build up of seaweed which sometimes almost chokes the beaches north of Mombasa and Shelly beach just south of the city. There is however, one drawback to Malindi and that is the brown silt which flows down the Sabaki river at the north end of the bay during the rainy season and makes the sea very muddy. For the rest of the year it's perfect.

Information

Tourist Office There is a tourist office in Malindi past the Stardust Club, but they don't have a lot of material.

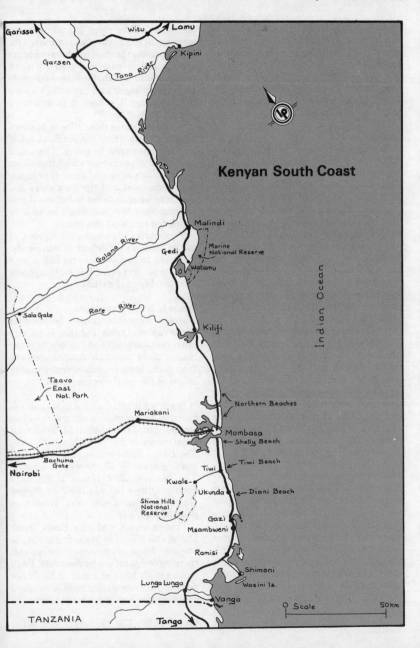

Bank Barclays Bank is open Monday to Friday from 8.30 am to 1 pm and 2.30 to 5 pm and on Saturday from 8.30 am to 12 noon.

Immigration There is an office next to the Juma Mosque and Pillar Tombs on the waterfront (see street map for location).

Malindi Town

Malindi has a pedigree going back to the 12th century and was one of the ports visited by the Chinese junks of Cheng Ho between 1417 and 1419 before the emperor of China prohibited further overseas voyages. It was one of the few places on the coast to offer a friendly welcome to the early Portuguese mariners and to this day the pillar erected by Vasco da Gama as a navigational aid still stands on the promontory at the south end of the bay. The cross which surmounts this pillar is of Lisbon stone (and therefore original) but the supporting pillar is of local coral.

There's also the partial remains of a Portuguese chapel, which is undoubtedly the one which St Francis Xavier visited on his way to India. A painting of the crucifixion is still faintly visible. Not far to the north, are a number of pillar tombs and the remains of a mosque and a palace. Other than this, however, little remains of the old town. The nearest substantial ruins from pre-Portuguese days are at Gedi, south of Malindi.

Malindi Marine National Park

The most popular excursion from Malindi is to the Marine National Park to the south of town past Silver Sands. Here you can rent a glass-bottomed boat to take you out to the coral reef. Snorkelling gear is provided though there generally aren't enough sets for everyone at the same time. The variety and colours of the coral and the fish are simply amazing and you'll be surprised how close you can get to the fish without alarming them.

The best time to go is at low tide when the water will be clear. It's advisable to wear a pair of canvas shoes or thongs for wading across the coral to where the boats are moored in case you step on a sea urchin or a stone fish, these are extremely well camouflaged and can inflict a very painful sting. The boat trips generally last an hour.

You can arrange these trips in Malindi – people come round the hotels to ask if you are interested in going. The usual price is Sh 90 per person which includes a taxi to take you to and from your hotel, hire of the boat and the park entry fee. You may be able to get it for less if you bargain hard but you won't be able to knock too much off this price.

If you'd like to go scuba diving see Bill at the Driftwood Club at Silver Sands. It's going to cost you an arm and a leg – Sh 2500 per dive plus Sh 10 for temporary membership of the club!

Places to Stay – bottom end

There are a number of cheap, basic lodges in the centre of town, but they're usually fairly noisy at night and you don't get the benefit of sea breezes or instant access to the beach. Most travellers prefer to stay in one of the hotels on the beach.

In the Town If you do have to stay in the centre of town the *New Safari Hotel* has singles at Sh 35, doubles at Sh 50 without a bathroom or Sh 70 with a bathroom. The *Lamu Hotel* is clean and basic and has doubles at Sh 50, there are no singles. The *Malindi Rest House* is Sh 45 a double. Others include the *New Kenya Hotel*, *Salama Lodge* and *Wananchi Boarding & Lodging*.

There's a cool and very clean *Youth Hostel* (tel 20531) in Malindi next to the hospital. Mosquito nets are provided and there's a fridge for use by residents. Each room has six beds at a cost of Sh 30 per person. No membership card is required and it's quite a popular place to stay.

On the Beach The *Travellers' Inn* is the

best value for money of the beach hotels. It's a fairly new place, very clean with pleasant rooms, excellent showers and mosquito netting on the windows. It costs Sh 70 a single and Sh 100 a double between September and April, Sh 65 a single and Sh 80 a double for the rest of the year. The staff are very friendly and soft drinks and food are available. It's very popular so you may find it's full during the high season.

Also very popular is the *Metro Hotel*, although it's hard to see why since all but one of the rooms (a triple at Sh 110 which overlooks the ocean and gets the sea breezes) are dingy, hardboard-partitioned cells. It costs Sh 35 a single and Sh 80 a double with mosquito coils and towels provided. The showers are hopeless and the water supply is totally inadequate. What redeems this place is the friendliness of the Asian owner who really tries hard to please, the excellent, reasonably-priced food and the lively beer garden at the front of the property which is staffed by some very pleasant Africans who deserve to be paid much more than they are getting.

Other places on, or very close to, the beach front include *Gilani's Hotel* and the *Lucky Lodge*, both similarly priced to the Metro. *Ozi's Bed & Breakfast* is a mid-range hotel. It's very clean, fairly new and costs Sh 122 a single and Sh 183 a double including breakfast with separate showers and toilets.

About 1½ km south of the hotels along the coast road is the very popular *Silver Sands Camp Site* (and the *Hotel Silver Sands*) which is used by long-distance overland safari trucks whenever they come through. It costs Sh 20 per person to camp here and there are good toilets and showers but very little shade. If you haven't got a tent then you can you can rent a large double room (with a shower, toilet and kitchen sink) at the hotel for just Sh 50 (cheaper than two beds at the Youth Hostel).

They also have two sorts of *bandas* –

the cheaper ones cost Sh 50, the others Sh 80 to Sh 95. The prices depend on the season and how long you plan to stay. They're comfortable. You can rent bicycles for Sh 35 per day (and you'll need them if you are going to spend much time in Malindi itself) and baggage can be left safely. The beach here is excellent and is protected by a coral reef. The only drawback is that there's no bar or restaurant except for the *Cold House* at the southern end of the camp, which offers cold drinks and snacks such as hamburgers (Sh 25).

Places to Stay – top end

All of Malindi's tourist-class hotels are strung out along the beach, north of the centre of town. They cater for affluent European (mostly German and Italian) tourists on two-week holidays and British Army soldiers on R&R from the joint exercises which they conduct with the Kenyan armed forces each year. Prices are much the same as the tourist resort hotels north and south of Mombasa. They include *Lawford's Hotel*, the *Sindibad Hotel* and the *Eden Roc Hotel*. If I were going to stay in any of them I'd choose the Sindibad if only for its beautiful architecture. The *Blue Marlin Hotel* is presently closed.

Places to Eat

Cheap Eats For snacks or a cheap breakfast, try the *Bahrain Tea House* which offers such things as mandazi, baji, samosas and chappatis. If you want something more substantial the *Bahari Restaurant* has the same sort of things plus fish & chips and fruit salad. Or there's the *Metro Hotel* which offers breakfasts for Sh 18 plus Indian curries which can't be beat. They have a range of good-sized dishes for between Sh 40 and Sh 80 plus the best lime juice in town.

Reasonably priced and very good breakfasts can also be found at the *Baobab Café* – they have fried/boiled eggs, toast, butter and jam, tea or coffee.

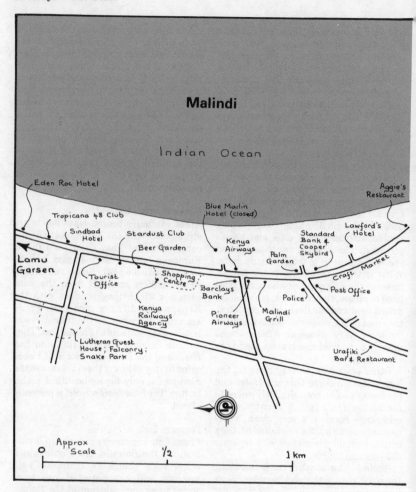

The Baobab also has cheap African food and does western-style dishes. Cheap meals (beans and vegetables for Sh 13) and fruit juices can also be found at the *Palatine Bar & Restaurant* which is very popular with local people. The *Malindi Fruit Juice Garden* in the market is definitely worth visiting for its excellent milk shakes and fruit juices which cost, on average, Sh 8.

For lunch or dinner there are a whole range of restaurants serving seafood and western-style food and their prices are remarkably similar despite, in some cases, the ritzy setting. One of the cheapest is *Aggie's Restaurant*, a fairly new place which offers Goan specialities. It's open daily until 7 pm. You're looking at Sh 20 to Sh 30 here or at the equally popular *Malindi Grill*.

For cheaper African food, try the *Urafiki Bar & Restaurant* which has

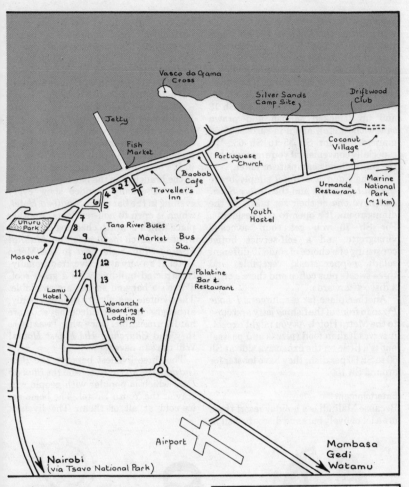

ugali and meat stew for less than Sh 20. The bar here gets very lively later on in the evening.

For German-style food you can eat among the palms and rock gardens at the *Beer Garden*. If you choose wisely and don't opt for the steaks – go for the wurst and kartofflensalat or the sea food with salad – it's possible to eat here for Sh 40 to Sh 60.

1	I Love Pizza
2	Sea Fishing Club
3	Metro Hotel
4	Gilani's Hotel
5	Ozi's Bed & Breakfast
6	Juma Mosque & Pillar Tombs
7	Bahari Restaurant
8	Lucky Lodge
9	Bahrain Tea House
10	New Safari Hotel
11	Malindi Rest House
12	New Kenya Hotel & Tawakal Buses
13	Salama Lodge

Expensive Restaurants For a splurge it's worth trying the *Driftwood Club* where you have to pay Sh 10 per day for temporary membership. This entitles you to the use of the swimming pool, hot showers, bar and restaurant. The prices are very reasonable – lunch for Sh 55, dinner for Sh 66, good snacks for Sh 18 and up (smoked sailfish and prawn sandwiches, etc), and à la carte seafood main dishes for Sh 35 to Sh 65. It's especially convenient if you are staying at the Silver Sands campsite or hotel.

At the *Eden Roc Hotel* simply brave the *haute couture* and the *Ambre Soleil* and have one of their set meals in the dining room. It's open to non-residents. For Sh 70 you get soup, avocado vinaigrette and a self-service buffet consisting of a choice of some 10 different salads, pepper steak, vegetables and three sweets plus coffee and there's often a disco afterwards.

Another place for a splurge is *I Love Pizza* in front of the fishing jetty and close to the Metro Hotel. As you might expect, it serves Italian food (pizzas and pastas) but is a little on the expensive side at Sh 50 to Sh 60 per dish; they have lobster for around Sh 150.

Entertainment

Because Malindi is a holiday resort there are a lot of lively bars and discos to visit in the evening, some of which rock away until dawn. The most famous of them is the *Stardust Club* which generally doesn't get started until late (10 or 11 pm) and costs Sh 40 entry. You can also get a meal here. The *Tropicana 48 Club* is similar.

There's also a disco at least once a week – usually on Wednesdays – at *Coconut Village* past the Driftwood Club and, if you get there early enough, you won't have to pay the entry charge. The bar is incredible and is worth a visit just to see it. It's built around a living tree with one of the branches as the bar top!

There is usually a video show every evening in the bar of the *Sindibad Hotel*, which is open to non-residents. Another place which is worth checking out if you want to catch a film is the *Malindi Fishing Club*, right next to the Metro Hotel. It's a very attractive, traditionally-constructed building with a grass roof. There's a bar and snacks are available. The clientele, mainly British, are friendly, although some of the videos they show are hardly irresistible. Once when I was there they had *Churchill: His Finest Hours*! Will the sun never set?

The three liveliest bars are the *Beer Garden*, the *Metro Hotel* and the *Baobab Café* which is popular with people who stay at the Youth Hostel. The beers are ice-cold at all of them. The liveliest

wrist knife

thumb knife

ivory earring

African bar is the *Urafiki* with its deafening juke box that seems to play Franco non-stop. It closes by 11.30 pm and the beers are often luke-warm.

A Warning Don't walk back to your hotel along the beach at night. Many people have been mugged at knife point. Go back along the main road (which has street lighting) or take a taxi. You also need to exercise caution if returning from the Baobab Café to the Youth Hostel late at night – people have even been mugged along that short stretch of road, although you're probably safe if you're part of a group.

Getting There
Air There are 10 or 11 flights per week in either direction between Nairobi and Malindi and between Mombasa and Malindi with Kenya Airways.

Cooper Skybird flies Lamu-Malindi daily at 10 am and 4 pm (Sh 400 one-way). The 4 pm flight continues to Mombasa. Return tickets are twice the price of one-way tickets. Cooper Skybird's booking offices (tel 20860/1) are on Government Rd near Lawford's Hotel in Malindi.

Pioneer Airlines fly Lamu-Malindi at 10 am and 12 noon (half an hour, Sh 400 one-way); Return tickets are double the cost of one-way tickets. Phone number in Malindi is 20585.

Bus There are many departures daily from Mombasa from early morning until late afternoon by several bus companies and *matatus*. A bus costs Sh 25 and takes up to three hours. A *matatu* costs Sh 40 and takes about two hours. In Malindi they depart from the bus station.

A group of five or six people can hire a private taxi for about Sh 50 each which will take you door-to-door in about 1½ hours. You can arrange these at the hotel you are staying at in Mombasa or Malindi. On this route there is a ferry crossing at Kilifi where you will have to disembark. You'll come across many

people here selling cashew nuts cheaply.

The best company to travel with from Malindi to Lamu is the Tana River Bus Company which has its terminus on Sir Ali Rd opposite the Habib Bank. They go to Lamu on Monday, Wednesday and Friday. Other companies making this trip are Lamy Bus and Tawakal. The fare is Sh 85 and journey takes about six hours. See the Lamu section for more details.

Rail You can make advance reservations for Kenyan Railways at the travel agent in the shopping centre along the Lamu road (indicated on the street map).

Getting Around
Bicycle Rental You can rent bicycles from the Silver Sands booking agency on the top side of Uhuru Gardens. They cost Sh 10 for the first hour and Sh 6 for each subsequent hour or Sh 45 per day.

Things to Buy
There are many craft shops lining both sides of the road between Uhuru Park and the post office. Prices are reasonable (though you must, of course, bargain) and the quality is high. They offer *makonde* carvings, wooden animal carvings, stone and wooden chess sets, basketware and the like. If you have unwanted or excess gear (T-shirts, jeans, cameras) you can often do a part-exchange deal with these people. Apart from Nairobi, it's probably the best collection of such shops in Kenya.

WATAMU
About 24 km south of Malindi, Watamu is a smaller beach resort with its own National Marine Park – part of the Marine National Reserve which stretches south from Malindi. The coral reef here is even more spectacular than at Malindi since it has been much less exploited and poached by shell hunters. It is not, however, as easy to get to and you will probably have to utilise the boats laid on

by the large hotels and they're usually more expensive than at Malindi. The beach is excellent and not as crowded as Malindi.

You can use the facilities at the large hotels even if you're not a resident – most of them have a bar, restaurant, swimming pool, disco and water-sport facilities. Scuba diving at the Seafarer Hotel is very expensive.

Places to Stay

The only trouble with Watamu is the lack of budget accommodation. The village itself has only a few bars and restaurants, many craft shops, local people's houses and a large disco/night club but no lodges. You could possibly rent a room in one of the private houses if you asked around. Otherwise, there is the *Seventh Day Adventist Youth Camp* where you can get a bed in one of the three rooms (each with two or three beds) or camp. The campsite is pretty basic and the facilities aren't up to much but there's a kitchen with a gas cooker (which works) and it's close to the beach, about 10-minutes' walk from the village. The beds cost Sh 45 each though you may initially be quoted up to Sh 80.

Getting There

There are plenty of *matatus* from the bus station in Malindi to Watamu throughout the day. They cost Sh 5 and take 20-30 minutes.

GEDI

Some three to four km from Watamu, just off the main road from Malindi, are the famous Gedi ruins, one of the principal historical monuments on the coast. Though the ruins are extensive, this Arab-Swahili town is something of a mystery since it's not mentioned in any of the Portuguese or Arab chronicles of the time.

Excavations, which have uncovered such things as Ming Chinese porcelain and glass and glazed earthenware from Persia, have indicated the 13th century as

the time of its foundation but it was inexplicably abandoned in the 17th or 18th century, possibly because the sea receded and left the town high and dry, or because of marauding Galla tribesmen from the north. The forest took over and the site was not rediscovered until the 1920s. These days you can see the remains of several mosques, a palace, several large pillar tombs, many houses and wells. If you're interested in archaeology it's worth a visit.

Entry costs Sh 30 (Sh 10 for student card holders). A good guidebook with map is for sale at the entrance.

Getting There

Take the same *matatus* as you would to Watamu but get off at Gedi village, where the *matatus* turn off from the main Malindi-Mombasa road. From there it's about a one km signposted walk to the monument along a gravel road.

MOMBASA

Mombasa is the largest port on the coast of East Africa. It has a population of nearly half a million of which about 70% are African, the rest being mainly Asian with a small minority of Europeans. Its docks not only serve Kenya, but also Uganda, Rwanda and Burundi. The bulk of the town sprawls over Mombasa Island which is connected to the mainland by an artificial causeway which carries the rail and road links. In recent years Mombasa has spread onto the mainland both north and south of the island.

Large Mombasa may be but, like Dar es Salaam to the south, it has retained its low-level traditional character and there are few high-rise buildings. The old town between the massive, Portuguese-built Fort Jesus and the old dhow careening dock remains much the same as it was in the mid-19th century, asphalt streets and craft shops apart. It's a hot and steamy town, as you might expect being so close to the equator, but an interesting place to visit.

Top: Balloons, Masai Mara National Park, Kenya (HF)
Left: On safari, Marsabit National Park, Kenya (GC)
Right: The Lamu bus, Mombasa, Kenya (GC)

Top: Shop, Equator, Kenya (RA)
Bottom: Dhow, Kenya (JS)

History

Mombasa's history goes back to at least the 12th century when it was described by Arab chroniclers as being a small town and the residence of the King of the Zenj – Arabic for black Africans. It later became an important settlement for the Shirazi and remained so until the arrival of the Portuguese in the early 16th century. Determined to destroy the Arab monopoly over maritime trade in the Indian Ocean, especially with regard to spices, the Portuguese, under Dom Francisco de Almeida, attacked Mombasa with a fleet of 16 ships in 1505. After a day and half it was all over and the town was burnt to the ground. So great was the quantity of loot that much of it had to be left behind, for fear of overloading the ships, when the fleet sailed for India

The town was quickly rebuilt and it wasn't long before it regained its commanding position over trade in the area, but peace didn't last long. In 1528, another Portuguese fleet under Nuña da Cunha arrived on the East African coast too late to catch the south-western monsoon which would take them to India, so they were forced to look around for temporary quarters. Naturally, Mombasa was in no mood to welcome them but, unfortunately, Mombasa was at that time engaged in bitter disputes with the kings of Malindi, Pemba and Zanzibar. An alliance was patched together and the Portuguese were again able to take Mombasa, but sickness and constant skirmishing over many months eventually decided the outcome. The city was again burnt to the ground and the Portuguese sailed for India.

The Portuguese finally made a bid for permanency in 1593 when the construction of Fort Jesus was begun, but in 1631 they were massacred to the last person in an uprising by the townspeople. The following year a Portuguese fleet was sent from Goa and Muscat to avenge the killings but was unable to re-take the town. By this time, however, the Mombasan ruler had decided that further resistance was useless and having reduced the town to rubble and cut down all the fruit trees and palms he withdrew to the mainland. It was re-occupied without a fight by the Portuguese the following year.

Portuguese hegemony of the Indian Ocean was on the wane by this time, not only because of corruption and nepotism within their own ranks, but because of Dutch, French and English activity in India and South-East Asia. The 17th century also saw the rise of Oman as a naval power and it was the Omanis who, in 1698, were the next to drive the Portuguese from Mombasa, after a 33-month siege in which all the defenders were slaughtered. Even this disaster wasn't enough to convince the Portuguese that their days were over. Mombasa was re-occupied yet again but the end finally came in 1729 following an invasion by an Arab fleet, a general uprising of the population in which Portuguese settlers were slaughtered and an abortive counter-offensive which involved the entire military resources of the Viceroyalty of Goa.

In 1832 the Sultan of Oman moved his capital from Muscat to Zanzibar and from then until Kenya's independence in 1963 the red flag of Zanzibar fluttered over Fort Jesus. Meanwhile, the British became active along the East African coast. In their attempts to suppress the slave trade, they interfered increasingly in the affairs of Zanzibar until, in 1895, the British East Africa Protectorate was set up with Mombasa as the capital (until it was moved to Nairobi) and the Sultan of Oman's possessions were administered as a part of it. When independence came, the Sultan's coastal possessions were attached to the new republic.

During the protectorate years the British confirmed Mombasa's status as East Africa's most important port by constructing a railway from Mombasa to Uganda. It was completed in 1901 using indentured labourers from Gujarat and

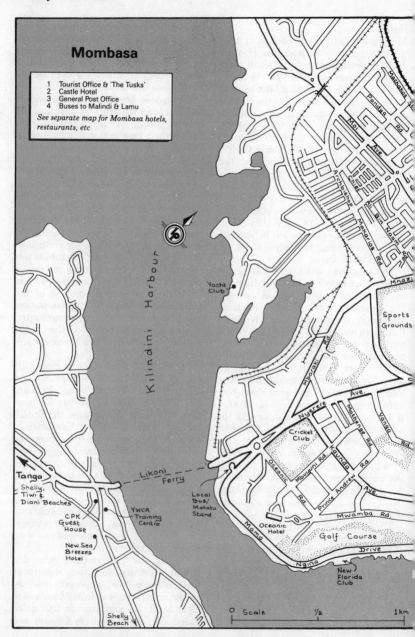

Mombasa

1 Tourist Office & 'The Tusks'
2 Castle Hotel
3 General Post Office
4 Buses to Malindi & Lamu

See separate map for Mombasa hotels, restaurants, etc

Kilindini Harbour

Yacht Club

Sports Grounds

Mnazi

Archbishop Cavel

Makaros Rd

Nkrumah Rd

Pandka Rd

Mbalakas Rd

Moi Ave

Rbaraki Rd

Nyerere Ave

Mablu.e Rd

Yanga Rd

Cricket Club

Oceanic Rd

Kaunda Rd

Mbuyuni Rd

Prince Andrew Ave

Mwamba Rd.

Golf Course

Oceanic Hotel

Mama

Ngina

Drive

New Florida Club

Tanga

Shelly, Tiwi & Diani Beaches

CPK Guest House

YWCA Training Centre

New Sea Breezes Hotel

Likoni Ferry

Local Bus/ Matatu Stand

Shelly Beach

O   Scale   ½   1km

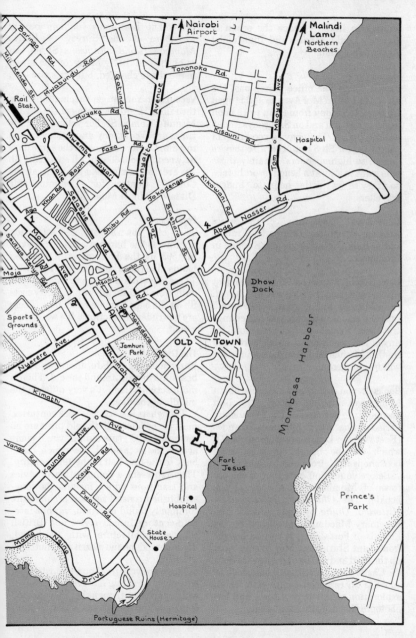

Punjab in India – hence the origin of Kenya's (and Uganda's and Tanzania's) Asian population.

Information

Tourist Office The office is just past the famous tusks on Moi Avenue and is open Monday to Friday from 8 am to 12 noon and 2 to 4.30 pm and on Saturdays from 8 am to 12 noon. They have a good map of Mombasa for Sh 3 but otherwise they're geared to high spenders – mainly those who want to stay at a beach resort hotel – so they're of little help to budget travellers.

Consulates There are consulates of Austria, Belgium, Denmark, France, India, Italy, Netherlands and Sweden in Mombasa.

Bank Barclays Bank on Moi Avenue, just up the road from the Castle Hotel, is open from Monday to Saturday, 8.30 am to 5 pm. Outside these hours you can change travellers' cheques at the Castle Hotel (or any of the beach resort hotels north and south of Mombasa) although a commission will be charged.

Books If you'd like more details about Mombasa's stirring history, the best account is to be found in *The Portuguese Period in East Africa* by Justus Strandes (East African Literature Bureau, 1971), which can be bought in most good bookshops in Nairobi and Mombasa.

Before you set off on a tour of the old town of Mombasa get a copy of the booklet *The Old Town Mombasa: A Historical Guide* by Judy Aldrick and Rosemary Macdonald published by the Friends of Fort Jesus. It can be bought from Kant Stationers, Moi Avenue, just up the road and on the opposite side from the Castle Hotel, for Sh 25. This excellent guide is an essential companion for an exploration of this part of town and has photographs, drawings and a map.

Maps The best map you can buy of Mombasa is the Survey of Kenya *Mombasa Island & Environs* (Sh 54), last published in 1977. Many of the street names have changed, but little else.

Vaccination You can get vaccinations from the Public Health Department (tel 26791), Msanifu Kombo St. For yellow fever the times are Wednesday and Friday from 8 to 9 am. Cholera is done on the same days between 2 and 3.30 pm. All shots cost Sh 20. Free bilharzia tests are done at the Control Centre for Communicable Diseases, Mnazi Moja Rd.

Fort Jesus

The old town's biggest attraction dominates the harbour entrance. Begun in 1593 by the Portuguese, it changed hands nine times between 1631 and 1875. These days it's a museum and is open daily from 8.30 am to 6.30 pm. Entry costs Sh 30 (Sh 5 for Kenyan residents). There are no student reductions. It's well worth a visit.

The Old Town

Early morning or late afternoon is the best time to walk around the old. There's more activity then, it's very quiet in the middle of the day.

Though its history goes back centuries, most of the houses in the old town are no more than 100 years old but you'll come across the occasional one which dates back to the first half of the 19th century. They represent a combination of styles and traditions which include the long-established coastal Swahili architecture commonly found in Lamu, various late-19th-century Indian styles and British colonial architecture with its broad, shady verandahs and glazed and shuttered windows.

There are very few houses constructed entirely of coral rag, however. Most are of wattle and daub though they may include coral here and there. Most of the old palm thatch or tile roofing has been replaced

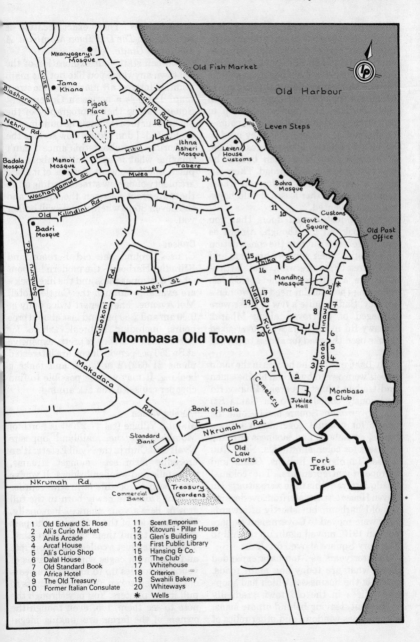

Mombasa Old Town

Mkanyagenyi Mosque
Jama Khana
Old Fish Market
Old Harbour
Biashara St.
Kuze Rd.
Pigott Place
Mzizima Rd.
Leven Steps
Nehru Rd.
13
Kitui Rd.
12
Ithna Asheri Mosque
Leven House Customs
Badala Mosque
Memon Mosque
Tabere
Mwea
14
Bohra Mosque
Wachangamwe St.
Old Kilindini Rd.
11
10
Customs
Govt. Square
Old Post Office
Badri Mosque
9
Samburu Rd.
15
Jinka St.
16
Mandhry Mosque
Nyeri St.
17
18
19
20
KCC
1
2
Kibokoni Rd.
Makadara Rd.
Mbarak Hinawy Rd.
7
8
6
5
4
Cemetery
Jubilee Hall
Mombasa Club
Bank of India
Nkrumah Rd.
Standard Bank
Old Law Courts
Fort Jesus
Nkrumah Rd.
Commercial Bank
Treasury Gardens

1	Old Edward St. Rose	11	Scent Emporium
2	Ali's Curio Market	12	Kitovuni - Pillar House
3	Anils Arcade	13	Glen's Building
4	Arcaf House	14	First Public Library
5	Ali's Curio Shop	15	Hansing & Co.
6	Dalal House	16	'The Club'
7	Old Standard Book	17	Whitehouse
8	Africa Hotel	18	Criterion
9	The Old Treasury	19	Swahili Bakery
10	Former Italian Consulate	20	Whiteways
		✳	Wells

with corrugated iron as well. What does remain are many examples of the massive, intricately-carved doors and door frames characteristic of Swahili houses in Lamu and Zanzibar. It seems that when anyone of importance moved from these towns to Mombasa they brought their doors with them or had them newly made up to reflect their financial status. Of course, they're not as numerous as they used to be, either because of the ravages of time, or because they have been bought by collectors and shipped abroad. There is a now a preservation order on those remaining so further losses should hopefully be prevented.

It's not just carved doors that you should look out for, though. Almost as much effort was put into the construction of balconies, their support brackets and enclosures. Fine fretwork and lattice-work are a feature of the enclosures, reflecting the Muslim need for women's privacy. Sadly, quite a few of these were damaged or destroyed along Mbarak Hinawy Rd in the days when over-sized trucks used the road for access to the old port.

By 1900, most of the houses in the main streets were owned by Indian businessmen and traders whilst Mbarak Hinawy Rd (previously called Vasco da Gama St) and Government Square had become the centre for colonial government offices, banks, consulates and business or living quarters for colonial officials. Ndia Kuu housed immigrant Indians, Goans and European entrepreneurs. The colonial headquarters at this time were situated in
• Leven House on the waterfront overlooking the old harbour, but shortly afterwards they were moved to Government Square and, in 1910, moved again up the hill to Treasury Square above Fort Jesus.

In later years as Mombasa expanded along what are today the main roads, many of the businesses which had shops and offices in the old town gradually moved out, leaving behind ornate signs, etched glass windows and other relics of former times. Their exact location is described in *The Old Town Mombasa: A Historical Guide*.

You can start your exploration of the old town anywhere you like but the main points of interest are marked on the street map. There is a notice in Government Square saying that photography of the old harbour area (but not the buildings) is prohibited. I don't know how serious the authorities are about this since I can't imagine what is so sensitive about the place, but if you want pictures of it there are plenty of narrow streets leading off to the waterfront between the square and the Leven Steps where no-one will bother you.

Cruises

Cruises around the old harbour and Kilindini Harbour – the modern harbour where container ships and the like dock – are available through the Castle Hotel, Moi Avenue. They depart twice daily at 9.30 am and 2.30 pm and last about three hours, including a break ashore for refreshment, but they're pretty expensive at Sh 250 per person. If you are interested phone 31 6391/2 or 25230 and make a booking. It may well be possible to find cheaper cruises if you ask around.

Mamba Village

Mamba Village (tel 47 2709) is north of Mombasa on the mainland opposite Nyali Golf Club in the Nyali Estate. It's a crocodile farm set amongst streams, waterfalls and wooden bridges. If you've never seen a crocodile farm with reptiles ranging from the newly born to the full grown, here's your chance. Personally, I've seen a lot of these farms in the past and I don't find them that interesting. They're often just a collection of concrete and wire-mesh cages with thousands of young crocodiles up to four to five years old and a few token, full-grown adults to pull in the punters. You pay through the nose to see them, too, even though the owners of the farms are making megabucks selling skins to Gucci and the like.

Bamburi Quarry Nature Trail

Further up the coast this nature trail (tel 48 5729) has been created on reclaimed and reforested areas damaged by cement-production activities which ceased in 1971. Once the forest was established, the area was restocked with plants and animals in an attempt to create a mini-replica of the wildlife parks of Kenya. At present, animal species represented include eland, oryx, waterbuck, buffalo, warthog, bush pig, various monkeys and many different varieties of birds. There's also what the owners claim to be an 'orphan' hippo which was introduced as a baby from Naivasha and which has remained bottle-fed ever since. A likely story!

The complex also includes a fish farm, crocodile farm, reptile pit and plant nursery. The centre is open daily from 2 to 5.30 pm. Feeding time is at 4 pm. To get there take a public bus to Bamburi Quarry Nature Trail stop (signposted) on the main Mombasa-Malindi road.

Places to Stay

There's a lot of choice for budget travellers and for those who want something slightly better, both in the centre of the city and on the mainland to the north and south. Accommodation up and down the coast from Mombasa Island itself is dealt with separately.

Places to Stay – bottom end

By far the best value for money in this category is the *Mvita Hotel*, on the corner of Hospital St and Turkana Rd. The entrance is on the first alley on the left hand side on Turkana Rd or through the bar on the ground floor on Hospital St. It's Indian-run, very clean and quiet, secure, friendly, all the rooms have fans, a hand basin and the beds are comfortable. Even toilet paper is provided. The showers and toilets are scrubbed out daily. All this for

just Sh 69 a double. There's a lively bar downstairs (which you can't hear in the rooms upstairs) and at lunch and dinner times barbecued meat and other snacks are available in the back yard.

Equally good value and popular with travellers is the *Cozy Guest House*, Haile Selassie Rd, which costs Sh 45 a single, Sh 70 a double and Sh 110 a triple. It's a clean place and all the rooms have fans. It will most likely be full if you get there late in the day. On the opposite side of the road from the Cozy Guest House is the *Midnight Guest House* which is a reasonable alternative at Sh 60 a single and Sh 70 a double with common showers and toilets or Sh 100 a double with a bathroom.

If these two are full then try the *Balgis Hotel*, Digo Rd, which is very friendly and good value for Sh 55 a single and Sh 70 a double. Also worth trying is the *New Britannia Board & Lodging*, Gusii St, which is very clean and tidy, has pleasant rooms with fans and water and costs Sh 60 a double. The staff here are friendly.

Another budget hotel which has been popular for years is the *New People's Hotel*, Abdel Nasser Rd right next to where the buses leave for Malindi and Lamu. Some travellers rate this place very highly and it certainly compares very well in price with the others but it is a little tatty and the rooms which face onto the main road are very noisy and the air stinks of diesel fumes. This is mainly because of the bus drivers who seem to have a fetish about revving their engines for anything up to an hour before they actually leave. The management are friendly and gear left in the rooms is safe. It costs Sh 36.50 a single, Sh 61.50 a double and Sh 75 a triple for a room with common showers and toilets, and Sh 59.50 a single, Sh 119 a double and Sh 178.50 a triple with a bathroom. All the rooms have fans, the sheets are clean and the water in the showers is generally lukewarm. It's a large place, rarely full and has a good restaurant downstairs.

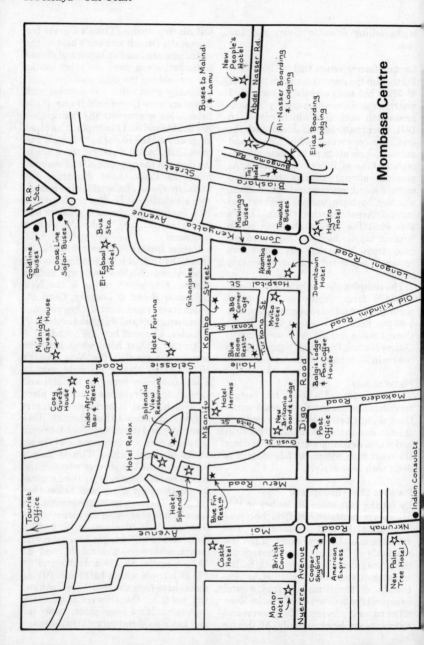

Mombasa Centre

Close to the Mvita and Balgis are two other places worth checking out if you can't find a room. The first is the *Downtown Hotel*, Hospital St, opposite the Mvita. It costs Sh 25 per person in a room with four beds, Sh 60 a single and Sh 70 a double with common showers and toilets. It's scruffy and some of the back rooms are dingy. The other is the *Hydro Hotel*, Digo Rd at the junction with Kenyatta Avenue. This place has been a popular budget hotel for years but it's very run-down these days. It costs Sh 25 per person in the dormitory, Sh 50 a single and Sh 75 a double with common showers and toilets. There's a reasonable restaurant on the 1st floor. Both the Downtown and the Hydro are relatively poor value in comparison to the Mvita and Balgis.

Somewhat more expensive than the above (but not necessarily better value) is the *Hotel Fortuna*, Haile Selassie Rd, which costs Sh 125 a single and Sh 150 a double both with private showers and toilets.

Places to Stay – middle
One of the cheapest in this range is the *Hotel Relax*, Meru Rd, which is clean and good value at Sh 160 a single and Sh 200 a double including private shower, toilet and breakfast. All the rooms have fans. Next door is the *Hotel Splendid*, a huge place which is rarely full. It costs Sh 122 a single and Sh 243 a double with private bathroom and breakfast. It's a very clean and modern place and there's a popular rooftop restaurant which gets sea breezes in the evenings.

Close to these two hotels is the *Hotel Hermes*, Msanifu Kombo St, which costs Sh 235 a single and Sh 280 a double with private bathrooms and including breakfast.

Perhaps the best place to stay in this range is the beautiful *New Palm Tree Hotel*, Nkrumah Rd, which I'd rate as being very similar in quality to the much more expensive Castle Hotel. A very comfortable room here costs Sh 163-234 a single and Sh 245-292 a double with a shower and toilet and including breakfast. The hotel has its own bar and restaurant.

The *Taj Hotel*, Bungoma Rd, is priced as a mid-range hotel but I cannot see how it justifies its prices since the quality is no better than some of the better budget hotels. It's quiet and clean but costs Sh 150 a single and Sh 200 a double without private bathroom and Sh 250 a double with a bathroom. On the other hand, the restaurant here serves some of the best Indian food in Mombasa.

Places to Stay – top end
In the centre of town the very popular *Castle Hotel* (tel 23403/21683), Moi Avenue, costs Sh 480-560 a single and Sh 700 to Sh 780 a double, including breakfast. You'll find all the comforts and facilities you would expect at the Castle Hotel and at the *Oceanic Hotel*, between Oceanic Rd and Mama Ngina Drive facing the Indian Ocean.

The older, colonial-style *Manor Hotel* (tel 21821/2), Nyerere Avenue, with a wide verandah and surrounding garden, is cheaper at Sh 260 to Sh 330 a single and Sh 430 to Sh 500 a double with a private bathroom and including breakfast.

Places to Eat
Indian Food Since many of the restaurants in Mombasa are Indian-owned you can find excellent curries and thalis and at lunch times (12.30 to around 3 pm) there is often a cheap, substantial set meal available. One which you'll hear nothing but praise for is the *Geetanjalee*, Msanifu Kombo St, which offers a 'deluxe' thali for Sh 35. Both the food and service are excellent.

Similar is the *New Chetna Restaurant*, Haile Selassie Rd directly under the Cozy Guest House. Here it's South Indian vegetarian food (masala dosa, idli, etc) and sweets, plus they offer an all-you-can-eat set vegetarian lunch for Sh 35. It's a very popular restaurant. Also reasonable is the *Taj Hotel*, Bungoma St, which offers curries (Sh 24-30), biriyanis (Sh 40-45) and fresh fruit juices (Sh 5). Like the other places it offers specials of the day.

Excellent tandoori specialities can be found at the very popular *Splendid View Café*, opposite, but not part of, the Hotel Splendid. They have things like chicken, lamb, fruit juices and lassis and you can eat well here for around Sh 35. There are tables outside and inside. The *Barbeque Corner Café*, Konzi St near the Mvita Hotel, is similar. This is a new place and the food is very good.

Swahili Food For coastal Swahili dishes made with coconut and coconut milk, the *Swahili Curry Bowl*, Tangere Rd off Moi Avenue, is recommended. Prices are reasonable. It's also one of *the* places for coffee and ice cream.

Cheap Eats If you are looking for seafood or western food then one of the cheapest is the *Blue Fin Restaurant*, on the corner of Meru Rd and Msanifu Kombo St. There's a fairly extensive menu but fish & chips or omelette & chips cost Sh 14 and two fried eggs & chips cost Sh 12. I thought this place was very good value considering the prices and the quality of the food but it has come in for adverse criticism in the past from some travellers – perhaps it didn't compare too well with their favourite chippie back home?.

Roshne's Cafe, Meru St, is similar – fish & chips, omelettes, samosas, etc. They also offer breakfasts for Sh 20. Good, self-service breakfasts can also be found at the *Blue Room Restaurant*, Haile Selassie Rd at the junction with Turkana St.

Medium Price Restaurants Going up slightly in price, try the *Indo-Africa Bar & Restaurant*, Haile Selassie Rd next door to the Cozy Guest House, for excellent Indian Mughlai dishes at reasonable prices. The *Masumin*, Digo Rd on the opposite side from the post office, is very good for things like prawns masala (about Sh 40), chicken curry, meat curries, fish & chips, fruit juices and lassi.

Expensive Restaurants For a splurge you could try a dinner one evening at the rooftop restaurant at the *Hotel Splendid*. There are good views over the city and the restaurant catches the evening sea breezes. For a more expensive splurge try either the *New Palm Tree Hotel* or the *Castle Hotel* but check prices first and take note of hidden extras such as tax and service charges which can increase your bill by up to 25%.

Entertainment
For an ice-cold beer in the heat of the day many people go to the terrace of the *Castle Hotel* which overlooks Moi Avenue. It's the nearest thing you'll find to the Thorn Tree Café in Nairobi but the comparison isn't really valid. If you prefer more local colour and a livelier place then there's a similar bar almost opposite the Castle Hotel. There's no name on the place but it's known as the *Istanbul Bar*. You can also get cheap snacks. The bar at the *Mvita Hotel* was very lively most nights – it takes a while to get used to seeing Swahili women dressed in *bui bui* drinking bottles of White Cap beer.

The *Rainbow Hotel* is a popular disco/African reggae club which is always filled with local ragers, seamen, whores and travellers. There are plenty of other excellent reggae clubs in the suburbs which are very cheap and good fun – ask around.

Getting There
Air There are 47 flights per week in either direction between Nairobi and Mombasa with Kenya Airways. There are a further 10 or 11 flights between Mombasa and Malindi. Flights to Kisumu go via Nairobi.

The Cooper Skybird Lamu-Malindi flight at 4 pm daily continues to

Mombasa. Their office in Mombasa is at Ambalal House (tel 21456/21443) on Nkrumah Rd. Pioneer Airlines fly Lamu-Mombasa at 4 pm (1½ hours, Sh 600 one-way). Return tickets are double the cost of one-way tickets. Pioneer Airlines' phone number in Mombasa is 43 2355.

Bus In Mombasa bus stations are mainly along Jomo Kenyatta Avenue/Mwembe Tayari Rd. For Nairobi-Mombasa buses there are many departures daily in either direction (mostly in the early morning and late evening) by, among others, Akamba, Coastline Safari, Goldline and Mawingo. The fare is Sh 100 and the trip takes seven to eight hours including a lunch break about half way.

Mombasa-Malindi there are also many departures daily in either direction from early morning until late afternoon by several bus companies and *matatus*. A bus costs Sh 25 and takes up to three hours. A *matatu* costs Sh 40 and takes about two hours. In Mombasa they all depart from outside the New People's Hotel, Abdel Nasser Rd. See the Malindi section for more details and for the alternative of hiring a taxi.

It's possible to go straight through from Mombasa to Lamu but most travellers stop en route at Malindi.

Rail Trains Nairobi-Mombasa operate in either direction at 5 and 7 pm. The journey takes about 13 hours. The fares are 1st class – Sh 321; 2nd class – Sh 138; 3rd class – Sh 60. If you're travelling alone and want a 1st class compartment to yourself it costs Sh 420.

Boat If you're interested in yachts or boats to India or the Seychelles it's worth getting out to Kilibi Creek. Most of the people with yachts moor at Kilibi Creek because mooring berths at the Mombasa Yacht Club are very expensive. If you want to make enquiries you can get to Kilibi by going to Tom's Beach, 1½ km from the centre, near the Seahorse Hotel.

Getting Around

Likoni Ferry This ferry connects Mombasa Island with the southern mainland and runs at frequent intervals throughout the night and day. There's a crossing every 20 minutes on average between 5 and 12.30 am; less frequently between 12.30 and 5 am. It's free to pedestrians.

Things to Buy

Mombasa isn't the craft entrepôt you might expect it to be, but it's not too bad either. The trouble is that there are a lot of tourists and seamen who pass through this port with lots of dollars to shed in a hurry. Bargains, therefore, can take a long time to negotiate. There are a lot of craft stalls along Msanifu Kombo St near the junction with Moi Avenue; along Moi Avenue itself from the Castle Hotel down to the roundabout with Nyerere Avenue; along Jomo Kenyatta Avenue close to the junction with Digo Rd; and in the old town close to Fort Jesus.

Have a look around – you might find something. *Makonde* wood carvings, stone chess sets and animal/human figurines, basketwork, drums and other musical instruments and paintings are the sorts of things that are sold.

Biashara St above Digo Rd is the centre for fabrics and those colourful, beautifully patterned, wrap-around skirts complete with Swahili proverbs (known as *kangas*) which most East African women wear (other than Hindus) even if they do it under a *bui bui*. You may need to bargain a little over the price (but not too much). What you get is generally what you pay for and, as a rule, they range in price from as little as Sh 35 to Sh 80. Assuming you are willing to bargain, the price you pay for one will reflect the quality of the cloth. Buy them in Mombasa if possible. You can often get them as cheaply in Nairobi but elsewhere prices escalate prohibitively.

SOUTH OF MOMBASA

The south coast is perhaps the most

highly developed of the mainland beaches which stretch north and south of Mombasa and there is very little cheap accommodation available. From the Likoni ferry going south the beaches are Shelly, Tiwi and Diani with another one at Shimoni much further down the coast near the border with Tanzania. There is also a National Marine Reserve there. All the beaches are white coral sand and are protected by a coral reef so there is no danger from sharks when you go swimming. Most of the way the beaches are fringed with coconut palms so you can always find shade if you want to get out of the sun.

Shelly Beach

Shelly Beach can suffer from an accumulation of seaweed between the reef and the shore. It gets so bad at times that there's no way you would want to go swimming in the sea.

Places to Stay Almost as soon as you turn off the main road after the Likoni ferry you come to one of the few relatively cheap places to stay; this is the *CPK Guest House* on the right hand side. It's a beautiful place and you can get a comfortable room for about Sh 160 per day with full board. The food is excellent and there's a very large swimming pool for use by residents.

Closer to the beach itself you will have to ask around for rooms to rent. There are quite a few of these (some of them in private houses) but expect to pay around Sh 200 a double per day without food. Try the *Rocking Boat Inn* about a km past the Shelly Beach Hotel.

At the *Shelly Beach Hotel* itself you are looking at Sh 370 to Sh 425 a single and Sh 555 to Sh 840 a double for bed and breakfast and Sh 385 to Sh 440 a single and Sh 585 to Sh 870 a double for half board.

Getting There To get to Shelly beach you need to turn left at the first major turn-off

after getting off the Likoni ferry. This is near the top of the rise past where the buses and *matatus* park. There are no public buses to Shelly beach so you will either have to hire a *matatu* (about Sh 30 per person), hitch (easy depending on the time of day) or walk (about 30 minutes).

Tiwi Beach

Tiwi beach can also suffer from the same seaweed problem as Shelly, but not usually to the same extent.

Places to Stay The only relatively cheap place to stay on Tiwi is the very popular *Twiga Lodge* which costs Sh 20 per person to camp or Sh 30 per person to camp if you want to hire a tent. You'll meet a lot of travellers and it's a very beautiful place to stay. The restaurant is quite expensive but the shop nearby sells most basics and people will come round everyday offering fish and fruit which you can cook yourself. Whatever you do when you get off the bus, *do not* walk from the main road to Tiwi (about three km). Many people have been mugged doing this. Wait on the main road until you get a lift. The Twiga Lodge is signposted on the main road to Ukunda.

Getting There To get to Tiwi or Diani beaches from the Likoni ferry take either a KRS bus with a 'Diani Beach' sign ('Likoni' in the opposite direction) or a *matatu* with a 'Ukunda' sign. Both cost Sh 6. If you're going to Tiwi it doesn't matter which you take since you will have to get off about half way.

Diani Beach

Diani is the longest and best of the beaches and doesn't suffer from the seaweed problem, but it is the most developed. Virtually the whole of the ocean frontage is taken up by expensive beach resorts.

Places to Stay – bottom end The only cheap place to stay on Diani beach is the well-

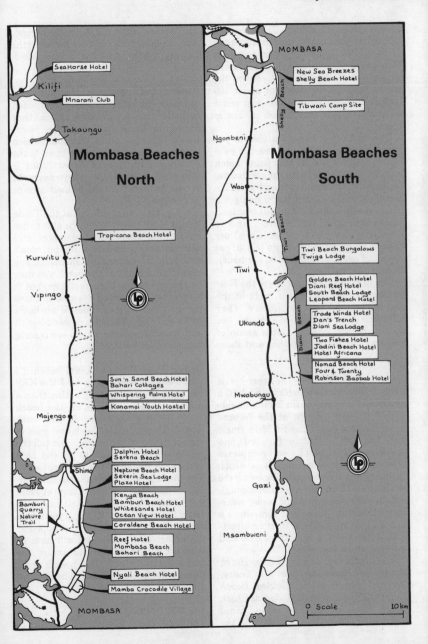

SeaHorse Hotel

Kilifi

Mnarani Club

Takaungu

Mombasa Beaches

North

Tropicana Beach Hotel

Kurwitu

Vipingo

Sun 'n Sand Beach Hotel
Bahari Cottages

Whispering Palms Hotel

Kanamai Youth Hostel

Majengo

Dolphin Hotel
Serena Beach

Shimo

Neptune Beach Hotel
Severin Sea Lodge
Plaza Hotel

Bamburi
Quarry
Nature
Trail

Kenya Beach
Bamburi Beach Hotel
Whitesands Hotel
Ocean View Hotel

Coraldene Beach Hotel

Reef Hotel
Mombasa Beach
Bahari Beach

Nyali Beach Hotel

Mamba Crocodile Village

MOMBASA

MOMBASA

New Sea Breezes
Shelly Beach Hotel

Tibwani Camp Site

Ngombeni

Shelly Beach

Mombasa Beaches

South

Waa

Tiwi Beach

Tiwi Beach Bungalows
Twiga Lodge

Tiwi

Golden Beach Hotel
Diani Reef Hotel
South Beach Lodge
Leopard Beach Hotel

Ukunda

Diani Beach

Trade Winds Hotel
Dan's Trench
Diani Sea Lodge

Two Fishes Hotel
Jadini Beach Hotel
Hotel Africana

Nomad Beach Hotel
Four & Twenty
Robinson Baobab Hotel

Mwabungu

Gazi

Msambweni

O Scale 10 km

known and popular *Dan's Trench* which shares the same access road as the *Trade Winds Hotel*. You won't see any signs for Dan's on the beach road so look out for the Trade Winds Hotel. Walk down the access road for the hotel for about 100 metres and you'll see a blue and white sign with 'Dan's' written on it. You're there.

It's basically a campsite (Sh 15 per person) and a collection of rustic, two-storey, concrete *bandas* with palm-thatch roofs (Sh 50 per bed) with simple cooking facilities. People are very friendly and it's a mellow place to stay but it can get a little crowded when long-haul overland trucks turn up as they do from time to time. You can hire bicycles (Sh 20 per hour or Sh 80 per day), tents (Sh 20 per day) and catamarans (Sh 100 per hour). Bring your own food.

The next cheapest places are the *Four 'n Twenty Beach Cottages*, right at the end of the road past Robinson's. They offer small, self-contained cottages but they're hardly 'cheap'. Get a group of three to five people together and share one.

Places to Stay - top end The other hotels along this beach cost Sh 800 to Sh 1000 a single and Sh 1200 to Sh 2550 a double with full board, except at the *Nomad* beach *bandas* which cost Sh 550 a single and Sh 880 a double for bed and breakfast. All the beach resort complexes offer much the same amenities which include spacious rooms usually facing the sea (some of them with air-conditioning), restaurants, bars, swimming pools, water-sports facilities, video and sometimes a disco. They only differ in their architectural styles and the quality of food and services which they offer.

The hotels are: *Leisure Lodge Hotel, Diani Reef Hotel, Africana Sea Lodge, Leopard Beach Hotel, Golden Beach Hotel* (all five-star hotels), *Jadini Beach Hotel, Robinson Baobab Hotel, Diani Sea Lodge, Trade Winds Hotel* and the *Two Fishes Hotel* (all four-star hotels). The hotels with discos include the Leisure Lodge and the Diani Beach Hotel.

Places to Eat There are also a number of independent restaurants along this beach (usually pretty expensive since they appeal to those staying at the resort hotels). They include *Ali Barbours* which specialises in sea food and is open in the evenings only. *Nomad's Restaurant* is also popular for Sunday all-you-can-eat curries for Sh 80. Get there about noon or just before.

If you are prepared to eat at the Trade Winds Hotel then you *may* be able to use the facilities there (swimming pool, etc) without having to pay a fee but don't count on it. Depending on how many people are staying at the hotel, you may be charged to use their facilities, but it seems they've clamped down on this now and won't allow you in unless it's to buy a drink or a meal. Money is money after all and, if you are spending it, no-one is going to make you unwelcome.

Getting There Going to Diani beach it's much more convenient to take the KRS bus from the Likoni ferry rather than a *matatu*. The bus serves all the beach resort hotels along Diani. It goes north first and then doubles back and goes to the south end of the beach – just tell the driver where you want to go and he'll make sure you get off at the right stop. The buses go every 40 minutes throughout the day – the first from Likoni at 5 and from Diani at 6 am. The last bus from Diani to Likoni is at 7.20 pm. If you take a *matatu* from Likoni you'll be dropped at the village of Ukunda and will have to take the bus from there to any of the beach hotels (Sh 2). Don't walk from Ukunda to the beach hotels. The chances are you will be mugged.

THE NORTH COAST

The north coast, like the south coast, is

well developed, with much of the ocean frontage taken up with hotel-resort complexes.

Kanamai

The beach near the Kanamai Youth Hostel is a seaweed disaster. It's completely choked with the stuff and the sea is extremely shallow between the beach and the reef – you can hardly swim, even if you could move for the seaweed. It's also hard to get to by public transport so it's definitely not recommended unless you have your own transport.

Places to Stay There are very few cheap places to stay along the north coast. The *Kanamai Youth Hostel* costs Sh 20 per bed in the dormitory, Sh 60 or Sh 120 a double (depending on what you take) for a self-contained chalet with a bedroom, shower, living room, kitchen and verandah. Cooking gas is provided if you want to put your own food together but otherwise you can buy meals at the canteen for Sh 25 (breakfast) and Sh 40 (lunch or dinner).

Getting There To get there you first take a *matatu* (Sh 5) to Majengo on the Mombasa-Kilifi road from where the buses leave for Malindi and Lamu outside the New People's Hotel in Mombasa. Get off when you see a yellow sign saying 'Camping Kanamai'. Go down the dirt track by this sign for about 300 metres and then turn left at the fork. Continue for about three km and you'll find it on the left hand side. It's a long, hot walk and lifts are few and far between. I wouldn't even attempt to come here if I had to walk with a backpack.

Along the Coast to Takaungu

Right up at the top end of this long line of beaches close to Kilifi is the village of Takaungu. It's supposedly the oldest slave port on the Kenyan coast – Zanzibar is the oldest. It's worth a visit if you have the time. The local people are very superstitious and no-one goes down to the beach at night except the fishermen. If you can speak Swahili you'll hear many weird stories going around which date back to the slaving days. It's an interesting place right off the beaten track where you won't meet any other travellers.

Places to Stay – bottom end Rooms can be rented in private houses in Takaungu for around Sh 25 per night. Ask around in the tea shops.

Places to Stay – top end The beach resort complexes along the north coast fall into the same price categories as those on the south coast. They include the *Nyali Beach Hotel, Mombasa Beach Hotel, Plaza Hotel, Serena Beach Hotel, Reef Hotel* (all five-star hotels), *Severin Sea Lodge, Bahari Beach Hotel, Silver Beach Hotel, Whitesands Hotel* (all four-star hotels), *Whispering Palms, Bamburi Beach Hotel, Dolphin Beach Hotel, Neptune Beach Hotel, Kenya Beach Hotel, Hotel Malaika, Ocean View Hotel* and *Sun 'n' Sand Beach Hotel* (all three-star hotels).

The Rift Valley

The towns and lakes of the Rift Valley stretch north-south, slightly to the west of Nairobi. The vast Lake Turkana, far to the north, is also a Rift Valley lake and is covered in the Northern Kenya section.

All the Rift Valley lakes with the exception of Naivasha and Baringo are highly saline soda lakes and most are very shallow. Their alkaline waters support high concentrations of microscopic blue-green algae and diatoms which provide an ideal environment for tiny crustaceans and insect larvae. They in turn are eaten by certain species of soda-resistant fish.

The water of these lakes might feel strange to the touch (it's soapy) and it often doesn't smell too pleasant (though this is mostly due to bird droppings) but it's simply heaven to many species of water bird which flock to them in their millions. Foremost among them are the deep-pink Lesser Flamingo (Phoenicopterus minor), which feed on the blue-green algae, and the pale-pink Greater Flamingo (Phoenicopterus ruber), which feed on the tiny crustaceans and insect larvae. Also numerous are various species of duck, pelican and stork. The highest concentrations of these birds are found where food is most abundant and this can vary from lake to lake.

No one really knows why Naivasha and Baringo should be freshwater lakes when all the others are highly saline and none of them have any outlets. The theory is that they somehow avoid accumulating soda because of massive underground seepage which has the same effect as a river flowing out of the lake. The ecology of these two freshwater lakes is very different from the soda lakes.

Getting There & Around

Lakes Naivasha, Nakuru, Elmenteita and, to a lesser extent, Baringo are readily accessible to independent travellers without their own vehicle. There are plenty of buses and matatus and a rail link between Nairobi, Naivasha and Nakuru and less frequent buses and matatus between Nakuru and Marigat (for Lake Baringo). The other lakes, however, are more remote and there's no public transport. Hitching is very difficult and can be impossible. There's also the problem that both Lakes Nakuru and Bogoria are in national parks, which you are not allowed to walk in. You must tour them in a vehicle.

Renting a vehicle may be expensive for budget travellers but it would certainly work out cheaper for four people to hire a vehicle to visit Naivasha, Nakuru, Bogoria and Baringo than for them all to pay individually for safari company tours. A one-day tour of Lake Nakuru

starting from Nairobi goes for around US$40. A two-day tour of Lakes Nakuru, Bogoria and Baringo will cost about US$150 per person. A car hired for several days and shared between four people would probably cost considerably less than the total cost of two-day tours for four people.

NAIVASHA

The town of Naivasha is of little interest in itself. Most travellers simply use it as a base or pass through it on the way to Lake Naivasha, Longonot Volcano and Hell's Gate National Park.

Places to Stay

The friendly Lake View Hotel costs Sh 35 a single or Sh 60 a double. The very clean Naivasha Super Lodge is Sh 25 a single and Sh 45 a double. Other reasonable budget hotels include the New Dryland Hotel and Silent Lodging.

Somewhat more expensive are the Kilimanjaro Hotel and the Equator Inn. Top of the range is the Bell Inn.

Places to Eat

Most of the cheapies have their own restaurants where you can get a good, simple meal. You can't beat the breakfasts at the Bell Inn. Sit out on the verandah and enjoy a substantial Sh 35 breakfast of juice, croissants, eggs, bacon, sausage, toast and marmalade and tea or coffee. They also serve excellent lunches and dinners.

Getting Around

The usual access to Lake Naivasha is along South Lake Rd. This also goes past the entrance to Hells' Gate National Park. There are fairly frequent matatus between Naivasha town and Kongoni for a few shillings. This road has to be one of the worst in Kenya! It's also extremely dusty in the dry season. It seems, however, that something is finally going to be done to improve it. Not before time!

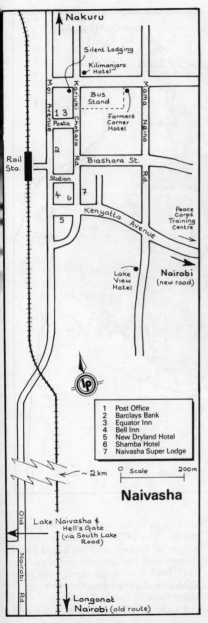

LAKE NAIVASHA

The best overall views of Lake Naivasha are from the top of the escarpment which you crest about half way between Nairobi and Naivasha town. There are also excellent views of Longonot Volcano.

Naivasha is one of the Rift Valley's freshwater lakes and its ecology is quite different from that of the soda lakes. It's home to an incredible variety of bird species and one of the main focii of conservation efforts in Kenya. Not everyone supports these efforts, however, and the ecology of the lake has been interfered with on a number of occasions, the most notable introductions being sport fish, commercial fish, the North American red swamp crayfish, the South American coypu or nutria (an escapee from a fur farm) and various aquatic plants including *Salvinia* which is a menace on Lake Kariba in southern Africa.

The lake has ebbed and flowed over the years as half-submerged fencing posts indicate. Early in the 1890s it dried up almost completely but then it rose a phenomenal 15 metres and inundated a far larger area than it presently occupies. It has receded since then and currently covers about 170 square km.

Since it's a freshwater lake which can be used for irrigation purposes, the surrounding countryside is a major producer of fresh fruit and vegetables as well as beef cattle both for domestic consumption and export.

On the west side of Naivasha Lake, past the village of Kongoni, there is a crater lake with lush vegetation at the bottom of a beautiful but small volcanic crater. If you have transport, it's worth visiting. You have to cross private land for about a half km in order to get there, so close all gates behind you or ask permission if necessary.

Places to Stay – bottom end

There are several budget accommodation possibilities on the lake shore. For those

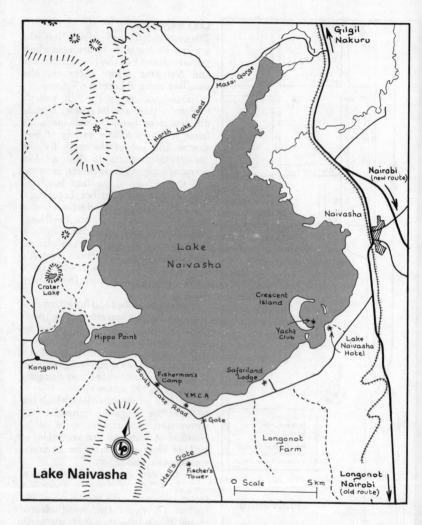

Lake Naivasha

without camping equipment, the *YMCA* is probably the best choice. You can rent a bed in a *banda* here for Sh 35 per night plus Sh 5 for temporary membership of the YMCA. Camping is also possible for Sh 15 but it's not the best site. The *bandas* have kitchens but no firewood or charcoal although you can buy this for Sh 5. Cooking utensils are provided free of charge. The office here has a limited supply of canned and packaged foods (corned beef, biscuits, soft drinks and the like). Look out for the sign on the right hand side after you pass the entrance for Hells' Gate.

It's also possible to camp or rent an old

boat anchored close to the shore for Sh 50 per boat per night (the boats sleep two people) at *Burch's Farm*. The Burches are very friendly and hospitable people. Hot showers are available and you can buy vegetables from their garden. The farm is about four km down South Lake Rd from the old Nairobi road turn-off. It's signposted on the right hand side.

The most popular place to stay, however, is *Fisherman's Camp*, some distance past the YMCA. You can camp here for Sh 20 with your own tent or rent a tent for Sh 30 per person. Rowing boats are available free to campers.

Near Fisherman's Camp is *Top Camp* where you can rent a *banda* for Sh 60 per person including cooking facilities. It's a very pleasant site and there's a tiny wooden shack nearby called the *Kanjiraini Hotel* which offers simple cooked meals and tea. If you are buying in your own supplies, there's a small village about 1½ km away where you can buy basic supplies and fresh meat.

Another place worth considering if you have your own camping equipment (no tents for hire) is the *Safariland Lodge* (tel 0311 20241). Camping here costs Sh 42 per person per night (children half price).

Places to Stay - top end

The *Safariland Lodge* (tel 0311 20241) is a top range hotel with all the facilities you might expect. A room here costs Sh 1093 a single and Sh 1329 a double with full board. Bookings can be made through UTC Safari Trail (tel Nairobi 27930), PO Box 41178, Nairobi. Facilities are free to residents but campers and non-residents must pay a daily fee of Sh 21 to use the horse riding, tennis, archery and indoor sports facilities.

The *Lake Naivasha Hotel* is very similar and can be booked through New Stanley House Arcade (tel Nairobi 335807), Standard St, PO Box 47557, Nairobi. Rooms cost Sh 1030 a single and Sh 1455 a double with full board except

between 1 April and 30 June when it's Sh 530 per person for full board.

Getting Around

Boat Trips Boats for game viewing can be hired from the Safariland Lodge for Sh 180 (four people), Sh 250 (seven people) and Sh 545 (12 people) per hour. The Lake Naivasha Hotel offers trips to Crescent Island (a game sanctuary) for Sh 80 per person, plus a charge of Sh 50 per person if you wish to get off there for a while, and other boat trips at Sh 350 per hour shared by up to eight people.

HELL'S GATE NATIONAL PARK

This park is a very recent creation and it may still be possible to walk through it although this will undoubtedly change before very long. Close to the entrance to Hell's Gate itself, which is some considerable distance from the entrance gate on South Lake Rd, is Fischer's Tower, a lone 25-metre high outcrop of rock. Further on, there is a geothermal power project in operation. The park has zebra, Thomson's gazelle, antelope, leopard, cheetah, baboon, Lammegayer eagle and ostrich among other species. It's of principal interest for the topography of the area. Entry costs Sh 30 per person plus Sh 10 for a vehicle.

LONGONOT VOLCANO

Hill climbers and view seekers shouldn't miss the opportunity of climbing to the rim of dormant Longonot (2777 metres), a fairly young volcano which still retains the uneroded, typical shape of these mountains.

To get to the start of the climb go first to the village of Longonot on the Nairobi-Nakuru railway line or the old road between Nakuru and Nairobi. If coming from Nakuru, walk or drive to the point where the railway crosses the road and then take the road off to the right. Follow this for about 6½ km to the base of the mountain. You may at times be able to drive about 1½ km further than this

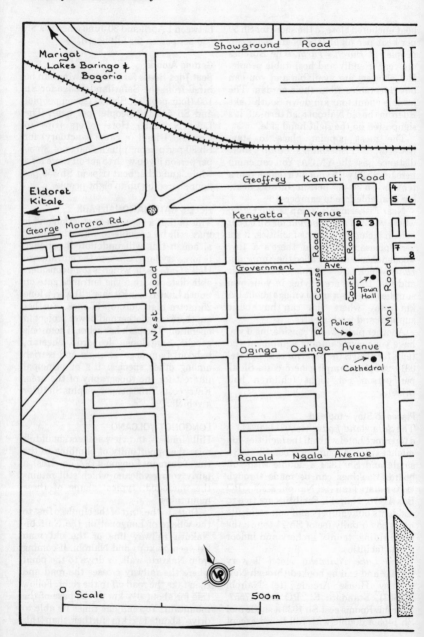

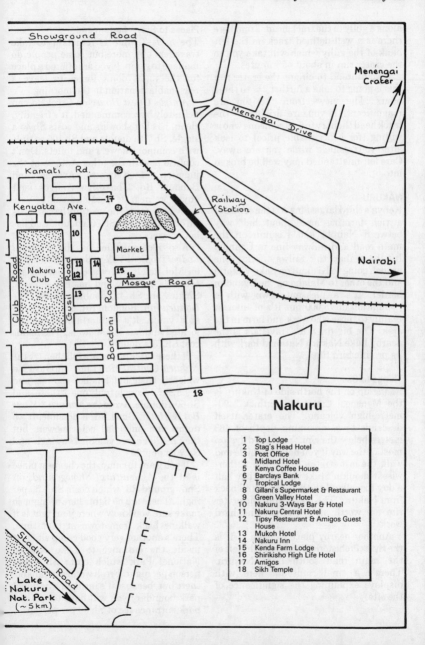

Nakuru

1   Top Lodge
2   Stag's Head Hotel
3   Post Office
4   Midland Hotel
5   Kenya Coffee House
6   Barclays Bank
7   Tropical Lodge
8   Gillani's Supermarket & Restaurant
9   Green Valley Hotel
10 Nakuru 3-Ways Bar & Hotel
11 Nakuru Central Hotel
12 Tipsy Restaurant & Amigos Guest
    House
13 Mukoh Hotel
14 Nakuru Inn
15 Kenda Farm Lodge
16 Shirikisho High Life Hotel
17 Amigos
18 Sikh Temple

along a gully to the track head. From here there is a well-defined track on the left bank of the gully which will take you to the crater rim in about 45 minutes.

If you intend to circuit the crater rim this is going to take a further 2½ to three hours. The views from the top are magnificent. If you are driving to the track head then try to find someone who is willing (for a negotiable price) to look after your vehicle while you are away. Cars left unattended may well be broken into.

NAKURU

Kenya's third largest town is the centre of a rich farming area about half way between Nairobi and Kisumu on the main road and railway line to Uganda. It's here that the railway forks, one branch going to Kisumu on Lake Victoria and the other to Malaba on the Ugandan border. It's a pleasant town with a population of 75,000 but it's of interest mainly to those who work and farm in the area. The big draw for travellers is the nearby Lake Nakuru National Park with its prolific bird life.

Things to See

Rising up on the north side of Nakuru is the **Menengai Crater**, an extinct 2490-metre-high volcano. The crater itself descends to a maximum depth of 483 metres below the rim. You can drive up most of the way if you have a vehicle and walk the last stretch to the rim. Otherwise it shouldn't take you more than half a day to walk all the way there and back from Nakuru. The views from the crater rim are worth all the sweat and hard work!

Another nearby place worth a visit is the **Hyrax Prehistoric Site**, just to the left of the main road south from Nakuru. There's a small museum here with displays explaining the significance of the site.

Places to Stay - bottom end

The *Sikh Temple* is reluctant to take travellers any more but some people do manage to get in. If you are offered a place for the night don't forget to leave a reasonable donation in the morning.

Amigos Guest House on Gusil Rd can definitely be recommended. It's friendly, clean, has hot showers and costs Sh 45 a single, Sh 70 a double and Sh 105 a triple with common showers and toilets. Don't confuse it with the other Amigos at the junction of Kenyatta Avenue and Bondoni Rd. The other *Amigos* isn't anywhere near as good and can be very noisy because of the upstairs bar. It costs Sh 50 a single and Sh 60 a double and has hot showers.

Also recommended is the *Tropical Lodge/Tropical Valley Board & Lodging* on Moi Rd. It's very good value, clean, spacious, friendly and has hot showers. Singles are Sh 42, doubles Sh 68. The *Nakuru Inn*, Bondoni Rd, is also reasonable value. It's comfortable, centrally located and has hot showers. The rooms cost Sh 60 a double.

If these three places are full then try the *Nakuru Central Hotel* just off Gusil Rd which is basic but has hot showers and costs Sh 50 a single (only one of these) and Sh 60 a double. Avoid the *Nakuru 3-Ways Bar & Hotel*, Gusil Rd, if possible. It's a dump and only has cold showers but they'll still charge you Sh 47 a single and Sh 70 a double.

If you want to camp, the cheapest place is at the *Agricultural Showground*, off Showground Rd, which costs Sh 7.50 per night. There are no lights here at night so make sure you know where your tent is if walking back from town at that time. There's another very good camp site just inside the entrance to Lake Nakuru National Park which costs Sh 5 per person per night. Fresh water is available there but, because it's inside the national park boundary you will have to pay the park entrance fee of Sh 30 per person.

Places to Stay - middle

Going up in price, the *Mukoh Hotel*, Gusil Rd, is very clean, quiet and comfortable. It costs Sh 60 a single and Sh 120 a double without own bathroom and Sh 85 a single and Sh 170 a double with own bathroom. There are hot showers.

Some 15 km south-east of Nakuru at Lanet there's another mid-range hotel, *The Stern Hotel* which has chalet-style rooms with own bathroom and hot water. It costs Sh 155 a double (though they'll initially ask for Sh 200) for bed and breakfast. The breakfast is substantial and, if you have a car, it gets washed, too! Excellent lunches and dinners are available at Sh 10 for soups and desserts and Sh 40-60 for a main course.

Places to Stay - top end

The *Stag's Head Hotel* on Kenyatta Avenue at Court Rd is a huge, old, colonial-style hotel with large, spacious, very clean rooms and pleasant furnishings and decor. It costs Sh 260 a single and Sh 320 a double (with a double bed) or Sh 400 a double (with two beds). All the rooms have their own bathroom and hot water. Prices include a substantial English-style cooked breakfast. The *Midland Hotel*, Moi Rd, is similar in price but a more modern building.

Places to Eat

For the price and quality of food, the best place to eat here is the *Tipsy Restaurant*, Gusil Rd. It's very popular with local people especially at lunch times. They offer Indian curries, western food and lake fish. A curry with salad and rice will cost Sh 25 and up depending on what you have. It's very tasty food. The restaurant in *Gillani's Supermarket*, corner Club Rd and Government Avenue, is also very good though more expensive than the Tipsy.

Other restaurants which can be recommended are the *Kabeer Restaurant*, behind the Post Office (excellent curries), and the *Skyways Restaurant*, Kenyatta Avenue close to the junction with Bondoni Rd, though it's a little pricey these days.

LAKE NAKURU NATIONAL PARK

Created in 1961 the park has since been considerably increased in size and now covers an area of some 200 square km. Like most of the other Rift Valley lakes, it is a shallow soda lake. A few years ago, the level of the lake rose and this resulted in a mass migration of the flamingoes to other Rift Valley lakes, principally Bogoria, Magadi and Natron. What had been dubbed 'the world's greatest ornithological spectacle' suddenly wasn't anywhere near as spectacular. Since then the lake has receded and the flamingoes have returned. Once again you have the opportunity of seeing up to two million flamingoes along with tens of thousands of other birds.

It's an ornithologists' paradise and one of the world's most magnificent sights. Those of you who have seen the film, *Out of Africa*, and remember the footage of the flight over the vast flocks of flamingoes are in for a very similar treat. Simply go up to the lookout on the top of Baboon Rocks on the west side of the lake and feast your eyes on the endless pink masses which fringe the lake.

Don't blame us, though, if the birds are not there in such profusion or even if the lake dries up! The flamingoes migrate from time to time if food gets scarce and there's a better supply elsewhere – usually to Lake Bogoria further north or to Lakes Magadi and Natron further south.

The lake is very shallow and fluctuates by up to four metres annually. When the water is low, the soda crystallises out along the shoreline as a blinding white band of powder which is going to severely test your skills as a photographer. Lake Nakuru last dried up in the late 1950s and, at that time, soda dust storms whipped up by high winds and dust devils made life unbearable for people in the

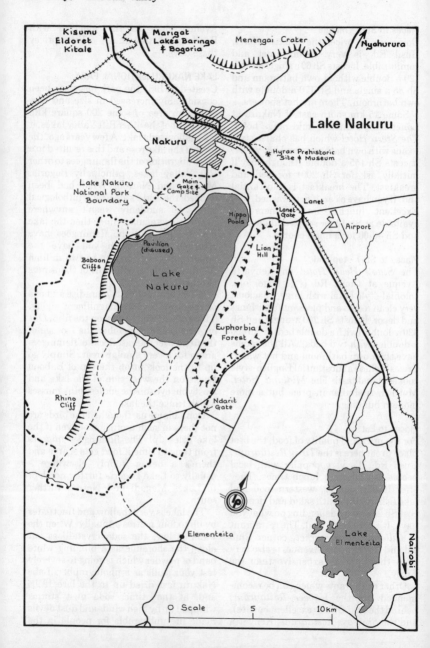

town and surrounding area. In the dry season you'll see these dust devils (like tiny tornadoes) whipping up soda into the air as they course along the shore line.

Since the park also has areas of grassland, bush, forest and rocky cliffs, there are many other animals to be seen apart from birds. One species you'll see plenty of are warthogs with their amusing way of running with their tails erect. Further into the bush are Thomson's gazelle, waterbuck, reedbuck and buffalo. Around the cliffs you may catch sight of hyrax and birds of prey and, if you're very lucky, you may come across an occasional rhino. There's even a small herd of hippos which generally lives along the north shore of the lake.

The national park entrance is about six km from the centre of Nakuru. Entry costs Sh 30 per person plus Sh 10 per vehicle. As in all game parks, you must be in a vehicle. You are not allowed to walk so you will either have to hitch a ride with other tourists, rent your own vehicle or go on a tour. It's possible to hire a taxi in Nakuru to take you round the park for around three hours for about Sh 250 though the starting price may well be Sh 400-500.

You can get out of your vehicle on the lake shore and at certain view points – but only there. It's a memorable experience being in the proximity of several hundred thousand flamingoes feeding, preening, grunting and honking and even more memorable when several thousand of them decide that you're a little too close for comfort and they take off to find a more congenial spot. Don't drive too close to the water's edge, the mud is very soft!

Places to Stay

There is a good camp site just inside the park gate which costs Sh 5 per person per night. Fresh water is available but you need to bring all your own food. Make sure tents are securely zipped up when you're away from them otherwise the

baboons will steal everything inside them.

If you have no camping equipment there's the very basic *Florida Day & Night Bar & Boarding* just before the entrance gate.

LAKE ELMENTEITA

Like Lake Nakuru, Elmenteita is a shallow, soda lake with a similar ecology. Flamingoes live here too, but in nowhere near the same numbers as Nakuru. It does have the advantage, though, that it's not a national park so you can walk around it and you don't have to pay to get in. The easiest way to get there is to take a *matatu* along the Naivasha-Nakuru road and get off at one of the viewpoints (signposted) on the escarpment above the lake. Walk down from there or hitch a ride if there's anything going.

NYAHURURU (Thomson's Falls)

These falls, about 70 km from Nakuru, are named after Joseph Thomson who was the first European to walk from Mombasa to Lake Victoria in the early 1880s. They're about 30 minutes' walk from the town and entry costs Sh 4 but most of the time there's no-one there to collect the entry fee. The best time to see them is in the wet season in the early morning.

Places to Stay – bottom end

There's a very pleasant camp site at the falls themselves for Sh 20 per person if you have your own equipment. Bring food and drink with you. There's also a camp site at the *Thomson's Falls Lodge* (tel 22006) which costs Sh 20 and is very clean.

For those without camping equipment there are several budget hotels available. The *Muthengera Farmers' Lodge* is very popular and costs just Sh 50 a single with own bathroom. Good food at reasonable prices is available here. Also highly recommended is the *Good Shepherd's Lodge* which at Sh 45 per room (one or two people) with own shower and toilet, towels and soap is a bargain. It's on the left hand side of the road on the way to the falls.

Others which have been recommended include the *Nyahururu Hotel Boarding & Lodging* at the north end of town which has clean, comfortable rooms and hot showers and the *Nyandarwa County Council Hostel* next to the post office. Both have their own restaurants and prices are reasonable.

Places to Stay – top end
The *Thomson's Falls Lodge* (tel 22006) offers bed and breakfast for Sh 265 a double with own shower and toilet. There's a log fire in your room which is lit about 6 pm. Meals here are excellent and the restaurant is open to non-residents. An English-style breakfast costs Sh 35 and lunch/dinner Sh 60 (four courses). They have a very rustic dining room.

Getting Around
There is a daily bus to Maralal between 11 am and 12 noon which costs Sh 50.

LAKE BOGORIA
The two completely dissimilar lakes Bogoria and Baringo are north of Nakuru off the B4 highway to Marigat and Lodwar. Lake Bogoria is a shallow soda lake, Lake Baringo is a deeper freshwater lake. The B4 is a superb, sealed highway all the way. Bogoria is now a National Park so there's an entry fee of Sh 30 per person plus Sh 10 per vehicle.

Most of the bird life on Bogoria has migrated to the (presently) richer pastures of Lake Nakuru but the stalwarts (of all species) remain. It's a very peaceful area but it doesn't currently compare with the ornithological spectacle of Nakuru. There are, however, the Hot Springs and geysers about ¾ of the way down the lake going south. They don't compare with Rotorua in New Zealand but if you've never seen geysers before then this is the place. The springs are boiling hot so don't

put your bare foot or hand into them unless you want to nurse scalds for the next week.

Places to Stay
There are two camp sites at the southern end of the lake – *Acacia* and *Riverside* – but there are no facilities whatsoever and the lake water is totally unpalatable. Bring all water and food with you if you are intending to stay at either site. Otherwise, the camp sites are very pleasant.

There's another camp site just outside the northern entrance gate which costs Sh 5 per person per night. Drinking water is available here and there's a small shop nearby which sells basic supplies (canned food, jam, biscuits, washing powder, soft drinks, etc). A top-range lodge is being built near the entrance but will not be completed for a while.

LAKE BARINGO
Some 15 km north of the town of Marigat you come to the village of Kampi-ya-Samaki which is the centre for exploring Lake Baringo. This lake, like Naivasha, is a freshwater lake with a very different ecology from Lake Bogoria. It supports many different species of aquatic and bird life as well as herds of hippos which invade the grassy shore every evening to browse. You'll hear their characteristic grunt as you walk back to your tent or *banda* after dark or settle down for the night. They might even decide to crop the grass right next to your tent. If they do, stay where you are. They're not aggressive animals – they don't need to be with a bulk and jaws like that! – but if you frighten them or annoy them they might go for you. And, despite all appearances, they can *move*!

Places to Stay – bottom end
There's a superb place to stay here just before the village called *Robert's Camp* where you can camp for Sh 30 per person per night or rent a *banda* for Sh 60 per

person. I'd strongly recommend the *bandas* if there is one available – there are only a few and demand is heavy. They are beautiful, circular, grass-thatched traditionally-styled houses which are clean as a new pin and furnished with comfortable beds, table and chairs and mosquito netting at the windows. Showers and toilets are separate and cooking facilities are available for a small extra charge. They are superb value. If you can, book in advance through David Roberts Wildlife, PO Box 1051, Nakuru. The people here are very friendly and there's a huge land tortoise which ambles around the grounds and appears to be used to the attention it receives.

If this place is full and you have no camping equipment then try the *Bahari Lodge* in Kampi-ya-Samaki which costs Sh 30 a single and Sh 50 a double. It's basic. This village is also the only place you will find beer apart from the lodge next door to the Roberts'. There's a lively bar at the end of the road facing you as you enter the village. The beer is cheap but lukewarm and the clientele isn't used to seeing *mazungu* but it's a good crowd. It's also one of the few places with electric lights.

There are also places to stay in Marigat if you prefer. At the crossroads of the B4 and the village is the *Wananchi Lodge* which costs Sh 50 a double and is basic but provides towels, soap and mosquito nets. More expensive is the *Marigat Inn* about 1½ km from the main road turn-off (no signs so you must ask). It costs Sh 70 a double and is very pleasant with its own bar and restaurant.

Places to Stay – top end

Right next door to the Roberts' the *Lake Baringo Club* costs Sh 860 a single and Sh 1315 a double for full board except between 1 April and 30 June when it costs Sh 530 per person per night for full board. The Club offers a swimming pool, darts, table tennis, badminton, a library and a whole range of local excursions such as

boat trips (Sh 100-350 per hour for up to eight people), bird-watching trips accompanied by an expert for Sh 50 per person or Sh 75 per person with transport and camel rides at Sh 30 per half hour. If you want to use the facilities as a non-resident it will cost you Sh 20 per day on weekdays and Sh 50 at weekends except for the swimming pool which is a standard Sh 50 per day. It's the only place on the mainland at Lake Baringo you will find ice-cold beers. It's also the only place you will be able to buy petrol since there is no petrol pump in Marigat. Prices are normal and the pumps are open to the public.

The alternative to the Lake Baringo Club is the *Island Camp*, PO Box 1141, Nakuru, which, as its name suggests, is located on an island in Lake Baringo. This is a luxury tented lodge which is rated highly by those who have stayed there. There are 25 double tents each with their own shower and toilet, two bars, a swimming pool and water sports facilities. It costs Sh 600 a single and Sh 800 a double for Kenyan residents and Sh 800 a single and Sh 1050 a double for foreigners with full board. Vehicles have to be left on the lake side and the boat transfer fare is Sh 50 return. To get to the boat jetty, drive into Kampi-ya-Samaki and turn left at the junction. Continue down the only feasible track (very rough) and you'll get there.

Getting There

Visiting Lake Bogoria *don't* take the first signposted road to the right about 38 km past Nakuru heading north. You will regret it – most of this road is good smooth dust/gravel but there is about five km of it which leads down to the southern park entrance which will certainly rip apart any tyres and destroy any vehicle driven at more than a few kilometres per hour. Without four-wheel-drive you'd be wasting your time. These razor-sharp lava beds don't end once you reach the park gate but continue for at least as far on the other side. In addition, signposting along the route from the turn-off is almost non-existent.

Give yourself a break! Continue along the B4 until you are close to Marigat and look for the 'Loboi Gate' turn-off. The gravel road from here to the northern park entrance is excellent all the way and continues like this until just after the main part of the lake and the hot springs.

LAKE MAGADI

Lake Magadi is the most southerly of the Rift Valley lakes in Kenya and is very rarely visited by tourists to Kenya because of its remoteness. Like most of the Rift Valley lakes, it is a soda lake and supports many flamingoes and other water birds. It also has a soda extraction factory, hence the railway line here. A few years ago it was the site of a major rescue operation of young flamingoes when drought threatened hundreds of thousands of them because of soda encrustation on their feathers – this doesn't affect the adults.

Magadi is quite different from the lakes to the north as it lies in semi-desert. Temperatures hover around the 38°C mark during the day and much of the lake is a semi-solid sludge of water and soda salts. There is a series of hot springs around the periphery of the lake.

Getting There

There is a rail link to the lake shore which branches off from the main Nairobi-Mombasa line but there are no passenger services along it. There's also a minor road from Nairobi (the C58) but there's no public transport along it so you will either have to hitch or have your own vehicle.

KISUMU

Kisumu is Kenya's main port on Lake Victoria and a rail head which is connected to the rest of the Kenyan system via Nakuru. It's a hot, steamy town but pleasant all the same. It's strongly Asian-influenced especially by those Muslims who are followers of the Aga Khan – there are schools, a hospital, a community centre and a mosque all bearing his name.

Information

Bank Barclays Bank is open Monday to Friday from 8.30 am to 1 pm and Saturday from 8.30 to 11 am; Standard Chartered Bank is open Monday to Friday from 8.30 to 2 pm and Saturday from 8.30 to 11 am.

Immigration Immigration is in Alpha House, Oginga Odinga Rd. It may be necessary to visit this office if you are taking the Lake Victoria ferry to Tanzania.

Library The British Council, Oginga Odinga Rd close to the junction with Jomo Kenyatta Highway, has a good library with current magazines and periodicals.

Kisumu Museum

About 15 minutes' walk up Jomo Kenyatta Highway on the way to Eldoret, the Kisumu Museum is one of the best in Kenya and is well worth a visit. It has the usual natural history displays plus a life-size recreation of a tribal homestead with six mud and grass huts, an aquarium, a snake pit and a compound of amorous tortoises.

Places to Stay – bottom end

There's a very good choice of pleasant budget hotels in Kisumu. One of the cheapest is the *YWCA*, on the corner of Omolo Agar Rd and Nairobi Rd. It takes both men and women and costs Sh 35 per person, plus Sh 20 per day temporary membership, in triple-bedded rooms. Breakfast is available.

If you want your own room then the *New Rozy Lodge*, Ogada St, is excellent value at Sh 55 a single and Sh 75 a double.

It's small, very pleasant, clean, the staff are friendly and it has hot water. If it's full, try the *Kisumu Lodge* next door. Another which is worth checking out in this price range is the *Mirukas Lodge*, Apindi St, which costs Sh 52 a single, Sh 65 a double and Sh 98 a triple, but it's not as good as the two previous places.

At the very bottom end of the market, mostly along Accra St, are the usual collection of brothels and noisy bars where you can find a room for less (although not always) but the facilities are very primitive and no-one is in a hurry to clean them. They include the rough *Sam's Hotel* at Sh 50 a single, Sh 60 a double. Others are the amusingly named *New Clean PVU Hotel* (!), the *Farid Hotel*, the *Mazamil Lodge* and the *Tivoli Boarding & Lodging*. You'd have to be desperate or of a particular proclivity to want to stay in most of them.

Going up slightly in price the *Razbi Guest House*, on the corner of Kendu Lane and Oginga Odinga Rd, is popular with Peace Corps volunteers and costs Sh 60 a single, Sh 100 a double and Sh 200 for a room with four beds. It's very clean, secure, friendly and there's hot water. A towel and soap are provided in each room and breakfast is available if you want it. The very similar *Mona Lisa Boarding & Lodging*, Oginga Odinga Rd is also very clean, pleasant and friendly and has hot water. Singles are Sh 75, doubles Sh 105.

Places to Stay – middle
The *Lake View Hotel*, Kendu Lane, is very pleasant and if you get a room in the front wing you'll have views over Lake Victoria. It costs Sh 100 a single and Sh 187 a double including breakfast. There is a bar and restaurant on the ground floor. The *New Victoria Hotel* costs the same for bed and breakfast plus they have triple rooms for Sh 281. All the rooms have their own bathroom and most of them have a balcony. The hotel has its own restaurant but no bar since it's Muslim-owned.

The *Black & Black Boarding & Lodging*, Accra Rd, is slightly cheaper at Sh 92 a single and Sh 138 a double for bed and breakfast and is relatively good value.

Places to Stay – top end
Kisumu's top-range hotel is the *Imperial Hotel*, Jomo Kenyatta Highway.

Places to Eat
There are several restaurants where you can get a good feed at a reasonable price. Some are only open for lunch or dinner, most are open for both. They include the *Mona Lisa Restaurant* and the *New Victoria Hotel* where you can get breakfast for Sh 23 (fruit juice, fruit, two eggs and sausage, toast and butter, tea or coffee) and lunch or dinner for between Sh 18 and Sh 28 per dish. The food is good and tasty though the atmosphere is subdued.

Much livelier is the *Octopus Club*, Ogada St, where you can eat and drink either on the verandah overlooking the street or inside. A good meal will cost you between Sh 22 and Sh 38. Those suffering withdrawal symptoms from fast food, hamburgers and the like should get along to *Wimpy*, on the corner of Jomo Kenyatta Highway and Anaawa Avenue. It's a fairly pleasant place to have a snack or meal and you have the choice of inside or outside tables.

For a splurge, give Kisumu's only Chinese restaurant a go. This is the *Katai Restaurant* next to the *Flamingo Casino & Disco*, Jomo Kenyatta Highway. It's only open in the evenings.

Getting There
Air There are nine flights a week in either direction between Nairobi and Kisumu. All flights between Kisumu and either Mombasa or Malindi go via Nairobi.

Rail The Railway Reservations office is open daily from 8 am to 12 noon and 2 to 4 pm. On the Nairobi-Kisumu line trains

Kisumu

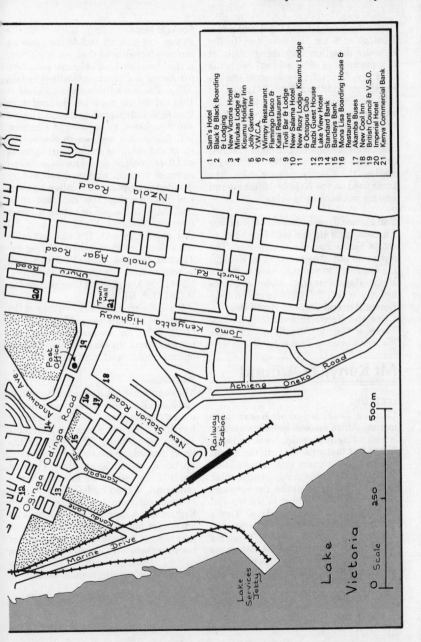

1 Sam's Hotel
2 Black & Black Boarding
  Lodging
3 New Victoria Hotel
4 Minkus Lodge &
  Kisumu Holiday Inn
5 Jolly Garden Inn
6 Y.W.C.A.
7 Wimpy Restaurant
8 Flamingo Disco &
  Katai Restaurant
9 Tivoli Bar & Lodge
10 New Salama Hotel
11 New Rozy Lodge, Kisumu Lodge
   & Octopus Club
12 Razbi Guest House
13 Lake View Hotel
14 Standard Bank
15 Barclays Bank
16 Mona Lisa Boarding House &
   Restaurant
17 Akamba Buses
18 New Cool Inn
19 British Council & V.S.O.
20 Imperial Hotel
21 Kenya Commercial Bank

depart Nairobi daily at 6 pm and arrive Kisumu at 8 am the next day. In the opposite direction they depart daily at 6.30 pm arriving at Nairobi at 7.35 am the next day. Depending on demand there is usually an additional train ('express') at 5.30 pm from Nairobi daily for the 1st week of every month (and sometimes for the second week too) which arrives at Kisumu at 6 am the next day. The fares are: 1st class – Sh 242; 2nd class – Sh 104; 3rd class – Sh 45. As a rule, the carriages used on the Kisumu run are older than those used on the Nairobi-Mombasa run and are not such good value.

Boat Ferries depart Kisumu daily except Thursday at 9 am and take four hours to get to Homa Bay via Kendu Bay. The ferries do not always return to Kisumu the same day so you may have to stay in Homa Bay overnight. Make enquiries before you set off. The fares are Sh 19 to Kendu Bay and Sh 24 to Homa Bay.

See the Kenya introductory Getting There section for details of the Lake Victoria ferries to Tanzania.

Mt Kenya & Around

MT KENYA

Climbing to the top of Mt Kenya (5199 metres), Africa's second highest mountain, is high on many travellers' priority list in Kenya but many people rush the ascent and end up with very little appreciation of what the mountain has to offer other than a thumping headache. I've even met people who have been up to the top and back again in just two days! That's inviting altitude sickness problems.

Since all the land above 3200 metres plus salients down to the Park HQ on the Naro Moru route and down to the entrance gate on the Sirimon route are part of the Mt Kenya National Park, you have to pay an entrance fee of Sh 30 per person plus Sh 5 per person for every night you spend on the mountain.

Books & Maps

Before you rush off and do the same we strongly recommend that you buy a copy of the Mountain Club of Kenya's *Guide to Mt Kenya & Kilimanjaro* edited by Iain Allan. The last edition was published in 1981 but not too much has changed since then especially regarding the main routes which trekkers, as opposed to climbers, will follow. It's well worth the money spent and contains sections on the fauna and flora, geology, access routes, huts and essential medical advice as well as very detailed descriptions of climbs with maps and photographs. You can find it in bookshops in Nairobi or obtain it direct from the Mountain Club of Kenya, PO Box 45741, Nairobi. It's also available from West Col Productions, Goring-on-Thames, Reading, Berks RG8 9AA, UK, as well as from Stanford's Map Centre, 12/14 Long Acre, Covent Garden, London WC2E 9LP, UK.

It's also a good idea to buy a copy of the Survey of Kenya's map, *Mount Kenya* (1:125,000), for an overall view. It's available from the Map Office in Nairobi or from bookshops for Sh 35.

Preparations

The summits of Mt Kenya are covered in glaciers and snow so you are going to need a good sleeping bag, lots of warm clothes including a hat and gloves and preferably waterproof clothing. The need for the latter depends on the time of year you go up, but it can rain at any time. The best times to go, as far as fair weather is concerned, is from mid-January to late-February or from late-August through September. A decent pair of boots is an advantage but not strictly necessary. A pair of joggers is quite adequate most of the time though it's a good idea to have a pair of thongs or canvas tennis shoes available for evening wear if your main shoes get wet.

A tent is a very good idea if you don't want to or can't pay the lodge and hut fees. It's more or less essential if you are

Top: At work, Lamu, Kenya (GC)
Bottom: At leisure, Lamu, Kenya (GC)

Top: Lamu, Kenya (GC)
Bottom: Takwa ruins, Manda Island near Lamu, Kenya (GC)

planning to use the Chogoria route. A stove and a billy are very useful not only for cooking up dried soups but for that hot drink when the night descends. You should also have a water container with a capacity of at least one litre per person and water purifying tablets for the lower levels of the mountain. All this sort of gear can be hired in Nairobi – see under National Parks & Game Reserves for details.

Accommodation on the Mountain

All the huts on the mountain where people stay for the night, except the National Park Rangers Station in Teleki Valley and the Meteorological Station lodge, belong to the Mountain Club of Kenya but some of them are reserved exclusively for use by members. Their agent on the mountain is the *Naro Moru River Lodge* (tel 23), PO Box 18, Naro Moru, which is about two km from the town of Naro Moru on the west side of the main road to Nanyuki. In theory, you are supposed to book and pay for the use of these huts beforehand. This is surely fair since the club has to pay for maintenance and repairs – or, at least, it would be if the overnight fees were reasonable. Many hikers, however, consider the Sh 75 per person per night fee to be a rip-off. Since most of the huts are unlocked and don't have a caretaker, you are presented with a moral choice. A lot of people don't even see it that way and consider the decision to be an entirely practical one. Mackinder's hut, owned exclusively by the Naro Moru River Lodge, costs even more – Sh 160 per night. The alternative is to take your own tent and, on some routes, this is almost essential. Camping fees, where they are charged, are usually only Sh 15.

Getting to the Trail Heads

There are seven different routes to the summit but only the three main routes are covered here – Maro Moru, Sirimon and Chogoria. Details of where to stay in the towns and villages on or just off the main roads circling Mt Kenya are at the end of this section. With your own transport you can get much closer to the trail heads on the Naro Moru and Sirimon tracks than you can using public transport so this gives you a head start.

Naro Moru Route Your starting point here is the town of Naro Moru on the Nairobi-Nanyuki road. There is at least one daily OTC bus per day from Nairobi to Naro Moru which costs Sh 39. The depot in Nairobi is at the junction of Cross Rd and Racecourse Rd.

You can also take a public bus from the country bus station in Nairobi to Nyeri for Sh 30 and a *matatu* from there to Naro Moru for Sh 10 (they often ask for Sh 15-20 because they see a lot of tourists). This two-stage journey is not recommended. The buses are very crowded and you end up hurtling down hills at high speed and crawling up them at a snail's pace.

Sirimon Route Take the same OTC bus as to Naro Moru but continue on to Nanyuki or do the same two-stage journey except that on the final leg you need a *matatu* to Nanyuki (Sh 15). If you want to start out up the mountain the same day as you leave Nairobi, on this route you need to take the earliest possible bus leaving Nairobi otherwise you'll probably have to stay in Nanyuki for the night and leave the following day.

To get from Nanyuki to the start of the Sirimon track take one of the frequent *matatus* going to Timau and tell the driver you want to be dropped off at the start of the track (signposted). If you go over a fairly large river (the Sirimon River) then you've gone too far. It's about 15 km out of Nanyuki and the fare should be Sh 5.

Chogoria Route Take an OTC bus from Nairobi direct to Chogoria village or one first to Embu and then another to Chogoria. The fares for the latter combination are Sh 30 and Sh 20 respectively. You will probably have to spend the night in Chogoria before setting off up the mountain as the first day's hike is a long slog up the forest track with nowhere to stay en route.

The Trails

The normal weather pattern is for clear mornings with the mist closing in between 11 am and 1 pm. The mist sometimes clears again in the early evening for a while. This means that if you want to make the most of the trek you should set off early every morning and for the final assault on Point Lenana (the highest point for walkers) you need to make a 5 am start if you want to see the sunrise from the top.

In describing the routes below it's assumed that you are reliant on public transport.

The Naro Moru Trail This is the most popular route and the quickest. It's also the steepest and the one on which you are most likely to come down with altitude sickness if you rush the hike. It can be done in three or even two days starting from the Meteorological Station but what's the point in climbing up to the top and back down again just so you can say you've done it? If you take four or five days you can adopt a far more leisurely pace and see something en route, too.

Day 1 The first day is spent walking from Naro Moru to the Meteorological Station at 3050 metres, a distance of 26 km. On the way there you will pass the *Youth Hostel* (tel 2471) (about 10 km out of Naro Moru). If you decide to stay there it will cost Sh 35 but you must have a membership card. It's a beautiful old converted farmhouse with kerosene lanterns and log fires. Cooking facilities are provided and, although it's a good idea to bring food along, you can buy things like eggs, milk, carrots, cabbages as well as prepared food nearby. You can also rent essential camping gear here. Tents cost Sh 125 per

day and boots and stoves cost Sh 25 each per day. *Minto's Safaris* also have a rest house nearby where it's possible to find a bed. Half way between the Youth Hostel and the Meteorological Station is the park entrance gate where there is a camp site. It's sometimes possible to get a lift all the way from Naro Moru to the Meteorological Station.

At the Meteorological Station, which is where most people stay, you can camp for Sh 15 per person or rent a bunk in the lodge there for Sh 100 per person.

Day 2 The second day you start out for Teleki Valley (4000 metres) which will take five to six hours. About one hour out of the Meteorological Station you come to the so-called 'vertical bog' which, if you have ever been up the Ruwenzori, is by comparison little more than a gentle slope with occasional wet patches. Once you reach the crest of the ridge overlooking Teleki Valley, the trail veers off to the right above Teleki Hut and down to the valley floor and on to Mackinder's Camp. This camp is just a series of tents set up on platforms and if you haven't got your own equipment it's going to cost you Sh 80 per person for a bunk in one of these. If you have your own tent the fee is Sh 15. The warden here is very friendly and may let you cook on his stove.

Day 3 The third day takes you from Mackinder's Camp to the rocky bluff on which the Austrian Hut sits below Point Lenana. It's a steep four-hour climb. Next to the Austrian Hut is Top Hut but the latter is for the exclusive use of Kenya Mountain Club members. In theory, you're supposed to pay the normal fee for use of the Austrian Hut at the Naro Moru River Lodge but the hut is unattended.

Day 4 On the fourth day you need to get up very early – at the latest by 5 am – in order to make the hour-long trek to Point Lenana (4985 metres) which is the highest you can go without specialist climbing equipment. Most of this walk is on a snow-covered glacier but it's fairly easy going. When you have taken in the sunrise and the views you can either return the same way you came or descend along either the Chogoria or Sirimon trails.

The Sirimon Trail This is the least used of the three trails which we cover.

Day 1 On the first day you walk from the start of the track on the Nanyuki-Timau road to the park entrance gate (about 10 km) and on from there to the camp site (3350 metres) which is a further 11 km. It's a fairly easy stroll and you don't gain much in altitude. If you prefer, you can stay at the park entrance gate and continue on the next day.

Day 2 On the second day you walk from the camp site to Liki North Hut (3993 metres). It's an easy morning's walk. This hut belongs to the Mountain Club but is unattended. If it's still early in the day and you prefer to continue then don't take the trail off to the left at the Liki North stream (which takes you to Liki North Hut) but cross the stream and the ridge beyond and descend into Mackinder Valley. There is a clearly defined track from here which follows the eastern side of the valley, eventually crosses the main Liki stream and leads you to Shipton's Cave – a formation of obvious rock overhangs where you can camp for the night. From the camp site to Shipton's Cave takes about seven hours.

Day 3 On the third day (assuming you start from Liki North Hut) you descend into the main Liki valley and pick up the track mentioned above which takes you past Shipton's Cave and on to Kami Hut. The last part of this walk is heavy going as it's steep but there are cairns to guide you. Kami Hut is another Mountain Club hut but, again, unattended.

Day 4 On the fourth day you go from Kami Hut to the Austrian Hut. There are two possibilities here and unless you have experience of rock climbing it's not recommended that you take the direct route since it involves a fairly precipitous rock scramble. Instead, cut left into the head of the Gorges Valley and then round the east side of Point Lenana to the Austrian Hut along a well-defined track.

Day 5 On the fifth day your options are the same as on the Naro Moru route.

The Chogoria Trail This trail, from the eastern side of the mountain, is perhaps the most beautiful of the access routes to the summit and certainly the easiest as far as gradients go. From Minto Hut there are breathtaking views of the head of the Gorges Valley and the glaciers beyond.

Day 1 On the first day you need to set off from Chogoria village early because it's a long 24 km slog to the park entrance gate where there is a lodge with *bandas* where you can stay for Sh 80 per person. If you have a tent and prefer to camp there is a camp site two km beyond the park entrance gate. This is free unless the park warden comes round to collect fees in which case it will cost you Sh 10 per person. En route you will pass the Chogoria Forest Station a few km past Chogoria village. If you can't make it as far as the park entrance gate the first day it's possible to camp at the Bairunyi Clearing (2700 metres) – indicated simply as 'Clearing' on the tourist map of Mt Kenya.

It's possible to get a lift all the way from Chogoria village to the park entrance. There is at least one vehicle per day which goes between the Forest Station and the park entrance lodge. It generally leaves the forest station between 6.30 and 7 am and returns between 9 and 10 am. There may also be people staying at the lodge who can help out with lifts.

Day 2 The second day is spent walking from either the lodge or the camp site to Minto Hut with spectacular views all the way. The hut belongs to the Mountain Club but is unattended.

Day 3 On the third day you walk from Minto Hut to the Austrian Hut (about 3½ hours) up to the head of the Gorges Valley and then round the head of the Hobley Valley.

Day 4 From the Austrian Hut your options are the same as on the Naro Moru trail.

EMBU

On the south-eastern slopes of Mt Kenya, Embu is an important provincial centre but spread out over many km along the main road. It has a famous school and hotel and is set in a very hilly area which is intensively cultivated. Most of the people who live here are Kikuyu. Not many travellers stay here overnight except those planning to scale Mt Kenya from the eastern side along the Chogoria trail.

Places to Stay & Eat

There are many cheap hotels spread out along the main road especially near to where the buses stop. One that can be recommended is the *Kwiremia Guest House* which is clean and costs Sh 35 a single or Sh 40 for a room which sleeps two people.

Those who want to splurge might like to consider a night in what must be one of Kenya's most beautiful and memorable colonial-style hotels – the *Izaak Walton Inn* (tel 20128/9). It's on the main road several km north of the main part of town and set in landscaped gardens. It costs Sh 373 a single and Sh 467 a double with own bathroom and all the comforts you would expect for that price. Even if you don't stay here, it's worth coming for a meal. Breakfast is Sh 45 and lunch or dinner Sh 80. If you can't afford the meals then call in for tea (Sh 8) or a beer (usual prices).

NANYUKI

Nanyuki is a small town on the western side of Mt Kenya which services the predominantly agricultural activities of the surrounding area. For travellers it's an overnight stop either on the way to Lake Turkana or for those who are planning to climb Mt Kenya along the Sirimon trail.

Places to Stay & Eat

The best place to stay is the *Sirimon Guest House* near the *matatu* park which costs Sh 45 for a room (one or two people). Soap and towels are provided and it's spotlessly clean including the showers and toilets. They also have rooms with their own shower and toilet for Sh 70 a single and Sh 90 a double. There is hot water 24 hours a day. The meals here are also very good. Steak/chicken, chips and vegetables cost Sh 25. Breakfasts of eggs, sausage, toast, tea/coffee are also excellent value.

There's also a *Youth Hostel* (tel 2112) at the Emmanuel Parish Centre, Market Rd near the post office, which costs Sh 35 for a bed. People who have stayed there report that no membership card is needed to stay here and the staff are very friendly.

NARO MORU

The *Naro Moru River Lodge* (tel 23), about two km from the town on the west side of the main Nairobi-Nanyuki road, maintains a bunk house for budget travellers where you can rent a bed for Sh 60 per night. The private rooms cost considerably more. Meals are available here.

In the town itself there is the *Naro Moru 82 Bar & Restaurant* which costs Sh 35 a single and Sh 55 a double but we don't recommend that you stay here. It's a scruffy, poorly maintained place and the mattresses often stink of urine.

Northern Kenya

This vast area, covering thousands of square km to the borders with Sudan, Ethiopia and Somalia, is an explorer's paradise hardly touched by the 20th century. The tribes which live here – the Samburu, Turkana, Rendille, Boran, Gabra, Merille and el-Molo – are some of the most colourful and fascinating people in the world. The whole area is a living ethnology museum. Like the Maasai, most of them have little contact with the modern world preferring their own centuries-old traditional lifestyles and customs which bind members of a tribe together and ensure that each individual has a part to play. Many have strong warrior traditions and, in the past, it was the balance of power between the tribes which defined their respective areas.

As late as 1980 there was a clash between the Samburu and the Turkana over grazing land near South Horr which required army intervention. Since most of the tribes are nomadic pastoralists these sort of conflicts have a long history. Nevertheless, the settlement of disputes between the tribes is based on compensation rather than retribution so wholesale violence is a rare occurrence. Change is slowly coming to these people as a result of missionary activity (there are an incredible number of different Christian missions, schools and aid agencies, many of them in very remote areas), employment as rangers and anti-poaching patrols in national parks and game reserves and the tourist trade. It will be a long, long time, however, before there is a McDonald's in Loyangalani.

Not only are the people another world away from Nairobi and the more developed areas of the country but the landscapes are tremendous. Perhaps no other country in Africa offers such diversity. Much of it is scrub desert dissected by *luggas* (dry river beds which burst into brief but violent life whenever there is a cloud burst) and peppered with acacia thorn trees which are often festooned with weaver bird nests. But there are also extinct and dormant volcanos, barren, shattered lava beds, canyons through which cool, clear streams flow, oases of lush vegetation hemmed in by craggy mountains and huge islands of forested mountains surrounded by sand deserts. And, of course, the legendary 'Jade Sea' (Lake Turkana) – Kenya's largest lake and, as a result of the Leakeys' archeological digs, regarded by many as the birthplace of mankind.

The contrasts are incredible and the climate mirrors this. By midday on the plains the temperature can touch top 50°C without a breath of wind to relieve the sweat pouring from your brow. Mirages shimmer in the distance on all sides. Nothing moves. Yet in the evening, the calm can suddenly be shattered as the most violent thunderstorm you have ever experienced tears through the place taking all before it. And, just as suddenly, it can all be over leaving you with the clearest, star-studded skies you have ever seen. It's adventure country *par excellence*.

A remote region like this with such diverse geographical and climatic features naturally supports a varied fauna. Two species you will see a lot of here (but not elsewhere) are Grevy's zebra, with their much denser pattern of stripes and saucer-like ears, and the reticulated giraffe. Herds of domestic camel are commonplace in the area and often miraculously emerge from a mirage along with their owner when you are bogged down to the axles in soft sand or mud in the middle of the desert. A rope is all you need, although it's a seller's market of course. Lake Turkana also supports the largest population of Nile crocodile in Kenya which feed mainly on the fish living in the lake but which will quite happily dine on incautious humans swimming there. Giant elands find sanctuary in the forested hills around Marsabit.

There are several national parks and game sanctuaries in the area, three of them along the Ewaso Ngiro River just north of Isiolo. Further north are the national reserves of Maralal, Losai and Marsabit and right up near the Ethiopian border on the eastern shores of Lake Turkana is the Sibilot National Park. Others are in the planning stages particularly one in the Mathew's range north of Wamba which is currently a rhino and elephant sanctuary.

Getting There & Around

Hitching Apart from three routes – Kitale-Lodwar, Nyahururu-Maralal and Isiolo-Marsabit-Moyale – there is no public transport in this area of Kenya. You can certainly hitch as far as Lodwar (from Kitale) on the western side of Lake Turkana and Maralal or Marsabit (from Nyahururu or Isiolo) on the western side of Lake Turkana but that's about the limit of reliable hitching possibilities. Other routes have *very* little traffic.

The mission stations/schools invariably have their own Land-Rovers (and some have their own light aircraft) but they usually only go in to regional centres of population once a week or once a fortnight. Even so, although most will try to help out if you're stuck, you cannot be guaranteed a lift. The vehicle might be full of people who need urgent medical assistance or (on the return journey) full of supplies. It can be done, of course, but you must have no deadlines to meet and you must be the sort of person who is quite happy to wait around for days for a ride. In some ways, this could be a very interesting way of getting around and you'd certainly meet a lot of local people but if it is lifts you want you can only do this along the main routes.

You could, of course, buy a camel and do a John Hillaby but this isn't something to approach lightly. It is, however, a distinct possibility especially if you are part of a small group. You'd have the adventure of your life!

Own Vehicle For most travellers who want freedom of movement and to see a lot of places it comes down to hiring a vehicle or going on a tour. Remember if you are taking your own vehicle to bring a high-rise jack, sand ladders, a shovel, a long, strong rope (that you can hitch up to camels) plus enough fuel and water. The only regular petrol pumps you will find are at Isiolo, Maralal, Marsabit and Lodwar. Elsewhere there's nothing except religious mission stations which will reluctantly sell you limited amounts of fuel at up to three times the price in Nairobi. You can't blame them – they have to truck it in in barrels in the back of their Land-Rovers or pay for someone else to do it in a truck. A four-wheel-drive is obligatory. Don't attempt this area in anything else.

Tours Most of the tours last eight to nine days and they all seem to follow much the same route. Starting from Nairobi, they head up the Rift Valley to Lake Baringo, over to Maralal and then up the main route to Loyangalani on Lake Turkana via Baragoi and South Horr. On the return journey, again via Maralal, they take in Samburu National Reserve/Buffalo Springs National Reserve. Only one or two of them take in Marsabit National Reserve since the only way of getting there from Loyangalani is directly across the Koroli Desert (hazardous after rain) or via the long loop north through North Horr and Maikona. Even this involves crossing the Chalbi Desert which, like the Koroli, is hazardous after rain. There are also the restrictions on the Marsabit-Isiolo road to contend with – all transport must go in convoy at a certain time of day, usually 10 to 11 am.

The cost of the tours varies between Sh 2750 and Sh 3300 which includes transport, all meals, park fees and necessary camping equipment. There are all-camping safaris which use open-sided four-wheel-drive trucks and are not, therefore, for those in search of luxury. Everyone has their favourite company but a lot depends on the people you find yourself with, what you see en route and the drivers and guides. The following companies all offer Turkana tours, usually once a week but sometimes once a fortnight:

Safari Camp Services (tel 28936/330130), PO Box 44801, corner Koinange St & Moktar Daddah St, Nairobi.
Best Camping (tel 28091/27203), PO Box 40223, Nanak House, 2nd floor, corner Kimathi St & Banda St, Nairobi.
Zirkuli Expeditions (tel 23949/20848), PO Box 34548, Banda St, Nairobi.
Birds Paradise Tours & Travel (tel 25898), PO Box 22121, Nairobi.
Special Camping Safaris (tel 338325), PO Box 51512, Gilfillan House, 3rd floor, Kenyatta Avenue, Nairobi.

Some companies also offer flying safaris to Lake Turkana using twin-engined aircraft but they cost more than the truck tours. Two companies which offer this are Birds Paradise Tours & Travel Ltd (address above) and Turkana Air Safaris (tel 26623/26808), PO Box 41078, Nairobi. These usually go to the west side of the lake and use Lake Turkana Lodge on Ferguson's Gulf as a base. A five-day tour costs Sh 5800. You can also combine the Turkana safari with one to Masai Mara but the five-day safari then goes up to Sh 7700.

ELDORET

Eldoret is a small railway junction town on the main road between Nairobi and the Ugandan border, set among fertile, rolling hills above Lake Victoria. Numerous different crops are produced in this area and are brought here for distribution. If you're heading for Lodwar on the western side of Lake Turkana, you may well have to spend a night here.

Places to Stay – bottom end

Probably the cheapest place to stay is the *African Inland Church Training & Conference Centre* but it's about half an hour's walk out of town on the Kisumu Rd. You can get a single room here for Sh 30. There are no double rooms but they will usually allow two people to share a single room. Hot showers are available.

In town itself, there's not a large choice of decent budget hotels. The *New Paradise Bar & Lodging, Mayfair Board & Lodging* and the *International Top Lodge* are really just brothels and are very basic, scruffy and noisy. The *Highway Café & Hotel* and the *Korosiot Super Lodge* aren't much better, but they are tolerable.

Places to Stay – middle

This is one town where you may feel inclined to spend a little extra and stay in a decent place. There are several which aren't going to burn a large hole in your pocket. The cheapest is the *Miyako Hotel*, close to the bus and matatu park, which costs Sh 80 a single without a bathroom, Sh 100 a single and Sh 120 a double with a bathroom. It's a clean place and it has its own bar and restaurant.

Slightly better, but often full, is the *New Lincoln Hotel*, Oloo St, where the rooms surround a shady courtyard and beer garden. Room cost Sh 97 a single and Sh 171 a double both with bathrooms and including breakfast. The hotel has its own bar and restaurant.

Also very good value in this range is the *Mahindi Hotel*, Uganda Rd, which costs Sh 80 a single without a bathroom and Sh 100 a single and Sh 140 a double with a bathroom. It's a large place so there will usually be room here. The hotel has its own restaurant.

A delightful place to stay, if you have the money, is the *New Wagon Wheel Hotel*, Oloo St. It's a huge, old, rambling, colonial-style wooden building with a large verandah and beer garden and it's popular with African travellers. The rooms are in a separate wing to the bar so there are no problems with noise. It costs Sh 98 a single and Sh 171 a double without a bathroom and Sh 116 a single and Sh

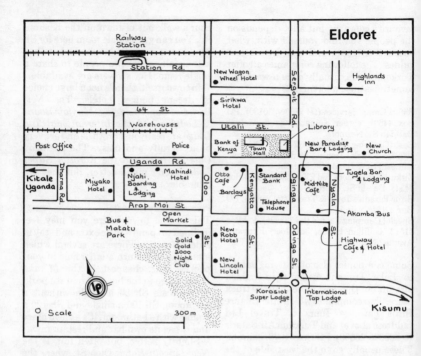

Eldoret

195 a double with a bathroom. The beds are comfortable, the rooms secure and the staff are friendly. There's hot water 24 hours a day and soap and towels are provided. The prices include a substantial cooked breakfast. Lunches and dinners are available at very reasonable prices – large, tasty portions of keema curry, rice and salad cost Sh 36, for instance. The hotel has one of the liveliest bars in town.

Places to Stay – top end
Top-range hotels include the *Highlands Inn* and the *Sirikwa Hotel*. The latter is Eldoret's best hotel and one of the focal points for the annual East African Motor Rally.

Places to Eat
If you're not eating at one of the hotels there are two other good restaurants in Eldoret. The *Remember Otto Cafe*, Uganda Rd opposite the Bank of Kenya, is very popular at lunch time. It offers good, cheap, western-style meals such as steak, chicken, sausages, eggs, chips and other snacks.

Also very popular is the *Mid-Nite Café/Mid-Nite Cave*, Oginga Odinga St. It offers good, cheap food and has outside as well as inside tables. It's a popular bar outside meal times.

Getting There
Kitale buses from Nairobi (see below) run through Eldoret.

KITALE
Kitale, like Eldoret, is set in fertile, rolling hills and the area around it is intensively cultivated. It's a jumping-off point for a visit to the west side of Lake Turkana and Mt Elgon (4321 metres)

which is visible to the west of town, straddling the border between Kenya and Uganda. The Museum of Western Kenya is worth visiting if you are passing through.

Museum of Western Kenya

The museum is open daily from 9.30 am to 6 pm. Entry costs Sh 10. There are displays of stuffed animals' heads and skulls and an ethnology section (Pokot, Turkana and Nandi), but perhaps the most enjoyable part of the museum is the nature trail through a remnant of rain forest at the rear and the compound full of the inevitable copulating tortoises. There's also a craft shop.

Mt Elgon

To explore the Mt Elgon region you first need to get to Enderbess, west of Kitale. There was, at one time, a lodge and camping site in the Mt Elgon National Reserve but it has apparently been closed for a number of years so make enquiries before you set off. The best place to do this is at the Youth Hostel in Kitale (the police in Kitale know very little about what is going on).

Places to Stay - bottom end

Blue Skies Farm (or Blue Skies Shamba) used to be a youth hostel and you can still camp there for Sh 15 per person per night. There are hardly any facilities and you need to bring your own food. It's about 10 km outside Kitale on the Eldoret road. Take a *matatu* to Mailet Saba village and then walk back 400 metres or so towards Kitale. You'll see a gate on your left. Go through it and the camp site is about 300 metres down the track through the field at the second farm.

Sirikwa Campsite & Safaris is a better place for camping. Camping with your own tent costs Sh 35 per person per night plus they have tents for hire at Sh 60 per person. There are hot showers, flush toilets, food is available and it's a beautiful site. The people who run it (the

Barnsley family) are friendly and hospitable. Take a *matatu* there, it's several km out of town on the road to Lodwar.

In Kitale itself the pleasant *Star Lodge* has hot water and costs Sh 34.50 a single and Sh 50.60 a double without a bathroom. The *Rock Hotel* has hot water in the mornings only and costs Sh 35 a single and Sh 70 a double without a bathroom. It's pretty scruffy and the bar can be noisy. The *Njoro Hotel* at Sh 30 a single and Sh 50 a double and the *Kimberu Rising Sun Hotel* are similar in quality.

There are plenty of other budget hotels up the rise past the bus station and covered market, including the *Balima Boarding & Lodging*, the *Salama Boarding & Lodging*, the *Bismaliha Hotel*, the *Safari Hotel* and the *Wananchi Hotel*. They're all rock-bottom establishments and there's not much to choose between them.

Places to Stay - middle

My own favourite is the *Kahuroko Boarding & Lodging* which offers very pleasant rooms on the first floor at Sh 65 for a room with one bed (one or two people) and Sh 120 for a room with two beds, both with bathrooms (shower and toilet). The bed in the cheaper rooms is quite large enough for two people. It's very clean and your gear is safe. There's a bar and restaurant downstairs with traditional African fare.

Two mid-range hotels to try if the Kahuroko is full are the *Hotel Mamboleo*, Moi Avenue, and the *Executive Lodge*, Kenyatta St.

Places to Stay - top end

Kitale's top hotel is the *New Kitale Hotel*, on the corner of Kenyatta St and Askari Rd, which must, at one time, have been the white planters' watering hole. It's an old colonial-style building and is comfortable, although it has seen better days.

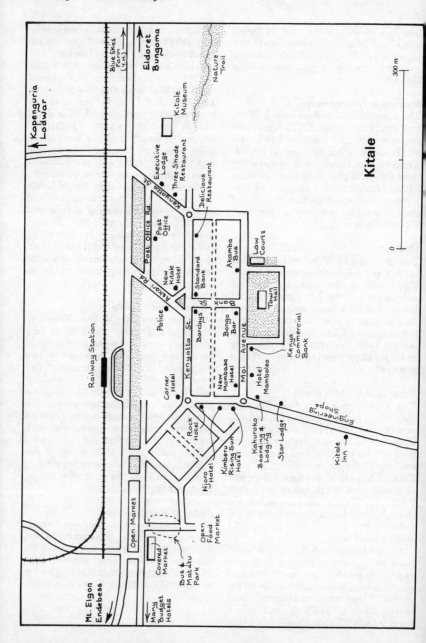

Kitale

Places to Eat

The most popular place to eat is the *Bongo Bar* at the junction of Moi Avenue and Bank St which does both lunches and dinners (Indian and western-style dishes). If you want a reasonable choice of dishes at dinner you need to get there early – there will be very little left by 8 pm. This restaurant actually consists of three parts: restaurant, a take-away counter for French fries, and a bar. The food isn't bad, but it's not exceptional.

Two other places you might like to try for a reasonably-priced meal are the *Delicious Restaurant* and the *Three Shade Restaurant*, both on Kenyatta St. For a splurge try a lunch or dinner at the *New Kitale Hotel*.

Getting There

From Nairobi there are daily departures in either direction by several bus companies. An ordinary bus will cost as little as Sh 75 whereas a luxury bus will cost Sh 120. The journey takes about 5½ hours. Buses to Kitale go via Eldoret so you can use them to get to either place.

To Lodwar there are two or three daily buses in either direction by different companies which leave at about 8 am although they often drive around town for another hour picking up passengers. The fare varies between Sh 70 and Sh 90 and the journey takes about eight hours, some of it over rough roads. It's also possible to hitch a ride with trucks for about Sh 60.

WEST OF TURKANA

The main route is from Kitale to Kapenguria and then along the A1 to the junction with the B4 highway and then north along the B4 to Lodwar and Ferguson's Gulf on Lake Turkana. It's also possible to go much further north on the C47 from Lodwar to Lokitaung.

Getting There

There are daily buses in either direction between Kitale and Lodwar. The trip costs Sh 70 to 90, depending on the

company, and takes about eight hours. You can also hitch trucks for about Sh 60 but they generally take longer than the buses. The road is now sealed all the way so it's a comfortable journey.

North or east of Lodwar, transport and cheap accommodation are rare commodities. The main routes which travellers take are to the lake shore at Kalekol or to Eliye Springs. There is an infrequent *matatu* service (Sh 25) from Lodwar to Kalekol which is usually an open-backed Land-Rover or Land Cruiser with bench seats. By Turkana standards this road is quite busy and most people will manage to get a lift if they are prepared to wait around for a day or two.

Saiwa Swamp National Park

If you are in your own vehicle there are a number of interesting stops you can make en route. The first is Saiwa Swamp National Park about 15 km north of Kitale to the east of the main road. The entrance fee is Sh 30 as usual. It's a very small park and one of the few that you are allowed to walk around. The main attraction is the shy and elusive Sitatunga swamp antelope.

Cherangani Hills

Further north the road passes over the beautiful Cherangani Hills and simple accommodation is available at Ortum in the Marich Pass for around Sh 25 per person. This is one of the great unknown trekking areas in the world. It's possible to climb up to over 3030 metres in the vicinity of Ortum and the views are really stunning. The area is inhabited by the Pokot tribe which, like many others in northern Kenya, have been virtually untouched by the 20th century. It's a superb area for trekking in.

Lodwar

In the junction town of Lodwar there's a good choice of accommodation. If you are interested in Turkana handicrafts, the best places to buy them are either in

Lokichar, 75 km south of Lodwar, or in Lodwar itself at the Diocesan Handicrafts shop. Prices are five to six times more expensive in Nairobi.

Places to Stay The *Mombasa Hotel* costs Sh 28.75 a single and Sh 40 a double but doesn't have fans. At the *Ngonda Hotel* singles are Sh 28 without a fan and Sh 40 with a fan. Doubles are Sh 70 with a fan. For those who would prefer something slightly better, the relatively new *Turkwel Lodge* is worth the extra at Sh 75 a single and Sh 105 a double, both with fan. You might also be able to get a very cheap bed (Sh 10 per person) at the *TRP Guesthouse* but it's supposedly only for those working on the Turkana Rehabilitation Project.

Places to Eat One of the cheapest places to eat in Lodwar is the *New Loima Hotel* which offers very filling meals. The *Turkwel Lodge* is also popular if you prefer western-style food (steak and chips, mixed grills, beef stew and rice, etc). Prices are reasonable.

Kalekol
From Lodwar many travellers head to Kalekol, (the village about three km from the lake shore at Ferguson's Gulf). The Safari Hotel is a good place to enquire about lifts back to Lodwar.

Places to Stay & Eat There are two fairly primitive lodges in Kalekol. One of them is the unnamed guest house across the main street from the *Safari Hotel*. It costs Sh 30 a single and good cheap meals are available. The other is the *Ojavo-Mieni Hotel* which is otherwise known as George's Hotel because it's owned by George Ojavo. It's a grass hut with kerosene lamps and many travellers have found a welcome with the extremely friendly people here. It costs Sh 25 a single or Sh 50 a double and they will prepare food for you very cheaply if you make arrangements in advance – subject to what's available.

The *Lake Turkana Fishing Lodge* is for well-heeled tourists and you are looking at Sh 550 a single and Sh 850 a double with full board though they offer considerable discounts in the low season (early March to the end of May). To get there you also have to take a boat from the lake shore across Ferguson's Gulf which costs Sh 40 return. It's definitely worth a visit for a meal – lunch is Sh 70, dinner Sh 90. Meals are based around lake fish and are excellent. It's also the only place where you can find a cold beer.

Central Island National Park
If you want to visit Central Island National Park the Lake Turkana Fishing Lodge lays on a launch which costs Sh 250 per person or Sh 850 for four people for a four-hour trip. The island is a dormant volcano and the three crater lakes provide a breeding ground for large numbers of Nile crocodile and water birds. It's worth the trip if you have the time and the money.

Eliye Springs
Getting to Eliye Springs is far more difficult and demands a four-wheel-drive vehicle as there is soft sand in places. There is very little traffic and what little there is, is reluctant to pick up extra passengers. It's a beautiful place with palm trees, white sand and, of course, the lake but the lodge here is very run-down these days.

Places to Stay & Eat Despite its run down state the lodge quotes ridiculous prices for a room although, depending on the season, you can haggle this down to Sh 50 for a very basic double. You can camp on the beach close to the lodge but they'll still charge you Sh 40 for this dubious privilege. Food is very limited and consists mainly of *ugali*, chips and fish. Bring your own with you if you want to be sure. They have a refrigerator where it can be stored and they'll cook for you if you make arrangements.

Other Places

There are other areas west of Lake Turkana which are worth visiting but you'll need your own transport and accommodation is hard to find so you'll have to camp. In the far north near Lokitaung the **Lokitaung Gorge** is very wild and beautiful and it may be possible to find accommodation if you ask around.

West of Lodwar the **Loima Hills** are an interesting area to explore. They rise up to 2121 metres out of the desert and are topped with cedar forests inhabited by elephant, lion, buffalo and other game. If you are thinking of going there, bring all your supplies with you, including camping equipment, and hire a Turkana guide at the Forestry Camp at the base of the hills.

ISIOLO

Isiolo is north of Mt Kenya on the road to Marsabit and Moyale and is close to both the Buffalo Springs and Shaba National Game Reserves. This is where the tarmac ends and the gravel begins if you are heading north. If you don't have your own vehicle and are heading to either Loyangalani (on Lake Turkana) or Marsabit you may have to spend the night here.

It's quite a friendly place with a colourful market and you will come across many Samburu and Turkana tribespeople here. Good quality copper and steel, and copper, steel and brass bracelets can be bought here. There is a bank (Barclays) and two petrol stations.

Places to Stay & Eat

The *Jamhuri Guest House* is a good place to stay and has been recommended by many travellers. It's at the back of Barclays Bank on the street parallel to the main street. It costs Sh 50 a double, mosquito nets, soap and towels are provided, there are hot showers and it's very clean.

Two other good hotels are the *Highway Lodge* and the *Al Hilal Hotel* which both cost Sh 30 a single. They are both on the main street, as is the *National Hotel* (where the Akamba buses stop), the *Frontier Lodge*, the *Tawakal Hotel Boarding & Lodging*, the *Isiolo Hotel* and the very small *Coffee Tree Hotel*.

Getting There

Continuing from Isiolo there are buses to Marsabit three times per week. They depart at 10 am on Wednesday, Friday and Sunday, cost Sh 100 and take about six hours. There are no buses to Loyangalani or the small towns en route. If you're taking the latter route you will have to hitch.

EAST OF TURKANA

There are two main routes here. The first is the A2 highway from Nanyuki to Marsabit via Isiolo and Laisamis and north from there to Moyale on the Ethiopian border. The other is from

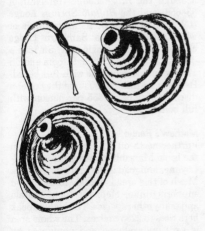

Pokot coiled wire earrings

Nakuru to Maralal via Nyahururu and north from there to Loyangalani on Lake Turkana via Baragoi and South Horr. From Loyangalani you can make a loop all the way round the top of the Chalbi Desert to Marsabit via North Horr and Maikona.

Getting There

None of the roads in this region are surfaced and the main A2 route is corrugated *piste* which will shake the guts out of both you and your vehicle. The road from Maralal to Loyangalani, however, is surprisingly smooth though there are bad patches here and there. The main cross route between the two is via Wamba and Parsaloi. This road leaves the main A2 about 20 km north of Archer's Post and rejoins the Maralal-Loyangalani road about 15 km south of Baragoi. This latter road, though a very minor route, is very smooth most of the way though there are occasional rough patches. You'll probably only use it if you want to visit the Mathew's Range.

There are public buses three times per week in either direction between Isiolo and Marsabit (at 11 am on Wednesday, Friday and Sunday from Marsabit) and between Marsabit and Moyale (at the same time on the same days from Marsabit). The fare is Sh 100 on either route and the journey takes about six hours. A convoy system is in operation in order to deter *shifta* (bandits) from stopping and robbing trucks, buses and cars.

Hitching is definitely possible between Isiolo, Marsabit and Moyale and between Nyahururu and Maralal but on the Maralal-Loyangalani road you are unlikely to get beyond Baragoi or South Horr.

National Reserves

Just north of Isiolo are three national reserves, **Samburu National Reserve, Buffalo Springs National Reserve** and **Shaba National Reserve**, all of them along

the banks of the Ewaso Ngiro River and covering an area of some 300 square km. They are mainly scrub desert and open savannah plain, broken here and there by small rugged hills. The river, however, which is permanent, supports a wide variety of game and you can see rhino, elephant, buffalo, cheetah, leopard and lion as well as dik dik and Grevy's zebra and the reticulated giraffe. Crocodiles can also be seen on certain sandy stretches of the river bank.

If you are driving round these parks in your own vehicle it's useful to have a copy of the Survey of Kenya map, *Samburu & Buffalo Springs Game Reserves* (SK 85) which costs Sh 30.

Places to Stay There are four public camp sites close to the Gare Mara entrance gate of the Buffalo Springs Reserve and three other special camp sites spread between this reserve and the Samburu Reserve.

There are also three lodges but they are outside the range of budget travellers. They are the *Samburu Lodge* (tel Nairobi 335807), the *River Lodge* (tel Nairobi 338656) and the *Buffalo Springs Lodge* (tel Nairobi 336858). As an example of what they cost, the Samburu Lodge charges Sh 1120 a single tent, Sh 1635 a double tent, Sh 1170 a single room and Sh 1735 a double room all with full board. Between 1 April and 30 June they offer a discount rate of Sh 555 per person with full board.

Mathew's Range

Further north off the link road between the Isiolo-Marsabit road and the Maralal-Loyangalani road is the Mathew's Range. Much of this area is thickly forested and supports rhino, elephant, lion, buffalo and many other species. The highest peak here rises to 2285 metres. The whole area is very undeveloped and populated by Samburu tribespeople but the government is in the process of making it into a game sanctuary especially for the rhino. Some of the tribesmen are already employed to protect the rhino from poachers and there's a game warden's centre.

A few km from this centre (which you have to report to on the way in though there are no charges as yet) is a camp site with no facilities other than river water and firewood. At one time it was a well set-up research centre, as the derelict huts indicate. It's a superb site and a genuine African bush experience. You are miles from the nearest village and elephants are quite likely to trundle through your camp in the middle of the night, lions too. During the day, traditionally-dressed Samburu warriors will probably visit you to see if you need a guide (which you will if you want to see game or climb to the top of the range as we did). Agree on a reasonable price beforehand (about Sh 50 per person per day) plus a similar amount for the one who stays behind to guard your vehicle. Don't forget that the rules of hospitality will oblige you to provide them with a beer, soft drink or cup of tea, a few cigarettes and perhaps a snack when you get back to camp. They're extremely friendly people. One or two will be able to speak English (the nearest school is in Wamba) but most can converse in Swahili as well as Samburu.

Getting to this camp site is not at all easy even with four-wheel-drive. There are many different tracks going all over the place and you are going to have to stop many times to ask the way. Perhaps the best approach is from the Wamba-Parsaloi road. Just before Wamba you will get to a T-junction. Instead of going into Wamba, continue north and take the first obvious main track off to the right after there (several km). If there are tyre tracks in the sand – follow them. There are two religious mission stations down this track and both have vehicles. You will be able to ask the way at either. One of them is right next to a large river course which generally has some water flowing through it and which you have to ford. If you get lost, ask a local tribesman to come

along and guide you but remember that you will have to drive him back to his *manyatta* after you have found the place. No-one in their right mind walks around in the bush after dark except in large groups – it's too dangerous. It might sound like a *tour de force* getting to this place but it's well worth it!

Parsaloi

Further north, Parsaloi (sometimes spelt Barsaloi) is a small scattered settlement with a few very basic shops but no petrol station and a large Catholic Mission which may or may not offer to accommodate you or allow you to camp. There are no lodges.

Baragoi

Next on is Baragoi, a more substantial settlement full of tribespeople, a couple of lodges, a few shops and petrol available (sometimes). You'll probably be the only white person/people in town and therefore an object of considerable curiosity. Quite a few people speak English around here. The town seems to get rain when everywhere else is dry so the surroundings are quite green.

Places to Stay & Eat If you have to stay in Baragoi the *Mt Ngiro Lodging* at Sh 25 a single is probably the best although facilities are primitive. It's the first building on the left as you enter the town from the south. For food, eat at *Hussein Mohammed's Hotel* across the street. They have tea and *mandazi* for breakfast, meat and potato *karanga* with rice or chappatis for lunch and dinner.

South Horr

The next village is South Horr which is set in a beautiful lush canyon between the craggy peaks of Mt Nyiro (2752 metres) and Mts Porale (1990 metres) and Supuko (2066 metres). There's no petrol available.

Places to Stay There is one small, basic

hotel in the centre of the village and a large Catholic Mission opposite which is unlikely to offer you accommodation. They have been hostile to travellers in the past.

The best place to stay, however, is the *Kurungu Camp Site*, a few km out of the village on the road to Loyangalani on the right hand side (signposted). This is the place where a lot of Turkana tour trucks put their people up for the night. There's also a lodge here but it's semi-defunct because the person who owns it is having problems with the government. There are, however, three double *bandas* with beds which you can rent, rates are negotiable. The camp site still functions (pitch your tent on the sand under trees) and there are staff. It costs Sh 20 per person per night. Whenever a large group stays here (a tour truck) the local tribespeople will put on a traditional dance for them (at a price). Local people here are used to tourists taking photographs but it's going to cost you money.

Lake Turkana – The Jade Sea
Going further north, the lushness of the Horr Valley gradually peters out until, finally, you reach the totally barren, shattered lava beds at the southern end of Lake Turkana. Top the ridge here and there it is in front of you – the Jade Sea. It's a breath-taking sight – vast and yet apparently totally barren. You'll see nothing living here except a few brave, stunted thorn trees. When you reach the lake shore, you'll know why – it's a soda lake and, at this end, highly saline. The north end of the lake isn't anywhere near as saline because it's fed by the Omo River from Ethiopia (is that where the name of the washing powder came from!?). At this point, most people abandon whatever vehicle they're in and plunge into the lake. If you do this watch out for crocodiles. They're quite partial to a meal of red meat as a change from *tilapia*.

Loyangalani
A little further up the lake shore and you are in Loyangalani – Turkana 'city'. There is an airstrip, post office, fishing station, luxury lodge (with the only cold, cleansing ales for hundreds of km), two camp sites, a Catholic Mission (which sells petrol for Sh 17 per litre, and reluctantly) and all of it surrounded by the yurt-like, stick-and-doum-palm dwellings of the Turkana tribespeople. Taking photographs of people or their houses here will attract 'fees'.

The Oasis Lodge can organise trips to the village where the el-Molo live. They're one of the smallest tribes in Africa and quite different from the Turkana. They also have trips to Mt Kulal and Mt Porr. Mt Kulal is a part drive/part walking trip up to the forest there and Mt Porr is a well-known fossicking spot. The Lodge will ask for Sh 22.50 per km for these trips so you'd better find some good gem stones at Mt Porr.

A better thing to do would be to get in touch with Francis Langachar who is a very friendly young Turkana man and ask him to organise something similar for you. He speaks fluent English and his father went on John Hillaby's 'Journey to the Jade Sea' saga.

Places to Stay
Of the two camp sites, it's hard to favour one over the other. Both are staffed by very friendly people but the *Sunset Camp* is the cheaper of the two. Camping costs Sh 20 per person with good showers and toilets plus they also have nine simple *bandas* at Sh 100 per person with sheets and blankets provided. Safari Camp Services utilise this camp site for their Turkana buses.

The other site, *El Molo Camping*, costs Sh 30 per person to camp plus they have several *bandas* for Sh 200 per person (singles, doubles and triples). There are good shower and toilet facilities. Best Camping put their people here on the Turkana bus. Both camp sites are fenced but neither have electricity or firewood though they do have kerosene lanterns.

'Improvements' are in progress at both camps. The Sunset is constructing a bar and there is already a covered dining area but they don't offer meals. El Molo is being more ambitious. A bar and a kitchen are being constructed and there's already a covered dining area. Whichever place you camp at, beware of the sudden storms which can descend from Mt Kulal. If there is a storm, stay with your tent otherwise it won't be there when you get back and neither will anything else.

Other than the camp sites there is the luxury *Oasis Lodge* (bookings through PO Box 14829, Nairobi, or phone 332713/ 332717) which has 25 self-contained double bungalows with electricity costing Sh 1100 a single and Sh 1450 a double with full board. It's a beautiful place with two spring-fed swimming pools, ice-cold beers and meals available. The only trouble is, if you are not staying there but want to use the facilities, it's going to cost you Sh 100 entrance fee which gives you the use of the bar and swimming pools. Buying a meal there doesn't entitle you to the use of the pools! Breakfast costs Sh 100, lunch Sh 150 and dinner Sh 180. A fishing boat is available for hire at Sh 350 per hour plus a fishing licence (?!) for Sh 50 per week. American Express will do nicely, *thankyouverymuch*. The Lodge is closed during June.

North Horr

North of Loyangalani the road loops over the lava beds to North Horr. There is a short cut across the desert through the village of Gus.

Places to Stay There are no lodges here and no petrol available but the Catholic Mission is very friendly and will probably offer you somewhere to stay for the night if you are stuck. It's staffed by German and Dutch people.

Maikona

Next down the line is Maikona where there is a large village with basic shops (but no lodges) and a very friendly Catholic Mission and school, staffed by Italian people, where you will undoubtedly be offered a place to stay for the night. Please leave a donation before you go if you stay here. The mission usually has electricity and the Father goes into Marsabit once a fortnight in his Land-Rover.

Marsabit National Park & Reserve

South of Maikona is Marsabit and you are back in relative civilisation. Here there are three petrol stations, a bank, dry cleaners, shops, bars and lodges, buses and an airport. The main attraction here though is the Marsabit National Park & Reserve centred around Mt Marsabit (1702 metres).

The hills here are thickly forested and in stark contrast to the desert on all sides. Mist often envelopes them in the early morning. The views from the communications tower on the summit above town are magnificent in all directions. In fact, they're probably as spectacular as any of the views from Mt Kenya or Kilimanjaro. The whole area is peppered with extinct volcanoes and volcanic craters (called *gofs*), some of which have a lake on the crater floor.

The National Park & Reserve is home to a wide variety of the larger mammals including lion, leopard, cheetah, elephant, rhino, buffalo, warthog, Grevy's zebra, the reticulated giraffe, hyena, Grant's gazelle, oryx, dik dik and greater kudu among others. Because the area is thickly forested, however, you won't see too much game unless you spend quite some time here and, preferably, camp at Lake Paradise. The lake, which occupies much of the crater floor of Gof Sokorte Guda, is appropriately named. It's an enchanting place and right out in the bush. Entry to the park, which is open from 6 am to 7.15 pm, costs the usual Sh 30 per person.

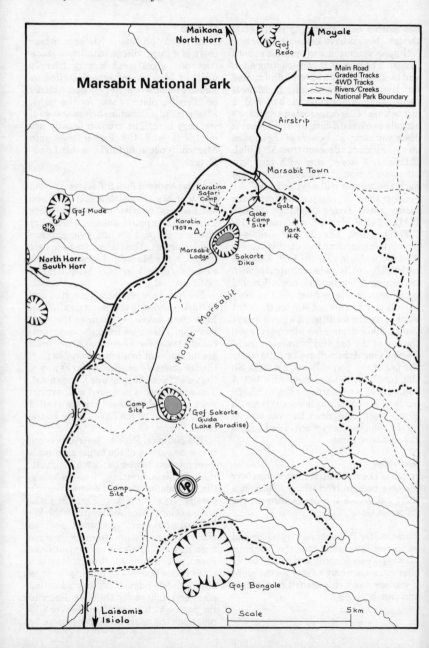

Marsabit National Park

The Survey of Kenya's map, *Marsabit National Park & Reserve* (SK 84), Sh 35, is a good buy if you are touring this park.

Places to Stay – in the Park Few camp sites in Kenya would rival the one at Lake Paradise. There are no facilities (except lake water and firewood) so bring everything with you. A ranger has to be present when you camp here so it costs more than an ordinary site (Sh 300 per group and

only one group at a time) but you can arrange all this at the park entrance gate. There's also another good camp site next to the entrance gate (water and plenty of firewood) but the so-called showers are a joke. You would die of thirst waiting for enough water to wet the back of your ears here. Camping at this site costs Sh 5 per person.

There's also a luxury safari lodge overlooking a lake in another *gof*, Sokorte Dika. This costs Sh 600 a single, Sh 950 a

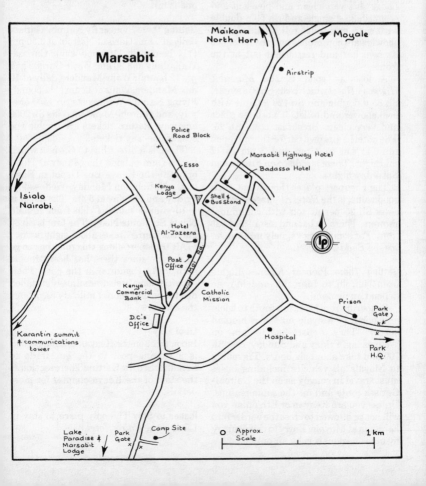

double and Sh 1250 a triple with full board except from 1 April to 15 July when the charges are Sh 415 a single, Sh 825 a double and Sh 1050 a triple. Bookings can be made at Msafiri Inns (tel 29751/ 330820), 11th floor, Utalii House, Uhuru Highway, Nairobi.

Places to Stay - in the Town If you have no camping equipment there's a good choice of lodges available in the town of Marsabit. One of the best is the *Kenya Lodge*. It's very clean and pleasant and costs Sh 35 a single and Sh 60 a double with soap and toilet roll provided. The showers are communal and the hotel has its own bar and restaurant out at the front.

Almost as good is the *Marsabit Highway Hotel* which costs Sh 50 a single, Sh 85 a double and Sh 120 a triple with own shower and toilet. It's a large place and very clean. Breakfast costs Sh 25. The hotel has its own bar/restaurant open from 11 am to 2 pm and 5 pm to 12 midnight. There is a disco on Friday and Saturday nights.

The cheapest place, though not such good value, is the *Hotel Al-Jazeera* which costs Sh 25 per person with communal showers. There's a bar and restaurant out front. For something vaguely mid-range, try the *Badassa Hotel*.

Getting There Pioneer Airlines flights from Nairobi to Marsabit and Moyale depend on demand.

Buses run from Marsabit south to Isiolo and north to Moyale on the Ethiopian border. They depart at 10 am on Wednesday, Friday and Sunday, cost Sh 100 and take about six hours. Travelling to Moyale all vehicles including buses must travel in convoy as on the Nairobi-Garissa route and for the same reasons. Unless you are Kenyan or Ethiopian you will not be allowed to cross the border into Ethiopia at Moyale. Entry to this country by other nationals is by air only.

NORTH TO SOMALIA
Garissa
The route north to Somalia passes through Garissa and Libio on the Kenya/ Somalia border. Wajir is further north of Garissa.

Places to Stay The best place to stay overnight in Garissa is the *Garissa Highlife Lodging*, Mosque St, which costs Sh 50 a double and has a good restaurant. There are other hotels if this one is full.

Getting There Pioneer fly Nairobi-Garissa daily at 7 am, Garissa-Nairobi at 3.30 pm (1¼ hours, Sh 1150 one-way); Garissa-Wajir daily at 8.30 am, Wajir-Garissa at 1 pm (2 hours); Wajir-Mandera daily at 10 am, Mandera-Wajir at 12 am (1¼ hours). Flying Nairobi-Wajir costs Sh 1400 one-way, and Nairobi-Mandera costs Sh 2000 one-way. Return tickets are double the cost of one-way tickets.

There is a direct bus to Garissa which leaves from outside the Munawar Hotel opposite the Kenya Bus Depot in Eastleigh, Nairobi, on Monday, Wednesday, Friday and Sunday at 8 am. The depot is a 10-minute *matatu* ride from Ronald Ngala St (Route No 9). The fare is Sh 80 and the journey takes about eight hours.

All transport along this road has to go in convoy since there has been trouble with *shifta* (bandits) in the past. Their activities have been dramatically curtailed due to the provision of military escorts for the convoys.

Liboi
Liboi, right on the Kenya/Somalia border, is a staging post in the *qat* trade to Somalia. See the Getting There section at the start of the Kenya chapter for more details.

Places to Stay The only place to stay in Liboi is the *Cairo Hotel*.

National Parks & Game Reserves

Kenya is East Africa's premier safari country. It's national parks may not be as large as those in Tanzania, Zambia, Namibia or South Africa but you'll be hard pressed to better the variety and numbers of wild game to be found here. National parks have a long history here and they haven't suffered – at least in recent years – from bitter, defeated, trigger-happy remnants of military factions which have decimated the wild life in many other parts of Africa particularly in Uganda. It's alive and well here and competently managed and protected, although poaching (especially for elephant and rhino) is a problem in some parks. Poaching aside, the only serious enemy of the wild life in Kenya is drought, although if the human population continues to expand at the current rate, land will have to be added to the list.

Nairobi, Lake Nakuru, Bogoria, Mt Kenya, Samburu, Buffalo Springs and Shaba, Marsabit and the marine national parks are covered in previous sections. Here we detail the most famous of the Kenyan parks, most of which lie along the border with Tanzania.

Most of the parks have a standard entry fee of Sh 30 per person plus Sh 30 per vehicle but Masai Mara costs Sh 50 per person plus Sh 50 per vehicle. If you are driving your own vehicle it's a good idea to equip yourself with maps of the parks before you set out. The best are all published by the Survey of Kenya and obtainable either from the Map Office or bookshops in Nairobi. The ones you will need are SK 87 *Amboseli National Park* (Sh 35), SK 86 *Masai Mara Game Reserve* (Sh 35), SK 82 *Tsavo East National Park* (Sh 30) and SK 78 *Tsavo West National Park* (Sh 30).

If you are travelling independently you will also need camping equipment unless you can afford to stay at the (very expensive) lodges, of which there are several in each park. Camping equipment can be rented from several places in Nairobi though the main places are Atul's (tel 25935), Biashara St, Nairobi, which is mainly a fabric shop, and Habib's Cars (tel 20463/23816), Agip House, Haile Selassie Avenue, Nairobi. Rental charges are less, proportionally, the longer you rent equipment but typical short-term charges per day would be:

Tent (two person): Sh 75 (deposit Sh 900)
Tent (three person): Sh 120 (deposit Sh 1200)
Sleeping Bag: Sh 30 (deposit Sh 500)
Mattress: Sh 12-16 (deposit Sh 200-300)
Mosquito Net: Sh 10-15 (deposit Sh 300-450)
Blankets: Sh 8-15 (deposit Sh 80-200)
Gas Stove: Sh 15-50 (deposit Sh 400)
Gas Tank (3 kg): Sh 45 – indefinite period (deposit Sh 500)
Kerosene Lamp: Sh 8 (deposit Sh 120)
Rucksack: Sh 25 (deposit Sh 300)

You are not allowed to walk in the national parks in Kenya (except in certain designated areas) so you will have to hitch a ride with other tourists, hire a vehicle or join an organised tour.

Hitching

Hitching is really only feasible if the people you get a ride with are going to be camping. Since this requires some considerable preparation in terms of food, drink and equipment, people with their own cars are naturally reluctant to pick up hitch hikers. If they are going to be staying at the lodges then you have the problem of how to get from the lodge to the camp site at the end of the day. Lodges and camp sites are often a long way apart and driving in the parks is not allowed between 7 pm and dawn.

Renting a Vehicle

An alternative is to get a group together and rent a car. If you're looking for other people to join you on a safari using a

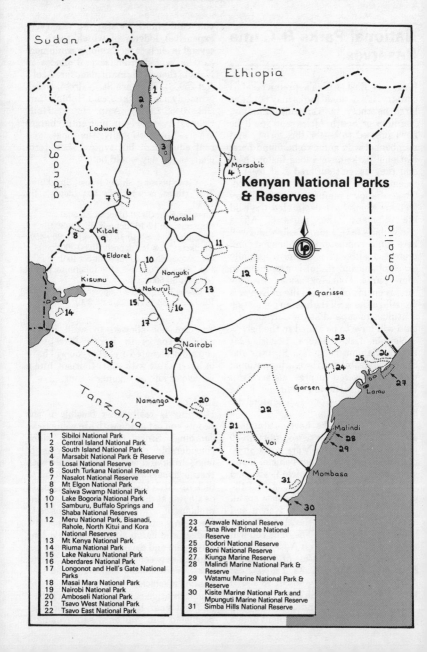

Kenyan National Parks & Reserves

1	Sibiloi National Park
2	Central Island National Park
3	South Island National Park
4	Marsabit National Park & Reserve
5	Losai National Reserve
6	South Turkana National Reserve
7	Nasalot National Reserve
8	Mt Elgon National Park
9	Saiwa Swamp National Park
10	Lake Bogoria National Park
11	Samburu, Buffalo Springs and Shaba National Reserves
12	Meru National Park, Bisanadi, Rahole, North Kitui and Kora National Reserves
13	Mt Kenya National Park
14	Riuma National Park
15	Lake Nakuru National Park
16	Aberdares National Park
17	Longonot and Hell's Gate National Parks
18	Masai Mara National Park
19	Nairobi National Park
20	Amboseli National Park
21	Tsavo West National Park
22	Tsavo East National Park
23	Arawale National Reserve
24	Tana River Primate National Reserve
25	Dodori National Reserve
26	Boni National Reserve
27	Kiunga Marine Reserve
28	Malindi Marine National Park & Reserve
29	Watamu Marine National Park & Reserve
30	Kisite Marine National Park and Mpunguti Marine National Reserve
31	Simba Hills National Reserve

rented vehicle then check out the notice boards at the YHA or Mrs Roche's in Nairobi.

Safari Tours

Most travellers opt to go on organised safaris. There are scores of different companies offering safaris and they cater for all pockets and tastes. The cheaper ones involve camping and a degree of self-help (erect your own tent, help with the catering, etc) and are for people who don't expect great comforts. You may not get hot showers or even any showers at all, the buses won't be well-sprung or air-conditioned, conditions may not be dust-free, there may not be refrigerators, etc.

Camping out in the bush is, of course, the authentic way of going about a safari. There's nothing quite like having just a sheet of canvas between you and what you would normally see only on the other side of a cage's bars. Full-on contact with the bush, its dangers and rewards is surely what you are looking for. Anything more luxurious than this is going to dilute the experience and remove the immediacy of it all. It's true there are some beautifully conceived and constructed game lodges and no doubt there is a case to be made out for staying at them but they are mainly for those who prefer to keep the bush at arm's length and a glass of ice-cold beer within arm's reach – or are simply too old at heart or accustomed to comfort to hack camping.

Which Park? There are all manner of different safari combinations to choose from depending on how long you want to be away and how many parks you want to explore. Masai Mara definitely has the edge on sheer numbers and variety of game but you can find the same variety in Amboseli and, of course, you have the magnificent backdrop of snow-capped Mt Kilimanjaro. Game in the Tsavo parks is much sparser (this is where much of the poaching goes on) but, because it's hilly country, you will see species here which you won't find in the plains parks of Amboseli and Masai Mara.

Which Safari Company? There is no doubt that some safari companies are better than others. The main factors which make for the difference are the quality and type of vehicles used, the standard of the food and the skills and knowledge of the drivers/guides. It's equally true that any particular company can take a bunch of people on safari one week and bring them back fully satisfied and yet the following week take a different set of people on the same safari and end up with a virtual mutiny. That's an extreme example, but whether a company gets praised or condemned can hinge on something as simple as a puncture which takes half a day to fix and for which there are no tools on board. Or a broken spring which involves having to wait around for most of the day whilst a replacement vehicle is sent out from Nairobi. There's obviously a lot which companies can do to head off unnecessary delays but a broken spring, for example, isn't one of them, so when you are deciding which company to go with make sure you know the basis for complaints, if that's what you are hearing.

Companies offering camping safaris which can be recommended are:

Best Camping Tours
    Nanak House, 2nd floor, corner Kimathi St
    & Banda St, Nairobi (tel 28091/27203)
Special Camping Safaris
    Gilfillan House, 3rd floor, Kenyatta
    Avenue, Nairobi (tel 338325)
Safari-Camp Services
    corner Koinange St & Moktar Daddah St,
    Nairobi (tel 289336/330130)
Zirkuli Expeditions
    Banda St, Nairobi (tel 23949/20848)
Gametrackers
    Elite Arcade, Kimathi St, Nairobi (tel
    335825)
Ahmedi Expeditions
    NCM House, 1st floor, Tom Mboya St,
    Nairobi (tel 334480)

Let's Go Travel
Caxton House, Standard St, Nairobi (tel 29539/40)

If you want to stay in a lodge rather than camp check out:

Birds Paradise Tours & Travel
PO Box 22121, Nairobi (tel 25898)
African Tours & Hotels
Utalii House, Uhuru Highway, Nairobi (tel 23285/21855)
Crossways Car Hire Tours & Travel
Banda St, Nairobi (tel 23949)

How Much? There's a lot of competition for the tourist dollar among the safari companies and prices for the same tour are very similar. Most offer a range of possibilities and combinations taking in one or more of Amboseli, Tsavo, Masai Mara, Nakuru, Naivasha, Baringo, Mt Kenya, Samburu and Buffalo Springs. The longer you go for, the less it costs per day. For camping safaris you are looking at Sh 583 (US$36.50) per day for three days down to as little as Sh 343 (US$21.50) per day for eight days. This will include camping equipment, transport, camping site and park entry fees and three cooked meals a day. You will be expected to provide a sleeping bag. Safari companies which are based on renting rooms for the night rather than camping generally charge about double these rates for the same trip and they normally expect two people to share a room. If you are a single traveller and want a room to yourself then there is a supplement of between 15-20% to pay.

Balloon Tours A final safari possibility is a hot-air balloon trip over Masai Mara. It certainly isn't cheap at Sh 2400 for an hour's trip but then it does include a champagne and chicken picnic at the end of the ride! There are daily flights but it's a good idea to book in advance at Balloon Safaris (tel 22860/22869), Nairobi. The flights take off about 7.30 am from Keekorok Lodge.

AMBOSELI NATIONAL PARK

This park must have one of the world's most stunning settings. Right there on the plain in front of Mt Kilimanjaro with nothing in the way to interrupt the views! It might be a somewhat clichéd shot these days (Mohamed Amin, one of Kenya's best photographers, must have taken it a thousand times) but you are going to cherish that photograph of a herd of elephant or wildebeeste in front of Kilimanjaro for the rest of your life. Game is very easy to see in Amboseli because of the terrain and the lack of forest. It's a small park, too, so you don't have to do too much driving. The lake which covers much of the western section of the park is generally dry except during a prolonged wet season.

Places to Stay

There used to be a camp site near the Ol Tukai Lodge but it's been moved outside the boundaries of the park south-west of the Amboseli Serena Lodge. It's run by friendly Maasai who live in a small house on the site but there are no facilities other than a plentiful supply of firewood for collection nearby. It's used principally by safari tour groups. Camping costs Sh 30 per person per night which is a bit of a rip-off considering there are no facilities. Warm beers and soft drinks can be bought from the Maasai in the house at normal prices. Elephant, leopard and lion wander through this camp site at night when everything has gone quiet but no-one has ever been eaten or crushed, although it's food for thought in the mornings when you see how close the piles of dung and footprints are to your tent!

There are two lodges in the park, the *Amboseli Serena Lodge* (tel Nairobi 338656/7), which costs Sh 600 a single and Sh 920 a double with own bathroom and full board, and the *Amboseli Lodge* (tel Nairobi 27136/332334), which costs Sh 1275 a single and Sh 1700 a double with own bathroom and full board. Both places have a restaurant and bar open to

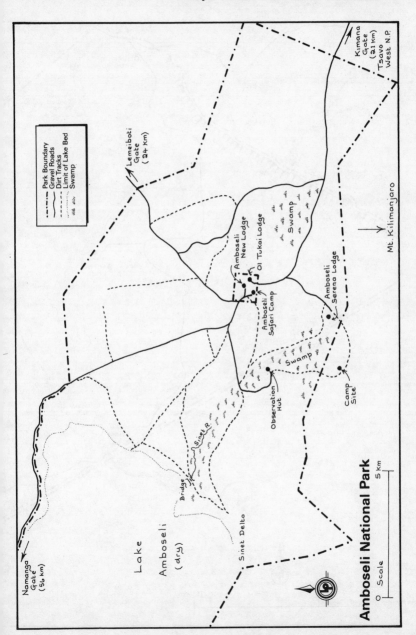

Amboseli National Park

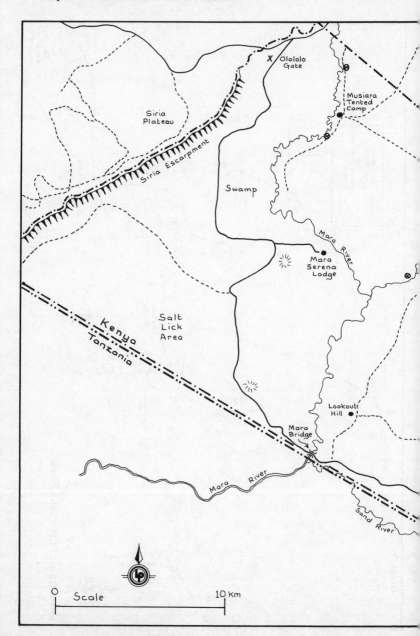

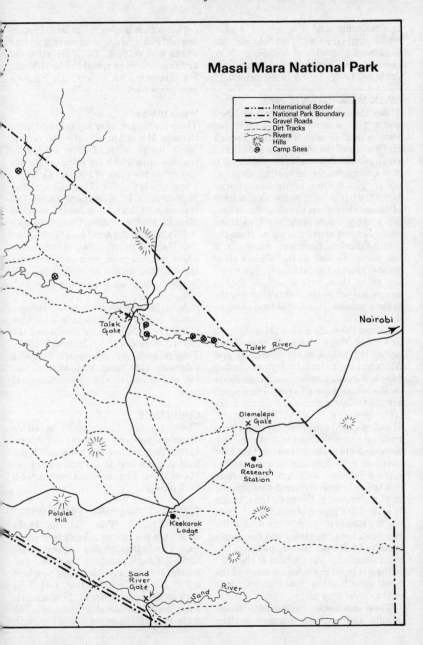

Masai Mara National Park

Legend:
- ·–··–·· International Border
- –·–·– National Park Boundary
- ——— Gravel Roads
- - - - - Dirt Tracks
- Rivers
- Hills
- ⊗ Camp Sites

Talek Gate

Talek River

Nairobi

Olemelepo Gate

Mara Research Station

Pololet Hill

Keekorok Lodge

Sand River Gate

Sand River

non-residents and the Serena Lodge, which overlooks a watering hole, also has a swimming pool and bookshop. Non-residents can have a hot shower at the Amboseli Lodge for Sh 15 per person.

MASAI MARA NATIONAL PARK

Masai Mara is much larger than Amboseli and is contiguous with Serengeti National Park in neighbouring Tanzania. Though it offers one of the widest range of big and small game to be found in East Africa it is also famous for the annual migration of up to two million wildebeeste (gnu). Since the herds are mixed with hundreds of thousands of zebra, gazelle and antelope, it's a truly magnificent sight as these animals move across the plain. Since the North American bison were wiped out, it has to be the last of the world's great animal spectacles. Naturally, you won't see all of them at one time – they're spread out across the plains wherever the grass is greenest – but that isn't going to diminish the sight.

During the rainy season (March, April and early May), the herds spread out across the plains of the Serengeti and Mara but as it starts to dry out (during May and June) they begin to concentrate on the better watered areas. Huge herds are gradually formed which finally move off westwards in search of better pasture. Hundreds can be drowned fording a large river on some of these migrations. The animals mate at about the same time that the herds begin to gather so there is a lot of rutting activity with bull wildebeeste defending temporary territories against rival males and, at the same time, trying to assemble a harem of females. Much of the dry season is spent in the west of the Serengeti but towards the end they begin to move back west in anticipation of the rainy season. Calves are born at the start of the wet but if the rains are late and the herds are still on the move then up to 80% of the calves may die.

These vast herds of wildebeeste, zebra, gazelle and antelope support healthy populations of predators like lion, cheetah, leopard and wild dogs and scavengers like hyena and vulture. You'll see all these and much more on a visit to Masai Mara. For numbers and variety, it's Kenya's best game park.

Places to Stay

There are numerous camp sites scattered through Masai Mara (indicated on the map) though many of them are luxury tented camps which are going to cost you about half the price of a room in a lodge. These include *Fig Tree Camp* (tel Nairobi 332170), *Governors' Camp* (tel Nairobi 331871/2), *Mara River Camp* (tel Nairobi 331228), *Mara Cottar's Camp* (tel Nairobi 27932) and *Mara Sara Camp* (tel Nairobi 21716). The other camps where you can pitch your own tent offer few facilities except for river water and firewood so bring everything else with you.

As in the other national parks, there are luxury lodges which include *Keekorok Game Lodge* (tel Nairobi 22860) and the *Mara Serena Lodge* (tel Nairobi 338656). They're both very expensive but, like lodges in other parks, non-residents can eat and drink in the restaurants and bars.

Getting There

There are two flights daily in either direction between Nairobi and Masai Mara. They depart at 10 am and 2 pm from Nairobi and 11 am and 3 pm from Masai Mara. The one hour flight costs Sh 1050 return.

TSAVO NATIONAL PARK – EAST & WEST

Tsavo East & West National Parks constitute the largest wildlife reserves in Kenya and although you can see a wide variety of game poaching has been – and continues to be – a problem. The poachers are mainly interested in ivory and rhino horn so the populations of these animals have been considerably reduced. The main area which people visit is the north end of Tsavo West where most of the game lodges and camp sites are located but it's also worth a visit to the **Taita Hills** which are sandwiched between the two parks although they are not themselves a national park. There's a famous salt lick here – and the inevitable lodge.

In Tsavo West, probably the most famous spot is **Mzima Springs** where there is a glass-panelled under-water observation chamber which some inspired soul once set up so that visitors could observe the private lives of the hippos which live here. It would appear, however, that the hippos were not too impressed by this invasion of their privacy since they've moved to the far end of the pool and you'll be very lucky to catch sight of them from the under-water chamber. There are plenty of fish to distract your attention in the meantime.

Not far from Mzima Springs is the interesting and recent **Shetani Lava Flow** which sweeps right across the road close to the Chyulu gate on the road from Amboseli. It's also worth visiting the high point of **Roaring Rocks** in this same area for the magnificent views over the surrounding countryside.

Places to Stay

There are a number of public camp sites where you can stay, most of them close to a park entrance gate and most of them pretty dilapidated. Water connected to a make-shift shower, one or two open-sided shelters and firewood for the gathering is usually all there is but, in most cases, no-one comes round to collect a camping fee. This is certainly true at the Chyulu gate but not at the Mtito Andei gate. The latter is a noisy site due to the proximity of the main Mombasa-Nairobi highway. Chyulu is peaceful and quiet but there is a mob of baboons which live here and if there's anything they can steal they will. Make sure tents are securely closed and food put into sealed containers when you go out game viewing.

As in the other parks, there are a number of lodges in Tsavo. In the western side they are concentrated in the north and include *Kilaguni Lodge* (tel Nairobi 336858) – a beautiful lodge with floodlit waterhole. Other places in that area are the *Ngulia Safari Lodge* (tel Nairobi 336858) and *Tsavo Safari Camp* (tel Nairobi 332334). In the Taita Hills there is a choice of the *Taita Hills Lodge* and the *Salt Lick Lodge* (both booked by phoning Nairobi 334000). In the eastern side of the park the lodges are concentrated just outside the town of Voi and include the *Voi Safari Lodge* (tel Voi 17 or Nairobi 336858).

Uganda

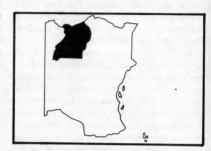

Uganda's long string of tragedies since independence in 1962 have featured in western newspapers to such an extent that most people probably regard the country as dangerously unstable and to be avoided. Despite the fact that previous predictions of stability have proven premature, the victory of Yoweri Museveni's National Resistance Army in early 1986 offers new hope for the future. If the policies and practices of Museveni's government can be made to stick, Uganda will have the cleanest administration it has ever had and there's a good chance it can be nursed back to stability and health.

Before independence Uganda was a prosperous and cohesive country. Winston Churchill referred to it as the 'Pearl of Africa' due to its great beauty, but by early 1986 Uganda lay shattered and bankrupt, broken by tribal animosity, nepotism, politicians who had gone mad on power and military tyranny. Though much of the blame can be laid squarely at the feet of the sordid and brutal military dictatorship of Idi Amin, who was overthrown in 1979, others have much to answer for. Indeed, all things considered, there was little difference between any of Uganda's pre-1986 rulers. All appear to have been spawned from the same degenerative mould.

Yet despite the killings and disappearances, the brutality, and the fear and destruction of the past, Ugandans appear to have weathered the storm remarkably well. You will not meet a sullen, bitter or cowed people, although the fact that they can still smile and find the enthusiasm to carry on and rebuild after the nightmare years is hard to believe – but they do. Undoubtedly, part of the reason is the new government headed by Museveni, which seems intent on making a clean sweep of the government, the civil service

and the army. Despite the huge odds against him and an empty treasury, Museveni has made a lot of effort to get the country back on its feet. There has been a clamp-down on corruption, political meetings have been banned to prevent a resurgence of inter-tribal rivalry and squabbling among power-brokers, and a real effort has been made to reassure tribal elders that his administration will be a balanced one. Perhaps most importantly, his army is the best disciplined that Uganda has ever experienced, despite the astonishing (to westerners) sight of many fatigue-clad teenagers among the ranks – some of them as young as 14 years old. Gone are the days when every road was littered with checkpoints manned by drunken, surly soldiers intent on squeezing every last penny out of civilians or when soldiers took anything they wanted from the stores at gunpoint. It's easy to be cynical, of course, but there's a distinct feeling that a genuine change has occurred. Even the Ugandans acknowledge it and they'd be the last people to be naively optimistic.

Recent Ugandan history may well dissuade you from going within a thousand miles of the country. Don't let it – although it would be prudent to keep an eye on developments. You will find most Ugandans friendly and hospitable regardless of your colour, creed or citizenship, and genuinely happy and relieved that their nightmare has finally ended. Don't be afraid to go there. It's a beautiful country and it has a great deal to offer.

HISTORY
Early Settlers

Until the 19th century, there was very little penetration of Uganda from outside and despite the fertility of the land and its capacity to grow surplus crops there were virtually no trading links with the coast. A number of indigenous kingdoms came into being from the 14th century onwards, among them Buganda, Bunyoro, Toro, Ankole and Busoga with Bunyoro initially being the most powerful. Over the following centuries, however, the Baganda (the people of the Buganda tribe) eventually created the dominant kingdom. The Baganda make up some 20% of Uganda's population and were ruled by a *kabaka* (the equivalent of a king).

During the reign of Kabaka Mwanga in the mid-19th century, contacts were finally made with Arab traders from the coast and European explorers. The Christian missionaries who followed the explorers made themselves very unpopular with the rulers of Buganda and Toro, and there were wholesale massacres of both Christians and Muslims.

The Colonial Era

After the Treaty of Berlin in 1890, which defined the various European countries' spheres of influence in Africa, Uganda was declared a British Protectorate in 1894 along with Kenya and the islands of Zanzibar and Pemba. The colonial administrators adopted a policy of indirect rule giving the traditional kingdoms a considerable degree of autonomy but, at the same time, they also favoured the Baganda in their recruitment for the civil service. The other tribes, faced with their inability to acquire responsible jobs in the colonial administration or to make inroads on the Baganda-dominated commercial sector, were forced to seek other ways of joining the mainstream. The Acholi and Lango, for example, chose the army and became the tribal majority in the military. Thus were planted the seeds of the inter-tribal conflicts which were to tear Uganda apart following independence.

Independence

Unlike Kenya and, to a lesser extent, Tanzania, Uganda never experienced a large influx of European settlers and the expropriation of land which went with it. Instead, the tribespeople were encouraged to grow cash crops for export through their own cooperative organisations. As a result, nationalist organisations were much later arriving on the scene than in neighbouring countries and when they did it was on a tribal basis. So exclusive were some of these that when independence began to be discussed the Baganda even considered secession. By the mid-1950s, however, a Lango schoolteacher, Milton Obote, managed to put together a loose coalition which led Uganda to independence in 1962 on the promise that the Baganda would have autonomy. The kabaka was the new nation's president and Milton Obote was its prime minister.

It wasn't a particularly propitious time for Uganda to come to grips with independence. Civil wars were raging in neighbouring southern Sudan, Zaïre and Rwanda and refugees streamed into the country adding to its problems. In addition, it soon became obvious that Obote had no intention of sharing power with the kabaka. A confrontation was inevitable. Obote moved fast, arresting a number of cabinet ministers and ordering his army chief of staff, Idi Amin, to storm the kabaka's palace. The raid resulted in the flight of the kabaka and his exile in London, where he died some five years later. Obote had himself made president, the Bagandan monarchy was abolished and Idi Amin's star was on the rise.

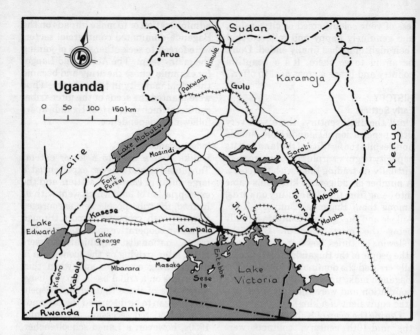

The Amin Years

Things started to go seriously wrong after that. Obote had his attorney general, Godfrey Binaisa (a Bagandan), rewrite the constitution to consolidate virtually all powers in the presidency and began to nationalise foreign assets. Then, in 1969, a scandal surfaced with the revelation that some US$5 million in funds and weapons allocated to the Ministry of Defence could not be accounted for. An explanation was demanded from Amin. When it wasn't forthcoming his deputy, Colonel Okoya, and a number of junior officers demanded his resignation. Shortly afterwards Okoya and his wife were shot to death in their Gulu home and rumours began to circulate about Amin's imminent arrest. It never came. Instead, when Obote left for Singapore to attend the Commonwealth Heads of Government conference in January 1971, Amin staged a coup. The British, who had probably suffered most from Obote's nationalisa-

tion programme, were one of the first countries to recognise the new regime. Obote returned from Singapore to exile in Tanzania.

So began Uganda's first reign of terror. All political activities were quickly suspended and the army was empowered to shoot anyone suspected of opposition to the regime on sight. Over the next eight years an estimated 300,000 Ugandans lost their lives, many of them in horrifying ways, bludgeoned to death with sledge hammers and iron bars or tortured to death in prisons and police stations all over the country. Nile Mansions next to the Conference Centre in Kampala was particularly notorious. The screams of those who were being tortured or beaten to death there could often be heard round-the-clock for days on end. Prime targets of Amin's death squads were the Acholi and Lango who were decimated in waves of massacres. Whole villages were wiped out. Then he turned on the

professional classes. University professors and lecturers, doctors, cabinet ministers, lawyers, businessmen and even military officers who might have posed a threat to Amin were dragged from their offices and shot or simply never seen again.

Next in line was the 70,000-strong Asian community. In 1972 they were given 90 days to leave the country with virtually nothing more than the clothes they stood in. Amin and his cronies grabbed the US$1000 million booty they had been forced to leave behind and quickly squandered it on new toys for the army and frivolous luxury items. The empty 'Departed Asians Property Custodial Board' offices which you'll come across in many Ugandan cities are both a sick joke and a legacy of those days. Amin then turned on the British and nationalised, without compensation, US$500 million worth of investments in tea plantations and other industries. Again the booty was squandered.

Meanwhile the economy collapsed, industrial activity ground to a halt, hospitals and rural health clinics closed, the roads cracked and filled with pot-holes, the cities became garbage dumps and their utilities fell apart, the prolific wildlife was machine-gunned down by soldiers for meat, ivory and skins and the tourist industry evaporated. The stream of refugees across the border became a flood.

Faced with chaos and an inflation rate which hit 1000%, Amin was forced to delegate more and more powers to the provincial governors who became virtual warlords in their own areas. Towards the end, the treasury was so bereft of funds that it was unable to pay soldiers' wages. At the same time, international condemnation of the sordid regime was getting stronger by the day as more and more news of massacres, torture and summary executions leaked out of the country.

Just about the only source of support for Amin at this time was coming from Libya under the increasingly idiosyncratic leadership of Qadafi. Libya bailed out the Ugandan economy, supposedly in the name of Islamic brotherhood (Amin had conveniently become a Muslim by this time), and began an intensive drive to equip the Ugandan forces with sophisticated weapons. The rot had spread too far, however, and was way past the point where it could be arrested by a few million dollars worth of Libyan largesse. Faced with a restless army in which inter-tribal fighting had broken out, Amin was forced to seek a diversion. He chose a war with Tanzania, ostensibly to teach that country a lesson for supporting anti-Amin dissidents. It was his last major act of insanity and in it were the seeds of his downfall.

Post-Amin Chaos

On 30 October 1978, the Ugandan army rolled across north-west Tanzania virtually unopposed and annexed over 1200 square km of territory. The air force meanwhile bombed the Lake Victoria ports of Bukoba and Musoma. Nyerere ordered a full-scale counterattack but it took months to mobilise his ill-equipped and poorly-trained forces. By the following spring, however, he had managed to scrape together a 50,000-strong people's militia composed mainly of illiterate youths from the bush. With these and the many exiled Ugandan liberation groups, who were united only in their determination to rid Uganda of Amin, the two armies met. East Africa's supposedly best equipped and best-trained army threw down its weapons and fled and the Tanzanians pushed on into the heart of Uganda. Kampala fell without a fight and by the end of April organised resistance had effectively ceased. Amin fled to Libya where he remained until Qadafi threw him out following a shoot-out with Libyan soldiers. He now lives in Jeddah on a Saudi Arabian pension.

The Tanzanian action was criticised, somewhat half-heartedly, by the OAU at the time, but it's probably true to say that most African countries breathed a sigh of relief to see the madman finally thrown out. All the same, Tanzania was forced to foot the entire bill for the war – estimated at US$500 million. This was a crushing blow for an already desperately poor country. No other country came forward with a contribution nor has any since.

The rejoicing in Uganda was short-lived. The 12,000 or so Tanzanian troops who remained in the country, supposedly to assist with reconstruction and to maintain law and order, turned on the Ugandans as soon as their pay wasn't forthcoming. They took what they wanted from shops at gun-point, hijacked trucks coming in from Kenya with international relief aid and slaughtered more of the already decimated wildlife. Once again the country slid into chaos and gangs of armed bandits began to roam the cities, killing and looting. Food supplies ran out and hospitals could no longer function. Nevertheless, thousands of exiled Ugandans began to answer the new president's call to return home and help with reconstruction. Usefu Lule, a modest and unambitious man, had been installed as president with Nyerere's blessing, but when he began speaking out against Nyerere, he was replaced by Godfrey Binaisa, sparking off riots in Kampala supporting Lule. Meanwhile, Milton Obote was biding his time in Dar es Salaam.

Binaisa quickly came under pressure to set a date for general elections and a return to civilian rule. Although this was done, he found himself at odds with other powerful members of the provisional government on ideological, constitutional and personal grounds, and particularly over his insistence that the old political parties that had been in existence before Amin's coup should not be allowed to contest the elections. The strongest criticism came from two senior members of the army, Tito Okello and David Ojok, who were supporters of Milton Obote. Fearing a coup, Binaisa attempted to

dismiss Ojok but the latter refused to step down and instead placed Binaisa under house arrest. The government was taken over by a military commission which set elections for later that year. Obote returned home from exile to an enthusiastic welcome in many parts of the country and swept to victory in the elections which were blatantly rigged in his favour. Binaisa returned to exile in the USA.

The honeymoon with Obote proved to be relatively short. Like Amin, Obote leaned heavily in favour of certain tribes. Large numbers of civil servants, and army and police commanders belonging to the tribes of the south were replaced with Obote supporters belonging to the tribes of the north. The State Research Bureau, a euphemism for the secret police, was re-established and the prisons began to fill up once more. Obote was about to complete the destruction that Amin had initiated. More and more reports leaked out of the country of atrocities and killings. Mass graves were unearthed that were unrelated to the Amin era. The press was muzzled and western journalists were expelled. It was obvious that Obote was once again attempting to achieve absolute power. Inter-tribal tension was again on the rise and in mid-1985 Obote was overthrown in a coup staged by the army under the leadership of Tito Okello.

The NRA Takeover

Okello was not the only opponent of Obote, however. Shortly after Obote had become president for the second time, a guerrilla army opposed to his tribally-biased government had been formed in western Uganda. It was led by Yoweri Museveni who had lived in exile in Tanzania during Amin's regime and who had served for a time as Defence Minister during the chaotic administrations of 1979-80. Though only 27 men strong when they first formed, the guerrillas eventually grew to a force of around 20,000, many of them orphaned teenagers. Yet, in the early days, few gave the guerrillas, known as the National Resistance Army, much of a chance. Government troops frequently made murderous sweeps across the notorious Luwero Triangle and artillery supplied by North Korea pounded areas where the guerrillas were thought to be hiding. Few people outside Uganda even knew of the existence of the NRA due to Obote's success in muzzling the press and expelling journalists. It seemed, at times, that Museveni might give up the fight – he spent several months in London at one point – but his dedicated young lieutenants never stopped fighting.

The NRA was not a bunch of drunken thugs like Amin's and Obote's armies. New recruits were indoctrinated in the bush by political commissars and taught they had to be the servants of the people not their oppressors. Discipline was tough. Anyone who got seriously out of line was executed. Museveni was determined that the army would never again disgrace Uganda. In addition, one of the main thrusts of the NRA was to win the hearts and minds of the people. They learned to identify totally with the persecuted Bagandans in the infamous Triangle.

By the time Obote was ousted and Okello had taken over, the NRA was in control of a large slice of western Uganda and was a power to be reckoned with. Recognising this, Okello attempted to arrange a truce while negotiations over sharing power took place between the leaders of both sides. The peace talks were held in Nairobi but were a complete failure. Museveni, wisely, didn't trust a man who had been one of Obote's closest military aides for over 15 years or his prime minister, Paulo Mwanga, who was formerly Obote's vice-president and minister of defence. Okello's army, too, was notorious for its indiscipline and brutality. Even units of Amin's former army had returned from exile in Zaïre and Sudan and thrown their lot in with

Okello. What Museveni wanted was a clean sweep of the administration, the army and the police. He wanted corruption stamped out and those who had been involved in atrocities during the Amin and Obote regimes brought to trial. These demands were, of course, anathema to Okello who was up to his neck in corruption and responsible for many atrocities.

The fighting continued in earnest and by late January 1986 it was obvious that Okello's days were numbered. The surrender of 1600 government soldiers holed up in their barracks in the southern town of Mbarara, which was controlled by the NRA, brought the NRA to the outskirts of Kampala itself. With the morale of the government troops at a low ebb, the NRA launched an all-out offensive to take the capital in February. Okello's troops fled, almost without a fight, although they somehow found the time to loot whatever remained and load it up inside commandeered buses before they left. It was an entirely typical parting gesture. As was the gratuitous shooting-up of many of Kampala's high-rise offices.

Over the next few weeks the NRA pursued Okello's rabble further and further north until they were finally pushed right over the border into Sudan. The civil war was effectively over apart from a few mopping-up operations here and there in the extreme north-west and Karamoja province. The long nightmare was finally over. Although there are occasional reports of units of Okello's army raiding frontier areas, it's a spent force. There is no mistaking which of the two armies Ugandan civilians prefer.

Despite Museveni's Marxist leanings (he studied political science at Dar es Salaam Univerity in the early 1970s and trained with the anti-Portuguese guerrillas in Mozambique), he has proved to be pragmatic since taking over from Okello. Despite many of his officers' radical stands on certain issues, he has appointed several arch-conservatives to his Cabinet and made an effort to reassure the country's influential Catholic community. Newspapers have reappeared on the streets and a big drive has been launched to clean up Kampala and get its public utilities repaired and working again. So far, things have gone smoothly and Museveni is riding a wave of popular adulation. Even the bankrupt economy doesn't daunt him. He believes the fertility of the soil is sufficient to pull Uganda out of the mire, if consciousness is raised and corruption is eliminated.

POPULATION

Uganda has a population of over 14 million people made up of a complex and diverse range of tribes. Lake Kyoga forms the northern boundary for the Bantu-speaking peoples who dominate much of east, central and southern Africa, and, in Uganda, include the Bagandans and a number of other tribes. In the north live the Lango (near Lake Kyoga) and the Acholi (towards the Sudan border) who speak Nilotic languages. To the east are the Teso and Karamojong who are related to the Maasai and who also speak Nilotic languages. Pygmies live in the forests of the south-west.

ECONOMY

Before Amin's coup, Uganda was close to being self-sufficient in food, had a small but vital industrial sector, profitable copper mines, and, to provide further export income, thriving coffee, sugar and tourist industries. Under Amin the country reverted, almost completely, to a subsistence economy. The managerial and technical elite was either expelled, killed or exiled and the country's infrastructure was virtually destroyed. Some cash crops made a tentative recovery under Obote, but Museveni's government has inherited massive problems. The land is rich and fertile and the situation has definitely begun to improve, but there is still a long way to go

before Uganda reaches pre-Amin levels of prosperity.

GEOGRAPHY

Uganda has an area of 236,860 square km. Approximately 25% of the total area is fertile arable land capable of providing a surplus of food. Lake Victoria, and the Victoria Nile, which flows through much of the country, create one of the best-watered areas of Africa. The land varies from semi-desert in the north-east, to the lush and fertile shores of the lake, to the Ruwenzori Mountains in the west, and the beautiful, mountainous south-west. The tropical heat is tempered by the altitude, which averages over 1000 metres.

FESTIVALS & HOLIDAYS

Public holidays are 1 January (New Year's Day), 11 April (Liberation Day), Good Friday, Easter Monday, 1 May (Labour Day), 7 May, 9 October (Independence Day), 25 December (Christmas Day) and 26 December (Boxing Day).

LANGUAGE

The official language is English and you'll find most people can speak it. The other major languages are Luganda and Swahili although the latter isn't spoken much in Kampala.

VISAS

Visas are required by everyone except nationals of Commonwealth countries, Denmark, Finland, West Germany, Iceland, the Irish Republic, Italy, Norway, Spain, Sweden and Turkey. Visas cost about US$20 and generally allow for a stay of two weeks in the first instance (renewable). Some travellers have reported that six-day transit visas are available free of charge. There are Ugandan embassies in Addis Ababa (Ethiopia), Beijing (China), Bonn (West Germany), Brussels (Belgium), Cairo (Egypt), Canberra (Australia),

Copenhagen (Denmark), Khartoum (Sudan), Kigali (Rwanda), Kinshasa (Zaïre), London (UK), Nairobi (Kenya), New Delhi (India), Ottawa (Canada), Paris (France), Tokyo (Japan), and Washington DC (USA).

In Kigali (Rwanda) the embassy is on Rue de Kalisimbi opposite the post office and is open Monday to Friday from 8 am to 12 noon and 2 to 5 pm but they will only deal with visa applications on Monday, Wednesday and Friday. A single or multiple entry tourist visa good for three months costs RFr 1934, requires two photographs and is issued in 24 hours. In Nairobi (Kenya) the embassy is on the 5th floor, Baring Arcade, Phoenix House, Kenyatta Avenue, and is open Monday to Friday from 9 am to 12.45 pm. A single entry tourist visa valid for a stay of two weeks costs KenSh 330, requires two photographs and is issued while you wait.

If you need a visa but can't get to a Ugandan embassy it's often worth just turning up at the border (eg from Zaïre). Most of the time you'll be allowed in on payment of the usual visa fee but don't blame us if you're not!

Those not requiring visas are issued with a free Visitor's Pass valid for one month (more if you request it) at the border.

Visas can be renewed at any District Commissioner's office free of charge. At the Kasese office, however, they'll tell you that you have to go to the Uganda/Zaïre border post at Mpondwe to have it renewed. It shouldn't take you more than a day to go there and back again. *Matatus* are available.

Visas for Other Countries

Burundi Visas The embassy is at 2 Katego Rd near the Uganda Museum (tel 545840). It's open Monday to Friday from 8.30 am to 12.30 pm and 2.30 to 5 pm but they will only issue visas on Wednesday and Friday and they take 48 hours so you have to make your application on Monday or Wednesday. One-month tourist visas cost Sh 3000 and two photos.

Egyptian Visas The embassy is on the 5th floor, Standard Bank Building, 2 Nile Avenue on the corner of Pilkington Avenue opposite Jubilee Park (tel 254525). It's open Monday to Friday from 10 am to 3 pm (ring the door bell if it looks closed). Single entry visas cost Sh 12,484 and multiple entry visas Sh 12,992, require one photograph and are issued in 24 hours (the same day if you get there early and ask them pleasantly to expedite the matter). There's no fuss and no onward ticket is asked for.

Kenyan Visas The High Commission is at Plot No 60, Kira Rd near the Uganda Museum (tel 31861). It's open Monday to Friday from 8.30 am to 12.30 pm and 2 to 4.30 pm. Visas cost Sh 3500 and are issued in 24 hours. No photographs are required.

Rwandan Visas The embassy is on the 2nd floor, Baumann House, Obote Avenue (Parliament Avenue) (tel 241105). One month, multiple entry tourist visas cost Sh 3600, require two photographs and take 24 hours.

Sudan Visas The embassy is on the 4th floor, Embassy House, King George VI Way on the corner of Obote Avenue (Parliament Avenue) (tel 243518). It's open Monday to Friday from 9 am to 3 pm and on Saturday from 10 am to 12 noon. Visa applications are only accepted on Monday and Thursday. A one month tourist visa costs US$9 (shillings not accepted), requires two photos, a letter of introduction from your own embassy, an onward ticket and may be issued in 24 hours if the application does not have to be referred to Khartoum. If it does it will take about three weeks to issue. The situation depends to a large extent on the course of the civil war in the south. The British High Commission charge Sh 6600 for the letters of introduction.

Tanzanian Visas The High Commission is at 6 Kagera Rd (tel 56755). It's open Monday to Friday from 9 am to 3 pm. Visas cost Sh 1500, require two photographs and are generally issued the same day. There's no fuss and they don't want to know how much money you have (very different from Nairobi).

Zaïre Visas The embassy is at 20 Philip Rd, Kololo District (tel 233777). It's open Monday to Friday from 8 am to 3 pm. Letters of introduction are required from your own embassy and four photographs.

MONEY

In early 1985 the official exchange rate for the Ugandan shilling was US$1 = Sh 550. By mid-1986 it was US$1 = Sh 1470 and going up all the time. Throughout this time there was a thriving black market (US$1 = Sh 1200 in early 1985; US$1 = Sh 7500 in late-1986) and few people with a choice in the matter were changing hard currency in the banks. So, until the new government gets the economy under control, there is no point in quoting hard and fast exchange rates. Probably by the time you read this the above exchange rates will look very much out of date, but they may stabilise to some extent as the government announced that it was setting up a two-tier official foreign exchange system in late 1986. The idea of this is to draw foreign currency away from the black market by offering the same rates to travellers at the banks. It's more or less the same system as the old 'Window 1' and 'Window 2' which used to operate a few years back.

The other trouble with the continuing devaluation of the Ugandan shilling is the sheer volume of bank notes it's necessary to carry around with you. The largest of them (at the time of writing) was Sh 1000. Change US$20 and that's a *minimum* of 100 Ugandan bank notes but most of the time a lot more. A visit to a bank is an unforgettable sight – truck loads of Sh 100 and Sh 500 bank notes roughly bundled up with elastic bands stacked two metres high and two metres wide against the counter. Carting them around and counting them is the only major growth sector of the economy. The only other country where I've seen anything comparable to this is Bolivia which I last visited when there were no less than 1,150,000 pesos to the US dollar! The smallest note in use there was 1000 pesos (less than 0.001 US cents!).

You won't have any trouble finding someone to change your money and you can change both cash and travellers' cheques on the street market, though you should expect at least Sh 1000 less for cheques per US dollar than cash. It's worth shopping around for the best rates. These are usually to be found in clothing stores, automobile parts shops, photographic shops and any store which sells imported goods, especially electronic appliances. Simply go in and ask.

Kampala is by far the best place to change money. Anywhere else and you're looking at lower rates (when the rate in Kampala was US$1 = Sh 5000 the rate in Kasese was only Sh 4000). At the Malaba (Uganda/Kenya) border the rates are generally poor because the money changers operate on the assumption that tourists won't know the current maximum rates (often true). Change only enough to get you to your next destination and make a point of asking other travellers who have been to Uganda recently what the rates are. Kenyan shillings are almost as good as other 'hard' currency though it is illegal to export them from Kenya. When the US dollar was worth Ugandan Sh 5000, the Kenyan shilling was worth Ugandan Sh 200. Rwandan francs aren't anywhere near as good (RFr 25 = Sh 1000 at the border).

Currency declaration forms are usually issued at the border on entry but it's very unlikely you'll be asked to show the money which you declare. However, if what you write on the form is a gross underestimate of the amount of money you actually have, then it would be prudent to hide the rest. These forms are hardly ever collected or even asked for when you exit the country (this is certainly true on the Rwandan and Zaïre borders) so whether you change a minimal amount of money at a bank just to get a bank stamp on the currency form is entirely up to you. Personally, I don't think it's worth worrying about. I still have my Ugandan currency form looking at me as this is written and there isn't a single transaction recorded on it. Regulations and particularly the enforcement of them do change from time to time, however, so ask around among other travellers who have been to Uganda recently before you go to the country. Don't be tempted to have a bank stamp made up by one of the many rubber-stamp-making stalls that you will see all over Kampala. It's not only totally unnecessary but, if you're caught, you'll probably be sent to jail (it rates as fraud and magistrates come down heavily on it). There's money to be made by informing the authorities about tourists who get up to these tricks.

There are some Ugandan borders where they don't even issue currency declaration forms (for example, Katuna on the Uganda/Rwanda border, and Nimule on the Uganda/Sudan border) and they even run out of forms at times at Malaba on the Uganda/Kenya border. This sort of thing makes nonsense of the whole operation. At Malaba, the office that deals with currency forms is across the road from customs and immigration and there are often large trucks parked between the two. If you simply walked out of customs and immigration and onto a waiting minibus you could hardly be blamed for not knowing there was a currency form office there at all.

Another piece of absurdity regarding currency forms is that the Ugandan Hotels Corporation, which runs a chain of top range hotels throughout the country, demands payment in hard currency. They won't accept shillings, even with sufficient bank stamps on your currency form to prove that you've changed money in a bank at the official rate. Naturally, if you don't happen to have the exact amount in hard currency to pay your bill at these hotels they'll give you the change in shillings (not hard currency!) at the official rate of exchange.

Much the same is true when buying airline tickets in Uganda. You must pay for these in hard currency and that goes for Ugandan Airlines' internal flights too. There are no cheap deals either. This makes flying out of Uganda an expensive business (over US$1000 to London, US$190 to Dar es Salaam and US$88 to Nairobi, for example). Likewise, many embassies will no longer accept shillings for visa fees so there's no advantage in buying visas in Kampala. However, you can still pay for postage and telephone calls in shillings, as is evident from the queue of bedraggled travellers calling home from the main post office in Kampala.

Banking hours are Monday to Friday from 8.30 am to 12.30 pm.

COSTS

Because of the very favourable street exchange rate for hard currency, Uganda is a very cheap country to visit at present. You can pay for all the necessities of life with shillings – hotels, food, drink, transport, national park entrance fees, post and telecommunications. The only exceptions are hotels belonging to the Ugandan Hotels Corporation and air fares. Transport and food are especially cheap since the prices must, to some extent, reflect the capacity of the average Ugandan to pay for them. Hotel prices are proportionally higher because they obviously cater for a somewhat more affluent clientele. Nevertheless, in comparison with Kenya, Rwanda and Burundi, for the same quality you pay much less in Uganda. Because of the high inflation rates all Ugandan prices in this chapter are quoted in US dollars changed at the street rate. If you change at the official rate, prices will be three to four times higher.

SECURITY

More than any other East African country, Uganda has suffered incredibly from misgovernment, corruption, civil war, coups and badly disciplined armies. As a result it has an image as a dangerous and unstable country to visit. Few tourists have come here since Idi Amin was thrown out in 1979. However, that image is no longer deserved since Yoweri Museveni and his National Resistance Army threw out Okello's rag-bag and undisciplined troops and took over the country. Order has been restored and there's a firm commitment to put the country back on its feet. The troops of the NRA are incredibly well disciplined. The numerous army checkpoints which used to clutter every main highway (where money was extracted from every man and his dog), have largely disappeared and those that remain are manned politely.

You no longer need to have any fears about travelling in Uganda despite what embassy officials may tell you to the contrary. It's true that there are still certain areas of the country where your safety cannot be guaranteed – Karamoja along the border with Kenya and certain areas in the extreme north of the country – but the situation can only improve. If you're thinking of visiting these areas, make enquiries before you set off. As for the rest of the country, it's safe to travel. Ugandans are generally very friendly people.

CLIMATE

Since most of Uganda is fairly flat with mountains only in the extreme east (Mt Elgon), extreme west (Ruwenzori) and close to the border with Rwanda, the bulk of the country enjoys the same tropical climate with temperatures averaging around 26°C during the day and 16°C at night. The hottest months are December to February when the daytime range is 27 to 29°C. The rainy seasons are March to May and October to November, the wettest month being April. During the wet seasons the average rainfall is 175 mm per month. Humidity is generally low outside the wet seasons.

NEWSPAPERS & MEDIA

Quite a few English-language newspapers have appeared (or re-appeared) now that order has been established. They include the *Uganda Times*, *Weekly Topic* and *The New Vision*.

FILM & PHOTOGRAPHY

Bring all your own equipment and film with you. There's almost nothing available in Uganda since everything was looted when Okello's troops were pushed out of the country by the NRA. It will be a long time before commodities such as these become generally available again.

There are no restrictions on photography. This is not Zaïre. Most Ugandans, in fact, are more than willing to be photographed and will request you to send them copies once you get back home. There are quite a few Ugandan homes which are proudly displaying family portraits which I took for them. And they always write back to you and wish you every happiness in the world. So, if you do promise them a copy, please send it. Even NRA soldiers are willing to pose for photographs, although some of the 14-year-old, AK 47-toting guerilla fighters can be a little shy.

HEALTH

You must take precautions against malaria. Bilharzia is a serious risk in any of Uganda's lakes (Victoria, Kyoga, etc) and rivers, so avoid swimming, or walking around without footwear, especially where there are a lot of reeds (the snails which are the intermediate host for the bilharzia parasite live in areas like these).

AIDS (known colloquially as 'slim') is a serious problem in Uganda as in neighbouring Rwanda and Zaïre. A recent study of prostitutes in Rwanda revealed that some 80% carried the AIDS antibody in their blood. No similar study has been done in Uganda but if local sob stories about 'no social life anymore' are anything to go by you'd be wise to assume the worst and leave prostitutes well alone. It's probably also unwise to get yourself involved in any medical treatment which might require a blood transfusion, for the same reason. If you're going to need any injections, carry your own disposable syringes unless you're absolutely certain the one that is being used hasn't been used on anyone else.

GENERAL INFORMATION
Post & Telecommunications

Despite the ravages of the civil wars, international postal and telephone services are excellent – at least from Kampala. I sent several letters and parcels back to Australia from Kampala and they all arrived. Poste restante also functions efficiently.

Kampala is also a good place to make international telephone calls. Internal telephone connections are a different matter. Many of the lines and poles were cut down during the civil wars and it will take a long time to replace them all. The line from Kampala to Kasese, for instance, was out in mid-1986.

Time
The time is GMT plus three hours.

INFORMATION
There is a tourist office in Kampala.

GETTING THERE
Possible access routes into Uganda are by air, road and lake ferry. There are railways in Uganda but there are no international trains even though the line is continuous with the Kenyan system. Service may one day be restored so it may again become possible to travel all the way from Kampala to Mombasa by train.

Air
International airlines serving Uganda include Aeroflot, Air Tanzania, Ethiopian Airlines, Kenya Airways, Sabena and Uganda Airlines.

Few travellers enter Uganda by air because most of the discounted air tickets available in Europe and North America use Nairobi as the gateway to East Africa. International airline tickets bought in Uganda have to be paid for in hard currency (Ugandan shillings are not acceptable). This, coupled with the fact that there are no discounted tickets available in Kampala, makes flying out of Uganda an expensive affair. You're looking at a minimum of US$1070 to London, US$190 to Dar es Salaam and US$88 to Nairobi. It is just possible, however, that you might find a cheap ticket with Aeroflot to a European city via Moscow for around US$450 but they don't fly very often. Flights to Kenya may be booked up for a week or two in advance because they're used a lot by international aid workers, banking officials and government delegations.

To/From Kenya
Road & Rail The two main border posts which most overland travellers use are Malaba and Busia with Malaba being by far the most commonly used. You would probably only use Busia if you were coming directly from Kisumu and wishing to go directly to Jinja or Kampala by-passing Tororo.

There are trains from Nairobi to Malaba via Nakuru and Eldoret on Tuesday, Friday and Saturday, leaving at 3 pm and arriving at 8.30 am the next day. In the opposite direction they depart Malaba on Wednesday, Saturday and Sunday at 4 pm and arrive at 9.30 am the next day. The fares are Ken Sh 336 (1st Class), Ken Sh 145 (2nd Class) and Ken Sh 63 (3rd Class). The trains do not connect with the Ugandan system so you must go by road between Malaba and Tororo (and beyond unless you want to take the train from Tororo to Jinja or Kampala).

If you don't want to take the train, there are daily buses by different companies between Nairobi and Malaba which depart both places at around 7.30 pm arriving at about 5.30 am the next day. The fare is Ken Sh 110. If you prefer to travel by day there are several daily buses in either direction between Nairobi and Bungoma which leave both places about 8 am and arrive about 5 pm the same day. The fare is Ken Sh 90. There are plenty of *matatus* between Bungoma and Malaba which cost Ken Sh 15 and take about 45 minutes. If you stay in Bungoma overnight there are plenty of cheap hotels to choose from.

The Kenyan and Ugandan border posts are about one km from each other at Malaba and you will have to walk. If you are leaving Kenya you will be asked for your currency declaration form and whether you have any Kenyan shillings in your possession (it's officially illegal to export them) but otherwise there's no fuss or baggage searches. Entering Uganda (customs/immigration usually closed for an hour at lunch time) you first go through immigration (no fuss – office on the right hand side coming from Kenya) and then across the road to the currency declaration form office. There's usually no baggage search. The currency form office sometimes runs out of forms in which case you won't get one! Otherwise it's little more than a formality and it's unlikely they'll want to actually see the money which you declare. If, however, what you write on the form is pure Mickey Mouse it would be prudent to hide the rest. If you are leaving Uganda at Malaba they may ask for your currency form but as they're often not issued at the Uganda/Zaïre, Uganda/Rwanda and Uganda/Sudan borders you may as well tell them you weren't issued with one (if asked).

There are plenty of money changers at both border posts but rates are poor, so only change as much as you need to get you to the next town or city. The nearest banks are at Bungoma (Kenya) and Tororo (Uganda). There are no banks at Malaba on either side.

There are frequent *matatus* in either direction between Malaba (Uganda) and Tororo which cost US$0.15 and take less than one hour. Between Tororo and Jinja or Kampala there are frequent *matatus* until the late afternoon. There's also a train but it's very slow.

If you're driving your own transport across the Malaba border you should expect the process to take several hours. Almost the whole road between the two border posts is lined with trucks and they're all trying to do exactly the same as you are.

To/From Rwanda

Road The two crossing points between Uganda and Rwanda are at Gatuna/Katuna south of Kabale and Cyanika south of Kisoro. Both border posts on the Ugandan side are very easy-going and it's very unlikely you will be asked for a currency form (if leaving) or issued with one (if arriving). Entering or leaving Rwanda is much the same.

There are frequent daily *matatus* between Kabale and the Gatuna border post which cost US$0.40 and take about half an hour. They leave Kabale from the road junction in front of the Skyline Hotel. It's also possible to find *matatus* here all the way to Kigali. The two border posts are about 100 metres apart. From the Rwandan side of the border there are frequent minibuses to Kigali until mid-afternoon for RFr 250 which take about 2½ hours. If you're coming from Kigali you need to set off early in the morning because there's a one hour time difference between Rwanda and Uganda; at 11 am Rwandan time you'll find the Ugandan border closed for lunch – and they take their time getting back.

Kisoro is about 12 km from the Uganda/Rwanda border at Cyanika. Not a lot of traffic uses this route so you may have to walk unless you can find a *matatu* or a lift. From the border, however, there are several minibuses daily to Ruhengeri which cost RFr 100 and take about an hour.

To/From Zaïre

Road The two main crossing points are

south from Kasese to Rutshuru via Ishasha and north-west from Kasese to Beni via Katwe and Kasindi though there are less used border posts further north between Mahagi and Pakwach and between Aru and Arua. If you're thinking of crossing Aru to Arua, you'd be wise to make enquiries about security before setting off. Rag-bag remnants of Amin's, Obote's and Okello's troops may still be making a nuisance of themselves in this area. It's also possible to cross the border between Kisoro and Rutshuru (about 30 km) but the road is rough and there's very little traffic. You may have to walk most of the way.

The Ishasha border is probably the most reliable to cross in terms of available transport, but there are no regular *matatus* between Ishasha and the Katunguru junction on the main Kasese-Mbarara road so you'll probably have to hitch. Depending on the day you go, this could involve a considerable wait. There is a market on Fridays at Ishasha so this is probably the best day to go. It's certainly the best day if you're coming from Zaïre to Uganda since there are trucks from Rutshuru to Ishasha which leave early in the morning (around 5.30 am) and return in the evening. There's also a market at Isharo (about half way between Rutshuru and Ishasha) on Saturdays so there are trucks from Rutshuru early on Saturday mornings. If you're coming into Uganda on this route you first pass through the customs hut where there may be a very cursory baggage check after which you register at the police hut down the road. The officials here may not be aware that Commonwealth citizens do not require visas so if you have problems you'll have to ask them to check with the immigration officer in the third hut. Otherwise there are no hassles coming in through this border.

A variation on this route involves a side trip to the Ugandan fishing village of Rwenshama on the shores of Lake Idi Amin (Edward). There is a turn-off to the village about half way between Ishasha (the border) and Katunguru on the main Kasese-Mbarara road. There's a rest house here where you can stay for US$0.20 a single and US$0.30 a double; it's very clean, provides soap and towels, has bucket showers and kerosene lanterns. You can find good food at the *Friend's Corner Hotel* (fish and *matoke* for around US$0.10). There are plenty of hippos wallowing just off-shore and the fishing boats put out around 4 pm and return around 6.30 am. It's possible to change money in the village but at a very poor rate if you only have US dollars. Zaïres are more useful as many people from the village go to the market at Ishasha, so they can use this currency. There are occasional vehicles direct to Kasese, but if you'd like to drive through a different part of the Ruwenzori National Park, there are *matatus* from outside the rest house to Rukungiri (about US$0.60, about four hours), others from there to Ishaka (about the same price) and then buses and *matatus* from there to Kasese (about the same price, three hours).

The route from Kasese to Beni via Katwe, Mpondwe and Kasindi likewise involves hitching unless you can find a *matatu*. Again, depending on the day you go, this could involve a considerable wait (hours rather than days) whichever of the two turn-offs you take going west. If you want to take this route it would be a good idea to make enquiries in Kasese before you set off.

To/From Sudan

Road The only point of entry into Sudan is via Nimule north of Gulu, but this is the area into which the retreating troops of Amin/Okello were pushed by the NRA in early 1986 so it may not be safe to go there. Make enquiries before you set off. Not only that, but there is a civil war going on in southern Sudan between the Muslim north and the Christian/animist south, so it may be impossible to get from Nimule to Juba. At present, it's certainly impossible to go overland from Juba to Khartoum without risking your life, so if you're heading north from Uganda you need to do a lot of serious thinking and asking around before you set off. There are a few intrepid travellers who make it through between Nimule and Juba when hostilities are on the back burner but don't undertake it lightly.

To/From Tanzania

Road The only practicable direct route between Uganda and Tanzania at present is the Lake Victoria ferry between Jinja and Mwanza. Attempting to go overland across the Kagera salient from Masaka to Bukoba via Kyaka will prove extremely frustrating. The road has been in extremely bad condition ever since Tanzanian troops repelled Idi Amin's forces in 1979 and went on to take Kampala. Very few vehicles use the route though there are discussions going on between Uganda, Tanzania and Rwanda to do something about improving the roads in this area. There's even talk of a railway between Tanzania and Rwanda but that's a long way off.

Boats The ferry service between Jinja and Mwanza (Tanzania) across Lake Victoria has been restored. The boats are modern and, although primarily for freight and railway cars, have room for about 30 passengers. The schedule varies so you'll have to make enquiries at the dock, but there is usually one a week in either direction. The fare is US$5 and the journey takes about 16 hours.

GETTING AROUND

Air

Uganda Airlines, the national airline, covers internal routes. Tickets must be paid for in hard currency. Ugandan shillings are not acceptable even with a currency form and bank stamps to prove that you have changed money officially at a bank. There are usually several flights per week between Entebbe and most major centres of population but they're often cancelled at short notice. Service should improve as the country gets back on its feet. As an example of prices, Entebbe-Kasese costs US$44.

Road

There's an excellent system of sealed roads between most major centres of population though there are sections here and there which were neglected or destroyed during the civil wars. Work is going ahead on repairing and improving major routes. The main road between the Uganda/Kenya border at Malaba and Kampala is excellent. Uganda is the land of minibuses and shared taxis (*matatus*) and there's never any shortage of them. Fares are fixed and they leave when full. The only trouble is that 'full' is usually the equivalent of 'way beyond capacity'. Most *matatus* are like sardine cans, but this isn't always the case. Many drivers are speed-maniacs who go much too fast to leave any leeway for emergencies. 'Accidents' are frequent.

There are also normal buses which connect the major towns. They're cheaper than minibuses but they are much slower because they stop a great deal to pick up and set down passengers. On the other hand, they are a lot safer.

Most towns and cities have a bus station/*matatu* park so simply turn up and tell people where you want to go. On the open road just put out your hand.

Hitching is possible and in some situations, such as getting into national parks, it's virtually obligatory since there's no public transport. Most of the lifts you will get will be with international aid workers, missionaries, businessmen and the occasional diplomat but you may have to wait a long time in some places before anyone comes along. There were not many privately-owned vehicles that were not 'requisitioned' by Okello's retreating troops. There must be a lot of rotting vehicles lying by the side of the road in northern Uganda.

Rail

There are two main lines in Uganda. The first starts at Tororo and runs west all the way to Kasese via Jinja and Kampala. The other line runs from Tororo northwest to Pakwach via Mbale, Soroti, Lira and Gulu. At the time of writing, the second track was only open as far as Soroti but by now this service should have been restored to Pakwach.

Travelling by train is a good way of getting around Uganda except perhaps between Tororo and Kampala where the service is extremely slow. It's certainly cheaper and much safer than going by *matatu* and there's obviously much more room. There are three classes on most trains, four classes on others. They are: 1st Class Special (new carriages with two-bunk compartments and hand basins which work and communal toilets which are usually well maintained); 1st Class (old carriages with two-bunk compartments which have seen better days, hand basins that generally don't work and communal toilets that often don't flush); Upper Class (the equivalent of 2nd class elsewhere; old carriages with four to six-berth compartments), and Economy (the equivalent of 3rd class elsewhere; seats only and often crowded). Even 1st Class Special works out more cheaply than going by bus but ordinary 1st Class is very acceptable. Sexes are separated in the upper three classes unless your group fills a compartment.

It's advisable to book in advance for the train if you want a ticket in one of the bunk classes though two days in advance is generally sufficient. When buying a ticket, first get a reservation (not necessary in Economy) and then join the queue to pay for your ticket. There's usually some semblance of order at the ticket offices and I've actually seen ticket clerks refuse to sell any more tickets until the queue got itself into an orderly line!

There are dining cars on some trains otherwise you can rely on food sellers at most stations. The latter are usually very cheap and offer things like barbecued meat (*mishkaki*), roast maize, *ugali*, stewed meat dishes, fruit, tea and coffee.

Kampala

The capital of Uganda, Kampala, naturally suffered a great deal during the years of civil strife that began with Idi Amin's defeat in 1979 at the hands of the Tanzanian army and (hopefully) ended with the victory of Yoweri Museveni's NRA in early 1986. The city is slowly getting back onto its feet and services are gradually being restored. For the moment, however, it still bears the scars of street fighting, the enforced departure of its Asian population, looting and years of corruption.

Unless you've had previous experience of upheavals like these, it's hard to believe the amount of gratuitous destruction and looting which has gone on: office blocks and government offices have had the bulk of their windows shattered, the buildings are pock-marked with rifle fire; plumbing and electrical fittings and telephone receivers have been ripped from walls; buses were shot up and abandoned; stores were looted of everything down to the last bottle of aspirin or the last pair of odd shoes which no-one could match up. It's incredible that the city still functions and that people can still smile. But smile they do. In fact, it's probably true to say that there's a general feeling of relief and hope that it might all finally be over. There's an almost tongue-in-cheek optimism that the new government will bring back order and deliver on its pledges. This heady atmosphere makes Kampala a very interesting city to visit so long as you can put up with inconveniences. It's quite safe to walk around, even at night. There are no longer any of Amin's, Obote's or Okello's drunken, undisciplined, unprincipled rabble to have to contend with.

The city is said to be built on seven hills though it's more than likely you will spend the bulk of your time on just one of them – Nakasero Hill – right in the centre of the city. The top half of this hill is a kind of garden city with wide, quiet avenues lined with flowering trees and large, detached houses behind imposing fences and hedges. It's where you find many of the embassies, international aid organisations, top-class hotels, rich people's houses, the High Court and government buildings. Between it and the lower part of the city is Kampala's main thoroughfare – Kampala Rd (which turns into Jinja Rd at one end and Bombo Rd at the other). On this road are the main banks, the post and telecommunications office, the railway station, the immigration office and a few hotels and restaurants.

Below Kampala Rd, going down to the valley bottom, are a million different shops and small businesses, budget hotels and restaurants, the market, the immense *gurdwaras* (temples) of the very much depleted Sikh community (one of them has been converted into a school) and the bus and *matatu* stations. It's a completely different world to that on the top side of Kampala Rd. There are potholed, congested streets thronged with people, battered old cars and minibuses, overflowing garbage skips, impromptu street markets and pavement stalls offering everything from rubber stamps to radio repairs, hawkers, husslers, newspaper sellers and one of the most mind-boggling and chaotic *matatu* stands you're ever likely to see. This is Nairobi's River Rd all over again.

The other hills of Kampala, except for Kololo (a fairly exclusive residential area), tend to be a mixture of the two.

Information

Tourist Office The Tourist Office (Ministry of Tourism & Wildlife) (tel 32971) is on Obote Avenue (Parliament Avenue), PO Box 4241, opposite the British High Commission and the American Embassy. The staff here are very friendly and helpful and do their best under trying circumstances. They usually have a free booklet about the country, *Uganda: The Pearl of Africa*, an excellent large-scale street map of Kampala for Sh 400, and a free, but out-of-date, leaflet containing details about trekking in the Ruwenzori, *Guiding Notes to the Ruwenzori*. They may also have a free leaflet detailing the prices and current state of repair of hotels belonging to the Ugandan Hotels Corporation and of the National Park lodges.

Maps Excellent large-scale maps of Uganda (Series 1301, Sheet NA-36) with much more detail on them than any of the usual maps of East Africa (Michelin, Bartholomew's, etc) can be bought from one or other of the Ugandan Bookshops stores in Kampala. If they have sold out then try the Map Sales Office, ground floor, Department of Lands & Surveys, further up Obote Avenue (Parliament Avenue) from the tourist office. This is one place which Okello's troops forgot to loot. They also have a large selection of other detailed maps. If any of the maps which they normally have are out of stock there's a good chance of finding them at the branch office in Entebbe – ask directions.

Books & Bookshops For English language publications the best two places to try are the Ugandan Bookshops. There is one branch at the junction of Colvile St and Kimathi Avenue and another at the junction of Buganda Rd and The Square (The Square is the small park in front of the High Court building and the bookshop is on the left hand side of the park as you face it). There is another bookshop on Kampala Rd between Pilkington Rd and Colvile St.

Post The main post office is on Kampala Rd at Speke Rd. The poste restante service is well organised and there's no charge for collecting letters. There's even a reasonable philately department in the building.

Telecommunications The post office also houses the international telephone department and, because it's so cheap to make an international call, it's always thronged with travellers. The service is usually very efficient – expect 5 to 10 minutes' wait for a call to the USA or Australia. To make a call, go to the cashier first, pay for the call and get a receipt. Then take the receipt to the dialling desk with the number you want to call written on another piece of paper. If you want longer than you paid for just indicate this when your time is up (the phones are just opposite the dialling desk). Half the time you won't even be disconnected.

Embassies There are embassies or High Commissions for Algeria, France (Embassy House, King George VI Way – issue visas for Central African Republic, Chad, etc), West Germany, India, Italy, Kenya, South Korea (South), Nigeria, Rwanda, Somalia, Sudan, Tanzania, UK, USA and Zaïre.

Uganda Museum

The Uganda Museum on Kira Rd is officially closed at present while renovations are undertaken, but that doesn't mean you can't get in. It's worth turning up and asking one of the staff if it's alright for you to have a quick look around. The people who work here are friendly and amenable. The museum has good ethnological exhibits which cover hunting, agriculture, war, religion and witchcraft as well as archeological and natural history displays. Perhaps its most interesting feature, however, is the collection of traditional musical instruments which the attendants will play for you (or even allow you to play). Entry is free while renovations are incomplete.

Kabaka's Palace

Another 'must' for a visit is the Kabaka's Palace and the **Kasubi Tombs** on Kasubi Hill just off Masiro Rd (otherwise known as the Ssekabaka's Tombs). Here you will find the huge traditional reed and bark-cloth buildings of the Kabakas (kings) of the Baganda people. The group of buildings contain the tombs of Muteesa I, his son Mwanga, Sir Daudi Chwa and his son Edward Muteesa II, who was the last of the Kabakas. He died in London in 1969 three years after being deposed by Idi Amin who, at that time, was the army commander in Obote's first government.

It may be that in the near future the palace will again be occupied by the last Kabaka's son, Prince Ronald Mutebi, who returned to Uganda in September 1986 from exile in England with the agreement of the new government.

Entry to the tombs costs US$0.20 (less for students) and this includes a guide, although a tip is half expected. Take your shoes off before you enter the main building. You can get to the tombs by minibus, either from the *matatu* park in the centre of the city (ask for Hoima Rd), or from the junction of Bombo Rd and Makerere Hill Rd (US$0.10). The minibuses you want are the ones which terminate at the market at the junction of Hoima Rd and Masiro Rd. The tombs are a few hundred metres' walk up the hill from here (signposted).

Religious Buildings

Also worth a visit, if you have the time, are the four main religious buildings in Kampala – the gleaming white **Kibuli Mosque** dominating Kibuli Hill on the other side of the railway station from Nakasero Hill; the huge Roman Catholic **Rubaga Cathedral** on Rubaga Hill; the Anglican **Namirembe Cathedral** where the congregation is called to worship by the beating of drums, and the enormous **Sikh Temple** right in the centre of the city.

Bats

Bat Valley between Bombo Rd and Makerere Rd used to be famous for its bats which you could see hanging from trees during the day. Most of them have now moved to Makerere University campus at the top of the hill.

Botanical Gardens

Outside Kampala at Entebbe are the Botanical Gardens which are well worth a half day's visit. They're situated along the lake side between the Sailing Club and the centre of Entebbe and were laid out in 1901. Even if you're not particularly interested in botany, there are some interesting and unusual trees and shrubs to be seen and the grounds are well maintained. There's also a zoo close by.

There are frequent minibuses from the central *matatu* park in Kampala to Entebbe which cost US$0.20 and take about 25 minutes. Get off before you reach the end of the line. If you need a meal, snack or drink while you're in the area, try the *Nakabugo Ajjuddo Restaurant* on the main street into the centre, close to the junction with Hill Lane. They offer good food at reasonable prices.

Entebbe Airport

There's little else of great interest in Entebbe unless you have a yen to see the airport where Israeli commandos once stormed a hijacked jet and liberated the hostages, much to the chagrin of Idi Amin.

Places to Stay - bottom end

Finding a cheap place to stay, especially if you arrive late in the day, can be difficult in Kampala since many of the budget hotels have semi-permanent residents. You may have to check out quite a few places before you find a room.

At the very bottom of the market you may still find a welcome at one of the Sikh temples but you shouldn't count on it.

They have been turning people away although they can be quite helpful about finding you alternative cheap accommodation. If they do let you stay, please make sure you leave a reasonable donation – accommodation at Sikh temples is generally free.

The next cheapest possibility is the *YMCA*, Bombo Rd, close to the UNICEF Headquarters, which has the cheapest rates for accommodation in Kampala. The director, Franco Ntambi, wrote to us recently saying, 'Accommodation for the moment is still fairly austere but this is compensated by a friendly and cooperative staff who will keep gear safe during the day. We hope to buy beds soon and we have already begun to build showers. We also plan to have a canteen that will serve good cheap meals. Because of the high inflation rate it is impossible to tell you what the price will be at any given time. All we can say is that we pledge to undercut the price of all other cheap lodging in Kampala.' You'll find quite a lot of travellers staying here. It's a popular place and they'll always find room for you.

Similar to the YMCA but with beds and showers (assuming water is available) is the *Namirembe Guest House*, close to the Mengo Hospital, which is part of the Anglican Cathedral complex on Namirembe Hill. They have a dormitory for US$0.50 per person, singles for US$0.60 and doubles for US$1. Good meals are available here for about US$1. It's a long walk from the centre so you need to take a *matatu*.

At the bottom of the budget-hotel market are three hotels. The one which many travellers rate as the best is the *Bombay Inn*, Nakivubo Rd, which costs US$0.60 per person including clean sheets. There is electricity and water and the staff are very pleasant. The rooms don't lock but there are no problems. They'll cook a meal for you in the evening at a very reasonable price (*matoke*, fish/chicken, potatoes/*ugali*). It's not an easy

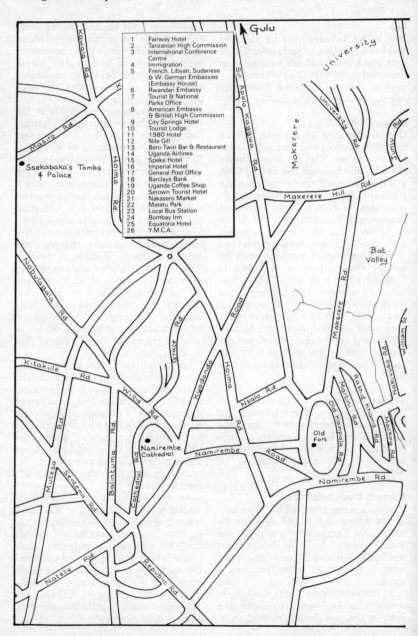

Gulu ↑

University

1   Fairway Hotel
2   Tanzanian High Commission
3   International Conference
    Centre
4   Immigration
5   French, Libyan, Sudanese
    & W. German Embassies
    (Embassy House)
6   Rwandan Embassy
7   Tourist & National
    Parks Office
8   American Embassy
    & British High Commission
9   City Springs Hotel
10 Tourist Lodge
11 1980 Hotel
12 Nile Gill
13 Bero Twin Bar & Restaurant
14 Uganda Airlines
15 Speke Hotel
16 Imperial Hotel
17 General Post Office
18 Barclays Bank
19 Uganda Coffee Shop
20 Serown Tourist Hotel
21 Nakasero Market
22 Matatu Park
23 Local Bus Station
24 Bombay Inn
25 Equatoria Hotel
26 Y.M.C.A.

Ssekabaka's Tombs
& Palace

Makerere

Makerere Hill Rd

Bat
Valley

Nabulagala Rd

Kitakule Rd

Grace Rd

Kyadondo Road

Hoima Rd

Nsalo Rd

Makerere Rd

Rashid Khamis Rd

William St

Nakivubo Pl

Willis Rd

Mutesa Rd

Sentema Rd

Balintuma Rd

Cathedral Rd

Namirembe
Cathedral

Namirembe Road

Old Fort

Old Kampala Rd

Martini Rd

Mackay Rd

Namirembe Rd

Natete Rd

Republic Rd

Masiro Rd

Hoima Rd

Kawala Rd

Sir Apolo Kaggwa Rd

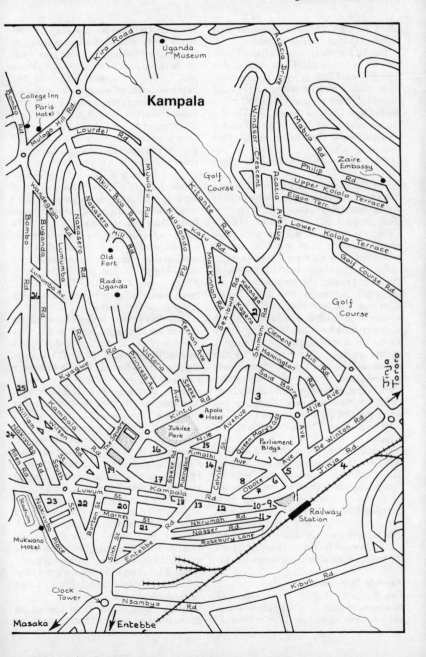

place to find and the street is very crowded during the day so ask.

The *Mukwano Hotel*, Nakivubu Place, very close to the local bus station, has friendly staff but is very scruffy with filthy toilets and no showers worth the mention. They charge US$0.50 for the dormitory, US$1 a single, US$1.50 a double and US$1.80 a triple. It's in a rough area and there's often a bad smell pervading the place because of the garbage-strewn creek on the other side of the road.

The *Nakasero Hotel*, Market St next to the Nakasero Market, is mainly a brothel and is often full (or reserved). It charges local people US$1.10 a double, but it's unlikely a traveller will get that price because there's more profit in renting rooms out to locals several times a day.

Another hotel that ought to belong to the budget range in terms of what you get for your money is the *1980 Hotel*, Nkrumah Rd, very close to the railway station. It costs US$2.30 a double without your own bathroom but including a very simple breakfast (hygiene is very suspect in the kitchen). Maintenance on the communal showers was abandoned years ago and the water pressure is very weak – start filling a bucket about half an hour before you want a shower. There's no hot water but there's a bar on the first floor with cold beers. The manager here is a creep.

A little better, although it's a *matatu* ride from the centre, is the *Paris Hotel*, Mulago Hill Rd, close to the junction with Bombo Rd where there's a large roundabout and a mosque. They are now charging US$3 for a double without your own bathroom but local people pay less. The showers, as elsewhere, depend on available water pressure. There is a bar on the ground floor which also serves snacks.

Places to Stay – middle

The *Serown Tourist Hotel*, opposite Nakasero Market, is a huge place and is likely to have rooms until later in the day.

It's been a popular place to stay for years but is badly in need of major renovation. The staff are friendly and your gear is safe left in the rooms. It costs US$3.50 a single and US$4.50 a double with your own bathroom. Clean sheets are provided. The bathrooms are actually a joke in most cases since the plumbing fittings have been ripped out and most of the time you have to go onto the roof with a bucket and get water from the tank up there (and there isn't much in the tanks).

If the Serown is full, try the *Tourist Lodge*, Kampala Rd/Jinja Rd, just round the corner from the railway station. It's a small place and often full, but services are better than in the Serown. It costs US$3 a single and US$5 a double with a bathroom – which works! The rooms are clean and comfortable although, in common with most places, it has seen better days. There's a snack bar on the 1st floor but it rarely seems to function. Like the Serown, it's popular with travellers.

Two doors down towards the railway station on the same street is the *City Springs Hotel* which has double rooms with bathrooms for US$4.40. There are no singles. This is the only hotel in this range that has hot water. It has its own very good bar and restaurant on the 1st floor. The only trouble with this place is that reception often doesn't know what's happening with vacancies upstairs so they'll tell you there's a room and ask you to wait and then, when you've been there for an hour, inform you that it's full! Perhaps it's a question of slipping reception a tip when you first ask?

Another hotel worth trying and one where you're likely to get a room (it's a large place) is the *Equatoria Hotel*, Kyagwe Rd, between South St and William St. Rooms cost US$2.70 a single and US$3.50 a double, both with bathrooms. Like everywhere else, it's tatty but reasonable value. The hotel has its own bar and restaurant.

In late 1986, a new hotel opened its doors. It would be a good bet if everything else is full. It is the *Rena Hotel*, Namirembe St, which costs US$5 per night.

Places to Stay – top end

All the top-range hotels in Kampala demand payment in hard currency – so they're not worth considering unless you have money to throw away. The most pretentious of them, the *Apolo Hotel* adjacent to Jubilee Park, is a near-wreck with windows smashed and furniture gone. The same goes for the *Nile Mansions* on Nile Avenue next to the International Conference Centre which is similarly wrecked. Only the *Imperial Hotel*, the *Speke Hotel* (both close to each other on Nile Avenue), and the *Fairway Hotel*, Mackinnon Rd, still function. At any of these you're looking at US$30 to US$45 a single and US$50 to US$55 a double. They both have their own bars and restaurants.

Places to Eat

For street stall food, there's a good choice around the local bus station and *matatu* park and around the stadium on Nakivubo Place. What's available can be seen cooking in pots on charcoal (fish, meat, matoke, cabbage, beans, chappatis, rice, etc). They're very popular with local people but it's a lunch time thing only. The hygiene wouldn't win too many prizes and there are a lot of flies and piles of stinking garbage; it's probably alright for strong stomachs.

You can get a good, cheap, traditional lunch (meat, fish and chicken with matoke and sauce) at the *Nakasero Hotel* next to the Nakasero Market. Similar is the *Mascot Restaurant*, Speke Rd, round the corner from the post office. They also offer excellent breakfasts.

Sooner or later, most travellers turn up at the *Nile Grill* on Kampala Rd opposite Obote Avenue (Parliament Avenue) which is open from 9 am to 9 pm daily. It's the equivalent of the *Thorn Tree Cafe* in Nairobi (except it's not part of a hotel)

and is very popular with local office workers and expatriates as a meeting place and restaurant. It consists of a bar, an inside restaurant and what is almost the equivalent of an Australian beer garden. The food is very good and it's worth a splurge – a meal costs under US$1 (at street exchange rates). They have roast chicken, T-bone steaks, fried/grilled fish, curries, hamburgers, etc. Many people just use it as a coffee house and bar.

The *Bero Twin Bar & Restaurant*, Kampala Rd, at the junction with Entebbe Rd, is also a good place for a splurge. Like the Nile Grill, it serves excellent western-style food but has no outside tables so it's best visited in the evening.

Outside the centre of town, the *College Inn Restaurant & Hotel*, Bombo Rd, just beyond the roundabout at the top of the hill, is well worth a visit. It has a very pleasant atmosphere, friendly staff and the food is good. It's also considerably cheaper than the Nile Grill and Bero Twin.

For coffee and snacks, the *Uganda Coffee Shop*, Kampala Rd, near the junction with Burton St and opposite the park in front of the High Court, is very popular. It's on the 1st floor and has a balcony from which you can watch the street below. A lot of civil servants use this place. There's another of these cafes on a side street linking Kampala Rd with Nkrumah Rd past the Nile Grill and before you reach the Tourist Lodge.

Entertainment

There was a long period of time before the present government came to power when Ugandans scurried home at dusk and didn't venture out at night for fear of being shot, raped, arrested or relieved of their valuables. As a result, there was little demand for night life. That has all changed and Kampala is getting much livelier, but there are still very few places to go if you're looking for action. There used to be a well-known disco on

Nkrumah Rd where dancers sweated until dawn but it was undergoing major renovations and may still be closed. It will be a good night out when it opens again. Until it does, night life is mainly bars and restaurants.

A very lively bar with cheap cold beer and African music is the *California Bar & Restaurant* on Luwum St just round the corner from the Serown Tourist Hotel. The clientele here are very friendly and you won't get hassled if you're a woman.

A good place for a cold beer during the day is the *Slow Boat Pub* on the top side of Kampala Rd opposite the Bero Twin Restaurant. It's mainly a concreted beer garden though there is a small inside section, too. Beers are cheaper here than at the Nile Grill. There are lots of other bars on Kampala Rd between The Square and Kyagwe Rd but they're mainly pick-up joints.

Getting There

Road By *matatu* Tororo-Kampala costs US$1.80 and the journey takes about 3½ hours. Jinja-Kampala by *matatu* is US$0.60 and the journey takes about 1½ hours. By ordinary bus the fare is US$0.40 and the journey takes over two hours.

Entebbe-Kampala by *matatu* costs US$0.20 and the journey takes 20 to 25 minutes. An ordinary taxi (which private cars suddenly turn into as soon as their drivers clap eyes on white people) costs US$0.40. Mbarara-Kampala by *matatu* is US$2 and the journey takes 4½ to five hours.

There are three buses per week in either direction between Kasese and Kampala – on Monday, Wednesday and Friday in the early evening – which cost US$3.20 and take about 12 hours. It's advisable to buy a ticket before the day of departure if possible as there's considerable demand for them. They are more expensive than the train, even in 1st Class Special, but the train does take longer.

Rail A train departs Tororo daily at 6 am and Kampala daily at 9 am on the Tororo-Jinja-Kampala route. The journey takes about 9½ hours. The fares are:

Tororo-Kampala: US$1.50 (1st Class); US$0.75 (Upper Class); US$0.35 (Economy).

Tororo-Jinja: US$1 (1st class); US$0.50 (Upper Class); US$0.26 (Economy)

Jinja-Kampala: US$0.79 (1st class); US$0.37 (Upper Class); US$0.20 (Economy)

There are two trains per day in either direction between Kasese and Kampala. One of them is an Economy Class-only train and the other is a 1st/Upper Class-only train. The Economy train departs Kampala and Kasese at 4 pm and arrives at 7 am the next day. The 1st/Upper Class train departs Kampala at 7 pm and arrives at 10 am the next day; and departs from Kasese at 8.30 pm arriving at Kampala at 11.30 am. These trains can be up to 2½ hours late at their final destination so don't rely on official arrival times. The fares are US$3 (1st Class Special); US$2.20 (1st Class); US$1.20 (Upper Class); US$0.50 (Economy).

Getting Around

Airport Transport The international airport is at Entebbe, 35 km from Kampala. It has a duty-free shop, restaurant, bank, post office and a hotel/car hire reservations office. There are public minibuses (*matatus*) between Kampala and Entebbe but only taxis service the last three km between the airport and Entebbe centre.

South-Eastern Uganda

TORORO

Just over the border from Kenya and the eastern railhead of Uganda, Tororo, with its many flowering trees, must have been

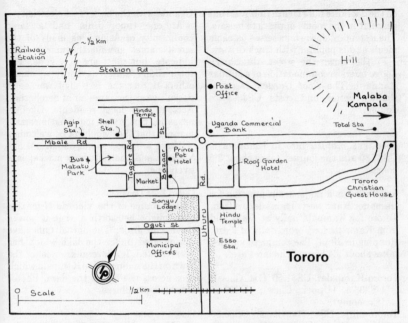

a particularly beautiful town. It must also have had a substantial Asian community as the two large Hindu temples suggest. One of them has been taken over by the Muslim community for use as an educational centre! Sadly, these days it's semi-derelict with empty, boarded-up shops, shabby hotels, vacant lots and few restaurants with precious little choice of food. Its only redeeming feature is the intriguing, forest-covered volcanic plug which rises up abruptly from an otherwise flat plain at the back of town. The views from the top would be well worth the climb.

Information

It's difficult to change money in Tororo after bank hours, even if you have cash. This is one place where you will have to go looking for money changers rather than the other way around.

Places to Stay & Eat

The only place worth considering in is the *Tororo Christian Guest House* on Mbale Rd diagonally opposite the Total petrol station on the way into town from Malaba. It's very clean and the people who run it are very friendly. It costs US$1 for a bed in the dormitory, US$1.30 a double and US$1.60 a triple, all without bathrooms. There are clean communal showers and excellent meals are available at reasonable prices.

The other hotels in town are in an execrable state though the people who run and staff them are often very friendly. The *Prince Pot Hotel*, Bazaar St, is virtually derelict but somehow staggers on and even manages to provide clean sheets, although precious little else. The showers don't work and the toilet stinks to high heaven since there are only buckets of dirty water available, The bar downstairs can also be noisy until late. Rooms cost US$1.20 a double. The locks on the doors are pure Heath Robinson but gear left in the rooms appears to be safe. The restaurant downstairs serves passable meals and is popular with truck drivers.

Further down the street, the *Sanyu Lodge* offers accommodation of a similar standard. The *Roof Garden Hotel* is slightly better and costs US$3.30 a double.

Getting There
Road The *matatu* fare to Kampala is US$1.80 and the journey takes about 3½ hours.

Rail Tororo is a major train junction for trains north and west. Trains depart from Tororo for Kampala daily at 6 am and from Kampala for Tororo daily at 9 am, stopping in Jinja. The complete journey takes about 9½ hours. The fares are:

Tororo-Kampala: US$1.50 (1st Class); US$0.75 (Upper Class); US$0.35 (Economy).

Tororo-Jinja: US$1 (1st Class); US$0.50 (Upper Class); US$0.25 (Economy).

Jinja-Kampala: US$0.80 (1st Class); US$0.40 (Upper Class); US$0.20 (Economy).

Another line runs north-west to Pakwach via Mbale and Gulu. When service is restored there should be a daily train in either direction at 5 pm. The fares are:

Tororo-Pakwach: US$3.10 (1st Class); US$1.70 (Upper Class); US$0.80 (Economy).

Tororo-Soroti: US$1.20 (1st Class); US$0.65 (Upper Class); US$0.30 (Economy).

JINJA
Jinja lies on the shores of Lake Victoria and is a major marketing and industrial centre for southern Uganda. It's close to what used to be the Owen Falls, where the Victoria Nile leaves the lake. Now there is a hydro-electric station which supplies Uganda with the bulk of its electricity.

At one time, Jinja had a large community of Asians, as many of the street names around the market area indicate, but most are now gone. The town didn't suffer as badly as many others during the last civil war so it doesn't wear the same air of dereliction. According to local residents, Okello's retreating troops were told in no uncertain manner that they wouldn't be welcome.

There are good views out over Lake Victoria and the Saturday market is a lively one.

Owen Falls Dam
At the source of the Victoria Nile, this dam might be worth a visit if you're staying in Jinja. The actual falls have disappeared under the lake which has been created. It's several km west of the town on the main road to Kampala which goes across the top of the dam. Photography is prohibited.

Places to Stay
The *Victoria View Hotel's* name might be wishful thinking, but it is very pleasant and clean and offers doubles for US$2 with bathrooms (there are no singles). The hotel is on Kutch Rd and has its own restaurant.

The *Market View Hotel* is equally pleasant and clean and offers rooms for US$1.55 a single and US$1.75 a double, both with shared bathrooms. It also has its own restaurant and is also on Kutch Rd. Its name is much more appropriate!

If you're looking for something cheaper then ask at the *Blue Cat Bar* for a spare room.

More expensive, but good value, is the *Belle View Hotel*, Kutch Rd. It's a very comfortable place to stay and spotlessly clean. Unfortunately they have no hot water. Rooms cost US$2.60 a single without a bathroom and US$3 a double with a bathroom. There's an excellent bar and restaurant downstairs.

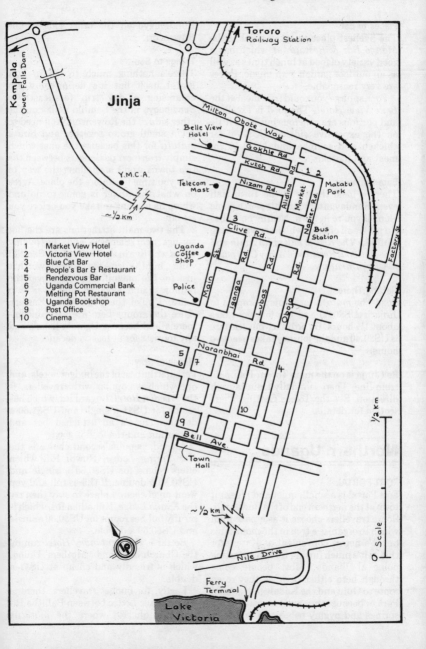

Jinja

1　Market View Hotel
2　Victoria View Hotel
3　Blue Cat Bar
4　People's Bar & Restaurant
5　Rendezvous Bar
6　Uganda Commercial Bank
7　Melting Pot Restaurant
8　Uganda Bookshop
9　Post Office
10　Cinema

Places to Eat

The liveliest place to eat or drink is the *Mango Bar & Restaurant* which has a good variety of food at lunch times as well as an outdoor garden with music. Prices are very reasonable.

For a splurge you could try a meal at the *Belle View Hotel*. The food is excellent and portions are generous but it's a little on the expensive side at US$0.80 for chicken and matoke and US$1.60 for meat and matoke.

Entertainment

There is local theatre at the Town Hall every Sunday afternoon. It's worth going along if you're in town. Nearby on Lubas Rd is a small cinema which shows stirring stuff like *The Rise & Fall of Idi Amin* and *The National Resistance Army Campaign – A Documentary*.

Getting There

Road The *matatu* fare from Kampala to Jinja is US$0.60 and the journey takes about 1½ hours. By ordinary bus the fare is US$0.40 and the journey takes over two hours.

Rail Jinja is on the main Tororo-Kampala train line. There is a daily train in each direction. See the Tororo Getting There section for details.

Northern Uganda

FORT PORTAL

Fort Portal is a small, quiet and pleasant town at the northern end of the Ruwenzori. Some travellers choose it as a base from which to organise a trek in the mountains but it's not as convenient as Kasese for this as it's much further from the starting point at Ibanda. Most people come through here either because they're en route to Gulu and the Kabalega National Park or because they want to visit the hot springs and pygmy tribes on the way to Bundibugyo on the other side of the Ruwenzori.

Things to See

There's nothing much to see in Fort Portal itself but it's definitely worth organising a day trip (at least) to **Bundibugyo** in the Semliki valley on the other side of the Ruwenzori. You need to get a small group together and hire a *matatu* for this because the ones which simply transport passengers between the two towns won't stop along the way to give you time to explore the place. Agree on what the driver is going to do and where he is going to take you before you set off.

The two main attractions are the hot springs near **Sempaya** and the pygmy tribes who live in the forest of the Semliki valley, but the drive over there is worth it just for the magnificent views over the rainforest and savanna and over into Zaïre. Unlike the pygmies in Eastern Zaïre the groups here are very uncommercialised because Uganda hasn't had any tourists for at least a decade.

Places to Stay

Perhaps the best of the budget hotels, and one which is popular with travellers, is the *Wooden Hotel*, Lugard Rd, which has rooms for US$1 a single and US$1.60 a double. There's an attached bar and restaurant and the food is good.

A good, popular second choice is the *Hot Spring Lodge*, Ruwdi Rd, which offers rooms for US$0.60 a single and US$0.80 a double. If this is full and you want an *el cheapo* place to stay then try the *Kyaka Lodge*, Kuhadika Rd, which is scruffy but has rooms for US$0.30 a single and US$0.50 a double.

Better is the *Centenary Hotel* run by the Church of Uganda Mothers' Union, which is friendly and cheap at US$1 a double.

Lastly, for budget travellers, there is the *Mwenge Lodge* between Babitha Rd and Kahinju Rd where the *matatus*

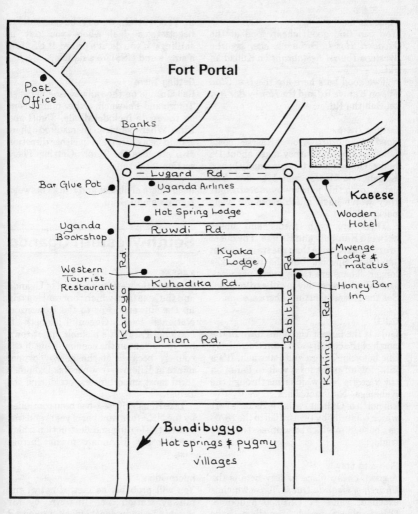

Fort Portal

Post Office

Banks

Bar Glue Pot

— Lugard Rd. — —

Uganda Airlines

Hot Spring Lodge

Uganda Bookshop

Ruwdi Rd.

Karoyo Rd.

Kyaka Lodge

Western Tourist Restaurant

Kuhadika Rd.

Union Rd.

Babitha Rd.

Kahinju Rd.

Kasese

Wooden Hotel

Mwenge Lodge & matatus

Honey Bar Inn

Bundibugyo
Hot springs & pygmy villages

arrive and depart. They have tiny singles for US$0.70, larger singles for US$1 and doubles for US$2. It's poor value considering what you can get for your money in this part of Uganda and the hotel is pretty scruffy.

Those with more commodious accommodation and services in mind should go to the *Mountains of the Moon Hotel*, one of the Ugandan Hotels Corporation chain, but you have to pay in hard currency so it works out to be very expensive. If there are very few guests, however, it may be possible to negotiate a deal where you pay in shillings. After all, it makes sense to have *someone* staying there rather than no-one, even if they are paying in shillings.

Places to Eat

You can find good, cheap food at the *Wooden Hotel*. For a change, try the *Western Tourist Restaurant* on Kuhadika Rd.

Two good bars here are the *Bar Glue Pot* on Karoye Rd and the *Honey Bar Inn* on Babitha Rd.

Getting There

Road A *matatu* from Kasese costs US$0.60 and the journey takes about 1½ hours. Going south, there is a daily bus to Kabale, via Kasese and Mbarara. You can also do this journey by *matatu*, but they won't have much room for your backpack.

There are both trains and buses between Kampala and Kasese. The buses are more expensive than the train, even in 1st Class Special, but the train takes longer. There are three buses per week and two trains per day in either direction. See the Kasese Getting There section.

GULU

Gulu is the largest Ugandan town in the north of the country and is on the railway line between Tororo and Pakwach. It's a jumping off point for a visit to Paraa on the Victoria Nile which runs through the Kabalega National Park. Twenty-five km north of Gulu at Patiko is Baker's Fort which was built by the British in the 1870s as a base from which to suppress the slave trade.

Places to Stay

A good, cheap place to stay here is the *Church of Uganda Guest House* which is excellent value at US$0.50 a double. Other places which travellers have recommended in the past are the *New Gulu Restaurant*, Pakwach Rd, and the *Luxxor Lodge* opposite the truck park.

The top-range hotel here is the *Acholi Inn* which is part of the Uganda Hotel Corporation, so you must pay for accommodation in hard currency though, as with the Mountains of the Moon Hotel

in Fort Portal, it may be possible to negotiate a deal where you pay in shillings. If you do, it's priced at US$1.30 a single and US$1.75 a double.

Getting There

Rail Gulu is on the railway line between Tororo and Pakwach. Other main towns on the route include Mbale, Soroti and Lira When service is restored there should be a daily train in either direction at 5 pm. See the Tororo Getting There section for details.

Road There are buses and trucks between Kampala and Gulu.

South-Western Uganda

KASESE

Kasese is the western railhead of Uganda and the base from which to organise a trip up the Ruwenzori or to the Ruwenzori National Park (Queen Elizabeth II National Park). It's a small, quiet town but important in the economic life of the country because of the nearby copper mines at Kilembe (copper was Uganda's third most important export during the 1970s).

Like Kabale, Kasese has been controlled by the NRA for a number of years and was spared the looting and destruction which befell other Ugandan towns further east.

Information

You will probably be met, if not at the railway station then in town, by Mr Singhi who has made it his self-appointed task to approach all incoming tourists and travellers and explain what there is to see and do in the area. He's very friendly and doesn't expect payment for his services so do talk to him if you have the chance. He's a mine of information about mountain climbing and visits to the copper mine, hot springs and pygmies.

Places to Stay

By far the best place to stay (in fact, I'd nominate it as the best value for money in Uganda) is the *Saad Hotel* (tel 157/9), Ruwenzori Rd. The staff are very friendly indeed, and the rooms are extremely pleasant and spotlessly clean. They only have double rooms (two single beds) with attached showers and toilets which cost US$3, but they will accept three people to a room. If hot water is not available on tap it will be brought to your room in buckets. Videos are sometimes shown in the lounge next to reception. This hotel is very popular with travellers and rightly so.

If it's full (unlikely) and you'd like something of a similar standard then the next best is the *Kaghesera Hotel*, Speke St, which is pleasant, very clean and has hot water. It costs US$1.10 a single and US$1.55 a double with a shower and toilet.

For something cheaper, try the *Highway Lodging*, Margherita Rd, which costs US$1 a single or double without bathrooms. It's a bit scruffy but clean sheets are provided and the manager is friendly. Two other similar places are the *Paradise Bar & Lodging* and the *Rwenzori Guest House*, both on Speke St. The *Moonlight Lodgings*, Margherita Rd, ought to be similarly priced considering the standard of accommodation which it offers but if the prices which I was quoted are correct (US$1 a single and US$2 a double) then it's very poor value for money. They do, however, serve reasonable food in the restaurant.

Considering the excellent value for money which the *Saad Hotel* offers I can't imagine anyone bothering to look further. There is, however, the *Hotel Margherita* some three km out of town on the road up towards the mountains. It's part of the Uganda Hotels Corporation and once again you must pay in hard currency. The setting is certainly beautiful – looking out towards the Ruwenzori on one side and the golf course on the other and surrounded by flowering trees – but it's hardly value for money, plus it's a long way to walk with a backpack.

Places to Eat

There are several inexpensive restaurants around the *matatu* park and market where you can get traditional staples like meat stews, matoke, beans and rice for less than US$0.20.

Otherwise, try one of the set lunches or the menu at either the *Saad Hotel* or the *Kaghesera Hotel*. The restaurant downstairs in the *Saad* is equally good value for breakfasts, lunch and dinner. Lunch is a huge, set-menu meal which you will be unable to finish (US$0.60) though you can also order a la carte (spicey liver and vegetables for US$0.25 or chicken stew for US$0.35, for example). The *Kaghesera* has its own restaurant with set lunches and a menu which is slightly cheaper than the Saad.

If you don't mind walking, you might also like to try a meal at the *Margherita Hotel*. The lunches are similar to those served at the Saad and you can pay for meals in shillings.

Entertainment

Kasese has two good bars if you want to enjoy a cold beer. One is the *Summit Club Bar* on Speke St and the other is an unnamed place on Stanley St opposite the Uganda Commercial Bank (indicated on the street map). The *Saad Hotel* does not serve beer since it's owned by Muslims.

At one time the *Golf Club* (on the other side of the golf course from the Margherita Hotel) used to have a bar and a disco on Saturday nights but it had been badly vandalised and was closed in mid-1986. The golf course itself is well maintained so it's likely the club house will be repaired before long. It would be worth making enquiries to see if there's anything going on there.

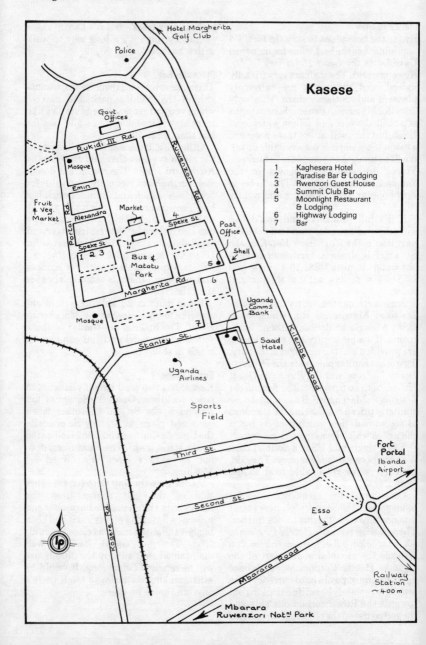

Kasese

1 Kaghesera Hotel
2 Paradise Bar & Lodging
3 Rwenzori Guest House
4 Summit Club Bar
5 Moonlight Restaurant & Lodging
6 Highway Lodging
7 Bar

Getting There

Road Between Kampala and Kasese, there are three buses per week in either direction (on Monday, Wednesday and Friday in the early evening) which cost US$3.20 and take about 12 hours. It's advisable to buy a ticket before the day of departure if possible as there's considerable demand for them. They are more expensive than the train, even in 1st Class Special, but the train takes longer.

Matatus run between Kasese and Fort Portal; the fare is US$0.60 and the journey takes about 1½ hours.

There is now a daily bus in either direction between Fort Portal and Kabale via Kasese and Mbarara. Going south, it leaves Kasese at about 9 am. The fare is US$2 and the journey takes about 9½ hours between Kasese and Kabale. You can also do the journey by *matatu* but there's much less room (important if you have a backpack) and they're not as safe as the buses. The last part of the journey going south crosses a mountain pass from which, weather permitting, you'll be rewarded with spectacular views to the west of the volcanoes along the Uganda/Rwanda border.

Rail There are two trains per day between Kampala and Kasese, in either direction. One of them is an Economy Class-only train and the other is a 1st/Upper Class-only train. The Economy train departs Kampala and Kasese at 4 pm and arrives at 7 am the next day. The 1st/Upper Class train departs Kampala at 7 pm (arriving at 10 am the next day) and departs Kasese at 8.30 pm (arriving at 11.30 am the next day). These trains can be up to 2½ hours late at their final destination so don't rely on the official arrival times. The fares are US$3 (1st Class Special); US$2.20 (1st Class); US$1.20 (Upper Class); US$0.50 (Economy).

MASAKA

In 1979 Masaka was virtually destroyed by the Tanzanian army in the closing stages of the war which ousted Idi Amin. Rebuilding is gradually taking place but most of the remaining lodges are on the main street.

There's very little to do in Masaka and for most travellers it's just a way station; it's from here that you can visit the Sese Islands in Lake Victoria.

Places to Stay & Eat

A good place to stay in Masaka is the *Masaka Safari Lodge* about three minutes' walk from the bus station. It's very clean and costs US$0.70 a double.

About 20 km east of Masaka is Lake Nabugabo where you can stay at the *Church of Uganda Holiday & Conference Centre* where there are bandas for hire for US$1.20 per night. The proprietors are very pleasant and there's also a beautiful camp site.

SESE ISLANDS

These islands lie off the north-western shores of Lake Victoria. Masaka is the jumping-off point if you want to visit them.

Places to Stay

For somewhere to stay, ask at the missions in Kalangula or take a room in one of the few simple lodges.

Getting There

To get to them you must first go by *matatu* from Masaka to Bukakata on the lake shore from where there is a daily ferry (except weekends) to Bugala Island where the main town, Kalangula, stands. The ferry generally leaves about 8 am. If you miss the ferry at Bukakata and have to stay the night, ask around for somewhere to stay. There *may* be a bus from the ferry jetty on Bugala Island to Kalangula but otherwise you will have to walk or hire a bicycle.

MBARARA

There's little of interest in Mbarara itself and there was a lot of destruction during the war but you may find yourself staying overnight if you're coming from or going to Kampala.

Places to Stay

Perhaps the best place to stay, and certainly one of the cheapest, is the *Church of Uganda Hostel* which many travellers have recommended. It's next to the bus station and near the market and costs US$0.20 for a bed in the dormitory.

If you don't want dormitory accommodation, try the *New Ankole Hotel* on the main road past the police station which costs US$1.20 a double with a bathroom and (usually) hot water. The hotel is set in beautiful grounds and has it's own good restaurant.

Getting There

Road The *matatu* fare from Kampala is US$2 and the journey takes 4½ to five hours. Mbarara is also on the route from Kampala to Kabale, and Fort Portal, so see the respective Getting There sections for more details.

KABALE

The tourist literature is fond of referring to Kigeza, the area in which Kabale stands, as the 'Little Switzerland of Africa', but it's not an appropriate description. This south-west corner of Uganda is certainly very beautiful with its intensively cultivated and terraced hills, forests and lakes but it reminded me much more of the hill stations of West Bengal, India. It doesn't, of course, offer breath-taking views of an endless range of massive, snow-capped mountains like you would find in Darjeeling, but there are equally impressive views of the Virunga chain of volcanoes from the summits of various passes (such as the one just before you drop down into Kabale on the road from Mbarara and from the Kanaba Gap, 60 km from Kabale on the road to Kisoro). There are also tea-growing estates all the way from Kabale to the Rwandan border at Gatuna.

The Kigeza is superb hiking country and the area is honeycombed with tracks and paths, hamlets and farms. A visit to Lake Bunyonyi is particularly recommended.

Kabale is Uganda's highest town (about 2000 metres) so it gets cool at night. Have warm clothes handy. Unlike many Ugandan towns further east, Kabale has been controlled by the NRA for a long time so it is in better shape than towns which were controlled by Obote's or Okello's troops.

Information

The Uganda Commercial Bank next to the post office won't change travellers' cheques so you'll have to ask around in the shops. Money changers (for cash) hang around at the Highlands Hotel and at the petrol stations opposite the Skyline Hotel.

Things to See

You can set off walking down any of the tracks in this area and let them take you where they will. There are always good views over the surrounding countryside and local people are very friendly and keen to stop and talk with you.

Perhaps the best trip you can make, however, is the one to **Lake Bunyonyi**, a famous beauty spot, over the ridge to the west of Kabale. It's a large and irregularly shaped lake with many islands and the surrounding hillsides, as elsewhere in this region, are intensively cultivated. Many of the villagers have boats and you shouldn't have any difficulty arranging a trip out onto the lake. There are two ways of getting to the lake. You can either walk all the way up and over the ridge from Kabale by picking your way through the tracks on the hillside (about three hours if you pick the right tracks) or you can hitch a ride on the road to Kisoro and get off where the road touches the lake (about half way). It isn't always easy to hitch to Kisoro but there are usually one or two *matatus* going there from outside the

Top: Hindu temple, Kampala, Uganda (GC)
Bottom: Street scene, Kampala, Uganda (GC)

Top: Kabale, Uganda (GC)
Bottom: Potholes, Kampala, Uganda (GC)

Capital Motel or post office in Kabale each morning. The fare to Kisoro is US$1.60.

Places to Stay – bottom end

If you are camping, there is a site close to the *White Horse Inn* which is free, but there are no facilities.

The cheapest place to stay in Kabale is *St Paul's Training Centre & Hostel* which is very friendly and costs US$0.30 for a bed in the dormitory and US$0.60 a double, but there are no showers. The Centre has been popular with budget travellers for a number of years.

Similar in price but fairly noisy because of the bar is the *Kabale Bar & Lodge* at the far end of the main street. It's a small place and very basic but you can get a cold shower.

For something better I'd nominate the *Capital Motel*, close to the post office, as the best value. Rooms cost US$2 a double and, although basic, clean sheets are provided and the communal showers have hot water in the mornings and evenings. There are clothes-washing facilities in the courtyard and clothes left to dry on the line don't disappear. There is an upstairs bar (usual prices) but the hotel doesn't have its own restaurant. If you have your own vehicle there's a compound where you can park which is locked at night.

Both the *Rubanza Restaurant & Lodge* and the *Paradise Hotel* are similar to the Capital and are on the main street. The *Rubanza Restaurant & Lodge* has its own good, cheap restaurant. More expensive, but convenient if you're taking a *matatu* to Rwanda in the morning, is the *Skyline Hotel* opposite the Shell and Agip stations on the town's main road junction.

Places to Stay – middle

The *Highlands Hotel*, at the far end of town, charges US$3 a double with a bathroom and toilet, and hot water is available. If there's no hot water in the taps, inform reception and they'll bring buckets of it to your room. It's a large place and will almost always have rooms available. The *Victoria Guest House*, at the back of the sports ground, is also popular with travellers. It is similarly priced to the *Highlands* and is equally comfortable. Both hotels have their own bar and restaurant.

Places to Stay – top end

Kabale's best hotel is the *White Horse Inn* up on the hill overlooking the town. It's one of the Uganda Hotels Corporation chain so theoretically you should pay in hard currency (US$27 a single!). Some travellers do manage to pay in shillings but this is not easy. It's perhaps one of the most attractive of the hotels belonging to this chain so it's worth staying if you can pay in local currency. The hotel has its own bar and restaurant.

Places to Eat

You can find a good breakfast (omelette, bread, tea/coffee) for US$0.15 at *Twincos* opposite the post office. They also serve lunches and dinners for around US$0.20. Many travellers recommend the *Rubanza Restaurant & Lodge* for good, cheap meals.

Perhaps the best value, however, given the street exchange rate, are the meals at the *Highlands Hotel* where there's often an open log fire burning in the evenings. Here you get a starched-white tablecloth and full waiter service in the dining hall. It's open to non-residents. The food is excellent and there's a choice of several main courses. A soup, main course and sweet will cost around US$0.60. Breakfasts aren't such good value, however. There's also a large, separate bar where you can get the usual drinks as well as the house speciality – *banapo*, a banana wine said to be made by the hotel owner. It's worth trying and much cheaper than beer! The *White Horse Inn* also has a pleasant, comfortable bar.

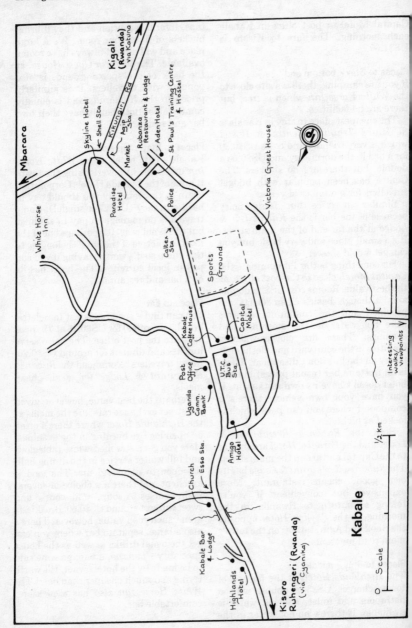

Kigali (Rwanda) via Katuna

Mbarara

Kikungiri Rd

Skyline Hotel

Shell Sta.

Market

A.S.P.

Rubanza Restaurant & Lodge

Aden Hotel

St Paul's Training Centre & Hostel

White Horse Inn

Paradise Hotel

Police

Caltex Sta.

Victoria Guest House

Sports Ground

Interesting walking viewpoints

Kabale Coffee House

Capital Motel

Post Office

U.T.C. Bus Sta.

Uganda Comm. Bank

Church

Esso Sta.

Amigo Hotel

Kabale Bar & Lodge

Highlands Hotel

Kisoro Ruhengeri (Rwanda) via Cyanika

Kabale

Scale

0   ½ km

Getting There

Road There is now a daily bus in either direction between Fort Portal and Kabale via Kasese and Mbarara (going south it leaves Kasese at about 9 am). The fare is US$2 and the journey takes about 9½ hours between Kasese and Kabale.

You can also do the journey by *matatu* but there's much less room (important if you have a backpack) and they're not as safe as the buses. The last part of the journey crosses a mountain pass from which, weather permitting, you'll be rewarded with spectacular views to the west of the volcanos along the Uganda/Rwanda border.

Between Kabale and Kisoro there are usually a few *matatus*/pick-up trucks daily in either direction which cost US$1.60 and take about six hours. They leave from outside the Capital Motel/post office in Kabale. It's a spectacular route but rough in parts.

KISORO

Kisoro is in the extreme south-western tip of Uganda on the other side of the Virunga mountains from Ruhengeri in neighbouring Rwanda. Many travellers prefer to enter Rwanda this way rather than direct from Kabale. It's a beautiful area and the journey, on a rough road from Kabale, is both spectacular and, at times, hair-raising. Kisoro is also the place to come if you want to see mountain gorillas in Uganda. It works out much cheaper than in Rwanda but very few people have seen them here recently so don't build up your hopes too high.

Things to See

If you're interested in trying to see gorillas, get in touch with a man called Zacharia who has been taking travellers up the mountains in search of gorillas for years. He lives about two hours' walk from Kisoro at a village called Giterderi. To get there, take the road which goes to Rwanda past the Travellers' Rest and turn first right past the hotel. Carry on past the Rafiki Hotel and then take the left fork. This will lead you to Giterderi. Zacharia charges US$0.40 per day for his guide services which is excellent value, but you can't be guaranteed a gorilla sighting. If you have no tent he'll probably let you sleep on his floor the day before you set off.

Another man called Sahan Erizahari has also started to offer guide services recently, he lives at a village which you get to by taking the right fork in the road past the Rafiki Hotel. Make enquiries about him before you leave Kisoro.

Places to Stay

One of the cheapest places to stay is the *Centenary Hotel* which costs US$0.40 a single (there are only three of these rooms) and US$0.60 a double. It's popular with budget travellers. You can also find cheap rooms at the *Rafiki Hotel*.

For something more up-market go to the *Mubano Hotel* where you can rent a VIP suite (lounge and bedroom) for US$2 a double.

Kisoro's top-range hotel is the *Travellers' Rest*, one of the Uganda Hotels Corporation chain. As usual, payment must be in hard currency.

Places to Eat

You can get a very good breakfast at *Bufumbira's Bakery* for about US$0.30 (scrambled eggs, bread, margarine, tea/coffee). For lunch or dinner go to the *Mubano Hotel* which has its own restaurant and serves excellent food – about US$0.60 for lunch or dinner.

Getting There

Road Between Kabale and Kisoro, there are usually a few *matatus*/pick-up trucks daily in either direction. See the Kabale Getting There section for details.

The National Parks & Ruwenzori Mountains

KABALEGA NATIONAL PARK

Encompassing an area of 3900 square km, through which the Victoria Nile flows on its way to Lake Mobutu Sese Seko (formerly Lake Albert), Kabalega National Park used to contain some of the largest concentrations of game in Uganda. Unfortunately, poachers and the retreating troops of Idi Amin and then of Okello, both armed with automatic weapons, almost wiped out most species except the most numerous (or less sought-after) herd species. There are now no lions, only a few rhinos and one herd of elephants numbering around 20 individuals, although there are still plenty of Ugandan kobs, buffaloes, hippos and crocodiles. The game is recovering slowly from the onslaught but it will be a long time before it returns to its former state – if ever. Not only that, but many of the lodges were vandalised at the same time and the *Pakuba Lodge* is still unserviceable.

Despite all this it's probably still worth visiting Kabalega if only for the animals which are left and for the **Murchison and Karuma Falls** on the Victoria Nile within the park boundaries. Entry to the park is US$0.40 per day.

One of the big drawcards for a visit to Paraa is the boat trip up the Victoria Nile to the Murchison Falls where the river is constricted into a narrow crevice some seven metres wide from which it roars and cascades onto the rocks 45 metres below. Fish swept over the falls support a healthy community of crocodiles in the gorge below. The cost of the boat is US$6.50 (payable in shillings) so you need to get a group together to share the cost. Otherwise it's a 25 km walk with nothing much but buffaloes to keep you company. All the locals walk through the park so it's probably relatively safe to do this. You'd have to camp somewhere for the night. Some travellers do walk but you may have to overcome the objections of park officials.

Places to Stay

There are presently two places to stay within the park. The first is *Paraa Lodge* south of Pakwach. There is no regular transport to this lodge from Pakwach so you will have to hitch. Coming up from the south, you should be able to find transport (for example, a *matatu*) from Masindi to the lakeside town of Butiaba. From here there may be a ferry to Paraa but try to confirm this before you set off. If it's not operating you'll have to hitch the rest of the way.

The cheapest place to stay at Paraa is the *Education Centre* where you can get a dormitory bed for US$0.30 including the use of cooking facilities. Apart from this you'll have to stay at the *Paraa Lodge* itself but that's going to be very expensive because it's part of the Uganda Hotels Corporation and you must pay in hard currency. Bring food with you unless you want to eat at the lodge – its relatively

Ugandan wooden bicycle

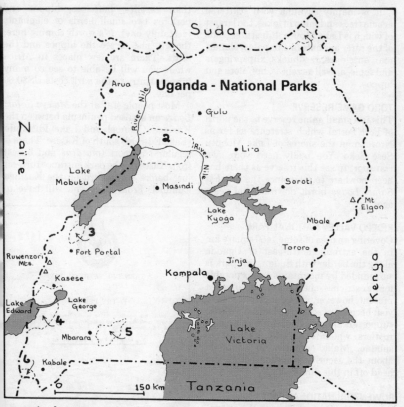

Uganda - National Parks

1. Kidepo National Park
2. Murchison Falls/Kabalego National Park
3. Toro Game Reserve
4. Queen Elizabeth/Ruwenzori National Park
5. Lake Mburo National Park
6. Gorilla Sanctuary

expensive but you can pay for meals in shillings.

The other place to stay is the *Chobe Lodge* on the east side of the park. The turn-off for the lodge is a little over half way between Masindi and Gulu and you will have to hitch since there's no regular transport. At Chobe you have the choice of sleeping on the floor of the museum for US$0.10 or camping for US$0.06. The *Chobe Lodge* itself is part of the Uganda Hotels Corporation so you have to pay in hard currency. Meals are available at the lodge and you can pay in shillings.

The *Chobe Lodge* overlooks Goragung Falls which are about 15 km downstream from the Karuma Falls.

LAKE MBURO NATIONAL PARK

Situated between Mbarara and Masaka and covering an area of 290 square km, this is Uganda's newest national park. It was gazetted in 1983.

It is mainly savanna with scattered acacia trees and some 14 lakes, the largest of which is Lake Mburo. It features some of the rarer animals like impalas, elands, roan antelopes, reedbucks, klipspringers and topis, as well as zebras, buffaloes and hippos.

TORO GAME RESERVE

This is a small game reserve to the north of Fort Portal which stretches as far as Ntoroko on the shores of Lake Mobutu Sese Seko. You really need your own transport to see this reserve as there has been nowhere to stay since the *Semliki Safari Lodge* burnt down several years ago.

KIDEPO VALLEY NATIONAL PARK

Covering an area of some 1450 square km in the extreme north-east of Uganda along the border with Sudan, this park is surrounded by mountains and is notable for its ostriches, cheetahs and giraffes. At present, however, it's a dangerous area to visit because of scattered bands of Okello supporters and so-called Karamoja cattle rustlers which the NRA has yet to subdue. Make enquiries in Kampala about the security situation before you head off in this direction.

RUWENZORI NATIONAL PARK

Formerly the Queen Elizabeth II National Park this reserve covers an area of 2000 square km and bordered to the north by the Ruwenzori mountains and to the west by Lake Idi Amin (Lake Edward). The Ruwenzori National Park used to be a magnificent place to visit. It used to have great herds of elephants, buffaloes, kobs, waterbucks, hippos, topis and, in the south around Ishasha, tree-climbing lions. Like Kabalega, however, much of the game was wiped out by Amin's and Okello's retreating troops. The Tanzanian army, which occupied the country for a while after Amin's demise, also did their ivory and trophy hunting best. There's now very little game in the park other

than gazelles, buffaloes, hippos and perhaps two small herds of elephants (certainly one). It's worth coming here, though, just to see the hippos and the birds. There are few places in Africa where you will be able to see so many hippos. Entry to the park costs US$0.60 per day.

Most people stay at the *Mweya Safari Lodge* on a raised peninsula between the Kazinga Channel and Lake Idi Amin (Lake Edward) south of Kasese. There is regular transport (*matatus* and buses) from Kasese to the park entrance turn-off just before Katunguru on the Kazinga Channel. From there you will have to

RWENZORI NATIONAL PARK

ENTRY PERMIT

The bearer has permission to be in the Rwenzori National Park subject to the conditions as set out in the National Parks Act, 1964, and the Bye-laws of the Rwenzori National Park (under section 12 of the Act).

You enter this Park at your own risk

Non-Resident
Adult Fee   *Signed* ....
Shs. 30 1000/-   *Warden, Rwenzori National Park.*

Date 18/4/85

GPRU—P. 508—200 bks.x100—8-74.

1422

hitch and there's not a lot of traffic (this is the road to Katwe, Mpondwe, Kasindi and Beni – the latter two in Zaïre). There's even less traffic from the turn-off, on this road, to the Lodge. The entry gate is at the turn-off to the lodge. Local people walk the last stretch (about seven km) but park officials are extremely reluctant to allow visitors to do this. Nevertheless, most travellers seem to make it in a morning or an afternoon.

Every visitor here takes a launch trip

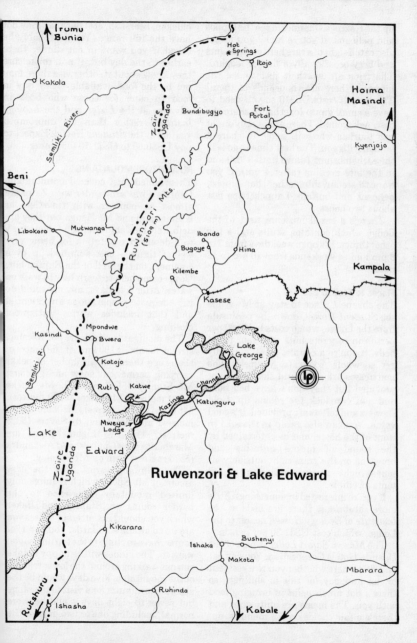

Ruwenzori & Lake Edward

up the Kazinga Channel to see the hippos and pelicans. If you're lucky you might also catch sight of a rare herd of elephants and *very* occasionally a lion or leopard. The trips are worth it just to see the hippos – there are thousands of them! The launch costs US$10 so you need to have a small group together to share the cost. Ask around. There are usually one or two tourists who will agree to share a launch with you. The best time to go is in the early morning (dawn until 9 am) and in the late evening (after 4 pm), if you want to see anything other than hippos, pelicans and buffalo. Launch trips last about two hours.

There's a small museum next to the Lodge which contains skulls and a few other things. It's open weekdays from 3 to 6 pm and at weekends from 10 am to 12 noon.

Places to Stay to Eat
The cheapest place to stay at Mweya is the *Student Hostel*, down the peninsula from the Lodge, which costs US$0.60 per person in concrete huts with four to six beds. If you're a couple, you'll normally get a whole room to yourself. The mattresses are dirty and sheets are not provided but they don't have bed bugs and you can lock the rooms up. Cold showers and toilets are provided. It's good value. You can also camp in the area in front of the hostel and be entertained by the sound of hippos grunting and browsing on the grass right outside your tent at night – they generally don't regard tents as edible.

If you're interested in something a little more salubrious, there are beds at the *Institute of Ecology Hostel*, nearer to the Lodge, which cost US$1.30 per person.

The *Mweya Safari Lodge* is part of the Uganda Hotels Corporation. You can eat and drink here whether you're a resident or not and pay for this in shillings, so there's not much point in bringing food with you. The meals are quite good and there's a fair choice on the menu (soup,

chicken, beef, fish, etc) but they may not have the full range. You'll probably be asked if you want to eat dinner there earlier in the day but, if not, make sure they know about it, otherwise there may not be the food available. They buy in food to cater for those who book in advance at the *Lodge* and the *Ecology Institute* rather than for impromptu visitors at the *Student Hostel*. Expect to pay US$0.60 to US$1.10 for dinner.

RUWENZORI MOUNTAINS
These fabled, mist-covered mountains on Uganda's western border with Zaïre are almost as popular with travellers as Kilimanjaro and Mt Kenya but they are definitely harder to climb and they have a well-deserved reputation for being very wet at times – best summed up by a comment on the wall of the Bujuku hut, 'Jesus came here to learn how to walk on water. After five days, anyone could do it.' Adequate preparations are essential and that includes warm, waterproof clothing.

The mountains, which are not volcanic, stretch for about 100 km. At the centre of the range there are a number of peaks carrying permanent snow and glaciers: Mt Stanley (5590 metres), Mt Speke (5340 metres), Mt Baker (5290 metres), Mt Gessi (5156 metres), Mt Emui (5240 metres) and Mt Luigi di Savoia (5028 metres). The two highest peaks are Margherita (5590 metres) and Alexandra (5570 metres) both on Mt Stanley.

The climbing varies from the easy ascent of Mt Speke which requires only limited mountain experience to the harder routes on Stanley and Baker which you should not attempt unless you are up to alpine standards. You don't, of course, have to climb to the top unless you want to. The guides will be happy to take you out walking around the lower reaches of the mountains. Five days would be the absolute minimum for a visit to the range but seven to eight days would be more normal, including one or two days at the top huts. The best times to go climbing are from late December to the end of February and mid-June to mid-August when there's little rain. Even at these times, however, the higher reaches of the mountains are frequently covered in mist, although this generally clears for a short time each day.

General Information

If you're a serious climber it would be worth buying a copy of, *Guide to the Ruwenzori* by Osmaston and Pasteur (Mountain Club of Uganda, 1972), before you come to Uganda. The only two places I know where you can buy this at present are the publishers, West Col Productions, 1 Meadow Close, Goring-on-Thames, Reading, Berks, UK, and at Stanfords Map Centre, Long Acre, Covent Garden, London WC2, UK. It costs £8.95 plus postage.

To set up a climb you first need to get in touch with John Matte, the Mountain Club agent who is in charge of arrangements for huts, guides and porters. It's best to book at least one week in advance if you want to be sure of starting on a certain day but, if it's not busy, treks can usually be arranged with just a few days' notice. The address is John Matte, PO Box 276, Kilimbe, via Kasese, Uganda.

Having made arrangements for the climb you need to assemble all the food, equipment and medicine which both your party and the guides and porters will need. All that's available at the starting point, Ibanda, is an extremely limited choice of local foodstuffs and even these are in short supply. You must get supplies in either Kasese or Fort Portal. Current food requirements for each guide/porter are: one kg of casava per day; one kg of smoked fish per day; one pint of powdered milk; one pint of cooking oil; about 200 grams of sugar per day, increasing to 1½ kg for a week; 500 grams of ground nuts for a four-day trip, increasing to 1½ kg for a week; 50 grams of tea for four days, increasing to 100 grams for five days to a

week; and 60 grams of salt for four days, increasing to 120 grams for five days to a week.

You also need to supply cigarettes (minimum of four per day per guide/ porter – 'Sportsman' are the preferred brand) as well as a blanket and pullover. These can be rented from John Matte (blankets US$0.40 and pullovers for US$0.15). No footwear is necessary for guides/porters as far as Bujuku hut (4400 metres) but above this level any of them who wear their own boots are entitled to an allowance of US$0.05 per day.

Suggested medicines are aspirin (for headaches and insomnia caused by mountain sickness), adhesive plaster and bandages, an antiseptic lotion (eg Dettol).

Be aware of the dangers of high altitude sickness. In extreme cases it can be fatal. High altitude sickness usually becomes noticeable above 3000 metres, and is a sign of your body adjusting to lower oxygen levels. Mild symptoms include headaches, mild nausea, and a slight loss of coordination. Symptoms of severe altitude sickness include marked loss of coordination, severe nausea, severe headaches, abnormal speech and behaviour and persistent coughing spasms. When any combination of these severe symptoms occurs, the afflicted person should descend 300 to 1000 metres *immediately*. When trekking, such a descent may even have to take place at night. There are no known indicators as to who might suffer from altitude sickness (fitness, age and previous high altitude experience all seem to be irrelevant), and the only cure is immediate descent to lower altitudes.

Your own equipment should include plenty of warm and waterproof clothing, sleeping bags, strong boots (John Matte has some very old and very heavy climbing boots for hire – definitely not recommended), a compass, primus stove and lamps. Guides and porters will not go onto the glaciers without being provided with proper clothing and footwear and, if you're going to do this, you'll also need to provide ice axes, ropes and crampons (which can be hired from John Matte for US$0.15, US$0.30 and US$0.15 respectively per trip).

Wages are: Guide (US$0.40 per day); Interpreter (US$0.35 per day); Porters (US$0.20 per day). Work on glaciers qualifies for double pay. Any porters discharged on the climb are entitled to the following compensation rates: from Nyabitaba (½ day); from Gigo or Nyamuleju (one day); from Bujuku (two days). Watchmen are available to look after motorcycles and vehicles at the Mountain Club at Ibanda at US$0.35 per day. Porters carry a maximum of 22 kg excluding the weight of their own blankets and clothing. Guides do not carry loads.

The total cost of going up the Ruwenzori shared between a party of five or six people is about US$12 per person per day, assuming you don't have to rent sleeping bags, waterproof clothing, boots, etc, and you change money at the prevailing street rate of exchange.

Ibanda

The take-off point for a climb is the Mountain Club at Ibanda about 22 km from Kasese. To get there you need to head down the road to Fort Portal for about 10 km and then turn left where you see a sign for 'Rwenzori High School' and 'Bugoye Sub-Dispensary'. There's also an electrical sub-station by the turn-off. There's plenty of transport as far as the turn-off but the remaining 12 km along a gravel road to Ibanda are very difficult to hitch. You may have to walk. People along this road are very friendly and there is warm beer (but no sodas) available at the tailor's shop in Bugoye. If you're bringing everything with you for a trek it would be worth hiring a *matatu* from Kasese to take you to Ibanda.

The *Mountain Club* is actually a very grandiose title for what is, in effect, little more than a filthy hovel with even filthier beds full of bed bugs which will cost you

US$0.20 for a bed or US$0.10 to sleep on the floor. If you can possibly bring a tent with you then do so and camp next to the 'Club' (US$0.10). Isn't it time you cleaned up the 'Club', John? Mrs Matte will cook reasonable meals for visitors depending on what's available. There's a clean river which runs close to the back of the 'Club' which is alright for washing in. Bags and excess gear left at the 'Club' can be safely locked up. There is electricity at Ibanda but no telephone.

The Huts

Most parties walk up the Mubuku and Bujuku valleys to the central peaks staying overnight at various huts. Some of these are in relatively poor shape and the lower huts no longer have any equipment in them because of past thefts. Starting from Ibanda the huts are:

Nyabitaba hut (2651 metres) This is the first stage. It's a two-room aluminium hut, built in 1951, with a wooden floor but no bunks. There's a rock shelter nearby and an aluminium lean-to for cooking. Firewood and water may not be available and you may have to walk a long way to find it.

Nyamuleju hut (3322 metres) This is the second stage. It's a single-room Nissen-type hut with bunks which will sleep up to eight people. There's a rock shelter and water supply close by.

Bigo hut (3707 metres) This is an alternative second stage hut. It's a round aluminium hut erected in 1951 with floor and bunks added nine years later. It will sleep up to 12 people. There's a good rock shelter and water supply close by. Firewood is available in the vicinity for open-air cooking in fine weather.

Bujuku hut (4281 metres) This is the third stage. There are two huts here – an older Nissen-type hut with four wooden bunks built in 1948 and another with large double-tier wooden bunks built in 1957 and extended in 1967. Apart from the bunks there is room for four to sleep on the floor of the first hut and six on the floor of the new hut. Each hut is provided with a wood stove but firewood is often very damp. There's a good water supply and the porters' rockshelter is about 10 minutes' walk below the hut.

Rwanda

Many travellers come to Rwanda, principally to visit the Parc National des Volcans in the north, where the borders of Rwanda, Uganda and Zaïre meet. The thickly forested slopes are one of the last remaining sanctuaries of the mountain gorilla. Like Burundi, Rwanda is one of the most densely populated countries on earth and in order to feed the people, almost every available piece of land, except for the Akagera along the border with Tanzania and the higher slopes of the volcanoes, is under cultivation. Since most of the country is mountainous, this involves a good deal of terracing and the banded hillsides may well remind you of Nepal or the Philippines. Tea plantations take up considerable areas of land in certain parts.

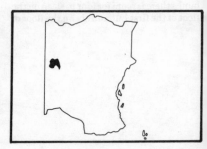

HISTORY
Early Settlement
As in neighbouring Burundi, the original inhabitants of Rwanda, the Twa pygmies, were gradually displaced from 1000 AD onwards by migrating Hutu tribespeople who, in turn, came to be dominated by the Watutsi from the 15th century onwards. The Watutsi used the same methods for securing domination over the Hutu as in Burundi, namely, the introduction of a feudal land system and a lord-peasant relationship with regard to services and the ownership of cattle which represented wealth. However, the similarities with Burundi end there. The Rwandan *mwami's* (king's) authority was far greater than his opposite number in Burundi and the system of feudal overlordship which developed was unsurpassed outside of Ethiopia.

Not only was the Rwandan *mwami* an absolute ruler in every sense of the word with the power to exact forced Hutu labour and to allocate land to peasants or evict them from it but the Watutsi

overlordship was reinforced by ceremonial and religious observances. Military organisation, likewise, was the sole preserve of the Watutsi. Rwanda, however, was more intensively farmed than Burundi and, in the process of growing food on all available land, the Hutu eventually denuded the hills of tree cover. The consequent land erosion, lack of fuel and competition for land with the Watutsi pastoralists, frequently threatened the Hutu with famine. Indeed, in the 20th century alone there have been no less than six famines.

Faced with such a narrow margin of security, something was bound to give sooner or later among the Hutu who, in this country, account for some 89% of the population. The process was interrupted, however, by the colonial period.

The Colonial Era
In 1890 the Germans took the country and held it until 1916 when their garrisons surrendered to the Belgian forces during WW I. At the end of the war, Rwanda was mandated to the Belgians along with Burundi, by the League of Nations. From then until independence, the power and privileges of the Watutsi were increased as the Belgians found it convenient to rule indirectly through the *mwami* and his princes. They were not only trained to run the bureaucracy but had a monopoly on

the educational system operated by the Catholic missionaries. The condition of the Hutu peasantry meanwhile deteriorated and led to a series of urgent demands for radical reform in 1957. Power and its props are rarely given up voluntarily in Africa, however, and in 1959, following the death of Mwami Matara III, a ruthless Watutsi clan seized power and set about murdering Hutu leaders.

Independence

The Watutsi power grab was a serious miscalculation and it led to a massive Hutu uprising. Some 100,000 Watutsi were butchered in the bloodletting which followed and many thousands more fled into neighbouring countries. The new *mwami* likewise fled into exile. Faced with carnage on this scale, the Belgian colonial authorities were forced to introduce political reforms and when independence was granted in 1962 it brought the Hutu majority to power under Prime Minister Gregoire Kayibanda.

Certain sections of the Watutsi, however, were unwilling to accept the loss of their privileged position. They formed a number of guerilla groups which mounted raids on Hutu communities but this only provoked further Hutu reprisals. In the bloodshed which followed, thousands more Watutsi were killed and tens of thousands of their fellow tribespeople fled to Uganda and Burundi. Since those dark days, things have cooled down though there was a resurgence of anti-Watutsi feeling in 1972 when Hutu tribespeople were being massacred in neighbouring Burundi. Disturbances in Rwanda during this time prompted the army commander, Juvenal Habyarimana, to oust Kayibanda. He has ruled the country ever since.

POPULATION

The population is something over five million.

ECONOMY

The economy is agriculture based with coffee by far the largest export, accounting for about 80% of export income. Tea is also important. The country is a major recipient of international aid, particularly from the Peoples Republic of China and you may well come across Chinese aid

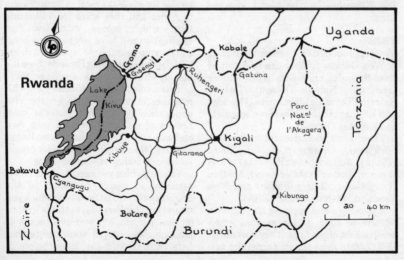

workers engaged on various projects, usually agricultural or hydro-electric.

GEOGRAPHY

Rwanda's mountainous terrain occupies a total area of 26,338 square km.

FESTIVALS & HOLIDAYS

1 January (New Year), 28 January (Democracy Day), Easter Monday, 1 May (Labour Day), Ascension Day, Whit Monday, 1 July (National Day), 5 July (Peace and National Unity Day), 15 August, 25 September (Kamarampaka Day), 26 October (Armed Forces Day), 1 November (All Saints Day), 25 December (Christmas).

Many shops and offices tend to be closed between 1 July and 5 July.

LANGUAGE

The national language is Kinyarwanda. The official languages are Kinyarwanda and French and you'll be able to get along in most areas with French. Kinyarwanda is the medium of school instruction at primary level; French at secondary level (only some 8% of the population reach secondary level). Little English is spoken but KiSwahili can be useful in some areas.

VISAS

Visas are required by all except nationals of West Germany. Visas can be obtained from Rwandan embassies in Bujumbura (Burundi), Nairobi (Kenya), Dar es Salaam (Tanzania), Kampala (Uganda) and Kinshasa (Zaïre). There is a consulate in Mombasa (Kenya).

There are also embassies in Brussels (Belgium), Ottawa (Canada), Cairo (Egypt), Addis Ababa (Ethiopia), Paris (France), Bonn (West Germany), Abidjan (Ivory Coast), Tokyo (Japan) and New York and Washington DC (USA).

If possible avoid applying for your visa outside of East Africa as they often involve a lot of red tape. They cost about US$12.50 in most countries, require two

photos, allow a one month stay and generally take 24 hours to issue. In Tanzania they're a bit cheaper if you're paying in local shillings bought on the street market. If you are intending to go to Zaïre and Burundi it's a good idea to request a multiple entry visa on the application form (no extra cost for this). The reason being that the most convenient route between Bukavu (Zaïre) and Bujumbura (Burundi) is via Rwanda and – even though only one-third of the road is through Rwanda and you have no intention of getting off the bus, truck or car you are in – you *may* need a Rwandan visa to pass through. Rwandan transit visas cost about US$10 so you might as well apply for a tourist visa in the first place.

Tourist visas can be extended in the capital, Kigali, at the Immigration office, Rue du Commerce, next to the Air France office for about US$17.

Rwanda may be one of the smallest African countries but they like their red tape in large portions and in French. Visa application forms are like attempting *Lord of the Rings* on a one-hour lunch break. Don't be put off. You are, after all, paying for one of the most expensive visas in Africa and they know it. A separate form which comes with the visa application will have you signing a bond where you promise to spend at least US$20 per day whilst in Rwanda. Sign it – nobody wants to know when you get there or when you leave. The same goes with mistakes or 'don't knows' on the visa application form. You'll get the visa. Letters of introduction from your own embassy and onward tickets are no longer required. No-one will ask to see (or count) how much money you are carrying.

The only thing you need to think about carefully in regard to filling in the application form, is the date on which you intend to enter Rwanda, as this is written on the visa which is stamped into your passport. You cannot enter before that date (though you can leave before it

No. **57**   Date...1 4 - 3 - 19 86

Received from M .GEOFFREY CROWTHER.

the sum of Shillings...Quatre cents.............

(.Four hundred only.)

being payment of..visas n? 0555 x 0558/86

WITH THE... [REPUBLIQUE RWANDAISE]

By Cash/Cheque— For

Shs. ■■■■■■

[stamp: AMBASSADE DE ... NAIROBI]

---

expires). This *may* not be strictly enforced and I would imagine from my own and other's experiences at Gatuna (Rwanda/Uganda) that it isn't. But I wouldn't rely on that.

There are no Rwandan consulates at either Bukavu or Goma in Eastern Zaïre so it's advisable to get your visa in Kinshasa (or elsewhere) if you're coming from the west. Although, several travellers have reported that it's possible to get a *permit provisoir*, valid for one week (a sort of transit visa), for about US$46 on demand at the Goma/Gisenyi border or, assuming you have the time, a tourist visa from the Belgian Consulate in Goma for about US$17. The latter takes two weeks to issue and you have to leave your passport with them. The same may be true for the Belgian Consulate in Bukavu. The regulations about these things change constantly so don't rely on this possibility.

If you are travelling between Bukavu (Zaïre) and Bujumbura (Burundi), the most convenient (and comfortable) route is via Rwanda. You don't have to go this way as there is a road all the way through Zairois territory to Uvira, at the head of

Lake Tanganyika, where both routes converge. Many trucks use this route but the road isn't in good shape – Rwandan roads are surfaced most of the way, Zairois roads are not. Nevertheless, many travellers use the all-Zaïre route and in the past we've had a lot of letters from travellers who have taken the Rwandan route and been fleeced for a US$10 Rwandan transit visa at the border (in the absence of a Rwandan multiple-entry visa).

I took this route in a minibus from Bukavu to Uvira without a multiple-entry Rwandan visa. Not only did the Zairois authorities not want to stamp my passport on exit or re-entry – or the Rwandans on entry or exit – but I was never asked for a Rwandan visa (or a Zaïre visa for that matter). And I stood out as I was the only white person on the bus. I would suggest, though I cannot confirm, that the no-visa deal is connected with the minibus alone. It may be different if you are in a private car or hitching a ride on a truck. The driver of the minibus had a list of names and passport/ID numbers on a clip-board which had to be completed before we left

Bukavu but that was the extent of the red tape. We also had to state how much cash and travellers' cheques we each carried, but this was not checked. This could change.

Visas for Other Countries

Kigali, the capital, is a small city and most of the embassies are within easy walking distance of the centre.

Burundi Visas The embassy is on Rue de Ntaruka off Avenue de Rusumo. The staff here are abrupt and unhelpful. Visas must be applied for one week in advance and are only issued on Fridays. They cost about US$17 (Rfr 1500), require two photographs and are valid for a stay of one month.

Kenyan Visas The embassy is on the Boulevard de Nyabugogo just off the Place de l'Unite Nationale next to the Panafrique Hotel and is open Monday to Friday from 8.30 am to 12 noon and 2 to 4.30 pm. Visas cost about US$5, require two photographs and are issued in 15 minutes to one hour. No onward tickets or minimum funds are asked for.

Tanzanian Visas The embassy is on Avenue Paul VI close to the junction of Avenue de Rusumo. Visas generally take a week to issue though you can often get one in 24 hours if you enlist the assistance of your own embassy (some embassies will do this; others won't). Other travellers who have spent a lot of time hassling on their own generally make it in less than a week but, if you do this, you may need to show an onward ticket. There is a scale of charges for visas depending on your nationality. They are cheaper for French nationals at about US$8, a little higher for Germans and Swiss, between US$15 and US$17 for other nationalities. Two photographs are needed and the visas are usually for a three-month stay and single entry.

Ugandan Visas The embassy is on Rue de Kalisimbi opposite the Post Office. It's open Monday to Friday from 8 am to 12 noon and 2 to 5 pm but visa applications are only accepted on Monday, Wednesday and Friday. They are issued in 24 hours, cost about US$22, require two photographs and are valid for three months (multiple entry). Transit visas (valid

for six days) are free. Visas may be available at the Gatuna border (very easy-going) for about US$15 on demand but don't count on it.

Zaïre Visas The embassy is on Rue Depute Kamuzinzi off Avenue de Rusumo. One-month single-entry visas cost US$10; two-month multiple-entry visas cost US$17.50 and three-month multiple-entry visas cost US$22.50. Four photographs are required for any visa and they are generally issued in 24 hours. A letter of recommendation from your own embassy is generally not needed nor is an onward ticket, but these regulations change from time to time.

MONEY

US$1 = RFr 80

The unit of currency is the Rwandan Franc (RFr). It's divided into 100 centimes but you're very unlikely to come across centimes.

Travellers with only travellers' cheques are at a considerable disadvantage in Rwanda since the bank commission rates are little short of outright banditry. Even at the Banque Commerciale de Rwanda in Kigali it is RFr 250 (about US$2.80) per transaction. In other banks you can expect RFr 370 (about US$4.25) per transaction. On one occasion, my travelling companion was charged RFr 440 (about US$5) for changing a US$20 travellers' cheque at the Banque Commerciale de Rwanda in Gisenyi. The moral of the story is to bring cash to Rwanda and change it on the street market or in the shops. The best rates are to be found in Kigali and Cyangugu (around US$1 = RFr 115 to 120) and Gatuna (US$1 = RFr 110). The rates in Gisenyi are relatively poor (around US$1 = RFr 105) probably because there are a lot of rich expatriate Belgians who come here for their holidays and they have more money than sense.

The street market in Kigali is more or less controlled by a few individuals and, if you find it, you'll get about 10% above the rates quoted, though we obviously can't identify exactly where you will find those people. Try walking around the Rue de Travail or the Boulevard de la Revolution. You can often change money in *matatus* on the way to Kigali. You'll find quite a few people around the petrol station on the main street in Gisenyi who offer to change US dollars, Rwandan francs, Zaïres, etc but their rates are poor. If you desperately need money then make it a small transaction (Zaïre banking hours are 8 am to 12 noon Mondays to Fridays and there is no effective black market).

Expatriate residents report that travellers' cheques and bank cheques/drafts (US dollars preferred) can be changed on the street market and that if you have a US bank account some Indian merchants will even take personal cheques in US dollars. Expect RFr 110 to 120 to the US dollar.

The Banque National de Kigali will change US dollar bank cheques into Bank America US dollar travellers' cheques for a 1% commission. Rwandan banking hours are Monday to Friday from 8 to 11 am. Outside of these hours armed only with travellers' cheques you are in dire straits. Only the banks want them. Don't come to Rwanda without at least *some* cash.

Currency declaration forms are not issued at the border.

Credit cards are generally acceptable only in relatively expensive hotels and restaurants in such places as Kigali and Gisenyi. The most useful cards are American Express, Diners Club and Visa.

COSTS

Rwanda is expensive – possibly because of the dense population and the many expatriates. A lot of export earnings are spent importing food, drink and transport requirements for the expats. As a budget traveller you will be hard pressed even if you stay in mission hostels. There is no way you can exist here on a Kenyan,

Tanzanian or Ugandan budget and student cards are no use in Rwanda.

If you don't mind dormitory accommodation then you're looking at US$2.50 to US$3.50 per night without food. Accommodation in the national parks is more expensive. If you want a private room at the same places you're looking at US$7 to US$12.50 per night a double. Hotels, as opposed to mission hostels, are considerably more expensive and rarely worth the extra – at least at the bottom end of the market where hotels are little better than squalid flea pits. You're also likely to be woken up at dawn by the sound of chickens being strangled in preparation for lunch. There are exceptions, but not many.

Mission hostels seem to attract an exceptionally conscientious brand of people who take the old adage that 'Cleanliness is next to Godliness' almost like a Maoist slogan. It shows – you might not get hot water but your bed and room will be spotless. The one catch with mission hostels is that they're often full, particularly on weekends or in places where there is only one mission hostel in town.

The national parks will burn a hole in your pocket unless you have your own tent and, unlike Kenya or Tanzania, organised safaris don't cater for budget travellers. They cater for intrepid mega-dollar travellers with two or three weeks to spare and to whom expense is no object. A trip to the gorillas in the Parc National des Volcans is going to cost you an arm and a leg. You're looking at US$60 park entry fee including a guide plus about US$3 per person to camp (with your own tent – none for hire) or US$9 per person to rent a bed in one of the cottages at the park HQ (firewood extra). Add on food (no local restaurants) and transport (no buses – hitch and pay) and it works out at a very expensive, though memorable, three to four hours tête-à-tête with a family of mountain gorillas.

Transport (by minibus or *matatu*) and

food in a road-side restaurant is much the same price as in the rest of East Africa so long as you don't want meat with your meal. Meat will just about double the price. Anything on which culinary expertise has been lavished will cost you a week's budget living. If you have a yen for French cuisine, however, there are some excellent restaurants or so I'm told.

CLIMATE

The average daytime temperature is 24°C with a possible maximum of 34°C except in the highland areas where the daytime range is between 12 and 15°C. There are four discernible seasons: the long rains from mid-March to mid-May, the long dry from mid-May to mid-September, the short rains from mid-September to mid-December and the short dry from mid-December to mid-March.

It rains more frequently and heavily in rainforest covered volcano area of the north-east. The summit of Kalisimbi (4507 metres), the highest of these volcanoes, is often covered with sleet or snow.

NEWSPAPERS & MEDIA

There are two AM and five FM radio stations which generally broadcast in either Kinyarwanda or French. There are also programmes in KiSwahili. Newspapers and periodicals are published in the same two languages.

FILM & PHOTOGRAPHY

Bring plenty of film with you as it is very expensive and the choice will be extremely limited – usually only 64 and 100 ASA colour-negative film and then only in places like Kigali and Gisenyi. Slide film is almost impossible to find. If you do buy film check the expiry dates carefully.

If you are going to take photographs of the gorillas in the Parc National des Volcans you will need high speed film. It's often very dark in the jungle where they live so if you use normal film you're going to be very disappointed when it's developed. Film of 800 ASA which is capable of being 'pushed' to 1600 ASA is worth trying but it's not available anywhere in East Africa.

Don't take photographs of anything connected with the government or the military (post offices, banks, bridges, border posts, barracks, prisons, dams, etc). If anyone sees you doing this your film and maybe also your equipment will be confiscated. I walked up the hill at the back of the prison in Ruhengeri to take shots of the volcanoes late one afternoon (not knowing the prison was at the base of the hill) and before I knew it was escorted at gunpoint by three soldiers down to the prison to see the commandant. What did I think I was doing? Didn't I know it was strictly forbidden to take photographs of the prison? Was I a spy? Luckily, I speak reasonable French (and, on this occasion, necessity was the mother of invention where my memory failed me) and was able to convince the commandant that there was no subversive intent in my activities. Nevertheless, he wanted to see all my documents, retained my camera and film and told me to come back the next morning to see his superior.

I ended up talking to the lower echelons of the general staff the next day and, credit where it is due, they were as helpful as they could be given the constraints of their position. In the end, not only were they happy with just the film from the camera but they even promised to return to me any frames which didn't include the prison at the base of the hill. Unfortunately, I couldn't wait that long (the film had to be sent to Kigali for processing) so I asked the person who ended up dealing with this if he would forward them to me in Australia so long as I paid his expenses. I never expected to see them again but there they were when I returned home! That's quite something in Africa. I've heard stories of travellers who were not so fortunate. Be careful!

HEALTH

As with most African countries you should take precautions against malaria whilst in Rwanda but mosquitoes in general, are not a problem.

Expatriate residents suggest that you should take special care in Rwanda to avoid illness and/or treatment which could require a blood transfusion. A recent study of prostitutes in this country indicated that around 80% of them carry the AIDS antibody. If you think you'll need any injections whilst you're there buy your own brand new disposable syringe.

There is a lack of good dentists in Rwanda and they are very expensive. This may change soon as the Seventh Day Adventists are setting up a clinic in Kigali.

There are certain parts of Lake Kivu where it is very dangerous to swim as volcanic gases are released continuously from the bottom and, in the absence of a wind, tend to collect on the surface of the lake. Quite a few people have been asphyxiated as a result. Make inquiries or watch where the local people swim and you'll probably be safe. Bilharzia is also a risk in Lake Kivu. Stay away from shore areas where there is a lot of reedy vegetation and from slow-moving rivers.

It's advisable not to drink tap water. Purify all water you intend to drink except for water that you get from mountain streams and springs which you can be sure are above any human

habitation. Soft drinks, fruit and beer are available in the smallest places.

Other than the above precautions, you'll find Rwanda a fairly healthy place to live as much of the country is considerably higher than neighbouring Tanzania, Uganda and Zaïre. Cholera vaccination certificates are compulsory for entry/exit by air. Entering overland the check is cursory but they do ask about it.

GENERAL INFORMATION
Post
Overseas postal rates are relatively high. A postcard, for instance, will cost RFr 60 (well over US$0.50 at the official exchange rate).

Time
Rwanda time is GMT plus two hours.

GETTING THERE
You can enter Rwanda by air or road. There are lake ferries on both the Rwandan and Zairois sides of Lake Kivu but they connect only their respective sides of the lake.

Air
International airlines flying into Rwanda are Air Burundi, Air France, Air Tanzania, Air Zaire, Ethiopian Airlines and Sabena.

Air Rwanda flies internationally to Brussels (Belgium), Goma (Zaire) (once per week), Bujumbura (Burundi) (three times per week) and Mwanza (Tanzania) (once per week) from Kigali. There are occasional flights (subject to demand) to various places in Kenya, Uganda and other cities in Tanzania. Their main office (tel 3793) is on Avenue de la Revolution (BP 808, Kigali) opposite the USA embassy. They also have offices at Kigali airport (tel 5472), Butare (c/o SORIMEX, tel 274), Gisenyi (c/o Hotel Edelweiss, tel 282), Kamembe (c/o Garage Ruzimeca, tel 407), and Ruhengeri (c/o Umubano Tours Agency, tel 217). Air tickets bought in Rwanda for international flights are very expensive and compare poorly with what is on offer in Nairobi.

Road

To/From Burundi The main crossing point between Rwanda and Burundi is via Kayanza on the Butare-Bujumbura road. The road is sealed all the way. There are Peugeot shared taxis between Butare and the border for about US$4, minibuses from there to Kayanza on Tuesday, Friday and Sunday for about US$1.25 (otherwise hire a taxi), and daily minibuses from Kayanza to Bujumbura for about US$2.90.

To/From Tanzania From Rwanda to Tanzania you may encounter problems – at least in terms of time and frustration. There are no direct buses between Kigali or Rusumo and Mwanza. The nearest places in Tanzania that you can pick up buses to Mwanza are Ngara (25 km from the Rwandan border) and Biharamulo (110 km from the border). From Kigali you have two choices. Either you take a minibus to Kibungo (RFr 350) and from there a shared taxi to the border (RFr 200) or take the bus from Kigali at 7 am to Rusumo. From Rusumo (the border) you will have to hitch a ride to Ngara. From Ngara there is (petrol willing) a daily bus (except on Saturday or Sunday) to Mwanza. It leaves about 6 am and takes about 14 hours for the approximately 400 km trip.

Other travellers, with less regard for comfort, have suggested it is much easier to arrange all this in Kigali at the truck park. If you're interested, take a 'Gikondo' minibus from the Place de l'Unite National in Kigali about three km down the Boulevard de l'OUA (RFr 20) to the STIR truck park and ask around there. There are a lot of trucks which leave daily around 9 am for Tanzania from this place. Most of the drivers are Somalis and, if you strike up a rapport with them, then you may well get a free lift all the way to a

major city in Tanzania. If not, you're looking at about US$20 from Kigali to Mwanza. Attempting to hitch from Rusumo without an arranged lift is like heaving yourself out of quicksand without assistance.

To/From Uganda Between Rwanda and Uganda there are two main crossing points – Katuna/Gatuna (from Kabale) to Kigali and Cyanika (from Kisoro) to Ruhengeri. If going from Rwanda to Uganda, make sure you get there before 11 am as there is a one hour time difference between Rwanda and Uganda (so 11 am in Rwanda is 12 noon in Uganda) and the Ugandans take a *long* lunch break. The Gatuna border is very easy-going and is only 100 metres from the Ugandan post. There are frequent minibuses from the border to Kabale which take about 30 minutes and cost about US$0.30 (at the street exchange rate). From Kigali to Gatuna is a 2½ hour minibus journey at a cost of RFr 250. It's a beautiful trip passing through many tea plantations.

To/From Zaire The two main crossing points between Rwanda and Zaire are between Gisenyi and Goma (at the northern end of Lake Kivu) and Cyangugu and Bukavu (at the southern end of Lake Kivu). These borders are open (for non-Africans) between 6 am and 6 pm. For Africans they are open from 6 am until 12 midnight. There are two border crossing points between Gisenyi and Goma – the *Poids Lourds* crossing (a rough road) along the main road north of the ritzy part of town, and a sealed road along the lake shore. It's only two to three km either way. Minibuses run to the border along the Poids Lourds route but not along the lake shore. Along the latter you will have to hitch or walk.

If you have a camera the Zairois officials may try to extract a 'fee' for this. We suggest you ask a lot of questions and sweat this one out. The 'fee' is nonsense, it goes straight into their back pockets. If you pay, you'll be handed a 'receipt' written on official paper headed 'Republic of the Congo' with 'Congo' crossed out and 'Zaire' substituted in handwriting. Buy them a bottle of beer instead.

GETTING AROUND
Air
Internally, Air Rwanda flies from Kigali to Butare, Gisenyi, Kamembe and Ruhengeri, using Twin Otters but the flights to Butare and Gisenyi are subject to demand (you go on stand-by and, if there are enough passengers, the plane will leave). There is at least one daily flight to Kamembe and flights to Ruhengeri on Tuesday, Friday and Saturday.

Road
Rwanda used to be a rough country to travel through by road. This is no longer the case. There are now excellent sealed roads from the Gatuna and Cyanika (Uganda) borders to Kigali; Kigali to Ruhengeri and Gisenyi, Kigali to Bujumbura (Burundi) via Butare and Kayanza and Kigali to the Tanzanian border. The Butare to Cyangugu road was two-thirds sealed at the time this book was researched and due for completion in the next two years. The government has placed a high priority on sealing the Ruhengeri-Gitarama and Gitarama-Kibuye roads.

There are plenty of modern, well-maintained minibuses serving all these routes (many of them bearing the Japan-Rwanda assistance programme logo). You can almost always find one going the way you want to go between dawn and about 3 pm (depending on the distance) from the Gare Routiere in any town. Destinations are displayed in the front window and the fares are fixed (ask other passengers if you're not sure). Minibuses leave when full and this means when all the seats are occupied unlike in Kenya, Uganda, and Tanzania where most of the time they won't leave until you can't breathe for the people sitting on your lap and jamming the aisle. You should not be charged for baggage. Many of these minibuses have decent sound-systems so you might hear some good African music which isn't ear-splitting. There are also shared and private taxis though there's often little advantage in taking the former rather than a minibus. Private taxis are expensive.

Hitching
If you are hitching in Rwanda you may find a list of vehicle licence plates useful since they indicate the province of origin of the vehicle (though that doesn't mean they are going there!). They are: AB (Kigali); BB (Gitarama); CB (Butare); DB (Gikongoro); EB (Cyangugu); FB (Kibuye); GB (Gisenyi); HB (Ruhengeri); IB (Byumba); JB (Kibungo).

If looking for lifts on trucks to Uganda, Kenya, Burundi or Zaire from Kigali go out to MAGERWA (short for Magasins Generaux de Rwanda) in the Gikondo suburb about two to three km from the centre. You can have your pick of scores of trucks at the customs clearance depot here. To get there head down the Boulevard de l'OUA and turn right when you see the sign. It's sometimes possible to find a free lift all the way to Mombasa. Otherwise you're looking at RFr 5000 and to Bujumbura about RFr 500 including meals and maybe a few beers.

Lake Ferries
The ferries on Lake Kivu used to connect Rwandan ports with Zairois ports but these days Rwandan ferries only call at Rwandan ports and Zairois ferries only at Zairois ports. The small modern motor ferry, *Nyungwe*, covers the route Cyangugu, Kirambo, Kibuye, Gisenyi leaving Cyangugu at 7 am on Wednesday and Saturday (in the opposite direction make inquiries at the Hotel Izuba-Meridien. Gisenyi to Cyangugu costs RFr 780 and takes 9½ hours; Gisenyi to

Kibuye costs RFr 215 and takes about three hours; Kibuye to Cyangugu costs RFr 520 and takes about 6½ hours.

Kigali

The tourist organisation describes Rwanda as the 'Land of Eternal Spring'. It's a very appropriate motto and Kigali, the capital, displays it to the full. Built on a ridge and extending down into the valley bottoms on either side, it's a small but beautiful city with an incredible variety of flowering trees and shrubs. From various points on the ridge there are superb views over the surrounding intensively-cultivated and terraced countryside. The mountains and hills seem to stretch forever and the abundant rainfall keeps them a lush green. The area might remind you of such places as Sikkim in north-east India.

Many international organisations have bases here – the UN, FAO, EEC, for instance – and there is a large number of resident expatriates, mainly from Europe and the Far East so it's a fairly cosmopolitan city. Don't miss the Chinese embassy – it's one of the largest and most impressive buildings in the country and puts both the American and Russian embassies to shame. China funds a lot of aid projects here.

The only trouble with Kigali is that, unless you have friends or contacts who will introduce you to the social life of the city, there isn't much to do. Restaurants, bars and cafés where, in surrounding countries, you'd almost always be drawn into whatever was happening, are few and far between. European-style restaurants, in particular, tend to be well outside most travellers' budgets.

Information
Tourist Office The National Tourist Office (tel 6514) is on the Place de l'Independence on the opposite side from the Post Office

(PTT). It's open daily including Sundays and public holidays from 7 am to 9 pm. They have a lot of free leaflets (all in French) about the mountain gorillas, the volcanoes and other areas of interest as well as other booklets/leaflets for sale such as the *Passeport Touristique* (about US$3 – not worth it) and the *Parc National de l'Akagera* (worth it if you are going there). There's also a video of the volcanoes and the mountain gorillas which runs continuously.

Detailed maps of Rwanda (but not of Kigali) can be bought here though they're pretty expensive. If you want to be dealt with in a civil manner you must speak French. Budget travellers are often virtually ignored. Except for those groups which do not require prior reservations it is here that you must make your reservations to see the mountain gorillas in the Parc National des Volcans.

Bookshops & Libraries There are a few bookshops in Kigali, predominantly French language publications. The best is probably that on the Avenue de la Paix close to the junction with the Avenue des Milles Collines. Street maps of Kigali can be bought from bookshops for about US$1. The USA embassy has a library (English language books only) and will exchange books on weekdays from 8 am to 12 noon and 2 to 4 pm.

Embassies Diplomatic offices in Kigali include Burundi, Kenya, Tanzania, Uganda and Zaïre – see the visa section above. There are also embassies for Belgium, Peoples' Republic of China, Egypt, France, West Germany and the USA. There's a British consulate at 55 Avenue Paul VI.

Immigration Immigration is on the Avenue du Commerce next door to the Air France office in a building set back from the road.

Post The poste restante in Kigali is quite

well organised. They'll give you piles of letters corresponding to the first letters of both your given and surname to sort through. It's unlikely you'd miss anything which was sent to you for collection including parcels. Each letter you collect will cost you RFr 20.

Things to See
Apart from the tremendous views and pleasant walks available there's very little else to see or do in Kigali.

Places to Stay - bottom end
Mission Hostels Most travellers stay at the *Auberge d'Accueil* (tel 5625) at the Eglise Presbyterienne au Rwanda, 2 Rue Depute Kayuku. The staff are very friendly and the accommodation is excellent but they only have cold water showers. It costs RFr 300 for a bed in the dormitory, RFr 550 a single and RFr 1100 a double. The private rooms have their own wash basin and clean sheets are provided. They don't object to you doing your own laundry. Breakfast is available for RFr 150 (good value). Soft drinks and beer are available from the bar which is usually open in the early evening (otherwise ask one of the staff). The Auberge closes at 10 pm except by prior arrangement.

Equally popular, though a considerable way from the centre of town, is the guest house at the *Eglise Episcopale au Rwanda* (tel 6340), 32 Avenue Paul VI. The rooms are clean and bright and there are plenty of them so you should always be able to find accommodation. There's hot water in the showers and a large laundry area. A bed in one of the six triple rooms costs RFr 500 including breakfast (eggs, bread, coffee/tea). The three double rooms cost RFr 800 without breakfast. Lunch and dinner are available for RFr 350 and there's a small shop in the compound.

The *Mission Catholique*, Boulevard de l'OUA, no longer accepts travellers. *CCF Bornefonden*, Avenue de Rusumo beside the Tanzanian embassy, is a Scandinavian children's aid organisation but some travellers with a particular interest in the work they do have stayed there although it is not a hostel as such.

Hotels The cheapest hotel is the *Lodgement Metropole* (part of the restaurant of the same name), Rue de Travail, which costs RFr 550 a single and RFr 750 a double without own bathroom but it's a filthy place. Other travellers go to the *Town Hotel Restaurant* (tel 6690), Avenue du Commerce, which costs RFr 750 a single and RFr 1000 a double but, again, it's grubby and poor value in comparison to the mission guest houses. It does, however, have hot water showers. The *Bonjour Bar* is similar at RFr 500 a single and RFr 1000 a double.

Much better value, though more expensive, is the *Gloria Hotel* (tel 2268), Rue du Travail at the junction with Avenue du Commerce. This is a large place with clean, pleasant rooms costing RFr 1200 a single and RFr 1600 a double both with their own shower and toilet. There's hot and cold running water.

Two other mid-range hotels you might like to try are the *Panafrique Hotel* (tel 5056) and the *Hotel Bienvenue* on the Boulevard de Nyabugogo below the Place de l'Unite Nationale. The Panafrique costs RFr 1500 a double with own bathroom and hot water.

Places to Stay - top end
The rest of the hotels in Kigali are all top range. They are the *Hotel des Diplomates* (tel 5111/2), 43 Boulevard de la Revolution; *Hotel Kiyovu* (tel 5106), 6 Avenue de Kiyovu; *Hotel des Milles Collines* (tel 6530), 1 Avenue de la Republique; *Hotel Umubano-Meridien* (tel 2176), Boulevard de l'Umuganda, and the *Village Urugwiro* (tel 6656), Boulevard de l'Umuganda. Except for the Kiyovu (RFr 1800 a single and RFr 2400 a double), you're looking at RFr 4500 a single and RFr 5500 a double for these.

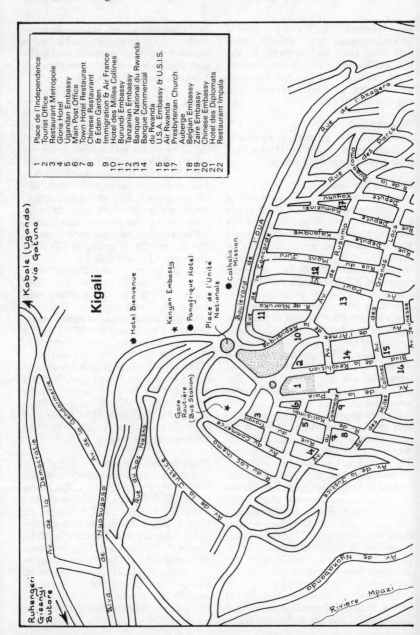

Kigali

Kabale (Uganda) via Gatuna

Ruhengeri / Gisenyi / Butare

● Hotel Bienvenue
★ Kenyan Embassy
● Panafrique Hotel
● Place de l'Unité Nationale
● Catholic Mission

Gare Routière (Bus Station)

Rivière Mpazi

1 Place de l'Independence
2 Tourist Office
3 Restaurant Metropole
4 Gloria Hotel
5 Ugandan Embassy
6 Main Post Office
7 Town Hotel Restaurant
8 Chinese Restaurant & Eden Garden
9 Immigration & Air France
10 Hotel des Milles Collines
11 Burundi Embassy
12 Tanzanian Embassy
13 Banque National du Rwanda
14 Banque Commercial du Rwanda
15 U.S.A. Embassy & U.S.I.S.
16 Air Rwanda
17 Presbyterian Church
18 Auberge
19 Belgian Embassy
20 Zaire Embassy
21 Chinese Embassy
22 Hotel des Diplomats
23 Restaurant Impala

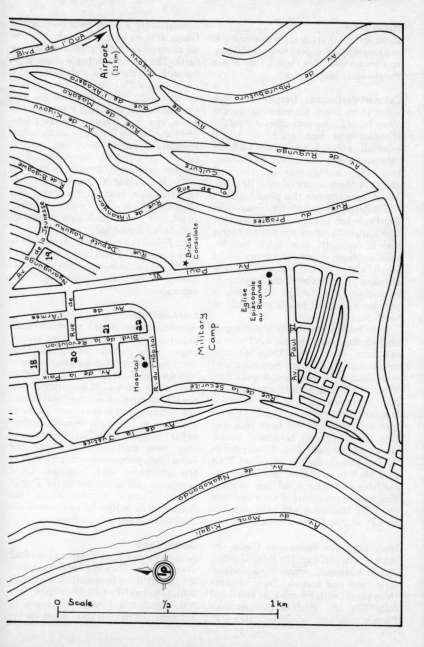

Places to Eat

If you're staying at one of the missions you can generally arrange all your meals there at a reasonable price though they're not the cheapest places to eat.

Cheaper Restaurants Despite the poor value of its hotel accommodation, the *Town Hotel Restaurant* offers some of the cheapest and best meals in Kigali especially at lunch time. There's a fairly extensive menu which includes chicken, beef, goat, beans, potatoes, rice and chips. Nothing is priced over RFr 100. Many travellers rate this place highly.

Similar places include the *Umuganda*, Rue Prefecture near the junction with the Rue Karisimbi, where you can get a large dish of spaghetti, rice, chips, *matoke*, peas, cabbage, carrots and sauce all for just RFr 100. Chicken is also available at the same price. Or there's the *Restaurant Metropole*, Rue du Travail, which is popular with local people especially at lunch time.

If you're staying at the Eglise Episcopale au Rwanda guest house but don't want to eat there, some good, cheap bars and restaurants are close by. Recommended is the *Restaurant Bambou*, Avenue Paul VI about 500 metres from the guest house. It's a fairly new place and the service is fast and friendly. Plates of stewed beef or goat with chappati and fresh peas cost RFr 125. They also have rice, beans, omelettes, tea and coffee. A lively bar in the same area is the *Bar Deviniere*. It's a good place to meet local people and you can have a lot of fun. Cold beers cost less here than in the centre of town and they also offer *brochettes* and roast potatoes for RFr 40. Ask for directions.

More Expensive Restaurants Going up-market, you could try the *Eden Garden*, Rue de Karisimbi, which offers western-style food and bamboo decor. Tilapia (Nile perch) with French fries and salad costs RFr 550. Beef or chicken with French fries and salad costs RFr 650.

Similar is the rooftop restaurant at the *Gloria Hotel* which offers a four-course set menu dinner for RFr 500 as well as a la carte. The Gloria also has a street level bar with outside tables and chairs.

Chinese food is expensive. *Le Yoyi*, Rue de Karisimbi, is the place to go. The Chinese menu (soup, fish, meat with hot sauce, rice and crepes) costs RFr 800. They also have a European menu (soup, chicken Provencal, French fries, crepes) for RFr 500 and an African menu (a chicken concoction) for slightly less.

The *Restaurant Impala*, Boulevard de la Revolution next to the Hotel des Diplomates, is also worth visiting. *Brochettes* are a lunch time speciality and there's a good bar.

La Fringale Restaurant, Avenue de la Paix close to the junction with Avenue des Milles Collines, is popular with well-heeled expatriate gourmets. It's expensive.

Entertainment

Apart from bars, there is not much cheap entertainment available. There are, of course, night clubs in the big hotels but apart from being expensive you need to be well dressed to get in. Jeans and T-shirts don't make it. It's worth enquiring at both the *US Information Service* (next door to the embassy) and at the *Centre Culturel Français*, Avenue de la Republique close to the Place de l'Unite Nationale to see if they have anything happening. The latter often puts on concerts and films in the afternoons and evenings. Local events are also advertised at the Tourist Office. There's a cinema on the Boulevard de la Revolution opposite the Banque Commerciale du Rwanda.

Getting There

Minibuses run from Kigali to towns all over Rwanda. They include Butare (RFr 400, about three hours), Gitarama (RFr 200), Kibuye (RFr 400), Ruhengeri (RFr 300, about two hours). Minibuses to Kibungo cost RFr 300 and take about 2½ hours, a backpack may cost half as much again on this route. See the various towns for more information.

Getting Around

Airport Transport The international airport is at Kanombe, 12 km from the city centre. A taxi there will cost RFr 1000 but you can get there cheaper by taking a minibus to Kabuga (RFr 30) and getting off at the airport turn-off. It's a 500 metre walk from there.

Lake Kivu

GISENYI

Gisenyi is a resort town for rich Rwandans and expatriate workers and residents. Their beautifully landscaped villas, plush hotels and clubs take up virtually the whole of the Lake Kivu frontage and are quite a contrast to the African township on the hillside above.

For those with the money, there's a wide variety of water sports available plus night clubs and restaurants. For those without, there are magnificent views over Lake Kivu and, looking north-west, the 3470 metre-high volcano of Nyiragongo. Swimming and sun-bathing on the sandy beach are also free. It's a pleasant town to stay in but, as you might expect, expensive, especially if you want some action.

Information

Visas There is no Zairois consulate here so you must obtain your visa elsewhere if intending to go to Zaïre. The nearest embassy is in Kigali.

Money If you are carrying only travellers' cheques, try to avoid having to change money at the banks here. Commission rates are outrageous (up to US$5 per transaction). Money changers (cash transactions only) approach all incoming minibuses. The rest of the time they can be found around the petrol station on the main street close to the market and the craft shops at the back of the Hotel Izuba-Meridien. The rates they offer are poor, about RFr 100 to the US dollar

Places to Stay – bottom end

There are a few small hotels up in the African part of town but they're hard to find (no signs) and the standard of accommodation is low. Most travellers stay at the Mission Presbyterienne's *Centre de Formation et d'accueil* (tel 397) about 100 metres from the market which costs RFr 300 per person. It's good value for money, clean and meals are available. The trouble with this place is that it's often full at the weekends – try to make a telephone booking in advance. If it is full, ask the staff about a Dutch family who live nearby and may offer accommodation if the centre is full.

Places to Stay – middle

Apart from the hostel there is nowhere cheap to stay in Gisenyi. Crossing the border to Goma in Zaïre would be the best proposition if you have a visa and want to save money. If you have to stay in Gisenyi, however, all the other hotels are down near the lake front. The most reasonably priced of them is the *Hotel Edelweiss* (tel 282) run by a Belgian and his Zairois wife. As the name suggests, it's built in the style of an alpine cottage and, although a fairly old building, it's homely and clean and the verandah is a delightful place to sit and have a beer and watch the lake. Rooms cost RFr 1300 a single and RFr 1700 a double with private toilet and hot shower.

Next up in price are the *Hotel Palm Beach* (tel 304) and the *Hotel Regina* (tel 263) both of them on the Avenue de la Cooperation – the palm-shaded lakeshore drive. They cost RFr 2200 a double with private toilet and hot shower. The Palm Beach doesn't have single rooms and the staff treat backpackers with considerable disdain (as do the clientele).

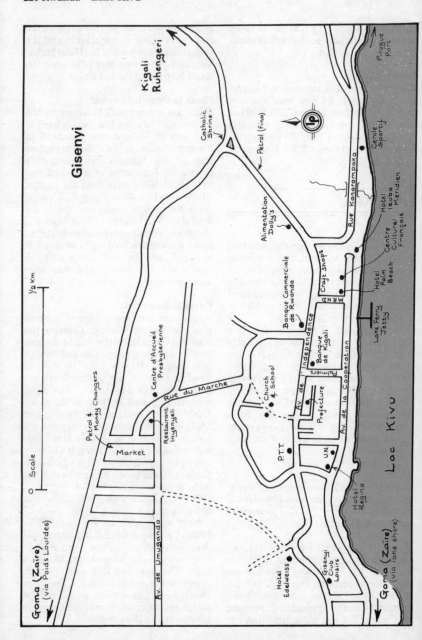

Places to Stay – top end

At the top end of the market is the *Hotel Izuba-Meridien* (tel 381). It's the equivalent of the Hotel des Diplomates in Kigali.

Places to Eat

There are a number of simple restaurants on the main road in the African part of town where you can get cheap meals (usually *matoke*, rice, beans and a little meat) but the standard isn't up to much. Much better is the *Restaurant Inyenyeli* opposite the Centre d'Accueil which has a reasonably priced, varied menu. Excellent, though expensive meals are available at the *Hotel Edelweiss* – RFr 1100 for a four-course lunch or dinner.

Alternatively you could put your own food together from the wide variety of fruit and vegetables available in the main market. Those suffering from super-market and delicatessen withdrawal symptoms should head off to *Alimentation Dolly's*, Avenue de l'Independence, if only to drool at the goodies for sale there. They also stock European cigarettes and liquor.

Entertainment

Check out the *Centre Culturel Français* next to the Hotel Palm Beach. They have a library, information about what's happening in and around Gisenyi and videos every Wednesday (at 3 pm) and Saturday (at 7 pm). Entry is free.

The *Cercle Sportif* right on the waterfront is worth visiting. You may find someone who will take you sailing. There's a bar where you can sit and enjoy the views across the lake. Entry for non-members costs RFr 100.

If you're looking for action at night, the *Gisenyi Club Loisirs*, close to the Hotel Edelweiss, is open to non-members and puts on rock bands on Saturday nights. Entry to the hall where the band plays costs RFr 400 but you can go into the bar free of charge if you want to check the music out first before paying.

Getting There

Air The Hotel Edelweiss is the agency for Air Rwanda.

Road Coming from Ruhengeri to Gisenyi a minibus takes about 1½ hours at a fare of RFr 150. It's a beautiful journey through upland forests and villages and finally there are panoramic views of Lake Kivu as you descend into Gisenyi.

KIBUYE

Kibuye is a small town about half way up Lake Kivu with an excellent beach and water sports facilities. It's a pleasant place to relax for a few days. If coming here from Gisenyi by road try not to miss the waterfall at Ndaba (Les Chutes de Ndaba) which is over 100 metres high.

Places to Stay

A very popular place among travellers is the *Hôme St Jean* about two km from town up the Kigali road. If you're not sure of the way ask at the Catholic church in town. The Hôme is on a superb site overlooking the lake and is excellent value at RFr 100 for a bed in the dormitory (RFr 50 for subsequent nights). They also have small singles without a view for RFr 400, beautiful upstairs singles with incredible views for RFr 600, upstairs doubles for RFr 800, triples for RFr 900 and rooms with four beds for RFr 1000.

The only other place to stay is the *Guest House Kibuye* (tel 181) which is right on the lake front. It's expensive at RFr 2200 a single, RFr 3100 a double and RFr 4200 a triple but it does have a good outdoor bar with cold beers for RFr 115 and a diving board which anyone can use.

Places to Eat

Excellent meals are available at the *Hôme St Jean* for RFr 300 (fish, potatoes and vegetables) and RFr 200 (meat, potatoes and vegetables). If you just want vegetables these cost RFr 80. Cold beers are available for RFr 100.

Otherwise there are two cheap places, the *Restaurant Nouveaute* and *Restaurant Moderne*, at the eastern end of town. They have the same menu (goat stew, beans, rice, potatoes, omelettes) and you can eat well from RFr 30. Cold beers are RFr 100 and soda RFr 25.

Getting There
From Kigali the road is partly sealed and minibuses cost RFr 400. The fare from Gitarama is RFr 250.

CYANGUGU
At the southern end of Lake Kivu and close to Bukavu (Zaire), Cyangugu is an attractively located town and an important centre for the processing of tea and cotton. Nearby is the Rugege forest, home for elephant, buffalo, leopard, chimpanzee and many other mammals as well as numerous birds. The waterfalls of the Rusizi river and the hot springs of Nyakabuye are also here and it's also the ferry departure point for other Rwandan towns on Lake Kivu – Kibuye and Gisenyi.

Places to Stay
A convenient place to stay if you're taking the ferry to Kibuye or Gisenyi (which departs at 7 am) is the *Hotel des Chutes* though it's quite expensive at RFr 1300 a single.

Getting There
From Butare the minibus fare is RFr 700 but it should become cheaper when the road is sealed.

North & South of Kigali

RUHENGERI
Most travellers come to Ruhengeri on their way to or from the Parc National des Volcans. It's a small town with two army barracks, a very busy hospital and magnificent views of the volcanoes to the north and west – Karisimbi, Visoke, Mikeno, Muside, Sabinyo, Gahinga and Muhabura.

Information
Money The banks here are open Monday to Friday from 7.45 to 11 am and 2 to 3 pm. Commission rates for travellers' cheques are about the same as in Kigali.

Post The post office is open Monday to Friday from 7.30 am to 12 noon and 2 to 3.30 pm. Service can be slow.

Places to Stay – bottom end
The cheapest place to stay and the one recommended by most travellers is the *Centre d'Accueil*, Avenue de la Nutrition close to the grass airstrip. The staff here are very friendly. A bed in the dormitory costs RFr 200 plus there are singles for RFr 400 and doubles for RFr 600. The private rooms are small and don't have their own toilet or shower but are very clean. The communal showers (cold water only) and toilets are scrubbed out daily. Excellent dinners are available (stewed meat, beans, cabbage, sauteed potatoes) for RFr 250 but the breakfasts aren't such good value at RFr 100 (tea, bread, margarine, jam). Cold beers are available (RFr 80) and there's a common room for residents. It's often full at weekends so if you're going to arrive there at that time try to make a booking by telephone.

Similar in price is the *Hôme d'Accueil*, Avenue du 5 Juillet, in the centre of town which has eight rooms. Meals are fairly expensive here at RFr 500 to RFr 650 for lunch or dinner.

If you want to camp enquire at the *Dutch Reformed Mission* at the northwest end of Avenue Mikeno.

Places to Stay – middle
Going somewhat upmarket there is the *Hotel Un, Deux, Trois* (tel 373), Rue Muhabura which costs RFr 650 a single. Doubles are also available. Meals cost

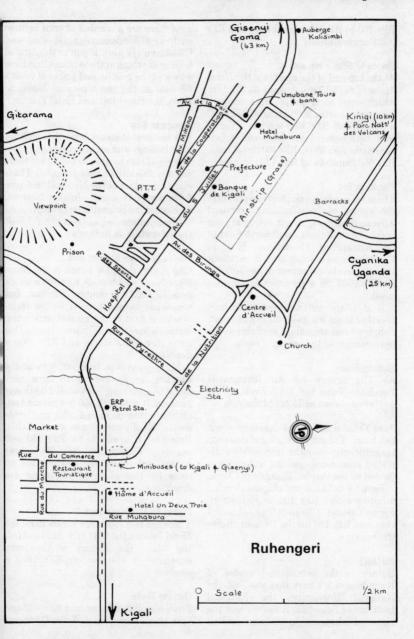

Ruhengeri

RFr 200 to RFr 300 (breakfast) and RFr 600 (lunch/dinner).

Places to Stay – top end

At the top end of the market is the *Hotel Muhabura* (tel 296), Avenue du 5 Juillet which even local people rate as very overpriced at RFr 2500 a single, RFr 3000 a double and RFr 3500 a triple all with own bathroom (hot water) and toilet. Meals cost RFr 250 to RFr 400 (breakfast), RFr 850 (lunch) and RFr 1200 (dinner).

Places to Eat

There are one or two simple restaurants in the centre of town offering standard African food if you're not eating at your hotel. For a splurge it's well worth going to the *Restaurant Touristique*, Rue du Commerce, where the food is excellent though you should expect to pay RFr 800 to RFr 1000 for a generous four-course meal.

If you are putting your own food together there's a good variety of meat, fish, fruit and vegetables available at the open market in the centre of town.

Getting There

Air The agency for Air Rwanda is Umubano Tours (tel 217), Avenue 5 de Juillet opposite the Hotel Muhabura.

Road From Kigali minibuses take about two hours. The road ascends and descends magnificently over the intensively cultivated mountains, passing aid projects funded by the Peoples' Republic of China.

From Cyanika (Rwanda/Uganda border) minibuses cost RFr 100 to Ruhengeri. From Gisenyi (Rwanda/Zaire border) they cost RFr 150 for the 1½ hour trip to Ruhengeri.

BUTARE

Butare is the intellectual centre of Rwanda and it's here that you find the National University, the National Institute of Scientific Research and the National Museum. In the surrounding area there are a number of craft centres such as Gihindamuyaga (10 km) and Gishamvu (12 km). If you're thinking of buying anything at these places first have a look at the quality and prices of what's for sale at the two top-range hotels in town, the Hotel Ibis and Hotel Faucon.

Things to See

The **National Museum** is worth a visit for its ethnology and archeological displays. They will also be able to tell you if there are any folklore dances planned. These often take place at the National Institute for Scientific Research – Institut National de Recherche Scientifique (INRS).

Those interested in trees should visit the **Arboretum de Ruhande**.

Places to Stay – bottom end

One of the cheapest hotels is the *Hotel Chez Nous* which costs RFr 500 a single and RFr 600 a double. Similar, but somewhat more expensive, is the *Hotel Weekend* next to the market and petrol station where the minibuses depart. This costs RFr 600 a single and RFr 1000 a double.

Many travellers, however, stay at the *Procure de Butare* which is a very attractive building surrounded by flower gardens. It costs RFr 400 per person and, although they do have double and triple rooms, usually only singles are available. Breakfast is available for RFr 150 and excellent dinners for RFr 250 (three courses, all-you-can-eat). There are no signs for this place so you must ask directions.

Places to Stay – top end

There are two top range hotels here, the *Hotel Faucon* (tel 391) and the *Hotel Ibis* (tel 335). The Faucon is the more expensive of the two at RFr 1800 a single.

Getting There

From Kigali minibuses cost RFr 400 and take about three hours. From Gitarama

It's about RFr 200 or from Cyangugu about RFr 700, perhaps less if the road has been sealed.

The National Parks

PARC NATIONAL DE L'AKAGERA

Created in 1934 and covering an area of 2500 square km, Akagera is one of the least visited but most interesting wildlife parks in Africa. One of the reasons for this is that it has three distinct types of environment. Large areas of the park are covered with tree-less savanna but there is an immense swampy area some 95 km long and between two and 20 km wide along the border with Tanzania. This contains six lakes and numerous islands, some of them covered with savanna, others with forest. Lastly, there is a chain of low mountains (ranging from 1618 metres to 1825 metres high) which stretches through much of the length of the park. The vegetation here is variable ranging from short grasses on the summits to wooded savanna and dense thickets of xerophitic forest on the flanks.

There's an extraordinary variety of animals to be seen here and they're often much easier to find than in other wildlife parks. In just a two to three day trip you can usually come across topi, impala, roan antelope, giant eland, bushbuck, oribi, various types of duiker, buffalo, warthog, red river hog, baboon, vervet monkeys, lion, leopard, hyena, zebra, hippo, crocodile and, at night, hare, palm civet, genet, galago (bushbaby) and giant crested porcupine. There are also herds of elephant. The best time to visit the park in terms of access is between mid-May and mid-September (the dry season). November and April are the wettest months.

The only trouble with getting to Akagera is that you need your own transport or to join an organised safari. The latter do not, as in Kenya and Tanzania, cater to budget travellers but, before you give the park a miss, check out current car hire and safari prices in Kigali. Rwanda Travel Service (tel 2210), Hotel des Diplomates, 45 Boulevard de la Revolution, Kigali; Umubano Tours Agency (tel 2176), B P 1160, Kigali and Agence Solliard (tel 5660), 2 Avenue de la Republique, Kigali, all offer car hire and safaris.

The park entry fees are RFr 1500 per person plus RFr 800 for a vehicle.

Waiting for a lift...

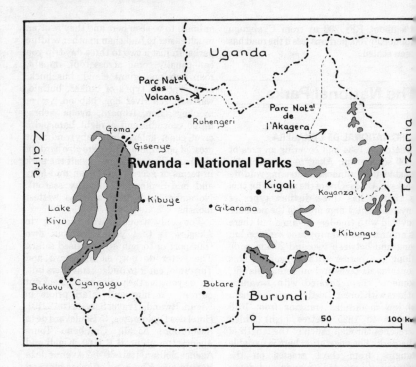

Camping costs RFr 1000 per person. If you want a guide these cost RFr 500 per day. A fishing licence costs RFr 1500 per day.

The best entry into the park is either at the Gabiro Hotel in the mid-north or the Akagera Hotel in the south but the quickest is the Nyamiyaga entrance about 16 km from the sealed road going through Kayonza. The hotels in the park are very expensive (RFr 3100 a single and RFr 4300 a double) so if you want to keep costs down you'll have to camp. You can do this on good sites at both of the hotels. There are also designated camping sites at various other points inside the park but that's all they are – 'designated'. There are no facilities and no protection. Some people do camp out but it's not really recommended and can be dangerous (sleep in the car instead).

One exception to this is at Plage Hippos, half way up the park close to the Tanzanian border. Here there are covered picnic tables, good waste bins and toilets but the site is no more protected than anywhere else. It's a beautiful site and there are plenty of hippos and crocodiles, monkeys and birdlife. Don't swim here – not only because of the hippos and crocodiles but because there's a fair chance of catching bilharzia.

Hiring a guide is a waste of money. You won't find any more animals with a guide than you will without. All you need is a map of the park (for sale at the Tourist Office in Kigali and remarkably accurate despite appearances – you can't buy these at the park), your eyes and a pair of binoculars. A wildlife handbook is also useful. Take all your own food, drinking and washing water and fuel. It's best to ssume you won't be able to get these in he park (fuel *may* be available at the otels sometimes but they're very eluctant to sell it). Tsetse flies can be roublesome in the north and east but you ould be bothered by the odd one nywhere in the park so bring a fly swat rith you and/or insect repellent.

ARC NATIONAL DES VOLCANS

This area along the border with Zaïre and Uganda with its chain of no less than even volcanos, one of them over 4500 metres high, has to be one of the most eautiful sights in Africa. But it's not just he mountains which attract travellers. On the bamboo and rainforest covered lopes is one of the last remaining anctuaries of the mountain gorilla. These animals were studied in depth first y George Schaller and, more recently, by Dian Fossey. Fossey spent the best part of 3 years living at a remote camp high up n the slopes of Visoke in order to study he gorillas and to habituate them to uman contact.

She'd probably still be there now had he not been murdered in December 1985, robably by poachers with whom she nade herself very unpopular. Without her tenacious efforts to have poaching tamped out, however, there probably vouldn't be any gorillas left in Rwanda by 1ow. It remains to be seen what will 1appen to the four known groups which re left.

It isn't just poaching which threatens hem. Another major factor which is clawing away at their existence is local pressure for grazing and agricultural land and the European Common Market's pyrethrum project – daisy-like flowers processed into a natural insecticide. This project was responsible for the removal, n 1969, of over 8900 hectares from the National Park – almost half the park! It 10w covers only 0.5% of the total land area of Rwanda.

Fossey's account of her years with the gorillas and her battle with the poachers

and government officials, *Gorillas in the Mist* (Penguin Books, 1985), makes fascinating reading. Pick up a copy before you come here.

Visiting the Gorillas

Many travellers rate a visit to the gorillas as one of the highlights of their trip to Africa. It isn't, however, a joy ride. The guides can generally find them within one to four hours from the departure points but it often involves a lot of strenuous effort scrambling through dense vegetation up steep, muddy hillsides sometimes to over 3000 metres. It also rains a lot in this area. If you don't have the right footwear and clothing then you're in for a hard time. An encounter with a silver-back alpha male gorilla at close quarters can also be a hair-raising experience if you've only ever seen large wild animals in the safety of a zoo. Some people return with a lot of nasty, soiled underwear to clean. (Gorillas actually do much the same thing when they're fleeing from danger!). Despite their size, however, they're remarkably non-aggressive animals and it's usually quite safe to be close to them. For most people it's a magical encounter but Tarzan myths die hard.

The only drawback to seeing the gorillas in Rwanda is the cost (around US$60 plus accommodation and food) and the fact that there's no transport between Ruhengeri and the park headquarters at Kinigi (you must hitch or walk). If you can't afford this sort of money for what amounts to a day-trip then you'll have to go to Zaïre to see gorillas – considerably cheaper though the cost is creeping up all the time. Details about this in the Eastern Zaïre chapter.

There are four groups of gorillas which you can visit known as Groups 9, 11 (Bisoke), 13 (Muside) and SUSA. Any of the first three can be seen in one day though Group 9 moves around a lot and may not be available. The SUSA group involves a more rugged trip lasting two days with an overnight stop in a metal hut (or your own tent if you prefer) at Cundura at about 3000 metres. You need to take warm clothes, a sleeping bag, foam mattress, food for two days, cooking utensils, a torch and preferably waterproof clothing. You can buy charcoal at Cundura and water is available there (though it's a good idea to purify it).

You must make advance reservations to visit Groups 11, 13 and SUSA at the Tourist Office in Kigali (Office Rwandais du Tourisme et des Parcs Nationaux, BP 905, Kigali) otherwise you can not be guaranteed a place on the day you want to go. Group 9 can only be booked at the park headquarters in Kinigi the afternoon before you want to go since no one can be sure what your chances of being able to see them in advance are. Groups 11 and 13 can be booked up weeks in advance especially during the European summer holiday season but there are many cancellations so it's usually possible to join another group of visitors if you are at the park headquarters before 8 am. The maximum group size for all the above is six people. There are restrictions on children joining gorilla-viewing groups. For the SUSA group, for example, the minimum age is 15 years.

Park fees are RFr 5000 per person for a gorilla visit (including guide – compulsory) plus RFr 1000 per person park entrance. Porters (optional) are available (20 kg maximum) at RFr 300 per day plus RFr 500 per night.

Having made a booking you must present yourself at the park headquarters between 7 and 8 am on the day of the visit to pay fees or have your permit checked and then reach the various take-off points by 9.15 am. This can be problematical without your own transport. The park doesn't lay any on and tourists with cars are often reluctant to take you. There's also very little local transport so it may not be possible to hitch. One possible solution to the transport problem is to hire a bicycle. These are available from a

shop near the market place in the centr of Ruhengeri for RFr 400 to RFr 500 fo two days. Whatever else you do it' obvious that if you are on foot, riding bicycle or hitching you'll have to stay a the park headquarters the night befor your intended visit if you're going to hav any chance of getting to the take-of points on the day. Journey times from Kinigi headquarters to the take-off point are as follows: Group 13 (Karandagi) – 2 minutes by car; 1½ hours on foot; Group (Point 9) – 45 minutes by car; two hour on foot; Group 11 (Parking Bisoke) – 4 minutes by car; 3½ hours on foot. For th SUSA group you must pay your fees a the park headquarters by 12 noon and b at Parking Bisoke by 3 pm. At 4 pm yo start walking to the overnight camp a Cundura (1½ to two hours). The par headquarters opens daily at 7 am.

Kinigi village is about 18 km from Ruhengeri and the park headquarters further two km from there (signposte 'Bureau du PNV'). It's not too difficult t hitch from Ruhengeri to the turn-off fo the park headquarters (expect to pa about RFr 50 for a lift).

Places to Stay If you have your own ten (none for hire) you can camp at th partially covered site 100 metres from th park headquarters for RFr 250 per perso per night and use the same facilities a the chalets across the road. Be ver careful about thieves on the camp site If you leave anything of value in a unguarded tent it won't be there whe you get back. Thieves even steal from tents in which the occupants are sleeping

If you have no tent you'll have to stay i one of the newly-built chalets opposit the camp site. There are four of these eac with five beds and a fireplace (a coupl often get a whole chalet to themselves) They cost RFr 800 per person. Clea sheets are provided but firewood cost RFr 200 per bundle. Toilets and shower (hot water) are communal but kept ver clean.

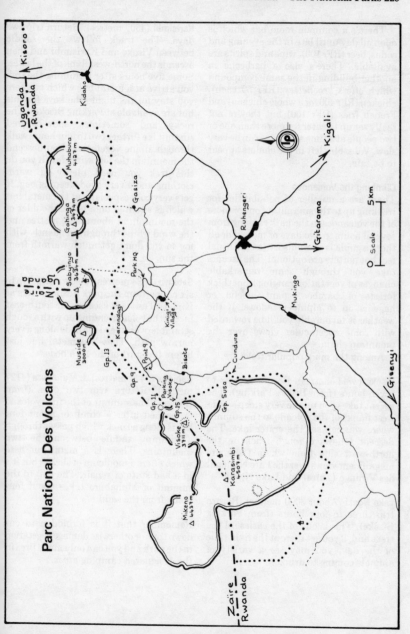

Parc National Des Volcans

There's a common room/bar which is open all day until late in the evening and sodas, beer (RFr 100), wine and spirits are available. There's also a barbecue in another building in the same compound which offers *brochettes* (RFr 50 each), chicken (RFr 400 for a whole chicken) and French fries (RFr 100) but they're not really set up to cater for more than one or two people at a time so service can be very slow. Valuables left in the chalets appear to be safe.

Climbing the Volcanoes

There are a number of possibilities for trekking up to the summits of one or more of the volcanoes in the park ranging from several hours to two days or more. For all these a guide is compulsory (at the usual fee) but porters are optional. The ascents take you through some remarkable changes of vegetation ranging from thick forests of bamboo, giant lobelia or hagenia on to alpine meadows. If the weather is favourable you'll be rewarded with some spectacular views over the mountain chain.

Among the more popular treks are:

Visoke (3711 metres). Return trip six to seven hours (from Bisoke Parking). The ascent takes you up the very steep south-west flanks of the volcano to the summit where you can see the crater lake. The descent follows a rough track on the north-west side from which there are magnificent views over the Parc National des Virunga (Zaïre) and Lake Ngezi.

Lake Ngezi (About 3000 metres). Return trip three to four hours (from Parking Bisoke). This is one of the easiest of the treks and, if you get there at the right time of the day, you may see a variety of animals coming to drink.

Karisimbi (4507 metres). Return trip two days. The track follows the saddle between Visoke and Karisimbi and then ascends the north-west flank of the latter. Some five hours after beginning the trek you arrive at a metal hut which is where you stay for the night (the keys for this hut are available at Parking Bisoke). The rocky and sometimes snow-covered summit is a further two to four hours walk through alpine vegetation. You descend the mountain the following day. If you do this trek you need plenty of warm clothing and a very good sleeping bag. It gets very cold especially at the metal hut which is situated on a bleak shoulder of the mountain at about 3660 metres and the wind whips through, frequently with fog so you don't get much warmth from the sun.

Sabinyo (3634 metres). Return trip five to six hours (from the park headquarters at Kinigi). The track ascends the south-east face of the volcano ending up with a rough scramble over steep lava beds along a very narrow path. There's a metal hut just before the start of the lava beds.

Gahinga (3474 metres) & **Muhabura** (4127 metres). Return trip two days (from Gasiza). The summit of the first volcano is reached after a climb of about four hours along a track which passes through a swampy saddle between the two mountains. There is a metal hut here which offers a modicum of shelter but it's in a bad state of repair. The trip to the summit of Muhabura takes about four hours from the saddle.

Remember that it is forbidden to cut down trees or otherwise damage vegetation in the park and you can only make fires in the designated camping areas.

Burundi

Burundi is a small but beautiful mountainous country sandwiched between Tanzania, Rwanda and Zaïre with magnificent views over Lake Tanganyika. It has had a stormy history full of tribal wars and factional struggles between the ruling families, further complicated in recent times by colonisation, firstly by the Germans and later by the Belgians. It is one of the most densely populated countries in the world with some 145 persons per square km yet, despite this, there are few urban centres. The only towns of any size are the capital, Bujumbura, and Gitega. Most people live in family compounds known as *rugos*.

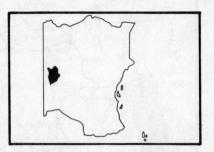

HISTORY
Early Settlement
The original inhabitants of the area, the Twa pygmies (who now comprise only 1% of the population), were gradually displaced from about 1000 AD onwards by migrating Hutu, mostly farmers of Bantu stock who now make up some 85% of the population. In the 16th and 17th centuries, however, the country experienced another wave of migration. This time it was the tall, pastoralist Watutsi from Ethiopia and Uganda – they now comprise 14% of the population. The Watutsi gradually subjugated the Hutu into a feudal system of sorts, very similar to the one in medieval Europe, with the Watutsi becoming a loosely organised aristocracy with a *mwami*, or king, at the top of each social pyramid. Under this system the Hutu relinquished their land and mortgaged their services to the nobility in return for cattle – the symbol of wealth and status in Burundi.

The Colonial Era
At the end of the 19th century, Burundi and Rwanda were colonised by the Germans but it was so thinly garrisoned

that the Belgians were easily able to oust the German forces during WW I. After the war, the League of Nations mandated Burundi (then known as Urundi) and Rwanda to Belgium. Taking advantage of the feudal structure, the Belgians ruled indirectly through the Watutsi chiefs and princes, granting them wide-ranging powers to recruit labour and raise taxes – powers they were not averse to abusing whenever it suited them. The Watutsi, after all, considered themselves to be a superior, intelligent people, born to rule, and the Hutu merely hard-working but dumb peasants. The Christian missions encouraged this view by concentrating on educating the Watutsi and virtually ignoring the Hutu and since the missions had been granted a monopoly on education, this policy remained unchallenged.

The establishment of coffee plantations and the subsequent concentration of wealth derived from its sale in the hands of the Watutsi urban elite further exacerbated tensions between the two tribal groups.

Independence
In the 1950s a nationalist organisation based on unity between the tribes was founded under the leadership of the *mwami's* eldest son, Prince Rwagasore, but in the run-up to independence the prince was assassinated with the con-

231

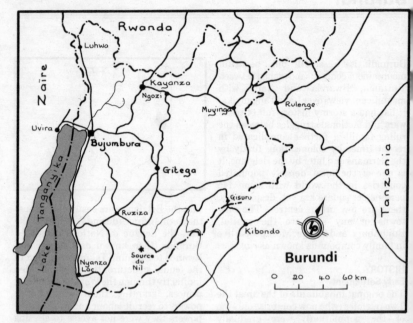

nivance of the colonial authorities who feared their commercial interests would be threatened if he came to power. Despite this setback, when independence was granted in 1962, challenges were raised about the concentration of power in Watutsi hands and it appeared that the country was headed for a majority government. This had already happened in neighbouring Rwanda where a similar tribal imbalance existed.

In elections in 1964 Hutu candidates collected the majority of votes but the *mwami* refused to appoint a Hutu prime minister. Hutu frustration boiled over a year later in an attempted coup by Hutu military officers and politicians. Though it failed it led to the flight of the *mwami* into exile in Switzerland and a Watutsi military junta takeover. A wholesale purge of Hutu from the army and bureaucracy followed but in 1972 there was another revolt in which over 1000 Watutsi were killed.

The military junta responded to this challenge with what was nothing less than selected genocide. Any Hutu who had received a formal education, had a job in the government or was wealthy was rooted out and murdered often in the most horrifying way. Certainly few bullets were used and convoys of army trucks full of the mutilated bodies of Hutu rumbled through the streets of Bujumbura for days on end and even in broad daylight at the beginning of the campaign. Many of the Hutu were taken from their homes at night while others received summonses to report to a police station.

It is hard to believe how subservient the Hutus had become to their Watutsi overlords since even the most uninformed peasant was aware of what was going on, but, three months later some 200,000 had lost their lives and over 100,000 fled to Tanzania, Rwanda and Zaïre. More refugees have poured into Tanzania since then. Neither the Christian missions inside the country nor the international community outside raised any voices of protest about this carnage. Indeed, whilst it was in full swing, an official of the OAU visited Bujumbura to congratulate President Michel Micombero on the orderly way the country was being run!

Little has changed since those times. The Watutsi continue to rule and the Hutu, despite their numbers, are a destroyed and cowed people. There have been half-hearted attempts by the government to remove some of the main causes of inter-tribal conflict but they're mostly cosmetic. The army and the bureaucracy are totally dominated by the Watutsi and the Hutu confined to menial jobs, agriculture and cattle raising. The government has even vetoed international aid at times where they suspect that it might be used to educate or enrich the Hutu and so eventually breed opposition. Religious missions have been regarded with equal suspicion and many missionaries have been told to leave, often at very short notice.

It's unlikely, as a visitor, that you will become aware of all this. Outwardly the country appears calm and seems destined to stay that way for the forseeable future. Few travellers stay long in Burundi in any case, it's mainly a place passed through to or from Tanzania or Rwanda.

POPULATION
The population of Burundi is something over four million, made up of about 14% the ruling Watutsi and about 85% the ruled Hutu.

ECONOMY
Burundi's economy is predominantly agricultural with coffee the main commercial crop.

GEOGRAPHY
Burundi occupies a mountainous 27,834 square km.

FESTIVALS & HOLIDAYS
Public holidays are 1 January, 1 May, Ascension Day, 1 July, 15 August, 18 September, 1 November and 25 December (Christmas).

LANGUAGE
The official languages are Kirundi and French. KiSwahili is also useful but hardly anyone speaks English in this country.

VISAS
Visas are required by all. Citizens of South Africa are not admitted. Visas can be obtained from Burundi embassies in Addis Ababa (Ethiopia), Algiers (Algeria), Cairo (Egypt), Dar es Salaam (Tanzania), Kampala (Uganda), Kigali (Rwanda), Kinshasa (Zaïre), Nairobi (Kenya) and Tripoli (Libya).

Outside of Africa there are embassies in Beijing (Peoples Republic of China), Bonn (West Germany), Brussels (Belgium), Bucharest (Romania), Geneva (Switzerland), Moscow (USSR), New York and Washington DC (USA), Ottawa (Canada) and Paris (France). There are Burundi consulates in Bukavu (Zaïre) and Kigoma (Tanzania).

The cost of visas varies depending on where you apply. It is least expensive in Tanzania and Uganda (paying with local shillings exchanged at the street rate) followed by Kenya and then Zaïre. Tourist visas allow for a stay of one month single entry, but there are also cheaper two-day transit visas available. The time it takes to obtain visas also varies but they generally take two days and are only issued on certain days of the week.

If you arrive at Bujumbura international airport without a visa you may be deported on the next available flight. Arriving by ferry on Lake Tanganyika, the authorities are more accommodating. What normally happens is that you pay BFr 1000 for an entry permit and leave your passport with immigration. You pick up your passport 24 hours later and pay a further BFr 1000 for your visa.

Visa extensions can be obtained from immigration in Bujumbura. They cost BFr 1000 per month and take 24 hours. The visa application story is as follows:

Kenya At the embassy in Nairobi, 14th Floor Development House, Moi Avenue (tel 3387735) they cost Sh 100, two photographs and take 24 hours but you can only apply on Mondays and Wednesdays. The embassy is open Monday to Thursday from 8.30 am to 12.30 pm and 2 to 5 pm. The staff are helpful and there's even some tourist literature available.

Rwanda At the embassy in Kigali (Rue de Ntaruka) they cost RFr 1500 and two photographs but you need to apply a week in advance and they are only issued on Fridays. The staff are not particularly helpful but it is possible to speed things up if you enlist the support of your own embassy (some will do this; others won't).

Tanzania At the consulate in Kigoma they cost Sh 200, two photographs and take three days but you can only apply on Mondays and Wednesdays between 8 am and 3 pm (pick up on Thursdays and Saturdays respectively). This will present problems if you do not already have a visa and are on the Lake Tanzania ferry coming up from Mpulungu (Zambia).

Uganda At the embassy in Kampala, 2 Katego Rd near the Uganda Museum (tel 54584), they cost Sh 3000, two photographs and take two days but they're only issued on Wednesdays and Fridays so you must apply on Monday or Wednesday. The embassy is open Monday to Friday from 8.30 am to 12.30 pm and 2.30 to 5 pm.

Zaïre At the consulate in Bukavu (SINELAC Building, 184 Avenue du President Mobutu) they cost Z510, two photographs and take 24 hours to issue. The consulate is open Monday to Friday from 7.30 am to 12 noon and 2.30 to 5 pm but visa applications are only accepted between 3 and 5 pm Monday to Thursday. The consulate is closed on Saturday and Sunday.

Visas for Other Countries

Embassies for neighbouring African countries include:

Rwandan Visas The embassy (tel 26865), is at 24 Avenue Zaïre, Bujumbura next to the Zaïre embassy. One month multiple-entry tourist visas cost BFr 1800, two photographs and are issued in 24 to 48 hours but they are only issued on Tuesdays and Fridays (try to get in there as early as possible on the day before visas are issued and it will probably be given to you the following day). Transit visas cost BFr 900.

Tanzanian Visas The embassy is on Avenue Patrice Lumumba opposite the main post office (PTT). Visa costs vary depending on your nationality and take 24 hours but applications are only accepted in the mornings. The embassy is open Monday to Friday from 8 to 11.30 am and 2 to 4.30 pm. The staff are helpful.

Zaïre Visas The embassy is on Avenue Zaïre next to the Rwandan embassy. The staff are friendly and helpful and you can usually get a visa within 24 hours.

MONEY

US$1 = BFr 104

The Burundi Franc (BFr) is divided into 100 centimes but you're very unlikely to see any centimes. The exchange value of the Burundi franc fluctuates according to the international currency market, particularly the value of the US dollar and the French franc. Currency declaration forms are not issued on arrival.

Commission rates for changing travellers' cheques at most banks are outright banditry – sometimes up to 7%! The Banque de la République du Burundi and the banks at the international airport do not, according to most travellers, charge commission. Banking hours are Monday to Friday from 8 to 11.30 am. Outside of these hours you can change travellers' cheques at one or another of the large hotels in Bujumbura (eg Novotel, Chaussée du Peuple Burundi) but their rates are fractionally below those offered by the banks though they charge no commission.

There's a relatively open street market

in Bujumbura so you're at a considerable advantage bringing hard currency with you to Burundi. Dealers generally hang around in front of the petrol station next to the central market on the Avenue Prince Louis Rwagasore, half a block down from the Banque Commerciale du Burundi. Rates obviously vary according to the official exchange rate and the amount you want to change (large bills are preferred) but you can usually expect 35% above the bank rate. You can also buy Tanzanian shillings here at a rate which is usually better than the rate in Kigoma but not as good as the rate in Dar es Salaam or Arusha. If you're taking the

Lake Tanganyika steamer down as far as Mpulungu (Zambia) or thinking of flying internally on Air Tanzania from Kigoma then you need to think about this carefully.

At the border post between Uvira (Zaïre) and Bujumbura you'll run into a lot of money changers. Their rates (Zaïres to Burundi francs but not hard currency to Burundi francs) are quite reasonable so long as you know the current street rates for the Burundi franc.

Some travellers have reported that the Banque de la République du Burundi will convert Burundi francs into US dollars cash if you produce a bank receipt for the

original transaction at a rate which works out better than the official exchange rate. I had my doubts about this so I checked it out. They weren't interested. Not surprising! It is possible to buy US dollars cash in Bujumbura but it's only worth doing that if you're heading into Tanzania.

COSTS
Burundi can be an expensive place to stay if you want to be near the town centre in Bujumbura but there are cheap places in the suburbs. Elsewhere meals can usually be found at a reasonable price and transport costs are about the same as in Rwanda.

CLIMATE
The climate is hot and humid especially around Lake Tanganyika with temperatures varying between 23 and 30°C. The average temperature in the mountains to the east of the lake is 20°C. The rainy season runs from October to May with a brief dry period during December and January.

NEWSPAPERS & MEDIA
The main newspaper is *Le Renouveau du Burundi* – a French language daily. Local radio stations broadcast in Kirundi, French and KiSwahili. There are occasional broadcasts in English.

HEALTH
As with most African countries you should take precautions against malaria in Burundi. There is a good beach (with expensive hotels and restaurants) at the northern end of Lake Tanganyika between Bujumbura and the Burundi/Zaïre border. It's probably safe to swim there but you should avoid bathing in this lake wherever there is reedy vegetation due to the risk of contracting bilharzia.

GENERAL INFORMATION
Time
The time in Burundi is GMT plus two hours.

Business Hours
Official business hours (other than banks) are Monday to Saturday from 8 am to 12 noon and 2 to 4.30 pm.

GETTING THERE
You can enter Burundi by air, road and lake ferry.

Air
International airlines servicing Burundi are Aeroflot, Air Burundi, Air France, Air Tanzania, Air Zaïre, Cameroon Airlines, Ethiopian Airlines, Kenya Airways and Sabena.

If you're heading for Tanzania and thinking of flying internally from Kigoma it's worth going to the Air Tanzania office in Bujumbura and making a reservation. You don't have to pay for the ticket until you get to Kigoma but they'll give you written confirmation of the reservation. This way you can pay in Tanzanian shillings at the street rate rather than in Burundi francs (a big saving!).

Road
To/From Rwanda There is a choice of two routes. The one you take will depend on whether you want to go direct to Kigali or via Lake Kivu. Going direct to Kigali you first take a minibus to Kayanza from Bujumbura (BFr 350, about 2½ hours), a minibus from there to the border for BFr 150 (these only go on Tuesday, Friday and Sunday; the rest of the week you will have to hitch or hire a taxi), a Peugeot shared taxi from the border to Butare (BFr 500), and a minibus from Butare to Kigali (RFr 400, frequent).

To Cyangugu on Lake Kivu you first take a minibus from Bujumbura to Rugombo (BFr 200, about 1½ hours). The next 12 km to the Burundi border post at Luhwa and the following eight km to the Rwandan border post at Bugarama you will probably have to hitch (trucks and cars). From the Rwandan border post to Cyangugu there are shared taxis but it's also fairly easy to hitch.

To/From Tanzania There are two routes, both using Lake Tanganyika at different points (see Lake Ferries). You'll be extremely lucky to find road transport from the Burundi border into Tanzania and it's not recommended that you try. You could be stuck for weeks.

To/From Zaïre There are also two routes to Zaïre. The first goes from Bujumbura to Cyangugu in Rwanda (described above) and then from there to Bukavu.

The direct route into Zaïre is from Bujumbura to Uvira across the top of Lake Tanganyika. You may be able to find a minibus going from Bujumbura to the Burundi border post but usually you will have to get a shared taxi (BFr 50, 10 to 15 minutes). From the Burundi border post to the Zaïre border post it's about one km and you will probably have to walk. From the Zaïre border post to Uvira there are shared taxis until late in the afternoon which cost Z50 (local people pay Z25) and take about 10 to 15 minutes.

Before you take this route, read about getting from Uvira to Bukavu in either the Rwandan or Eastern Zaïre chapters.

Lake Ferries
Lake Tanganyika Steamers The *MV Liemba* connects Burundi with Tanzania and Zambia. It used to operate in conjunction with a sister ship, the *MV Mwongozo*, so that there were two ferries in either direction every week but the *MV Mwongozo* now only services ports on the Tanzanian part of the lake. Like everything else in Africa, this may change so it's worth making enquiries.

The schedule for the *MV Liemba* is more or less regular but it can be delayed for up to 24 hours at either end depending on how much cargo there is to on-load or off-load. Engine trouble can also delay it at any point though not usually for more than a few hours. Officially, it departs once a week from Bujumbura on Mondays at about 4 pm, arrives Kigoma (Tanzania) on Tuesday at 8 am and Mpulungu (Zambia) on Thursday at 8 am. It calls at many small Tanzanian ports en route between Kigoma and Mpulungu but rarely for more than half an hour. In the opposite direction it departs Mpulungu on Friday at about 5 pm, arrives Kigoma on Sunday at 10 am and Bujumbura on Monday at 7.30 am.

The fares from Bujumbura to Kigoma are BFr 2430 (1st class – two-bunk cabin), BFr 1920 (2nd class – four-bunk cabin) and BFr 870 (3rd class – seats only). In the opposite direction the fares are Tan Sh 257 (1st class), Tan Sh 203 (2nd class) and Tan Sh 92 (3rd class). In addition there are port fees (at the port of embarkation only) of BFr 200 (at Bujumbura) and Tan Sh 40 (at Kigoma). If you are going all the way from Bujumbura to Mpulungu you can, of course, buy a ticket for the whole journey in Bujumbura in local currency but the trip will work out very expensive this way. You can save a lot of money by buying a ticket first to Kigoma and then, once the boat sails, buying a ticket for the rest of the journey to Mpulungu from the purser using Tanzanian shillings bought on the street market in Bujumbura. Do this as soon as possible if you want a cabin between Kigoma and Mpulungu. The fares from Kigoma to Mpulungu are Tan Sh 856 (1st class), Tan Sh 679 (2nd class) and Tan Sh 308 (3rd class).

Some travellers have reported that tickets bought in Mpulungu for travel up the lake have to be paid for in hard currency. This may no longer be true since the Zambian currency was effectively floated against the US dollar in mid-1986. Make enquiries. The *MV Liemba* is operated by the Tanzanian Railways Corporation so, in theory, they should accept Tanzanian shillings.

Tickets for the ferry can be bought from SONACO, Rue des Usines off the Avenue du Port, Bujumbura (signposted), on Monday, Tuesday, Wednesday and Saturday from 7.30 am to 12 noon and on Thursday and Friday from 2 to 5 pm. In Kigoma you buy tickets from the railway station. In Mpulungu you buy tickets on the boat.

Third class is not usually crowded between Bujumbura and Kigoma so, if you want to save money, this is a reasonable possibility. Between Kigoma and Mpulungu, however, it is very crowded. The choice is yours. Meals and drinks are available on board and have to be paid for in Tanzanian shillings. Bring sufficient shillings with you to cover this – exchange rates on board are naturally poor. A huge plate of rice and beef curry will cost you about Tan Sh 80. If you want soup and dessert as well this will cost you about Tan Sh 150. The breakfasts are also very good value; the boat from Bujumbura arrives at Kigoma about 6 am but you can't get off until 8 am when customs and immigration officials arrive. So, instead of packing your bags and hanging around it's a good idea to have breakfast.

To/From Tanzania via Banda Over the last few years another route into Tanzania has become very popular with travellers since it takes in the Gombe Stream National Park chimpanzee sanctuary half way between Bujumbura and Kigoma.

Going this way you first take a minibus from Bujumbura to either Nyanza Lac (Burundi customs and immigration) or Banda (the Burundi/Tanzania border village). There are daily minibuses which cost BFr 500 and take about three to four hours to either place. If you get off at Nyanza Lac you can continue on to Banda by minibus or take a small boat from there to Banda for Tan Sh 100 taking between one and three hours. It's probably best to carry on to Banda by minibus and clear Tanzanian customs there. The office is on the track which joins the villages on either side of the border. If you bought Tanzanian shillings in Burundi then hide them well. You may have to empty your pockets. If you miss this office then go through formalities when you get to Kigoma (though this involves a lot of walking).

Around the headland south of Banda there are daily boats to Kigoma via Gombe Stream National Park which leave about 7 am and take about six hours. The fare is Tan Sh 100. If you get stuck in Banda there are a couple of restaurants which take both Burundi francs and Tanzanian shillings and will probably let you sleep there for the night. These boats are small, partially covered, wooden affairs, often overcrowded not only with people but their produce and they offer no creature comforts whatsoever. They're good fun when the weather is fine. If there's a squall on the lake then you may be in for a rough time although it doesn't get as bad as Indian Ocean dhow trips can become.

If you're coming in the opposite direction from Kigoma to Banda the boats leave between 11 am and 12 noon and arrive about 6 pm. If you're white, immigration in Kigoma *may* tell you that it's illegal to leave Tanzania this way – that's nonsense. Be polite, determined and sit it out until you get that exit stamp.

GETTING AROUND
Air
There are no regular internal flights by the national airline, Air Burundi.

Road
Like Rwanda, Burundi used to be a difficult country to travel in especially during the rainy season because of the lack of decent roads and public transport. This has now changed and most of the major routes are sealed. The roads from Bujumbura through Kayanza, Butare, Kigali, Bujumbura, Ijenda, Source du Nil and Rutana; from Bujumbura through Gitega to Rutana and from Kayanza through Ngozi to Muyinga are now sealed all the way and only a small section of the Bujumbura-Rugombo-Cyangugu road remains to be sealed.

There are also plenty of modern, Japanese minibuses which are fairly frequent, not overcrowded and cheaper than shared taxis. Destinations are displayed in the front window and they go when full. You can usually find one going your direction from early morning to early afternoon from the *gare routière* (bus stand) in any town or city.

Also there's the OTRACO Bus Company which operates normal buses and has a ticket office on the bottom side of the *gare routière* in Bujumbura. In the window of this office there is a detailed map of the country and a timetable of all the routes they cover. Their buses are not as frequent as the minibuses and generally only go several days a week.

Bujumbura

Sprawling up the mountainside on the north-eastern tip of Lake Tanganyika and itself overlooking the the vast wall of mountains in Zaïre on the other side of the lake, the capital of Burundi is a mixture of grandiose colonial-style town planning with wide boulevards and imposing public buildings and dusty crowded suburbs of the type which surround many an African city. It's also one of the most important ports on Lake Tanganyika.

Like Kigali in neighbouring Rwanda, it hosts a sizeable expatriate population of international aid organisation workers, medics, missionaries and businessmen. Even Colonel Qadafi has made his mark here in the form of a large and beautifully-conceived Islamic Cultural Centre and mosque which must have cost a small fortune. You will also be in for a pleasant botanical surprise – like many other places along Lake Tanganyika, Bujumbura sports coconut palms! There are not many places where they are found well over 1000 km from the sea.

Information
Tourist Office The Tourist Office is on the

Avenue de l'Uprona near the Rue de la Mission but the information available is limited.

Embassies Diplomatic offices in Bujumbura include Rwanda, Tanzania and Zaïre – see the Visa section above. There are also consular offices for Belgium, Denmark, France, Netherlands, West Germany, USA and various other countries.

Post The main post office (PTT) in Bujumbura is open Monday to Friday from 8 am to 12 noon and 2 to 4 pm and on Saturday from 8 to 11 am.

Museums
Bujumbura has three museums within a block of each other on the Avenue du 13 Octobre which leads down to the Cercle Nautique on the lake front. The first is the **Musée Vivant**, a reconstructed traditional Burundian village with basket, pottery, drum and photographic displays. There are traditional drum shows daily – check the museum for times. Entry to the museum costs BFr 50 (BFr 20 for students) and it's open daily from 9 am to 12 noon and 2.30 to 5 pm, except Mondays.

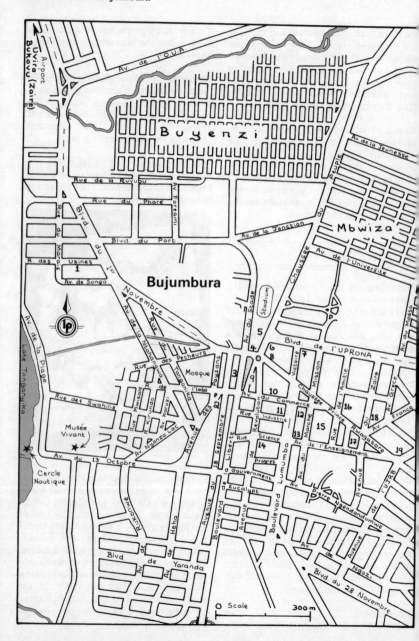

1	Sonaco (Lake Tanganyika boats)
2	Tourist Hotel
3	Hotel Central
4	Air Tanzania
5	Novotel
6	Hotel Burundi Palace
7	Restaurant Oasis
8	Aux Delices
9	Air Zaire
10	Au Beau Lilas Restaurant
11	Tanzanian Embassy
12	Main Post Office (PTT)
13	Banque due Credit du Burundi
14	Banque de la Republique du Burundi
15	Bus Station & Market
16	American Embassy & American Club
17	Banque Commercial du Burundi
18	Zaïre & Rwandan Embassies
19	Hotel Le Residence & Restaurant Stavros

Adjacent to this museum is the **Parc du Reptiles** (tel 25374) which is what you might expect it to be. Entry costs BFr 200 but it's only open on Saturdays from 2 to 4 pm or by appointment during the rest of the week. Across the street from the reptile park is the **Musée du Géologie du Burundi** (Geology Museum). It's dusty and run-down but has a good collection of fossils. Entry is free and it's open on weekdays from 7 am to 12 noon and 2 to 5 pm.

Islamic Cultural Centre & Mosque

This beautiful building is near the main square and was paid for by the Libyan government. There are often public performances of dance troupes, drummers and singers. Drum performances cost BFr 300 but there are half price discounts for students.

Places to Stay - bottom end

It can be difficult to find a reasonably-priced place to stay in Bujumbura, especially at weekends or if you arrive late in the day. Also many of the cheaper places are more or less permanently filled with expatriate aid workers. You may have to do some leg work!

For years budget travellers have found a warm welcome at the *Vugizu Mission* run by the Johnson family. They have a two-bed caravan and a tent (which sleeps two) in the garden of the mission for travellers' use. These facilities, as well as an excellent breakfast, are all free of charge and there are no chores to perform. The mission is on a beautiful site overlooking the lake but it's a considerable distance from the centre so you'll need to take a taxi there. Unfortunately, the government has been putting a lot of pressure on the missions in recent years and it's possible that the Johnsons may have been forced to leave Burundi by the time you read this. Make enquiries at the American Embassy or the American Cultural Center, Rue de l'Amitie opposite the market and bus stand.

If the Vugizu Mission is closed, there are a number of budget hotels in the Mbwiza (sometimes spelt Mubwiza) district to the north-east of the centre, down the Chaussée du Peuple Burundi. There are no street signs in this district so you'll have to ask where the various places are. In this area quite a few travellers go to *Au Bon Accueil* which costs BFr 800 a single and BFr 1500 a double. To get there, go down Chaussée du Peuple Burundi as far as the BP gas station, turn right and carry on for 150 metres. Similar is the *Panama Guest House* on the street before Au Bon Accueil and then turn right for 300 metres. It costs BFr 850 a single and BFr 1050 a double. Also nearby are the *Hotel Escottise*, which costs BFr 640 a single and the *Hotel New Bwiza*.

If you'd prefer to stay in the centre of town then it's worth checking out the *Hotel Central*, Place de l'Indépendence (the main square). It's scruffy and run-down and the staff are indifferent but it is the cheapest place in the centre at BFr

1000 a single and BFr 2000 a double. Showers and toilets are communal. The attached restaurant and bar at the front of the hotel is usually closed between 12 noon and 7 pm so between these times you'll have to go round the back of the place (Avenue du 18 Septembre) if you're looking for a room.

Campers should check out the *Cercle Nautique* on the lake front at the end of Avenue du 13 Octobre. It's usually free but watch out for the hippos!

Places to Stay – middle

If you don't find a place at one of the above hotels, then it's going to cost you a lot of money. The *Hotel Paguidas* (tel 2251), Chaussée du Peuple Burundi next door to the Novotel, has been used by travellers in the past but when I was there it was no longer being used as a hotel and was full of permanent residents.

The *Hotel Burundi Palace* (tel 2920), corner Boulevard de l'Uprona and Chaussée du Peuple Burundi, costs BFr 1570 a single and BFr 2610 a double with own bath but without air-conditioning and BFr 2320 a single and BFr 3480 a double with own bath and air-conditioning. Checkout time is 11 am.

The *Tourist Hotel* on Rue du Paysans facing the Islamic Cultural Centre costs BFr 2320 a single and BFr 2900 a double with own bathroom (hot and cold water) and fan. The beds are huge and very comfortable but checkout time is 9 am! You're more likely to get a room here than at the Burundi Palace. Other similar hotels are the *Hotel Grillon* (tel 2519), Avenue du Zaïre, and the *Hotel Le Résidence* (tel 2773), Avenue de Stanley close to the Avenue Prince Rwagasore.

Places to Stay – top end

At the top end of the market is the *Novotel*, Chaussée du Peuple Burundi, which is everything you would expect a hotel of this type to be at BFr 6000 a single and BFr 6500 a double.

Places to Eat

Best value for money is the *Restaurant Aux Beau Lilas*, Avenue du Commerce about half way between the Rue de la Poste and Avenue Patrice Lumumba. It's easy to miss this place as there's no sign outside but look for a red and white sign saying 'Foto'. The food here is excellent, attractively served in a pleasant atmosphere and the staff are friendly. You can eat very well for around BFr 600 but you can only get a beer during licencing hours.

Also very popular is *Aux Delices*, opposite the roundabout on the Place de l'Indépendence, where the soups and yogurt are recommended. It's a good place to meet local people too. Others have recommended the *Patisserie Snack à la Chez Michel* which offers very reasonably-priced meals, excellent garnished sandwiches from BFr 150, omelettes from BFr 100, soups, salads and cold beers. It's closed on Sundays.

If you want to splurge there are couple of good places to go though they are relatively expensive. The first is the *Cercle Nautique* (tel 2559) on the lake front at the end of Avenue du 13 Octobre which is very popular with expatriates especially at the weekends when it can be full to overflowing. You can eat very well here and *al fresco* for between BFr 800 and BFr 1000 whilst enjoying the views and the antics of the hippos (which are said to occasionally *eat* boats – though I didn't see them do this). It's a great place to sip a cold beer even if you don't want to eat. The Cercle is open daily except Tuesdays from 5 pm and all day on Sundays from 11 am. Memorise the number of the waiter here if you require change when paying the bill (otherwise you may not get it).

The other place for a splurge is the *Restaurant Oasis* (tel 2944), corner Avenue de l'Uprona and Avenue de la Victoire. It's a popular place and offers excellent multi-course lunches and dinners from BFr 900 and up. It's open

Burundi – Around Burundi 243

daily except Sundays (though I've seen it open on Sunday, too). Other restaurants in a similar price bracket include the *Restaurant Stavros*, Avenue Prince Rwagasore, the *Restaurant Olympia*, Avenue de la Victoire, and the restaurant at the *Hotel Burundi Palace*. The latter two specialise in Greek and Continental dishes.

Entertainment

Both the *American Cultural Center* and the *Centre Culturel Français*, opposite each other on Avenue Prince Rwagasore, have videos, films and other activities. The former shows videos of the ABC news on Mondays and Wednesdays at 5.30 pm and on Saturdays at 2.30 pm. They also have a reading room.

The *American Club*, next to the US embassy on Rue de l'Amitie, used to have two film and two chili and hamburger nights each week but when I was there it was closed for some reason. They also have a bar in the club. It would be worth checking to see if it's back in business. The *Bureau de Tourisme*, Avenue de l'Uprona, often puts on a disco in the evenings but the drinks there are expensive.

The swimming pool at the Novotel is open to non-residents for BFr 300 per day. There's no charge for using the poolside bar!

Getting Around

Airport Transport The international airport is 11 km from city.

Around Burundi

GITEGA

Gitega is the second largest town in Burundi and it's here that you find the **National Museum**. Though small, it's well worth a visit and very educational. Entry is free. There may also be a folklore performance – ask if the *tambourinaires* are playing.

Places to Stay

The *Mission Catholique* is probably the best place to inquire for budget accommodation as they have a huge guest house.

KAYANZA

Kayanza is on the road north to Kigali and not far from the Rwanda border. There's a good market here on Monday, Wednesday and Saturday.

Places to Stay

The missions here don't take guests so stay at the *Auberge de Kayanza* which costs BFr 960 a double.

Getting There

Minibuses from Bujumbura cost BFr 350 and take about 2½ hours. See the Getting There section for details of transport from Kyanza to the Rwanda border.

KILEMBA

The principal attraction here is the **Kibabi Hot Springs**, about 16 km from town, where there are several pools of differing temperature, the main one hovering around 100°C. A little further uphill is a waterfall and another deep pool where it's safe to swim.

Places to Stay

Most people stay at the *Swedish Pentecostal Mission* which has a very good guest house. A bed in the dormitory costs BFr 150. They also have private rooms with own shower and toilet and use of a fully equipped kitchen for BFr 600 per person.

OTHER PLACES

If you decide to visit the **Source du Nil** (the southernmost possible source of the Nile) it's possible to stay at the *Mission Catholique* in Rutavu seven km away.

Eastern Zaïre

This chapter covers a narrow strip of eastern Zaïre from the northern tip of Lake Tanganyika to Lake Mobutu Sese Seko, along the borders with Burundi, Rwanda and Uganda. It is included because it is an integral part of the mountainous area that forms the western wall of the Rift Valley. It is also considerably easier to get to from East Africa than it is from the west coast, which entails a journey through the jungles of the Congo basin. A full history of Zaïre would not be appropriate since only a small part of Kivu province is covered and many of the historical events which have taken place in the western parts of Zaïre have had no connection with events on the eastern borders.

There's some magnificent countryside and a lot of things to see and do in eastern Zaïre. They include mountain climbing, and visiting gorilla sanctuaries, pygmy settlements and remote fishing villages on Lakes Idi Amin (Edward) and Mobutu Sese Seko.

HISTORY
Because of the altitude and the fertile nature of the soil in this area, the Belgian colonialists developed many coffee plantations during the early part of the 20th century. They also built up the lake resort towns of Bukavu and Goma as well as a number of mountain retreats further north. These days it is Mobutu, president of Zaïre since 1965, and his cronies who maintain summer palaces here, although part of the reason is to ensure that their presence is felt in this far-flung corner of their vast country.

It isn't just Mobutu, however, who is keen to maintain a presence here. In few other areas of East Africa will you encounter so much Christian-missionary activity. The number of different sects hard at work saving souls is little short of

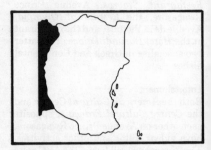

amazing. The whole range of Catholic and Protestant sects are involved, as well as the ubiquitous Seventh Day Adventists, Mormons and Jehovah's Witnesses. It's probably a good idea that they have chosen to work this area so intensively as their schools and hospitals provide many people with their only educational and medical facilities. Few funds are available for these sorts of facilities from the central government and because Mobutu's regime is so corrupt and is only interested in hanging onto power the funds shrink every year.

In the early years following independence, there was very little direct control of Kivu province by the central government in Kinshasa and local governors enjoyed virtual autonomy. The attempted secession by the southern province of Shaba (formerly known as Katanga) under Moise Tshombe, and the subsequent intervention by the United Nations is well known. These events prompted the overthrow and murder of Zaïre's first prime minister, Patrice Lumumba, and his replacement by Joseph Kasavubu with assistance from Mobutu, the army commander at the time. What is less well-known is that after the Katangan secession had been crushed, Kasavubu was faced with armed revolt by the governors of the eastern provinces including Kivu province. His failure to crush the rebellion and bring the governors to book led to his overthrow by Mobutu in 1965.

Mobutu has certainly restored a high level of centralised control to Zaïre since he came to power but the costs in terms of wasted resources, repression, jailings, executions, corruption and a decaying infrastructure have been enormous.

It is unlikely, however, that Mobutu will be replaced until he dies. He is a cunning and ruthless politician who has perfected the cult of personality in a way few other African presidents have been able to match. These days he rules as a half-god, half-chieftain, combining the sophisticated techniques of 20th century communication with traditional tribal symbolism. His photograph is to be seen everywhere, often accompanied by one of the many slogans underlining his indispensibility and benevolence – 'Mobutu: The Unifier'; 'Mobutu: The Pacifier'; 'Mobutu: The Guide', and many others. It would almost be a comic opera if it wasn't so serious – one day the people of Zaïre are going to have to pay for all the extravagance and neglect.

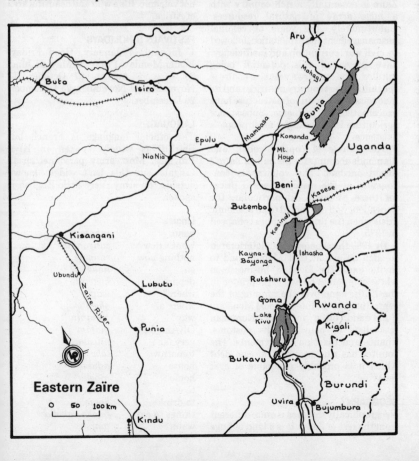

Eastern Zaïre

0   50   100 km

POPULATION
Zaïre's population of approximately 30 million people is divided between more than 200 tribes, several of which extend into neighbouring countries. Eastern Zaïre is one of the few areas in Africa where there are significant numbers of Twa people (the pygmies). The forest-dwelling Twa have resisted attempts to integrate them into the wider economy and many continue their nomadic, hunting-and-gathering existence.

ECONOMY
Zaïre is potentially a rich country with a huge array of natural resources. Unfortunately, the years of colonial mismanagement and exploitation, followed by civil war, corruption and inefficiency, have prevented this potential being fulfilled. The country's vast size (Zaïre is the third largest country in Africa) and its inadequate transport infrastructure have exacerbated the problems. Subsistence agriculture is the basis for most people's existence.

The mining of copper, cobalt and diamonds accounts for the bulk of Zaïre's export income. The country is consequently at the mercy of world prices for these products. In particular, the dependency on copper led to an economic crisis when the price for copper collapsed in 1975.

By 1980 the economy had deteriorated to such an extent that Mobutu had to invite back the Belgian businessmen whose companies he had expropriated in the 1970s, hand over the running of the central bank to the International Monetary Fund and bring in other European specialists to help run the customs, finance and taxation departments. The country has run up a vast foreign debt which it is probably incapable of ever repaying.

GEOGRAPHY
Geographically this area is quite different from the rest of Zaïre. It is a land of huge volcanoes and vast, deep lakes. Some of the volcanoes, such as those at the northern end of Lake Kivu, have erupted in the last decade though they are presently dormant. Others, where the three borders of Zaïre, Rwanda and Uganda meet, haven't erupted in living memory and their upper slopes are among the last remaining sanctuaries for the rare mountain gorilla. The Ruwenzori mountains along the border with Uganda – the highest in the region and the only ones with permanent snow cover on the peaks – are not typical at all since they are not volcanic. It's a wild and beautiful area of Africa.

FESTIVALS & HOLIDAYS
1 January, 4 January, Good Friday, Easter Monday, 1 May, 20 May, 24 June, 30 June, 1 August, 27 October, 17 November, 24 November, 25 December, 26 December.

LANGUAGE
The official language is French but Swahili is widely spoken in Kivu Province. Most army personnel speak Lingala but this isn't widely known outside the army. Very little English is spoken.

Lingala
hello	*mbote*
what's new?	*sangonini*
nothing new	*sangote*
go	*nake*
depart	*kokende*
where?	*wapi*
where are?	*okeyi wapi*
why?	*ponanini*
OK/thanks	*malam*
very far	*musika*
tomorrow	*lobi*
house	*ndako*
home	*mboka*
to eat	*kolia*
to drink	*komela*
things to eat	*biloko yakolia*
water	*mai*

manioc	songo
bananas	makemba
rice	loso
beans	madeso
salted fish	makaibo
fresh fish	mbisi
meat	nyama
peanuts	injunga karanga
market	nazondo
strong	makasi
a lot	mingi
new	sango
dog	mbwa

VISAS

Visas are required by everyone. They can be obtained from Zairois embassies in Abidjan (Ivory Coast), Accra (Ghana), Addis Ababa (Ethiopia), Algiers (Algeria), Bangui (Central African Republic), Brazzaville (Congo), Bujumbura (Burundi), Cairo (Egypt), Conakry (Guinea), Cotonou (Benin), Dakar (Senegal), Dar es Salaam (Tanzania), Harare (Zimbabwe), Kampala (Uganda), Khartoum (Sudan), Kigali (Rwanda), Lagos (Nigeria), Libreville (Gabon), Lome (Togo), Luanda (Angola), Lusaka (Zambia), Maputo (Mozambique), Monrovia (Liberia), Nairobi (Kenya), Nouakchott (Mauritania), N'Djamena (Chad), Rabat (Morocco), Tripoli (Libya), Tunis (Tunisia), Yaounde (Cameroon) and from the Zairois consulate in Kigoma (Tanzania).

The cost of a visa depends on whether you want a one-month, single-entry visa; a two-month, multiple-entry visa; or a three-month, multiple-entry visa. If there's any chance you are going to need a multiple-entry visa get it at the start. You'll save a lot of hassle this way. All visa applications must be accompanied by a letter of introduction from your own embassy (except in Bangui and Harare). Some embassies issue these free, others charge for them. British embassies charge about US$7.50! You may also be asked for an onward ticket and vaccination certificates (cholera and yellow fever).

On the visa application form it may say, 'Entry through Kinshasa only', but this isn't stamped in your passport so it doesn't make any difference.

Visa extensions can be obtained in Bukavu. Travellers who have got them here report that extensions for up to three months are easy to get and there's no fuss.

Tanzania In Dar es Salaam (the embassy is on Malik Rd off Upanga Rd) visas cost Tan Sh 300, require four photographs, a letter of introduction from your own embassy and they take 24 hours to issue. It's difficult to get anything other than a one-month, single-entry visa.

Avoid applying for a visa at the consulate in Kigoma as they take *two weeks* to issue one! It's open for applications on Monday, Wednesday and Friday from 9 am to 12.30 pm and 3 to 6.30 pm. Visas cost Tan Sh 200 and require four photographs. Kigoma is not a place to be stuck in for two weeks, although you could go and sit out the time at the Gombe Stream National Park.

Uganda There is an embassy in Kampala at 20 Philip Rd, Kololo (tel 233777), open Monday to Friday from 8 am to 3 pm. There are no other Zairois consulates in Uganda.

Kenya In Nairobi the embassy is in Electricity House, Harambee Avenue (tel 29771); a one-month, single-entry visa costs Ken Sh 160, a two-month, multiple-entry visa costs Ken Sh 280 and a three-month, multiple-entry visa costs Ken Sh 360. Four photographs, a letter of introduction and vaccination certificates are required and they take 24 hours to issue. You may also be asked for an onward ticket but it doesn't have to start in Zaïre. The staff are pleasant and the embassy is open Monday to Friday from 10 am to 12 noon.

Rwanda There is no Zairois consulate in either Gisenyi or Cyangugu.

Visas for Other Countries

Burundi Visas Visas can be obtained from the Burundi consulate in Bukavu (SINELAC Building, 184 Avenue du Président Mobutu). They cost Z510, require two photographs and are issued in 24 hours. You must apply for visas in the afternoon between 3 and 5 pm, Monday to Thursday. The consulate is closed on Saturdays and Sundays.

Rwandan Visas There are no consulates in either Bukavu or Goma. If you have no visa it's possible to obtain a *permit provisoir* (a kind of transit visa) at the border for RFr 4000 (!) valid for one week. The alternative is to go to the Belgian consulate in either Bukavu or Goma and ask them if they can help. Some travellers have reported that they can get a Rwandan visa for RFr 1500 but it takes two weeks. The consulate in Goma is very helpful.

Although it doesn't seem to be necessary at the moment, it's probably wise to have both Rwandan and Zairois multiple-entry visas if you intend to go by road between Bukavu and Uvira via Rwanda. This is the most convenient route in terms of the state of the road. Circumstances may well change (see the Uvira and Bukavu sections for details).

Kenyan, Tanzanian & Ugandan Visas There are no consulates for these countries in eastern Zaïre. The nearest embassies are in Kigali (Rwanda) and Bujumbura (Burundi).

MONEY

US$1 = Z65

The unit of currency is the Zaïre, which is made up of 100 makutas, although you're not likely to see anything smaller than 50 makutas these days.

There are both old and new bank notes in circulation. They're all legal tender but the design on them is different and the old notes are huge and usually in an advanced state of decrepitude. Most of them ought to carry a government health warning. Banks love giving them to you, perhaps as a joke, but more probably because they're usually low denominations so it's easy for them to miss a few out here and there without you noticing.

Since Zaïre devalued by a massive 520% in 1983, there has been very little difference between the bank rate and the street rate. Changing cash on the street does, however, save you a lot of time and you don't pay commission. You can expect up to Z60 for the US dollar. It's not always easy to find someone who wants to change money (Asian and European shopkeepers are your best bet) but most people can be persuaded if you accept something near the bank rate.

If you have travellers' cheques you need to shop around before you change them. Commission can vary from 1% to 20%! Some banks won't even change travellers' cheques (the Banque de Kinshasa in Goma and the Banque de Zaïre in Bukavu, for example). The Banque Commerciale Zairoise is probably the best bet as their commission is only Z38 per transaction and you can usually have your cheque cashed in half an hour. Avoid the Union des Banques Zairoises – this is where some travellers have been charged 20% commission. Banking hours are Monday to Friday from 8 am to 12 noon, but if you're changing travellers' cheques, you must arrive before 11 am. They won't entertain you after that.

There are a lot of hilarious stories circulating about banks and travellers' cheques in eastern Zaïre. One traveller spent all day at a bank in Bukavu (he didn't say which one) trying to change a travellers' cheque. They wouldn't change it because it didn't have 'Specimen' printed across it like the bank's sample! We heard another story about a manager who wouldn't change a US$100 cheque because his sample was a US$50 cheque. Others may refuse if your cheque is issued by a company which has a different name to the manager's sample. You should not run into anything as silly as this at either Banque Commerciale Zairoise in either Goma or Bukavu but you cannot change travellers' cheques at the bank in Uvira.

Currency declaration forms were abolished in May 1986 but that doesn't mean that this information will have percolated down to every customs and immigration officer at every border post. If you're issued with one, you can safely ignore it.

The import or export of local currency

is officially prohibited and you may well be asked if you have any when you are leaving Zaïre. It's very unlikely that you will be searched. Moreover, there will be some occasions when you simply have to take Zaïres into Zaïre (at weekends, for instance, if you only have travellers' cheques, or any day of the week if you're crossing to Uvira from Bujumbura where banks won't change cheques). You must hide them though.

COSTS

It's usually fairly cheap to travel in Zaïre and there's a much better selection of budget hotels and restaurants in most towns than you would find in neighbouring Burundi or Rwanda. Where there are no public buses (and there are not many) you will have to hitch rides on trucks. The fares are negotiable but you shouldn't have to pay more than the local people. It's certainly considerably cheaper to visit gorilla sanctuaries in Zaïre than it is in Rwanda.

CLIMATE

Eastern Zaïre enjoys a Mediterranean climate and this is one reason, aside from the magnificent views and water sports, why those with sufficient money (including the president) have made Goma and Bukavu on Lake Kivu into resort towns. The seasons are similar to those in Rwanda and Burundi. The main rainy season is from mid-March to mid-May and the dry season is from mid-May to mid-September. The short rains last from mid-September to mid-December and the short dry season from mid-December to mid-March.

FILM & PHOTOGRAPHY

Bring all your film requirements with you. Just about the only places where you will be able to find film are in Bukavu and Goma and it's expensive. If you do buy it here, check the expiry date carefully.

When you enter Zaïre, customs may demand that you buy a photography

permit for each camera that you have. The usual charge is about US$3. It's my firm belief that these 'permits' are an unbridled act of creativity on the part of the customs officers and that the money they fleece from travellers merely supplements their pay. I've seen receipts issued on Republic of the Congo official notepaper (Zaïre hasn't been called the Congo since 1971!). I'm not sure what the answer to this is. After all, who do you complain to? Crossing from Gisenyi to Goma they only spring this one on you at the Poids Lourds post, not at the lake shore post.

Don't take photographs of anything vaguely connected with the military, or of government buildings, banks, bridges, border posts, post offices or ports. If anyone sees you, the chances are you'll lose your film. There is intense paranoia about spies in some places (Uvira is one of them) because Zaïre doesn't get on well with Burundi, Rwanda or Tanzania. On a visit to Burundi and Rwanda in 1985, Colonel Qadafi stated that Mobutu's assassin would be guaranteed a place in paradise! They also haven't forgotten the Katanga secession in the 1960s, the invasions from Angola in the 1970s and the more recent raids from Tanzania. If you don't want to run into problems, get a written OK to take pictures from the Sous-Regional Commissioner before going ahead. You may have to cross his palm to get it but don't offer unless it's strongly indicated. Travellers have been arrested for taking pictures of such innocent scenes as markets.

HEALTH

You must take precautions against malaria. If you stay in Zaïre a long time, you could still pick it up. I've met very few American Peace Corps volunteers in Zaïre who haven't had at least one bout of malaria.

Tap water is not safe to drink – purify it first.

The other things you might pick up,

especially if you only wear thongs on your feet, are jiggers (tropical fleas which burrow under your skin). Go and get them pulled out at a clinic. They're easy to remove if you know what you're doing.

No matter how strong that urge in your groin might get, if you have any sense at all you'll stay well clear of prostitutes in Zaïre. If a recent study in Rwanda is anything to go by, the majority of them will be carrying the AIDS antibody.

GENERAL INFORMATION
Post
There's a charge of Z7.50 for each letter collected from poste restante.

Time
Eastern Zaïre is GMT plus two hours.

GETTING THERE
Air
The national airline, Air Zaïre, flies into Goma from Kinshasa and Kisangani on a fairly regular basis but it can be diverted from time to time, depending on cargo requirements. The jet is also sometimes commandeered by the president on his visits to Goma and Bukavu. You *may* be able to get student discounts if you're

under 26 years old, but it usually involves a lot of talking!

Air Rwanda flies Twin Otters between Kigali and Goma, on Saturdays only.

Road
To/from Burundi There are two routes to Zaïre. The first goes from Bujumbura to Cyangugu in Rwanda and then to Bukavu in Zaïre. The most direct route is from Bujumbura to Uvira. See the Getting There section in the Burundi chapter, and the Uvira section in this chapter for details.

To/from Rwanda The two main crossing points between Rwanda and Zaïre are between Gisenyi and Goma and between Cyangugu and Bukavu. See the Getting There section in the Rwanda chapter and the appropriate cities in this chapter for details.

To/from Uganda There are three main crossing points: Rutshuru-Kisoro; Rutshuru-Ishasha-Kasese; Beni-Kasindi-Katwe-Kasese. You may experience considerable difficulty using the first route as the road is rough and there's little traffic but you shouldn't have problems with the last two. See the Getting There section in the Uganda chapter for details.

To/from Western Zaïre The main route between eastern Zaïre and Kisangani on the Zaïre River is from Komanda on the Beni to Bunia road via Mambasa, Epulu, Nia Nia and Bafwasende. There are some diabolical stretches of road en route but it's generally passable even in the wet season. Trucks cover the route regularly. The journey can take as little as 2½ days but three would be usual at the best of times. In the wet season you should count on six days or even more (without breakdowns). In terms of cost, Z600 would be very generous. Z800-1000 would be more likely.

There's also the occasional possibility

of negotiating a lift with one of those overland trucks which cart yuppies from one end of the continent to the other in conditions of pseudo-bohemia at vast expense. If you're an independent traveller it might be barely tolerable for a few days. For further details of this route you'll need a copy of *Africa on a Shoestring*.

Lake Ferries

There are two ferries which ply between Goma and Bukavu on Lake Kivu, the *Matadi* and *Karisimbi*, but neither of them call at Rwandan ports, nor do the Rwandan ferries call any longer at Zairois ports. See the Getting Around, Lake Ferries section.

It used to be possible to find boats between Kalemie and Kigoma (Tanzania), on opposite sides of Lake Tanganyika, and you'll certainly see Zairois cargo boats tied up at Kigoma, but it's very difficult to persuade captains to take you.

GETTING AROUND
Air

There are quite a number of private airline companies operating small planes between various places in eastern Zaïre. If you're in a desperate hurry for any reason, they might be of interest. VAC flies between Goma and Bukavu twice daily for Z2020 taking half an hour. *Broussair* flies from Bukavu to Goma, Beni, Bunia, Kindu, Isiro and Kisangani. See the section on Goma.

Road

With a few exceptions, getting around Zaïre is an exercise in initiative, imagination, patience, persistence and endurance. It's archetypal Africa. And it promises some of the most memorable adventures you're ever likely to experience. To enjoy it and not end up with a frazzled brain, you need to forget your fetish for getting from A to B in a certain time, or eating food and staying in accommodation

of a particular standard. Few things can be guaranteed, nothing runs on time and, in the wet season, you could be stranded for days or even weeks waiting for a lift, or for the road to dry out sufficiently to give you a fighting chance of getting through. On the other hand, the beer rarely runs out. Aside from Australia and Germany, there are few other countries which place such a high priority on their beer supplies.

Roads are often in a diabolical state of repair, with potholes large enough to swallow a truck, but they do tend to get smoothed out somewhat as the dry season progresses. There are very few regular buses of any description and most of the time you will have to hitch lifts on trucks. Free lifts are the exception unless you meet the occasional Somali or Kenyan driver. Usually you will have to pay for lifts and the price often reflects the difficulty of the journey rather than the distance but it's more or less 'fixed'. This doesn't mean you'll be quoted the price local people pay straight away. Negotiation is the name of the game. There's generally a truck park in every town where drivers congregate and it's here that you'll have to go to find a lift. In small places it's usually around the petrol (gas) station.

Transport on the main route (between Bunia on Lake Mobutu Sese Seko and Uvira on Lake Tanganyika) is more or less guaranteed but once you get off it you may well have to do a lot of walking. You must be in the right frame of mind to do this and it helps if you have a light pack. It's quite safe to walk around in this area (no one has ever been mugged, maimed or murdered that we've heard about), hospitality is usually excellent so long as you observe village protocol, and the rewards are well worth the discomforts. Many places haven't seen a tourist for years, if ever.

Although it's safe to travel in the north, don't attempt to go by road south from Uvira to Kalemie. The road over the mountains via Fizi and Baraka is reportedly the hideout for the remnants of the *Simbas* from the 1965-67 insurgency.

There's little point in quoting hitching costs on trucks since these will change and, to some extent, they'll depend on your bargaining ability. To get the best price, don't be in a hurry and ask around before you have to leave. Free lifts are available in some places if you can make the contacts.

Lake Ferries

There are two ferries which ply between Goma and Bukavu on Lake Kivu, the *Matadi* and *Karisimbi*. The *Matadi* is simply a passenger boat, although it will take motorcycles. The *Karisimbi* carries both cargo and passengers and takes longer. Neither of them call at Rwandan ports nor do the Rwandan ferries call at Zairois ports. It's a pleasant trip with incomparable views of the Virunga volcanos across the lake. See the Goma and Bukavu sections for more details.

Eastern Zaïre from South to North

UVIRA

Uvira is situated on the north-west tip of Lake Tanganyika facing Bujumbura across the lake. It's not a particularly attractive or interesting place. Avoid army personnel if possible and keep that camera out of sight – there's a lot of mercenary paranoia in the area. The actual port area, Kalundu, is some four km south of Uvira (taxis for Z30). You'll be very lucky to find a boat going south – most travellers have drawn a blank – and the road south from here is not safe.

Places to Stay

One of the cheapest places to stay is the *Hotel Babyo 'La Patience'*, Avenue Bas-Zaïre near the mosque, which has rooms

for Z70 a single. If it's full, try the *Pole Pole* which costs Z150 a single. There's no running water but there's a bar and good *brochettes* for sale. Another good place which is clean and quiet is the *Hotel Rafiki* which costs Z150 to Z180 with an air cooler.

Places to Eat

A good place to eat is the *Tanganyika Restaurant*, just down the road from La Patience, which is run by Ugandan refugees. The food is good, the staff are pleasant and English is spoken. For a splurge, try the *Hotel La Côte* which offers very good three-course meals for around Z300.

For nightlife, try the *Lobe Disco* which gets very crowded after 9.30 pm. The *Nyanda au Grand Lac* also has music sometimes.

Getting There

Taxis to the Zaïre border post run all day until late afternoon, cost Z50 (local people pay Z25) and take 10 minutes. It's a very easy-going border. Although they will probably ask you if you have any Zairois currency there's no baggage search. From here it's a one km walk to the Burundi border post unless you can find a lift. The Burundi post is also very easy-going. There are no baggage searches, no currency forms and there are money changers outside the office who offer a reasonable rate for Zaïres (Z50 = BFr 130). There may be taxis from the border post to Bujumbura (BFr 50) otherwise you'll have to hitch.

There are two possible routes between Uvira and Bukavu. The first goes entirely through Zairois territory and involves finding a lift on a truck (there are usually several daily). The route takes a mountain road on the western side of the Rusizi River via Kamanyola and Nya-Ngezi through stunning countryside. Minibuses are available between Uvira and Kamanyola for about Z100 if you can't find a truck.

The second route goes partially through Rwanda to take advantage of the excellent Rwandan road system which is sealed. There's one daily bus in either direction which leaves when full (usually between 7.30 and 8 am), costs Z250 and takes about 5½ hours. In the past, travellers who have used this route were required to have a Rwandan visa (at a cost of US$7-10 if they didn't have one) and a Zairois re-entry visa (which also cost money if they didn't have a multiple-entry visa). When I took this route I wasn't asked for either a Rwandan visa or a Zairois re-entry visa (I didn't have either). The only bit of bureaucracy I had to go through was to fill in a form at the first Zairois frontier stating how much money I was carrying but they didn't want to see it. They were not interested in stamping passports. It's possible this is a special deal which only relates to the bus. If you're hitching or driving your own car it may be different. To avoid any possible hassles or a change of rules make sure you have both Rwandan and Zairois multiple entry visas.

BUKAVU

Built over several lush tongues of land which jut out into Lake Kivu and sprawling back up the steep mountainside behind, Bukavu is a large but very attractive city with a fairly cosmopolitan population. It's effectively divided into two parts following the lines of the Avenue des Martyrs de la Révolution, which heads south straight up a valley from the lake shore, and the Avenue du Président Mobutu, which winds its way east above the lake shore. The two parts are separated by the grassy saddle of a hill. Most of the budget hotels and restaurants, the main market (Marché Maman Mobutu) and truck parks are to be found in the south of the city. The business centre, government offices, consulates, the huge cathedral and the ritzier parts of the city are to be found along the Avenue du Président Mobutu.

Information

National Parks Office The Institut Zairois pour la Conservation de la Nature is at 185 Avenue du President Mobutu and is open Monday to Friday from 8.30 am to 3 pm and on Saturday from 8.30 am to 12 noon. It's run by a very friendly German director who speaks fluent French and English (the institute is actually a joint Zairo-German project).

The director will tell you that you must make a booking here if you want to visit the plains gorillas in the Parc National de Kahuzi-Biega north of Bukavu but this isn't strictly necessary except on Sundays when there may be a lot of visitors. During the rest of the week it's unlikely you'll be turned down if you're at the take-off point by 9 am.

Consulates The Burundi consulate is on the top floor of the SINELAC Building, 184 Avenue du President Mobutu (look for the three flags of Burundi, Rwanda and Zaïre). It's open Monday to Friday from 7.30 am to 12 noon and 2.30 to 5 pm but you can only apply for visas Monday to Thursday from 3 to 5 pm. They take 24 hours.

There is no Rwandan consulate here. If you're stuck it's worth making enquiries at the Belgian consulate (see map). They may be able to help though it could take two weeks.

Bank If you need to change travellers' cheques here, the Banque Commerciale Zairoise is probably the best.

Places to Stay - bottom end

Most of the budget hotels are along the Avenue des Martyrs de la Révolution. If you stay in this area you should be prepared for the electricity to be cut off during the evening (sometimes all night). As soon as the system gets over-loaded, this is the first area to be cut off. It doesn't happen on the other side of town.

One of the cheapest hotels is the *Hotel Taifa* which is fairly pleasant and costs

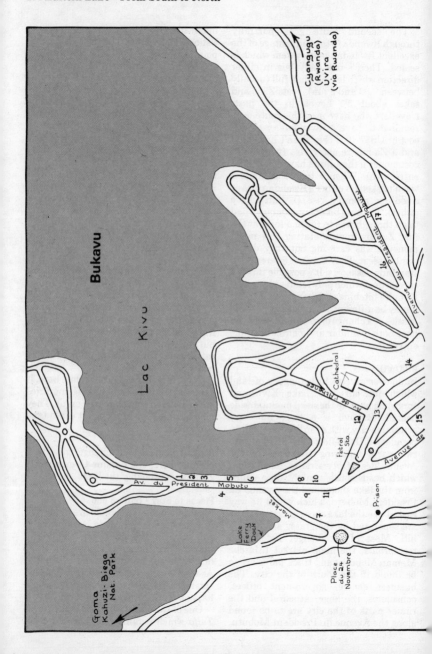

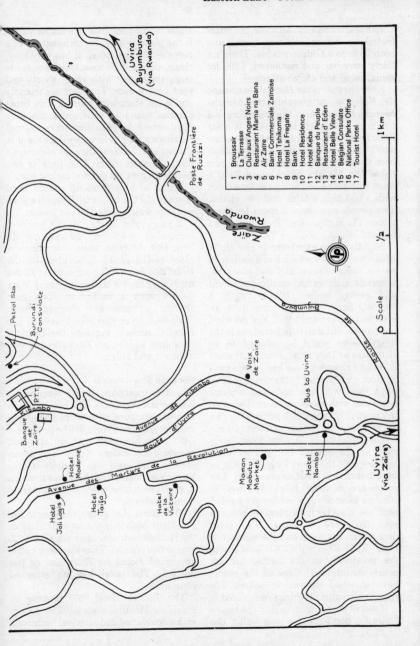

1 Broussair
2 La Terrasse
3 Club aux Anges Noirs
4 Restaurant Mama na Bana
5 Air Zaïre
6 Bank Commerciale Zaïroise
7 Hotel Tshikoma
8 Hotel La Fregate
9 Bank
10 Hotel Residence
11 Hotel Keba
12 Banque du Peuple
13 Restaurant d' Eden
14 Hotel Belle View
15 Belgian Consulate
16 National Parks Office
17 Tourist Hotel

1 km

Uvira
Bujumbura (via Rwanda)

Poste Frontiere
de Ruzizi

Zaïre
Rwanda

½

0   Scale

Petrol Sta.

Burundi
Consulate

P.T.T.

Banque de
Kibombo

Route de Bujumbura

Voix
de Zaïre

Avenue de Kibombo

Route d'Uvira

Bus to Uvira

Uvira (via Zaïre)

Hotel
Nambo

Mamu
Mobutu
Market

Hotel Moderne

Avenue des Martyrs de la Revolution

Hotel
Joli Logis

Hotel
Taïfa

Hotel
de la Victoire

Z150 a single and Z225 a double, the latter includes a shower (cold water only) and both include a Gideon's bible. There's a fairly busy bar and restaurant (Z60 for steak, salad and chips) attached.

Even cheaper is the *Hotel de la Groupe de Kalemie* up towards the Marché Maman Mobutu past the green concrete columns on the left hand side. It costs Z130 for a room with two beds but often won't take travellers. If you draw a blank here then try the *Hotel Mu-Unga* just below the Marche which costs Z150 a room with just a bed and Z180 for a room with a bed plus a table and two chairs. Two people can share a room for these prices. The staff are friendly and there's a bar and bibles.

Slightly more expensive is the *Hotel Moderne/Mareza* which has a variety of rooms, some of them airy and pleasant, others dark, dingy and smelling of mould and sweaty bodies. It's primarily a brothel. Some of the rooms have an attached shower and toilet. You get what you pay for, but if all they have left are the dingy rooms you'd be advised to go elsewhere as they're poor value. It costs Z180 for a room with one bed (sleeps two) without an attached bathroom and Z250 for a room with two beds and a share bathroom with one other room. Two men in a room get charged 50% extra. There's a fairly noisy attached bar and restaurant.

The *Hotel de la Victoire* looks fairly ritzy on the outside but is very tatty inside – half the doors look like they've been kicked in at one time or another. The rooms are, however, bright and well-lit (though most of the windows are welded shut!) so it's a far more pleasant place to stay than the Moderne. The price depends on the room and the number of beds – Z150, Z175 and Z205. Clean sheets are provided but the bathrooms are poorly maintained. None of the rooms have attached showers or toilets. It's reasonable value all things considered.

If you're planning on taking the bus to Uvira (or don't mind a long walk), the *Hotel Nambo* on the Place Major Vangu is the place to stay. It reminded me of a Nepalese budget hotel. It has very cosy, clean, simple little rooms with one fairly large single bed with clean sheets and your gear is safe. The staff are friendly and if the electricity goes off they bring candles round to your room. Showers (cold water only) and toilets are communal – although they're in a very dark room at the back of the hotel they are reasonably clean. A room costs Z200 (one or two people). There's a quiet attached bar.

Those wishing to camp should head down to the *Club Sportif*. There's a good site here which costs Z30 per person.

If you prefer to stay in the business section of town on the Avenue du Président Mobutu then the cheapest place is the *Hotel Keba* opposite the Hotel Résidence. It's good value at Z246 a double without a bathroom and Z303 a double with a bathroom. Two men sharing a room are charged more. Travellers have also recommended the *Hotel Canadien*, opposite the Burundi consulate, which costs Z315 a double with a shower and toilet.

Places to Stay – middle

One of the most popular mid-range hotels is the *Hotel Joli Logis*. The hotel is set in its own compound with lawns and ample parking space and costs Z357 a single and Z497 a double, both with an attached shower (hot water), toilet and clean sheets. The staff are friendly (some English is spoken) and there's a bar which is attached to the office but is separate from the rooms.

The *Hotel La Frégate*, Avenue du Président Mobutu, almost next door to the Hotel Résidence, has rooms for Z420 (one or two people). They also have better appointed rooms for Z720 (one or two people). The hotel has no attached restaurant.

The *Tourist Hotel*, 260 Avenue du Président Mobutu, costs Z400 for a room with a double bed and attached bathroom.

Top: Drinking home-brew, Uganda (GC)
Bottom: Volcanoes, Zaïre/Rwanda border (GC)

Top: Bujumbura, Burundi (GC)
Bottom: Bukavu, Zaïre (GC)

The only trouble with this hotel is its distance from the centre and the lake ferry dock.

In terms of quality, the *Hotel Tshikoma* near the Place du 24 Novembre, should be graded as mid-range but it's actually quite expensive – perhaps because it's the nearest hotel to the ferry dock? It costs Z730 a single and Z840 a double, both with attached bathrooms. There's a bar and restaurant.

Places to Stay – top end

Bukavu's most luxurious hotel is the *Hotel Résidence*. If you want to see how the other half live go for a beer in the air-conditioned luxury bar/restaurant underneath the hotel. The entrance is at street level through the Martini-umbrellared outdoor tables).

Places to Eat

There's a good choice of cheap, African-style restaurants in Bukavu. Two of the simplest are the *Unity Restaurant* and the *Café du Peuple*, both of which you'll find at the back of the small meat and vegetable market overlooking the lake ferry dock (marked 'Market' on the map). The *Café du Peuple* is highly recommended and very popular with local people. Some travellers rate it as the best restaurant in Bukavu. The food is very good and the portions are large. Rice and roast beef in tomato and onion sauce costs Z40. If you want potatoes the price goes up to Z45. A cup of milk coffee will cost you Z7. The *Unity Restaurant* isn't quite so good but offers rice and meat for Z30 and rice and beans for Z25.

Also very good is the *ABC Restaurant* next to the entrance to the Hotel Joli Logis. The food here is very tasty and the staff are friendly. Rice and beans in sauce costs Z35, meat, sauce and rice Z55 and chicken, sauce and rice Z65. If you want chips instead of rice the meal costs Z10 extra. A large pot of coffee or tea with milk costs Z10. It's open from 8 am to 4 pm daily.

Further up the hill near Maman Mobutu market, the *Tua Tugaure Restaurant* is reasonably good. Rice and beans cost Z20, meat and rice Z25 and omelettes Z30. The tea house below this restaurant next to Chez Abou hairdressers offers excellent curd-type yoghurt for Z7 a glass.

In the centre of town, the *Mama Na Bana*, Avenue du Président Mobutu, is good value and very friendly. It offers rice, *ugali* or *fou fou* served with chicken, fish or beef as well as *brochettes* and omelettes. You can eat from Z30.

Also recommended is the *Café de l'Avenue* on Avenue du Président Mobutu opposite the electricity office. They offer large, spicy *brochettes* (Z25) as well as salads, rice and beef. It's a pleasant place to eat, overlooking the valley.

There's an excellent patisserie selling yoghurt and cheap breakfasts (omelette, bread, jam and tea/coffee) about 200 metres from the Mama Na Bana on the opposite side of the road.

Entertainment

There are hundreds of small bars in Bukavu and though most of them are just beer-swilling places or brothels they can be great fun if you're in the mood. Some of them get pretty wild as the night wears on. There's usually African music playing (as there is in most bars in Zaïre). Other than these you could give the *Club aux Anges Noirs*, Avenue du Président Mobutu, a try.

The *Club Sportif* has a pleasant bar overlooking the lake and you may meet someone who is prepared to take you out sailing.

Getting There

Air There are quite a number of private airline companies operating small planes between various places in eastern Zaïre and there are several flights a day between Goma and Bukavu, amongst others. See the Goma section.

Road The main truck parks are around the Marché Maman Mobutu, the Place Major Vangu (at the very top of the Avenue des Martyrs de la Revolution opposite the Hotel Nambo) and on the Avenue de l'Athenée close to the cathedral. You can also pick up trucks going north from the BRALIMA brewery about two km from the Place du 24 Novembre along the Goma road. Minibuses going north usually start from the Place du 24 Novembre but they often do at least one run up the Avenue de la Révolution to collect passengers. The bus to Uvira (via Rwanda) leaves from the Place Major Vangu.

It is possible to go south from Bukavu to Cyangugu (Rwanda), then to the Rwanda/ Burundi border at Luhwa and then on to Bujumbura (the capital of Burundi). There are minibuses and taxis all the way. See the Burundi chapter for details.

Most travellers who simply want to get from Bukavu to Goma take the Lake Kivu ferry since it's quicker, cheaper and smoother than going by road. If you prefer to go by road or you want to visit the Kahuzi-Biega National Park then you will have to hitch. A truck will cost about Z400 and take about 10 hours (longer in the wet season). Other travellers, however, have reported that you can find a truck to Goma from the BRALIMA brewery for as little as Z250 and that it could take only eight hours. The road is partially sealed.

Lake Ferries There are two ferries which ply between Bukavu and Goma on Lake Kivu: the *Matadi* and *Karisimbi*. The *Matadi* is simply a passenger boat, although it will take motorcycles. The *Karisimbi* carries both cargo and passengers and takes longer. Neither of them call at Rwandan ports nor do the Rwandan ferries call at Zairois ports. The *Matadi* sails from Bukavu on Tuesdays and Fridays at 7.30 am. The fare is Z260 plus Z10 for 'validation' and the journey takes about six hours. All the seats are numbered. You need to be at the dock at least half an hour before departure. Breakfast (omelette, bread and coffee) is available for Z100 (reasonable value) and 'Primus' beer for Z35.

The boat stops two or three times for 10 minutes en route to set down/take on passengers and, in the meantime, fruit sellers in dug-outs surround the boat selling their wares. Be careful taking photographs of these people. You'll get an orange in your face before you have time to focus! It's a pleasant trip with incomparable views of the Virunga volcanos across the lake.

The *Karisimbi* leaves Bukavu on Wednesdays, costs Z85 plus Z25 tax and takes about 10-12 hours.

Buying tickets for these boats is usually simple. Turn up at the ticket office (at the dock) the previous day before 9.30 am and join the queue, after having made your presence known (this is important otherwise you'll wait all day!). It shouldn't take more than half an hour and you don't usually have to bribe anyone. Having got your ticket you need to have it 'validated' by customs at the port gates. This is where the other Z10 goes.

There are times when buying a ticket can be like getting a front seat at Bishop Tutu's enthronement. This is when there's a large government party going from one side to the other. At such times government officials, police, army personnel, other important people, their friends and friends of friends get priority. Chaos erupts and it can take all morning to get a ticket. Make sure you have your passport with you when you go to buy a ticket as they won't sell you one without it. An individual can buy several tickets so long as he/she has the passports for everyone who wants a ticket.

GOMA

Goma sits at the foot of the brooding Nyiragongo volcano at the northern end of Lake Kivu and not very far from the chain of volcanoes which make up the Parc National des Virunga on the border between Zaïre and Rwanda. Like Bukavu, it's an important business, government and resort town with a fairly cosmopolitan population and there's quite a contrast between the ritzy landscaped villas down by the lake shore and the *cité* behind it. The president maintains a palatial villa here – and you're advised to keep away from it. Nevertheless, it's a dusty, somewhat run-down town with many unsealed roads. Goma has the only international airport in this part of Zaïre.

Information

National Parks Office The Institut Zairois pour la Conservation de la Nature has an office next door to the Banque Commerciale Zairoise one street back from the main street (see the map) but it's not easy to find. Look for two large corrugated iron doors which take you through into a metalworkers' yard. The office is a small concrete building on the right-hand side. It's open daily from 9 to 11 am (sometimes later). You must make advance bookings to see the mountain gorillas at Djomba near Rutshuru. It's also possible to book at Rwindi at the radio shack but you may have to wait a week for confirmation.

Bank If you're changing travellers' cheques, the best bank to go to is the Banque Commerciale Zairoise. It shouldn't take longer than half an hour and commission is minimal.

Places to Stay – bottom end

Although many travellers prefer to stay in one of the budget hotels around the market area, my own nomination for best value in Goma is the *Catholic Mission Guest House*, an unmarked yellow building close to the Hotel Tuneko. It's comfortable, spotlessly clean, sheets and towels are provided and *boiled* after use!), there's hot water in the showers, a library, and it's totally secure. This little haven of peace and quiet costs just Z150 a single and Z350 a double. All the rooms have a wash basin and breakfast is included in the price. It's popular with travellers but what puts some people off is the *mère* (?) who rules with a hand of phosphor-bronze steel. On the other hand, you only see her at breakfast. There's also a 10 pm curfew.

Cheaper than the Catholic Guest House and recommended by many travellers is the *Chambres Aspro*. Despite the unusual name, it's not subsidised by a drug company but run by a very friendly family. They will let you use their stove to warm up water or to cook on and they charge only Z100 per room. Similar and also very friendly is the *Hotel Abki* next to the football field which costs Z150 per room (one or two people). There are bucket showers but the water supply is erratic. You can leave excess gear safely if you want to climb Nyiragongo. Try to get a room in the main part of the hotel. The *Macho Kwa Macho* is the same price.

Many travellers have stayed at the *Hotel Haut Zaïre* in the past but I personally think it's poor value for money in comparison to what else is available. It costs Z225 for a room with one bed (one or two people) and Z250 for a room with two beds (the beds are single size). The rooms are very basic and cell-like and the showers are intermittent. There are also quite a lot of mosquitos and the locks on the doors and windows are a joke. It has an attached restaurant. Better value at this price would be the *Hotel Tuneko* next to the Catholic Guest House which costs Z200 a single. It's pleasant but there's an attached bar which can get noisy.

Other travellers have suggested the *Guest House Mutara* near the market which costs Z180 for a room (one or two people) and is clean but has no electricity.

There's a camp site at the *Cercle Sportif* which costs Z100 per tent per night, plus they have cabins for Z250 per

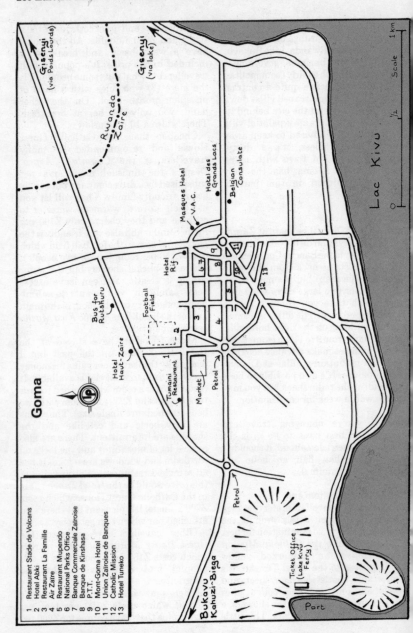

Goma

1 Restaurant Stade de Volcans
2 Hotel Abki
3 Restaurant La Famille
4 Air Zaïre
5 Restaurant Mupendo
6 National Parks Office
7 Banque Commerciale Zairoise
8 Banque de Kinshasa
9 P.T.T.
10 Mont-Goma Hotel
11 Union Zairoise de Banques
12 Catholic Mission
13 Hotel Tuneko

Lac Kivu

Scale
1 km
½
0

Rwanda
Zaïre

Grisenyi (via Poids Lourds)
Grisenyi (via lake)

Hotel des Grands Lacs
Belgian Consulate
Masques Hotel
V.A.C.
Hotel Rif

Bus for Rutshuru

Football Field

Hotel Haut-Zaïre

Tomaini Restaurant

Market

Petrol

Bukavu
Kahuzi-Biega

Petrol

Ticket Office (Lake Kivu Ferry)

Port

night. There's only one shower, lots of mosquitos and it's filthy according to those who have stayed there.

Places to Stay - middle

There is little choice in terms of mid-range hotels. Probably the best place is the *Mont-Goma Hotel* at the back of the Banque du Peuple which fronts onto the main roundabout. Rooms cost Z490 a single and Z990 a double with an attached bathroom (hot water) and, if you're lucky, a balcony. The *Hotel Rif* is similar.

Places to Stay - top end

The only top-range hotels in Goma are the *Masques Hotel* and the *Hotel des Grands Lacs*, close to each other near the main roundabout.

Places to Eat

There are three good places where you can pick up a cheap African-style meal. *Restaurant La Famille* is run by a very friendly family who will do everything possible to cook you what you want. They offer both traditional African and western staples like omelettes with various fillings. It's highly recommended. The *Restaurant Tumaini*, next to the market in a building with a low overhanging roof, is also very good. It has large portions of potatoes and rice or cabbage and beans for Z30 and potatoes, rice and meat for Z40. The restaurant at the *Hotel Abki* offers large portions of beans, potatoes and rice for Z30, rice, potatoes and meat for Z80, rice and sauce for Z50 and potatoes and sauce for Z60.

For western food, the *Restaurant Mupendo* which takes up a part of the *Boulangerie/Patisserie Mupendo* on the main street is highly recommended and very popular. It's run by a Frenchman and offers things like steak and chips (Z110) and portions of pizza (Z70) – you need two of them if you're hungry. The set menu breakfasts are very good value – a two-egg omelette, bread, butter, jam and two cups of coffee with milk for Z65. They also have cakes and meat pies.

If you want to splurge try the set meal at the *Mont-Goma Hotel*.

Avoid eating at the restaurant in the *Hotel Rif*. It's not only expensive (around Z260 for soup and a main course) but there are high taxes too (15%). The meal I was served there ranked as one of the worst I've come across in the whole of East Africa. I don't think the chicken had even passed by a cooking pot let alone been put in one. It was totally inedible.

One of the most pleasant surprises about Goma is the cheeses which are produced locally. You can buy them from street hawkers or general stores (*alimentations*) for about Z150 per kg. That's excellent value especially if you're putting your own food together. Salami and pâtes are also produced locally and sold for about Z10-15 per 100 gm.

The market in Goma has a good selection of food for those who want to do their own cooking.

Getting There

Air VAC, next to the Masques Hotel near the main roundabout, flies from Goma to Bukavu twice daily for Z2020 taking ½ an hour. Broussair, Avenue du Président Mobutu, flies from Bukavu to Goma, Beni, Bunia, Kindu, Isiro and Kisangani.

Road There is a daily bus in both directions between Goma and Rutshuru, which costs Z150 and takes about 2½ hours. From Goma it departs about 2 pm and from Rutshuru about 6.15 am. If you want a seat then you should be there about two hours before departure otherwise you'll be one of the 25 people standing on a 16-seat minibus. Resist paying outrageous baggage charges (local people will often intervene on your behalf if this happens). In Goma the bus departs from a private house between the *Hotel Haut Zaïre* and the main north/south road.

You can also hitch for about the same price – ask around at wholesale merchants and truck depots in either town.

There are two bus companies which cover the route from Goma to Bunia via Butembo – up to five days a week, season and mechanics permitting. The company most people use is the Butembo Safari Bus. The fare is Z550 and the journey should take about 12 hours (longer in the wet season). You need to buy your ticket the day before departure from the Hotel Tuneko in Goma. If it's full, ask at the Texaco petrol (gas) station on the roundabout on the main street in Goma. The bus departs Goma on Wednesday and Saturday and Butembo on Monday and Thursday.

The road goes through the Virunga National Park at one stage and you're likely to see quite a lot of animals (antelopes, hyaenas, buffaloes and hippos). You don't have to pay the entry fee for the National Park. There are quite a few military checkpoints en route. Hitching a truck along this stretch could take you up to two days because of stops en route.

Lake Ferries There are two ferries between Goma and Bukavu: the *Matadi* is a passenger boat, although it will take motorcycles; and the *Karisimbi* carries both cargo and passengers and is slower. Neither of them call at Rwandan ports. The *Matadi* sails from Goma on Wednesdays and Saturdays at 7.30 am. You need to buy your tickets the day before you depart and to be at the dock at least ½ an hour before departure. The fare is Z260 plus Z10 for 'validation' and the journey takes about six hours. The *Karisimbi* leaves Goma on Saturdays, costs Z85 plus Z25 tax and takes about 10-12 hours. See the Bukavu section for details about buying tickets, and the journey.

RUTSHURU

Rutshuru is perhaps the most convenient take-off point for a visit to the mountain gorillas in the Parc National des Virunga where they are found on the slopes of

Muside and Sabinyo volcanos (which Zaïre shares with Rwanda and Uganda). You first have to make your way to Djomba. The turn-off for this place is some two km south of Rutshuru and is clearly signposted.

If you're coming from or going to Uganda you will probably also come through Rutshuru unless you are going to cross the border further north between Beni and Kasese via Kasindi.

Places to Stay & Eat

Probably the best place to stay in Rutshuru is the *Catholic Mission* which has a guest house where you can stay for Z180 a double. There are showers, and meals are available for Z70. If you prefer to camp they may let you do this in the grounds of the mission without charge.

Cheaper is the unnamed lodging house about 50 metres north of the police station on the opposite side of the road which has rooms for Z100 (one or two people). It's simple but there are bucket showers, an earth toilet and the owner is very friendly. He may help you find transport.

Other hotels which have been recommended by travellers in the past are the *Hotel du Parc* and the *Katata Hotel*. The latter is very clean and has hot water but is more expensive than the other alternatives.

Getting There

There is a daily bus to and from Goma which costs Z150 and takes about 2½ hours. It departs from Rutshuru about 6.15 am. You can also hitch for about the same price – ask around at wholesale merchants and truck depots. See the Goma section for more details.

KAYNA-BAYONGA

This town is a truck-stop on the road between Goma and Butembo, especially going south since drivers are not allowed to travel through the Virunga National Park at night. As far as views are concerned, this is to your advantage since otherwise you would miss the Kabasha escarpment.

Places to Stay & Eat

Although there are a few small places in the town centre, most truck drivers (and therefore travellers looking for a lift) stay at the *Hotel Italie* about three km north of the town. Rooms with one bed cost Z100 (for one or two people) and rooms with two beds cost Z200. There are clean, concrete toilets, bucket showers (cold water). There's no electricity so kerosene lamps are provided.

If you stay at the Italie then you'll probably have to eat there too though the food is relatively expensive (omelettes for Z80, tea for Z30). On the other hand, they don't mind cooking late for those who arrive late (say, up to 10 pm).

If you stay in the town centre there are three places where you can pick up food. Two of them are on the main street but one of them is really only a bar which has bread. The restaurant on the main street offers the best value with meat and rice for Z60 and tea for Z10 though the proprietor may try to charge you a 'tourist price'. The other restaurant is down an alley off the main street and has meat and rice for Z80 and tea for Z10. There's a good daily market for those who want to put their own food together.

Getting There

Trucks leave for Goma early in the morning between 5.30 and 6 am, either from the Hotel Italie or from the market. After that you'll have to rely on transport passing through from elsewhere.

BUTEMBO

With a population of some 100,000, Butembo is another large town about half way between Goma and Bunia. There's a good market here and excellent views of the surrounding countryside.

Places to Stay

Two good cheap places to stay are the *Lodgement Apollo II*, which costs Z110 per room (one or two people), has electricity in the evenings and bucket showers, and the *Semuliki Hotel* which costs Z220 a double without a shower and toilet. The *Semuliki* has a good attached restaurant.

Somewhat more expensive is the *Hotel Ambiance* which costs Z300 a double. It's very pleasant, has electricity, running water, showers and washing facilities.

The *Oasis Hotel*, a colonial-style place displaying a delightful air of deteriorating elegance, used to be a popular and none too expensive hotel but, sadly, it has now closed. Perhaps someone will resurrect it?

Places to Eat

Apart from the *Semuliki Hotel*, the *Restaurant Cafeteria* near the market is recommended. Soup costs Z20, meat, rice and potatoes Z50 and coffee with milk Z20.

Getting There

There are two bus companies which cover the route between Goma and Bunia via Butembo up to five times a week. The most popular company is the Butembo Safari Bus. They have a bus which departs from Butembo for Bunia on Monday and Thursday. See the Goma section for more details.

Hitching a truck along this stretch could take you up to two days because of stops en route. If you do decide to hitch, trucks leave from 'Concorde' at the Goma end of town.

Between Butembo and Beni there are frequent pick-ups and minibuses available for around Z130.

BENI

Beni is the starting point for climbing the Ruwenzori Mountains from the Zairois side. They can also be climbed on the Uganda side (see the Uganda chapter).

Several of the hotels offer excess baggage storage facilities though you can also leave gear at the park warden's office in Mutsora.

Places to Stay

One of the best and cheapest places to stay is the *Hotel Walaba*, about 100 metres down the Kasindi road from the roundabout. It costs Z58 a room (sleeps two people) and has bucket showers. It's a good place to meet other travellers and the Somali owner, Mohammed, will change money for you if you're stuck. Both he and the predominantly Ugandan staff speak English. You can leave baggage safely while you climb the Ruwenzoris. They don't mind if you cook your own food but they also have their own good, cheap restaurant.

Similar and very friendly is the *Jumbo Hotel* at Z80 a single and Z100 a double. They also have an excess baggage store.

Other travellers have recommended the *Hotel Virunga* (Z80 per room – one or two people); the *Hotel Busa Beni* (Z100 a single and Z150 a double); the *Hotel Isale* (Z150 a single and Z200 a double – very clean and friendly), the *Hotel Bashu* (Z150 a single and Z200 a double), and the *Hotel Sina Makosa* (Z170 per room).

Places to Eat

The restaurant at the *Hotel Walaba* offers rice and beans for Z25, meat and rice for Z45 and omelettes for Z25-40. The bread they serve is baked on the premises.

Good breakfasts are available from the *Restaurant Ronde-Pointe* on the roundabout (omelettes, bread and tea, etc for Z70. The snacks outside the *Paradisio Club* (a disco) are also recommended.

Next to the Hotel Walaba there is a small well-stocked market. There are a number of similar shops (mostly Greek owned) in the centre of town. They're useful if you're organising a trek up the Ruwenzoris.

Getting There

Air Broussair flies to Beni as well as Bukavu, Goma, Bunia, Kindu, Isiro and Kisangani.

Road There are frequent pick-ups and minibuses available for around Z130 between Beni and Butembo. In Beni both the minibuses and trucks leave from the gas station just down the Komanda road from the roundabout.

For free trucks out of Beni ask at the CAPACO depot about trucks to Goma. The manager here is very friendly and may fix you up with a free lift. Otherwise you're looking at Z450. The journey often takes about 24 hours.

BUNIA

Bunia is a large town in the hills above Lake Mobutu Sese Seko. It's one of the starting points for the trip west to Kisangani via Komanda, Mambasa and Nia Nia. If you get this far up it's worth making a side trip to the fishing village of Tshoma.

Places to Stay

One of the most popular places to stay in Bunia is the *Chez Tout Bunia Hotel* which has rooms for Z70 a single. There's an attached restaurant.

Further down the hill in the city are plenty of other cheapies which have rooms from Z50. The *Hotel Rubi*, on the main street, is one of the best. Another hotel which has been recommended in Bunia is the *Butembo II* which is very friendly indeed and has great food.

Getting There

Air Broussair flies from Bunia, Bukavu, Goma, Beni, Bunia, Kindu, Isiro and Kisangani.

Road There are two bus companies which cover the route between Bunia and Goma. Season and mechanics permitting they leave up to five times a week. The fare is Z550 and the journey should take about 12 hours. Hitching a truck along this stretch could take you up to two days because of stops en route. See the Goma section.

Around Bunia

Tshoma Tshoma is a fishing village on the lake, reached via the border post town of Kasenye. It's a very lively village with bars open 24 hours a day to accommodate the fishermen's antisocial hours. The hospitality is excellent and fresh fish are very cheap indeed. Unfortunately, it's not safe to swim in the lake because of bilharzia. Transport is fairly easy to find and there are regular trucks from the fisheries in Tshoma to Beni (the fare is about Z300).

The National Parks

PARC NATIONAL DE KAHUZI-BIEGA

Lying between Bukavu and Goma, this park was created in 1970 with an initial area of 600 square km but was expanded to 6,000 square km in 1975. The principal reason for its creation was to preserve the habitat of the plains gorilla (*Gorilla gorilla graueri*) which was once distributed all the way from the right bank of the Zaïre River to the mountains on the borders with Uganda and Rwanda. These days, like the mountain gorillas which live on the slopes of the volcanos on the borders between Zaïre, Rwanda and Uganda, they're an endangered species. Many other animals, of course, live in this park including chimpanzees, many other kinds of monkeys, elephants, buffaloes, many kinds of antelopes, leopards, genets, servals and mongooses. The bird life is prolific.

The altitude in the park varies between 900 and 3308 metres (Mt Kahuzi) and the average annual rainfall is fairly heavy at 1900 mm with the heaviest falls in April and November. The dry season runs through the months of June, July and August. Most areas of the park have a temperate climate with a fairly constant average temperature of 15°C.

Because of the heavy rainfall and the varying altitude, there's a wide variety of vegetation in the park ranging from dense rain-forests at the lower levels, through bamboo forests between 2400 and 2600 metres and finally heath and alpine meadows on the summits of the highest mountains. A lot of the animals tend to live in the denser parts of the forest and they are often difficult to see. This is also true of the gorillas which are not nearly as used to human contact as their cousins in Rwanda and so tend to flee as soon as they hear you or catch sight of you.

Visiting the Gorillas

There are several groups of gorillas in the park though you will usually only see one of the groups which has become partially accustomed to human contact. They can be visited any day of the year including public holidays. Children under 15 years of age are not allowed to visit. The National Park office in Bukavu (Institut Zairois pour la Conservation de la Nature, 185 Avenue du Président Mobutu) will tell you that it's necessary to make a booking with them. This isn't really the case except on Sundays when demand can be high. The office is open Monday to Friday from 8.30 am to 3 pm and on Saturday from 8.30 am to 12 noon. If you don't make a booking you must be at the Station Tshivanga (park entrance and take-off point) by 8 am on the day you want to go. If you have a booking you don't need to be there until 9 am.

The park entry fee is Z1500 per person which includes the compulsory guide and trackers (who chop the vegetation to make a track). They all expect a tip at the end - so would I if I had to chop my way through thick jungle to take a bunch of tourists to see gorillas everyday! The average tip is Z25-30 for the guide and Z20 for each tracker. At current prices it is considerably cheaper to see gorillas in

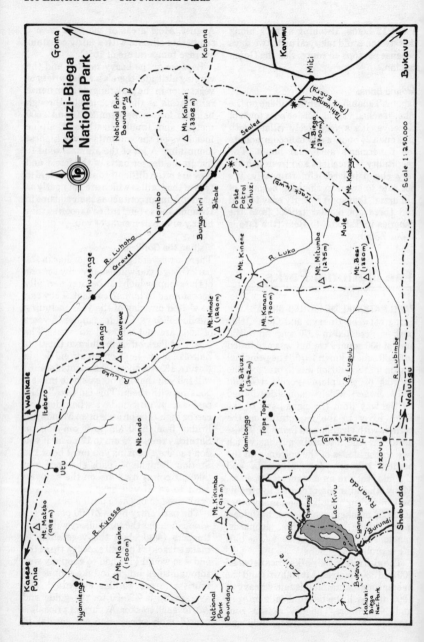

Kahuzi-Biega National Park

Scale 1 : 250,000

Zaïre than in Rwanda (about US$25 as opposed to US$60).

You must have appropriate footwear and clothing, preferably a pair of stout boots and waterproof clothing. This is not a picnic. It's often very muddy and hard going up steep slopes. You need to be careful what you grab hold of to pull yourself up – many vines and other plants carry thorns or will sting you. A pair of gloves would be an excellent idea. It can rain even in the dry season. The guides can generally locate a group of gorillas within two hours although it can be up to five hours or as little as five minutes (unusual). If you don't see any the first day your fee covers you for another attempt the next. No refunds are possible if you can't come back the next day.

If you have a camera there is an additional fee of Z50. Officially, movie cameras and video cassette recorders are prohibited but some people apparently manage to take movie cameras as they report being charged Z250 for them. It's also officially prohibited to publish photographs taken of the gorillas. Just how they plan to police this, goodness only knows. You need the fastest film you can get hold of – ASA 800/1600 would be the kind to go for. Anything less and you're going to be very disappointed when you get home. When you finally find a troop of gorillas, the trackers start hacking away at the bush to give you a better view. The troop retreats and the 'view' becomes a running hunt by the humans followed by a retreat of the gorillas. The silverback male makes mock charges to give the other members of his group time to retreat. You might find this exciting or frightening but either way it's hopeless for pictures. It doesn't contribute much to gorilla-human relations either.

To get to the take-off point at Station Tshivanga you have a choice of a combination bus trip and walk, or a taxi. A taxi is really only feasible if there's a group of you – you're looking at between Z1700 and Z2000 – although it would save time. You could probably set off from Bukavu in time to reach Tshivanga by 8 am, see the gorillas and be back in Bukavu by early or mid-afternoon. If you have to use public transport you'll need a minimum of two days. The first day you take a bus (frequent) from the Place du 24 Novembre in Bukavu to Miti along a sealed road. The fare is about Z50. From Miti it's seven km to Tshivanga and lifts are difficult to find. You may have to walk so it's best to plan on staying at Tshivanga for the night and seeing the gorillas the next day. Bring everything you need with you (tent, food, drinks). Occasionally the people at Tshivanga have a tent for hire, but don't count on it. Food and drink should be bought in Bukavu or in Miti. Miti has an adequate fruit and vegetable market though canned food, etc is limited. Camping at the park entrance costs Z40.

Climbing Mt Kahuzi

The take-off point for climbing this mountain is Poste Patrol Kahuzi which you get to by following the sealed road from the park entrance at Tshivanga. Guides, which are compulsory, can be found at Kahuzi. The climb to the summit takes about three hours and you pass through virtually all the park's different strata of vegetation. There are excellent views from the summit. Bring everything you need with you.

Treks in the Lowland Rainforest

It's possible to arrange a trek starting from the Irangi Research Station about 100 km from Tshivanga but it's very difficult to get there without your own four-wheel-drive transport as there's very little traffic beyond Hombo. You're advised to discuss this option at the national park office in Bukavu before attempting it.

PARC NATIONAL DES VIRUNGA

This park covers a sizeable area of the

Zaïre/Uganda and Zaïre/Rwanda borders, stretching all the way from Goma almost to Lake Mobutu Sese Seko via Lake Idi Amin (Edward). Much of it is continuous with national parks in Uganda and Rwanda. The Virunga was Zaïre's first national park and was created in 1925. It covers an area of 8,000 square km. For administrative purposes the park has been divided into four sections. From the south they are: Nyiragongo, Nyamulgira and Karisimbi; Rwindi and Vitshumbi; Ishango, and lastly the Ruwenzori. This is also the way they'll be dealt with in this book.

Entry to any part of the Virunga (except you're if passing straight through on transport between Rutshuru and Kayna-Bayonga) costs Z600 for a seven-day permit plus Z50 for a camera permit. You can go from one part of the park to another without paying twice so long as your permit is still valid.

Nyiragongo, Nyamulgira & Karisimbi

This section of the park includes the three volcanos which give it its name and also includes the gorilla sanctuary at Djomba on the slopes of Muside and Sabinyo volcanos along the border with Rwanda.

The Gorilla Sanctuary The sanctuary is managed by the Institut Zairois pour la Conservation de la Nature. If you want to be absolutely sure of getting onto a gorilla-viewing group, you must first make a booking at the IZCN office in Goma, before going to Djomba (the take-off point for visits). The office is open daily between 9 and 11 am and sometimes later, but it's not easy to find so refer to the Goma section for details. If you don't make a booking you can still go to see the gorillas if there is room on the one group per day which visits them. Usually there is, but if an overland truck arrives, you might have to wait several days before they manage to fit you in.

The fee is Z1000 per person and there's a hut where you can stay in Djomba for Z250 per person per night. There's a stove but you must take all your own food with you or have the villagers cook for you. The villagers have a limited range of food which they'll sell if you want to do your own cooking but the nearest stores are in Djomba. Camping costs Z100.

You must be at the take-off point by 8 am if you want to see the gorillas. The fee includes a guide (compulsory) but he will expect a tip at the end. Even so, it is considerably cheaper to see the gorillas here than in Rwanda. The guides can usually find a group of gorillas within an hour or two. There are two groups, one known as Oscar and the other known as Marcel. Only two people may visit the Oscar group at any one time but up to six may visit the Marcel group.

To get to Djomba you have to first get to Rutshuru (see the Rutshuru section). The turn-off for Djomba is about two km before Rutshuru and is clearly signposted. The Michelin map of this area is not very precise and on the map it appears that the road goes off from the centre of town. This isn't the case. The turn-off you want branches from a roundabout with a petrol station about four km from the actual centre of Rutshuru. The signposts saying you are already in Rutshuru are misleading – the city's boundaries start about two km from the roundabout and six km from the town centre.

There's another right fork in the centre of town which takes you to Uganda via Ishasha. The bus from Goma takes you right into the centre unless you request to be let down. From the turn-off on the Goma-Rutshuru road it's about 26 km to Djomba over a very rough road (four-wheel drive). Transport is sporadic. Finally, from Djomba it's a seven km walk, gradually uphill, to the starting point and the hut where you can stay overnight.

If you don't want to stay in the hut, there's a *Catholic Mission* in Djomba where you can get full board for Z400. There's also an *American Baptist*

Mission at Rwanguba which is five km uphill from Djomba.

Djoma is about seven km from the Ugandan border.

Nyiragongo

Nyiragongo (3470 metres) which broods over Goma used to be a spectacular sight when it was erupting but at present it's quiescent. It's still worth climbing to the top for the views. Since it only takes five hours up and three hours down it can be done in one day, so long as you set off very early. This isn't recommended because the summit is only clear of mist or cloud in the early morning and again, briefly, in the late afternoon. Make it a two-day event.

The take-off point is at Kibati about 15 km north of Goma on the Rutshuru road. Here you find the Camp des Guides which is a long, white, unmarked building set back above the road at the foot of the volcano. You can either hitch or walk to this place. Fees are paid at the camp (Z600 park entry plus Z50 for a camera). If you plan to spend the night in the hut about ½ an hour's walk from the crater rim, it will cost you Z40 extra per person. The huts are in bad shape but there is usually water close by. Bring all the food and firewood/charcoal you need from Kibati. The park entry fee is supposed to cover the cost of a guide (compulsory) but most people have to pay another Z100 'tip', though for this the guide will usually double as a porter.

It's possible to stay at the Camp des Guides the day before you go up the mountain but there's no regular accommodation. Many travellers buy the head guide a bottle of beer and end up sleeping on his floor – he's friendly and interesting. Otherwise you could camp.

On the first day you need to start off before 1 pm as it's a three-hour walk to the base of the crater cone proper and then another hour to the huts. On the way up you pass some interesting geology and vegetation – tropical forest, hardened lava flows (recent, old and ancient) and giant lobelia.

On the second day you need to get up early and put on some warm clothes so you can set off by 6.30 am. It's a half hour walk to the crater rim and the weather should be clear. Looking down into the base of the crater you'll probably still see wisps of steam and vapour coming from the walls while the base itself is an uneven cooled mass of lava. Sulphur fumes hang in the air. The views of Goma, Lake Kivu and over into Rwanda are terrific. By about 9.30 am the mist will start closing in for the day and you lose the views. The descent takes about three hours.

Nyamulgira

To climb Nyamulgira (3055 metres) you need a minimum of three days but you shouldn't have to pay the park entry fee again if you haven't used up your original seven days. As on Nyiragongo, you'll have to tip the guides extra. Bring all your food requirements and, as there's nowhere to stay at the Nyamulgira base camp, you'll need a tent.

The trip starts at Kibati (as for Nyiragongo) and the first part involves a 45 km walk to the base camp through beautiful countryside. The next day involves a six-hour climb through an incredibly varied landscape ranging from old and recent lava flows (some of them pocked with lava pools) to dense upland jungles. You may be lucky and catch sight of elephants, chimpanzees, buffaloes and antelopes but you'll definitely see and hear hundreds of different birds. The first night on the mountain is spent at a decaying but rambling hut (for which you pay extra) though it is possible to return to the base camp the same day if you set off early enough. Camping is an alternative. The guides generally cook their own food.

The next day you set off for the crater rim. It takes about one hour to reach the tree line and then another hour to get to the crater rim across recent lava flows (slippery when wet). As from Nyiragongo, the views from the summit are magnificent. You descend the mountain the same day.

Rwindi & Vitshumbi

The main attraction in this part of the park is the game – lions, elephants, hippos, giraffes, antelopes, hyenas, buffaloes and many others. The Ruwenzori National Park in neighbouring Uganda (which is contiguous with Virunga) used to be much the same but it was sadly depleted of wild life during that country's civil wars. If you come to this part of the Virunga you need to make enquiries beforehand to see if vehicles can be hired for a safari. If not, you're going to be reliant on tourists and they're not always very keen on picking up hitchers.

The lodge at Rwindi is somewhat expensive at Z1800 per person although if you wait until the bar closes it may be possible to bed down by the swimming pool. The more people do this, the sooner there will be a clampdown, as camping is officially forbidden in or around the lodge. If you can't afford to stay at the lodge, enquire about rooms in the drivers' quarters. You may be lucky and get a room with two beds for Z290. There's also a small guest house in the nearby village but they're not keen on taking tourists.

While you're in this area you should pay a visit to the fishing village of Vitshumbi at the southern end of Lake Idi Amin (Edward). A visit to the fishing village of Kiavinyonge at the northern end of the lake near Kasindi is also interesting (see the following section).

Ishango

This is similar to the Rwindi/Vitshumbi part of the park except you don't find elephants here. Ishango is just a park camping area with a small airstrip and a derelict lodge which you can use free of charge – it's usually filthy with bat droppings. Camping is preferable but you'll be charged Z200 per tent for this.

There are no fences so you're advised to be careful at night. Campers have encountered hyenas and leopards that have come too close for comfort.

Those who know the area well say that it's possible to swim in either Lake Idi Amin (Edward) or in the Semliki River which flows into it as there's apparently no danger of bilharzia. They do, however, warn strongly about hippos. If you do decide to go for a swim you need to watch closely for 10-15 minutes to make sure there are no hippos anywhere near you. One traveller who ignored the warnings had a buttock bitten off a few years ago. There are no hospitals close by in Zaïre, but he was lucky and survived because the Ugandans allowed him through to their nearest hospital (after a long hassle). The wildlife and particularly the bird life is prolific where the Semliki flows into the lake.

To get to Ishango you need to get to Kasindi, either from Beni (Zaïre) or Kasese (Uganda). There are usually a fair number of trucks on the road between the two places and you can hitch. Wait at the turn-off in Kasindi for a lift into the park. If you get stuck at the turn-off, it's three km to the park entrance and you can generally rent a bedroom in one of the buildings there for around Z50 per night for two people. You will have to pay another Z600 park entry fee if your seven-day permit has run out but there is a way around this *if* you don't want to go to Ishango. If that's the case, tell them you are going to Kiavinyonge which is 10 km beyond Ishango and is not strictly in the national park. No one else pays to get there as the only road in is through Kasindi and Ishango. The trip involves a ferry crossing over a river literally swarming with hippos.

Kiavinyonge

This large fishing village has a spectacular setting at the foot of a mountain range leading down to the lake. Herds of hippo wallow close to the beach and large marabou birds are to be seen everywhere. At about 6 am the village becomes a hive of activity as fishing boats land their catches on the sandy beach in front of the restaurant and houses. The men look after the nets and the women sort the fish which are smoked during the day. Few tourists visit so you're in for an off-the-beaten-track treat.

Stay at the *Lodgement Special* at the west end of the village where they have rooms for Z80 (one or two people). Don't be put off if they're not sure what to do with you when you turn up! There's a restaurant on the lake shore which sells coffee, tea, bread and hot corned beef (!) but the best thing to buy is fish and rice (about Z50 per person). You're not going to find it fresher anywhere else! It's open from 6 am to 8 pm.

When you want to leave Kiavinyonge enquire about trucks taking fish to Butembo. They leave about 8 am, cost about Z250 and take about four hours. It's an incredible journey up over the mountains on a dirt road with many hairpin bends. This is not the normal Kasindi-Butembo road.

Ruwenzori

This is the most northerly part of the Virunga and its major appeal for travellers is, of course, the climb up the Ruwenzori mountains. It is also possible to climb from the Ugandan side since the border between the two countries passes along the summits. Don't underestimate the difficulties of this trek from either side. It's much tougher than climbing up Kilimanjaro. True, some people do make it in joggers and normal clothes but they suffer for it. You can almost freeze to death without adequate clothes and a warm sleeping bag if you're anywhere above Hut 3 (about 4200 metres). Snow is not unusual either at or above this point. Prepare for it properly and it will be one of the most memorable trips in your life.

Before you even think about doing this trek get hold of the appropriate footwear,

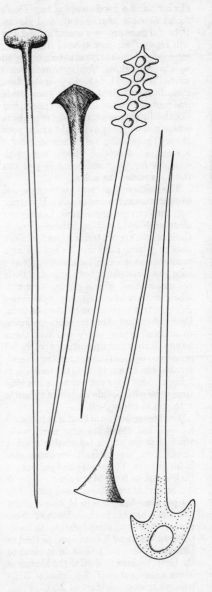

Zaïre hairpins

clothing and a good sleeping bag. Don't forget about a beanie (hat) and gloves. Pots and pans are very useful indeed and will repay their cost several times over, especially if you're trying to economise on weight by taking, for instance, dried soups. You need to take *all* your own food including sufficient to feed your guide and porters. A stove is also very useful but not absolutely essential. Many of the huts where you will stay overnight are in poor shape. There is no glass in the windows for a start, so sheets of plastic can work wonders for your wellbeing if you pin them up across the holes.

The guide and porters are very partial to cigarettes at the end of a day. If you run out, they can get unpleasant. Leave your clean-and-healthy-living fetishes at home, these people are not trekking for fun. Sure they're getting paid but it's not a king's ransom even in Zaïre. Before you go make sure you agree about both your and their responsibilities, who is paying for what, where exactly you are going, how many days the trip will take, and then be firm. Remember that other trekkers are going to come after you, so try and keep them happy. If they end up wishing they could string you up from the nearest tree then I, for one, don't want to be on the trek which follows yours. Five days or more is a long time to be with people who want to battle with you at every turn.

The best selection of food is to be found in Beni but there are also fairly well-stocked shops and a reasonable market (meat, fruit, vegetables, beer, sodas, etc) in Mutwanga. The guides and porters get their supplies from Mutwanga.

The actual trek starts when you get to the park headquarters in Mutsora, about four km from Mutwanga. Both of these places are situated about halfway between Beni and Kasindi on the road to Uganda. There are trucks from close to the Hotel Walaba in Beni to the Mutsora/Mutwanga turn-off for about Z150 (though they often start at Z200). From there you walk, although it is possible to

get a lift all the way to Mutwanga. It's about 13 km from the turn-off on the Beni-Kasindi road to either Mutsora or Mutwanga. At the park headquarters in Mutsora you pay the necessary fees and arrange for guides and porters: park entrance fee – Z600, guide – Z1600, guide's porter – Z800, additional porters for your gear – Z800 each, hut fees – Z100 per person per night, and camera fees – Z50 each. You pay for all the food but the guide and porters provide their own equipment.

If you like, you can stay at the park headquarters. Camping costs Z100 or you can rent a large, clean, well-furnished room for Z250 which they will allow three people to sleep in. Most budget travellers, however, go to Mutwanga, about four km away. Here you will find a place that has become a legend among the travelling *cognoscenti* – an abandoned hotel, variously called the *Hotel Ruwenzori* or the *Hotel Engles* with three swimming pools but no windows or furniture. No one, including the Belgian owner and the caretaker, minds if you stay here for the night and it's completely free of charge (but please leave a tip with the caretaker). You can also camp free of charge. It's a great place and anyone will tell you where it is. The caretaker will even chop wood for you (at a price) and sell you food. Don't forget that tip! When the revolution happened the authorities wouldn't talk sense about finance so the owner let it fall into disuse. The dispute is still going on.

As for going up the Ruwenzoris, the standard trek takes five days: Mutsora (1700 metres) to Hut 1 (2042 metres), known as Kalongi, takes about five hours; Hut 1 to Hut 2 (3333 metres), known as Mahungu, takes about 5½ hours; Hut 2 to Hut 3 (4303 metres), known as Kyondo, takes about 4½ hours; Hut 3 (4303 metres) to the summit and back to Hut 1 takes about seven hours; Hut 1 to Mutsora takes about four hours. It's possible to stay at Hut 3 if the weather is unfavourable for an assault on the summit. There's also a fourth hut (known as Moraine) at 4312 metres on the edge of the moraine but you'll probably be charged an extra Z100 for this and you have to sign an indemnity releasing the National Parks from any responsibility for you – part of the route is across bare rock with only a rope to hold onto. Properly equipped climbers can also make an ascent on the peaks of Mt Stanley.

There are beds (that have never seen cleaners – but what do you want!) at Huts 1 and 2 but none in the rest. Water is available at or near each of the huts except Hut 2 (where you may have to walk two km to find it). Be warned, too, that the climb from Hut 1 to Hut 2 is the worst of the lot. It's all uphill and is very hard going between roots and vines. For much of the way the ground is very wet and rain can be frequent even outside the wet season.

If the conditions described here give you second thoughts, don't let them. The views from Hut 3 and above will make it all worthwhile.

There are variations on the route and scheduling but you must arrange these before you set off.

Trekkers and climbers who would like more information on the various routes as well as detailed notes on the natural history of the mountains should get hold of a copy of *Guide to the Ruwenzori* by Osmaston and Pasteur which was last published in 1972. The only two places I know of where you can buy this book any longer are West Col Productions, 1 Meadow Close, Goring-on-Thames, Reading, Berks, UK, and Stanfords Map Centre, Long Acre, Covent Garden, London WC2, UK. It costs £8.95 (plus postage).

Mt Hoyo

Mt Hoyo is about 13 km off the Beni-Bunia road close to Komanda and its draw is the waterfalls known as the Chutes de Venus, the grottos and the pygmy villages nearby. It also used to be possible to climb Mt Hoyo (a two-day trek) but the track is now overgrown and there's no longer a hut at the top. This shouldn't deter those who are determined and guides can be found at the hotel.

The Chutes and grottos are managed as an extension of the Parc National des Virunga so you have to pay Z150 for a seven-day permit plus Z50 for a photography permit. This includes the services of a compulsory guide. The guide may tell you that you have to pay him direct but this isn't true. You must pay at the Auberge. The tour of the Chutes and grottos lasts about two hours and takes you to three different cavern systems (illuminated with a kerosene lantern) and finally down to the base of the waterfall.

Visits to one of the pygmy villages cost Z200 per group but too many tourists have been here and they're very commercialised. You'll be hassled to death and you'll have to pay for every photograph you take. If you have the time, it's better to spend a few days here and gradually build up a relationship with the pygmies by trading with them or buying food from them before going to visit their village.

If you come here on the Eka Massambe bus from Butembo (Monday and Thursday from Butembo, about seven hours, Z450) it will drop you at the Mt Hoyo turn-off at about 5 pm which means you'll have to complete the 13 km walk to the hotel at night. It's possible to hire porters for this three hour walk (the average charge is Z150). Seven km down the road is a fruit plantation which has pineapples, papaya, avocado and bananas for sale. Buy some while you have the chance because food at the hotel is very expensive.

The hotel, *Auberge de Mont Hoyo*, charges a minimum of Z880 for a room with three beds and you will literally have to beg for electricity. You can also camp for Z80 per person including the use of toilet and showers. If you have no tent and cannot afford the hotel there's a small room adjoining the toilet and bathroom which you can rent for Z80 each (it sleeps up to four people on the floor). Meals are very expensive. Some food can be bought from pygmies who come up to the hotel.

Tanzania

Tanzania, with its magnificent wildlife reserves, is East Africa at its best. Famous parks like Serengeti or the wonderful crater of Ngorongoro offer some of the best safari opportunities in the whole continent. These two may be the best known of the country's numerous parks and reserves but many others deserve a visit. They range from the tiny Gombe Stream chimpanzee reserve near the Burundi border to the huge and virtually untouched Selous Game Reserve in the south-east.

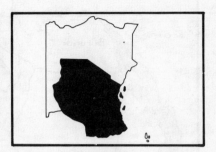

Parks and wildlife are not all Tanzania has to offer. In the north near the Kenya border is snow-capped Mt Kilimanjaro, the highest mountain in Africa. Scaling this 5895 metre peak is an African goal for many travellers. Offshore in the Indian Ocean there are a number of islands including exotic Zanzibar, one of those truly magic travel names like Kathmandu or Timbuktu.

All these sights and attractions are mixed in with Tanzania's single-minded and erratic system of government which, unfortunately, has recently led to some major price increases in park entry fees and costs. The wide disparity between the official bank rate of exchange and the widely utilised black market also adds to the confusion but it's a beautiful country and well worth seeing.

HISTORY

No other African country has been moulded so closely in the image of its president. Known as Mwalimu (teacher) in his own country and often referred to as the 'conscience of black Africa' elsewhere, Julius Nyerere is one of Africa's elder statesmen. He ruled his country as president for over 20 years until 1985 when he stepped down to become the chairman of the party. Like many other first presidents of post-colonial Africa

such as Nkrumah, Sekou Touré and Kaunda, Nyerere was firmly committed to radical socialism and non-alignment. He was always in the forefront of African liberation struggles and Dar es Salaam has been home to many a political exile or guerrilla fighter. Likewise, he has never missed an opportunity to condemn the South African regime.

Certainly his sincerity cannot be faulted, but a more pragmatic attitude to solving his country's problems might well have been more realistic than rigid adherence to ideology. On the other hand, his popularity among the people cannot be doubted. In 1975 and 1980 elections he picked up over 90% of the vote. None of his party colleagues have come even close to matching this performance. Since November 1985, Ali Hassan Mwinyi has been the president though, out of respect, both their photographs appear side by side in offices, hotels and restaurants.

Early History

Not a great deal is known about the early history of the Tanzanian interior, except that by 1800 AD the Maasai, who in previous centuries had grazed their cattle in the Lake Turkana region of Kenya, had migrated down the Rift Valley as far as Dodoma. Their advance was only stopped by the Gogo, who occupied an area west of the Rift Valley, and the Hehe

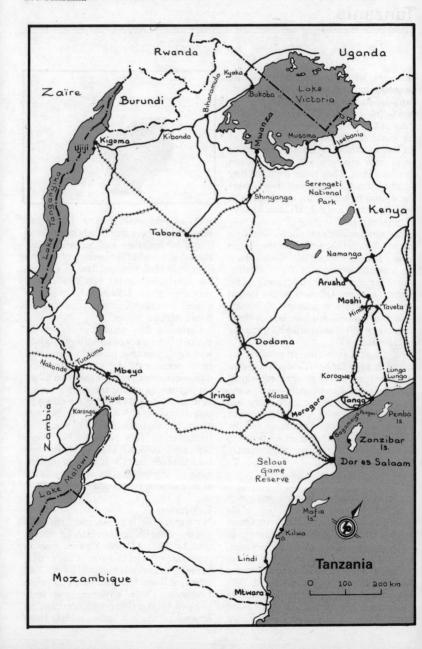

to the south of Dodoma. Because of their reputation as a warrior tribe, the Maasai were feared by the neighbouring Bantu tribes and avoided by the Arab traders, so the northern part of Tanzania was almost free from the depredations of the slave trade and the civil wars which destroyed so many villages and settlements in other areas of the country.

These days the Maasai occupy only a fraction of their former grazing grounds and have been forced to share it with some of Tanzania's most famous national parks and game reserves. Although some of the southern clans have now built permanent villages and planted crops, their northern cousins have retained their pastoral habits and are the least affected by, or interested in, the mainstream of modern Tanzania. Most of the other tribes of this country have more or less given up their traditional customs under pressure from Nyerere's drive to create a unified nation which cuts across tribal divisions.

Though the coastal area had long been the scene of maritime rivalry, first between the Portuguese and Arab traders and later between the various European powers, it was Arab traders and slavers who first penetrated the interior as far as Lake Tanganyika in the middle of the 18th century. Their main depots were at Ujiji on the shores of Lake Tanganyika and Tabora on the central plain. Their captives were generally acquired by commerce rather than force and were taken first to Bagamoyo and then to Zanzibar, where they were either put to work on the plantations there or on Pemba, or shipped to the Arabian peninsula for sale as domestic servants.

Zanzibar, which had been ruled for decades from Oman at the mouth of the Persian Gulf, had, by the first half of the 1800s, become so important as a slaving and spice entrepôt that the Omani Sultan, Seyyid Said, moved his capital there from Muscat in 1832. Though cloves had only been introduced to Zanzibar from the Moluccas in 1818, by the end of Seyyid Said's reign it was producing three-quarters of the world's supply.

British Influence

Britain's interest in this area stemmed from the beginning of the 19th century when a treaty had been signed with Seyyid Said's predecessor to forestall possible threats from Napoleonic France to British possessions in India. The British were only too pleased that a friendly oriental power should extend its dominion down the East African coast rather than leave it open to the French. When Seyyid Said moved to Zanzibar, the British set up their first consulate there.

These were the days when Britain was actively trying to suppress the slave trade and various treaties limiting the trade were signed with the Omani sultans but it wasn't until 1873, under the threat of a naval bombardment, that Sultan Barghash (Seyyid Said's successor) signed a decree outlawing the slave trade. The decree certainly abolished the sea-borne trade but the practice still continued on the mainland for many years since it was an integral part of the search for ivory. Indeed, it probably intensified the slaughter of elephants since ivory was now one of the few exportable commodities which would hold its value, despite the cost of transport to the coast. Slaves were used as the means of transport.

European explorers began arriving around the middle of the 19th century, the most famous of which were Livingstone and Stanley. Stanley's famous phrase, 'Dr Livingstone, I presume', stems from their meeting at Ujiji on Lake Tanganyika. Other notable explorers in this region included Burton and Speke who were sent to Lake Tanganyika in 1858 by the Royal Geographical Society.

The German Colonial Era

A little later, a German explorer, Carl Peters, set about persuading unsuspecting and generally illiterate chiefs to sign so-called treaties of friendship. On the strength of these the German East Africa Company was set up to exploit and colonise what was to become Tanganyika. Though much of the coastal area was part of the Sultan of Zanzibar's lands, German gunboats were used to ensure his compliance. The company's sphere of influence was soon declared a protectorate of the German state after an agreement was signed with Britain which gave the Germans Tanganyika while the British took Kenya and Uganda.

Like the British in Kenya, the Germans set about building railways to open their colony to commerce. Unlike Kenya's fertile and climatically pleasant highlands, eminently suitable for European farmers to colonise, much of Tanganyika was unsuitable for agriculture. Additionally the tsetse fly made cattle grazing or dairying over large areas of central and southern Tanganyika impossible. Most farming was done along the coast and around Mt Kilimanjaro and Mt Meru.

The detachment of the sultan's coastal mainland possessions didn't go down too well with his subjects and Bagamoyo, Pangani and Tanga rose in revolt. These revolts were crushed, as were other anti-German revolts in 1889, but the Maji Maji revolt in 1905 was only put down at a cost of some 120,000 African lives.

The British Era & Independence

The German occupation continued until the end of WW I after which the League of Nations mandated the territory to the British. Nationalist organisations came into being after WW II, but it wasn't until Julius Nyerere founded the Tanganyika African National Union (TANU) in 1954 that they became very effective. The British would have preferred to see a 'multi-racial' constitution adopted by the nationalists so as to protect the European and Asian minorities but this was opposed by Nyerere. Sensibly, the last British governor, Sir Richard Turnbull,

ditched the idea and Tanganyika attained independence in 1961 with Nyerere as the country's first president.

The island of Zanzibar had been a British Protectorate since 1890, along with a 16 km wide strip of the entire Kenyan coastline which was considered the sultan's. It remained that way until Zanzibar and Kenya attained independence in 1963. The Sultan of Zanzibar was toppled about a year after independence in a Communist-inspired revolution in which most of the Arab population of the island was either massacred or expelled, and he was replaced by a revolutionary council formed by the Afro-Shirazi Party. A short time later, Zanzibar and the other offshore island of Pemba merged with mainland Tanganyika to form Tanzania.

Socialist Tanzania

Nyerere inherited a country which had been largely ignored by the British colonial authorities since it had few exploitable resources and only one major export crop, sisal. Education had been neglected, too, so that at independence there were only 120 university graduates in the whole country.

It was an inauspicious beginning and the problems which it created eventually led to the Arusha Declaration of 1967. Based on the Communist Chinese model, the cornerstone of this policy was the *Ujamaa* village – a collective agricultural venture run along traditional African lines. The villages were intended to be socialist organisations created by the people and governed by those who lived and worked in them. Self-reliance was the keyword in the hundreds of villages that were set up. Basic goods and tools were to be held in common and shared among members while each individual had the obligation to work on the land.

Nyerere's proposals for education were seen as an essential part of this scheme and were designed to foster constructive attitudes to cooperative endeavor, stress the concept of social equality and responsibility and counter the tendency towards intellectual arrogance among the educated.

At the same time as the villages were set up, the economy and a great deal of rental property was nationalised and taxes were increased in an attempt to redistribute individual wealth. Nyerere also sought to ensure that those in political power did not develop into an exploitative class by banning government ministers and party officials from holding shares or directorships in companies or from receiving more than one salary. They were also prohibited from owning houses which were rented out, nevertheless corruption remained widespread.

In the early days of the *Ujamaa* movement progressive farmers were encouraged to expand in the hope that other peasants would follow their example. This resulted in little improvement in rural poverty and the enrichment of those who were the recipients of state funds. This approach was therefore abandoned in favour of direct state control, and peasants were resettled into planned villages with the object of modernising and monetising the agricultural sector of the economy. The settlements were to be well provided with potable water, clinics, schools, fertilizers, high-yielding seeds and, where possible, irrigation. Again they failed, since this was well beyond the country's financial resources and there was much hostility and resentment among the peasants to what they regarded as compulsory resettlement, without any consultation or influence over the decision-making process.

Following the second failure a third scheme was adopted. This was based on persuading the peasants to amalgamate their small holdings into large, communally owned farms using economic incentives and shifting the emphasis onto self-reliance. In this way, the benefits reaped by the members of such *Ujamaa* settlements would be a direct reflection of the dedication of those who lived there. This scheme has had its critics but has been relatively successful and has prompted the government to adopt a policy of compulsory villagisation of the entire rural population.

Despite lip-service to his policies there was little development aid from the west so Nyerere turned to the People's Republic of China as his foreign partners. They built Tanzania a brand-new, modern railway from Dar es Salaam to Kapiri Mposhi in the copper belt of Zambia (the TAZARA railway) costing some US$400 million. For a time it was the showpiece of eastern and southern Africa and considerably reduced Zambia's dependence on the Zimbabwean (at that time Rhodesian) and South African railway systems. OPEC's oil price hike at the beginning of the 1970s, however, led to a financial crisis and Tanzania was no longer able to afford any more than essential maintenance of the railway. There were also serious fuel shortages. As a result, the railway no longer functions anywhere near as well as it did when first built although recently things have been improving slightly.

Tanzania Today

Tanzania's experiment in radical socialism and self-reliance might have been a courageous path to follow in the heady days following independence, and even during the 1970s when not only Tanzania, but many other African countries were feeling the oil-price pinch, however only romantics would argue with the assessment that it has failed. The transport system is in tatters, agricultural production is stagnant, the industrial sector limps along at well under 50% capacity, the capital, Dar es Salaam , is dusty and down-at-heel and all economic incentives seem to have been eliminated. Obviously, many factors have contributed to Tanzania's woes and many of them have been beyond her control, not least that of being one of the world's poorest countries. At least, that is true of the mainland. Zanzibar was one of the most prosperous countries in Africa at the time of independence.

The trouble is, Nyerere has no intention of changing and he tolerates no dissent. In 1979, Tanzanian jails held more political prisoners than South Africa though over 6000 were freed late that year and a further 4400 the following year. Even now that Nyerere has stepped down as president, it is unlikely there will be any significant changes until after his death.

Tanzania has been one of the most consistently outspoken supporters of African liberation movements particularly in the south. Nyerere joined with Kaunda in supporting the guerrillas fighting for the independence of Angola and Mozambique against the Portuguese, and also those fighting to overthrow the white minority government of Rhodesia during Ian Smith's regime. This support has continued to cost both countries dearly now that the focus has moved to South Africa, though these days the cost is spread between the so-called Front Line States of Angola, Botswana, Mozambique, Tanzania, Zambia and Zimbabwe.

Tanzania also provided asylum to Ugandan exiles during Idi Amin's regime including Milton Obote and the current president, Yoweri Museveni. This support almost bankrupted Tanzania. In October 1978, Idi Amin sent his army into northern Tanzania and occupied the Kagera salient as well as bombing the Lake Victoria ports of Bukoba and Musoma. It was done, so he said, to teach Tanzania a lesson for supporting exiled groups hostile to his regime but it's more likely that it was a diversionary movement to head off a mutiny among his restless troops.

Since Tanzania had hardly any army worth mentioning it took several months to scrape together a people's militia of 50,000 men and get them to the front. They were ill-equipped and poorly trained but they utterly routed the Ugandans – supposedly one of Africa's best trained and equipped armies. The Ugandans threw down their weapons and fled and the Tanzanians pushed on into Uganda. A 12,000-strong Tanzanian contingent stayed in the country for some time to maintain law and order and to ensure that Nyerere could exert a strong influence over the choice of Amin's successor. The war cost Tanzania around US$500 million and it received not a single contribution from any source.

Not only that but it was half-heartedly condemned by other African countries at the OAU since one of the cardinal principles of the OAU is that African borders are inviolable and member states must not interfere in the internal affairs of others. It wasn't the first time that Tanzania had interfered in the affairs of its neighbours. Nyerere had helped to topple two other regimes, once in the Comoros Islands in 1975 and again in the Seychelles in 1977.

Perhaps Tanzania's economy wouldn't have got into such a parlous state if the East African Economic Community had been allowed to work. At independence, Kenya, Tanzania and Uganda were linked together in an economic union which shared a common airline, telecommunications and postal facilities, transportation and customs. Their currencies were freely convertible and there was freedom of movement. Any person from one country could work in another. It fell apart in 1977 due to political differences between socialistic Tanzania, capitalistic Kenya and the military chaos that went for government in Uganda.

As a result of Kenya's action in grabbing the bulk of the community's assets, Nyerere closed his country's border with Kenya. Though one of the ideas of this was to force tourists to fly directly to Tanzania rather than entering via Kenya, all it achieved was an alarming loss of tourism for Tanzania.

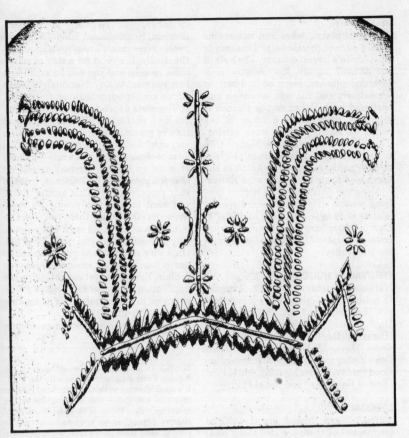

back tattoos

The border remained closed for years and although it is now open again the government continues to display a propensity for economic suicide.

POPULATION

The population of Tanzania is about 20 million. There are over 100 different tribal groups in the country but the majority of them are of Bantu origin. The Arab influence on Zanzibar and Pemba Islands is shown in the people who are a mix of Shirazis (from Persia), Arabs and Comorians (from the Comoros Islands).

ECONOMY

Tanzania, or Tanganyika as it then was, was always the poor cousin of the British colonial Kenya-Uganda-Tanganyika trio. Although it did not have the problem of a large influx of European settlers Tanzania was still a seriously underdeveloped country at the time of independence. Things have not improved, the economy is still overwhelmingly agricultural and overall it has been marked most by mismanagement and decline.

GEOGRAPHY

A land of plains, lakes and mountains with a narrow coastal belt, Tanzania is East Africa's largest country. The bulk of the 945,087 square km country is a highland plateau, some of it desert or semi-desert and the rest savannah and scattered bush. Much of the plateau is relatively uninhabited because of the tsetse fly which prevent stock raising. The highest mountains – Meru (4556 metres) and Kilimanjaro (Africa's highest at 5895 metres) – are to be found in the north-east along the border with Kenya.

Along the coast there is a narrow low-lying coastal strip and off-shore are the islands of Pemba, Zanzibar and Mafia. Over 53,000 square km of the country are covered by inland lakes, most of them in the Rift Valley.

FESTIVALS & HOLIDAYS

National holidays are: 12 January (Zanzibar Revolution Day), 5 February (CCM Foundation Day), 26 April (Union Day), 1 May (Workers' Day), 7 July (Peasants' Day), 9 December (Independence Day), 25 December (Christmas Day). Other variable public holidays are Good Friday, Easter Monday, Idd el Fitri (End of Ramadan) and Idd el Haji.

LANGUAGE

KiSwahili and English are the official languages but there are also many local African languages. Outside of the cities and towns far fewer local people speak English than you would find in comparable areas in Kenya. It's said that the KiSwahili spoken in Zanzibar is of a much purer form than that which you find in Kenya (at least, that's their story) and quite a few travellers come here to learn it since there's the Institute of KiSwahili & Foreign Languages on the island.

VISAS

Visas are required by all except nationals of Commonwealth countries, Scandinavian countries, the Republic of Ireland, Rwanda, Romania and Sudan. For these people a free visitor's pass is obtainable at the border. It's valid for a stay of one to three months and you will be asked how long you want to stay. Nationals of South Africa are not admitted.

Visa costs depend on your nationality but two photographs are required and they're generally issued in 24 hours. Be very careful when filling in the application form because there is now a rule (enforced at some embassies, ignored at others) that you must have US$80 for each day of your proposed stay! This means that if you want to stay two weeks you must write on the form that you have a minimum of US$1120 or, if you want to stay a month, that you have US$2400. Only very rarely would you be asked to prove you have the amount which you declare. Even if you get caught out on the application form you can always renew your visa in Dar es Salaam or at another immigration office.

The visa story in neighbouring countries is:

Burundi In Bujumbura the embassy is on Avenue Patrice Lumumba opposite the PTT. It's open Monday to Friday from 8 to 11.30 am and 2 to 4.30 pm – visa applications in the morning only. There is a varying scale of charges depending on your nationality, two photographs are required and they're issued in 24 hours.

Rwanda In Kigali the embassy is on Avenue Paul VI at the junction with Avenue de Rusumo. Visas cost RFr 715 to 1315, require two photographs and can take up to one week to issue though five days would be average. If you make a polite fuss or enlist the support of your own embassy you may get it in 24 hours but they may insist on you producing onward tickets in this case. Visas are for three months and single entry.

Kenya In Nairobi the embassy is on the 4th floor, Continental House on the corner of Harambee Avenue and Uhuru Highway (tel 331056/7). It's Monday to Thursday from 2 to 5 pm. Visas cost Ken Sh 35 to 139, require two photographs and take 48 hours to issue. The US$80 per day rule is enforced here but they don't ask to see the money. The woman on reception here is unhelpful to the point of being rude.

Uganda In Kampala the embassy is at 6 Kagera Rd (tel 56755) and it's open Monday to Friday from 9 am to 3 pm. Visas cost Ug Sh 1500, require two photographs and can be issued the same day if you're lucky. There's no fuss about sufficient funds.

Tanzanian embassies can also be found in Addis Ababa (Ethiopia), Bonn (West Germany), Brussels (Belgium), Cairo (Egypt), Conakry (Guinea), Geneva (Switzerland), The Hague (Netherlands), Harare (Zimbabwe), Khartoum (Sudan), Kinshasa (Zaire), Lagos (Nigeria), London (UK), Lusaka (Zambia), New Delhi (India), New York (USA), Ottawa (Canada), Paris (France), Rome (Italy), Stockholm (Sweden), Tokyo (Japan) and Washington DC (USA). Avoid getting your visa in Zambia if at all possible. They take three weeks to come through.

Some Tanzanian borders have acquired bad reputations for hassling travellers. At the Tunduma/Nakonde (Tanzania/Zambia) border you can expect hassles whether you cross by road or on the TAZARA railway. Make sure your papers are in order and everything else is hunky-dory. The Kyela/Karonga (Tanzania/Malawi) border is probably the worst. Your bag will be minutely searched and all your travellers' cheques and cash counted. The border crossing points into Kenya are generally a breeze (Namanga and Lunga Lunga) and take just a few minutes. They don't even collect currency forms at Namanga.

If you take a car across the border into Tanzania you will have to buy a road permit valid for 90 days which costs Sh 1000.

Warning You will probably be refused a visa or visitor's pass if you have South African stamps in your passport or the stamps of border posts to South Africa. This is especially true at the Malawi/Tanzania border and the Zambia/Tanzania border. If you think you are going to have problems you can hedge your bets by getting a visitor's pass at the High Commission in Harare, Zimbabwe. It's free, there's no fuss and it takes 48 hours to issue. Don't bother applying in Lusaka, Zambia, as it takes three weeks to come through!

Even with this pass you cannot be guaranteed entry. We have heard of people being refused after doing all the right things. You could be one of the unlucky few. New passports also evoke suspicion especially if issued in Botswana, Zambia or Zimbabwe. Even stamps showing that you entered *and* left Lesotho or Swaziland by air may evoke suspicion. If they're sure you've been to South Africa you passport may well be endorsed 'undesirable alien' or 'illegal immigrant'. Some travellers have had this stamped in their passports just for arguing too forcefully with immigration officials. If you have to convince them that you haven't been to South Africa then do it politely and don't get agitated.

Visas for Other Countries

Burundi Visas It's probably best to get your visa for Burundi in Dar es Salaam. The embassy is at 1007 Upanga Rd (tel 29282). You can also get them at the Burundi consulate in Kigoma on Lake Tanganyika. This consulate is open for applications on Monday and Wednesday only from 8 am to 3 pm. Visas cost Sh 200, are valid for a stay of one month and take three days to issue Pick them up on Thursday and Saturday respectively.

Kenya Visas The embassy is on the 14th floor, NIC Investment House, Samora Avenue at the junction with Mirambo St, Dar es Salaam. Visas cost Sh 120, require three photographs and take 24 hours to issue.

Rwanda Visas The embassy is at 32 Upanga Rd, Dar es Salaam (tel 20115). Visas cost Sh 250, require two photographs and take 24 hours to issue. They're valid for a stay of one month.

Zaïre Visas The embassy is at 438 Malik Rd, Dar es Salaam (tel 24181/2). Visas cost Sh 300, require four photographs, a letter of recommendation from your own embassy and are issued in 24 hours but they will only issue one-month, single entry visas.

There's also a consulate in Kigoma on Lake Tanganyika which is open for visa applications on Monday, Wednesday and Friday from 9 am to 12.20 pm and 3 to 6.30 pm. Visas there cost Sh 200 and require four photographs but they take *two weeks* to issue. No letter of recommendation from your own embassy is needed.

Dar es Salaam is a good place to stock up on Francophone country visas (Central African Republic, Chad, etc) since there are very few of these embassies in the capital so you have to get them all from the French embassy. They generally cost Sh 110 each, issued without fuss and are valid for a stay of one month. The French embassy is on Bagamoyo Rd (tel 68601/3).

MONEY

US$1 = Sh 40

The unit of currency is the Tanzanian shilling = 100 senti. Despite the mid-86 100% devaluation which took the official rate from Sh 20 to Sh 40 to the US dollar, the rate is still Mickey Mouse since the street rate is currently up to Sh 160. The devaluation has halted the rise in the blackmarket rate and may even have forced it down a little. Banking hours are Monday to Friday from 8.30 am to 12.30 pm and on Saturday from 8.30 to 11.30 am.

You can change both cash and travellers' cheques on the black market though you naturally get less for cheques. The rate not only depends on where you change your money but on how big the bills are – US$50 and US$100 bills are preferred. Dar es Salaam and Zanzibar are the best places followed by Arusha. The rates in Kigoma, Moshi, Tanga and Bujumbura (Burundi) are usually well below par so only change as much as you need to get you to Dar es Salaam. Be careful who you change money with on the black market especially in Dar. There are some very dubious characters hanging around Maktaba St whom you'd be well advised to stay clear of. Take your time and you'll get offers from much more reliable quarters.

As in Uganda, Kenyan shillings are almost as good as hard currency when you want to change money although it's officially illegal to take them out of the country. Expect Tan Sh 100 = Ken Sh 550 which amounts to about Tan Sh 126 to the US dollar.

Currency declaration forms are issued on arrival and officials may demand to see the cash and cheques which you declare on the form so you must hide any excess. It's very unlikely, however, that you'd be subjected to a body search and baggage searches are cursory.

It is probably a good idea to change *something* at a bank just to get a stamp on the currency form and a bank receipt in case anyone official wants to know where you have been changing money. This is important if you are crossing the Tanzania/Zambia border between Tunduma and Nakonde on the TAZARA train or the Tanzania/Malawi border between Kyela and Karonga. I get occasional letters from travellers who have been strip searched at these borders and that includes women. Crossing the Tanzania/Kenya border is a different matter. You probably won't even be asked for the currency form and, if you are, it won't be scrutinised. I'm still looking at my own currency form as this is written and the amount which I changed at the bank certainly wouldn't have got me through the country even with the wildest of imaginations at work.

In the past there used to be a lively trade on the black market in forged bank stamps and bank receipts which you paid for by a lower exchange rate. This was especially so in Arusha but now you're wasting your time and money getting involved in this since the authorities are wise to it.

Don't mix 'official' and 'black market' shillings when travelling in Tanzania especially by air. Make sure that any excess shillings not covered by bank receipts and stamps on your currency form as well as any undeclared hard currency is well hidden. Discovery would involve confiscation and other problems.

COSTS

All these schemes to make travelling in Tanzania affordable and to get realistic exchange rates for your hard-earned dollars are all very well but they only go so far. The Tanzanian authorities are not devoid of imagination either. In order to clamp down on the black market and bring in much needed foreign currency, you must now pay for all entry fees to national parks and (in theory – and often in practice) park lodges too in hard currency. Shillings are not acceptable even with bank receipts. And if you don't happen to have the exact amount in foreign currency then you'll get the change in shillings at the official rate of exchange. The same goes for the big hotels on the mainland and for all hotels on Zanzibar. Likewise, you must pay for all international flight tickets in hard currency. Zambia Airways was the only exception I discovered – they would accept shillings but only with appropriate bank receipts.

Where the authorities have really gone too far is in putting a blanket fee on the climbing of Kilimanjaro. Mountain climbing is essentially a young people's activity and these are not the people with dollars flowing out of their ears. It will now cost you US$380 just in fees and guides/porters wages, excluding food and transport to Marangu, for the five-day trek! That is, without doubt, over-kill. You'll be pleased to know that the authorities are being pressured to reduce the fees.

You can still pay for all your food (even at national park lodges), transport, accommodation at budget hotels, souvenirs and internal flights on Air Tanzania in shillings and you don't need to produce bank receipts for this.

CLIMATE

Tanzania's widely varying geography accounts for its variety of climatic conditions. Much of the country is a high plateau where the altitude considerably tempers what would otherwise be a tropical climate. In many places it can be quite cool at night.

The coastal strip along the Indian Ocean together with the off-shore islands of Pemba, Zanzibar and Mafia have a hot, humid tropical climate but tempered by sea breezes. The high mountains are in the north-east along the Kenyan border and this area enjoys an almost temperate climate for much of the year.

The long rainy season is from April to May when it rains almost every day. The short rains fall during November and December.

NEWSPAPERS & MEDIA

The only English-language daily newspaper is the *Daily News* which you can get in Dar es Salaam and one or two other cities. Foreign news coverage is minimal. International magazines and periodicals can be found in the same places.

FILM & PHOTOGRAPHY

Bring all your photographic requirements with you as very little is available outside of Dar es Salaam, Arusha and Zanzibar. Even here the choice is very limited and prices are high. Slide film is a rarity – most of what is available is colour negative and black and white. If you're desperate for film then the large hotels are probably your best bet. You'll be extremely lucky to find film at any of the national park lodges.

Don't take photographs of anything connected with the government or the military (government offices, post offices, banks, railway stations, bridges, airports, barracks, etc). You may well be arrested and your film confiscated if you do. People are worried about South African-instigated sabotage and spying (and with good reason after what happened in Zambia and Zimbabwe early in 1986). If you're on the TAZARA train from Dar es Salaam to Kapiri Mposhi (Zambia) and want to take photographs of game as you go through the Selous Game Reserve, get permission first from military personnel if possible or, failing that, from railway officials. You might think that what you are doing is completely innocuous; they may well think otherwise.

HEALTH

As in most African countries you must take precautions against malaria. Most of the lakes and rivers of Tanzania carry a risk of bilharzia if you bathe in them or walk along the shores without footwear especially where the vegetation is very reedy. Tsetse flies are distributed over large areas of the central plateau though only in a few places are they a real nuisance. Insect repellant and a fly whisk would be useful in such places.

GENERAL INFORMATION

Post

The poste restante is well organised and you should have no problems with expected letters not turning up. The same is true for telegrams. There's no charge for collecting letters. Because of the very favourable street exchange rate for hard currency posting parcels from Tanzania is much cheaper than doing it from Kenya. The approximate parcel post rates from Tanzania are:

Surface
 100 gm to 1 kg – Sh 60; 1 kg to 3 kg – Sh 90; 3 kg to 5 kg – Sh 131; 5 kg to 10 kg – Sh 205.
Air
 Up to 200 gm – Sh 63; each additional 200 gm – Sh 22.

Telephone

If you need to make an international telephone call try to do it from either a private house or from one of the large hotels although at the hotels there will be a surcharge, usually 25% of the cost of the call. The reason for this is that the Extelcoms office on Samora Avenue in Dar es Salaam has a grand total of *two* international lines for use by the public! If they're busy – and they often are – you'll be waiting for hours. Even Kampala does better than this!

Time

The time in Tanzania is GMT plus three hours.

INFORMATION

There are offices of the Tanzania Tourist Corporation in Dar es Salaam (PO Box 2485), Zanzibar and Arusha. The TTC

can make bookings for you at any of the large hotels in Tanzania and at most of the national park lodges but you must pay for these in hard currency. It's better to book for the national park lodges through a travel agency since some of them may be able to arrange a deal where you pay in shillings.

The TTC also has a number of overseas offices:

Italy
    Palazzo Africa, Largo Africa 1, Milano (tel 432870-464421)
West Germany
    Kaiserstrasse 13, 6000 Frankfurt Main 1 (tel (0611) 280154)
Sweden
    Oxtorgsgatan 2-4, PO Box 7627, 102 94 Stockholm (tel 08-21 6700)
UK
    77 South Audley St, London W1Y 5TA (tel 01-499 7727)
USA
    201 East 42nd St, New York, NY 10017 (tel (212) 986 7124)

The National Parks are managed by the Tanzania National Parks Authority (tel 3471), PO Box 3134, Arusha. Their main administrative office is on the 6th floor, Kilimanjaro Wing, Arusha International Conference Centre and if you call in they may well have a range of descriptive leaflets about the national parks and a reasonably good road map of the Serengeti National Park, there's a nominal charge for these. The Director is a hard-working but friendly man and may have copies of the *Quarterly Report* which the authority puts out. If you're interested in what they do this report makes fascinating reading. They have another office on India St close to the YMCA in Arusha but it doesn't deal with public enquiries.

If you're going to spend any length of time in Tanzania then it's worth buying a copy of *Tourist Guide to Tanzania* by Gratian Luhikula (1985), which is available from most of the large hotels in Dar es Salaam for Sh 75. The transport information in this booklet is somewhat out of date but it contains street maps of Dar, Arusha and Zanzibar as well as descriptions of most of the places of interest in the country and exhaustive lists of addresses and telephone numbers of government agencies, embassies, banks, businesses, travel agents and even a KiSwahili-English precis.

GETTING THERE

Possible access routes into Tanzania are by air, road, rail or lake ferry. Rail access is only from Zambia. Even though the Tanzanian system is continuous with the Kenyan system there are no through services any longer. This may change in the near future as the East African Community (Kenya, Uganda and Tanzania) gets itself back together again. It may also be possible to enter Tanzania by sea – there are occasional dhows which come down the coast from Kenya and call at Pemba, Zanzibar and Dar es Salaam. There are also occasional ferries between the Comoros Islands and Tanzania.

All fares translated into US dollar prices in this section are on the basis that US$1 = Sh 150 (the average street rate). If you're changing money exclusively at the official rate of exchange then the fare will obviously be considerably higher.

Air

International airlines serving Tanzania either through Kilimanjaro International Airport or Dar es Salaam International Airport include Aeroflot, Air France, Air India, Alitalia, British Airways, Egyptair, Ethiopian Airlines, Kenya Airways, KLM, Linhas Aereas Mocambique, Lufthansa, PIA, Sabena, SAS, Somali Airlines, Swissair and Uganda Airlines.

Quite a few travellers use Tanzania as a gateway to Africa although it is not as popular as Nairobi. There's not a lot of difference between Nairobi and Dar/Kilimanjaro in the one-way fare from the most price competitive agents in Europe (it's about £20) but, for some strange reason, there's a considerable difference between the return fares (up to £65). You're looking at around £260 one-way and £440-450 return from London.

International flight tickets bought in Tanzania have to be paid for in hard currency. You can not buy them in shillings even with bank receipts to prove that you have changed money officially. The only exception I found to this rule was with Zambia Airways which will accept shillings backed up by bank receipts. This may change, of course.

If you are flying to Europe from Dar with Aeroflot then contact Hit Holidays (tel 25835), NBC Building, Jamhuri St and ask about the possibility of a Moscow stop-over at around US$30 per day which includes hotel, breakfast and dinner, a tour of the city and transport to and from the airport. You can find the same deal in Nairobi but it will cost considerably more.

Airport Tax The international airport departure tax is US$10 – payable in cash dollars. Travellers' cheques are not acceptable. You have to change them at the airport bank and they'll only give you US$19 for a US$20 travellers' cheque!

To/From Burundi

There is no road or rail transport between the two countries. The only possibility is by boat along Lake Tanganyika.

Lake Tanganyika Ferry The main ferry on Lake Tanganyika is the historic *MV Liemba* which connects Tanzania with Burundi and Zambia. It's a legend amongst travellers and must be one of the oldest steamers in the world still operating on a regular basis. Built by the Germans in 1914 and assembled on the lake shore after having been transported in pieces on the railway from Dar es Salaam, it first saw service as the *Graf von Goetzn*. Not long afterwards, however, following Germany's defeat in WW I, it was greased and scuttled to prevent the British getting their hands on it. In 1927 the British colonial authorities raised it from the bottom, reconditioned it and put it back into service as the *MV Liemba*. That it's still going after all these years is a real credit to the engineers who maintain her.

The *Liemba* runs on a regular weekly schedule though it can be delayed if there is engine trouble or for up to 24 hours at any point if there is a lot of cargo to be loaded or off-loaded. It departs Bujumbura (Burundi) on Monday at about 4 pm and arrives Kigoma at 8 am the next day. It sets sail from Kigoma later on Tuesday and arrives at Mpulungu (Zambia) on Thursday at 8 am calling at many small Tanzanian ports en route (usually for not much more than half an hour). On the return journey, it departs Mpulungu at 5 pm on Friday and arrives at Kigoma at 10 am on Sunday. It leaves Kigoma again later on Sunday and arrives at Bujumbura at 7.30 am on Monday.

From Kigoma approximate fares to Bujumbura are 1st class US$1.70, 2nd class US$1.35, 3rd class US$0.60. To Mpulungu the fares are 1st class US$5.70, 2nd class US$4.50, 3rd class US$2. There's also a port fee of Sh 40 at Kigoma. Fares from Bujumbura can be found in the Burundi chapter. At one time, if you were buying your ticket in Mpulungu you had to pay in hard currency but it's unlikely that this is still the case since the Zambian kwacha was floated against the US dollar in mid-1986. The boat is operated by the Tanzanian Railways Corporation so there's no reason why you should not be able to pay in Tanzanian shillings.

First class is a cabin with two bunks; 2nd class is a cabin with four bunks, and 3rd class is deck space on the lower deck. It's well worth going 1st or 2nd class if only because you're on the upper deck but don't expect anything in the way of luxury. It's more quaint than luxurious. Third class is tolerable and rarely crowded between Kigoma and Bujumbura but between Kigoma and Mpulungu it's very crowded.

Meals can be bought on board and are good value. A huge plate of beef curry and rice costs Sh 80, add soup and dessert and it costs Sh 150. Breakfast is particularly good value (omelette, bread, tea/coffee).

Top: Tanga, Tanzania (GC)
Left: Mt Kilimanjaro, Tanzania (GC)
Right: Market, Kampala, Uganda (GC)

Beer can be bought on board but is much more expensive than buying it on the mainland (a large 'Primus' goes for Sh 120). All meals and drinks have to be paid for in shillings.

There used to be another ferry, the *MV Mwongozo*, which doubled up on the *Liemba's* schedule but this boat only operates services in Tanzania now.

Gombe Stream Boat The *MV Liemba* is not the only boat to Burundi, there's also a route via the Gombe Stream National Park to Banda/Nyanza Lac just over the border with Tanzania. Gombe Stream is mainly a chimpanzee sanctuary, just north of Kigoma beside Lake Tanganyika.

Small, motorised, wooden boats ply between Kigoma and Banda via Gombe Stream everyday and are used by local people to get to villages up the shore and to bring their produce in to market. They depart Kigoma between 11 am and 12 noon and arrive at Banda around 6 pm. In the opposite direction they depart Banda about 7 am and arrive in Kigoma between 12 noon and 1 pm. The fare is Sh 100. To get to the place where they dock in Kigoma you walk up the railway line from the railway station for about one km and you'll see them on the left hand side. If you get off at Gombe Stream it will still cost you Sh 100 and when you get back on to continue your journey or go back to Kigoma you will have to pay again.

The boats are partially covered, often overcrowded and offer hardly any creature comforts but they're fun in fine weather. In rough weather they might give you cause for concern.

If you intend leaving Tanzania on one of these small boats (whether you drop off at Gombe Stream or not) you will first have to get an exit stamp from immigration in Kigoma. They're sometimes reluctant to give you these (and may go as far as telling you that it's illegal to leave Tanzania this way). Be firm, polite and make it clear you have all day to wait. You'll get the stamp.

To/From Kenya
There are several points of entry into Kenya but the main overland routes are between Arusha and Nairobi via Namanga and between Dar/Tanga and Mombasa via Lunga Lunga. Other lesser used routes are between Musoma and Kisii via Isebania in the north-west and between Moshi and Voi via Taveta. There's also the Lake Victoria ferry from Mwanza and Musoma to Kisumu and occasional dhows between Zanzibar/Pemba and Mombasa – refer to the Kenyan chapter under Dhows.

Road Until early-86 there were several companies operating international buses between Dar and both Nairobi (via Arusha) and Mombasa (via Tanga) but by the middle of the year many had suspended services because of the fees imposed on commercial vehicles at the Tanzanian border. These services have now been resumed – at least by some companies.

There are certainly international buses on the Dar-Tanga-Mombasa run. Check out Cat Bus (Monday, Wednesday, Friday and Sunday at 3 pm) or Maranzana Bus (daily at 4 pm). Kidato's Bus Service at Livingstone and Somali Avenues and the country bus station on Libya St are other possibilities. The fare is usually about US$3 and the journey can last 14 to 20 hours. You go through the border in the middle of the night and since there's usually no electricity and it's all in semi-darkness there's no fuss about currency forms.

You can also do the journey in stages. On the Dar/Tanga to Mombasa run there are shared taxis and *matatus* from Tanga to the Lunga Lunga border for about US$1 which take about one hour. From the Tanzanian border post to the Kenyan border post it's five or six km and you may have to walk if there's no transport. In any case you have to hitch – there are no taxis or *matatus*. From the Kenyan side of the border there are frequent buses (Sh 30), shared taxis and *matatus* to the Likoni ferry on the southern side of the Mombasa mainland which take about 1½ hours. The border posts are fairly easy-going and there are no hassles about currency forms.

Going to Nairobi, there are frequent buses (about US$0.50), *matatus* (US$1) and shared taxis from Arusha to Namanga which take less than two hours. The two border posts here are right next to each other and the Tanzanian side often doesn't even ask for the currency form. From the Kenyan side there are frequent buses (Sh 30), *matatus* and shared taxis to Nairobi. It's much more convenient to take one of the shared taxis (five passengers per car) operated by East African Road Services which cost Sh 50 and take two hours. The buses take about four hours.

The crossing between Moshi and Voi via Taveta is also fairly reliable as far as transport goes but between Musoma and Kisii in the north you may well have problems and be forced to do a lot of walking.

Rail There are no international rail services between Tanzania and Kenya.

Boat On Lake Victoria the *MV Bukoba* connects Bukoba, Mwanza and Musoma in Tanzania with Kisumu in Kenya. See the Lake Victoria section for timetable and fare details.

It is sometimes possible to get dhows from Zanzibar, Pemba or Tanga to Mombasa but there's a lot of red tape involved. Tanganyika Coastal Shipping (see the Dar es Salaam section) occasionally has ships to Mombasa.

To/From Malawi
Road There's only one crossing point here and that is between Mbeya and Karonga at the top of Lake Malawi via Kyela. The Tanzanian side of this border is notorious for officialdom but it's the route most people are using these days between the

two countries rather than via Nakonde (Zambia) and Chitipa (Malawi) along which transport can be problematical. All the bridges along the Mbeya-Karonga route are now completed.

There is usually one bus daily from Mbeya to Kyela which costs about US$0.50 and takes about three hours. From here to the Tanzanian border post (four km) there are no buses and you will have to hitch or walk. Make sure your currency form is in order or there will be major hassles at the border post. From the Tanzanian post to the first Malawi border post it's a further four km and again you will have to hitch or walk. A brief passport check is done here after which you continue on to the second Malawi border post where immigration and currency formalities are completed. The distance between the two is 16 km and there is one local bus daily. If you miss it then you can usually find transport in a local pick-up truck. Otherwise hitch or walk. From the second Malawi border post there is a daily bus in either direction to Karonga.

Officials on the Malawi side are very pleasant in comparison to the Tanzanian side.

To/From Rwanda
Road You may have a lot of trouble finding transport direct from Tanzania to Rwanda. There are no direct buses between Mwanza and either Rusumo (Rwanda) or Kigali (Rwanda). The nearest place to the border that you can get by bus is Ngara (25 km from the border) or Biharamulo (110 km from the border) and even those depend on the availability of petrol. Hitching without a pre-arranged lift is definitely not recommended. You could be stuck for days. There are, however, trucks between Dar or Mwanza and Kigali often driven by Somalis. They're usually pretty good about giving lifts but they are not easy to track down. We wish you luck.

To/From Uganda

Road Road transport between Bukoba and either Masaka or Kampala is almost impossible to find. There are no buses and trucks are like hen's teeth. Ever since the Tanzanians invaded Uganda to push out Idi Amin, the roads have been atrocious. We haven't heard of anyone going this way for years.

Rail Ferry There is now a rail ferry across Lake Victoria from Mwanza to Jinja once per week which has room for about 30 passengers. Enquire in Mwanza for details as it doesn't go on the same day every week. The ferry is mainly for freight and railway freight cars but it has room for 30 passengers. The fare is Ugandan Sh 25,000/US$5 and the boats they are using are in good shape.

To/From Zaire

There is no land border between Tanzania and Zaire, the two are separated by Lake Tanganyika and there are no longer any ferries between Tanzania and Zaire. You will, however, see Zairois cargo boats tied up at Kigoma which come from Kalemie. The chances of getting a lift on one of them are very slim so the only practical route between Tanzania and Zaire is via Burundi.

To/From Zambia

Road The usual route is on the TAZARA railway but there's also road transport from Mbeya to Tunduma on the Tanzania/Zambia border. From there you walk to Nakonde on the Zambian side and take other buses from there to Kasama and Lusaka. Not many people use the road route. This border, like the one into Malawi, is notorious for officialdom.

Rail The TAZARA Railway runs between Dar es Salaam and Kapiri Mposhi. There are two and sometimes three trains in either direction per week (one express and two ordinary trains) but the actual days on which they go varies so much that the only way to find out is to go to the station and buy a ticket. It is usually on Wednesday and Saturday at 11 am or on Tuesday at 4 pm and Friday at 9.15 am. The journey takes 48 to 54 hours. It's about 24 hours to Mbeya, close to the border.

In Dar you need to go to the TAZARA station on Pugu Rd to buy tickets. This is not the same station as the one in central Dar where Central Line trains arrive and depart. The TAZARA station is about half way to the airport and you can get there on an airport bus from the junction of Sokoine Drive and Kivukoni Front opposite the Cenotaph and Lutheran Church (which looks vaguely like a recreation of Neuschwanstein).

You need to book tickets in advance, at least five days is advisable. Don't expect any 1st or 2nd class tickets to be left up to two days before departure. Third class tickets are only sold on the day of departure. Approximate fares are 1st class US$9, 2nd class US$6, 3rd class US$2.50. From Dar es Salaam only as far as Mbeya the fares are 1st class US$6, 2nd class US$3, 3rd class US$1.50. Student discounts of 50% are available for international student card holders but getting authorisation for this can be time consuming. The normal procedure is to pick up a form from the TAZARA station and take it to the Ministry of Education beside State House where you fill in more forms and get the appropriate rubber stamp. You then take the form back to the TAZARA station and buy your ticket. It's a lot of fuss for a few dollars!

Meals are usually available on the TAZARA train and can be served in your compartment. Otherwise, there are always plenty of food and drink vendors at the stations en route. Don't take photographs on this train unless you have discussed the matter beforehand with police.

If you're going all the way to Kapiri Mposhi then you have the Tunduma/

Nakonde border to contend with and it's notorious. It's best to expect the worst which is a very thorough search right down to your underwear, women included. The officials who do the searching would have no problem finding employment with the Mafia. And if they find anything which you shouldn't have or haven't got something which you should have, then you're in for a hard time. Fines and bribes are the order of the day. If they don't find anything that they can give you a hard time about you may well be hassled for 'presents' - I've had letters from a few travellers who have actually been thrown off the train for refusing to cross someone's palm. Beware!

Boat See the Burundi details above about the *MV Liemba's* services on Lake Tanganyika.

GETTING AROUND
Air
Air Tanzania, the national carrier, serves internal routes. Small jets are used between the main airports - Dar, Kilimanjaro, Mwanza and Zanzibar. Propeller planes are used on routes which service smaller airports such as Bukoba, Dodoma, Iringa, Kigoma, Kilwa, Lindi, Mafia, Mbeya, Musoma, Mtwara, Pemba, Shinyanga, Songea, Tabora and Tanga. There are usually several flights a day between the main airports and at least three flights a week through the smaller ones. Internal flights can be paid for in shillings without having to produce bank receipts or a currency form. This makes them an incomparable bargain if all you want to do is to get from A to B and you're changing your money at the unofficial rate. The departure tax for internal flights is Sh 140 - payable in shillings.

Road
Tanzania's economy is in dire straits and part of the reason for this is the crippling bill for oil imports, vehicles and spare parts. As a result, petrol and diesel are in short supply and buses often very ramshackle. Many services have been suspended indefinitely - there are no longer any buses, for example, between Arusha and Musoma through the Serengeti National Park - and other services are liable to cancellation at short notice. Breakdowns are frequent. This means that, where there is no train service to fall back on, there's a lot of competition for a place on a bus. Off the main routes (Dar-Moshi-Arusha and Dar-Iringa-Mbeya) it is possible to get stuck for days. Even safari company buses and Land-Rovers have been known to run out of fuel on occasion.

Given these circumstances. it's not surprising that there is a black market in diesel and petrol. In 1986 pump prices were Sh 17 (standard) and Sh 20 (premium) per litre but, in most places, you can only buy so much at these prices. If you want more then you'll have to pay for it at black market rates which can be up to three times the pump prices. Sunday is a virtually transportless day because only foreign registered vehicles and those with special plates are allowed to operate.

A few Tanzanian towns have central bus and *matatu* stations (Moshi and Arusha, for example) so it's easy to find the bus you want. Other places - and Dar is the prime example - don't have a central stand and buses depart from several locations, some of them not at all obvious. In circumstances like this you will have to ask around before you find the bus you want. Buses and *matatus* leave when full but pick up more people en route. Fares are usually fixed though you may be charged extra for baggage.

Don't, under any circumstances, allow your bag to be put on the roof if there's any possibility of other people travelling up there with it. There won't be much left in it by the time you arrive. The safest thing to do is to insist that it goes under your seat or in the aisle where you can keep your eye on it. Most of the time you won't have to dispute this with the driver. You also need to be very wary of pick-pockets at bus stations – there are usually hundreds of them and they're all waiting just for you! Arusha is supposedly notorious for them.

Rail

Most of Tanzania's major centres of population are connected by railway except for Arusha, Bagamoyo and Kilwa. The Central Line linking Dar es Salaam with Kigoma via Morogoro, Kilosa, Dodoma and Tabora was built by the German colonial authorities between 1905 and 1914 and subsequently extended by the British from Tabora to Mwanza. The extension of this line links Dar es Salaam with Moshi and Tanga via Korogwe.

The other major line is the TAZARA Railway linking Dar es Salaam with Kapiri Mposhi in the heartland of the Zambian copper belt via Morogoro, Mbeya and Tunduma/Nakonde. This line was built by the Chinese People's Republic in the 1960s and passes through some of the most remote country in Africa including part of the Selous Game Reserve. The line involved the construction of 147 stations, over 300 bridges and 23 tunnels. It was the most ambitious project ever undertaken by the Chinese outside of their own territory. Apart from rail links to the east and south, it is Zambia's most important link with the sea but, unfortunately, maintenance hasn't matched the energy with which the Chinese first constructed the railway, so schedules are often a figment of the imagination, though there are usually two trains in either direction each week.

There are three classes on Tanzanian trains – 1st Class (two-bunk compartments), 2nd Class (six-bunk compartments) and 3rd Class (wooden benches only). You'd have to be desperate to go any distance in 3rd – it's very uncomfortable, very crowded and there are thieves to contend with. It's definitely not recommended. Second class is several quantum levels above 3rd in terms of space and comfort (though the fans may not work) and it's an acceptable way to travel long distances. The only real difference between 2nd and 1st is that there are two people to a compartment instead of six. On some trains meals can be served in your compartment (the food is usually good). Otherwise there are always food and drink sellers on the platform at stations en route.

Even when you try to book a ticket several days in advance you may well be told that 1st and 2nd class is sold out. The Central Line station in Dar es Salaam is notorious for this. The claim is usually pure, unadulterated rubbish but it helps to secure 'presents' for ticket clerks. If you are told this then go to see the station master and beg, scrape and plead for his assistance. It may take some time but you'll get those supposedly 'booked' tickets in the end. The claim is generally true on the day of departure.

Boat

Lake Tanganyika See the section above about transport to Burundi for details on the *MV Liemba's* ferry services on Lake Tanganyika. This connects Tanzania with Burundi and Zambia and also operates between Tanzanian ports on the lake. The *MV Mwongozo* operates services only in Tanzania, connecting Kigoma with the small Tanzanian ports to the south.

Lake Victoria There are two ferries which serve ports on Lake Victoria. The *MV Victoria* connects Bukoba and Mwanza while the *MV Bukoba* serves Bukoba, Mwanza, Musoma and Kisumu in Kenya. See the Lake Victoria section for schedules and fare details.

Offshore Islands See the Dar es Salaam section and the Zanzibar section for details on the services out to the islands off the Tanzania coast.

Dhows Dhows have sailed the coastal waters of East Africa and across to Arabia and India for centuries and, although greatly reduced in numbers these days, they can still be found if you're looking for a romantic way of getting across to the islands off the coast. You need to be persistent and prepared to deal with red tape.

In the early 1980s foreigners were virtually prohibited from sailing on dhows after a number of accidents. Tourist drownings don't enhance the country's tourism image! The rules have been relaxed again but you still need to get the District Commissioner's permission before sailing on a dhow. This is little more than a formality and, if the captain of the dhow is prepared to help you, it can all be completed in a matter of minutes.

Since they rely entirely on the wind, dhows only sail when the winds are favourable otherwise too much tacking becomes necessary. This may mean that they sail at night but, on a full moon especially, this is pure magic. There's nothing to disturb the silence except for the lapping of the sea against the sides of the boat. Remember that they are open boats without bunks or any other luxuries, you simply have to bed down wherever there is space and where you won't get in the way of the crew. Fares are negotiable but are often more than you would pay on a modern ship for the same journey.

Most of the towns and cities on the coast and on the islands have their dhow docks which is where you will have to go to make enquiries. This dock is often in a different place to that where the modern shipping docks. In Dar es Salaam, for example, it is the Malindi Dock alongside Sokoine Drive. Well-used dhow routes on which captains are familiar with travellers include Dar-Zanzibar, Zanzibar-Pemba, Pemba-Tanga and sometimes to Mombasa in Kenya. See the Zanzibar section for more details.

Dar es Salaam

Dar es Salaam, the 'Haven of Peace' started out as a humble fishing village in the mid-19th century when the Sultan of Zanzibar decided to turn the inland creek, which is now the harbour, into a safe port and trading centre. It became the capital in 1891 when the German colonial authorities transferred their seat of government from Bagamoyo, a move prompted because the port there was unsuitable for steamships.

Since that time it has continued to grow and is now a city of almost 1½ million people. Although quite a few high-rise buildings have appeared in the centre and at various places in the suburbs, it remains substantially a low-rise city of red-tiled roofs with its colonial character intact. The harbour is still fringed with palms and mangroves and you can see Arab dhows and dugout canoes mingling with huge ocean-going freighters and liners. Dar has a long way to go before it matches the same frenzied pace of life in Nairobi.

Information

Tourist Office The TTC office (tel 2485) is on Maktaba Rd near the junction with Samora Avenue and opposite the New Africa Hotel. They're open Monday to Friday from 9 am to 5 pm and Saturday from 9 am to 12 noon. It has a limited range of glossy leaflets about the national parks and other places of interest, a map of the city and a 1:2 million scale map of Tanzania but they're often out of stock of all of these. If the maps are unavailable it can be difficult to find any street map of Dar but the road map is sometimes available from the Kilimanjaro Hotel shops.

The TTC can also make reservations at any of the larger hotels in Tanzania and at most of the national park lodges (payment in foreign currency only) but they can't help you with budget accom-

Tanzania – Dar es Salaam 295

modation. It's better to book national park lodges through a travel agency as you can often arrange a deal to pay in shillings.

Embassies Apart from embassies for neighbouring countries mentioned in the Visa section others include:

Algeria
    34 Upanga Rd (tel 20846)
Australia
    NIC Investment House, Samora Ave
    (tel 20244)
Belgium
    NIC Investment House (tel 20604)
Canada
    Pan African Insurance Co Building,
    Samora Ave (tel 20651)
Denmark
    Bank House, Samora Ave (tel 27077)
Finland
    NIC Investment House, Samora Ave
    (tel 30396)
West Germany
    NIC Investment House, Samora Ave
    (tel 23286)
Guinea
    35 Haile Selassie Rd, Oyster Bay
    (tel 68626)
India
    NIC Investment House, Samora Ave
    (tel 28197)
Italy
    316 Lugalo Rd (tel 29961)
Japan
    78 Bagamoyo Rd, Kinondoni (tel 68644)
Madagascar
    Magore St (tel 68229)
Mozambique
    25 Garden Avenue (tel 33062)
Netherlands
    IPS Building, Samora Ave (tel 26767)
Nigeria
    3 Bagamoyo Rd (tel 67746)
Norway
    Extelcoms Building, Samora Ave
    (tel 22301)
Somalia
    31 Upanga Rd (tel 32104)
Spain
    IPS Building, Samora Ave (tel 23203)
Sudan
    64 Upanga Rd (tel 32022)

Sweden
    Extelcoms Building, Samora Ave
    (tel 23501)
Switzerland
    17 Kenyatta Drive (tel 67801)
UK
    Hifiadhi House, Samora Ave (tel 29601)
USA
    36 Laibon Rd (tel 68894)
Zambia
    5/9 Sokoine Drive/Ohio St (tel 27261)
Zimbabwe
    Umoja wa Vijana Building, Morogoro Rd
    (tel 30455)

Airline Offices
Aeroflot
    Eminaz Mansion, Samora Avenue
    (tel 23577)
Air France
    Coronation House, Azikiwe St (tel 20356)
Air India
    corner of UWT St & Upanga Rd
    (tel 23525)
Air Tanzania
    ATC House, Ohio St (tel 38300)
Air Zaire
    IPS Building, Samora Avenue (tel 20836)
Alitalia
    AMI Building, Samora Avenue
    (tel 23621)
British Airways
    Coronation House, Samora Avenue
    (tel 20322)
Egyptair
    Matasalamat Mansion, Samora Avenue
    (tel 23425)
Ethiopian Airlines
    TDFL Building, Samora Avenue
    (tel 24174)
Kenya Airlines
    Tancot House, Sokoine Drive (tel 25352)
KLM
    TDFL Building, Samora Avenue
    (tel 33725)
Lufthansa
    Extelcoms Building, Samora Avenue
    (tel 22270)
Pakistan International Airlines
    IPS Building, Samora Avenue (tel 26944)
Pan Am
    Kilimanjaro Hotel, Kivukoni Front
    (tel 23526)
Sabena
    AMI Building, Samora Avenue
    (tel 30109)

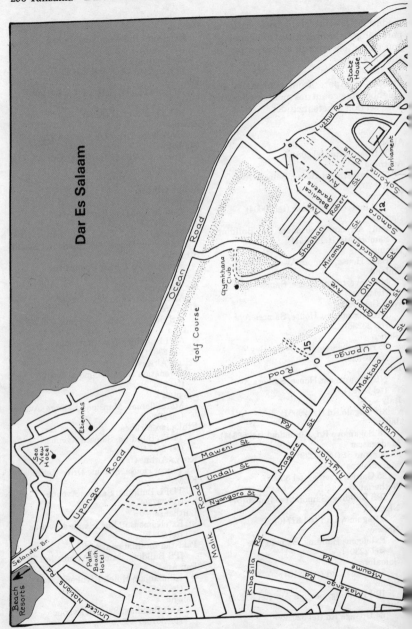

Dar Es Salaam

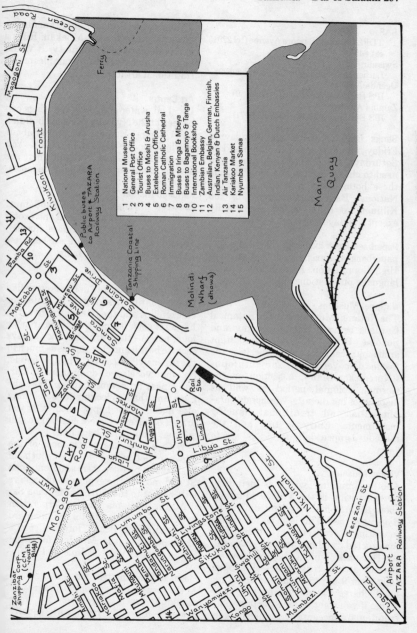

1   National Museum
2   General Post Office
3   Tourist Office
4   Buses to Moshi & Arusha
5   Extelecomms Office
6   Roman Catholic Cathedral
7   Immigration
8   Buses to Iringa & Mbeya
9   Buses to Bagamoyo & Tanga
10 International Bookshop
11 Zambian Embassy
12 Australian, Belgian, German, Finnish,
    Indian, Kenyan & Dutch Embassies
13 Air Tanzania
14 Kariakoo Market
15 Nyumba ya Sanaa

SAS
   TDFL Building, Samora Avenue (tel 22015
   ext 845)
Swissair
   Luther House, Sokoine Drive (tel 22539)
Uganda Airlines
   IPS Building, Azikiwe St (tel 30359)
Zambia Airways
   IPS Building, Azikiwe St (tel 29071)

Banks Banking hours are Monday to Friday from 8.30 am to 12.30 pm and on Saturdays from 8.30 to 11.30 am. If you need to change money at a bank outside these hours there is a branch of the National Bank of Commerce in the Kilimanjaro Hotel which opens daily except Sunday from 8 am to 8 pm.

Paperback Book Exchange There is a free paperback book exchange at the Canadian High Commission. English and French language publications only.

National Museum
The National Museum is in the Botanical Gardens between Samora Avenue and Sokoine Drive. It houses important archaeological collections especially the fossil discoveries of Zinjanthropus ('Nutcracker Man'), a section on the German colonial period as well as displays of handicrafts, witchcraft paraphernalia and traditional dancing instruments. Entry is free and the museum is open daily from 9.30 am to 7 pm.

Village Museum
Another museum which is definitely worth visiting is the Village Museum, about 10 km from the city centre along the Bagamoyo road. This is an actual village consisting of a collection of authentically constructed dwellings from various parts of Tanzania which display several distinct architectural styles. It's open daily from 9 am to 7 pm and there's a small charge for entry plus a further charge if you want to take photographs. Traditional dances are performed here on

Thursday and Sunday. Three km further down the same road at Mpakani Rd is a *makonde* carving community. It would be a good place to pick up examples of this traditional art form.

Art Centre
Local oil, water and chalk paintings can be seen at the Nyumba ya Sanaa building on Upanga Rd at the roundabout overlooking the Gymkhana Club. You can see the artists at work and there are also *makonde* carvers and batik designers.

Kariakoo Market
Between Mkunguni St and Tandamuti St this market has a colourful and exotic atmosphere – fruit, fish, spices, flowers, vegetables, etc – but there are very few handicrafts for sale any more.

Places to Stay
Finding a place to stay in Dar is often like trying to find rocking horse dung or chicken lips and the later you arrive, the harder it gets. It's not that there aren't a lot of hotels – there are – but they always seem to be full and this applies as much to the expensive places as the budget hotels. So, whatever else you do on arrival in Dar, *don't* pass up a vacant room. Take the room and then go looking for something else if you're not happy with it. If you draw a blank everywhere else you've still got that room to fall back on.

With a few exceptions, most of the cheaper hotels are to the south of Maktaba St between there and Lumumba St and most of the expensive places are either on or to the north of Maktaba St.

All the Tanzania Tourist Corporation hotels – New Africa Hotel, Kilimanjaro Hotel, Kunduchi Beach Hotel – offer 50% discounts from the Monday following Easter Sunday until 30 June each year.

Places to Stay – bottom end
At the very bottom end of the market you shouldn't expect too much for your money – a scruffy room with equally

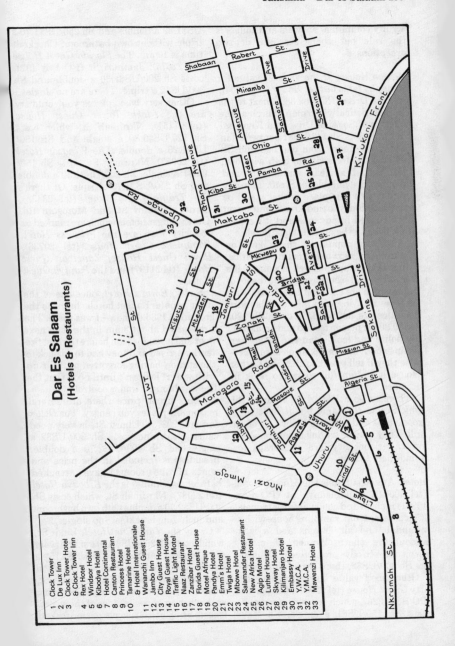

Dar Es Salaam
(Hotels & Restaurants)

1 Clock Tower
2 De Lux Inn
3 Clock Tower Hotel
   & Clock Tower Inn
4 Rex Hotel
5 Windsor Hotel
6 Kibodya Hotel
7 Hotel Continental
8 Canton Restaurant
9 Princess Hotel
10 Tamarine Hotel
11 Hotel Internationale
   & Wananchi Guest House
12 Jambo Inn
13 City Guest House
14 Royal Guest House
15 Traffic Light Motel
16 Naaz Restaurant
17 Zanzibar Hotel
18 Florida Guest House
19 Motel Afrique
20 Pandya Hotel
21 Emm's Hotel
22 Twiga Hotel
23 Mbowe Hotel
24 Salamander Restaurant
25 New Africa Hotel
26 Agip Motel
27 Luther House
28 Skyway Hotel
29 Kilimanjaro Hotel
30 Embassy Hotel
31 Y.W.C.A.
32 Y.M.C.A.
33 Mawenzi Hotel

scruffy communal showers and toilets is the rule but there are one or two exceptions.

Mission Houses & the Ys Best value for money by far is *Luther House* (tel 32154), Sokoine Drive (PO Box 389), next to the characteristically German church at the junction of Sokoine Drive and Kivukoni Front. It costs Sh 143/US$1 per person in rooms with more than one bed and Sh 200/US$1.30 for a single, both with own bathroom. It's clean and secure and breakfast is available for Sh 40. The only trouble with this place is that you'll be extremely lucky to find a room unless you have booked in advance and it's a long walk back to the other budget hotels.

Also very popular is the *YWCA* on Maktaba St, next to the main post office, which takes couples as well as women. It's very clean and secure and there are a lot of rules which are enforced but things work as a result. Mosquito nets and laundry facilities are provided. It costs Sh 120/US$0.80 per person for bed and breakfast. Be polite and look clean and tidy when asking about accommodation here otherwise they'll tell you it's full. Like Luther House it's often full so try to book in advance.

There's also a *YMCA* on Upanga Rd which costs the same but it isn't such good value and, like the YWCA, is often full. They may be willing to let you sleep on the floor if you're desperate for somewhere to stay.

Hotels Amongst hotels the *Mbowe Hotel* (tel 20501), Makunganya St (PO Box 15261) is clean and good value for money. It's a pleasant, old, rambling house with a verandah and airy rooms and a sign announcing that: 'Women of moral turpitude strictly prohibited'. Doubles are Sh 300/US$2, there are no singles.

Other good value hotels include the *City Guest House* (tel 22987), Chagga St (PO Box 1326), which is pretty clean and costs Sh 150/US$1 a single, Sh 200/

US$1.30 a double and Sh 250/US$1.70 a triple without own bathroom. Checkout time is 10 am. The *Florida Guest House* (tel 22675), Jamhuri St (PO Box 132), costs Sh 200/US$1.30 a double and Sh 300/US$2 a triple. There are no singles.

Other very basic places you could try are the *Clock Tower Guest House* (tel 21151), Nkrumah St, which costs Sh 120/US$0.80 a single and Sh 180/US$1.20 a double. The *Windsor Hotel* (tel 20353), Nkrumah St, costs Sh 150/US$1 a single, Sh 200/US$1.30 a double and Sh 250/US$1.70 a triple. Or there's the *Traffic Light Motel* (tel 23438), corner Jamhuri St and Morogoro Rd. Other budget hotels which are marked on the city map are the *Princess Hotel*, *Wananchi Guest House* (tel 20736), *Royal Guest House*, *Zanzibar Guest House* (tel 21197) and the *Pandya Guest House*.

Sadly, *Emm's Hotel*, once one of the most popular budget hotels, burnt to the ground in 1986. I know – I was there. The fire started about 3 am in the shop next door and it was 6.45 am before the first fire tender arrived and they had to go back to the station having forgotten to fill it up with water! It wasn't until noon that the fire was brought under control.

Going up in price there are several reasonable places you can try. The *Delux Inn* (tel 20873), Uhuru St, is very good value, clean and costs Sh 300/US$2 a single and Sh 400/US$2.70 a double. Breakfast is included in the price and some of the rooms have attached bathrooms. Similar is the *Kibodya Hotel* (tel 22987), Nkrumah St, which costs Sh 400/US$2.70 a double with own bathroom and including breakfast (no singles).

Or try the *Tamarine Hotel*, Lindi St, which costs Sh 250/US$1.70 a single (very few singles) and Sh 325/US$2.15 a double. Next to the Tamarine is the *Hotel Internationale* (tel 22785), Lindi St, which consists of two buildings facing each other on opposite sides of the street. It costs Sh 280/US$1.85 per person for bed and breakfast or Sh 580/US$3.85 per person for full board.

Going further up-market, the *Rex Hotel* (tel 21414), Nkrumah St, is clean and not bad value at Sh 350/US$2.30 a single and Sh 460/US$3.05 a double. There's a bar and restaurant downstairs.

Places to Stay – middle

In mid-range hotels my nomination for best value would be the *Jambo Inn* (tel 35359/21552), Libya St. This is a newly-built place which is very clean and pleasant and has its own reasonably-priced restaurant. It costs Sh 400/US$2.70 a single and Sh 500/US$3.40 a double without air-conditioning and Sh 450/US$3 a single and Sh 550/US$3.70 a double with air-conditioning. All prices include breakfast and taxes. It's very popular and so often full.

Similarly priced is the *Motel Afrique* (tel 31034), corner Kaluta St and Bridge St, which costs Sh 472/US$3.15 a double with own bathroom. The hotel has its own bar and restaurant. The *Mawenzi Hotel* (tel 27761), corner Upanga Rd and Maktaba St at the roundabout, is also worth trying. It costs Sh 400/US$2.70 a single, Sh 500/US$3.40 a double and Sh 600/US$4 a triple with own bathroom but excluding breakfast. Checkout time is 11 am.

The *Continental Hotel* (tel 22481), Nkrumah St, has a similar price structure at Sh 570/US$3.80 a single and Sh 674/US$4.50 a double with own bathroom, air-conditioning and including breakfast. Some travellers have had to pay in foreign currency though that may not always be the case. Lastly in this range there is the *Skyways Hotel* (tel 27061), corner Sokoine Drive and Ohio St, but I met several local people who advised against staying there as they said a lot of theft goes on from the rooms. I've not had this confirmed from other sources.

Places to Stay – top end

At all the top range hotels you must pay in foreign currency. This puts them well out of the range of most travellers' budgets.

The cheapest of the top end places is the *Twiga Hotel* (tel 22561), Samora Avenue, which costs about US$20 a double with bathroom, air-conditioning and breakfast. It's often full. Next comes the *New Africa Hotel* (tel 29611), Maktaba St, where you're looking at US$33 a single and US$42 a double with own bathroom and air-conditioning. After that it's the *Kilimanjaro Hotel* (tel 21281), Kivukoni Front, and the *Motel Agip* (tel 23511), Pamba Rd between Sokoine Drive and Samora Avenue, which cost US$45 a single and US$49 a double with own bathroom and air-conditioning.

The most expensive hotel is the *Hotel Embassy* (tel 30006), Garden Avenue, which is pure banditry at US$50 a single and US$80 a double with bathroom, air-conditioning and including breakfast.

Places to Eat

Cheap Eats There are many small restaurants in the city centre, some of them attached to hotels, where you can buy a cheap traditional African meal or Indian food. The *Naaz Restaurant*, Jamhuri St has good, clean, cheap Indian food. The *Royal Restaurant*, Jamhuri St between Mosque St and Kitumbini St, does vegetable curries and the like. *Nawaz Restaurant*, Msinhiri St between Mosque St and Morogoro Rd, has cheap rice and meat dishes.

There's a good Chinese restaurant in the basement of the NIC Investment House, Samora Avenue at Mirambo St. There's also a small, unnamed café¼ under the *Agip Motel* on Pamba St which is good value. They have chicken, roast potatoes, pizzas and coffee at very reasonable prices. One of the best vegetarian restaurants is the *Supreme Restaurant*, Nkrumah St, which serves Indian vegetarian food.

Slightly more expensive but very good is the restaurant at the *Jambo Inn*, Jamhuri St which has soups for Sh 20, chicken curry for Sh 80, ox liver, fish or chicken with rice or chips are all Sh 100. Similar and especially popular for its lunches is the *Salamander Coffee & Snack Bar*, Samora Avenue at Mkwepu St. At both of these places you have the choice of eating inside or outside though the verandah of the Salamander is particularly pleasant. An average lunch here costs around Sh 100/US$0.65.

Ice-cream freaks should make at least one visit to the *Sno-Cream Parlour*, Mansfield St near the junction with Bridge St. Mansfield St runs part of the way between Samora Avenue and Sokoine Drive. This place has the best ice cream in Tanzania and is well on the way to becoming a legend among travellers. You should see the number of Indian families who come here on Sundays! Lastly, for fruit juices, peanut brittle and gooey cakes go to *Siefee's Juice Shop*, Samora Avenue. They also have good samosas.

More Expensive Places For a not-too-expensive splurge, try a meal at the *New Africa Hotel* on the ground floor. Their cooking varies from average to good and a full meal will cost Sh 225/US$1.50 though you can buy just a main course for around Sh 180/US$1.20.

For a real splurge you should try the roof-top restaurants at either the *Twiga Hotel*, Samora Avenue, or the *Kilimanjaro Hotel*, Kivukoni Front. They're both popular with local businessmen, ex-patriates and well-heeled tourists but the food at both is excellent and the views over the city (especially at night) worth the extra you pay for a meal. You're looking at around Sh 250/US$1.70 plus drinks, coffee and tips.

VSOs and Peace Corps volunteers rate lunch at *Etiennes* and dinner at the *Sea View Hotel* highly though you'll need a taxi to get there from the centre. They're both on Ocean Rd close to Selander Bridge.

Entertainment

Probably the best place to go for a cold, cleansing ale is the street level patio of the *New Africa Hotel*, Maktaba St. This is the nearest place you will find in Dar es Salaam to the Thorn Tree Cafe at the New Stanley Hotel in Nairobi. Most travellers come here at one time or another and you can always get into a lively conversation with them, with local people or both. It gets very busy between 4.30 and 7 pm. Drinks without meals are only served in the outdoor part at lunch and dinner times. Later at night the roof-top restaurant at the *Twiga Hotel* may be worth checking out for a cold beer. Others have recommended the bar at the *Agip Motel*.

The British Council (tel 22716), Samora Avenue, has free film shows on Wednesday afternoons/evenings and sometimes on Mondays too. Similar social evenings are organised by the Goethe Institute (tel 22227), IPS Building, Samora Avenue, and the US Information Service (tel 26611), Samora Avenue.

There are occasional discos at the larger hotels in Dar and at the beach resort hotels.

Getting There

Air Dar es Salaam is the major international arrival point for flights from overseas. See the introductory Getting There section for more details and the Getting Around section for details on domestic flights with Air Tanzania.

The international departure tax is US$10 – payable in cash dollars. Travellers' cheques are not acceptable. You have to change them at the airport bank and they'll only give you US$19 for a US$20 travellers' cheque! The departure tax for internal flights is Sh 140 – payable in shillings.

Road Buses for Bagamoyo leave daily

from the Kariakoo Market. For Moshi and Arusha buses go from the bus station on the corner of Morogoro Rd and Libya St. It's a rough road to Moshi and the trip takes 12 to 14 hours. To Tanga buses take about seven to eight hours and go from the station bounded by Lumumba St, Uhuru St and Libya St. Mbeya buses take about 20 hours and go from the same station. See the relevant sections for more details on fares, departure times and so on.

Rail Booking rail tickets is complicated by the practice of claiming that tickets are sold out when they're actually not, in order to extract bribes. The Central Line station in Dar is particularly bad for this.

See the Getting There section on transport to and from Zambia for information about the TAZARA railway service. Trains also run from Dar es Salaam to Kigoma and Mwanza about four times a week and up the coast to Moshi and Tanga three times a week. See the relevant sections for timetable, travel time and fare details.

Boat The Zanzibar Shipping Corporation (tel 30749), Jengo la Vijana, Morogoro Rd (PO Box 1395) operates a service to Zanzibar. Their office is marked 'CCM Youth' on tourist maps of Dar es Salaam. See the Zanzibar section for fare and timetable details.

The Tanzanian Coastal Shipping Line (NASACO) (tel 26192), Sokoine Drive (PO Box 9461) operates boats which connect Dar with Tanga, Mafia Island, and to Kilwa, Lindi and Mtwara south of Dar. They normally sail to Tanga twice a week taking about 12 hours and, although passengers are rare, you are welcome on board (seats only) for Sh 150/US$1. They also sail to Mafia Island and Kilwa on average about once every two weeks. To Mafia takes about eight hours and costs Sh 40/US$0.25 (seats only). To Kilwa takes about 16 hours and costs Sh 80/US$0.55 (seats only). This same company

also occasionally sails to Mombasa and the Comoros Islands. There is no regular schedule for any of these boats so you need to enquire at the office at the junction of Sokoine Drive and Mission St. One of the managers is a friendly German who speaks English.

Dhows See the introductory Getting Around section for information about dhow travel. Dhows operate from the Malindi Dock alongside Sokoine Drive rather than the modern shipping docks. Dhow captains are familiar with travellers on the route to Zanzibar which typically costs Sh 170/US$1.15. It's sometimes possible to pick up a dhow from Dar to Mombasa but the red tape is likely to be involved.

Getting Around
Airport Transport Dar es Salaam airport is 13 km from the city centre. Bus No 67 connects the two but, if you get on at the airport, make sure that it is going right into the city centre. Some of them don't. Takim's Holidays, Tours & Safaris operate a shuttle bus service between the centre and the airport departing the city at 8 am, 10 am, 12 noon, 2 pm and 4 pm and the airport at 9 am, 11 am, 1 pm, 3 pm, 6 pm and 7 pm. Their terminus in the city is close to the Jambo Inn, Libya St. A taxi to or from the airport will cost Sh 300/US$2 shared by up to four people.

Local Transport Local buses are operated by both the government (UDA buses) and private firms (Dala Dala). Neither type are numbered but instead have their first and last stop indicated in the front window. The one to the TAZARA railway station is marked Posta-Vigunguti. Fares are fixed and cost only a few shillings.

If you need to hire a private taxi, for the day, for instance, go to Co-Cabs (tel 20177/8) at the corner of Lumumba and Nkrumah Sts.

BEACHES AROUND DAR ES SALAAM

Oyster Bay is the nearest beach, six km north of the city centre, but most people head up to the beaches around the Kunduchi Beach/Bahari Beach/Silver Sands/Rungwe Oceanic Hotels, 24 km north of the city. Be careful walking around on the beach between these hotels unless you're in a reasonable sized group. Armed gangs of five to six people roam the stretch and you'll get mugged. We've had many reports of this.

Boat trips are available from some of the hotels to off-shore islands such as Mbudya Island where you can go swimming, snorkelling or sunbathing. The Rungwe Oceanic Hotel charges Sh 1000/US$7 for a boat shared between up to eight people. From the Kunduchi Beach Hotel a boat costs Sh 150/US$1 per person. They take off in the early morning and return in the late afternoon. Grilled fish and warm sodas *may* be available on the island but if you want to be sure then take your own. There's very little shade, so bear this in mind if you're not well tanned.

The Kunduchi Hotel also offers longer boat trips to Zanzibar for Sh 1000/US$7 per person. They depart between 3.30 and 7 am depending on the tides and return in the evening. The journey in either direction takes four to five hours and leaves you with a few hours to wander around Zanzibar town. The man who operates this boat will only take groups – maximum size is 18 people.

Places to Stay

The resort hotels are all north of Dar es Salaam. The first is the *Oysterbay Hotel* (tel 68631), Toure Drive, about six km from the city centre facing the sea and palm-fringed beach. Rooms are about US$20.

All the other hotels are some 24 km north of the city centre. In order of appearance they are the *Kunduchi Beach Hotel* (tel 47261), the *Silver Sands Hotel* (tel 47231), the *Rungwe Oceanic Hotel* (tel 47021) and the *Bahari Beach Hotel* (tel 47101).

The Rungwe Oceanic Hotel is where all the overland trucks park because camping is possible here at Sh 20 per person per night. The facilities are minimal but the site is guarded 24 hours a day by a man armed with a bow and arrow! Water is pumped up from a well so the supply can be erratic. Some travellers have managed to pay for rooms here in shillings (Sh 300/US$2 a single and Sh 575/US$3.85). If that's no longer possible it's still the cheapest of the beach hotels at US$20 a single and US$34 a double. Rooms have attached bathrooms, air-conditioning and breakfast in included. There are also some slightly more expensive self-contained bungalows in the grounds.

Other travellers have reported that it's possible to camp free at the Silver Sands Hotel so long as you eat your meals at the hotel. Lunch or dinner costs Sh 200 to 250, payable in shillings.

Other than these possibilities all these hotels require payment in foreign currency. After the Rungwe Oceanic the Silver Sands is next cheapest. The Kunduchi and the Bahari both charge about US$40 for singles, US$50 for doubles with bathroom, air-con and continental breakfast (eggs are extra!). All meals, drinks and other services (boat trips, etc) can be paid for in shillings.

Places to Eat

At the beach resort hotels the *Rungwe Oceanic Hotel* has the cheapest meals at around Sh 150/US$1 for a main course and Sh 220/US$1.45 for a three-course meal. At the other three hotels you are looking at Sh 200-300 for a three-course meal. The *Bahari Beach Hotel* has an all-you-can-eat buffet for Sh 250/US$1.70 on Saturday evenings.

Getting There

To get to the beaches you can take a local bus from the centre but it's quite a walk from where it stops and you might get mugged. It's much safer to take the shuttle bus from the New Africa Hotel in the centre to the Rungwe Oceanic Hotel even though it costs more. The State Travel Service operates this service which departs the city Monday to Friday at 9 am, 12 noon, 2 pm and 5 pm and on Saturdays/Sundays at 9 am, 11 am, 1 pm, 3 pm and 5 pm. The fare is Sh 100/US$0.65.

The Coast

BAGAMOYO

The name of this coastal town, 75 km north of Dar es Salaam, derives from the word 'bwagamoyo' meaning 'lay down your heart'. It's a reminder that it was once the terminus of the slave trade caravan route from Lake Tanganyika. This was the point of no return where the captives were loaded onto dhows and shipped to Zanzibar for sale to Arab buyers. Bagamoyo hasn't entirely left it's infamous history behind either. These days, it's notorious for thieves and muggers. Be careful if you're on your own.

Bagamoyo was the headquarters of the German colonial administration and many of the buildings which they constructed still remain but its history goes back to the 14th century when the East African coast was being settled by Arabs and Shirazis from the Persian Gulf. The ruins they left at Kaole, just outside of Bagamoyo, are similar to those at Gedi and around the Lamu archipelago further north in Kenya.

Around Town

Like Lamu, Mombasa, Zanzibar, and other old coastal towns, Bagamoyo has its stone town of narrow, winding alleys, tiny mosques, cafes and whitewashed German colonial buildings. They're great to wander around. Don't miss the Old Prison (now the police station) which incorporates the tunnel through which slaves were driven to waiting dhows and the former German administrative headquarters on India St.

For more immediate pleasures, the evening market by the bus station is worth a visit if you'd like to sample local food from the many street stalls to be found here.

Out of Town

The Catholic Mission north of town maintains a museum with relics of the slave trade and displays about the early European explorers Burton, Speke and Stanley. The chapel where Livingstone's body was laid before being taken to Zanzibar en route to Westminster Abbey is also here. Don't walk to this museum alone as there's a good chance you'll get mugged. To visit the 14th century ruins at Kaole you'll need to hire a taxi.

Places to Stay & Eat

Almost all the travellers who come to Bagamoyo stay at the *Badeco Beach Hotel* which costs Sh 50/US$0.30 a single and Sh 90/US$0.60 a double without own bathroom. There are no mosquito nets but lots of mosquitoes. It's somewhat rundown and the water supply tends to be erratic but the excellent beach compensates for any hardship. The cook at the hotel will prepare food for a small fee but don't expect any fancy preparation. You can buy lobster (about Sh 125) or other seafood from the fishermen near the famous German Boma building. They land their catches there in the late morning and late afternoon.

Entertainment

Gloria's Bar in the town centre is a lively place to visit. It's run by a friendly Goan woman and her daughters. The *Police Club* is another interesting bar. Both have beers, spirits and sodas.

Getting There

There are several buses daily from Dar es

Salaam to Bagamoyo. They leave from the Kariakoo Market up to 3 pm, cost Sh 40/US$0.25 and take 2½ to three hours.

PANGANI

Pangani is a small village north of Bagamoyo and some 50 km south of Tanga. It's on a beautiful stretch of coast where there are many reefs and islands off-shore. From here you can organise fishing trips to the reefs and snorkelling at the two islands of Mawe Mdogo and Mwamba Mawe. There's also a small Marine Park on the island of Maziwi and boat trips are possible to see the wildlife up the Pangani River.

Places to Stay

Accommodation can be found at the YMCA on the opposite side of the river from the village. The prices are the same as at other YMCA establishments – Sh 245/US$1.60 a single and Sh 350/US$2.30 a double including breakfast.

TANGA

Strolling around Tanga, with its sleepy, colonial atmosphere, you'd hardly be aware that this is Tanzania's second largest seaport. It was founded by the Germans in the late 19th century and is a centre for the export of sisal. Not many travellers come here except those looking for a dhow to Pemba Island or heading north to Mombasa.

Amboni Caves

This area is predominantly a limestone district and not too far from town off the road to Lunga Lunga are the Amboni Caves.

Tongoni Ruins

The Tongoni Ruins are 20 km south of Tanga on the Pangani road. There's a large ruined mosque and over 40 tombs, the largest concentration of such tombs on the whole of the East African coast.

According to accounts which came into the hands of the Portuguese when they first arrived at Kilwa in 1505, both Kilwa and Tongoni were founded by Ali bin Hasan who was the son of Sultan Hasan of Shiraz in Persia at the end of the 10th century AD. Certainly the method of construction of the mosque is unlike that used by the Arabs who came from the Arabian Peninsula in later centuries but Persian script has only been found once and that is on one of the tombstones at Tongoni though Persian coins are common at other sites along the coast such as at Malindi.

Places to Stay – bottom end

Overlooking the harbour on Independence Avenue the *Bandorini Hotel* is a very twee place to stay which many travellers rate highly. It offers matchless English colonial-style living (reflecting the owner's nationality) but is often full because they only have seven rooms. Bed and breakfast costs Sh 125/US$0.80 per person.

The *Usabara Guest House* on Third St is similarly priced – Sh 125/US$0.80 gets you a fan, clean sheets and a towel. The staff are friendly and gear is secure left in the rooms. You can't miss this place as it's painted in large bright stripes.

If the Bandorini and the Usabara are full then try the *Planters Hotel* (tel 2041) on Market St. It's a huge, rambling, old wooden hotel surrounded by an enormous verandah with its own bar and restaurant downstairs. Aussies from Queensland will love this place – it's home from home. It costs Sh 265/US$1.75 a single and Sh 460/US$3 a double including breakfast. The rooms are clean and provided with a hand basin but the communal showers have cold water only. If these hotels are too expensive the *Mkwakwani Lodgings*, behind the maternity hospital and dispensary, has clean doubles with fans for Sh 100/US$0.65.

Other reasonable hotels in Tanga include the *Sunset Guest House*, the *Equator Guest House* (single rooms only at Sh 150/US$1) and the *Splendid Hotel* (tel 2031).

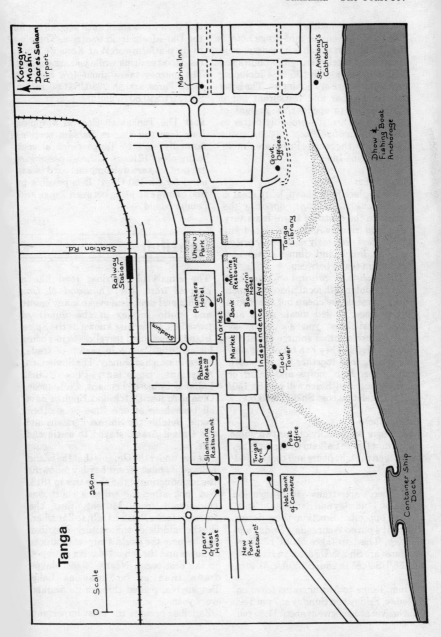

Tanga

Scale

0   250 m

Korogwe
Moshi
Dar es Salaam
Airport

Marina Inn

St. Anthony's Cathedral

Dhow &
Fishing Boat
Anchorage

Govt.
Offices

Station Rd.

Railway
Station

Uhuru Park

Tanga
Library

Stadium

Planters Hotel

Market St.

Marine Restaurant

Bandarini Hotel

Independence Ave.

Patwas Rest.

Bank

Market

Clock
Tower

Slamiana Restaurant

Twiga Grill

Post
Office

Upare Guest
House

New Park Restaurant

Nat. Bank
of Commerce

Container Ship
Dock

Places to Stay - middle

The most convenient mid-range hotel is the *Marina Inn* which is a modern, well-maintained hotel offering air-conditioned double rooms for Sh 595/US4 including breakfast. There are no singles. The hotel has its own bar and restaurant but if you're going to spend this amount of money, however, it's probably better to stay at the *Baobab Hotel* (40638), about five km from the centre. Prices are similar to the Marina Inn.

Places to Eat

The best place for a cheap, tasty meal is the *Patwas Restaurant*, opposite the market in the centre of town. It's a very clean, and friendly Asian-run restaurant which offers extremely reasonably priced meals at lunch and dinner times and snacks and tea in between.

The *Marine Restaurant* on Market St is very popular with local people at lunch time and meals are cheap but the food is only average. Boiled meat, sauce and potatoes will cost you about Sh 45/US$0.30. For a minor splurge eat at the Planters Hotel. They're a bit on the slow side getting food together but it's worth waiting for. Fish, chips and salad or curried prawns with rice will cost Sh 150/US$1. Omelettes cost Sh 80/US$0.50.

Getting There

Road There are usually one or two buses daily from Dar es Salaam to Tanga. They take seven to eight hours and cost Sh 160/$1.

Rail There are trains to Tanga on Tuesday, Thursday and Saturday at 3 pm. In the opposite direction they depart Tanga at 4 pm on Wednesday, Friday and Sunday. The trip takes about 13 hours and fares are Sh 283/US$1.90 in 1st class, Sh 128/US$0.85 in 2nd, Sh 59/US$0.40 in 3rd.

From Tanga to Moshi trains leave on Tuesday, Friday and Sunday at 7 pm The train arrives at Korogwe at about 11.30 pm and then waits there until about 3 am for the Dar-Moshi train to arrive. There's a lively platform cafe¼ at Korogwe if you need food or drink while you are waiting. The journey takes about 16½ hours in total. Fares are Sh 268/US$1.80 in 1st, Sh 123/US$0.80 in 2nd.

Boat The Tanzanian Coastal Shipping Line (see the Dar es Salaam section) normally sails to Tanga twice a week taking about 12 hours. Although passengers are rare, you are welcome on board (seats only) for Sh 150/US$1. It is possible to find dhows operating between Tanga and Pemba Island.

Zanzibar

The annals of Zanzibar read like a chapter from *The Thousand & One Nights* and doubtless evoke many exotic and erotic images in the minds of travellers. Otherwise known as the Spice Island, it has lured travellers to its shores for centuries, some in search of trade, others in search of plunder. The Sumerians, Assyrians, Egyptians, Phoenicians, Indians, Chinese, Persians, Portuguese, Omani Arabs, Dutch and English have all been here at one time or another. Some, notably the Shirazi Persians and the Omani Arabs, stayed to settle and rule.

It was under the Omanis that the island enjoyed its most recent heyday following the introduction of the clove tree in 1818. Not long after the sultan's court was transferred from Muscat, near the entrance to the Persian Gulf, to Zanzibar. By the middle of the century Zanzibar had become the world's largest producer of cloves and the largest slaving entrepôt on the east coast. Nearly 50,000 slaves drawn from as far away as Lake Tanganyika, passed through its market every year.

Zanzibar became the most important

town on the East African coast. All other centres were subject to it and all trade passed through it until the establishment of the European Protectorates towards the end of the 19th century and the construction of the Mombasa to Kampala railway. The Omani sultans continued to rule under a British Protectorate right down to 1963 when independence was granted but were overthrown the following year, prior to the union of Zanzibar with mainland Tanganyika.

The many centuries of occupation and influence by all these various peoples has left its mark and the old stone town of Zanzibar is one of the most fascinating places on the whole east coast. Much larger than Lamu or Bagamoyo it is honeycombed with narrow, winding streets lined with whitewashed houses and magnificently carved, brass-studded doors though, regrettably, many of these have disappeared in recent years. There are quaint little shops, bazaars, mosques, courtyards and squares, even a fortress and a sultan's palace.

Outside of town there are more palaces, Shirazi ruins, the famous Persian baths and that other perennial attraction – magnificent, palm-fringed beaches with warm, clear water ideal for swimming.

Information
The Tourist Office (Tanzania Friendship Tourist Bureau) (PO Box 216, tel 32344) has an excellent map of Zanzibar town. It's a worthwhile investment for exploring the alleys of the old town though you'll probably still get lost from time to time. They also have a good map of the island (DOS 608 Edition 1-DOS 1983) at 1:200,000 scale.

There is an American-sponsored Malaria Centre in the old American Embassy building near the Starehe Club right across from the Ministry of Education. If you think you have the disease or would like to get checked out, they'll do this free of charge and often give you an answer the same day.

Around Town
There are a number of interesting buildings around the old stone town. They include the Beit-el-Ajaib or House of Wonders which is one of the largest structures in Zanzibar. The People's Palace was formerly the Sultan's Palace, the Arab Fort was built by the Portuguese in 1700 and there's the Shirazi Mosque and the Old Slave Market on which was built the first Anglican Cathedral in East Africa. Livingstone House was the base for the missionary-explorer's last expedition before he died and don't miss the Dhow Harbour.

National Museum
The rather run down museum has displays cataloguing the history of the island. Entry cost is Sh 10.

Out of Town
On the outskirts of the town, it's worth visiting the Maruhubi Palace, built by Sultan Seyyid Bargash to house his harem. Further afield are the well-preserved Kidichi Persian Baths built by Sultan Seyyid Said for his Persian wife on the highest point on the island (153 metres).

The Old Slave Caves, near the famous Mangapwani beach about 15 km north of Zanzibar, were used for illegal slave trading after it was finally abolished by the British in the late 1800s. There are buses to within a km of the caves from the bus station in town or you can get there on a bicycle.

There are other ruins around the island, some of them Portuguese at Mvuleni, north of Mkokotoni. They date from the Portuguese maritime heyday when they abortively attempted to colonise the island.

Near Kizimkazi in the south the ruins of the Dimbani Mosque has an inscription round the *mihrab* dated 1107 – the oldest inscription found in East Africa. Excavations have indicated the existence of an earlier mosque on the same site.

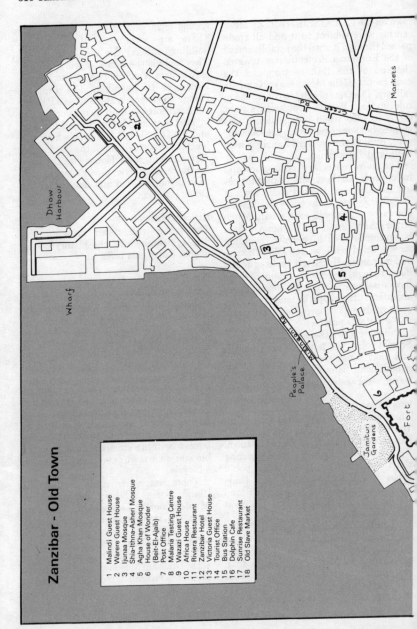

Zanzibar – Old Town

1 Malindi Guest House
2 Warere Guest House
3 Ijunaa Mosque
4 Shia-Ithna-Asheri Mosque
5 Agha Khan Mosque
6 House of Wonder
  (Beit-El-Ajaib)
7 Post Office
8 Malaria Testing Centre
9 Wazazi Guest House
10 Africa House
11 Riviera Restaurant
12 Zanzibar Hotel
13 Victoria Guest House
14 Tourist Office
15 Bus Station
16 Dolphin Cafe
17 Sunrise Restaurant
18 Old Slave Market

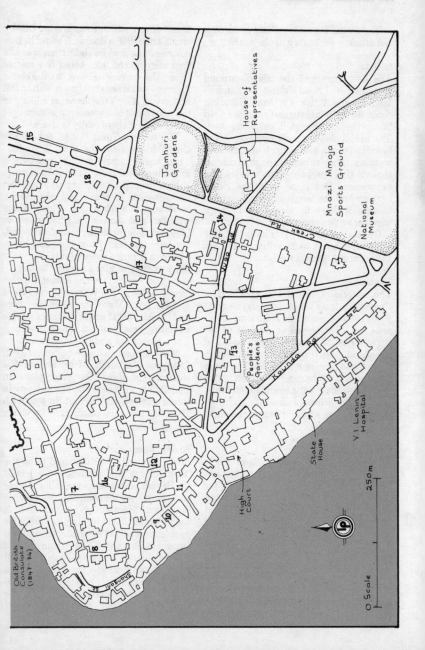

Old British Consulate (1847–74)

Jamhuri Gardens

House of Representatives

Mnazi Mmoja Sports Ground

National Museum

People's Gardens

Creek Rd

Vimo Rd

Kaunda

State House

High Court

V I Lenin Hospital

Shangan St

0 Scale

250 m

The Jozani Forest is the last remaining red monkey sanctuary in the world.

Islands

The best known of the islands around Zanzibar is Prison Island (Kibandiko Island), about five km from Zanzibar town. As the name suggest there is an old prison there, although it was never used. The island also has a disused hospital, a beautiful beach and a bunch of giant land tortoises. They're large enough to ride on though they probably don't enjoy the experience. Boats go from the dhow harbour and the fare is whatever you can bargain it down to. Get a small group together so you can share the costs.

On the island of Tumbatu, off the north-west coast of Zanzibar, there are 13th century Shirazi ruins.

Festivals

The festival of Idd el Fitr (the end of Ramadan) lasts about four days and if you visit the island at that time don't miss the Zanzibarian equivalent of the tug of war at Makunduchi in the south of the island. Men from the south challenge those from the north by beating each other silly with banana branches. After that the women of the town launch into a series of traditional folk songs and then the whole town eats and dances the night away.

Places to Stay

All accommodation on the island has to be paid for in foreign currency. This has been the case at most of the hotels for years, but until 1985 there was always one or other of the budget hotels which would allow you to pay in local currency. There are now no exceptions. Even staying with friends on the island requires a special permit though it's easily obtained. The prices quoted here may vary as the exchange rate floats.

Places to Stay – bottom end

The cheapest place to stay is the *Wazazi Guest House* which costs around US$4 a single and US$8 a double. To find it, face Africa House and go right then take the first alley on the left. About five metres from the corner above a darkened doorway you'll see the sign. It's often full and even if it isn't the manager is likely to tell you that it is. Perseverance might get you a room if there really is space.

The *Warere Guest House*, behind the Cine Afrique near the port, is similar. They have rooms for US$8 per person including breakfast. Next in line is the *Victoria Guest House*, half way between the Majestic Cinema and the Soviet consulate. It's often full. Clean rooms with fan and shower are US$5 single or US$10 double including breakfast (bread, omelette and tea). From the guest house Miti can arrange spice plantation visits but you have to hire a car for the day.

If these are full try the *Malindi Guest House*, close to the Warere Guest House and the port. Many travellers stay here and it costs US$11 single or US$18 double including breakfast but it's poor value – just a cup of tea and two *mandazi*.

Musa Maisara's house on Nyerere Rd, just past Abdallah Mzee Rd on the seafront, is about the only place in Zanzibar town where you can still pay in local currency. Rooms cost Sh 450 to Sh 700 and he's very pleasant. Everybody knows him.

Places to Stay – middle

Africa House (tel 30708) used to be the 'British Club' and esoteric reminders of the British presence are the billiard table and the toilets marked, 'Ladies Powder Room' and 'Gentlemens Cloak Room'! It has rooms at US$14 for singles, US$25 for doubles and US$33 for triples, all without bathroom. Rooms with bathroom are only a dollar or two more expensive and all these prices include breakfast. Africa House is owned and operated by the Afro-Shirazi Party which also owns the similarly priced *Zanzibar Hotel* (tel 30309).

The *Spice Inn* is more expensive at US$22 for singles and US$27 for doubles or US$28 and US$33 with air-con. All the rooms have their own bathroom.

Places to Stay – top end
At the *Bwawani Hotel* (tel 30200) overlooking Funguni Creek all the rooms are air-conditioned and have their own bathroom and colour TV. Rooms cost from US$30 a single and up. The hotel has a swimming pool, bars and restaurant. There is a disco here every Thursday, Saturday and Sunday which is open to non-residents. Western videos are occasionally shown in the bar.

Places to Eat
Cheap Eats The *Dolphin Restaurant*, the *Sunrise Restaurant* and the *Riviera Restaurant* are good cheap places which have been popular with travellers for years. Situated close to Africa House the Riviera is a fairly new establishment and serves excellent food at reasonable prices in a clean and pleasant atmosphere.

Another place to try is the *Falcon Restaurant* off Malawi Rd near the new apartments. It offers relatively good food and a pleasant terrace where you can sit and watch the street life. For hot, spicy food try the *Spice Inn*.

Don't miss *Jamituri Gardens* on the waterfront near the Beit-el-Ajaib (House of Wonders) one evening. The townspeople gather here at that time to socialise, talk about what's happened and watch the sun go down. Food stall vendors sell spicy curries, roasted meat and maize, cassava, smoked octopus, sugar-cane juice and ice-cream at extremely reasonable prices. It's one of the cheapest places to eat in Zanzibar.

More Expensive Restaurants *Africa House* and the *Zanzibar Hotel* both offer meals to residents and non-residents alike which you can pay for in local currency. In the past their meals haven't been up to much but they have improved considerably

of late. Africa House is good for a drink in the evening to watch the sun go down. The bar is on the first floor with a terrace overlooking the ocean.

For a splurge, try the *Bwawani Hotel* on Saturday evening when they have an all-you-can-eat buffet. It's a little expensive at Sh 250 but the food is superb.

Getting There
Air If you arrive by air you must compulsorily change US$30 per day of your intended stay into shillings at the official rate of exchange even though all accommodation on the island (no exceptions) must be paid for in foreign currency. Shillings bought on the mainland at the official rate of exchange and backed up by bank receipts are not acceptable. There is no compulsory change if you arrive by boat or dhow.

Boat Zanzibar Shipping Corporation (see the Dar es Salaam section) operate ships to Zanzibar. Their ship *MV Mandeleo* seems to be permanently out of operation due to lack of funds to repair it but they still have the *MV Mapinduzi* which, if fuel is available, sails from Dar to Zanzibar twice a week.

Departures are usually on Tuesday and Saturday at 12 noon arriving about four to five hours later but check with the office in Dar. In the opposite direction it sails from Zanzibar to Dar on Monday and Friday at 7 am. The fares are Sh 510/US$3.40 (1st Class); Sh 250/US$1.70 (2nd Class), and Sh 190/US$1.25 (3rd Class). In addition, there is a harbour tax of Sh 40.

Small boats cross between Zanzibar and Pemba Island. Ask around at the wharf in Zanzibar.

See the introductory Getting Around section for information about dhow travel. Dar-Zanzibar is a well-used dhow route on which captains are familiar with travellers. Fares are typically about Sh 170/US$1.15. Dhows also operate from

Zanzibar to Pemba. You may also be able to pick up a dhow from Zanzibar to Mombasa at times but the red tape is involved.

Getting Around
Airport Transport Municipal buses run between the airport and town for a few shillings. They're marked 'Uwanja wa Ndege'. A taxi will cost about Sh 200/US$1.30.

Bicycle Rental Bicycles can be hired near the market for Sh 85/US$0.55 per day. Otherwise it's possible to rent a bicycle for the day either from a shop close to the Malindi Guest House or from an old man named Isaac opposite the Air Tanzania office. The charge is usually Sh 10 per hour or Sh 60 per day. Bicycles can be put on the roofs of local buses if you get tired of pedalling.

THE BEACH RESORTS
There are some superb beaches, particularly on the east coast. Ask any traveller who has stayed there what they think of them and you're going to wonder whether they're describing some born-again paradise. 'Perfect honeymoon destination,' or 'I loved every minute of it. Fresh fish and lobster every day and a beautiful deserted beach less than six metres from the front step,' are typical of what we get through the mail.

Tranquil and beautiful they certainly are but they are not for those who cannot enjoy paradise without artificial sweeteners like electricity, hot and cold running water, luxury apartments, swimming pools and discos. Paradise here is simple and uncomplicated. That's why the beaches are largely deserted and unlike some places in Africa you don't have to give a second thought to getting mugged just by walking up the beach.

Places to Stay
The Tourist Office in Zanzibar maintains a number of bungalows at the best beaches – Bwejuu, Chwaka, Jambiani, Makunduchi and Uroa. Most of them are priced on the basis that they will sleep five people comfortably but will easily take six at a pinch. As with other accommodation on Zanzibar, you must pay for these bungalows in foreign currency though we have heard of travellers who have simply asked around the villages for accommodation in local houses and paid in local currency.

Most people rate Jambiani and Bwejuu as the best beaches. Rates for the tourist bungalows vary but are between US$12 to US$18 per night for a whole bungalow. Kerosene lanterns are provided and water is usually drawn from a well. At Jambiani, the caretaker, Hassan Haji, is very helpful and friendly. If you ask him, he'll catch crabs and fish during the day for you and his wife will cook them up with coconut rice and spicy sauces in the evening. Their charges are very reasonable indeed. During the day people will come round with coconuts and other fruits for sale. All you have to do is relax.

Getting There
There is one public bus daily in either direction between Zanzibar town and Jambiani.

Other Indian Ocean Islands

PEMBA
While many travellers make it to Zanzibar, very few ever make the journey to Pemba Island, north of Zanzibar. It's a very laid back, friendly place and completely untouched by tourism although the beaches tend to be difficult to get to. Cloves are the mainstay of its economy but the island was never as important as Zanzibar or other settlements on the coast although it has had some remarkable associations during its history.

At Pujini on the east coast there is a

fortified settlement and the remains of a palace destroyed by the Portuguese in 1520. They were apparently built by conquerors from the Maldive Islands! It seems they were not particularly welcome – one of the rulers of this town was known as Mkame Ndume ('Milker of Men') because of the amount of work he extracted from his subjects. Later, after the expulsion of the Portuguese from this part of East Africa, Pemba was taken over first by the rulers of Pate in the Lamu archipelago, then by the rulers of Mombasa, and finally by the sultans of Zanzibar.

Places to Stay

There is a government-owned hotel in each of the three main towns and they're all reasonably priced. All the rooms in these three hotels have their own bathroom though you shouldn't expect the services (water and electricity) to work too often.

Getting There

Air Air Tanzania flies Tanga to Chake Chake on Pemba three times a week.

Boat There are dhows from Tanga and from Zanzibar. The Tanga dhows usually dock at Wete, the most northerly of the island's three towns, while the Zanzibar dhows dock at Mkoani, the most southerly. From Tanga the fare is generally around Sh 200/US$1.30 and the boats take all night plus you need permission from the District Commissioner before you can sail. The boats from Zanzibar are fairly frequent, cost about Sh 250/US$1.70 and take about 12 hours. On rare occasions you may be able to get a dhow from Pemba to Mombasa but there is likely to be some red tape involved.

There are also small, motorised, passenger boats – often overcrowded – between Zanzibar and Mkoani on Pemba island. They take about 12 hours and cost Sh 250/US$1.70. Ask around at the wharf in Zanzibar.

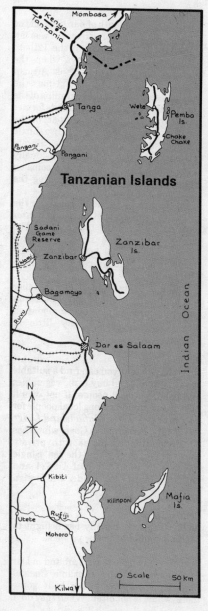

MAFIA

Mafia Island lies south of Zanzibar off the mouth of the Rufiji River. It was an important settlement from the 12th to 14th centuries in the days when the Shirazis ruled much of the East African coastal area but by the time the Portuguese arrived at the beginning of the 16th century it had lost much of its former importance and had become part of the territory ruled by the king of Kilwa. Little remains above ground of the Shirazi settlement though you may occasionally come across pottery shards and coins on the shore where the sea is eroding the ruins south of Kilindoni.

On the nearby island of Juani are the extensive remains of Kua, a much later town dating from the 18th century The largest structure here is thought to have been a palace. Kua was destroyed by raiders from Madagascar in the early 19th century.

You're unlikely to meet any traveller who has been to Mafia Island. The reason for this is fairly simple – accommodation and transport, there's very little of either.

Places to Stay

If you have a tent you can find a suitable spot to pitch it and buy fruit, vegetables and fish from local people. If not, you'll have to ask around among local people for a room or stay at the *Mafia Island Lodge* (tel 23491), Fisherman's Cove, which has 30 air-conditioned rooms with private showers, etc, overlooking the sea. Single rooms with breakfast cost US$24 and payment must be made in foreign currency.

Getting There

Air Air Tanzania usually has a flight to Mafia Island at least once a week.

Boat You may have to wait around in Dar es Salaam until the Tanzania Coastal Shipping Company has a boat going there, which is not often. When they do it takes about eight hours and costs Sh40/US$0.25 for a seat.

North towards Kenya

MOSHI

Moshi is the gateway to Kilimanjaro and the end of the northern railway line from Dar es Salaam but otherwise not a very interesting place. Rather than stay here, many travellers head straight out to Marangu and arrange a trek up the mountain from there but this might not always be the best thing to do. The pros and cons are discussed under National Parks.

Information

There is an immigration office in Moshi if you need to renew a visa or stay permit. It's in Kibo House close to the clocktower on the road which leads to the YMCA. Opening hours are Monday to Friday from 7.30 am to 2.30 pm and on Saturday from 7.30 am to 12.30 pm.

Places to Stay – bottom end

The cheapest place to stay is the *Sikh Community Centre* where you can sleep on the floor free of charge and use the showers. To get there, turn left out of the railway station and continue until you see a football pitch on the left hand side with a sign saying, 'Members Only'. That's the place. If it looks closed, see the caretaker. Make sure you leave a donation if you stay here, otherwise travellers won't be welcome for very much longer.

There are a number of cheap hotels in Moshi but most of them are right up at the south end of town and not very convenient if you arrive by bus or train. They include the *Arawa Hotel*, the *Korini Hotel*, *Mlay's Residential Hotel* and the *Hotel Taj Mahal*. There's another marked simply *Boarding & Lodging*. Other travellers have recommended the *Sunflower Resthouse* which

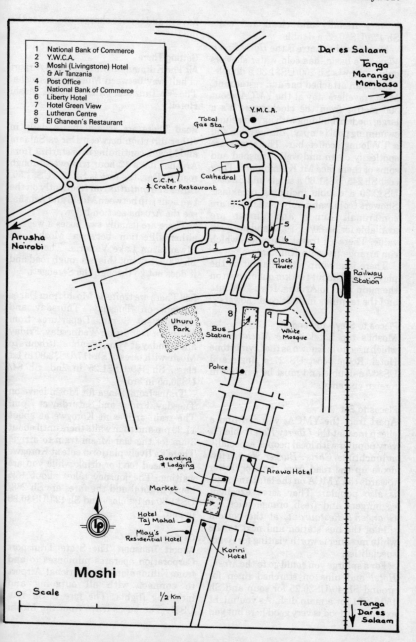

Moshi

Scale
0   1/2 Km

is very friendly and clean and costs Sh 125/US$0.85 a double.

Nearer to the centre is the *Hotel Green View*. It's basic, has cold water showers only and costs Sh 200/US$1.30 a double. There's an attached bar and restaurant. Most travellers stay at the *YMCA* about 300 metres from the clocktower. It's a large, modern building with a gymnasium, swimming pool (empty), dining room and a TV lounge/coffee bar. The rooms are spotlessly clean and well-furnished and some of them face Mt Kilimanjaro. They cost Sh 245/US$1.60 a single and Sh 350/US$2.30 a double including breakfast. Showers (cold water only) and toilets are communal. Lunch and dinner are available for Sh 80/US$0.55 and are good value. There's a travel office here which can arrange treks up Kilimanjaro.

There is a camp site adjacent to the playing field about two km out of town on the main road to Arusha. It's a good site and the facilities include cold showers.

Places to Stay - top end

Moshi's top hotel is the *Moshi Hotel* which used to be known as the Livingstone Hotel. Rooms cost US$27 a single and US$37 a double and must be paid for in foreign currency.

Places to Eat

Apart from the YMCA, you can find a cheap meal at the *Liberty Hotel* which is very popular with local people, especially at lunchtime. *Chris's Burger Shop*, a few doors up the road from the clocktower towards the YMCA on the left hand side, is also popular. They serve excellent eggburgers and fresh orange juice. *El Ghaneen's Restaurant*, at the bottom side of the bus station and next to the white mosque, is worth visiting for Asian specialities.

For a splurge you could go to the *Moshi Hotel* and dine on starched linen for around Sh 40/US$0.25 for soup and Sh 150/US$1 for a main dish. As you might expect, the food is very good here but you

have to add service charges and tax to the bill.

Getting There

Air The Kilimanjaro International Airport is half way between Moshi and Arusha. The Air Tanzania office is at the Moshi Hotel.

Road There are several buses daily in either direction between Dar es Salaam and Moshi, continuing to or starting from Arusha. It's a 12 hour trip over a rough road to Dar, the fare is Sh 225/US$1.50. Buses and *matatus* run frequently on the two hour trip between Moshi and Arusha, see the Arusha section below.

There are usually two buses a week in either direction between Moshi and Mwanza on Lake Victoria. The fare is Sh 300/US$2 but this is a rough road and it does not go through the Serengeti.

Rail There are trains to Moshi from Dar es Salaam on Tuesday, Thursday and Saturday at 3 pm. Departures from Moshi for Dar are on Wednesday, Friday and Sunday at 4 pm. It's about 15 hours to Moshi with fares of Sh 417/US$2.80 in 1st class, Sh 189/US$1.25 in 2nd, Sh 84/US$0.55 in 3rd.

Trains from Tanga for Moshi leave on Tuesday, Friday and Saturday at 7 pm. The train arrives at Korogwe at about 11.30 pm and then waits there until about 3 am for the Dar-Moshi train to arrive. There's a lively platform cafe at Korogwe if you need food or drink while you are waiting. The journey takes about 16½ hours in total and the fares are Sh 268/US$1.80 in 1st class and Sh 123/US$0.80 in 2nd.

Getting Around

Airport Transport The State Transport Corporation operates minibuses to and from Kilimanjaro International Airport to connect with all outgoing and incoming flights. The fare is Sh 150/US$1. The buses leave from the Moshi

Hotel in the centre of town. See the Arusha Airport Transport section below.

ARUSHA
Arusha is one of Tanzania's most attractive towns and was the headquarters of the East African Community in the days when Kenya, Tanzania and Uganda were members of an economic, communications and customs union. It sits in lush, green countryside at the foot of Mt Meru (4556 metres) and enjoys a temperate climate throughout the year. Surrounding it are many coffee, wheat and maize estates tended by the Waarusha and Wameru tribespeople whom you may occasionally see in the market area of town. For travellers, Arusha is the gateway to Serengeti, Lake Manyara and Tarangire National Parks and the Ngorongoro Conservation Area and it's here that you come to arrange a safari. Mt Meru can also be climbed from here.

Arusha is a pleasant town to walk around and take in the sights and the market area is particularly lively but most travellers' main concern will be arranging a safari and taking off for the national parks.

Information
The town is divided into two parts, separated by a small valley through which the Naura River runs. The upper part just off the main Moshi-Namanga road contains the government buildings, post office, the top class hotels, safari companies, airline offices, curio and craft shops and the huge International Conference Centre. Further down the hill and across the valley is the commercial and industrial area, the market, many small shops, most of the budget hotels and the bus station.

Tourist Office There is a Tourist Office (tel 3842) on Boma Rd just down from the New Safari Hotel. It generally has a few glossy leaflets about the national parks but its main function is to make bookings for the national park lodges which must be paid for in hard currency. Safari companies will generally also book the lodges and you may be able to pay them in local currency, especially in the low season.

National Parks The Tanzania National Parks headquarters (tel 3471) is on 6th Floor, Kilimanjaro Wing, International Conference Centre (PO Box 3134). They usually stock a few leaflets about the national parks for which there's a nominal charge. If you're interested in the work they do you may be able to talk with the friendly and hard-working director. The quarterly reports make interesting but often distressing reading especially as far as poaching goes.

Many of the safari companies have their offices in the International Conference Centre and the remainder you will find along Boma Rd, Sokoine Rd and India St.

Craft Shops There are a number of very good craft shops along the short street between the clock tower and Ngoliondoi Rd. They have superb examples of *makonde* carving at lower prices than Dar es Salaam. If I were looking to buy an example of this beautiful and traditional art form I would look for it here.

Places to Stay – bottom end
St Theresa's Catholic Guest House is the cheapest place to stay and has been popular for years. From the bridge over the river you can see it, the pink building next to the Catholic Church in the valley between the two parts of town. It costs Sh 50/US$0.40 for a bed in triple rooms or Sh 25/US$0.20 to sleep on the floor. There's no hot water in the showers and nowhere to lock up your gear during the day but it's unlikely anything will be stolen.

The *Anglican Guest House*, next to Christchurch off Moshi Rd, is very

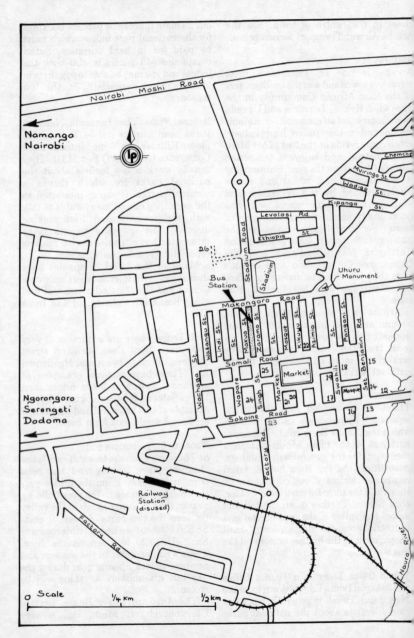

Nairobi Moshi Road

Namanga
Nairobi

Chemche

Mviringo St.

Wadigo St.

Kipanga St.

Levolasi Rd

Ethiopia St.

Uhuru
Monument

26

Bus
Station

Stadium
Road

Stadium

Makongoro Road

Watangu St.

Lindi St.

Makua St.

Zaramo St.

Mosque St.

Kikwaju St.

Azimio St.

Pangani St.

Benjamin Rd

Somali Road

Wachaga

Wapare St.

Singh St.

Market Street

Market

Sahili St.

Mosque St.

15

12

Ngorongoro
Serengeti
Dodoma

25

24

19
17

18

14

16

13

23

Sokoine Road

Factory Rd

Railway
Station
(disused)

Factory Rd

Naura River

Scale

0   1/4 Km   1/2 km

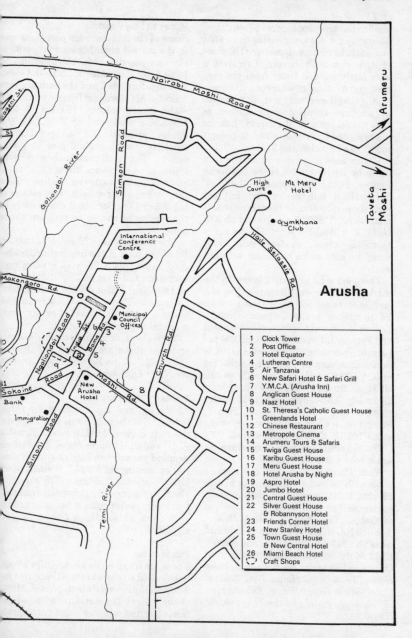

Arusha

1 Clock Tower
2 Post Office
3 Hotel Equator
4 Lutheran Centre
5 Air Tanzania
6 New Safari Hotel & Safari Grill
7 Y.M.C.A. (Arusha Inn)
8 Anglican Guest House
9 Naaz Hotel
10 St. Theresa's Catholic Guest House
11 Greenlands Hotel
12 Chinese Restaurant
13 Metropole Cinema
14 Arumeru Tours & Safaris
15 Twiga Guest House
16 Karibu Guest House
17 Meru Guest House
18 Hotel Arusha by Night
19 Aspro Hotel
20 Jumbo Hotel
21 Central Guest House
22 Silver Guest House
   & Robannyson Hotel
23 Friends Corner Hotel
24 New Stanley Hotel
25 Town Guest House
   & New Central Hotel
26 Miami Beach Hotel
⊟ Craft Shops

similar but few people seem to stay here. That may not be too surprising since a few years ago, having recommended the place in *Africa on a Shoestring*, I received a very tartly worded letter from the very reverend gentleman who runs the place saying that it was 'not for those who wish to scrounge cheap accommodation as they travel around the world, but for missionaries from the bush.' It doesn't sound like he's changed his tack.

If you want a private room the best value by far in Arusha is the *Lutheran Centre*, Boma Rd opposite the New Safari Hotel, but they're often full and sometimes reluctant to take travellers. It costs Sh 100/US$0.65 a single and Sh 200/US$1.30 a double. For this you get a spotlessly clean, modern room with mosquito nets and a bathroom with hot water.

There are a lot of budget hotels in the market area of town, all more or less of a similar standard and price – there's not a lot to choose between them. *Friends' Corner Hotel*, on the corner of Sokoine Rd and Factory Rd, costs Sh 50/US$0.30 per person. *Greenlands Hotel*, Sokoine Rd, is decaying somewhat but has singles for Sh 90/US$0.60 and large doubles for Sh 150/US$1 to Sh 240/US$1.60 without own bathroom and there are cold water showers only. *Central Guest House*, Market St, is clean and fairly good value at Sh 100/US$0.65 a single and Sh 200/US$1.30 a double without own bathroom, again cold water showers only.

Naaz Hotel, Sokoine Rd, is a strange place with its own restaurant which costs Sh 150/US$1 a double without own bathroom but hot water is sometimes available. The *Karibu Guest House*, Sokoine Rd, is fairly rough and ready and costs Sh 100/US$0.65 a single and Sh 200/US$1.30 a double without own bathroom. Others in this range are the *Meru Guest House*, *Town Guest House*, *New Central Hotel*, *Silver Guest House*, *Robannyson Hotel*, *Aspro Hotel* and the *Twiga Guest House*.

Places to Stay – middle

Some of the middle range places are also in the market area. My own favourite is the very popular *YMCA/Arusha Inn* on India St. It's an older building but clean and well-furnished and the staff are very friendly. Mt Meru is in front of you as you stand on the balcony. It costs Sh 250/US$1.70 a single and Sh 350/US$2.30 a double for bed and a breakfast of omelette, toast, butter, jam and tea/coffee. The communal showers and toilets are kept clean, there's hot water and clothes left to dry on the line will be there when you get back. Downstairs is the *Silver City Bar* but it closes early in the evening so there's no problem about noise.

The *Miami Beach Hotel*, off Stadium Rd at the back of the bus station, is also good value. It's a fairly new place and very clean and costs Sh 150/US$1 a single and Sh 300/US$2 a double without own bathroom. There is hot water in the showers and the hotel has its own reasonably-priced restaurant.

Two other hotels which would be worth trying if these are full are the *Jumbo Hotel* off Sokoine Rd and *Hotel Arusha By Night* on Swahili St.

Places to Stay – top end

At the top end of the market are three hotels, all of them on Boma Rd. They are the *New Safari Hotel*, the *New Arusha Hotel* and the *Equator Hotel*. All of them demand payment in foreign currency so you're looking at US$17 a single and US$28 a double minimum. The Equator Hotel is often used by European overland truck companies since it has a large car park from which things frequently get ripped off!

Places to Eat

There are quite a few cheap cafés along Sokoine Rd all the way from the bridge to well past the *Friends' Corner Hotel*. Most of them serve the standard Afro-Indian fare – curries, *ugali* or *ndizi* with meat stew and beans, *sambusa*, biriyani and the like. The restaurant at the *Naaz Hotel* is similar and recommended by many travellers. The *Silver City Bar* in the YMCA/Arusha Inn has a pleasant, shady courtyard and offers tasty, cheap barbecued meat but it closes early.

For a splurge, most travellers go to the *Safari Grill* next to the New Safari Hotel. The food here is usually very good and there's a range of meat and fish dishes as well as soups and desserts. Main courses cost Sh 140 to Sh 160, about US$1. Soup is extra. They also serve *very* cold beers.

The *Chinese Restaurant*, Sokoine Rd close to the bridge, is also worth a splurge and is somewhat cheaper than the Safari Grill. The *New Arusha Hotel* has a (relatively) fast-food grill and griddle which is reasonably good value and popular with local people and tourists.

Entertainment

There are a number of lively bars in Arusha which are very popular with local people and travellers. You can always get into a conversation at any of them. The best are probably those at the *YMCA/Arusha Inn* (the cheapest but it closes early), the *Equator Hotel* and the beer garden at the *New Safari Hotel*.

The *Cave Disco* at the New Safari Hotel rages until the early hours and is described in one of the tourist brochures as 'a sensation'. Whether you agree may well depend on how long you've spent in the bush! There are disco nights at the New Arusha Hotel too.

Getting There

Air The major Kilimanjaro International Airport is between Arusha and Moshi. Air Tanzania, Ethiopian Airlines and KLM all have offices on Boma Rd close to the New Safari Hotel.

Road There are several buses daily in either direction between Dar es Salaam via Moshi to Arusha. It takes about 12 hours on the rough road to Moshi and

another two on to Arusha. Dar-Arusha is Sh 300/US$2.

There are plenty of buses and *matatus* between Moshi and Arusha from early morning until late afternoon. They leave when full, take about two hours and cost Sh 50/US$0.30. It's relatively easy to hitch along this road but you'll generally be charged more than the bus fare.

There are no longer any buses between Arusha and Musoma on Lake Victoria which means there is no public transport through the Serengeti.

Getting Around

Airport Transport The State Transport Corporation, corner Temi Rd and Sokoine Rd, runs minibuses which connect Arusha and Moshi with all incoming and outgoing flights at Kilimanjaro International Airport. The fare is Sh 150/US$1. These buses used to go beyond Moshi to the hotels at Marangu (on the slopes of Kilimanjaro) and beyond Arusha in the other direction to the lodge at Lake Manyara and the lodges at Ngorongoro Crater. These services are suspended at present because of the shortage of vehicles and fuel.

Lake Victoria

Lake Victoria is bordered by Kenya, Uganda and Tanzania and there are ferry services between the main Tanzanian ports on the lake and to Kisumu in Kenya.

Getting Around the Lake

Schedules for the lakes ferries are:

MV Victoria

day	port	arrive	depart
Sunday	Mwanza	–	9 pm
Monday	Bukoba	6 pm	9 pm
Tuesday	Mwanza	6 pm	9 pm
Wednesday	Bukoba	6 pm	9 pm
Thursday	Mwanza	6 pm	-
Friday	Mwanza	–	9 pm

| Saturday | Bukoba | 6 pm | 9 pm |
| Sunday | Mwanza | 6 pm | 9 pm |

MV Bukoba

day	*port*	*arrive*	*depart*
Monday	Mwanza	–	9 pm
Tuesday	Musoma	6 am	9 pm
Wednesday	Mwanza	6 am	–
Thursday	Mwanza	–	9 am
–	Musoma	7 pm	9 pm
Friday	Kisumu	6 am	9 pm
Saturday	Musoma	6 am	9 am
–	Mwanza	6 pm	9 pm
Sunday	Bukoba	7 am	9 pm
Monday	Mwanza	7 am	–

	1st class	2nd class	3rd class
Bukoba- Mwanza	Sh 257 US$1.70	Sh 203 US$1.35	Sh 97 US$0.65
Mwanza- Musoma	Sh 283 US$1.90	Sh 226 US$1.50	Sh 103 US$0.70
Mwanza- Kisumu	Sh 571 US$3.80	Sh 453 US$3.00	Sh 206 US$1.35

First class on these boats is a four-bunk cabin on the upper deck. Second class is a four-bunk cabin on the lower deck. Third class is simply wooden seats. Meals on board are Sh 80 for a main course and Sh 150 for a three-course meal.

MWANZA

Mwanza is Tanzania's most important port on the shore of Lake Victoria and the terminus of a branch of the central railway line from Dar es Salaam. It's a fairly attractive town flanked by rocky hills and its port handles the cotton, tea and coffee grown in the fertile western part of the country. In the area live the Wasukuma people who make up the largest tribe in the country. There are lake ferries from Mwanza to the other Tanzanian ports of Bukoba and Musoma as well as to Kisumu (Kenya) and Jinja (Uganda).

Sukuma Museum

About 15 km east of Mwanza on the Musoma road the Sukuma Museum (sometimes called the Bujora Museum) was originally put together by a Quebeçois missionary. It contains displays about the culture and traditions of the Wasukuma tribe as well as an excellent drum collection and once a week, on average, it puts on traditional dances of this tribe including the spectacular Bugobogobo, the Sukuma Snake Dance. It's well worth making enquiries in town as to when the next performance is due. To get there take a local bus from the bus station in Mwanza to Kisessa (Sh 20) and from there it's about a km walk. It's possible to camp at the museum or rent a *banda*.

North of Mwanza

There are regular ferries from Mwanza to Ukerewe Island further north if you'd like to explore the surrounding area.

Places to Stay

You can generally camp for free at the Sukuma Museum but if you have no tent there are two-bed *bandas* for rent for just Sh 80/US$0.55. It's a lovely spot and many travellers stay here. You can also camp free of charge at the *Saba Saba Showground* near the airport. Facilities consist of a tap and toilet only, there are no showers.

In Mwanza itself there's quite a choice of reasonably priced hotels. The *Zimbabwe Guest House* near the bus station, is adequate for most budget travellers' needs and the staff are friendly. It costs Sh 135/US$0.90 per room (one or two people) and mosquito nets and towels are provided.

Similar places include the *Shinyanga Guest House* at Sh 160/US$1 a double. The *Furaha Guest House* at the railway station and *Wageni Salim's Guest House* both cost Sh 100/US$0.65 a single and Sh 120/US$0.80 a double. *Jafferies Hotel* costs Sh 120/US$0.80 a single and Sh 160/US$1 a double or there's the *New Safari Lodge* which costs Sh 150/US$1 a single and Sh 200/US$1.30 a double.

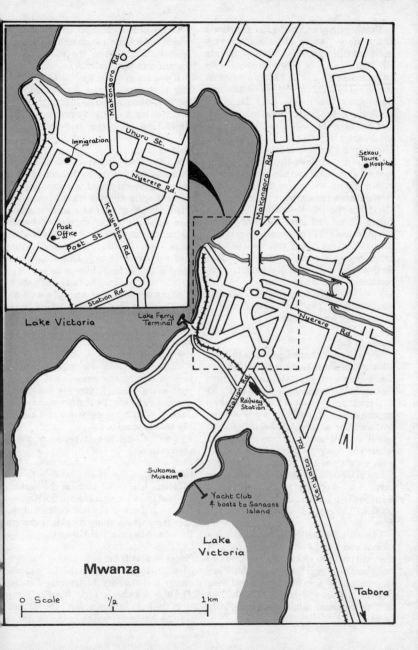

Mwanza

Going up in price, try the *Kishinapanda Guest House*, a new place which is very good but fills up early in the day. It costs Sh 200/US$1.30 a single without own bathroom or Sh 250/US$1.70 a single and Sh 350/US$2.30 a double with own bathroom. The rooms have fans and mosquito nets. To get there from the bus station, take the first street on the right (on Nyerere Rd) after the Mutimba Guest House and then the second on the left. About 50 metres down this road you come to the Delux Hotel and the Kishinapanda is just round the corner from there. If coming from the harbour, take the first street on the left before the Mutimba Guest House and after that the second street on the left. The *Delux Hotel* is also worth checking out if you want a mid-range hotel. It costs Sh 350/US$2.30 a double for bed and breakfast. The restaurant here is excellent.

The *Victoria Hotel* at Sh 200/US$1.30 a single and Sh 255/US$1.70 a double is pretty tatty for the price.

Places to Eat

There are a number of good cheap local restaurants along Lumumba St. Try the *Cairo* next to the Shinyanga Guest House. In the evenings between 5.30 and 6.30 pm there are a lot of food stalls set up opposite the Victoria Hotel where you can eat well for a song. A favourite with travellers is *Al Shah's African Restaurant* where you can get a meal of fish or meat with vegetables and potatoes or rice for Sh 100/US$0.65. At the rear of this place there is a lively disco on Saturdays and Sundays (African music) which costs Sh 100/US$0.65 entry or if you eat there it's free.

The *Delux Hotel* is definitely worth a visit if you like Indian Moghlai food. A dish will cost you around Sh 215/US$1.50 but there's enough for two people. They have cheaper dishes like kebabs and fried chicken for around Sh 130/US$0.90 as well as samosas, other snacks and cold beers.

Other reasonably priced restaurants which have been recommended are the *Kunaris Restaurant*, the *Furaha Restaurant* and the *Rex Hotel*.

If you are catering for yourself you can buy cheap fish at the market near the ferry terminal. A fish large enough to feed seven or eight shouldn't cost more than Sh 75/US$0.50, gutted and cleaned.

Getting There

Rail The railway line from Dar es Salaam runs due west as far as Tabora where it splits, one line continuing west to Kigoma while the other runs north to Mwanza. In theory, there should be a train in either direction daily but fuel shortages generally reduce the service to four trains per week, usually on Tuesday, Thursday, Friday and Sunday at 8 pm. Dar to Mwanza takes about 36 hours but trains can be up to four hours late at the final destination.

Fares between Dar and Mwanza are Sh 922/US$6.15 in 1st, Sh 418/US$2.80 in 2nd, Sh 185/US$1.20 in 3rd.

Travelling from Mwanza to Kigoma you can only get 1st and 2nd class reservations as far as Tabora. Beyond that you cannot be guaranteed a reservation in the same class on the connecting train. If you are doing this journey go to see the station manager at Tabora as soon as you arrive and ask for his assistance. He's a very helpful man and will do his best to get you onward reservations.

MUSOMA

Musoma is a small port on the eastern shore of Lake Victoria close to the Kenyan border. It's one of the ports of call of the lake ferry which connects this port with Bukoba, Mwanza and Kisumu.

Places to Stay & Eat

Most travellers stay at the very clean, cheap and friendly *Mennonite Centre*. The only drawback is that it's a long way from the ferry terminal. If it's too far then try the *Embassy Lodge* in the centre of town which costs Sh 90/US$0.60 a double or the slightly more expensive *Musambura Guest House* round the corner.

The *Sengerema Guest House* close to the market and bus station has also been recommended by travellers in the past. For a mid-range hotel the *Railway Hotel*, about half an hour's walk from the centre of town, is probably the best value. It's worth coming here for a meal whilst you're in town even if you don't stay. Breakfasts are Sh 40/US$0.25, a main course at lunch or dinner Sh 75/US$0.50 and a three-course meal Sh 150/US$1.

BUKOBA

Bukoba is one of Tanzania's principle ports on Lake Victoria but few travellers come here these days because it's something of a dead end – there's hardly any transport north to Uganda and getting to Rwanda involves back-tracking to Biharamulo.

Places to Stay

One of the cheapest places to stay is the *Nyumba na Vijana* (Youth Centre) at the Evangelical Lutheran Church on the road to the hospital. It costs Sh 50/US$0.30 for a dorm bed. Your bags are safe here. The *Catholic Mission* has a similar place.

For a cheap private room there are many budget hotels around the bus station. If you don't mind spending the money, however, it's worth staying at the *Lake Hotel* (tel 237), a beautiful old colonial building with a verandah overlooking the lake. The hotel is about two km from the centre of town past the police station and the council offices. It costs Sh 225/US$1.50 a double with own bathroom and including breakfast. Lunch or dinner costs Sh 150/US$1. The *Coffee Tree Inn* (tel 412) is similar.

Getting Around

The lake ferries jetty is about 2½ km from the centre of town.

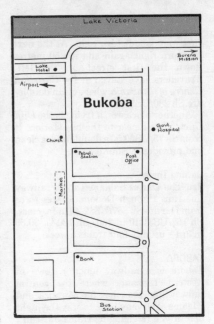

Western Tanzania

DODOMA

Dodoma is the party political headquarters and slated to become the capital of Tanzania sometime towards the end of the century though economic constraints may delay implementation of that plan. In the meantime there's little of interest here for the traveller. It is, on the other hand, the only wine-producing area of Africa south of Morocco and north of South Africa. Bacchanalians shouldn't get too excited though – Tanzanian viniculture has a *long* way to go before they'll interest anyone but a Bowery bum in their product.

Places to Stay

The *Central Province Hotel* (tel 21177) is a reasonable place which costs Sh 100/US$0.65 a double. To get there, leave the front of the railway station, turn right along the road by the tracks and at the first roundabout turn right. At the next one turn right again and it's 50 metres down the first street on the left. Travellers have stayed at the *Christian Centre of Tanzania* where clean doubles are Sh 280/US$1.90.

Another place worth trying is the *Ujiji Guest House* near to the bus station. It costs Sh 75/US$0.50 a double and is clean and provides mosquito nets.

Getting There

Rail The Dar es Salaam-Tabora railway line runs through Dodoma. Fares to or from Dar are Sh 357/US$2.40 in 1st class, Sh 162/US$1.10 in 2nd, Sh 120/US$0.80 in 3rd – usually four trains a week.

TABORA

Tabora is a railway junction town in western Tanzania where the central railway line branches for Mwanza and Kigoma. You may have to stay the night here if you're changing trains but can't get immediate onward reservations.

Places to Stay

The *Moravian Guest House* is probably the best place to stay and is certainly cheap at Sh 25/US$0.20 per person. It's pleasant and the staff are friendly. If the accommodation isn't to your liking you could try the somewhat expensive *Railway Hotel*. Meals there are reasonable.

Getting There

The railway line west from Dar es Salaam splits at Tabora, one line continuing west to Kigoma on Lake Tanganyika, the other heading north to Mwanza on Lake Victoria. There are usually four trains a week and fares from Dar es Salaam are Sh 640/US$4.25 in 1st class, Sh 290/US$2 in 2nd, Sh 128/US$0.90 in 3rd.

If you're travelling between Mwanza and Kigoma note the comment in the Mwanza section on onward reservations beyond Tabora.

KIGOMA

Kigoma is the most important Tanzanian port on Lake Tanganyika and the terminus of the railway from Dar es Salaam. Many travellers come through here en route to or coming from Bujumbura (Burundi) or Mpulungu (Zambia) on the Lake Tanganyika steamer *MV Liemba*. The town has little of interest in itself but it is a jumping off point for visits to Ujiji and the Gombe Stream National Park. See the parks section for information on Gombe Stream.

Information

There are consulates for Burundi and Zaire in Kigoma but don't apply for a Zairois visa here as it takes at least two weeks to issue – see Visas.

Ujiji

Just down the coast from Kigoma, Ujiji is one of Africa's oldest market villages and it's a good deal more interesting than Kigoma itself. This is also where the famous words, 'Dr Livingstone, I presume', were spoken by the explorer and journalist, Stanley. There's the inevitable plaque. There are occasional buses there from the railway station in Kigoma for a few shillings or you can hire a car for Sh 200/US$1.30. Boat building and repairs go on down by the lake shore. If you need a meal the *Kudra Hotel* has good food and fruit salads.

Places to Stay

The *Kigoma Community Centre* is the cheapest place to stay but they're not very friendly towards travellers. Singles are Sh 45/US$0.30, doubles Sh 65/US$0.45, with hand basin and running water. To find it, turn left out of the railway station, go over the bridge and then look for the sign 'Tanzania Electrical Supply Co' on the left hand side. The Community Centre is the last door of this building.

The best value for money in normal

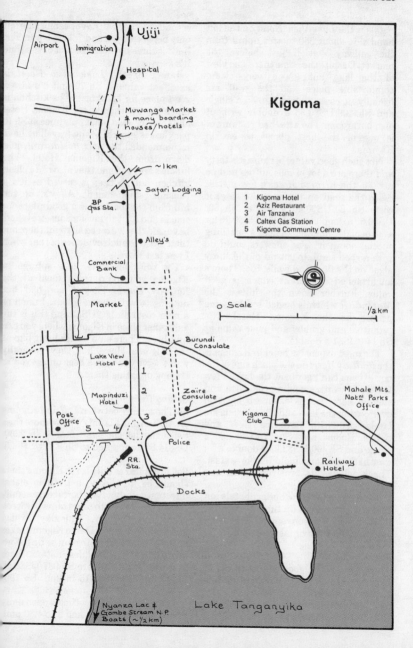

Kigoma

1 Kigoma Hotel
2 Aziz Restaurant
3 Air Tanzania
4 Caltex Gas Station
5 Kigoma Community Centre

hotels is the *Lake View Hotel* on the left hand side about 350 metres uphill from the railway station just before the market. Despite the name there's no view of the lake but it's a very clean, comfortable place and the staff are friendly. It costs Sh 80/US$0.55 a single and Sh 100/US$0.65 a double without own bathroom. The attached restaurant is one of the best places to eat in Kigoma.

Not such good value, because it's tatty and there are a lot of mosquitoes and no nets, is the *Kigoma Hotel* a few metres down the road on the opposite side. It costs Sh 60/US$0.40 a single, Sh 80/US$0.55 a double and Sh 115/US$0.75 for a 'special' double. There's nothing special about it! The showers could do with a good scrub to get rid of the slimy algae on the floor and walls, too. There's an attached restaurant which is good value. Further down the hill is the *Mapinduzi* which is owned by the same people as the Kigoma Hotel. It's primitive and grubby and poor value at Sh 140/US$1 a double.

The most expensive hotel in Kigoma is the *Railway Hotel* on the south side of the port. If you can't get in at the Lake View Hotel it's worth spending the extra and staying here. It has a superb location overlooking the lake and the grounds are landscaped with flowering trees and palms. Rooms cost Sh 270/US$1.80 a single and Sh 490/US$3.25 a double with own bathroom and including breakfast. The hotel has its own restaurant and bar.

There are a lot more budget hotels but they are several km up the hill from the market – very inconvenient if you are catching the train or lake steamer.

Places to Eat

There are several good places to eat in Kigoma. One of the cheapest is the *Kigoma Hotel* where you can get a meal of fish, sauce and fried rice for Sh 40. Breakfasts are good value, too. Every

second day they will have beer for sale but only between 6 pm and 7.30 to 8 pm. The limit is three bottles. The rest of the time it's *konyagi*.

Lunch at the *Lake View Hotel* i excellent value at Sh 70 and it's also good place for breakfast. The kitchen i much cleaner than at the Kigoma Hote and their ice-cold pineapple juice at Sh 1 per glass is superb. Many travellers have recommended the *Aziz Restaurant*, jus down from the Kigoma Hotel. The lunches are good and they also run a clea kitchen but no beer is served as it's a Muslim establishment. *Alley's*, up the hill from the market, is a good place for snacks and African music. Some travellers have said they've raged all night there bu there wasn't much evidence of that when I was last there.

For what amounts to a splurge i Kigoma you could try a meal at the *Railway Hotel*. They're not bad but nothing to write home about. Lunch or dinner costs Sh 150/US$1 and this is the only other place in Kigoma where you car find beer. There's no bottle limit like at the Kigoma Hotel but they generally won't serve you with a beer unless you're staying or eating there.

Getting There

Air The air fare between Dar and Kigoma on Air Tanzania is only a little more than twice the 1st class rail fare – Sh 2230, US$14.85 as opposed to Sh 937/US$6.25

Rail From Dar es Salaam to Kigoma there should be, in theory, a train in either direction daily but fuel shortages generally reduce the service to four trains per week usually on Tuesday, Thursday, Friday and Sunday at 8 pm. Dar to Kigoma takes about 38 hours but trains can be up to four hours late at the final destination. Fares from Dar es Salaam are Sh 937/US$6.25 in 1st, Sh 480/US$3.15 in 2nd, Sh 190/ US$1.25 in 3rd.

The railway booking office is open daily from 8 am to 12.30 pm and 2 to 4.30 pm.

If you're coming from Mwanza to Kigoma by rail note the warning in the Mwanza section about reservations beyond Tabora.

Boat The 'dock' for boats to the Gombe Stream National Park is about a km up the railway tracks from the station.

Getting Around
Airport Transport Air Tanzania runs a minibus from their office in town to the airport. There's a small charge for the service.

MBEYA
Until recently, few travellers stayed overnight in Mbeya but since the opening up of the direct route to Karonga in Malawi via Kyela it has become a busy one-night stop-over town. The surrounding area is very fertile and bananas, tea, coffee and cocoa are grown here but there's little of interest for the traveller.

Places to Stay & Eat
If at all possible you should try to arrive early in the day as places fill up rapidly as late afternoon. One of the best places is the very clean and friendly *Moravian*

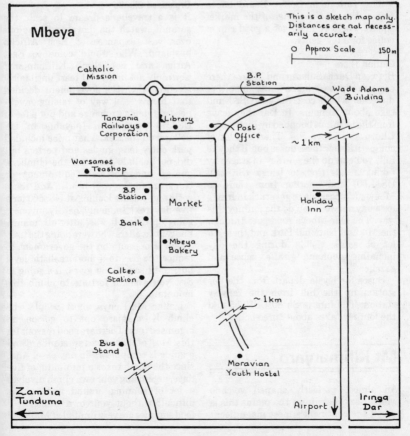

Mbeya

This is a sketch map only. Distances are not necessarily accurate.

0 Approx Scale 150 m

Catholic Mission

B.P. Station

Wade Adams Building

Tanzania Railways Corporation

Library

Post Office

~1 km

Warsames Teashop

B.P. Station

Market

Holiday Inn

Bank

Mbeya Bakery

Caltex Station

~1 km

Bus Stand

Moravian Youth Hostel

Zambia Tunduma

Airport ↓

Iringa Dar

Church Hostel near the radio tower which costs Sh 150/US$1 a double. Breakfast and dinner are very reasonably priced at Sh 80/US$0.55. Cheaper rooms are available at guest houses but they're nothing special.

For a mid-range hotel, the *Mbeya Hotel* opposite the football stadium and managed by the Tanzanian Railways Corporation is recommended. It's a very pleasant, colonial-style hotel with comfortable rooms, clean sheets, mosquito nets and hot showers. It costs Sh 200/US$1.30 a single and Sh 300/US$2 a double.

The Tanzanian Coffee Board has a coffee shop on the corner of the market square where you can get a good cup of coffee for a few cents.

Getting There

Between Dar es Salaam and Mbeya there are usually two buses daily in either direction which cost Sh 440/US$3 and take about 20 hours. In Dar they leave from the terminus bounded by Lumumba, Uhuru and Libya Sts. There's a lot of competition for these buses but, if they're full, you can do the journey in stages by taking a bus first to Iringa (Sh 240/US$1.60) and another from there to Mbeya. It's possible to get stuck in Iringa for a day or two if you do the journey this way. The Dar-Mbeya road goes through the Mikumi National Park and there's a lot of game visible during the day including elephant, giraffe, zebra and gazelle.

Buses for Kyela depart from the bus station up the hill from the railway station. The fare is Sh 80/US$0.55 and the journey takes about three hours.

Mt Kilimanjaro

An almost perfectly shaped volcano which rises sheer from the plains this is one of the continent's most magnificent sights. The snow-capped and not yet extinct peak is, at 5894 metres, the highest in Africa.

From cultivated farmlands on the lower levels, it rises through lush rainforest to alpine meadow and finally across a barren lunar landscape to the snow and ice-capped summit. The rainforest is home to many animals including elephants, buffaloes, rhino, leopards and monkeys and you may even encounter herds of eland on the saddle between the summits of Mawenzi and Kibo.

Organised Climbs

It is a traveller's dream to scale the summit, watch the dawn and gaze out over vast expanses of East African bushland. Who would come to East Africa and not climb Kilimanjaro? Certainly not many – at least until fairly recently when the government decided that here was a way of raising much-needed foreign exchange and put a fee of US$380 per person (payable in US dollars) on the trek. That price included park entry fees, guides and porters but did not include food (for the climbers, guides and porters), equipment or transport to the trail heads. Add those costs and you are looking at US$500 for a five-day trek! Suddenly, hardly anyone is going up there. It was, after all, mainly budget travellers who were doing the trek. There is pressure on the government to reduce the fees to a more realistic level but, until something gives, it's going to cost you a small fortune to climb this mountain.

Unlike Mt Kenya, most people who climb Kilimanjaro opt to go on an organised tour. There are good reasons for this. Most of the charges are standard and a guide is compulsory in any case. And, since the climb takes a minimum of five days, organising your own climb involves a lot of running around and this is difficult without your own transport – food supplies are very limited at Marangu

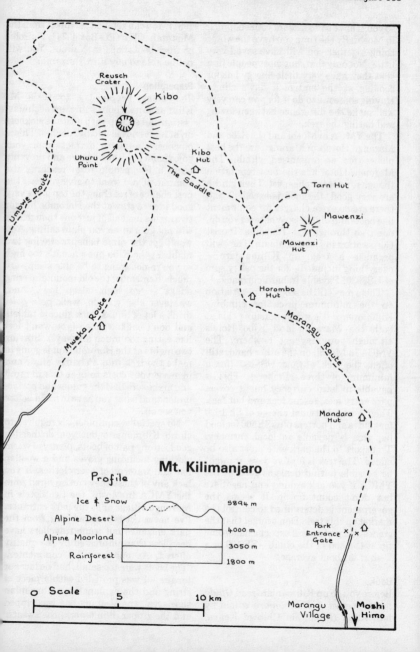

Reusch
Crater

Kibo

Uhuru
Point

Kibo
Hut

The Saddle

Tarn Hut

Mawenzi

Mawenzi
Hut

Umbwe Route

Horombo
Hut

Marangu Route

Mweka Route

Mandara
Hut

Mt. Kilimanjaro

Profile

Ice & Snow   5894 m

Alpine Desert   4000 m

Alpine Moorland   3050 m

Rainforest   1800 m

Park
Entrance
Gate

Scale

0   5   10 km

Marangu
Village

Moshi
Himo

so you'll have to do most of your shopping in Moshi. By the time you have the whole thing together you will have saved very little. Not only that, but most people find that they have very little energy left for cooking at the end of a day's climb. Having someone to do it for you can very well make the difference between loving and hating the trek.

The YMCA in Moshi and the Kibo and Marangu Hotels in Marangu are the best places for an organised climb. The Marangu Hotel has the best reputation though it's not the cheapest. Their guides are very good, the food is excellent and there are no extra charges for equipment like boots and blankets. Whatever you do, don't go through the Tanzania Tourist Corporation in Dar es Salaam. They will organise a trek up Kilimanjaro – everything included – for the paltry sum of US$930! Payable in hard currency.

There may still be scope for negotiation on the minimum price for climbing Kilimanjaro. It's worth pursuing this at both the Marangu and Kibo Hotels although you may get nowhere. The YMCA in Moshi, on the other hand, still offers the trek at just US$180 (for a minimum of three climbers). This is payable in hard currency but it covers park entry fees, rescue fees and hut fees. There's an additional charge of Sh 1620 for guides and porters plus Sh 500 for food but this is payable in local currency. Transport to the park gate must also be added. The trek is for five days. It might be possible to find deals as good as the YMCA if you ask around and negotiate but don't count on it. It seems the government is determined to control the market on this trek. Don't forget that the guides and porters will expect a handsome tip at the end of the climb – Sh 100 or a T-shirt is about average.

Books

Before you go up Kilimanjaro read *Guide to Mt Kenya & Kilimanjaro* edited by Iain Allan (Mountain Club of Kenya,

1981). You can get it either direct from the Mountain Club (PO Box 45741, Nairobi) or from bookshops in Nairobi. You will not be able to buy it in Tanzania.

Preparation

Too many people try to scale Mt Kilimanjaro without sufficient acclimatisation and end up with altitude sickness or, at least nausea and headaches. This is obviously going to detract from your enjoyment of going up there and prevents quite a few people from reaching the summit. If you want to give yourself the best chance of reaching the top it is a very good idea to stay at the Horombo hut for two nights instead of just one though this will not guarantee you plain sailing. You won't get the same benefits staying two nights at the Kibo hut since it's too high so you're not going to be able sleep very much. Remember the old mountaineering adage – 'go high, sleep low'. And, whatever else you do, walk *pole pole*, drink a lot of liquid, suck glucose tablets and don't eat too much (you won't feel like eating too much anyway!). Staying two nights at the Horombo hut is going to make the trek into a six-day affair and increase your costs so bear this in mind and make sure that the guides and porters understand what you have in mind before you set off.

No specialist equipment is required to climb Kilimanjaro but you do need a good, strong pair of boots, plenty of warm clothing including gloves and a woollen hat and waterproof over-clothes. If you lack any of these they can be hired from the YMCA in Moshi, the two hotels in Marangu village or at the park entrance. I've never actually hired gear from the park entrance but some travellers have been less than impressed by the quality offered. As one traveller commented: 'The boots were too small, had no laces or tongue – I was provided with a piece of string and the explanation: 'Tanzanian shoelaces', the sleeping bag was ripped and the zipper didn't work, the sweater was patched in five or six places, the jacket was too small and soaked from the previous wearer but I had no complaints about the gloves or hat.'

You can climb Kilimanjaro at any time of year but you will probably encounter a lot of rain during April, May and November.

Accommodation on the Mountain

There are huts where you stay for the night on all these routes except the northern ones. The Mandara (about 2700 metres) and Horombo (3720 metres) huts might be better described as lodges in some ways since they consist of a large central chalet surrounded by many smaller huts and both can accommodate up to 200 people at a time. They almost constitute villages. The Kibo hut (4703 metres) further up is more like a mountain hut of the type you are likely to find on Mt Kenya.

The Trails

As on Mt Kenya, there are a number of routes to the summit but the most usual is the Marangu Trail (starting at Marangu village). The Mweka Trail (direct from Moshi), the Umbwe Trail (west of Moshi), the Machame Trail (west again from the Umbwe Trail) and the Shira Trail (from west of the mountain) are other possibilities. You are strongly advised to avoid the northern routes from Loitokitok in Kenya as there are stories doing the rounds in Nairobi of murders along these routes.

Getting to the Marangu Trail Head

If you're doing the climb with the YMCA and don't mind paying for their expensive transport to the park entrance you can stay at their Moshi hostel the night before departing.

If you want to save money and have camping equipment you can stay at the park entrance gate. It costs Sh 20 to camp or, if you don't have a tent, there's a national park hostel which costs Sh 60 per

person per night. Add Sh 20 to the camping or hostel cost if you want hot water in the showers. The hostel cook turns out delicious lunches and dinner for Sh 60 to 70.

It's also possible to camp at the *Marangu Hotel* (tel Marangu 11), 32 km from Moshi. Camping costs Sh 20 per person plus Sh 20 extra if you want a hot shower, however the Marangu Hotel isn't too friendly to campers these day. If you need a good rest and comfort before or after the climb the Marangu Hotel has rooms with attached bathrooms and hot water for Sh 350 single or Sh 700 double including half board. The *Kibo Hotel* (tel Marangu 4), 40 km from Moshi, is about 30% more expensive. You will probably have to pay in foreign currency though there may be scope for negotiation if you are organising the Kilimanjaro trek through them.

The Marangu Trail

This is the trail which most visitors take.

Day 1 Starting from the Marangu National Park gate at 1800 metres it's a fairly easy three to four hours' walk through thick rainforest to the Mandara hut. There's often quite a lot of mud along this route so wear good boots.

Day 2 Next day the route climbs steeply through giant heath forest and out across moorlands onto the slopes of Mawenzi and finally to the Horombo hut. It's a difficult 14 km walk and you need to take it slowly. If your clothes are soaked through by the time you arrive at the Horombo hut, don't assume you will be able to dry them there. Firewood is relatively scarce and reserved for cooking.

Day 3 & 4 If possible, spend two nights at this hut and on the fourth day go to Kibo hut – about six to seven hours. Porters don't go beyond the Kibo hut so you'll have to carry your own essential gear from here to the summit and back. Don't skimp on plenty of warm clothing. It's extremely cold on the summit and you'll freeze to death if you're not adequately clothed.

Day 5 Most people find it difficult to sleep very much at Kibo and, since you have to start out for the summit very early (around 1 or 2 am) to get to the summit just before sunrise, it's a good idea to stay awake the evening before. You'll feel better if you do this than trying to grab a couple of hours of fitful sleep. The mist and cloud closes in and obscures the views by 9 am and sometimes earlier. The same day you descend from the summit to the Horombo hut and spend the night there.

Day 6 On the last day you return to the starting point at Marangu.

National Parks & Game Reserves

Kenya may well have the better stocked game parks and easier access to them but Tanzania has the world-famous Serengeti National Park and Ngorongoro Crater with the Olduvai Gorge sandwiched between them. Serengeti has a huge animal population and they're easy to see in the flat grassland of the park. At Ngorongoro the park is in the crater of a huge extinct volcano. Tanzania also has the very large, but completely undeveloped, Selous Game Reserve.

The long border closure with Kenya did a great deal of damage to Tanzania's tourist industry and facilities are nowhere near as numerous or as easily accessible as Kenya's except in the northern parks and game reserves. Travellers are once again visiting such places as Ngorongoro Crater and Serengeti National Park in greater numbers but the government continues to display a propensity for

cutting its own throat. In 1985, it increased park entry fees to US$15 per person per day (Kenya charges about US$2) and US$15 per person per day for camping. The park entry fees have subsequently been reduced to US$10 but this still makes it much more expensive to visit Tanzanian game parks than Kenya ones.

Park Fees

As with Mt Kilimanjaro, the government has excelled itself in squeezing the maximum number of tourist dollars out of visitors to the national parks. It now costs US$10 per person per day plus US$75 per day for a non-Tanzanian registered vehicle (but only about US$12.50 per day for a Tanzanian registered vehicle) plus the cost of camping which is US$15 per person per day for established sites and US$20 per person per day for non-established sites. All these fees are payable in foreign currency only.

Not only that, but if you pass through two park entry gates in one day (Lake Manyara/Ngorongoro or Ngorongoro/ Serengeti, for instance) then you pay twice. This means it's going to cost you US$50 just in park fees alone to go on a five-day safari of Lake Manyara, Ngorongoro and Serengeti. None of these fees are 'negotiable.' The national parks are open daily from 6 am to 7 pm.

Accommodation at all the lodges in the parks must also be paid for in foreign currency (they're all about US$40 for singles, US$50 for doubles including breakfast) though there is a 50% discount on these prices from the Monday following Easter Sunday until 30th June. However, unlike the park entry fees, there may be scope for negotiation in paying for the lodges in local currency depending on which safari company you go through. Certainly all meals and drinks at the lodges can be paid for in local currency so make sure that in booking and paying for lodges in advance

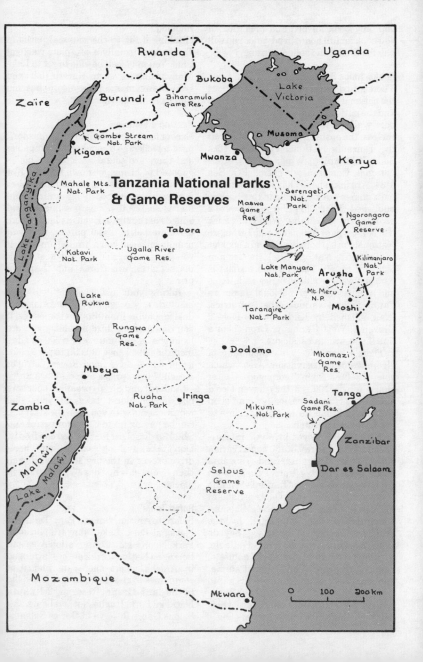

Rwanda

Uganda

Bukoba

Lake
Victoria

Zaïre

Burundi

Biharamulo
Game Res.

Gombe Stream
Nat. Park

Kigoma

Musoma

Mwanza

Kenya

Mahale Mts.
Nat. Park

**Tanzania National Parks
& Game Reserves**

Serengeti
Nat.
Park

Maswa
Game
Res.

Ngorongoro
Game
Reserve

Tabora

Katavi
Nat. Park

Ugalla River
Game Res.

Lake Manyara
Nat. Park

Arusha

Kilimanjaro
Nat. Park

Lake
Rukwa

Mt Meru
N.P.

Moshi

Tarangire
Nat. Park

Rungwa
Game
Res.

Dodoma

Mkomazi
Game
Res.

Mbeya

Zambia

Ruaha
Nat. Park

Iringa

Mikumi
Nat. Park

Tanga

Sadani
Game Res.

Zanzibar

Malawi

Dar es Salaam

Selous
Game
Reserve

Mozambique

Mtwara

0   100   200 km

you only book for bed and breakfast. If you book for full board in advance you will pay for the lot in foreign currency.

Books, Maps & Information

There's little literature available about the national parks. The tourist corporation and the national parks get a budget which barely allows them to tick over. Nevertheless, the enthusiastic people who staff the Tanzania National Parks HQ (6th floor, Kilimanjaro Wing, Arusha International Conference Centre, PO Box 3134, Arusha) should have new national park guides out by the time this book is published. Their old publications were a booklet titled *Ruaha National Park* (Sh 50), maps of Serengeti and Tarangire National Parks (both Sh 15) and a booklet on Tarangire National Park (in German only) for Sh 50. The German booklet is part of a well-produced series with maps and photographs of national parks in Tanzania and various other countries. It's published by Kilda-Verlag, D-4402 Greven 1, West Germany. Drop them a line if you want a catalogue.

There's also a very detailed map of Ngorongoro Conservation Area which you can buy from Ngorongoro Crater House for Sh 100 – if they haven't sold out. Crater House is basically a craft shop and it's on Boma Rd in Arusha, close to the New Safari Hotel.

If you'd like to get involved in anti-poaching measures and conservation activities in Tanzania (and Tanzania needs help in a big hurry) there is an organisation called the 'Tanzania Wildlife Protection Fund' (tel Dar es Salaam 27271), PO Box 1994, Dar es Salaam, which is partially supported by the Frankfurt Zoological Society. They do what they can, given the funds available, to protect wildlife and their habitats, help the recovery of endangered animal and plant species and fund research into the management of wildlife and the impact of human beings on their habitats. Enquiries are welcome.

Hitching

Hitching a lift to the national parks in Tanzania is usually a complete waste of time. You may well be able to get to Lake Manyara and even to Karatu (between Lake Manyara and Ngorongoro) but you won't get any further.

Renting a Vehicle

Except for those with their own transport, most travellers go through safari companies and there are sound reasons for this as opposed to hiring your own vehicle. Not only does rental cost an arm and a leg but most vehicles are poorly maintained and fuel is scarce if not impossible to find outside of the cities. Even in places where there are petrol/diesel pumps, they will usually only sell you a limited amount. If you want more, you pay for it at black market rates – up to three times the pump price.

Taking your own vehicle will also preclude any possibility of negotiating a deal for paying in shillings at the lodges. If you do decide to hire a vehicle you are looking at a minimum of Sh 500 per day including insurance plus Sh 20 per km for a four-wheel-drive Land-Rover (petrol or diesel). Pump prices for petrol are Sh 17 (standard) and Sh 20 (premium) per litre but if you don't take all your fuel requirements with you from the start you can be paying up to Sh 50 for petrol and Sh 25 for diesel per litre – *if* you can find it. Don't take anything less than four-wheel-drive except in the dry season and even then you might have problems in places.

Safari Tours

Safaris to Arusha National Park, Tarangire National Park, Lake Manyara National Park, Ngorongoro Conservation Area and Serengeti National Park are best arranged in Arusha where there are plenty of companies to choose from. Arrange visits to Sadani Game Reserve, Mikumu National Park, Ruaha National Park and Selous Game Reserve in Dar es Salaam.

Most of the safari companies offer a range of possibilities to suite all tastes and pockets though cost and reliability vary widely. To a large extent you get what you pay for.

If a bunch of people go on a safari with a certain company, have an excellent time and there are no hitches like vehicle breakdowns then they are going to recommend that company to others. If the company also fixes it for them to pay for accommodation at the park lodges in local currency then that's a double plus. The trouble is, for many travellers all that is required to convert an enthusiastic recommendation into a scathing condemnation is for the vehicle to break down for half a day, especially on a four to five day tour of Ngorongoro and Serengeti.

I get letters all the time with these two opposing views of particular companies. Some of the complaints are justified but others are simply bad luck. There's obviously a lot which companies can do to head off forseeable problems, in particular by having well-maintained vehicles. In Tanzania, however, this is often easier said than done. Spare parts require scarce foreign currency and there are harsh government restrictions on its use.

Also, if the company you go through is trying hard to cater for budget travellers and allowing you to pay in local currency without wanting to see your currency declaration form then it's hardly fair to be enthusiastic about this and then totally condemnatory when you lose half a day because of a breakdown.

All the same, you'd be surprised how many people want their bread buttered on both sides. Recently I received a lot of scathing letters about a certain company in Arusha whose vehicles were supposedly unreliable and their drivers/guides unable to do much more than change a wheel or put on a new fan belt. There were, it's true, a few more serious allegations, such as drivers substituting water for brake fluid in leaking hydraulic systems but it's impossible to substantiate this.

What I do know for certain is that I took a trip to Manyara, Ngorongoro and Serengeti with the same company in a full Land-Rover in the worst of the wet season when the road between Manyara and Serengeti was just a sea of mud and there were whole lines of bogged trucks and buses broadside across the road. We didn't have a single breakdown or delay; I would have been proud to recommend our driver/guide for the toughest motor rally in the world, and we all paid for the entire trip including lodges (though not, of course, park entry fees) in local currency. And it was all done with one bald back tyre. The only thing I was disappointed about was the parsimony of two or three of the passengers when it came to giving the driver a tip at the end of the safari. You wouldn't believe how tight-fisted some people can be!

OK, you can be lucky, but that's the name of the game in Tanzania. The moral of the story? If you break down, don't whinge, count your blessings, get out and help, get your hands dirty and get back on the road. This is a safari!

Bear the above in mind when you're choosing which safari company to go through and get several quotes first. At least in Arusha, you'll come across many companies which can offer budget prices at comparable rates – you pay your own park entrance fees (in foreign currency), the transport and driver/guide in local currency and maybe accommodation also in local currency.

Most, though not all, of the cheaper companies have offices in the Arusha International Conference Centre (AICC). Check the four companies listed below before deciding who to go with, they are the ones most used by budget travellers:

Arumeru Tours & Safaris
    PO Box 730, Seth Benjamin St, Arusha (tel 2780)
Star Tours
    PO Box 1099, Room 138/140, Ngorongoro Wing, AICC, Arusha (tel 3181 ext 2281 or 2285 after hours)

Taurus Tours & Safaris
  PO Box 1254, Boma St, Arusha (next door to the New Safari Hotel) (tel 2388 – 24 hours)
Wildersun Safaris & Tours
  PO Box 930, Sokoine Rd, Arusha (tel 3880)

Other cheap companies which can be found in the AICC include Sengo Safaris (Room 155), Wapa Safaris (Room 225), Ranger Safaris (Room 332), Lions Safaris (Room 435), Wilderness Safaris/Takims Holidays and Sable Safaris (Room 517). There are others scattered around town.

These companies will give you a fair spectrum of the prices which you'll have to pay to visit Manyara, Ngorongoro and Serengeti ranging from budget to relatively expensive. Whatever you do, don't go with African Wildlife Tours on India St close to the YMCA. The prices of their tours are pure banditry. For a one-day tour of Arusha National Park they charge between US$170 per person (for two people) and US$60 per person (for six people). For a five-day tour of Manyara, Ngorongoro, Olduvai and Serengeti they charge between US$1005 per person (for two people) and US$525 (for six people). Their prices include everything – but then so they should. In fact, I'd expect a free bottle of champagne every night at that price. It's nearly four times the cost of going on a comparable safari in Kenya.

For the cheapest safaris you are looking at a minimum of Sh 28,000/US$185 for transport and driver/guide for a five day, four night safari of Lake Manyara, Ngorongoro and Serengeti. This includes the compulsory accompanying guide down onto the crater floor at Ngorongoro. Shared between six people that's about Sh 4700/US$32 per person. This does not include the park entry fees or accommodation. Park entry fees will be US$60 per person and accommodation at the lodges, if you can pay for them in local currency, will be about Sh 2050/US$13.50

for accommodation, breakfast and dinner. A self-catered lunch (buy food in Arusha before leaving) will be extra as will drinks at the lodges. So will a tip for the driver/guide. All up, it comes to about US$125 per person. All the US dollar prices in this paragraph (except the park entry fees) assume that you are buying your local currency at the street rate of exchange. If that's what you are doing then the safari prices are comparable to those in Kenya. If you have to pay in dollars then you're going to need a rich uncle.

TARANGIRE NATIONAL PARK

This national park covers quite a large area south-east of Lake Manyara, mainly along the course of the Tarangire River and the swamp lands and flood plains which feed it to the east. During the dry season, the only water here flows along the Tarangire River and the park fills with herds of zebra, wildebeeste and kongoni which stay until October when the short rains allow them to move to new pastures. Throughout the year, however, you can see eland, lesser kudu, various species of gazelle, buffalo, giraffe, waterbuck, impala and elephant and you may see the occasional rhino. The animals are very timid because there are so few visitors. For ornithologists, the best season is from October to May.

Places to Stay

The only trouble with this park is that there is no cheap accommodation regardless of what you might be told in Arusha or Dar es Salaam. There's only a luxurious tented camp at Sh 500 a double with own shower and toilet. Meals are Sh 125 a pop.

LAKE MANYARA NATIONAL PARK

Manyara National Park is generally visited as the first stop on a safari which takes in this park and Ngorongoro and Serengeti. It's generally a bit of a letdown apart from the hippos since the large herds of elephant which used to nhabit the park have been decimated in recent years because basically the park is too small and so they invade adjoining farmland for fodder during the dry season. Naturally, local farmers have been none too pleased and, of course, once outside the park boundaries the elephants are fair game (and their ivory worth a lot of money).

Even the waterbirds which come to nest here (greater and lesser flamingoes in particular) can usually only be seen from a distance because there are no roads to the lake shore. You will certainly see wildebeeste, giraffe and baboon. What you see here really depends on how long you are prepared to stay and for most people (and most tours) that's just a day.

There is a reasonably interesting market in the nearby village of Mto-wa-Mbu – mainly fabrics and crafts – but they see a lot of tourists here so there are few bargains to be had that you can't find in Arusha.

Places to Stay

There are two camp sites just outside the park entrance which itself is just down the road from the village of Mto-wa-Mbu ('River of Gnats' or 'Mosquito Village' according to various translations and whichever one you choose, it's true). *Camp Site No 2* is probably the best. It costs Sh 40 per person plus they have *bandas* for Sh 200 which contain two beds, blankets and sheets and have running water, toilets and firewood. Insect repellent and/or a mosquito net would be very useful and you need to beware of thieving baboons.

There's also a *Youth Hostel* of sorts here but it can't be recommended unless you're in love with mosquitoes. *Fig Tree Farm*, about two km from the park entrance, has been recommended by some travellers. They offer accommodation for Sh 75 per person and excellent meals at Sh 65.

You can find budget accommodation in the Mto-wa-Mbu village. There are three very basic hotels here – the *Mzalendo Guest House* and the *Rombo Guest House*, both on the main road, and the *Rift Valley Bar & Guest House*, on the dirt 'square' next to the petrol station.

The best place to stay, however, especially if you don't have a tent and which I can recommend without any reservations, is the *Starehe Bar & Hotel* on the escarpment up above Lake Manyara. It's about 100 metres off to the left on the turn-off for Lake Manyara Hotel (signposted) on the main road from Mto-wa-Mbu to Ngorongoro. It's not an obvious place but there is a sign. It's rustic, very clean, very comfortable, there are no bugs, mosquitoes or electricity (though candles are provided) and it costs Sh 200 a single (without own bathroom) and Sh 300 a double (with own bathroom). There are only cold water showers but the staff are eager to please, very friendly and they'll cook you up superb, generous meals of tasty stewed chicken, sautee¼d potatoes, haricot beans, mung beans, gravy and rice for Sh 120 and great breakfasts of two eggs, bread, butter, jam and tea/coffee for Sh 80.

Lake Manyara Hotel (tel 3300/3113), which sits right on the edge of the escarpment overlooking Lake Manyara about three km along the same turn off on which the Starehe stands, is where the rich people stay. It costs US$38 a single and US$49 a double for bed and breakfast (foreign currency only accepted). There are flower gardens, a swimming pool, curio shop and what one guide to Tanzania calls a 'specious restaurant and bar' (sic).

NGORONGORO CONSERVATION AREA

There can be few people who have not heard, read or seen film or TV footage of this incredible 20 km-wide volcano crater packed with just about every species of wildlife to be found in East Africa. The views from the 700 metre-high crater rim are incredible and, though the wildlife

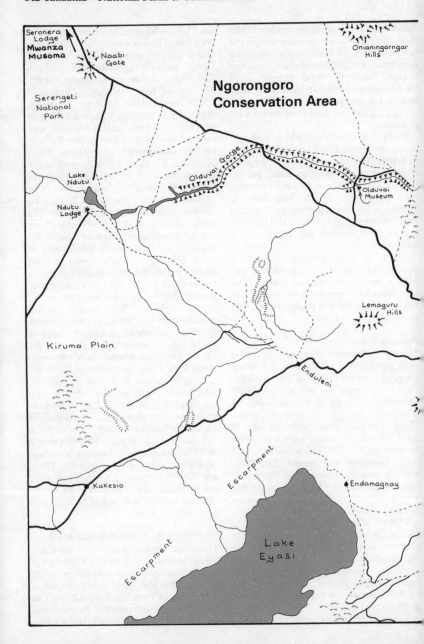

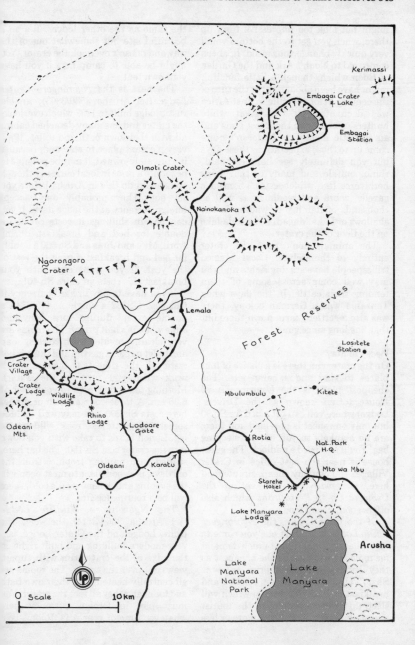

might not look too impressive from up there, when you get to the bottom you'll very quickly change your mind. It's been compared to Noah's Ark and the Garden of Eden which, though a little fanciful, might have been about right at the turn of the century before wildlife in East Africa was decimated by the 'great white hunters' armed with the latest guns and an egotistic mentality. It doesn't quite come up to those expectations these days but you definitely see lion, elephant, rhino, buffalo and many of the plains herbivores like wildebeeste, Thomson's gazelle, zebra and reedbuck as well as thousands of flamingoes wading in the shallows of Lake Magadi – the soda lake on the floor of the crater.

The animals don't have the crater entirely to themselves. Local Maasai tribespeople have grazing rights and you may well come across some of them tending their cattle. In the days when Tanzania was a German colony, there was also a settler's farm down there but that has long since gone.

Places to Stay

On the crater rim there is a choice of four places to stay and a camp site. The cheapest place is the *Usiwara Guest House* (often known as the Drivers' Lodge) where you can get a bed for Sh 90 but only one sheet is provided and there are no blankets so you need a sleeping bag. You'll also need a padlock. The guest house is near the post office in Crater Village. You can buy cheap, simple food here. Otherwise you can eat at the *Ushirika Co-op Restaurant* which also offers good, cheap food.

Of the three lodges, the *Ngorongoro Rhino Lodge* is the first one you come to off to the left. If there isn't much demand for rooms it will also be the cheapest as they'll offer you a 'special price' as low as Sh 175/US$1.15 per person for bed and breakfast or US$9 for a room which will sleep up to three people. In the tourist season, however, it will cost more or less

the same as the other lodges. It's on a beautiful site but somewhat out of the way and doesn't overlook the crater. You might be able to camp here if you have your own tent.

The next is the *Ngorongoro Crater Lodge* (tel Arusha 3530/3303), an old rustic lodge built in 1937 which overlooks the crater and has many detached cabins all with their own bath and toilet. It's a very pleasant place to stay and, because it's privately-owned, it may be possible to negotiate a price in local currency though you should do this in Arusha before you set out. They probably only accept foreign currency at the lodge itself. If you can pay in shillings it costs Sh 450 a double for bed and breakfast during April, May and June and Sh 900 a double for bed and breakfast during the rest of the year. If you want eggs with your breakfast this costs an extra Sh 40!

If you have to pay in hard currency it will cost US$32 a single and US$48 a double (except during April, May and June when it's half price). The rooms are very clean, provided with towels, soap and toilet paper, a gas fire and there is hot water all the time (gas heaters which work when you turn on the water) Morning tea is delivered to your door at 6.30 am. A three-course lunch or dinner here costs Sh 200 and may well include something exotic like roast wildebeeste leg. Lunch boxes to take with you down into the crater cost Sh 150. The bar here, stuffed with hunting trophies from the old days, is a good place to meet people in the evening and, whenever it's cold, there will be a roaring log fire.

The *Ngorongoro Wildlife Lodge* (tel Arusha 3300/3114), between the Rhino Lodge and the Crater Lodge, is a very modern building and built right on the edge of the crater rim with superb views out over the crater. The rooms are all centrally heated with their own bath and toilet and they all face the crater. You must pay in foreign currency here whatever time of year it is. Rooms cost

US$38 a single and US$49 a double for bed and breakfast. There is a 50% discount during April, May and June. Meals are excellent and you can pay for them in local currency. The bar is a good place to meet people and, like the one at the Crater Lodge, has a log fire.

Most campers stay at the *Simba* site on the crater rim about two km from Crater Village. The site costs US$15 per person and has hot showers, toilets and firewood and is guarded. There is also a camp site down in the crater but there are no facilities and you need a ranger with you if you are going to stay there. It costs US$30 per person. There's a general store at Crater Village but they only have a limited range of foodstuffs so bring food with you from Arusha or eat at the lodges.

At Karatu, about half way between Lake Manyara and Ngorongoro, is *Gibb's Farm* run by a white Tanzanian family who, according to most of the people who have stayed there, offer the best accommodation and meals to be found in the whole country. It costs Sh 750 a double for bed and breakfast or, if you don't want to stay there, you can have either lunch or dinner for Sh 200. The food is excellent and the farm is beautifully situated. Gibb's Farm is signposted on the main road as you drive into Karatu from Manyara.

Getting There

If you are trying to get to the Crater under your own steam, there are private buses from Arusha at least as far as Karatu but it may be difficult to find anything going beyond there. There are also plenty of trucks as far as Karatu. The State Transport Corporation in Arusha used to have buses to Lake Manyara, Ngorongoro and Seronera village in Serengeti but shortages of fuel and buses have led to the service being suspended.

Only four-wheel-drive vehicles are allowed down in the crater except at times during the dry season when the authorities *may* allow conventional vehicles to go down. The roads into the crater are very steep so if you are driving your own vehicle make sure it will handle the roads. It takes about 30 to 45 minutes to get down to the crater floor. Whether you are driving your own vehicle or on an organised tour, you must take a park ranger with you at a cost of Sh 75 per day although they expect more. You can pay this in local currency. It's also possible to hire a four-wheel-drive Land-Rover at Crater Village from the same place where you collect a ranger. They cost Sh 1750 for half a day and Sh 2400 for a whole day (payable in shillings) but there are often fuel shortages so don't count on being able to hire one. If they are not going down for this reason then enquire at the lodges about tours.

THE OLDUVAI GORGE

The Olduvai Gorge made world headlines in 1959 following the discovery by the Leakeys of fossil fragments of the skull of one of the ancestors of *Homo sapiens*. The fragments were dated at 1.8 million years old. The Leakeys were convinced by this and other finds that the fragments represented a third species of early man which they dubbed *habilis*. They proposed that the other two, known as *Australopithecus africanus* and *A robustus*, had died out and that *habilis* had given rise to modern man. The debate raged for two decades and is still unsettled.

Meanwhile, in 1979, Mary Leakey made another important discovery in the shape of footprints at Laetoli which she claimed were of a man, woman and child. They were dated to 3.5 million years old and, since they were made by creatures which walked upright, this pushed the dawn of mankind much further back than had previously been supposed.

The gorge itself isn't of great interest unless you are archaeologically inclined but it has acquired a kind of cult attraction among those who just want to visit the site where the evolution of early man presumably took place. There is a small museum on the site, which is only a 10-15 minute drive from the main road between Ngorongoro Crater and Serengeti. The museum closes at 3 pm and in the rainy season it's often not open at all. It's possible to go down into the gorge at certain times of year if you would like to see the sites of the digs.

Places to Stay

There is nowhere to stay at Olduvai but, at the western end of the gorge where the creek which flows through it empties into Lake Ndutu, there is the *Ndutu Safari Lodge* on the borders of the Serengeti National Park. There is both tented accommodation and chalets here with a total of 94 beds as well as a bar and restaurant. It costs approximately US$20 per person for bed and breakfast (payable in foreign currency). You can also camp here if you have your own tent in which case it costs Sh 75 per person but there are no facilities at the camp site.

SERENGETI NATIONAL PARK

Serengeti, which covers a total of 14,763 square km, is Tanzania's most famous game park and is continuous with that of Masai Mara in neighbouring Kenya. Here you can get a glimpse of what much of East Africa must have looked like in the days before the 'great white hunters'. Their mindless slaughter of the plains animals began in the late 19th century and more recently trophy hunters and poachers in search of ivory and rhino horn have added to the sickening toll. On the seemingly endless and almost tree-less plains of the Serengeti are literally millions of hooved animals. They're constantly on the move in search of pasture and watched and pursued by the predators which feed off them. It's one of the most incredible sights you will ever see and the numbers are simply mind-boggling.

Nowhere else will you see wildebeeste, gazelle, zebra and antelope in such concentrations. The wildebeeste, o which there are up to two million in tota is the chief herbivore of the Serengeti an also the main prey of the large carnivore such as lions and hyenas. The wildebeest are well-known for the annual migratio which they undertake – a trek with man hazards not least of which is the crossin of large rivers which can leave hundred drowned, maimed or taken by crocodiles During the rainy season the herds ar widely scattered over the eastern sectio of the Serengeti and Masai Mara in th north. These areas have few large river and streams and quickly dry out when th rains cease. When that happens th wildebeeste concentrate on the fe remaining green areas and graduall form huge herds which move off west i search of better pasture. At about th same time that the migration starts, th annual rut also begins. For a few days at time while the herds pause, bull establish territories which they defen against rivals and, meanwhile, try t assemble as many females as they ca with which they mate. As soon as th migration resumes, the female herd merge again.

The dry season is spent in the wester parts of the Serengeti at the end of whicl the herds move back east in anticipatio of the rains. Calving begins at the start o the rainy season but, if it arrives lat anything up to 80% of the new calves ma die due to lack of food.

Serengeti is also famous for its lions many of which have collars fitted witl transmitters so that their movements ca be studied and their location known, an its cheetahs. If you want to give yoursel the chance of being in on a 'kill', however then you are going to need a pair c binoculars. Distances are so great in thi park that you'd probably miss then unless they happened close to the road.

The main road from Ngorongoro t Seronera village is a good gravel roa which is well maintained with th occasional *kopje* to one side or another

Kopjes are slight rises strewn with huge, smooth boulders which generally support few trees and are often the lookouts of cheetahs. You'll see plenty of Maasai herding cattle all the way from Ngorongoro as far as the Olduvai Gorge.

A census taken in 1978 put the populations of the largest mammals in the Serengeti at: wildebeeste – 1,500,000; zebra – 200,000; impala – 75,000; Grant's and Thomson's gazelle – 1,000,000; buffalo – 74,000; topi – 5,000; eland – 18,000; giraffe – 9000; elephant 5000; hyena – 4000; lion – 3000; cheetah – 500 and rhino 100. There hasn't been too much change in the numbers since then except for rhino and elephant which have suffered badly from poaching. The hard-pressed but enthusiastic rangers can do little about poaching given the extremely limited resources provided them by the government. The animals are also very easy to see as the Serengeti is substantially flat grassland with bushes and trees only in clumps here and there, particularly along river banks.

Places to Stay

Most budget travellers stay at either the camp site or the hostel close to the lodge near Seronera village. The camp site normally costs US$15 per person but there is usually scope for negotiation. The hostel has dormitory-style rooms with old showers and toilets and it costs Sh 50 per person per night. You need to bring your own bedding. Candles and a torch are also useful since there's no electricity. Basic meals are available in the village but the quality of the food is poor.

The other place to stay is the *Seronera Lodge* (tel Arusha 3842). This is a stunningly beautiful and very imaginative building constructed on top of and around a *kopje* with hyrax (a small rodent-like creature) running around everywhere. They're so tame you can almost touch them. The bar and observation deck at this lodge is enormous and right on top of the *kopje* with the boulders incorporated into the design. Getting up to it on narrow stone steps between massive rocks is like entering Aladdin's Cave!

The rooms are very pleasantly furnished and decorated (though there seem to be a lack of electric light bulbs) and they all have their own bathroom with hot water. It costs US$38 a single and US$49 a double for bed and breakfast except during April, May and June when there is a 50% discount. It *may* be possible to arrange to pay in shillings in which case it's an absolute bargain, but you must arrange this in Arusha before you set off. The lodge has its own generator but they only switch it on between sunset and around 12 midnight. Three-course dinners are available and are good value. There are no guide books, maps, postcards or film for sale in the shop at the lodge.

North-east of Seronera village near the park border is another lodge – the *Lobo Wildlife Lodge* (tel Arusha 3842) which is built into the faults and contours of a massive rock promontory overlooking the plains. It's very similar to the Seronera Lodge in terms of what it offers but is somewhat cheaper at US$24 a single and US$33 a double for bed and breakfast except during April, May and June when there is a 50% discount.

MIKUMI NATIONAL PARK

Mikumi National Park covers an area of 3237 square km and sits astride the main Dar es Salaam-Mbeya highway about 300 km from Dar es Salaam. Not many budget travellers seem to visit this park probably because of the lack of cheap accommodation but there is a lot of wildlife to be seen. Elephant, lion, leopard, buffalo, zebra, impala, wildebeeste and warthog can be seen at any time of year.

One of the principal features of Mikumi is the Mkata River flood plain, an area of lush vegetation which attracts elephant and buffalo in particular. Hippos can also be seen at Hippo Pools about five km from the park entrance gate.

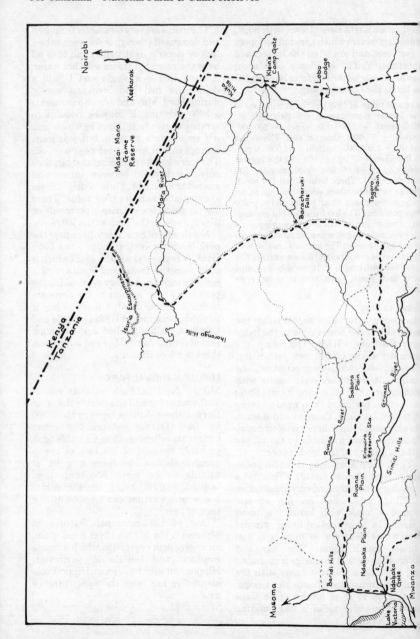

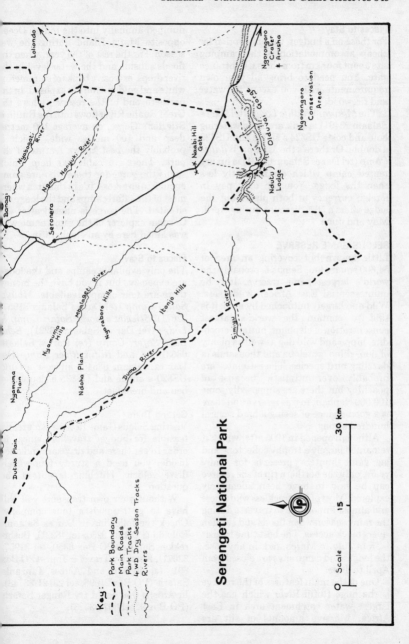

Serengeti National Park

Key:

— — — Park Boundary

———— Main Roads

········· Park Tracks

----- 4wd Dry Season Tracks

········· Rivers

Scale

0   15   30 km

Places to Stay

For those on a budget, the only option for cheap accommodation is the camping site about four km from the park entrance gate. You need to bring all your own requirements with you except for water and firewood.

The *Mikumi Wildlife Lodge* (tel Dar es Salaam 23491) is built around a watering hole and costs US$24 a single and US$33 a double. Or there's the *Mikumi Wildlife Camp* (tel Dar es Salaam 68631), a luxury tented camp which costs slightly less than the lodge. You can only pay in foreign currency at both places but the lodge offers a 50% discount during April, May and June.

SELOUS GAME RESERVE

Little known but covering an area of 54,600 square km, Selous is probably the world's largest game reserve. It's the quintessential East African wilderness. Wild and largely untouched by man, it is said to contain the world's largest concentration of elephant, buffalo, crocodile, hippo and wild dog as well as plenty of lion, rhino, antelope and thousands of dazzling bird species. The estimates are probably over-optimistic because of poaching but there are supposedly some 100,000 elephant in this reserve and there is a good chance of seeing a herd several hundred strong.

Although opened in 1905 after which it remained largely a trophy collectors' and big game hunters' preserve for many years, only the northern tip of the reserve can be said to have been adequately explored. Most of it is trackless wilderness and almost impossible to traverse during the rainy season when floods and swollen rivers block access. The best time to visit is from July to March and, in any case, the lodges and camp sites are closed from April to June.

One of the main features of the reserve is the huge Rufiji River which has the largest water catchment area in East Africa. Massive amounts of silt are dumped annually into the Indian Ocean opposite Mafia Island during the wet season. For the rest of the year, when the floods subside and the water level in the river drops, extensive banks of shimmering white and golden sand are exposed. In the northern end of the reserve, where the Great Ruaha River flows into the Rufiji, is Stiegler's Gorge, on average 100 metres deep and 100 metres wide, which is probably the best known feature of the park. There's a cable car here which spans the gorge for those who are game enough to go across. It's in this area where most of the safari camps and the lodge are situated. The gorge is named after the German explorer of the same name who was killed here by an elephant in 1907.

Places to Stay

The only available camps and the lodge are expensive but if you have the money there are four camps available. *Mbuyu Safari Camp* (tel Dar es Salaam 31957/32671), *Stiegler's Gorge Safari Camp & Lodge* (tel Dar es Salaam 48221), *Beho Beho Safari Camp* (tel Dar es Salaam 68631/33), and *Rufiji River Camp* (tel Dar es Salaam 63546) all cost around US$20 a single and US$35 a double for bed and breakfast.

Getting There

Visiting Selous Game Reserve isn't really feasible for budget travellers since, in order to get there and drive around once inside, you need a sturdy four-wheel-drive vehicle. Hitching is out of the question.

Without your own transport you will have to go through a tour company. Check the following in Dar es Salaam: Rubada (PO Box 9230, tel 48221), Bushtrekker Safaris (PO Box 5350, tel 31957/32671), Kearsley Travel & Tours (PO Box 801, tel 20807), and Across Tanzania Safaris (PO Box 21996, tel 23121/38748). In Arusha you could try Ranger Safaris (PO Box 9, tel 3074/3023).

RUAHA NATIONAL PARK

Ruaha National Park was created in 1964 from half of the Rungwa Game Reserve and it covers some 13,000 square km. Like the Selous, it's a wild, undeveloped area and access is difficult but there's a lot of wildlife here as a result. Elephant, kudu, roan and sable antelope, hippo and crocodile are particularly numerous. The Great Ruaha River, which forms the eastern boundary of the park, has spectacular gorges though much of the rest of the park is undulating plateau averaging 1000 metres in height with occasional rocky outcrops.

Visiting the park is only feasible in the dry season from July to December. During the rest of the year the tracks are virtually impassable.

Places to Stay

If you do manage to get there, you can find accommodation in rondavels equipped with beds, showers and kitchen at *Msembe Camp* – contact the Park Warden, Ruaha National Park, PO Box 369, Iringa.

Getting There

As with the Selous, you need your own sturdy four-wheel-drive vehicle or you have to go on an organised tour so it's not really a possibility for budget travellers.

GOMBE STREAM NATIONAL PARK

Primarily a chimpanzee sanctuary, this tiny park is on the shores of Lake Tanganyika between Kigoma and the Burundi border. In recent years it has become very popular with travellers going north to or coming south from Burundi. The park is the site of Jane Goodall's research station which was set up in 1960. It's a beautiful place and the chimps are great fun. A group of them usually come down to the research station every day but if they don't the rangers generally know where to find them. You must have a guide with you whenever you are away from the station or the lake shore. This only costs Sh 50 per party per day and the guides are mellow, interesting people.

Places to Stay

No camping is allowed but there are caged huts, each with six beds and a table and chairs. They're caged to keep the baboons out. A bed costs US$10 per night plus you will have to pay the standard

In the game parks one can get easily spooked...

park fee of US$10 per person – not a cheap visit these days!

You need to bring all your own food with you though eggs and fish are sometimes available at the station. If you do run out of food then you can get more at Mwangongo village about 10 km north of here where there is a market twice a week (enquire at the station as to the days). Be careful when walking between the cookhouse and the huts at the station especially if you are carrying food. Baboons have jumped on quite a few people and robbed them of their food. There's a well-stocked library at the hostel.

Getting There

There are no roads to Gombe Stream so the only way in is to take a small lake boat from either Kigoma or from Banda, the Tanzania/Burundi border village. The boats leave from the lake shore about one km up the railway line in Kigoma daily between 9 am and 1 pm (or when full). The fare is Sh 100 and the journey takes about 2½ hours. The fare and the journey time is about the same if you are coming down the lake from Banda. Try to get a boat with a canvas roof as it gets very hot out on the lake at midday.

MAHALE MOUNTAINS NATIONAL PARK

This national park, like Gombe Stream, is mainly a chimpanzee sanctuary but you won't find it marked on most maps since it was only created in mid-1985. It's on the knuckle-shaped area of land which protrudes into Lake Tanganyika about half way down the lake opposite the Zairois port of Kalemie. The highest peak in the park – Nkungwe – at 2460 metres ensures that moist air blowing in from the lake condenses there and falls as rain. This rain supports extensive montane forests, grasslands and alpine bamboo. Numerous valleys intersect the mountains and some of them have permanent streams which flow into the lake. The eastern side of the mountains are considerably drier and support what is known as miombo woodlands. It's a very isolated area.

The animals which live in this park show closer affinities with western rather than eastern Africa. They include chimpanzee, brush-tailed porcupine various species of colobus monkey including the Angolan black and white colobus, guinea fowl and mongoose. Scientists, mainly from Japan, have been studying the chimpanzees for 20 years and more than 100 of the animals have been habituated to human contact. The population has dramatically increased since 1975 when local people were moved to villages outside the park which put a stop to poaching and field-burning activities. This relocation has also led to the reappearance of leopard, lion and buffalo which were never or very rarely seen in the past.

Unlike other national parks in Tanzania this is one which you can walk around – there are no roads in any case. Very few tourists come here because of the remoteness of the area but it's well worth it if you have the time and initiative.

Places to Stay

Camping is allowed in specific areas if you have equipment (none for hire) and this costs US$15 per day. Otherwise a guest house was under construction at Kasiha village and should now be open. You need to bring all your food requirements with you from Kigoma since meals are not available. It's a good idea to check with the park headquarters in Kigoma about current conditions, transport and accommodation before you set off. The park entry fee is the usual US$10 per head.

Getting There

The only way to get to the park is by lake steamer from Kigoma using either the *MV Liemba* or the *MV Mwongozo*. You have to get off at Mugambo (usually in the middle of the night) and take a small boat to the shore. From Mugambo you eed to charter a small boat from either the local fishermen or merchants to Mahale (Kasiha village) which should take about three hours. The schedule for the *MV*

Liemba can be found the section on transport to and from Burundi. For the *MV Mwongozo* schedule you need to enquire in Kigoma.

Comoros

The Comoros consist of four main islands – Grande Comore, Moheli, Anjouan and Mayotte – as well as a number of islets. They lie between the northern tip of Madagascar and the African mainland. Despite the crazy years following independence, the violence and the xenophobia, life has returned to normal and the islands are quite safe to visit. The people are polite, friendly and honest and the islands are some of the most beautiful in the world and quite different from each other. There are coral reefs, sandy beaches, picturesque old Arab towns, luxuriant vegetation and even an active volcano (Mt Kartala). And not a tourist in sight. Visit them if you get the chance.

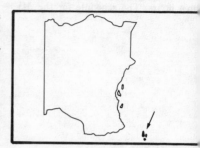

HISTORY
Early Settlement
Like Madagascar the Comoros Islands were originally settled by people of Malay-Polynesian origin around the 6th century AD. Since then the population has become much more racially mixed as a result of successive waves of immigration by Africans, Arabs and Shirazis. The latter were Persians from the Gulf area who came between the 10th and 15th centuries and were responsible for setting up a number of rival sultanates on the islands. Their wealth was based on the slave trade and spices which were grown on the islands.

The Colonial Era
The Portuguese largely ignored the islands in their 16th and 17th century rampages up and down the coast of East Africa except for the occasional re-victualing stop. They were scooped up by the French in the late 19th century during the European scramble for African colonies. The French conquest was made considerably easier by the rivalry between the sultans. The sultan of Mayotte sold his island to the French for a guaranteed annual payment. The rest succumbed quickly following naval bombardments.

Despite numerous peasant revolts, the French maintained an iron grip over the islands for well over a century. Political organisations and newspapers were banned and revolts suppressed with unrestrained military efficiency. No-one was allowed into or out of the islands without the approval of the colonial authorities.

Independence
In the early days of the colonial period the islands were administered from Madagascar but they became a separate territory in 1947 with a form of internal autonomy granted in 1961. Seven years later, however, a strike by local students led to mass demonstrations and the French were forced to allow the formation of political parties. Numerous parties were formed representing various factional interests ranging over the whole spectrum from those demanding immediate and unconditional independence to those who vigorously opposed independence.

Tensions between the various political parties grew steadily over the next few years and, in an attempt to contain it, the French staged a referendum in late 1974. Overall, 94% of the population was in

354

avour of independence though in Mayotte some 64% were against it. Less than one year later Ahmed Abdallah announced a unilateral declaration of independence while Mayotte's deputies cabled France requesting French intervention. The Federal Islamic Republic of the Comoros – minus Mayotte – were admitted to membership of the UN and the OAU barely two weeks later.

The French retaliated by withdrawing their US$18 million subsidy and 500 technicians. Economic collapse and political turmoil were virtually inevitable. Even before the French withdrew, the islands were barely ticking over on a subsistence economy, a threadbare administration and there were few auspicious signs to suggest optimism. The crunch came just one month later when Abdallah was overthrown in a coup by Ali Solih.

The Crazy Years

When he first came to power, Solih, an atheist despite his Muslim upbringing and something of an idealist, appeared to be quite normal and perhaps just what the Comoros needed. Determined to drag the islands screaming into the 20th century and away from colonial-induced attitudes, Solih set about his task with gusto. French citizens were expelled and their property nationalised, feudal institutions were attacked, women were unveiled, the traditionally elaborate and costly arrangements which were part of marriages and funerals were abolished, and the privileges of ancestry, based on dubious claims of direct descent from the Prophet's family, were likewise attacked.

Revolution was in the air and Solih seemed determined to outdo both Kemal Atatürk and Mao Tse Tung. The trouble was he brooked no opposition and used a rabble of illiterate youths, dubbed the 'Jeunesse Revolutionnaire', to enforce his ideas. He dismissed the 3500 members of the civil service and turned it over to the youth brigade and jailed or murdered

anyone with the intelligence or courage to speak out against his excesses. Petty criminals and anyone who could be labelled (rightly or wrongly) as 'counterrevolutionary' were dressed in rough sacking, their heads shaven and beaten through the narrow streets accompanied by megaphone announcements of their alleged crimes. Even old people were not immune from this kind of brutality. Any ideology that might have been defensible in the early days quickly turned into nothing more than the power of the gun, wielded by his teenage thugs.

Solih quickly turned into the living embodiment of the adage that 'Power corrupts; absolute power corrupts absolutely'. He had himself declared a prophet and was heard to tell his people at one rally, 'I am your god and teacher. I am the divine way, the torch that lights the dark. There is no god but Ali Solih'. He was clearly demented and, towards the end, refused to leave his palace for lengthy periods of time during which he went on whisky drinking binges and watched movies in the company of young girls drawn from the youth brigade.

And back to France

Though the Comoran people took it all with remarkable passivity, something had to give soon. It came in the form of 29 white mercenaries led by Bob Denard and recruited by Ahmed Abdallah, the former president, and Mohammed Ahmed, a wealthy Comoran businessman, both of whom were living in exile in Paris. They struck at dawn on 13 May 1978 whilst most of the 2000-man army were in Anjouan. Within a few hours it was all over. The army surrendered and people took to the streets to celebrate.

Abdallah returned to the islands two weeks later to a rousing welcome and Ali Solih was shot to death by the mercenaries, supposedly while trying to escape, and his body dumped in his mother's backyard on the slopes of Mt Kartala.

The OAU reacted with outrage and

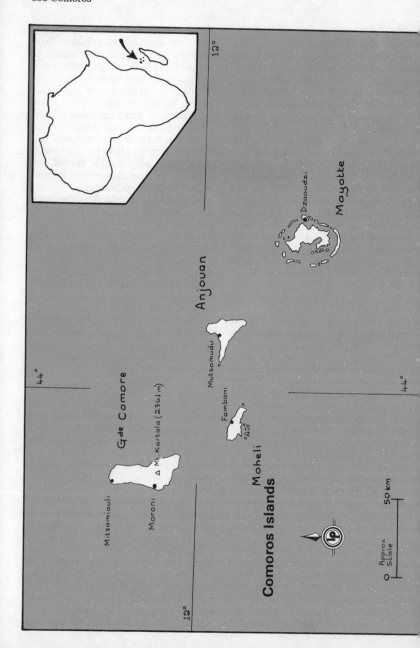

Mitsamiouli

Moroni

Gde Comore

△ Mt. Kartala (2361 m)

Mutsamudu

Anjouan

Fomboni

Moheli

Dzaoudzi

Mayotte

Comoros Islands

0   Approx   50 km
     Scale

44°

12°

12°

44°

refused to accept the new Comoran delegation to its summit conference that year. Meanwhile, Denard's mercenaries took over control of key ministries like defense and communications and began to get the country back onto the rails. The economy was denationalised, relations with France re-established and children sent back to school. The country quickly returned to some semblance of normality. Denard himself hung up his gun, took a Comoran wife and settled down to what he thought would become his home for the rest of his life. His dreams didn't last long. Though Abdallah had agreed to allow him to stay in the Comoros, Denard's presence was creating many problems of recognition for the new government among mainland African states and he was finally persuaded to leave following a lavish state banquet for him. Many of his fellow mercenaries, however, remain and this has not gone unnoticed in places like Madagascar, the Seychelles and Tanzania.

French aid to the island republic has been resumed but, despite all the changes, Mayotte still refuses to join the republic and remains to this day a French overseas territory. How long it will continue to tread this path is anyone's guess though it clearly benefitted from being outside Ali Solih's nightmare and is visibly more prosperous than the other three islands.

POPULATION

The population of the Comoros Islands is about 400,000.

ECONOMY

The Comoros Islands have an extremely shaky economy based on vanilla, ylang-ylang, copra and cloves. None of these commodities are doing very well and to make matters worse the republic is far from self sufficient, nearly 50% of the import bill is for food.

GEOGRAPHY

There are four main islands – Grande Comore, Anjouan, Moheli and Mayotte. The total area is 2171 square km.

LANGUAGE

The official languages are French and Arabic though most people speak Comoran which is a variant of KiSwahili. Comoran is pronounced very much like KiSwahili except that 'ou' is pronounced as in French. There are local variants of Comoran on each of the islands but the following phrases will be understood everywhere:

Good morning
 bariza soubouni
Good afternoon
 bariza djioni
Good evening
 bariza massihou
Goodbye
 namlala ounono
How are you?
 habar?
(Response to the above)
 salama or *njema*
How much is this?
 riyali gapvi?
I don't speak Comoran
 mimi tsidji ourogowa shi gazidja
Are you going to Moroni?
 gowedo Moroni?
I'm looking for a place to sleep
 gamtsaho pvahanou nilale
I'm looking for a place to eat
 gamtsaho pvahanou nililye
Have you anything to eat?
 kamtsina bahidrou ya houla?
Yes we have
 gassina
No we haven't
 karitsina
Do you have rice?
 gagnina sohole?
Meat
 gnama
Water
 madji

Bananas
  zikoudou
Coconut (fresh)
  idjavou
Coconut (dried)
  nazi

Numbers

1	*motsi*
2	*mbili*
3	*drarou*
4	*nne*
5	*tsanou*
6	*dradarou*
7	*mfoukaré*
8	*nané*
9	*sheda*
10	*koumé*
11	*koumé na motsi*
20	*shirini*
30	*megomirarou*
40	*megominne*
50	*megomitsanou*
100	*ojana*
200	*madjanamayli*
300	*madjanadrarou:*
1000	*shihwi*
2000	*shihwizyli*
3000	*shihwidrarou*

VISAS

Visas are required by all except French nationals arriving in Mayotte (since Mayotte is still a French overseas territory) but all travellers arriving by air are admitted with or without a visa. If you arrive without a visa, however, you must go to Immigration in either Moroni (Grande Comore) or Mutsamudu (Anjouan) as soon as possible to get a visa. These cost CFr 2000 for four weeks. Those visiting Mayotte must be in possession of a French visa where necessary. Travellers must have an onward ticket before they will be allowed to enter the Comoros.

There are hardly any Comoros Islands embassies around the world (Paris and Brussels are the only two but you can probably get one from their representative at the UN in New York) even in neighbouring countries. Where there is no embassy, the French embassy generally deals with their affairs.

There are embassies for Belgium, France and Senegal in Moroni.

MONEY

US$1 = CFr 450

The unit of currency is the Franc Comorien (CFr) which is linked to the French franc on the basis of CFr 50 = Fr fr 1. This is exactly the same as the west and central African CFA. There are no limits on the import or export of local currency and there is no blackmarket. BIC is the only international bank on the independent islands.

CLIMATE

The dry season runs from May to October when the average temperature is 24°C. The rainy season runs from November to April and the temperature can range from 27°C to 35°C. Sea breezes make the climate very pleasant for most of the year.

FILM & PHOTOGRAPHY

There are no restrictions on photography but you should ask people before taking photographs of them. Women, in particular, may object to photographs since this is a Muslim country. As elsewhere in Africa, don't take photographs of military installations.

HEALTH

Cholera and yellow fever vaccinations are mandatory. You are also strongly advised to be vaccinated against typhoid and tetanus.

As elsewhere in Africa, you must take precautions against malaria. Tap water is not safe to drink.

GENERAL INFORMATION
Post & Telecommunications

Under Ali Solih's regime, posts and telecommunications fell into disrepair and couldn't be relied on. They have now been rehabilitated and are reliable. A full range of services are available at the head post office in Moroni which is in the same square as the Friday Mosque.

Time
GMT plus 3 hours.

INFORMATION
See Comores Tours in the Moroni section below.

GETTING THERE
Air

Airlines serving the Comoros are Air France, Air Madagascar and Air Mauritius. There are twice-weekly flights by Air Madagascar and Air Mauritius on the route Kenya (Nairobi)-Grande Comore-Madagascar-Réunion-Mauritius. Air France flies once weekly in either direction from Paris to Grande Comore via Jeddah and Dar es Salaam. The best place to buy a ticket on Air Madagascar or Air Mauritius is in Nairobi where a number of relatively cheap deals are available (see the Kenya chapter).

Airport tax for international departures is CFr 5000.

Sea
There are no regular boats from the African mainland at present. If you are interested in sailing to the Comoros the only place you'll find a boat is in Dar es Salaam. Enquire at the Tanzanian Coastal Shipping Line (tel 26192), PO Box 9461, Sokoine Drive, Dar es Salaam. The office is at the junction of Sokoine Drive and Mission St. They do this run at the most once a month.

GETTING AROUND
Air
Air Comores services the internal routes

and Mayotte. Their office in Moroni is in the terminal building at the old airstrip opposite the Hotel Karthala.

Road
Land transport on each island is by taxi-brousse (Renaults, Peugeot 404s or 505s). These taxis are fairly frequent but there are very few sealed roads on the islands and you must bargain over the fares.

Sea
There are small boats which ply between the islands for very reasonable prices though they are often crowded. They usually sail at night. One of them is the *M'fano* which is operated by very friendly man named Jeanot. He sails from Moroni on Grande Comore to Moheli and Anjouan regularly; sometimes to Mayotte and once in a while to Majunga on Madagascar island. Information about these boats can be obtained down at the harbour in Moroni and at a small office on the first floor on the main square between the post office and the 'supermarket' in Mutsamudu (Anjouan).

There are also a number of orange-coloured outriggers (a gift from the Japanese government) which go from Shindini, south of Fumbuni on Grande Comore, to Bimbini near the western tip of Anjouan. They also sometimes sail from Bimbini to Moheli island. These outriggers only have a small sail area so an inter-island trip can take quite some time.

Grande Comore (Njazidja)

Njazidja is the Comoran name for this island. It's a pretty island, 65 km long with the islands' highest mountain, the dormant volcano Mt Kartala (2461 metres), roughly in the centre. The crater is one of the largest in Africa. There are several other volcanic cones over 1000

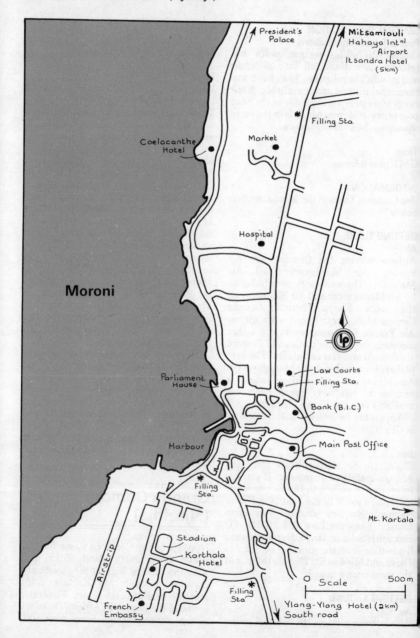

metres high at the northern end of the island.

Most of the coast is raw black lava with semi-submerged coral on the outer edge of that. At the northern tip of the island the coral reef is more extensive and there is a beach. There are also regular stretches of coral down the eastern side of the island. The vegetation is an interesting mixture of coconut and pandanus palm, bananas and baobab trees. Further up the slopes of Mt Kartala there are plantations of ylang-ylang whose trunks resemble overgrown grape vines. Further up still there is rainforest watered by almost constant cloud.

There's surprisingly little bird life on the island but many bats and spiders. The bats – with wing spans up to a metre across – often fly around even during the day. Mongoose may occasionally be sighted.

The villages outside of Moroni are very down-to-earth and services are few. There are no hotels outside the capital but you may be invited to stay with people.

MORONI

Moroni is a very small capital city with a population of just 15,000. The main part is the old Arab town clustered around the harbour with its tortuous alleyways and tiny courtyards. Ali Solih had the whole place whitewashed during his days in power and although mildew is again returning it's still very pretty. The waterfront itself is more Mediterranean than African with solid rock jetties enclosing a small harbour where wooden boats are tied up. All these boats are hand-built and they serve as dories to the ships which call at the island – larger boats cannot get through the coral reefs.

Information

Tourist Information The tourist agency Comores Tours, Services & Safaris (tel 2336), BP 974, Moroni, Grande Comore, puts out free information booklets on the Comoros in both French and English. These include a good map of both the four islands and of the capital, Moroni. If you write (in French) they'll send you a copy to your home address. Otherwise you can pick them up when you get there. The agency offers various tours around the islands.

Money BIC is the only international bank on the independent islands. It's on Grande Comore in Moroni and banking hours are Monday to Thursday from 7 am to 12 noon and on Friday from 7 to 11.30 am. They are closed on Saturday and Sunday.

Things to See

Moroni has little to see apart from the harbour and a walk around the old Arab quarter. There's more to see around the island, however.

Places to Stay

Finding budget accommodation in Moroni or anywhere else on the island is like looking for hen's teeth but there are possibilities. Private houses can be rented for as little as CFr 2000 per night if you ask around. Otherwise try the little restaurant called *Le Glacier* at the 'Place Caltex' which is run by a Malagasy couple. They offer good meals and have two rooms to rent at CFr 4000 a double. You may also be offered accommodation by French Canadian and Belgian volunteer workers since tourists are a rarity in the Comoros Islands and they'll probably be surprised to see you there and come over for a chat. The best place to meet them is at *La Grillade*, a bar and restaurant close to the Coelacanthe Hotel.

There are five hotels but they are all very expensive though usually empty. The *Hotel Karthala* costs CFr 9000 for singles including breakfast. The *Coelacanthe Hotel* costs CFr 18,500 a single and CFr 27,000 a double including breakfast and dinner for accommodation in one of their 12 bungalows. The prices include transport to and from the international airport.

Outside of Moroni there is the *Hotel Itsandra*, about seven km north of the capital, which costs much the same as the Coelacanthe and has a beach of sorts. The *Ylang-Ylang Hotel* is about two km south of the capital.

Places to Eat

Apart from the tourist hotels, there are a number of small, cheaper cafés along the road which runs from the football stadium to the 'Place Caltex' and in the area around the Friday Mosque. In the latter area, many travellers recommend the *Café Ikodjou* (sometimes known as the Café du Port) which is a small Muslim restaurant with a view over the harbour. Prices are reasonable but if you want to eat here you should order food in advance. The *Islam Restaurant* in the town centre is similar.

For Indian food, try the *Babou Restaurant*, close to the Belgian embassy which is just off our map of Moroni on the road to Mitsamiouli. You might also like to try the mess of the *French Military Assistance Mission* near the main post office which offers *brochettes* (skewered barbecued meat) and beer.

Entertainment

Movies are shown every day at *Al Camar* cinema. The *Alliance Franco-Comorienne*, near the Coelacanthe Hotel, shows movies five days a week. You can hear Comoran music every Wednesday at 7 pm at the Ylang-Ylang Hotel.

Getting Around

Airport Transport The international airport in Moroni is at Hahaya about 20 km from the capital. A taxi-brousse between the two should cost CFr 250-500 though the drivers often ask considerably more from foreigners. There may also still be an Air Comores minibus between the airport and Moroni so it's worth enquiring about this before taking a taxi. Taxi drivers will naturally hotly deny there is any such bus. True, it's mainly for staff but passengers can also use it if there is space.

Taxis The five km from the centre of Moroni to the Itsandra Hotel should be about CFr 150.

MT KARTALA

To climb Mt Kartala you need a guide as there are no obvious paths to the top. The best thing to do is to get a taxi-brousse to the village of Kurani (CFr 400 from Moroni) and ask around there. Initial quotes will be high because quite a few well-heeled tourists and geologists do the trip. You may be asked for CFr 15,000 for a full day but you can bargain this down. Make sure your guide can speak some French – many can't so you'll have problems of communication.

It will take you all day to go to the top and return so you need to make a very early start. You can climb down from the crater directly to Moroni in about four hours but you're not advised to climb directly up from there as it's very steep. Beware of small children throwing palm-sized spiders at you through villages on the way. It's a common joke and creates much laughter when the recipient freaks-out.

AROUND THE ISLAND

Itsandra, the ancient capital, has a fortress, royal tombs and a mosque. At Lac Sale there are hot sulphur springs. In the southern part of the island you might like to visit the 14th century village of Mbachile and a ylang-ylang distillery.

On the eastern side of the island is a place called Chomoni which has a spectacular beach and where you can rent small palm-tree huts for CFr 500. Take food and water with you. At weekends many expatriates come over here and the place takes on a party atmosphere but all the huts will be rented out days in advance. It's best to come here at the beginning of the week.

Moheli (Mwali)

Mwali is the Comoran name for Moheli. This is the least populated of the islands with only some 20,000 inhabitants. Off the south coast of this island are a number of smaller islands with beautiful beaches and many sea turtles. You can camp on the beaches here. Fishermen will take you over there and bring you back at a pre-arranged time. 'Fares' are negotiable.

FOMBONI

The chief town on Moheli has a population of 3000.

Places to Stay

M Legrand has one or two rooms to rent at a reasonable price, ask for him at the airstrip. Apart from this there is only the *Relais de Moroni* but it's expensive at around U$25 per room.

Anjouan (Ndzuani)

Ndzuani is the Comoran name for Anjouan. The population of the island is about 150,000 and the highest point is 1575 metres.

MUTSAMUDU

Mutsamudu has a population of 10,000 and is the chief town on the island. It's noted for its beautiful Arab architecture.

Places to Stay & Eat

One of the few places to stay in Mutsamudu is the *Hotel Al Amal* which has a restaurant, bar and swimming pool

but costs about US$25 per room.

For a cheap place to eat, try *La Paillotte*, a small café just behind the *Al-Quitar* cinema. There's also another cheap restaurant at the port end of the main alley.

DOMONI

Domoni, the second largest town on the island, is the birthplace of the president of the republic. It was formerly the capital of the islands and has a colourful market.

MOYA

At the south end of the island there's a very beautiful and deserted beach near this village. Except at weekends, when foreign volunteer workers come here, you'll be on your own.

Places to Stay

There's a very pleasant hotel of sorts with a number of 'bungalows' for rent at CFr 1500 a double and a restaurant.

Mayotte (Maore)

Maore is the Comoran name for Mayotte. Mayotte is, of course, still a French overseas territory and therefore not part of the independent island republic. It voted to stay this way in a referendum after the other islands unilaterally declared independence in 1975. The island, though largely surrounded by coral reefs, has the only deep-water harbour in the archipelago.

DZAOUDZI

The main point of interest on Mayotte is the island's capital of Dzaoudzi which is built on a small islet off the coast. It's very similar to Moroni in that it has an labyrinthine old Arab quarter which is worth exploring.

Index

Lonely Planet

Lonely Planet published its first book in 1973. Tony and Maureen Wheeler had made a lengthy overland trip from England to Australia and, in response to numerous 'how do you do it?' questions, Tony wrote and they published *Across Asia on the Cheap*. It became an instant local best-seller and inspired thoughts of a second travel guide. A year and a half in South-East Asia resulted in their second book, *South-East Asia on a Shoestring*, which they put together in a backstreet Chinese hotel in Singapore in 1975. The 'yellow book', as it quickly became known, soon became *the* guide to the region and has now gone through five editions, always with its familiar yellow cover.

Soon other writers started to come to them with ideas for similar books – books that went off the beaten track and took an adventurous approach to travel, books that 'assumed you knew how to get your luggage off the carousel,' as one reviewer described them. Lonely Planet soon grew from a kitchen table operation to a spare room and also started to develop an international reputation as the Lonely Planet logo began to appear in more and more countries.

By 1980 our list had crept up to more than a dozen titles, there was a full time office and Jim Hart, at one time the editor of *Student Guide to Asia*, had joined the company. Today there are over 40 titles in print, over 20 people work at the Lonely Planet office in Melbourne, Australia and there are another half dozen at the company's US office in Oakland, California.

At first Lonely Planet specialised in the Asia region but these days we are also developing major ranges of guidebooks to the Pacific region, to Latin America and to Africa. The list of walking guides is also growing and Lonely Planet is producing a unique series of phrasebooks to 'unusual' languages. In 1982 *India – a travel survival kit* won the Thomas Cook Guidebook of the Year award, the major international award for travel guidebooks, and the company's business achievements have been recognised by twice winning Australian Export Achievement Awards, in 1982 and 1986. Always the emphasis has been on travel for travellers and Tony and Maureen still manage to fit in a number of trips each year and play a very active part in the writing and updating of Lonely Planet's guides.

Keeping guidebooks up to date is a constant battle and although the basic element in that struggle is still an ear to the ground and lots of walking, modern technology also plays its part. All Lonely Planet guidebooks are now stored and updated on computer. In some cases authors take lap-top computers into the field with them. We are also using computers to draw maps and eventually most of the maps will also be stored on disk.

The people at Lonely Planet strongly feel that travellers can make a positive contribution to the countries they visit both by better appreciation of cultures and by the money they spend. In addition the company tries to make a direct contribution to the countries and regions it covers. Since 1986 a percentage of the income from each book has gone to aid groups and associations. This has included donations to famine relief in Africa, to aid projects in India, to agricultural projects in Nicaragua and other Central American countries and to Greenpeace's efforts to halt French nuclear testing in the Pacific. In 1987 $30,000 was donated by Lonely Planet to these projects.

Temperature

To convert °C to °F multipy by 1.8 and add 32

To convert °F to °C subtract 32 and multipy by 5/9

Length, Distance & Area

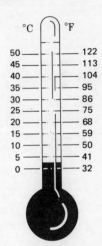

	multipy by
inches to centimetres	2.54
centimetres to inches	0.39
feet to metres	0.30
metres to feet	3.28
yards to metres	0.91
metres to yards	1.09
miles to kilometres	1.61
kilometres to miles	0.62
acres to hectares	0.40
hectares to acres	2.47

Weight

	multipy by
ounces to grams	28.35
grams to ounces	0.035
pounds to kilograms	0.45
kilograms to pounds	2.21
British tons to kilograms	1016
US tons to kilograms	907

A British ton is 2240 lbs, a US ton is 2000 lbs

Volume

	multipy by
imperial gallons to litres	4.55
litres to imperial gallons	0.22
US gallons to litres	3.79
litres to US gallons	0.26

5 imperial gallons equals 6 US gallons
a litre is slightly more than a US quart, slightly less
than a British one

Lonely Planet shoestring guides

South-East Asia on a shoestring
The best known and most widely used guide to the region since its first appearance 10 years ago. Completely updated information on Brunei, Burma, Hong Kong, Indonesia, Macau, Malaysia, Papua New Guinea, Philippines, Singapore, Thailand.

West Asia on a shoestring
A complete guide to the overland trip from Bangladesh to Turkey. Updated information on Afghanistan, Bangladesh, Bhutan, India, Iran, Maldives, Nepal, Pakistan, Sri Lanka, Turkey and the Middle East.

North-East Asia on a shoestring
Concise and up-to-date information on six unique states, including one of the largest countries in the world and one of the smallest colonies: China, Hong Kong, Japan, Korea, Macau, Taiwan.

South America on a shoestring
This extensively up-dated edition covers Central and South America from the USA-Mexico border all the way to Tierra del Fuego. There's background information and numerous maps; details on hotels, restaurants, buses, trains, things to do and hassles to avoid.

Africa on a shoestring
From Marrakesh to Kampala, Mozambique to Mauritania, Johannesburg to Cairo – this guidebook gives you all the facts on travelling in Africa. It provides comprehensive information on more than 50 African countries.

Lonely Planet Publications are available around the world – a list of distributors follows.

Lonely Planet Newsletter

We collect an enormous amount of information here at Lonely Planet. Apart from our research there's a steady stream of letters from people out on the road. To make the most of all this info we produce a quarterly Newsletter (approx Feb, May, Aug, and Nov).

The Newsletter is packed with down-to-earth information from the pens of hundreds of travellers who write from first-hand experience. Whether you want the latest facts, travel stories, or simply to reminisce, the Newsletter will keep you in touch with what is going on.

Where else could you find out:

- about boat trips on the Yalu River?
- where to stay if you want to live in a typical Thai village?
- how long it takes to get a Nepalese trekking permit?
- that Israeli youth hostel stamps will get you deported from Syria?

One year's subscription is $10.00 (that's US$ in the USA or A$ in Australia), payable by cheque, money order, Amex, Visa, Bankcard or MasterCard.

Order Form

Please send me four issues of the Lonely Planet Newsletter. (Subscription starts with next issue. 1987 price – subject to change.)

Name and address (print) ....

....

....

Tick one

☐ Cheque enclosed (payable to Lonely Planet Publications)
☐ Money Order enclosed (payable to Lonely Planet Publications)
Charge my ☐ Amex, ☐ Visa, ☐ Bankcard, ☐ MasterCard for the amount of $.............

Card No ....   Expiry Date ....

Cardholder's Name (print) ....

Signature ....   Date ....

Return this form to:
Lonely Planet Publications   *or*   Lonely Planet Publications
PO Box 2001A   PO Box 88
Berkeley   South Yarra
CA 94702   Victoria 3141
USA   Australia

Lonely Planet Distribution

Lonely Planet travel guides are available round the world. If you can't find them, ask your bookshop to order them from one of the distributors listed below. For countries not listed, or if you would like a free copy of our latest booklist write to Lonely Planet in Australia.

Australia
Lonely Planet Publications, PO Box 88, South Yarra, Victoria 3141.
Canada
Raincoast Books, 112 East 3rd Avenue, Vancouver, British Columbia V5T 1C8.
Denmark, Finland & Norway
Scanvik Books aps, Store Kongensgade 59 A, DK-1264 Copenhagen K.
Hong Kong
The Book Society, GPO Box 7804.
India & Nepal
UBS Distributors, 5 Ansari Rd, New Delhi - 110002.
Israel
Geographical Tours Ltd, 8 Tverya St, Tel Aviv 63144.
Japan
Intercontinental Marketing Corp, IPO Box 5056, Tokyo 100-31.
Netherlands
Nilsson & Lamm bv, Postbus 195, Pampuslaan 212, 1380 AD Weesp.
New Zealand
Roulston Greene Publishing Associates Ltd, Private Bag, Takapuna, Auckland 9.
Papua New Guinea see Australia.
Singapore & Malaysia
MPH Distributors, 601 Sims Drive #03-21, Singapore 1438.
Spain
Altair, Balmes 69, 08007 Barcelona.
Sweden
Esselte Kartcentrum AB, Vasagatan 16, S-111 20 Stockholm.
Thailand
Chalermnit, 108 Sukhumvit 53, Bangkok, 10110.
UK
Roger Lascelles, 47 York Rd, Brentford, Middlesex, TW8 OQP.
USA
Lonely Planet Publications, PO Box 2001A, Berkeley, CA 94702.
West Germany
Buchvertrieb Gerda Schettler, Postfach 64, D3415 Hattorf a H.

Lonely Planet travel guides

Africa on a Shoestring
Alaska – a travel survival kit
Australia – a travel survival kit
Bali & Lombok – a travel survival kit
Bangladesh – a travel survival kit
Burma – a travel survival kit
Bushwalking in Papua New Guinea
Canada – a travel survival kit
China – a travel survival kit
Chile & Easter Island – a travel survival kit
East Africa – a travel survival kit
Ecuador & the Galapagos Islands
Egypt & the Sudan – a travel survival kit
Fiji – a travel survival kit
Hong Kong, Macau & Canton – a travel survival kit
India – a travel survival kit
Indonesia – a travel survival kit
Japan – a travel survival kit
Kashmir, Ladakh & Zanskar – a travel survival kit
Kathmandu & the Kingdom of Nepal
Korea & Taiwan – a travel survival kit
Malaysia, Singapore & Brunei – a travel survival kit
Mexico – a travel survival kit
New Zealand – a travel survival kit
North-East Asia on a Shoestring
Pakistan – a travel survival kit kit
Papua New Guinea – a travel survival kit
Philippines – a travel survival kit
Raratonga & the Cook Islands – a travel survival kit
South America on a Shoestring
South-East Asia on a Shoestring
Sri Lanka – a travel survival kit
Tahiti – a travel survival kit
Thailand – a travel survival kit
Tibet – a travel survival kit
Tramping in New Zealand
Travel with Children
Travellers Tales
Trekking in the Indian Himalaya
Trekking in the Nepal Himalaya
Turkey – a travel survival kit
West Asia on a Shoestring

Lonely Planet phrasebooks

Indonesia Phrasebook
China Phrasebook
Nepal Phrasebook
Papua New Guinea Phrasebook
Sri Lanka Phrasebook
Thailand Phrasebook
Tibet Phrasebook